CIVIL APPEALS:
PRINCIPLE AND PROCEDURE

CIVIL APPEALS:
PRINCIPLE AND PROCEDURE

by
James Leabeater
MA (Oxon.), Barrister

Lynne McCafferty
BA (Oxon.), Barrister

Sean O'Sullivan
MA (Oxon.), Barrister

James Purchas
MA (Cantab.), Barrister

The authors all practise as barristers at
4 Pump Court, Temple, London EC4Y 7AN

SWEET & MAXWELL

 THOMSON REUTERS

First Edition 2010

Published in 2010 by Thomson Reuters (Legal) Limited
(Registered in England & Wales, Company No 1679046.
Registered Office and address for service:
100 Avenue Road, London NW3 3PF)
trading as Sweet & Maxwell

Computerset by YHT Ltd, London
Printed in England by CPI Antony Rowe, Chippenham, Wiltshire

For further information on our products and services, visit:
www.sweetandmaxwell.co.uk

ISBN 9780421960800

No natural forests were destroyed to make this product; only farmed timber
was used and replanted

A CIP catalogue record for this book is available from the British Library

©
Thomson Reuters (Legal) Limited
2010

FOREWORD

I welcome this new book on Civil Appeals, including appeals under the Arbitration Act 1996, written by four barristers at 4 Pump Court. Advising clients and representing them on appeals, either in the Court of Appeal or elsewhere, can be daunting for the junior barrister or solicitor advocate, and even for those more senior. The Courts rightly expect those representing appellants and respondents to appeals to understand and follow the rules, yet there is something of a shortage of good, up to date commentary available to assist them. It seems to me that this book will help to fill that gap.

I am pleased to see that this book considers many of the principles underlying appeals: what makes a decision wrong; when there may be an appeal because a decision was unjust because of a serious procedural or other irregularity; when new evidence may be admitted or appeals reopened. The principles underlying these issues can be complicated and are sometimes misunderstood. I welcome this new analysis of them. I am also pleased to see a discussion of arbitration appeals which recognises the similarities and differences between such appeals and those from the decisions of judges. The result is a book which will be useful for all civil practitioners.

The Right Honourable Sir Simon Tuckey
November 8, 2010

PREFACE

In 1955 Sir Robert Megarry explained that there was some merit to the principle, by then doubted, that books should not be cited as authority for any legal proposition unless the author had died. Whilst, he said, many books by dead authors represented mature views after a lifetime of studying and practising in the particular branch of law concerned,

> "...all too many books by the living are written by those who, laudably enough, have merely hoped to learn the rudiments of a subject by writing a book about it."[1]

A book on appeals written by four junior barristers invites exactly that criticism. All we can say in response is that the considerable time and energy this book has taken to write will not have been wasted if it is of use to those readers who, having found they have lost a trial, perhaps unexpectedly, need to advise their clients quickly about whether they can seek to appeal; their prospects of success of doing so; and how to do so.

Indeed, it was just such a predicament which led to the idea of writing this book. The principles upon which appellate courts approach appeals—to findings of fact, or to case management decisions, and so on—can, for the uninitiated, be difficult to ascertain and difficult fully to understand. Part 52 of the Civil Procedure Rules, supplemented as it is by its unwieldy practice direction, can be difficult to navigate. So we hope that this book may be of use to those who need to learn about appeals.

This book has taken a long time to write, and we have learnt much whilst doing so. We have relied considerably on *Civil Procedure* (the White Book) and Sir Henry Brooke's *Manual of Civil Appeals*.[2] Master Robert Hendy, Master of Civil Appeals, gave generously of his time to read and comment on Part 3 of this book, which deals with Practice and Procedure under the Civil Procedure Rules. We have also had help in writing this book from our colleagues in 4 Pump Court: in particular Anthony Speaight QC, Nicholas Vineall QC, Alex Potts (now at Conyers Dill & Pearman in Bermuda), Alex

---

[1] *Miscellany-at-Law: a diversion for lawyers and others* R.E. Megarry (1955) p.328
[2] Butterworths, 2nd Ed 2004.

Wright, Elspeth Owens, and Adam Temple. We are very grateful to them for their assistance.

We have tried to describe the law at August 1, 2010, though some later cases have been considered where possible. The errors in this book which no doubt remain—despite the assistance we have received—are of course our responsibility. The first edition of a book like this remains to some extent work in progress, and if you have any comments, clarifications or corrections, we would be most grateful if you could send an email to appealbook@4pumpcourt.com.

We would like to thank the clerks at 4 Pump Court—in particular Carolyn McCombe, Carl Wall and Rebecca Fenton—for their administrative assistance, encouragement and for helping us to find time to write; and to thank James Douse, Gregory Smith and Kacey Mann at Sweet & Maxwell for their assistance and patience over the years that have passed from the time we first agreed we would finish this book.

We would also like to thank Helen Vaughan-Jones and Elise and Shaka Purchas, for encouragement and proof-reading.

Finally, we would note that at the date of going to press, the Civil Procedure Rule Committee intends to re-write the Practice Direction to Part 52, which will come into force not before October 2011. We will seek to address the changes arising from the new Practice Direction either by a supplement or a new edition, depending upon the timing and ambit of the changes.

James Leabeater
Lynne McCafferty
Sean O'Sullivan
James Purchas
November 8, 2010

CONTENTS

PART 3: PRACTICE AND PROCEDURE FOR APPEALS UNDER THE CPR

PART 4: THE HIGHER APPELLATE COURTS

Chapter 18—Practice in the Supreme Court

PART 5: ARBITRATION APPEALS

Chapter 20—Background to Arbitration Appeals

Chapter 21—Appeal on Points of Law: Section 69

Chapter 21: Challenging the Substantive Jurisdiction: Section 67

TABLE OF CASES

l

TABLE OF STATUTES

TABLE OF STATUTORY INSTRUMENTS

PART 1

Introduction and History

CHAPTER 1

History of Appeals

INTRODUCTION

Why should a busy practitioner be interested in the history of appeals? It is   1–001
quite possible to read, understand, follow and apply the rules of procedure
and substantive laws which apply to appeals without any knowledge of
what came before them, or how they came about. Indeed, some might say
that it is better to read the rules without any preconceptions about what
they should mean or what the intentions were behind them, especially if
those preconceptions are obtained from previous appellate systems which
have since been reformed. But this chapter has been included in the belief
that there is some merit in understanding when, how and why the appellate
jurisdiction developed.

First, an understanding of the history of appeals assists the practitioner to
understand the jurisdiction of the various courts exercising appellate roles.
Historically appeals were either limited or non-existent. The appellate
jurisdiction is entirely the creature of statute, and an understanding of how
that statutory jurisdiction arose clarifies its ambit and the way its jurisdiction is exercised.

Secondly, an understanding of the history of appeals informs the way in
which appellate courts approach their tasks. A good example is the
approach the appellate court will take to appeals against findings of fact.
The jury has now all but disappeared from the arena of civil disputes, but its
footprint still remains in the approach the appellate court takes when
addressing findings of fact.

Thirdly, it is possible that an understanding of the history of appeals adds
to an understanding of the rules of appellate procedure. Maitland commented in 1909 that "[t]he forms of action we have buried, but they still
rule us from their graves".[1] This book deals with the principles applied by
the appellate courts within their jurisdiction, and it will be apparent, from
time to time, that some of the procedural and substantive principles which

---

[1] Maitland in A.H. Chaytor and W.J. Whittaker (eds), *The Forms of Action at Common
Law* (1969), p.1.

are still applied by appellate courts can be traced back to the curious way in which the appellate structure developed in the Court of Chancery; and the piecemeal manner in which it was transposed across the entire court system. Whilst the forms of action no longer bind Court procedure, this chapter will show that many of the procedural and substantive principles which are still applied by appellate courts pre-date the Judicature Acts.

Fourthly, an examination of the history of appeals elucidates how parliaments have struggled over time with the tensions between the various goals of perfecting justice, encouraging certainty in the law, providing some reasonable finality in litigation, and reducing the time and costs of litigation.

Finally, there might be some people who consider that the history of how the appellate system developed is a matter of interest to at least some practising lawyers in any event.

ROMAN LAW

1–002   Virtually nothing is known of pre-Roman British law. It was not written, and very little exists in recorded form of its oral traditions. We do not know who decided disputes; accordingly, nothing at all is known of any appellate system. The Romans brought written law to Britain. As it developed, Roman law had an appellate system of sorts. Where a case was commenced at provincial level, the case was heard by the governor or his deputy; and in the latter case, an appeal lay from the deputy to the governor. An appeal lay from the governor to the imperial vicar of the civil diocese in which the province lay—in Britain, the imperial vicar of London. From the imperial vicar an appeal lay to the praetorian prefect, and thence to one of the Augusti. There were two appeals for each case. When the Roman legions departed at the beginning of the 5th century, they probably took their legal system with them, though some traditions may have remained.

THE ORIGINS AND DEVELOPMENT OF THE COMMON LAW

1–003   After the Roman legions formally abandoned Britain in 410 the Angles and the Saxons invaded, establishing various different kingdoms in England. In Wales the Britons maintained their independence from the Germanic invaders, and some Roman traditions: in particular, Christianity, administrative structures, and, perhaps, some legal terminology.[2]

In England, change was more profound. The Anglo-Saxons brought their own religion and customs, valuing heroism and the giving of gifts and,

---

[2] Thomas Glyn Watkin, *The Legal History of Wales* (2007), Ch.3.

above all, loyalty to lord and family, which could be enforced, in principle at least, by the blood-feud.[3] At first the Anglo-Saxon kingdoms were fragmented into many regions. According to Bede, King Aethelberht of Kent had enacted written laws for his people, following the Roman example, at some point between 597 and 618.[4] This was the first written record of Anglo-Saxon law, but there is good reason to assume that the laws were well preserved before they were written down.[5]

The limitations of the ambit and cohesion of the Anglo-Saxon written codes have traditionally been regarded as illustrating a "feeble executive power".[6] More recent scholarship shows, however, that the orality of Anglo-Saxon law may have hidden its effectiveness from the historian's view. Anglo-Saxon law, operating through courts of the hundreds and of the shires under the king's jurisdiction, knew writs, the taking of evidence and, perhaps, decision by jury.[7] Above all, the law gained by the early centralisation of power of the English state.

By the 8th century the Anglo-Saxons had consolidated through the hegemony of the militarily successful and had become Christian. In the 9th century they came together under Alfred. In addition to military success, Alfred encouraged literacy and learning, and it seems the development of legal principles and practice.

1–004

The common law, it is now thought, commenced not with Henry II in the 12th century, but with Alfred in the 9th, or even earlier.

> "England's law is distinctive because it is as old as the English kingdom. What above all distinguishes the history of England from that of its neighbours and counterparts is that the power of government has been longer and more consistently felt throughout the area it has claimed to rule. English law has been the instrument and expression of that power ever since it was exercised by King Alfred (871-99) and his heirs. Henry II made law like no other twelfth-century king, because he inherited a system of royal justice that was already uniquely old and active."[8]

The procedures of the Anglo-Saxon courts, if they were fixed, are quite obscure. However there is some evidence of the possibility of an appeal against an unfair decision, in the sense of an appeal for clemency to the king. It appears that the king carried out an appellate review of decisions reached by lower judges. According to Asser's *Life of Alfred* the king heard

---

[3] Chris Wickham, *The Inheritance of Rome: A History of Europe 400–1000* (2009), p.159.
[4] Bede, *Hist. Eccl.* ii 5, p.150-1; Patrick Wormald, *The First Code of English Law* (2005), p.16.
[5] Patrick Wormald, *The First Code of English Law* (2005), p.15.
[6] T. Maitland and S. Pollock, *The History of English Law*, 2nd edn (1923) Vol.1, p.50.
[7] Patrick Wormald, *The Making of English Law: King Alfred to the Twelfth Century Vol 1: Legislation and its Limits* (1999), p.18 (juries), p.152 (depositions from witnesses) and pp.157–158 (writs).
[8] Wormald, *The Making of English Law: King Alfred to the Twelfth Century Vol 1: Legislation and its Limits*, 1999, p.xi.

appeals from both noblemen and commoners, where neither party accepted the judgment of ealdormen or reeves. Alfred was, according to his biographer, "an extremely astute investigator in judicial matters as in everything else". If the judges had passed an unfair sentence through ignorance or some other malpractice, they were given the choice between losing their office and being obliged to study the books so that they could acquire the wisdom necessary for a judge.[9] If Asser's account is correct, it indicates that the Anglo-Saxon courts were subject to review by the king.

1–005   Between the 9th century and the Norman arrival in the 11th century not much is known. However by 1066 there was a body of English law, albeit mostly oral, administered by a system of courts under the king.

In the next two centuries the application of the law by royal courts, the *aula regis*, was systemised, consolidated and reformed so that, by the reign of Edward I (1239–1307), the traditional starting date of the common law, there were courts of the King's Bench, Common Pleas and the Exchequer, each with their systems of procedure. In theory their jurisdiction was distinct: the King's Bench had jurisdiction over pleas of the Crown and criminal causes; the Common Pleas dealt with disputes between subjects; and the Exchequer with disputes about revenue. The Court of Chancery came a little later—though quite when is unclear. But if there had been a system of ad hoc appeals on the merits to Alfred and, perhaps, his successors, it was forgotten in the centuries that followed.

APPEALS FROM COMMON LAW COURTS OF RECORD

1–006   In the system as it existed from Edward I onwards there was no appeal from the decision of a common law court of record (King's Bench, Common Pleas or Exchequer) once the order had been entered in the record. The common law decision was final and binding, and the only way it could be challenged was by showing bad faith on the part of the original jury, or some mistake on the formal record of proceedings. That is not to say that the concept of an appeal was completely unknown. On the contrary, ecclesiastical courts operated a system of appeals which was based upon the Diocletian Roman model. Canon law allowed appeals from the archdeacon to the bishop; from the bishop to the archbishop; and from the archbishop to the pope. In the struggle for supremacy between local courts and the king's courts, the king's courts held themselves out as having appellate jurisdiction over the local courts. Bracton sought to compare the supremacy of the pope over matters spiritual, and over those to whom he had delegated his authority, to the supremacy of the king over matters temporal, and over

---

[9] Wormald, *The Making of English Law: King Alfred to the Twelfth Century Vol 1: Legislation and its Limits*, 1999, pp.119–120.

those courts to whom he had delegated that authority.[10] Nevertheless, it was a long path from Bracton's image of a line of delegated authority in the 12th century to a true system of appeals.

There were some procedures which, in Maitland's phrase, had something about them more or less of an appellate character[11]: among others, the writ of attaint; false judgment and writs of error. The last of these, described below, was the most significant. Of more practical importance, the common law judges sought to bolster the quality of their decision making by reserving difficult points of law to the consideration of judges sitting in banc. This was not an appeal, because the decision of the court was adjourned pending the consideration in banc. However, it rendered the decision more authoritative than otherwise it would have been, and presumably therefore contributed to certainty of the law—which, as we shall see, is nowadays said to be one of the main aims of the appellate jurisdiction.

Writs of attaint and of false judgment

Maitland commented that in the early development of the common law it was difficult to distinguish a complaint against a judgment from an accusation of personal failure on the part of the judge.[12] Modern theories of civil justice, focusing on the goals of efficacious and proportionate dispute resolution, take for granted the reality that perfect justice is unobtainable, and what is important is that a judicial determination is a fair application of the law reasonably founded upon the facts. However, pre-modern jurists may instead have assumed that there was in theory such a thing as perfect justice and truth, known to God. A system truly founded upon the will of God would dispense justice as it ought to be dispensed. Such a system could not, perhaps, admit of the possibility that errors might occur even if the system was functioning correctly. Accordingly, the earliest procedures to complain about a decision tended to be founded upon an accusation of bad faith on the part of the decision maker.

From the earliest times for which there are reasonable records it seems in theory to have been possible to bring a writ of attaint against a decision. The writ of attaint commenced an inquiry into whether the jury had given a false verdict.[13] The applicant had to show some form of bad faith on the part of the jury. Originally it had lain only in respect of verdicts in actions for personal injuries not amounting to trespass, but by the reign of Richard II (1367–1400) it was allowed in almost every action.

1–007

---

[10] Bracton, *De legibus et consuetudinibus Angliae*, Vol.4, p.281 (Bracton online: law.-harvard.edu), cited in Maitland and Pollock, *The History of English Law*, Vol.2, 1923, p.664, n.6.
[11] Maitland and Pollock, *The History of English Law*, Vol.2, 1923, p.665.
[12] Maitland and Pollock, *The History of English Law*, Vol.2, 1923, p.668.
[13] Bl Comm iii.402–404.

The inquiry was heard by a jury of 24. The applicant was not allowed to adduce any evidence other than that given to the original jury. However, new evidence might be adduced to resist the writ, if the original jury had considered evidence of their own knowledge.

1–008   If the grand jury found that the original verdict had been false, the punishments for the original jury were severe in the extreme: outlawry, loss of all assets and property; imprisonment and full reparations. Blackstone commented that the severity of the punishment had its usual effect: it prevented the law from being executed.[14] Although punishments were reduced in the 16th century, that seems to have been of little effect, since Blackstone noted that there was no record of any writ of attaint later than the 16th century.[15]

A complaint of false judgment could be brought only in the king's courts. The unsuccessful litigant obtained a writ (*breve de falso iudicio*) which commanded the lower court to cause a record to be made of the proceedings and to send four suitors of the court to bear the record before the king's justices. Then a fight or debate was held between the complainant and the four suitors. If the complainant was successful, the relevant power behind the local court was punished.[16] Like the writ of attaint, this appears to have fallen into disuse before the advent of law reporting. The writ that took their place, and became the closest thing the common law knew to an appeal, was the writ of error.

Writ of error

1–009   A writ of error was an original writ issued out of Chancery in the nature of a new proceeding, which lay for some error or defect in substance which appeared in the proceedings of a court of record. It appears that it first came into use after the reign of Edward I, when the king's court assumed its triple form of Common Pleas, King's Bench and King in Council (later Exchequer).[17]

The principle form of a writ of error was in the nature of a commission authorising the judges to whom it was directed to examine some record upon which a judgment had been given, and to affirm or reverse the judgment in accordance with the law.[18]

The writ was returnable at the "court of review" for all allegations of errors of law. Where the error alleged was one of fact or procedure, the writ was addressed to the Court which entered judgment, addressed *coram nobis* to the judges of the King's Bench or *coram vobis* to the judges of Common Pleas or the Exchequer. The grounds upon which errors of fact might ground a successful claim were extremely limited; indeed, they appear to

---

[14] Bl Comm iii.402.
[15] Bl Comm iii.403.
[16] Maitland and Pollock, *The History of English Law*, Vol.2, 1923, pp.667–668.
[17] Maitland and Pollock, *The History of English Law*, Vol.2, 1923, p.668.
[18] William Baggley, *The New Practice of the Courts of Law at Westminster* (1840).

have been limited to defects in the legal capacity of one of the parties to the litigation such as, for example, the fact that one of the parties was a married woman or was an infant not appearing by a guardian.[19]

The Court of King's Bench had jurisdiction in error over inferior courts of record and over the Court of Common Pleas. The first recorded writ of error in the King's Bench from the Common Pleas was in 1236.[20] In 1338 it also claimed the right to hear errors from the Court of Exchequer.[21] The Barons of the Exchequer strongly objected to review by the King's Bench and Edward III agreed. In 1357 a new court was enacted to hear alleged errors from the Court of Exchequer. Since the new court was to sit in "any council room nigh the exchequer" it became known as the "Exchequer Chamber". It was composed of the Chancellor and the Treasurer, who alone were the judges, though they could call upon the justices to the common law court as assessors, and could put questions to the Barons of the Exchequer. Such a system was apparently practically speaking unworkable.[22]

From the Court of the King's Bench a writ of error lay only to parliament. **1–010** This severely limited its efficacy, because parliament sat irregularly, at the pleasure of the crown, and when it was sitting, it was busy.[23]

In 1585 statute erected a new court to hear errors from the King's Bench.[24] The court consisted of the judges of the other two common law courts—the Common Pleas and the Barons of the Exchequer who were also Serjeants—sitting together in the Exchequer Chamber. At least six were necessary before judgment could be given. Their decision was subject to further proceedings on a writ in error in parliament. A party could still go directly from the King's Bench to parliament if he chose.

There were a number of very real difficulties with the writ of error.

- First, it lay only for errors appearing on the face of the court record: essentially, the form of action, and the verdict. It might be that important issues arising in the case did not appear on the court record and were therefore not amenable to review by error. For example some forms of action were highly stylised, or depended upon legal fictions. It may be that it was only with the rise of actions on the case that the writ of error became significant.

- Secondly, the writ could only be brought after the completion of the case. That was not only inconvenient, but could also lead to injustice: a party could note an error, but raise it only after the end of proceedings, when if

---

[19] Parliamentary Papers (*Common Law Commission*) (1851), Vol.XXII, p.53.
[20] Theodore Plunkett, *A Concise History of the Common Law*, 5th edn (1956), p.388, n.4, referring to *Bracton's Note Book*, No.1166.
[21] Plunkett, *A Concise History of the Common Law*, 1956, p.160.
[22] Plunkett, *A Concise History of the Common Law*, 1956, p.162
[23] Plunkett, *A Concise History of the Common Law*, 1956, p.171.
[24] 27 Eliz. C. 8 (1585) as amended by 31 Eliz.c.1 (1589).

it had been raised at an earlier date, it could have been corrected by the original court.[25]

- Thirdly, even if the action in error was successful, the most the complaining party could achieve was a setting aside of the original judgment. It would have to start a new action in order to obtain any further relief.

Motions in banc

1–011   From the 16th century the common law courts developed various motions which allowed difficult points of law to be argued "in banc", so that the litigants could have the benefit of judgments considered between judges, and so that the common law could benefit from more considered decisions.[26]

- First, there was the motion in arrest of judgment, in which the unsuccessful defendant alleged that even if the facts alleged by the plaintiff were true, as found by the jury, they disclosed no cause of action.

- Secondly, the plaintiff could raise a motion for judgment *non obtstante verdictio*, alleging that even though he had lost on the facts he should be entitled to a verdict on the law.

- Thirdly, the parties could request a special verdict or a case stated, for the consideration of a point of law on assumed facts.

These forms of motion were akin to applications to strike out or on preliminary points of law, and as such were distinct from what we now consider as appeals. Nevertheless, they allowed a degree of reconsideration by the judges in banc over and above the consideration of the jury at trial.

Motions for a new trial

1–012   Finally, a motion could be brought for a new trial, on the basis that the trial judge considered that the jury's verdict was contrary to the law or evidence, or that there had been misconduct by the jury. Such a motion could only be made before the decision of the court had been entered on the court record.

By the 17th century, a motion for a new trial could also be brought on the basis that the judge himself had erred in his direction to the jury, or in his ruling on the admissibility of evidence. Lord Mansfield C.J. in particular developed this procedure to allow full consideration of the case in banc, relying upon his own full notes of the evidence, rather than simply relying on the facts appearing on the court record.[27] Upon a motion for a new trial

---

[25] Parliamentary Papers (*Common Law Commission*) (1851), Vol.XXII, p.52.
[26] J.H. Baker, *An Introduction to English Legal History*, 4th edn (2002), pp.82–84.
[27] Baker, *An Introduction to English Legal History*, 2002, p.85.

the court had a discretion to grant the order. At the height of its popularity it appears that the discretion was exercised so as to do justice to the parties; it might be exercised on the basis that the jury had simply reached the wrong reason; though the party seeking the new trial would generally have to pay the costs of the party successful first time around.[28]

Although this motion was rather more similar to the modern appeal, the successful applicant could achieve only an order for a new trial and as such was quite distinct from a right of appeal, since the new trial was a trial afresh, without any consideration of the first decision. Nonetheless by at least the 18th century this was an important method of rectifying unjust results in the common law courts, in the absence of any substantive right of appeal.[29]

CHANCERY

The origins of the chancery as a court are obscure. Maitland said that under   **1–013**
Edward I it could not be called a court: "it was a great secretarial bureau, a home office, a foreign office and a ministry of justice."[30] The Lord Chancellor was holder of the great seal of England, which was used to authenticate royal grants of property, privilege, dignity or office, writs and commissions. Writs were issued in the Chancery.

The development of the Court is obscure because of a lack of records. However, it appears to have developed principally as the Chancellor— acting on behalf of the king—took jurisdiction to act against wrongs done by courts of law or other authorities.

The Chancellor acted on men's consciences, and his court was quite different in procedure from the courts of common law. Pleading was in English, and not subject to the constraints of common law writs. There was no jury; evidence was taken by interrogation or written deposition.[31]

Chancery practice allowed the review of enrolled decrees for error on their face by bill of review, which appears to have been a process very similar to the writ of error.[32] However, it also developed a system of appeals to review decisions made pursuant to powers delegated by the Chancellor to others.

The Chancellor was assisted by various administrative assistants known as Masters. As the judicial practice of the Chancery developed, it appears that the Chancellor delegated to them certain activities and powers, some of which encompassed a degree of judicial competence.

---

[28] *Bright v Eynon* (1757) 1 Burr. 390 at 394–395, per Lord Mansfield C.J.
[29] See the discussion in James Oldham, *English Common Law in the Age of Mansfield* (2004), pp.73–76.
[30] Maitland and Pollock, *The History of English Law*, Vol.1, 1923, p.193.
[31] Baker, *An Introduction to English Legal History*, 2002, Ch.6 generally.
[32] The procedure is explained in H. Maddock, *A Treatise on the Principles and Practice of the High Court of Chancery*, 3rd edn (1837), Vol.ii, pp.709–716.

1-014   One of those, the Master in charge of the Rolls, over time became the Chancellor's deputy, so that in his absence he would make decrees and orders. By 1623 orders relating to the practice of the Court were issued by both the Chancellor and the Master of the Rolls. However, the existence, nature and source of his authority was a matter of some dispute, perhaps provoked by jealousy of other masters.[33]

In 1730 the situation was clarified and made certain by statute. 3 Geo. II c.30, entitled "An Act to put an End to certain Disputes touching Orders and Decrees made in the Court of Chancery" recorded the existence of "questions and disputes touching the authority of the Master of the Rolls in the High Court of Chancery". The dispute was resolved by the provision that all orders and decrees made by the Master of the Rolls, either in the past or in the future, were deemed valid orders and decrees of the Court of Chancery; subject, nevertheless, "to be discharged, reversed or altered by the Lord Chancellor ... for the time being, and so as no such Orders or Decrees inrolled till the same are signed by the Lord Chancellor...".

Save perhaps for the jurisdiction exercised by the House of Lords, which is addressed further below, it is likely that this is the first example of a right of appeal within the courts of England and Wales, in that the appellate authority had the jurisdiction not just to examine the lower decision for errors, but also to alter it and replace it with its own decision.

It should, however, be noted that the right of appeal arose because as a matter of theory the Master of Rolls was exercising authority delegated to him from or by the Lord Chancellor. The Lord Chancellor could choose to exercise his jurisdiction in relation to the matter afresh, notwithstanding the fact that the Master of Rolls had already made a decision.

1-015   The authority of the Master of the Rolls was initially limited; in the 18th century he undertook motions and simple causes, whilst the more important cases were considered by the Lord Chancellor himself. Into the 19th century his caseload grew, as the volume of work in Chancery grew.

Some tasks were delegated to lower Masters, who might be given delegated inquires into trusts or partnerships which were simple or uncontested; but their decisions could similarly be the subject of appeals, first to the Master of the Rolls, and then to the Lord Chancellor.

In 1813 a Vice Chancellor was appointed to assist the Lord Chancellor; but from his decisions too there was an appeal to the Lord Chancellor, so shortly afterwards it appears that most of the Lord Chancellor's time was taken up hearing appeals from the Master of the Rolls or the Vice Chancellor, or hearing appeals in the House of Lords, or undertaking his political business.[34]

1-016   When a party sought to bring an appeal, a caveat had to be entered against the signing and enrolling of the decree, to stay it from being presented to the Chancellor. The court hearing the case did have jurisdiction to

---

[33] Holdsworth in Goodhart and Banbury (eds), *A History of English Law*, Vol.i, p.420.
[34] Michael Lobban, "Preparing for Fusion: Reforming the Nineteenth-Century Court of Chancery Part I" (2004) 22 *Law and History Review* 389, 390.

order a new hearing in respect of a dispute. Therefore a case before the Master of the Rolls could be the subject of two hearings, and then an appeal to the Chancellor[35]; and thereafter, once the Chancellor had enrolled a decree, the decision could be appealed to the House of Lords.

An appeal was brought by petition, which was supposed to be presented within one month of the declaration of the original decree. However, according to *Maddock* it had long been the practice to permit appeals beyond that time.[36] It appears that the petition could raise issues of fact or law, but in general it was limited to arguing about points that appeared in the pleadings or the evidence. The petition could not bring up new questions of fact.[37] It was not, in general, permissible to appeal questions of costs,[38] though if an appeal was allowed, costs were at large to be decided by the appellate court.

The appeal itself had to be signed by two counsel who had either argued the case below or were to argue the case on appeal; this was supposed to ensure that there was some proper ground for it to be argued. However, Lord Eldon, at least, thought the barrier for what was properly arguable was lower than whether the appeal was likely to succeed:

> "There have been so many cases in which I have, when at the Bar, succeeded, when I thought I was not entitled, and vice versa, that I agree ... that the case ought to be pretty clear before Counsel should refuse to give their sanction to an Appeal."[39]

THE ORIGINS OF THE APPELLATE JURISDICTION OF THE HOUSE OF LORDS

By 1410 Parliament exercised jurisdiction over writs of error from the Court of Common Pleas via the King's Bench. In 1485 the judges declared that the House of Lords rather than the House of Commons would entertain jurisdiction over writs of error.[40]   1–017

The most visible aspect of the Lords' judicial jurisdiction was that of impeachment; the appellate jurisdiction was less important, but nevertheless continued. It must always have been obvious that the burden of

---

[35] *Brown v Higgs*, 8 Ves. 561.
[36] *A Treatise on the Principles and Practice of the High Court of Chancery*, 3rd edn (1837), Vol.ii, p.758.
[37] *Woods v Griffiths*, 19 Ves. 550 at 551; *A Treatise on the Principles and Practice of the High Court of Chancery*, 3rd edn (1837), Vol.ii, pp.759, 764.
[38] *A Treatise on the Principles and Practice of the High Court of Chancery*, 3rd edn, 1837, Vol.ii, pp.758, 762: *Wirdman v Kent*, 1 Bro. C.C. 140; cf. *Gould v Grander*, Mos. 395.
[39] *Wood v Milner* 1 Jac. & Walk 636, cited in *A Treatise on the Principles and Practice of the High Court of Chancery*, 3rd edn, 1837, Vol.ii, p.756.
[40] Robert Stevens, *Law and Politics: The House of Lords as a Judicial Body 1800–1976* (1979), p.6, n.9.

reviewing decided cases was both onerous and difficult or even, for those peers who were not lawyers, impossible.

From the earliest stages, therefore, the Lords had delegated the jurisdiction to those properly qualified. Originally they were known as legal assistants; later, but by 1305, selected peers were appointed as "receivers and tryers". The Lords also consulted judges: according to Sir Matthew Hale, "since the time that the whole decision of errors have been practiced in the house of lords by their votes, the judges have been always consulted withal, and their opinion held so sacred, that the lords have ever confirmed their judgments thereunto unless in cases where all the judges were parties to the former judgement, as in the case of ship money". Hale had a personal preference for judicial precedence, but there was undoubtedly a practice of consulting judges before peers cast their votes.[41]

As set out above the appeal from the courts of common law was by writ of error and therefore all the shortcomings of the writ of error applied to the appeal in the House of Lords, just as in the courts below: only errors on the record could be considered, and the only remedy was an order for a new hearing.

There were also defects specific to the House of Lords. In particular, appeals could be heard only whilst Parliament was sitting, and when it might sit was in the discretion of the monarch. Appeals could be heard only when time was available; and it may be assumed that peers often had political concerns that were more pressing than the House's appellate jurisdiction. All in all, the possibility of an appeal to the House of Lords was, for nearly all litigants, a theoretical rather than a practical possibility.

1–018   The development of the appellate jurisdiction of the House of Lords over the Court of Chancery was much slower. The Court of Chancery was not a court of record, and so the writ of error did not run in respect of decrees or orders of the Chancellor or his Court. In 1675 it was held that the House of Lords could review decrees and orders of the Court of Chancery for error even without record.[42] Thereafter appeal lay to the House of Lords in respect of all decrees and interlocutory orders. However, there was an added disadvantage for Chancery appeals; there was the possibility, and in the 19th century even the probability, that the appeal would be heard in the House of Lords by a panel including the Lord Chancellor, from whose decision the appeal was being brought.

The original jurisdiction of the House of Lords in legal disputes was the jurisdiction of the entire house. There was no restriction on which lords could vote. In the 17th and 18th centuries lay peers voted in significant numbers on disputes of political or social interest.

Peers, whether legally qualified or not, were not required to give speeches explaining their decision; before the 19th century it appears that cases were decided by numbers of votes. In the 18th century the reporting of cases was

---

[41] Robert Stevens, *Law and Politics: The House of Lords as a Judicial Body 1800–1976* (1979), pp.11–12.

[42] *Shirley v Fagg* (1675) 6 St. Tr. 1121.

considered an infringement of the House's liberties; thereafter reports were meagre.

In the first quarter of the 19th century the judicial work was largely   1–019
carried out by Lord Eldon and Lord Redesdale. Between the retirement of Lord Eldon and the Judicature Acts the House made greater use of their right to call the judges to give their opinions on the matter. But the nature of the questions posed often ran beyond those that rose for consideration or argument in the particular case, as Mr Justice Maule pointed out when asked a series of questions in *McNaghten's* case.[43]

All in all, the House of Lords served as an unattractive prospect for any litigant, whether because the appeal had to proceed by writ of error or because he had to appeal to the House of Lords on which the Chancellor would sit against the Chancellor's earlier decision.

By the 19th century the vast bulk of the House's appellate work came in fact from Scotland. For Scottish litigants the prospect of an appeal to the House of Lords was much more attractive: first, the appeal was an appeal de novo; and secondly, it led to an automatic stay of execution.[44] Of the cases decided in 1801–02, only one was brought by writ of error from the courts of common law. 19 decisions concerned equity appeals. There were many more Scottish appeals; by 1808, 139 Scottish appeals were waiting to be heard.[45]

Delays increased as Irish appeals were also taken to the House from 1802 onwards; and there were calls for reform to mitigate the serious delays. But calls for reform were not just in relation to the appellate procedure of the jurisdiction of the House of Lords, but in relation to many aspects of civil litigation.

EARLY ATTEMPTS AT REFORM

Calls for law reform are probably as old as the law itself. Calls for pro-   1–020
cedural reform can be traced from at least the 17th century onwards. Early proposals for modest reforms were overtaken by the dangers posed by use of prerogative power and the threat of royal despotism: the Star Chamber; and the failure of the common law judges to stand up to Charles I over ship money.

During the interregnum, thoughts turned to how to reform the law so as to improve it for the general population, as parliamentarians, agitators from the New Model Army and other radicals sought to raise a new nation from the ashes of the 1649 revolution. Some of the most radical grounded

---

[43] 10 Cl. & F. 200. This paragraph relies on Van Vechten Veeder, "A Century of English Judicature 1800-1900" in *Select Essays in Anglo-American History* (1907) Vol.1, pp.756–763.

[44] Robert Stevens, *Law and Politics: The House of Lords as a Judicial Body 1800–1976* (1979), pp.8–9.

[45] Stevens, *Law and Politics: The House of Lords as a Judicial Body 1800–1976*, 1979, p.15.

their innovations on new ideals, but the majority turned to the Bible or romanticised notions of the supposed purity of the common law before it was tainted following the imposition of the Norman yoke.

There was certainly no shortage of ideas: "levellers", distrustful of lawyers, called for codification of the law, decentralisation of courts and more power for juries. "Diggers" identified the law itself as an instrument of economic oppression and regarded juries as likely to uphold the rights of the propertied classes. Some called for the adoption of continental civil law. More moderate reformers, including lawyers, proposed more specific and targeted improvements.

1–021 In 1652 calls for reform were appeased, not for the last time, by the setting up of a commission for law reform. Sir Matthew Hale was chairman, and although the commission contained some radicals it was dominated by lawyers and its meetings were technical.[46]

The Hale Commission's proposals were careful and wide-reaching.[47] Among other things, there was to be codification of the law. English should be used instead of Legal French. There was to be an end to the use of the court hand format of handwriting, illegible to all but a few learned in its arcane formalities.[48] More radically, there was to be wholesale reform of the court system, from county courts upwards, ending with review by a Court of Appeal enjoying jurisdiction over all lower courts. This was, it appears, the first serious proposal for the consolidation of the appellate structures into a comprehensive and cohesive format.

The proposals were not enacted by the Rump Parliament, and after the restoration of the monarchy in 1660 they became politically inexpedient, at least in England and Wales. The spirit of law reform was however carried over the Atlantic to the new colonies[49] and nearly two hundred years later law reformers in England sought ideas and inspiration from what had been achieved in reforming the common law in the United States; in particular, in relation to the fusion of common law and equity.

CALLS FOR REFORM IN THE EARLY 19TH CENTURY

1–022 With none of the Hale Commission's proposals enacted for political reasons, the legal system was left virtually unreformed to deal with the new and unprecedented demands posed by industrialisation and the growth of commercialism. By the 19th century the system was so chaotic it had become acceptable even for main stream politicians and lawyers to suggest

---

[46] Mary Cotterell, "Interregnum Law Reform: the Hale Commission of 1652" (1968) 83 *English Historical Review* 699.

[47] Veall, *Popular Movement for Law Reform*, Ch.4.

[48] Veall, *Popular Movement for Law Reform*, p.117.

[49] See, generally, G.B. Warden, "Law Reform in England and New England 1620–1660" (1978) *William and Mary Quarterly* 3d series, Vol.35, pp.668–690.

that it needed to be reformed. The problems were well known. Erskine May described the situation in this way.

"The noble principles of English law had been expounded by eminent judges, and applied to the varying circumstances of society, until they had expanded into a comprehensive system of jurisprudence, entitled to respect and veneration. But however admirable its principles, its practice had departed from the simplicity of former times, and, by manifold defects, went far to defeat the ends of justice. Lawyers, ever following precedents, were blind to principles. Legal fictions, technicalities, obsolete forms, intricate rules of procedure, accumulated. Fine intellects were wasted on the narrow subtleties of special pleading; and clients won or lost causes,—like a game of chess,—not by the force of truth and right, but by the skill and cunning of the players. Heartbreaking delays and ruinous costs were the lot of suitors. Justice was dilatory, expensive, uncertain, and remote. To the rich it was a costly lottery: to the poor a denial of right, or certain ruin. The class who profited most by its dark mysteries, were the lawyers themselves. A suitor might be reduced to beggary or madness: but his advisers revelled in the chicane and artifices of a life-long suit, and grew rich. Out of a multiplicity of forms and processes arose numberless fees and well-paid offices. Many subordinate functionaries, holding sinecure or superfluous appointments, enjoyed greater emoluments than the judges of the court; and upon the luckless suitors, again, fell the charge of these egregious establishments. If complaints were made, they were repelled as the promptings of ignorance: if amendments of the law were proposed, they were resisted as innovations. To question the perfection of English jurisprudence was to doubt the wisdom of our ancestors,—a political heresy, which could expect no toleration."

Erskine May, *Constitutional History*, Vol.III, Ch.XVIII, pp.387–388.

The most pressing concern was the state of the Court of Chancery, which **1–023** under the careful but slow stewardship of Lord Eldon suffered delays which became notorious. The political aspect of the Lord Chancellor's job meant that complaints about procedure were always close to party political intrigue. The result, as usual, was to send the problem to be considered by commissioners, who reported in 1826.

In addition to the specific concerns about delays in Chancery, there were calls for wider reforms of legal system as a whole. Jeremy Bentham was the most prolific and insistent reformer. He, like the Hale Commission in the 17th century, advocated the codification of laws, but came to realise that that was too radical a proposal to make much headway. He also considered in detail and from first principles whether there should be a system of appeal. If judges were fallible, what was the point of an appellate system, since that too was bound to be fallible? Why should an appellate judge have the power to reverse the decision of a judge of first instance on a question of fact, when the judge had the superior means of ascertaining facts? Bentham's answer, in both cases, was that an appeal would reduce the chance of the arbitrary or unfair use of power by the lower judge. The appellate court would form a check on the powers of the lower court. Why should there only be one level of appeal? Because one level of appeal would achieve the aim of forming a check on the judge at first instance; any further levels would increase expense and delay ("the evil opposite to the collateral ends of justice") without any benefit.[50]

Bentham corresponded with many in relation to his proposals, including Sir Robert Peel. Sir Henry (later Lord) Brougham, however, proved to be the most active and practically minded of Bentham's protégés in the arena of law reform.[51] Brougham was a Scot who moved from the Scottish bar to the English bar in 1803. His reputation was as a powerful jury advocate rather than for arguing difficult points of law; his most celebrated victory was his defence of Queen Caroline against a bill of pain and penalties in 1820.[52] He entered politics with considerable success and in April 1827, whilst out of power and in search of a cause, he took up the issue of law reform. His original plan appears to have been radical: the abolition of the common law. But he consulted Bentham and together they decided that it would be more prudent to take things more slowly: the first step should be the setting up of a Royal commission, "which would prove that large changes were needed".

1–024   To that end, on February 7, 1828 Brougham rose to deliver a six hour speech to the House of Commons, which itemised the serious flaws in the systems of the common law courts.[53] Bentham had sent Brougham copies of his work to assist him in preparing his speech[54]; but it is also clear that much of the speech arose from his own experience as a practising barrister.

Brougham did not advocate a reform of the court system to form a new court of appeal. His speech contained no mention of a wider philosophical basis or practical requirement for a systematic appellate system. Nor did he criticise the limited ambit of a writ of error. His criticisms were much narrower in scope and ambition. The principal evil of the courts of error, he said, was their practice of effecting a stay of execution, which thereby gave the losing party an interest in prosecuting groundless appeals. He proposed instead that the party who obtained judgment should be entitled to instant

---

[50] "Principles of Judicial Procedure", Ch.XXVIII ("Appeal and Quasi-Appeal") in John Bowring (ed.) *The Works of Jeremy Bentham*, Vol.ii, pp.161–168. The *Principles of Judicial Procedure* were not completed by Bentham; they were prepared for publication by his former secretary, Richard Douane: see J.H. Burns and H.L.A. Hart, *An Introduction to the Principles of Morals and Legislation* (1996) pp.xliii–xliv.

[51] Michael Lobban, "Henry Brougham and Law Reform" (2000) *English Historical Review* 1184.

[52] Michael Lobban, *Oxford Dictionary of National Biography* (2000) Vol.7, pp.970 and 974. His speech in defence of the Queen lasted two days, and was so powerful that Lord Erskine rushed out of the chamber in tears. Public houses throughout the country were renamed the Brougham's Head: ibid. p.974.

[53] HC Deb, February 7, 1828, Vol.18, cc128–258.

[54] Michael Lobban, "Henry Brougham and Law Reform" (2000) *English Historical Review* 1184, 1188–1189.

possession or execution, upon giving security for restitution should the decision be reversed.

Brougham's speech succeeded in its principle aim of having a commission set up to enquire into the practice and proceedings of the superior courts of common law. Their first report was delivered in February 1829. Amongst its very least controversial proposals[55] was the clarification of jurisdiction for writs of error from the superior courts of law. The proposal was swiftly enacted: in 1830 error jurisdiction of the King's Bench, Council Chamber and Exchequer Chamber was combined into a new Court of Exchequer Chamber, comprising the judges of all three superior common-law courts; error from any one court was heard by the judges of the other two.[56]

The purpose of the reform was to remove doubts about the correct   1–025
destination of writs from the King's Bench; to deprive the King's Bench of jurisdiction as court of error from the Common Pleas; and to remove the requirement for the attendance of the Chancellor and the Lord Treasurer for writs of error from the Plea side of the Exchequer.[57] The procedure remained by writ of error.

The commissioners' third report proposed simplification of the writ of error procedure. Practitioners' responses to their consultation disclosed widespread antipathy to the idea that error should lie in respect of findings of fact, largely because practitioners disliked the idea of considering facts on affidavits rather than orally. The commissioners' considerations followed Brougham's suggestions quite closely: they advocated any stay of judgment pending the hearing of a writ of error be made conditional upon security been given. They also proposed procedural reforms for writs of error for example, the form of the writ should be shortened; certificate of counsel that there be "probable ground in law" for bringing the writ of error should be a pre-condition of any stay of execution.[58]

These proposals were not, by and large, enacted until the Common Law Procedure Act of 1852, by which stage the appetite for reform had grown and, as we shall see, the ambit of the changes were more significant.

Is it surprising that the defects in the writ of error were not singled out by Brougham or his contemporaries in Parliament for reform? Holdsworth said that the writ of error was at once both too narrow and too wide: too narrow because in order to succeed one had to establish some error on the record; and too wide, because if there was error, the court was bound to give relief, whether the error was significant or not.[59] Success in an action

---

[55] The reforms appear to have excited very little interest: see, for example, (1829) 2 *Law Magazine* 151 commented that the reform did not "require further explanation" and (1831) 1 *Legal Observer* 19 and 60 stated that the reforms were less important than the other changes effected by the same Act: the admission of attorneys to the court of Exchequer, the abolition of the Courts of Wales and Chester, changes in terms and returns, and reforms to bail.

[56] 11 Geo IV and 1 Will. IV, c.70, s.8.

[57] (1831) 1 *Legal Observer* 60.

[58] (1831) Parlt. Papers, Vol.x, pp.407–409.

[59] Cited by Lord Evershed M.R. in *The Court of Appeal in England* (1950, Lecture before the University of London), p.5.

brought by writ of error depended upon an error being found on the record which might have little to do with whether or not the original decision was correct. It might well be thought that such defects would be obvious and lead to widespread demands for reform; but they did not.

1–026   Perhaps the reason that there were not greater calls for reform in the 19th century was that the system functioned reasonably well because the common law judges sat *in banc* at first instance. Certainly that was the view of the distinguished American Judge and legal historian Van Vechten Veeder, writing at the beginning of the 20th century:

> "The three great common law courts in banc administered the system then in force as well as any court could administer it. It was not until the breakdown of the common law courts in banc that more liberal rights of appeal became necessary."[60]

As we shall see, and contrary to Judge Veeder's assumption, the availability of an appellate jurisdiction led to the breakdown of the practice of sitting *in banc* at first instance, rather than the other way around. However, his opinion that sitting *in banc* at first instance might have avoided the need for an appeal—perhaps formed after discussions with lawyers who remembered the old system—may be correct. It may have been the case that the prestige attached to a considered decision of judges sitting *in banc* at first instance meant that the absence of a structured appellate system was not a source of dissatisfaction to practising lawyers or their clients.

Whether it was for that reason or another, or even as a result of a lack of imagination, the modern system of appeals did not come about as a result of principled or systematic calls for reform. Rather, the present system of a Court of Appeal, with a further appeal to the House of Lords, on points of fact as well as law, came about in a roundabout and unexpected manner, not as a desirable end in itself, but as an adjunct to the movement for the fusion of law and equity.

TOWARDS THE FUSION OF LAW AND EQUITY

1–027   As mentioned above while the 17th century spirit for reforming the law might have had little lasting success in England, it had been taken across the Atlantic to the new colonies, later the United States of America where it was taken up with vigour. Ironically, in due course, thoughts turned to a transfer of ideas in the other direction.

In 1848 the State of New York had adopted a new procedural code which, among other things, abolished the distinction between actions at law

---

[60] Van Vechten Veeder, "A Century of English Judicature 1800–1900" in *Select Essays in Anglo-American History* (1907), Vol.1, p.755.

and suits in equity and substituted a single form of action for all civil actions.[61] In 1850 the Law Amendment Society invited the New York code's author, Mr David Dudley Field, to come to England to address them on the reforms. Before the talk, and consistent with the resistance to reform, the *Law Times* declared that fusion would be "suicide". However following the talk in 1851, that same journal reported that there was "almost unanimity" that the distinction between law and equity was "the parent of most of the defects in the administration of our law".[62]

Fusion was first achieved in the County Courts. The old system of county and other local courts was swept away by the County Courts Act 1846.[63] In 1865 the County Courts were given an equitable jurisdiction,[64] although that jurisdiction was not widely used.[65]

There was at the same time a continuing pressure for specific procedural reforms. In Chancery, delays had again grown pressing[65a]; and it was obvious that the demands on the Chancellor's time were too great: he was a judge at first instance and on appeal in the Chancery Court, on appellate business in the House of Lords; and he also had political obligations. In 1851 the Prime Minister, Lord John Russell, introduced a bill to introduce a Court of Appeal in Chancery, so that appeals could be dealt with by other judges if the Chancellor was too busy.   1–028

The Court of Appeal in Chancery was formed, but existed for just over 20 years. For its early period it was dominated by Knight-Bruce and Turner L.JJ; for its last few years it was led by James and Mellish L.JJ. Mellish L.J. had a common law background.[66] It is possible that he was appointed by Lord Selbourne to the court in 1870 to make preparations for a new Court of Appeal with fused jurisdiction over common law and equity.

Commission reports in 1850 and 1851 into defects in common law courts and in Chancery recommended that the courts should have the power to deliver all remedies at law or in equity in the same action. Throughout the latter half of the 19th century there were statutes introduced to give, on the one hand, the court of Chancery the power to grant common law damages and to use common law procedures and on the other hand to give the courts of common law the power to grant equitable remedies and grant disclosure

---

[61] *Duely and Constantly Kept: A History of the New York Supreme Court, 1691–1847*, App.H.

[62] Michael Lobban, "Preparing for Fusion: Reforming the Nineteenth-Century Court of Chancery Part 2" (2004) 22 *Law and History Review* 29.

[63] 9 & 10 Vict c.95.

[64] County Courts (Equity Jurisdiction) Act 1865; Patrick Polden, *A History of the County Court, 1846–1971* (1999) p.59.

[65] Michael Lobban, "Preparing for Fusion: Reforming the Nineteenth-Century Court of Chancery Part 2" (2004) 22 *Law and History Review* 29.

[65a] The delays in Chancery were most famously satirised by Charles Dickens in his masterpiece *Bleak House*, published in 1853. Dickens, who was a reporter in the Lord Chancellor's court in the late 1820s, illustrated the point through the "interminable suit" in the Court of Chancery of the fictional case of *Jarndyce v Jarndyce*.

[66] Van Vechten Veeder, "A Century of English Judicature 1800–1900" in *Select Essays in Anglo-American History* (1907), Vol.1, p. 802. Veeder described the Court of Appeal in Chancery as "one of the most satisfactory courts that ever administered English law": ibid., p.800.

of documents.[67] But the systems still remained separate, and so long as they were separate, courts of competing jurisdictions were likely to give rise to conflicting decisions, confusion of procedure and duplicative costs.

1–029   Further reform was afoot. In 1852 the writ of error was abolished, and proceedings in error were brought by memorandum as a step in the cause rather than a separate action.[68] This meant that the parties did not have to wait until the conclusion of the proceedings to raise an error. They could bring error on a special case stated, or they could move for a new trial; and they could grant appeal to the Exchequer Chamber from the refusal to grant a new trial, unless the members of the court were unanimous in their refusal. The court on appeal had greater powers: it could take all circumstances into consideration, give judgment as ought to have been given below, and it could refuse a new trial if it considered that the misdirection was not in a material point.[69]

While these reforms of the 1850s brought important improvements to the appellate structure, but those who advocated the fusion of law and equity thought that a fused appellate structure required more fundamental change.

THE JUDICATURE COMMISSION

1–030   On February 22, 1867 Sir Roundell Palmer, at that time Attorney General and later Lord Selbourne L.C., brought a motion in the House of Commons for a commission of inquiry into the superior courts, their procedure, and courts error and of appeal.[70] The commissioners, led by Lord Cairns, reported in March 1869. They said that common law and equity had not been sufficiently fused and the appellate structures were needlessly confused. The new powers of the courts at common law to grant injunctions, and in chancery to have trial by jury, had been little used in practice. The old defects remained.[71]

In particular, there was a danger of different courts reaching inconsistent decisions. Railway disputes had led to litigation in different courts, causing expense, delay and the danger of conflicting decisions. Litigation between sellers of railway shares and jobbers on the stock exchange, by which the sellers sought to obtain an indemnity from the jobbers against calls, had been the subject of actions in courts of common law and equity. Both had gone to appeal, but to different appellate courts (the Court of Exchequer Chamber and Court of Appeal in Chancery).

---

[67] W.S. Holdsworth in A.L. Goodhart and H.G. Hansbury (eds), *A History of English Law*, Vol.15, (1965), pp.121–127.

[68] 15, 16 Victoria c.76, ss.148, 149, 152, 157, enacting proposals of the First Report of the Common Law Commission Parliamentary Papers 1851, Vol.XXII, pp.53–43.

[69] Holdsworth, *A History of English Law*, Vol.i, pp.245–246.

[70] Roundell Palmer, Earl of Selbourne, *Memorials Part II: Personal and Political* (1898), Vol.i, p.46.

[71] *Report from Judicature Commissioners* Parliamentary Papers (1868–1869), Vol.xxv, p.6.

Decisions of the Admiralty Court, by comparison, went on appeal to the Privy Council. In the County Courts, although the judge had jurisdiction at law and in equity, the litigant had to choose which form of procedure he wanted from the outset.

The commissioners recommended that all superior courts of law and equity, together with the courts of probate, divorce and admiralty, be consolidated into one Supreme Court.[72] Common law decisions which previously had been made *in banc* could, if there was a right of appeal, safely be entrusted to a single judge, as had always been the situation in Chancery.[73] The Supreme Court would include a new Court of Appeal. They proposed that an appeal should lie from all judgments, decrees, rules and orders in suits or proceedings not strictly criminal. They further commented:

> "It may hereafter deserve consideration, after experience of the working of the Court thus constituted, whether its decisions may not be made final, unless leave to appeal from them be given, either by the Court itself, or by the House of Lords. In the meantime, we recommend that there should be a right of appeal to the House of Lords."[74]

There was to be no writ of error; instead appeals would be brought by notice of motion, without any petition or formal procedure. Interlocutory orders could be appealed during the suit, subject to general orders. The right of appeal was to be conditional on substantial security given by the appellant for costs of the appeal. No appeal should operate as a stay of execution, or of any proceedings under the order appealed from unless the judge or Court of Appeal so ordered. Every appeal should be deemed to be in the nature of a rehearing.[75]   1–031

The commissioners' proposals were not enacted without difficulty.[76] The proposed changes were important and difficult, and chancery and common lawyers were concerned to protect their own interests. An initial attempt by Lord Hatherley L.C. to enact the proposals Bill of just 25 clauses was unsuccessful. Lord Cairns himself said it was not sufficiently detailed. Sir Alexander Cockburn L.C.J. was more partisan; the Bill would, he said, allow the Court of Chancery to reign exclusively supreme.

Lord Selbourne L.C., Lord Hatherley's successor, presented his Supreme Court of Judicature Bill to the House of Lords in February 1873, which was much more detailed. He had also taken the precaution of sending it in draft for comments to Lord Cairns, Lord Hatherley, Lord Westbury and Lord Romilly, Cockburn C.J. and Bovill C.J., Kelly C.B., James and Mellish

---

[72] ibid, p.9.
[73] ibid, p.10. See, in this regard Patrick Polden, "Mingling the Waters: Personalities, Politics and the Making of the Supreme Court of Judicature" [2002] C.L.J. 575, 584–585.
[74] ibid., pp.23–24.
[75] ibid., p.24.
[76] This paragraph relies heavily on Patrick Polden, "Mingling the Waters: Personalities, Politics and the Making of the Supreme Court of Judicature" [2002] C.L.J. 575.

L.JJ.; and the Attorney General and the Solicitor General.[77] It passed successfully.

The Judicature Act 1873 established a Supreme Court of two parts: the High Court of Justice, with original jurisdiction, and the Court of Appeal, with appellate jurisdiction. The Court of Appeal was given jurisdiction and power to hear and determine appeals from any judgment or order of the High Court; and for the purposes of and incidental to the hearing and determination of any appeal, the Court of Appeal was to have all the power, authority and jurisdiction vested in the High Court of Justice.

1–032   The identity of the judges of the new Court of Appeal was the subject of some discussion. Common lawyers thought that three judges would not be sufficient to command respect if they sought to overturn the decision of a lower common law court sitting *in banc*. Some equity lawyers pushed for the Court of Appeal to sit in two divisions: common law and equity. In fact, the Supreme Court of Judicature Act 1875 proposed a majority of equity judges; the Appeallate Jurisdiction Act 1876 added three further new Lord Justices of Appeal to increase the common law representation (Bramwell, Brett and Amphlett L.JJ.).[78]

The most controversial subject was not whether there should be a combined Court of Appeal, but whether the House of Lords should retain its appellate jurisdiction over the Court of Appeal. Lord Selbourne's intention was to end the expense and delay incident to the system of double appeals, with all appellate jurisdiction concentrated in one final Court of Appeal[79]; although, as noted above, the Judicature Commissioners had not gone so far as to make that recommendation. As enacted in August 1873, the Judicature Act provided that there would be no appeal from the new Court of Appeal either to the House of Lords or to the Privy Council; thus leaving the House of Lords with a judicial function only in respect of appeals from Ireland and Scotland. But that did not come to pass.

In fact, the new appellate structure, which was to subsist for over a century, was shaped by the politics of the day. There was a successful rearguard conservative defence to preserve the status quo. In February 1874 Gladstone's administration fell. Disraeli became Prime Minister with a comfortable conservative majority and he appointed Lord Cairns as Lord Chancellor. Lord Cairns introduced a Bill to send Irish and Scottish appeals to the Court of Appeal, to be renamed the Imperial Court of Appeal. This Imperial Court of Appeal would also take colonial and ecclesiastical appeals from the Privy Council. However the conservative support for retaining the judicial functions of the House of Lords was growing more confident. In July 1874 Disraeli agreed to drop the Bill, praying in aid

---

[77] Roundell Palmer, Earl of Selbourne, *Memorials Part II: Personal and Political* (1898), Vol.i, p.301.

[78] Amphlett L.J. had practised in bankruptcy law, but was then appointed to the Court of Exchequer: Patrick Polden, "Mingling the Waters: Personalities, Politics and the Making of the Supreme Court of Judicature" [2002] C.L.J. 575, 588.

[79] Roundell Palmer, Earl of Selbourne, *Memorials Part II: Personal and Political* (1898), Vol.i, p.305.

pressure of other business, and the fact that the new Rules of the Supreme Court were yet to be drawn up. A Bill was introduced and quickly passed postponing the date that the Judicature Act 1873 would come into force by a year to November 1875.[80] Cairns reintroduced his Bill the next year, but by that stage the Committee for Preserving the House of Lords had persuaded Conservative peers that the appellate jurisdiction of the House of Lords should be preserved. On April 8, 1875 Cairns was obliged to withdraw his Bill and consult once more. His new Bill, which received Royal assent in August 1876 as the Appellate Jurisdiction Act of 1876,[81] restored the House of Lords to be the final court of appeal, although with modifications: in particular, there were to be professional lawyers, called Lords of Appeal in Ordinary; and the procedure was not on a writ of error, but by petition.[82] It came into force on November 1, 1876. The House of Lords was to remain the pre-eminent appellate court for well over a century.[83]

THE APPELLATE SYSTEM AFTER NOVEMBER 1876

The Judicature Acts left significant areas of judicial practice to be developed by Orders, Rules of the Court and by the judges themselves.   1–033

First, the Judicature Acts had left too many divisions. On November 29, 1880 the Council of Judges of the Supreme Court resolved that the Common Pleas and Exchequer Divisions should be consolidated in the Queen's Bench, and the offices of the Chief Justice of the Common Pleas and the Chief Baron of the Exchequer be abolished. This was achieved by Order made on December 16, 1880.[84]

Secondly, the Acts left unclear the extent to which procedure should follow the old rules of the Queen's Bench or the Chancery Division.

Significant changes were made to the rules of procedure in 1883, enacted in the Rules of the Supreme Court 1883, following some of the recommendations of the Legal Procedure Committee of 1881. In particular it was decided that trial before a judge without jury was to be the usual mode of trial in the Queen's Bench—though an application for trial before jury could not be refused unless there would be prolonged examination of documents or accounts or there was to be any scientific or local investigation made, in which case the trial could be ordered before a referee.

---

[80] Supreme Court of Judicature Act (1873) Suspension Act 1874.

[81] 39 & 40 Vict. c.59.

[82] On the successful conservative backlash see Stevens, *Law and Politics: The House of Lords as a Judicial Body 1800–1976*, 1979, pp.57–67.

[83] The new Court of Appeal needed somewhere to sit. Royal Courts of Justice were opened by the Queen on December 4, 1882 and commenced business at the beginning of Hilary Sittings 1883. The buildings were funded in part by unclaimed funds standing in Court accounts.

[84] Notes from Lely and Foulkes, *The Judicature Acts, 1873 and 1875, the Appellate Jurisdiction Act 1876 and other statues... forming a Practice of the Supreme* Court, 4th edn (1883), p.lv.

Either party could appeal under s.19 of the Judicature Act 1873, though s.49 provided that there would be no appeal against any order as to costs only except by leave of the court or judge making such order.

1–034   The Rules of the Supreme Court provided for various different systems of appeals, or systems akin to appeals, which varied according to whether the decision was made by judge sitting alone or with a jury; or by a master.

Where a party sought to appeal judgment after a trial by jury, it might apply to set aside judgment on the basis that the finding of the jury upon the question submitted to them had not been properly entered, or because upon the finding as entered, the judgment so directed was wrong. Such an application had to be made to the Court of Appeal, unless the party sought a motion for a new trial, in which case the appeal was to the divisional court.[85] A motion for a new trial lay under Ord.39, where the party objected to a finding by a jury. Motions for new trials are discussed further below.

Where, on the other hand, a trial was held without jury, there was an appeal on law and fact to the Court of Appeal.[86] Order 58 r.1 provided that:

> "All appeals to the Court of Appeal shall be by way of rehearing, and shall be brought by notice of motion in a summary way, and no petition, case, or other formal proceeding other than such notice of motion appeal from the whole or any part of any judgment or order, and the notice of motion shall state whether the whole or part only of such judgment or order is complained of, and in the latter case shall specify such part."

1–035   Under Ord.58 r.4 the Court of Appeal had full discretionary power to receive further evidence upon questions of fact. However on appeals from a judgment after trial or hearing of any cause or matter upon the merits, such further evidence would be admitted on special grounds only, and not without special leave of the court. The Court of Appeal had power to draw inferences of fact and to give any judgment and make any order which ought to have been made, and to make such further order as the case might require. By Ord.58 r.16 an appeal would not operate as a stay of execution or of proceedings under the decision appealed from, save as the court appealed from or the Court of Appeal might order.

In all these regards the new Court of Appeal followed closely the practice of the Court of Appeal in Chancery; save for in relation to time limits. The new rules introduced much stricter time limits than had prevailed before. By Ord.58 r.15 an appeal had to be brought (unless with special permission) within 21 days of any order save for one made in an action, and otherwise

---

[85] RSC Ord.40. The provision for a motion for a new trial to be made to the divisional court was entered added in 1883. The motion to the Court of Appeal had to be on notice: *Jones v Davies* (CA) 36 L.T. 415.

[86] *Oatler v Henderson*, 2 Q.B.D. 575.

26

within one year. The Court of Appeal in Chancery had allowed five years for appeal, except by leave; at common law, six years for bringing error on a final judgment; though on appeals strictly so called notice had to be given in four days.[87]

Motions for a new trial

The new rules brought about the possibility of seeking to appeal findings of fact made by juries. Under the old rules motions for new trials were motions made whilst the cause was still extant, because judgment was not entered until later. As mentioned in para.1–006, the courts of common law allowed points to be argued *in banc* before judgment was entered.[88] Under the new rules, the hearings *in banc* ceased over time, and it became the norm for a decision that had been rendered on the merits to stand unless there was an appeal. Motions for new trials stood uneasily on the cusp of the old and the new.

1–036

From 1875 Ord.39 r.1 provided that:

> "Every motion for a new trial or to set aside a verdict, finding or judgment shall be made (1) in every cause or matter by the principal Act assigned to the Probate Divorce and Admiralty Division, where there has been a trial thereof or of any issue therein with a jury, to a Divisional Court of that Division, one of the judges of which shall (where practicable) sit on the hearing of such motion; (2) in every other cause or matter, where there has been a trial thereof or of any issue therein with a jury, to a Divisional Court of the Queen's Bench Division; and (3) where there has been a trial without a jury, by appeal to the Court of Appeal."

The Court of Appeal held that it had no jurisdiction to hear objection to the finding of the jury; it had objections only to the judgment entered by the judge. If, therefore, a litigant objected to a finding of a jury, it had to apply for a new trial under Ord.39: see *Davies v Felix*.[88a]

This system was, it appears, apt to give rise to double appeals. The Judicature Act 1890, introduced by Mr Robert Finlay MP, later Viscount Finlay L.C., provided that any motions for new trials should instead be

1–037

---

[87] Lely and Foulkes, *The Judicature Acts, 1873 and 1875, the Appellate Jurisdiction Act 1876 and other statues... forming a Practice of the Supreme Court*, 4th edn (1883), p.352.

[88] In this regard, Holdsworth explained that unless the question was one of law, it was very rare for judgment to be delivered by the court. Generally judgment was entered by the relevant court official signing judgment at the request of one of the party's attorneys, and it stood in place of its actual delivery by the judges themselves. The attorney, after judgment, took out a writ of execution, upon peril that if he took a wrong execution, the proceedings would be illegal and void and the opposite party entitled to redress: Sir William Holdsworth, *A History of English Law*, 3rd edn (1944), Vol.ix, pp.259–260, referring to Stephen, *Pleading*, pp.132–138.

[88a] (1878) 4 Ex. D. 32.

made to the Court of Appeal. The Court of Appeal held in *Heckscher v Crosley*[88b] that it would continue to hear such motions in a similar manner to the divisional court, and in that regard, they would follow the old practice in saying that no order for security for costs against the costs of a new trial should be granted. That principle was disapproved of in *Wightwick v Pope*,[88c] where at 99–100, Collins M.R. held that *Hecksher* should not be followed. The old practice had arisen because,

> "...judgment was never given by the judge at nisi prius, who has been described as "only the instrument of the Court to try the issues raised": see *Wells v. Abrahams* (1872) L. R. 7 Q. B. 554; and, where leave to move was reserved, the matter was suspended till the rule nisi could be moved for. Nowadays the judge has complete control of the cause, and can enter judgment as he thinks right. Hence there is now—unless the learned judge has declined to give judgment—a collateral or alternative application in every motion for a new trial asking the Court to deal with the judgment accordingly."

From 1909 motions for new trials were assimilated to the appellate system. They were entered in the same list as that for final appeals[89]; and on a motion for a new trial the court might give judgment, or direct issues, or accounts and inquiries.[90]

Appeals from masters

1–038   Appeals from masters also sat uneasily between the old and the new, for the Judicature Acts did not abolish the differences between practice and jurisdiction in the Chancery and the Queen's Bench Division. The differences in the jurisdiction of masters in the Chancery and the Queen's Bench Division and the substantive differences in appeals from their decisions reflected the different historical roots of the masters in each jurisdiction.[91]

In the Chancery division, the rules maintained the principle that a master exercised power delegated by the judge. A party had the right to ask the judge to make a decision instead of the master. Thus there was no appeal from a decision of the master; rather, the matter could be adjourned from the master to the judge. Thus RSC Ord.55 r.15, based upon provisions in the Court of Chancery Act 1852, gave powers to judges of the Chancery Division to order what matters should be heard and investigated by the masters. Order 55 r.69 provided that any party might, before proceedings before the master were concluded, take the opinion of the judge upon any

---

[88b] [1891] 1 Q.B. 224.
[88c] [1902] 2 K.B. 99.
[89] *Practice Note*, 1909 W.N. 6.
[90] RSC Ord.40 r.10.
[91] See in general para.512 of *Final Report of the Committee on Supreme Court Practice and Procedure* (1953) Cmd.8878 under Sir Raymond Evershed M.R., p.165.

matter arising in the course of the proceedings without any fresh summons for the purpose.[92] After an order had been passed and entered on the record a party dissatisfied with the master's decision was obliged to apply to the court to discharge it under Ord.55 r.71.[93]

By contrast, in the Queen's Bench Division, the master exercised the jurisdiction of the judge sitting in chambers (with certain significant exceptions): Ord.54 r.12. From the master there was an appeal to the judge: Ord.54 r.21 and 21A. "An appeal under this rule is an appeal in the fullest sense of the term, and both the law and the facts are open to review."[94]

County Courts[95]

The County Courts Act 1846 set up new system of County Courts. To begin with, there was no appeal. This gave rise to judgments widely considered absurd, including in particular the "My Aunt's Case", in which a judge, being told by a defendant that he could not pay, but that his aunt would, proceeded to make an order against his aunt.[96] The County Courts Extension Act 1850 s.14 provided for an appeal on point of law or admission or rejection of evidence in claims above £20 to a court of appeal of two puisne judges of the superior courts of common law at Westminster.   **1–039**

The County Courts Act 1875 provided by s.6 that any appeal could be by motion rather than case stated; and that if the court was not sitting, it could be made before any judge of superior court sitting in chambers. The judge was to make a note of any question of law, and of facts in evidence in relation thereto; and of his decision, and he should furnish a note of that at the parties' expense. Thereafter there was a variety of different rules about whether leave was required or not for an appeal from the County Court, addressed in a systematic manner by the Evershed committee in the 1950s, referred to below.

CONSOLIDATING THE NEW SYSTEM

In 1925 the Judicature Acts were consolidated in the Supreme Court of Judicature (Consolidation) Act 1925. But disquiet was growing that there were too many appeals; and that appeals were giving rise to serious delays   **1–040**

---

[92] per Byrne J. in *Lloyds Bank Ltd v Princess Royal Colliery Co Ltd* (1900) 48 W.R. 427 at 428: "the right of every suitor in the Chancery Division to have any question determined by the judge personally was beyond question, and that an adjournment to the judge was not in the nature of an appeal. All orders made in chambers are orders of the judge, though taken without the parties actually going before him." Affirmed by Megarry V.C. in *In re Caines, decd* [1978] 1 W.L.R. 540 at 544.

[93] On jurisdiction of masters now see CPR r.2.4 and PD 2B and the notes on p.30 (2009 version).

[94] *Scott v Walley* (1922) 38 Times Rep. 525.

[95] See, in general, Polden, *A History of the County Court, 1846–1971*, 1999.

[96] Polden, *A History of the County Court, 1846–1971*, 1999, p.50.

and extra expense. A committee was set up under Hanworth M.R. to consider (among other things) the elimination or restriction of the rights of appeal to or within or from the Supreme Court. They concluded in their report of December 13, 1933 that:

(a) The divisional courts should be abolished. They had hitherto heard appeals (until 1932) from official referees and from the County Court. Their jurisdiction was to be transferred to the Court of Appeal.

(b) Appeals to the House of Lords should be by leave only, either of the Court of Appeal or the House itself.

The report led to the Administration of Justice (Appeals) Act 1934 and s.105 of the County Courts Act 1934. The former provided that appeals to the House of Lords be by leave only; the latter provided that an appeal from a County Court lay to the Court of Appeal on any point of law or equity, or upon the admission or rejection of any evidence; save that there should be no appeal without the leave of the judge where the subject matter in dispute was below £20.

The Evershed Report

1–041 The restriction on two levels of appeals did not satisfy the voices of disquiet and the increasing belief that appeals were still leading to too much expense and delay. Again a committee was set up, under Sir Raymond Evershed. Its terms of reference, dated April 22, 1947, required the committee to consider whether any and if so what modifications should be made in respect of the rights of appeal to, from or within the Supreme Court. The committee reported in 1953.[97]

The report noted that about 600 appeals were heard by the Court of Appeal, about 400 of which came from the High Court. About 5 per cent then went to the House of Lords. The committee declined to limit the right to appeal decisions of fact, on the basis that it would not be possible precisely to explain the threshold for obtaining an appeal; as opposed to interlocutory appeals, where the test could be more simply whether or not there was an issue of principle at stake. In any event, they thought a judge would find it difficult to evaluate whether or not to give permission to appeal against his own decision of fact.

In relation to procedure, they recommended that orders 39 (motions for new trials) and 58 (appeals) be combined into one order. There was no requirement for the appellant to give the Court or the respondent any idea of the basis of the appeal—unless the appeal was brought under Ord.39 by way of motion for a new trial. They did recommend, however, reforming

---

[97] *Final Report of the Committee on Supreme Court Practice and Procedure* (1953) Cmd.8878 under Sir Raymond Evershed M.R.

notices of appeal so that they had to include the findings of fact or issues of law raised by the appeal, and setting out the precise order sought. These reforms were put in hand by amendments to the Rules of the Supreme Court.

At that time, the Court of Appeal did no pre-reading and counsel read to them the relevant documents, which took a great deal of time. In relation to judicial pre-reading, they were unconvinced that it would always lead to saving money—in particular, in appeals from County Courts the judges would probably have to be taken through the notes and evidence to explain them. They noted the "brief" system in the US, which could save court time, but had found "singularly little enthusiasm for it". They declined to recommend it, because they thought that: **1–042**

(1) the English procedure would be more likely to lead to common decisions, as opposed to dissenting ones;
(2) it led to a quicker decision;
(3) it would increase counsels' fees.

They recommended instead that the notice of appeal should have a statement specifying the documents and parts of evidence that counsel thought relevant, and the Court would then decide whether to pre-read. The Court of Appeal should have discretion whether or not to read reserved judgments. They also recommended that the Court of Appeal be given power to review the amount of damages awarded.

The committee recommended a leap frog appeal: this was enacted by the Administration of Justice Act 1969. See para 18–006 to 18–010.

In relation to the County Courts, the committee said that "[t]he question **1–043** of appeals from County Courts has proved to be one of obstinate difficulty and has given rise to a remarkable diversity of view amongst the witnesses whose opinions are sought".[98] The committee recommended an absolute right of appeal on cases worth more than £100, to remove the anomaly in cases which could be commenced in the High Court. County Court Judges would have to undertake the burden of making a sufficient note of the evidence for the purposes of the Court of Appeal.

It has been argued that the Evershed report failed to recommend wider reform in part because, although the case for reform was overwhelming, the Bar succeeded in resisting reform because it was easier to argue an appeal by oral process, without any written arguments, and the Court of Appeal judges liked the fact that they did not have to pre-read.[99] In due course change came about, but it was not until after Lord Denning had retired as Master of the Rolls.

---

[98] *Final Report of the Committee on Supreme Court Practice and Procedure* (1953) Cmd.8878 under Sir Raymond Evershed M.R., p.179.
[99] Gavin Drewry, Louis Blom-Cooper and Charles Blake, *The Court of Appeal* (2007), p.37.

Changes in procedure in the Court of Appeal

1–044   Under Lord Denning, who was Master of the Rolls from 1962 to 1982, the Court of Appeal had virtually no administrative staff. There was no registrar or central listing organisation. There were no skeleton arguments and the Court did little or no pre-reading. Counsel would read out relevant documents and passages from relevant authorities.[100] The life of the judge was still busy, trying to find time between busy sitting schedules to write reserved judgments, but not as hectic as it was later to become. Sir Michael Kerr described the work of the Court of Appeal as "hypnotically pleasant and rewarding", but oppressed by a "black cloud of overdue unwritten judgments".[101]

When Sir John Donaldson became Master of the Rolls in 1982, administration of the Court of Appeal was improved and the number of appeals heard increased. There was a registrar, with supporting staff, introduced by the Supreme Court Act 1981.[102]

Further, the Court of Appeal introduced the requirement for written advocacy, in the form of the skeleton argument. By practice direction issued in 1983 Sir John Donaldson M.R. said that the usual practice should be for counsel to provide skeleton arguments as soon as convenient before the hearing. The skeleton argument was "a very abbreviated note of the argument"; it should "in no way usurp any part of the function of oral argument in court". Rather, the skeleton argument was "an aide memoire for convenience of reference before and during the hearing". No-one was to be inhibited from departing from their terms; but skeleton arguments saved time because they reduced or obviated the need for the judges to take a longhand note, sometimes at dictation speed, of the submissions and authorities and other documents to which counsel referred.[103] In 1985 Sir John Donaldson M.R. indicated that skeleton arguments had "amply proved their worth"; and, further, that counsel should provide a written chronology of events relating to the appeal with the skeleton argument or in any event so that it was available as soon as the appeal was called on for hearing.[104] By the date of his retirement in 1992, the skeleton argument had become a document of primary importance in the advocacy in support of an appeal.

---

[100] Drewry, Blom-Cooper and Blake, *The Court of Appeal*, 2007, pp.37–38.
[101] Michael Kerr, *As Far As I Remember* (Hart Publishing, 2006), pp.316–317.
[102] Now Senior Courts Act 1981. This innovation was recommended by an unpublished report of a working party on the Court of Appeal chaired by Lord Scarman: Gavin Drewry, Louis Blom-Cooper and Charles Blake, *The Court of Appeal* (2007), p.52.
[103] *Practice Note (Court of Appeal: Skeleton Arguments)* [1983] 1 W.L.R. 1055.
[104] *Practice Note (Court of Appeal: Chronologies of Events)* [1985] 1 W.L.R. 1156.

THE WOOLF AND BOWMAN REPORTS

Lord Woolf, Master of the Rolls from 1996 to 2000, published his report   **1–045**
"Access to Justice" in 1995–1996 with the aim of simplifying and speeding
up civil procedure, reducing costs and improving access to justice. His
reforms were enacted in 1999 by the Access to Justice Act 1999 and the
Civil Procedure Rules, issued in 1999. Lord Woolf's reforms were not
predominantly concerned with appeals, but they did bring in widespread
changes in nomenclature, and encouraged judicial management of the
procedure for each case. The reforms undoubtedly assisted in speeding up
the time it took to hear and decide a case, though they probably increased
costs even more, and therefore reduced access to justice for all but the
richest of litigants.[105]

In 1996 Sir Jeffrey Bowman was asked to conduct a review of the Court
of Appeal (Civil Division), and he reported in November 1997. His suggestions, which were enacted in the Access to Justice Act 1999 and the
Access to Justice Act 1999 (Destination of Appeals) Order 2000, and by
amendments to Pt 52 of the CPR, affected the whole appellate structure
(save for the House of Lords), and were not limited to the Court of Appeal.

The Bowman report analysed appeals as having two different kinds of
rationale: private and public. The private purpose of appeals is to correct an
unjust result in particular case. The public purposes are to ensure public
confidence in the administration of justice; clarify and develop law, practice
and procedure; and help maintain standards at first instance. Relying upon
this analysis, and the principle of proportionality underlying the Civil
Procedure Rules, Bowman recommended that a party should not be entitled
to an appeal automatically, but only if a review indicated that there might
have been an injustice.[106]

Bowman's innovations were to require nearly all appellants first to obtain
permission to appeal; to introduce the principle that generally appeals were
to be heard by a judge on the next rung up of judicial seniority[107]; and to
limit second appeals to those raising important points of principle or
practice. Further, appeals were generally to be limited to reviews, so that
appeals from masters and district judges on matters of procedures were not
"*rehearings*" to be argued *de novo*, but reviews of whether or not the
original decision was wrong.

---

[105] This conclusion represents the broad consensus of speakers at a conference organised by
Oxford University on December 1 and 2, 2008 to discuss the first 10 years of the CPR. In
an article in the New Law Journal, March 13, 2009, "*Zander on Woolf*", Professor
Michael Zander QC quotes, with approval, Judge Michael Cook: "The idea of the Civil
Procedure Rules...was to cut the costs of civil litigation. But the scheme has been spec-
tacularly unsuccessful in achieving its aims of bringing control, certainty and
transparency."
[106] There is a helpful summary of the Bowman report at para.52.0.4 of the *White Book* 2010.
[107] The principle exception to this is in relation to final decisions in cases heard on the "multi-
track" in County Courts, which go to the Court of Appeal.

It is difficult to say whether the Bowman reforms have reduced appeals, or saved costs, because the lower court statistics are quite unreliable.[108] However they undoubtedly simplified appellate procedure, and harmonised the approaches of different courts to appeals.

THE SUPREME COURT

1–046   The Bowman reforms did not consider the House of Lords. Despite its long history in this role, the House of Lords, as an appellate court, came to an end in an extraordinary and abrupt manner. If the House of Lords had survived as an appellate court at the end of the 19th century due to politics, in the form of a successful rearguard conservative defence of the status quo, in the 21st century it was ditched and replaced by the Supreme Court in the wake of a messy cabinet reshuffle, in which the Prime Minister, Mr Tony Blair, removed his longstanding friend and mentor, Lord Irvine, from the position of Lord Chancellor.

The story is the more surprising given that in January 2000 a Royal Commission on the future of the House of Lords had recommended no reforms to the judicial practice of the House of Lords.[109] Consistent with this on April 2, 2003 the Lord Chancellor, Lord Irvine, said that there were no plans for a Supreme Court building; the old system worked well and should not be interfered with unless it was sure to achieve a better result.[110]

However, perhaps sensing a change in the air, on June 5, 2003 Lord Irvine asked Mr Blair whether there was any truth in newspaper stories that he was in fact considering the abolition of the office of Lord Chancellor. Mr Blair told him that there was. Lord Irvine expressed surprise that such a change could be considered without consultation, and thought it equally surprising that Mr Blair appeared to have no constitutional appreciation of the importance of such a step.[111]

On June 9, 2003 Mr Blair was considering appointing Mr Peter Hain to act as Secretary of State for Constitutional Affairs, and abolishing the office of Lord Chancellor as soon as possible; there would be an interim Lord

---

[108] *Should the Civil Courts be Unified?*, Sir Henry Brooke, Annex J. In relation to County Court statistics, HHJ Paul Collins CBE commented in his annual report on the state of civil justice in the London county courts 2006–2007: "The published statistics cannot be relied upon for any practical purpose": see p.4 of *http://www.hmcourts-service.gov.uk/docs/ annualreports_county06_07/Central-London-Civil-Annual-Report-2006-2007.pdf*

[109] *A House for the Future*, Cmd.4543.

[110] Cited in Andrew Le Sueur, "From Appellate Committee to Supreme Court: A Narrative" in Blom-Cooper, Dickson and Drewry (eds), *The Judicial House of Lords 1876–2009* (OUP, 2009), p.65.

[111] Evidence from Lord Irvine of Lairg to the House of Lords Select Committee on the Constitution, October 26, 2009, para.8: *http://www.parliament.uk/documents/upload/ ConstLordIrvineofLairg.pdf*

Chancellor with the status of a junior minister.[112] Lord Irvine advised Mr Blair to take the opportunity to create a Ministry of Justice.

Mr Blair accepted Lord Irvine's advice to create a Ministry of Justice, but appointed Lord Falconer as Secretary of State. On June 12, 2003 it was announced that Lord Irvine was retiring; that the House of Lords would be replaced, in its judicial form, by a Supreme Court; and the office of the Lord Chancellor would be abolished.

There was and to a certain degree remains considerable disquiet about the manner in which the reforms had been proclaimed.[113] A majority of the sitting Law Lords was against a new Supreme Court, Lord Hoffmann commenting in the House of Lords that it was "sad that a great constitutional change should be adopted as a quick fix for personal squabbles in the Cabinet".[114] Lord Neuberger suggested that the Supreme Court had been created pursuant to "a last-minute decision over a glass of whisky".[115]

1–047

Lord Woolf was concerned that the change was one of form only, since it would still be subordinate to the will of Parliament, and would have no jurisdiction over Scottish criminal appeals.[116] There was widespread concern about the premises in which the Supreme Court would be housed.

The Constitutional Reform Act 2005 passed into law on March 24, 2005, and on the completion of the renovation of the old Middlesex Crown Court into premises suitable for the Supreme Court, the judicial functions of the House of Lords were transferred to the Supreme Court. According to Lord Woolf, the change is largely symbolic, since the ambit of the powers of the Supreme Court is unchanged from that enjoyed by the House of Lords.[117] Lord Neuberger, however, has suggested that it is difficult to predict how the Supreme Court might develop its powers freed from the constitutional baggage of sitting in the House of Lords. It is a concern,

---

[112] Evidence from Lord Irvine of Lairg to the House of Lords Select Committee on the Constitution, October 26, 2009, para.10 *http://www.parliament.uk/documents/upload/ConstLordIrvineofLairg.pdf*.

[113] "I think that it is completely disgraceful that a constitutional position and constitutional office should suddenly be abolished at the whim of a Prime Minister. All other constitutions have checks and balances in them. How dare he treat this House with such contempt? ...How dare he behave as he has? We live in a parliamentary democracy. We live in a democracy honed by centuries of checks and balances. We cannot have arbitrary government, but this is arbitrary government at its absolute worst.": The Earl of Onslow, *Hansard* HL Vol.649, col.437–438 (June 12, 2003).

[114] *Hansard* HL Vol.657, col.1259, cited in Andrew Le Sueur, "From Appellate Committee to Supreme Court: A Narrative" in Blom-Cooper, Dickson and Drewry (eds) *The Judicial House of Lords 1876–2009* (OUP, 2009), p.65.

[115] Lord Neuberger talking on Radio 4's "Top Dogs: Britain's New Supreme Court", September 8, 2009; *http://news.bbc.co.uk/1/hi/uk/8237855.stm*.

[116] "Among the Supreme Courts of the world, our Supreme Court will, because of its more limited role, be a poor relation. We will be exchanging a first class Final Court of Appeal for a second class Supreme Court.": Lord Woolf, *The Pursuit of Justice* (OUP, 2008), p.126.

[117] Lord Woolf, *The Pursuit of Justice*, 2008, p.126.

perhaps, that "one unintended consequence of the Supreme Court's creation might be the eventual emergence of a constitutional court".[118]

One undoubted practical improvement is that the Supreme Court is now
housed in magnificent surroundings. Opening in October 2009, directly
opposite the Houses of Parliament in Westminster, the old Middlesex
Guildhall has been sympathetically restored and developed into a fine, well
equipped building with three courts and ample facilities for lawyers and
members of the public.

CONCLUSION

1–048   With the benefit of centuries of experience, it is now possible to understand
that a coherent system of judicial appeals brings a number of important
benefits: avoiding injustice in particular cases; developing court procedure;
and clarifying the law. But the more appeals, the greater the expense for
individual litigants; the longer a dispute may take to be finally determined;
and the greater the potential for contradictory decisions. A system of
appeals needs to balance the benefits of appeals against the perennial
problems of cost, delay and uncertainty.

Despite many attempts to limit the number and costs of appeals, it is still
possible for a case to have no fewer than three appeals. Despite many
attempts to simplify procedure, the procedure applying to appeals still
differs between the Senior Courts and the Supreme Court.

The development of the appellate system of the courts of England and
Wales has been marked by many centuries of slow development punctuated
by legislation, sometimes haphazard, often politically rather than theoretically inspired, leaving the detail to be worked through by the courts on a
case by case basis. That the judgments of those appellate courts remain
cited throughout the commonwealth is testimony to the calibre of the
judges who have sat in those courts, rather than the manner in which the
structure of and statutory basis for the courts has developed.

---

[118] Lord Neuberger "Supreme Court: Is the House of Lords 'Losing Part of Itself'?", December
2, 2009, para.23: *http://www.judiciary.gov.uk/docs/speeches/mr-supreme-court-lecture-
dec-2009.pdf*

PART 2

General Principles

CHAPTER 2

Jurisdiction and Powers on Appeal

INTRODUCTION

As Chapter 1 shows, there is no general, free-standing, or implied right to appeal. In the absence of an express source of a right to appeal, a decision of a court or tribunal is final. A right of appeal can only be granted by statute or with statutory authority. Neither the superior nor inferior tribunal, nor both combined, can create a right of appeal.[1]

2–001

JURISDICTION OF THE SUPREME COURT

The Supreme Court was established by s.23 of the Constitutional Reform Act 2005. By s.40 it is a superior court of record, so it will be presumed that it acts within its jurisdiction unless the contrary should appear either on the face of the proceedings or otherwise.[2] See para.18–004.

2–002

By s.40(2) of the Constitutional Reform Act 2005, an appeal lies from any order or judgment of the Court of Appeal in England and Wales in civil proceedings, though only, by s.40(6), with the permission of the Court of Appeal or the Supreme Court. The Supreme Court also has jurisdiction to hear appeals from the High Court under the leapfrog procedure, pursuant to Pt II of the Administration of Justice Act 1969. See paras 18–006 to 18–010.

By s.40(5) the Supreme Court has power to determine any question necessary to be determined for the purposes of doing justice to it under any enactment.

---

[1] *Att Gen v Sillem* (1864) 10 H.L. Cas. 704.
[2] *R. v Chancellor of St Edmundsbury and Ipswich Diocese Ex p. White* [1948] 1 K.B. 195 at 206, per Wrottesley L.J. On the distinction between superior and inferior courts, see *Halsbury's Laws of England* Vol.10 (Reissue) Courts, para.309.

JURISDICTION OF THE COURT OF APPEAL

2–003   The Court of Appeal is, by s.15 of the Senior Courts Act 1981, also a superior court of record. The Court of Appeal has all such jurisdiction (whether civil or criminal) as is conferred on it by statute; and all such other jurisdiction (whether civil or criminal) as was exercisable by it immediately before the commencement of the Senior Courts Act 1981. For all purposes of or incidental to the hearing and determination of any appeal to the civil division of the Court of Appeal, and the amendment, execution and enforcement of any judgment or order made on such an appeal, the Court of Appeal has all the authority and jurisdiction of the court or tribunal from which the appeal was brought.[3]

Section 81 of the County Courts Act 1984 provides that the Court of Appeal may draw any inference of fact and order a new trial on such terms as the court thinks just, or order judgment to be entered for any party, or make a final or other order on such terms as the court thinks proper to ensure the determination on the merits of the real question in controversy between the parties. This provision clarifies the powers of the Court of Appeal on appeals from County Courts as previously appeals on points of fact had been restricted.

The jurisdiction of the Court of Appeal is exclusively appellate and this cannot and should not be evaded.[4] However, in very unusual circumstances the judges of the Court of Appeal may be persuaded to hear a new issue or claim by sitting as a court of first instance.[5]

APPEALS FROM THE HIGH COURT TO THE COURT OF APPEAL

2–004   Section 16 of the Senior Courts Act 1981, as amended, confers jurisdiction on the Court of Appeal to hear appeals from the High Court to the Court of Appeal, subject to two provisos.[6]

> "(1) Subject as otherwise provided by this or any other Act (and in particular to the provision in s.13(2)(a) of the Administration of Justice Act 1969 excluding appeals to the Court of Appeal in cases where leave to appeal from the High Court directly to the [Supreme Court] is granted under Part II of that Act), [or as provided by any order made by the Lord Chancellor under section 56(1) of the Access to Justice Act

---

[3] Senior Courts Act 1981 s.15.

[4] *R. v Secretary of state for Trade and Industry Ex p. Eastway* [2001] 1 All E.R. 27.

[5] *Farley v Child Support Agency* [2005] EWCA Civ 869; [2006] C.P. Rep. 4.

[6] The section is based upon the Supreme Court of Judicature (Consolidation) Act 1925 s.27(1).

1999,] the Court of Appeal shall have jurisdiction to hear and determine appeals from any judgment or order of the High Court.

(2) An appeal from a judgment or order of the High Court when acting as a prize court shall not be to the Court of Appeal, but shall be to Her Majesty in Council in accordance with the Prize Acts 1864 to 1944."

The first proviso is that it is subject to contrary provision in any other Act; in particular, leapfrog appeals to the Supreme Court: see paras 13–039 to 13–042 and 18–006 to 18–010.

The second proviso is that the right of appeal to the Court of Appeal is subject to any order made under s.56(1) of the Access to Justice Act 1999. Under that section the Lord Chancellor may by order provide that appeals which would otherwise lie to the County Court, the High Court, or the Court of Appeal, shall instead lie to another of those courts. That section does not permit the Lord Chancellor to remove a right of appeal, nor to grant one where none exists otherwise[7]; merely to make that appeal lie to a different court.

Section 16(2) introduces a third and somewhat arcane proviso: appeals from the High Court sitting as a prize court shall lie to Her Majesty in Council.[8-9]

Section 16 of the Senior Courts Act therefore grants a very widely expressed right of appeal from the High Court to the Court of Appeal. It is, however, subject to the restrictions in s.18, considered below. They are a mixture of specific and general exceptions. It is important to note that they are not limited to restrictions on appeals to the Court of Appeal from the High Court: some of them are restrictions on appeals to the Court of Appeal, wherever they might come from.

APPEALS FROM THE COUNTY COURTS

The general rule is that appeals lie from the High Court to the Court of   **2–005**
Appeal. Appeals from the County Court may also proceed to the Court of Appeal, but it is more likely that it will lie to the High Court. The destination of appeals has been simplified and clarified recently, so that generally speaking an appeal will be to the next level of judge: see Chapter 12. But it may be necessary on occasion to consider in more detail the statutory basis of appeals from County Courts.

Section 77 of the County Court Act 1984 provides that:

---

[7] *Westminster City Council v O'Reilly* [2004] 1 W.L.R. 195 at [9].
[8-9] It is not entirely clear that this provision is strictly necessary. S.5 of the Naval Prize Act 1864 expressly provides that an appeal shall lie to Her Majesty in Council from any order or decree of a prize court, and it seems that appeals from a prize court would therefore caught within the first proviso in s.16(1) of the SCA 1981.

> "... if any party to any proceedings in the county court is dissatisfied with the determination of the judge or jury, he may appeal from it to the Court of Appeal in such manner and subject to such conditions as may be provided by Civil Procedure Rules."

But this general rule is subject to a large number of exceptions. The general right in s.77(1) is subject:

(a) to the provisions of the balance of section 77, of which there are essentially two:

    (i) section 77(6) which says that the section does not confer a right of appeal on any question of fact in proceedings for the possession of premises in cases where the court can only grant permission on being satisfied that it is reasonable to grant possession; and

    (ii) section 77(7) which says that section 77 does not confer any right of appeal where a right of appeal is conferred by some other enactment, does not take away any right of appeal where a right of appeal is so conferred; and shall have effect subject to any enactment other than the County Court Act

(b) to the other provisions in Part IV of the County Courts Act, and
(c) to any order made by the Lord Chancellor under section 56(1) of the Access to Justice Act 1999.

As already stated, and as explained in Chapter 12, by virtue of rules made under s.56(1) of the Access to Justice Act, most appeals from the County Court go to the High Court, or, if they are a decision of a district judge, to a County Court judge.

There is a difference between the wording of the statutory provisions which provide the basic source of the right of appeal from the High Court and from the County Courts. The High Court provision, shorn of exceptions and provisos, is that "the Court of Appeal may hear and determine appeals from any judgment or order of the High Court". The County Court provision is that "if any party to the proceedings in the county court is dissatisfied with the determination ... he may appeal from it to the Court of Appeal". The difference may be of significance in relation to non-parties who seek to appeal.[10]

---

[10] See paras 2–021 to 2–022 and Ch.9.

POWERS OF THE APPELLATE COURTS UNDER THE CIVIL PROCEDURE RULES

CPR r.52.10 is the main source for powers of appellate courts under the Civil Procedure Rules. It confirms that appellate courts have all the powers of the lower court.   2–006

> "(1) In relation to an appeal the appeal court has all the powers of the lower court.
>
> (Rule 52.1(4) provides that this Part is subject to any enactment that sets out special provisions with regard to any particular category of appeal—where such an enactment gives a statutory power to a tribunal, person or other body it may be the case that the appeal court may not exercise that power on an appeal)
>
> (2) The appeal court has power to—
>
>   (a) affirm, set aside or vary any order or judgment made or given by the lower court;
>
>   (b) refer any claim or issue for determination by the lower court;
>
>   (c) order a new trial or hearing;
>
>   (d) make orders for the payment of interest;
>
>   (e) make a costs order.
>
> (3) In an appeal from a claim tried with a jury the Court of Appeal may, instead of ordering a new trial—
>
>   (a) make an order for damages; or
>
>   (b) vary an award of damages made by the jury.
>
> (4) The appeal court may exercise its powers in relation to the whole or part of an order of the lower court."

RESTRICTIONS ON APPEALS TO THE COURT OF APPEAL UNDER SECTION 18 OF THE SENIOR COURTS ACT

Section 18(1) of the Senior Courts Act 1981 (as amended) provides that no appeal shall lie to the Court of Appeal in each of six circumstances. Two of those apply only in family proceedings and are beyond the scope of this work. The other four require comment. It is important to note that two of them impose restrictions that apply to appeals to the Court of Appeal wherever the appeal comes from.   2–007

Criminal cause or matter

2–008   Criminal appeals proceed generally to the Court of Appeal (Criminal Division). Criminal appeals are, of course, outside the ambit of this book, and what follows is concerned only with the relationship between criminal causes or matters and the jurisdiction of the Court of Appeal (Civil Division).

Section 18(1)(a) of the Senior Courts Act 1981 provides that no appeal shall lie to the Court of Appeal (Civil Division) "except as provided by the Administration of Justice Act 1960, from any judgment of the High Court in any criminal cause or matter".

What constitutes a judgment of the High Court in any criminal cause or matter? The words have been widely construed, with the emphasis on underlying substance rather than procedural technicalities.

The leading case is *Amand v Secretary of State for Home Affairs*.[11] A subject of the Netherlands residing in England was arrested, on the grounds that he was an absentee without leave from the Netherlands army, so that he could be handed over to the Netherlands authorities. He sought habeas corpus and the Divisional Court refused his application. The question for the House of Lords was whether that refusal was a judgment made in a criminal cause or matter, in which case it could not be appealed. The House of Lords held that it was a criminal cause or matter. Viscount Simon L.C. said, at 156, that, "[i]t is the nature and character of the proceeding in which habeas corpus is sought which provide the test. If the matter is one the direct outcome of which may be trial of the applicant and his possible punishment for an alleged offence by a court claiming jurisdiction to do so, the matter is criminal."[12] Lord Wright said that the principle was that "if the cause or matter is one which, if carried to its conclusion, might result in the conviction of the person charged and in a sentence of some punishment, such as imprisonment or fine, it is 'a criminal cause or matter' ".[13]

Accordingly, the Court should look "not to the particular order under appeal, but to the underlying proceedings in which the order was made, and those are the proceedings which have to be characterised as either criminal or non-criminal".[14]

2–009   The importance of identifying the underlying substance of the proceedings was emphasised in *R. (SW Yorkshire Mental Health NHS Trust) v Bradford Crown Court*.[15] A was found by the jury in a Crown Court trial to be unfit to stand trial, and subsequently found by another jury to have committed the act as charged. The Crown Court judge ordered A's

---

[11] [1943] A.C. 147.
[12] [1943] A.C. 147 at 156. This second sentence has been held to be an example, not a definition: per Lord Hoffmann in *Government of the United States of America v Montgomery* [2001] 1 W.L.R. 196 at [17].
[13] [1943] A.C. 147 at 162.
[14] *Day v Grant (Note)* [1987] Q.B. 972 at 976, per Sir John Donaldson M.R.
[15] [2004] 1 W.L.R. 1664. See also *R. (on the application of Mehmet) v Miskin, Cynon Valley & Merthyr Tydfill Justices* [2002] EWCA Civ 1248.

detention in hospital but made his order under the wrong legislation. The NHS trust applied by way of judicial review to quash that order. On the judicial review application the court quashed the order and remitted the matter for a Crown Court judge to make an order under the correct legislation. The NHS trust appealed from the Administrative Court to the Court of Appeal. The Court of Appeal held it had no jurisdiction because the appeal was an appeal in a "criminal cause or matter".

It is not necessary for the underlying criminal proceedings to have been commenced: an order or a refusal of an on order under Sch.1 to the Police and Criminal Evidence Act 1984 relating to excluded or special procedure material is made in a criminal context in aid of a criminal investigation. Hence, despite the fact that no proceedings have begun, any such order is made in a criminal cause or matter.[16]

In *R. (Aru) v Chief Constable of Merseyside Police*[17] the Court of Appeal held that where the issuing of a caution had been challenged by way of judicial review in the Administrative Division of the High Court, there was no appeal to the Court of Appeal because the Administrative Court decision related to a criminal cause or matter. The Court of Appeal (per Maurice Kay L.J.) suggested that the effective absence of an appeal (save where a point of law of public importance could go direct to the House of Lords) might be regrettable, and suggested that consideration be given to amending legislation permitting an appellate route from a criminal cause or matter in the Administrative Court to the Court of Appeal Criminal Division.

Despite the wide meaning given to "criminal cause or matter", the line   **2–010** has been drawn so that restraint and confiscation orders fall outside that definition. Hence an order made under Pt VI of the Criminal Justice Act 1988, albeit granted in consequence of criminal proceedings, was "essentially civil in character".[18]

Proceedings relating to anti-social behaviour orders also fall outside the s.18(1)(a) limitation, because no criminal offence need be established, no penalty ensues (unless and until they are breached) and the order does not go on the person's criminal record.[19]

Section 18(1)(a) applies to a judgment of the High Court, rather than a judgment or order of the High Court. But in *USA v Montgomery*[20] the House of Lords rejected a submission that the exception did not apply to orders. Although in civil proceedings there is a distinction between judgments and orders, the distinction is impossible to transpose into criminal proceedings, and s.18(1)(a) and its statutory predecessors had been

---

[16] *Carr v Atkins* [1987] Q.B. 963.

[17] [2004] 1 W.L.R. 1697.

[18] *Gov of USA v Montgomery* [2001] 1 W.L.R. 196; *In Re O (restraint Orders: Disclosure of Assts)* [1991] 2 Q.B. 520.

[19] *R. (McCann) v Manchester Crown Court* [2003] 1 A.C. 787.

[20] [2001] 1 W.L.R. 196.

"uniformly interpreted as applying generally to all orders made in a criminal cause or matter".[21]

Extensions of time for appealing

2–011   By section 18(1)(b) of the Senior Courts Act 1981 no appeal shall lie to the Court of Appeal from any order of the High Court or any other court or tribunal allowing an extension of time for appealing from a judgment or order. The Court of Appeal does however, have jurisdiction to hear an appeal against a refusal of an extension of time for appealing to the court below.[22]

No appeal from "final" decisions

2–012   Section 18(1)(c) of the Senior Courts Act 1981 provides that "no appeal shall lie to the Court of Appeal from any order, judgment or decision of the High Court or any other court or tribunal which by virtue of any provision (however expressed) of this or any other Act, is final".

The principle example of a "final" decision of the High Court comes from s.28A of the Senior Courts Act 1981. Section 28A provides that, where the High Court gives a decision on an appeal by way of a case stated by a magistrates' court under s.11 of the Magistrates' Courts Act 1980 or by the Crown Court under s.28(1) of the Senior Courts Act 1981, then "except as provided by the AJA 1960 (right of appeal to House of Lords in criminal cases) a decision of the High Court under this section is final".

The prohibition imposed by s.18(1)(c) applies to appeals on a point of law as much to appeals on points of fact.[23]

In exceptional circumstances the Court of Appeal has been prepared to take unusual procedural steps in order to overcome the restriction on appeals to the Court of Appeal from a case stated by the magistrates' court to the High Court. In *Farley v Child Support Agency*[24] the North Somerset Magistrates' Court made a liability order against Mr Farley under the Child Support Act. Mr Farley appealed to the High Court by way of case stated, and his appeal was dismissed. The Court of Appeal granted leave and then allowed the appeal—despite having no jurisdiction to do so. The House of Lords indicated its willingness to accept a further appeal. It was then realised that the Court of Appeal had had no jurisdiction to allow the appeal in the first place, and the matter was brought back to the Court of Appeal.

---

[21] [2001] 1 W.L.R. 196 at [13].
[22] *Rickards v Rickards* [1990] Fam 194; *Foenander v Bond Lewis & Co (A Firm)* [2002] 1 W.L.R. 525.
[23] *In Re Racal Communications Ltd* [1981] A.C. 374; *Maile v Manchester City Council* [1998] COD 19; *Westminster City Council v O'Reilly* [2004] 1 W.L.R. 195.
[24] [2005] EWCA Civ 869; [2006] C.P. Rep. 4. The House of Lords allowed the appeal: [2006] 1 W.L.R. 1817.

The Court of Appeal, having held that indeed the court had not had jurisdiction to allow the appeal, decided, with the consent of the parties, (a) to accept an undertaking by Mr Farley to apply for judicial review (rather than appealing by way of case stated), (b) to dispense with any procedural requirements as to the form of the application, (c) to sit, there and then, as a court of first instance and dismiss the application, but (d) to give permission to appeal, and (e) then to reconstitute itself as an appellate court and allow the appeal, giving a declaration in the same terms as the appeal that had been heard without jurisdiction.

Other examples of decisions which are expressed to be final, in whole or in part, are: decisions of the Lands Tribunal, which are final save as to errors in point of law[25]; and a decision of the High Court on an appeal from the committee of the Council for Licensed Conveyancers.[26]

ARBITRATION APPEALS

Section 18(1)(g) of the Senior Courts Act 1981 provides that no appeal shall lie to the Court of Appeal, except as provided by Pt I of the Arbitration Act 1996, from any decision of the High Court under that Part.[27]   **2–013**

GENERAL PROHIBITION ON APPEALS AGAINST DECISIONS GRANTING OR REFUSING PERMISSION TO APPEAL

Section 54(4) of the Access to Justice Act 1999 provides that no appeal may be made against a decision of a court to give or refuse permission to appeal. The reasons for this provision are obvious. First, the cost and time benefits of limiting hopeless appeals would be undermined if a dissatisfied party could appeal against the refusal of permission to appeal. Secondly, if an appellant has been granted permission to appeal, since the appeal itself still has to be determined, there is no need for a dissatisfied respondent to be able to appeal against the grant of permission.   **2–014**

CONTRACTING IN AND OUT OF APPEALS

Parties cannot contract into a judicial right of appeal which is not otherwise available. They can however contract out of rights of appeal they would otherwise have. The precise circumstances in which an agreement not to   **2–015**

---

[25] Land Tribunal Act 1949 s.3(2).
[26] Administration of Justice Act 1985 s.26(7).
[27] See Part 5 for appeals from arbitration awards.

appeal can be effective is clear in relation to appeals from the County Court, but unclear in relation to appeals from the High Court. It is therefore convenient to begin with the County Court position.

Contracting out of the right of appeal: County Court proceedings

2–016   By s.79 of the County Courts Act 1984, the parties may in effect contract out of the right of appeal before judgment is given: no appeal lies from the judgment, decision or order of a judge of the County Courts if, before the judgment, direction, order or decision was given or made, the parties had agreed, in writing signed by themselves or their legal representatives or agents, that it should be final.[28]

It is highly unusual for parties to take advantage of this right.

It is unclear what the position would be if the parties had agreed there should be no appeal but a non-party wished to exercise a right of appeal it would otherwise have had.[29] Although it might seem strange that the agreement of others should affect a non-party's right to appeal, the wording of s.79 of the County Courts Act is that "no appeal shall lie" in those circumstances, and it might be argued that that wording goes wider than simply preventing the parties to that agreement from appealing.

Contracting out of the right of appeal: High Court Proceedings

2–017   There is no statutory provision applicable to appeals from the High Court which is equivalent to the county court provision in s.79 of the County Courts Act 1984, and the CPR give no indication as to the High Court position.

There is some authority that suggests that it is only where the parties' agreement not to appeal is embodied in a court order[30] that it will be enforced; but it seems unlikely that this line of authority (some of which turns on pre-Judicature Act provisions) would be regarded nowadays as entirely compelling.

If an agreement not to appeal is made before the decision against which the appeal lies is known, then both parties give good consideration to the other: each gives up a contingent right of appeal. It is submitted that there is no reason in principle why they should not be held to their agreement, whether or not that agreement is embodied in an order, if necessary by restraining a party from acting in breach of his contract.

---

[28] See also para.12–003.
[29] See also paras 2–021 to 2–022 and Ch.9.
[30] *Jones v Victoria Graving Dock Co* (1877) 2 QBD 314; *West Devon Great Consols Mine, Re* (1888) 38 Ch. D. 51; *Hull and County Bank, Trotter's Claim, Re* (1880) 13 Ch. D. 261 CA.

Contracting out of rights of appeal: arbitrations

Section 69 of the Arbitration Act 1996 provides that unless otherwise 2–018
agreed by the parties, a party to arbitral proceedings may appeal to the
court on a question of law, and further provides that an agreement to
dispense with reasons for the tribunal's award shall be considered an
agreement to exclude the court's jurisdiction under the section. See
para.21–009.

Parties to arbitral proceedings can therefore contract out of the rights of
appeal they would otherwise have either expressly, or impliedly by agreeing
to dispense with the requirement for a reasoned decision. Such an agreement would however, have to be "in writing"[31]; although "in writing"
merely means "being recorded by any means".[32]

COMPROMISING AN APPEAL

Once judgment has been given the parties are of course free to compromise 2–019
their rights of appeal. If good consideration is given, such a contract is
enforceable.[33] Compromising an appeal is dealt with in more detail in paras
7–001 to 7–008.

Where a settlement has been reached disposing of the application or
appeal, the parties may make a joint request to the court stating that (1)
none of them is a child or protected party; and (2) the appeal or application
is not from a decision of the Court of Protection, and asking that the
application or appeal be dismissed by consent. If the request is granted the
application or appeal will be dismissed.[34]

Parties and their representatives should note that if a dispute has been
settled or is likely to settle, they must inform the appellate court forthwith,
or face the wrath of the court, whether it relates to an appeal or an
application for permission to appeal. If the case has settled, the parties or
their representatives[35] must tell the court immediately, even if that is at
night or over the weekend. There is a 24 hour switchboard facility at the
Royal Courts of Justice, and the parties should use it.[36] "There is nothing
more infuriating than spending the weekend preparing Monday's case only
to be told that it had settled late on Friday."[37]

---

[31] Arbitration Act 1996 s.5(1).
[32] Arbitration Act 1996 s.5(6).
[33] *National Benzole Co Ltd v Gooch* [1961] 1 W.L.R. 1489.
[34] CPR PD 52 12.4.
[35] It is a professional obligation for the lawyers involved to notify the Court: *Yell Ltd v Garton* [2004] [2004] EWCA Civ 87; [2004] C.P. Rep.29.
[36] *Taysurdu v SSHD* [2003] EWCA Civ 447; [2003] C.P. Rep. 61.
[37] *Taysurdu v SSHD* [2003] EWCA Civ 447; [2003] C.P. Rep. 61 at [14], per Lord Phillips.

If an appeal has partially settled, the courts should inform the appellate court of that fact, and if they fail to do so, they may find that their costs are disallowed.[38]

If a case is likely to settle, the Court of Appeal has said that it is helpful if the Civil Appeals Office can be informed of this. Such information will be treated as given on a without prejudice basis, which means that the listing will not be altered until it is confirmed that the application or appeal will be withdrawn.[39]

The fact that the dispute has settled does not necessarily mean that the Court of Appeal or, probably, the Supreme Court may not entertain an appeal[40]; and, in circumstances where the parties settle the dispute in the period between receipt of the draft judgment and the handing down of judgment, the court retains a discretion to hand down judgment.[41]

NO RIGHTS OF APPEAL UNDER THE EUROPEAN CONVENTION ON HUMAN RIGHTS

2–020   The European Convention on Human Rights does not give any right of appeal in civil cases, although where a right of appeal exists, art.6 of the convention applies to it.[42]

WHO MAY APPEAL?

2–021   Any party to an action may appeal. Interested parties may in certain circumstances make submissions in relation to an appeal: see Chapter 9. But are there circumstances in which parties other than the parties to the decision of the court or tribunal below may exercise a right of appeal?

CPR r.40.9 deals with the different but related circumstances of a party applying to have the judgment set aside or varied in the following way:

> "A person who is not a party but who is directly affected by a judgment or order may apply to have the judgment or order set aside or varied."

---

[38]   *Red River UK Ltd v Sheikh* [2009] EWCA Civ 643.
[39]   *Tasyurdu v Secretary of State for the Home Department* [2003] EWCA Civ 447; [2003] C.P. Rep. 61.
[40]   See para.17–072.
[41]   *Prudential Assurance Co Ltd v McBains Cooper* [2000] 1 W.L.R. 2000. See also *Gurney Consulting Engineers v Gleeds Health & Safety Ltd* [2006] EWHC 536 (TCC); 108 Con. L.R. 58.
[42]   *R. (Aru) v Chief Constable of Merseyside Police* [2004] 1 W.L.R. 1697.

The notes to the *White Book* suggest[43] that "sometimes an application [under this rule] will take the form of an appeal, sometimes not". If this provision is sufficient to ground an appeal, it gives no guidance as to the circumstances in which a non-party may appeal, save insofar as it stipulates that the non-party must be "directly affected".

Under the Civil Procedure Rules it has been held that appeals may be brought by non-parties, because "appellant" is defined as a person who brings or seeks to bring an appeal, and is not limited to the parties to the proceedings at first instance. Further, the definition of "respondent" includes not just the parties to the proceedings at first instance affected by the appeal, other than the appellant, but also "a person who is permitted by the appeal court to be a party to the appeal". These provisions are sufficient to give rise to a power to allow non-parties to be appellants or respondents to appeal, if sufficient reason is shown.[44]

Permission to appeal will not be granted to a non-party unless it has a real interest in the appeal; it will not be granted, for example, to a "mere busybody".[45]

Although the Civil Procedure Rules are a new procedural code, some practical guidance on when a non-party may appeal may perhaps be gained from the old rules.[46]

- A person could be joined to an appeal if he had a "legal interest" in the proceedings: if there was an issue between that person and someone already a party to the proceedings in respect of which some remedy or relief in the proceedings could be claimed. But a person who had no legal interest, but was merely a person who would be affected commercially or in some other respect by the outcome of the appeal, could not be joined as a party.[47]
- A non-party could appeal if an order had been made that he should be bound by the result of the proceedings.[48]
- A non-party could appeal, although he would require leave to do so, if "he could by any possibility have been made a party to the action by service".[49]

The last (pre-CPR) occasion on which the Court of Appeal dealt with what was in substance an appeal by a non-party was in *Astro Exito Navegacion SA v Southland Enterprise Co Ltd (No.2) (Chase Manhattan Bank intervening)*.[50] It is noteworthy that it did so without reference to any   **2–022**

---

[43] Civil Procedure Rules 2010 para.40.9.1.
[44] *George Wimpey v Tewksbury BC* [2008] EWCA Civ 12; [2008] 1 W.L.R. 1649.
[45] *George Wimpey v Tewksbury BC* [2008] EWCA Civ 12; [2008] 1 W.L.R. 1649 at [24].
[46] See the *Supreme Court Practice 1999* 59/3/3 and 59/8/2.
[47] *IG Farbenindustrie AG Agreement, Re* [1944] Ch 41; *Spelling Goldberg Productions v BPC Publishing Ltd*, 1981 R.P.C. 280.
[48] *The Millwall* [1905] P. 155.
[49] *Crawcourt v Slater* (1882) 30 W.R. 329; *Hambrough's Estate, Re* [1909] 2 Ch. 620 at 625; *B, Re* [1958] 1 Q.B. 12.
[50] [1982] Q.B. 1248.

of the elderly authorities referred to in the preceding paragraph, but that is because at the time of the application by the third party there was an extant appeal, so the case was argued on the basis of the court's power to join a party to existing proceedings, rather than the ability of a third party to mount an appeal when the parties to the decision had not appealed.

In those proceedings, which were between buyers and sellers of a ship, the buyers were ordered by the first instance judge to sign a notice of readiness, which would trigger payment under a letter of credit, failing which it would be signed by a master. The buyers failed to sign, so the master signed the notice of readiness, and the buyers presented the notice of readiness and the other documents necessary to operate the letter of credit. The bank rejected the letter of credit. The buyers appealed. The buyers then applied to withdraw from the appeal (the issue between them and the sellers having become academic as a result of an arbitration award), and the bank sought to intervene, applying to be joined as a defendant so that it could pursue the appeal.

The application was made under RSC Ord.15 r.6. The Court of Appeal held that the bank fell within the wide wording of RSC Ord.15. Although a third party could only be added to existing proceedings, the buyers' application to be released from the appeal had not yet been allowed, and it did not matter that they might subsequently be allowed to withdraw. Having allowed the bank to be joined, and released the buyers from the appeal, the Court of Appeal rejected the bank's appeal. The bank's further appeal to the House of Lords[51] was rejected, and it was doubted whether, in fact, the bank had had sufficient interest to be properly joined in the first place.

As noted in para.2–005, there is a difference between the wording of the statutory provisions which provide the basic source of the right of appeal from the High Court and from the County Courts. The High Court provision is that "the Court of Appeal may hear and determine appeals from any judgment or order of the High Court". The County Court provision is that "if any party to the proceedings in the county court is dissatisfied with the determination ... he may appeal from it to the Court of Appeal". This may indicate that the Court of Appeal has no jurisdiction under the County Courts Act 1984 to hear appeals from those who were not parties to the proceedings in the county court. If so, it is tentatively suggested that the Court of Appeal has a jurisdiction under Pt 52 for the reasons set out in *George Wimpey v Tewksbury BC*.[52] See Chapter 9.

---

[51] [1983] 2 A.C. 787 HL.
[52] *George Wimpey v Tewksbury BC* [2008] EWCA Civ 12; [2009] 1 W.L.R. 1649.

ACADEMIC APPEALS

The general rule is that an appeal will not be heard if it is academic, in that   **2–023**
its result will not affect the rights or obligations of the parties.[53] This issue is
also discussed in para.17–076

Courts decide disputes between the parties between them. They do not
pronounce on abstract questions of law.

However, in *R. v Secretary of State for the Home Department Ex p
Salem*[54] it was held that the court does have jurisdiction to decide points of
public law, although that jurisdiction should be exercised with caution only
where there is good reason in the public interest to do so. A good reason
might be where a discrete point of statutory construction arose which did
not involve detailed consideration of facts and where a large number of
similar cases existed, so that the issue would most likely need to be resolved
in the near future in any event. On the facts, the House of Lords declined to
hear the appeal.

In *Bowman v Fels*[55] former cohabitees were parties to a private law
dispute concerning their respective interests in a jointly acquired home. In
the course of the proceedings the claimant's solicitors, on the basis of
documents disclosed by the defendant, made a disclosure to NCIS under the
provisions of the Proceeds of Crime Act 2002. Because of the time it would
take NCIS to respond to that disclosure, and because they took the view
that they were not permitted to inform either their client or the defendant of
the disclosure, the claimant's solicitors applied ex parte to the county court
judge to adjourn the trial. The judge granted the application. The defendant's solicitors successfully applied to the county court to set aside that
order. The claimant appealed to the Court of Appeal that part of the order
below which had directed the claimant to disclose her original application
for an adjournment and the evidence relied upon. The Court of Appeal
allowed the Bar Council, the Law Society, and NCIS, to intervene. By the
time of the appeal hearing the claimant and defendant had settled the
action.

The Court of Appeal noted that the issue at the heart of the appeal—the   **2–024**
circumstances in which lawyers were obliged to make "authorised dis-
closures" under the Act—was an issue of public law of great importance.
Brooke L.J. reviewed the authorities. Accordingly, and notwithstanding the
fact that the underlying dispute had been settled, the court was anxious to
continue hearing the appeal if it possibly could. "To send them away empty
handed on an issue of such importance seemed to be not only churlish but
also in breach of the overriding objective which illuminates all civil court
practice today."[56]

---

[53] *Sun Life Assurance Co of Canada v Jervis* [1944] A.C. 111; *Ainsbury v Millington* [1987] 1
W.L.R. 379.
[54] [1999] 1 A.C. 450.
[55] [2005] 4 All E.R. 609. See Ch.16.
[56] [2005] 4 All E.R. 609 at [10].

The court accepted a submission that "an important point of public law, involving a public authority, where there was an additional public element arising out of the court's supervisory jurisdiction in connection with solicitors, made this par excellence an appeal over which the court should assume jurisdiction". The court held that "[i]f it is in the public interest for this court to decide an important point of law arising out the interpretation of a recent statute, when both the parties to the case and three interveners of the status of those who appeared before the court are anxious that the court should do so, it is in our judgment unnecessary for the court to resort to artificial devices to found its jurisdiction".

More recently, the Court of Appeal has confirmed that the exceptional jurisdiction to decide an academic point will only by exercised where it is in the public interest. Such cases are likely to have a number of characteristics in addition to the critical requirement that an academic appeal is in the public interest. They include the necessity that all sides of the argument will be fully and properly put, with counsel being instructed by solicitors instructed by those with a real interest in the outcome of the appeal. Before giving permission the court will wish to consider what the other options are and how the proposed issues could otherwise be resolved without doing so by way of academic appeal.[57]

THE NATURE OF THE HEARING BEFORE THE APPELLATE COURT: REVIEWS AND REHEARINGS

2–025 CPR r.52.11 provides that every appeal will be limited to a review of the decision below unless (a) a practice direction makes different provision for a particular category of hearing, or (b) the court considers that in the circumstances of an individual appeal it would be in the interests of justice to hold a rehearing.

Paragraph 9.1 of the Practice Direction to Pt 52 provides that the hearing of an appeal will be a rehearing if the appeal is from the decision of a minister, person or other body and that person (1) did not hold a hearing to come to that decision, or (2) held a hearing to come to that decision, but the procedure adopted did not provide for the consideration of evidence.

A distinction without importance?

2–026 The distinction between review and rehearing is a historical one which, it is suggested, may have outlived its usefulness. The rehearing, as originally and strictly conceived, is now unknown. It arose out of the historic development of appeals in Chancery as rehearings of disputes delegated by the Lord

---

[57] *Gawler v Raettig* [2007] EWCA Civ 1560. See also *Rolls Royce v Unite* [2010] 1 W.L.R. 318.

Chancellor to the lower judges, as discussed in para.1–014, whereby an appeal was a rehearing in the sense of a "trial over again, on the evidence used in the Court below"; albeit with a power to receive new evidence.[58]

The review, on the other hand, is more recent.

> "The review is closely akin to, although not conceptually identical with, the scope of an appeal to the Court of Appeal under the former RSC. The review will engage the merits of the appeal. It will accord appropriate respect to the decision of the lower court. Appropriate respect will be tempered by the nature of the lower court and its decision making process. There will also be a spectrum of appropriate respect depending on the nature of the decision of the lower court which is challenged. At one end of the spectrum will be decisions of primary fact reached after an evaluation of oral evidence where credibility is in issue and purely discretionary decisions. Further along the spectrum will be multi-factorial decisions often dependent on inferences and an analysis of documentary material. Rule 52.11(4) expressly empowers the court to draw inferences."[59]

The importance of labelling a hearing "review" or a "rehearing" can be overstated. May L.J. has said that the idea of a "rehearing" has a range of meaning, which, at the lesser end of the range merges with that of "review". At the margin, he said, attributing one label or the other is a semantic exercise which does not answer such questions of substance as arise in any appeal.[60]

Review or rehearing on appeals from exercises of discretion

Where the decision under appeal is one relating to the exercise of discretion, or is a case management or other interlocutory decision, then the difference between a review and a rehearing is significant. Brooke L.J. has said that under the old rules, an appeal to a judge was a rehearing in the fullest sense of the word, and the judge exercised his/her discretion afresh, while giving appropriate weight to the way the lower court had exercised its discretion in the matter. Under the new practice, the decision of the lower court will attract much greater significance. The appeal court's duty is now limited to a review of that decision, and it may only interfere in the quite limited circumstances set out in CPR r.52.11(3).[61]

2–027

---

[58] Quotation from *In Re Chennell* (1878) 8 Ch. D. 492 at 505. See the discussion in *Builders Licensing Board v Sperway Constructions (Syd) Pty Ltd* [1976] HCA 62; (1976) 135 C.L.R. 616 at 620.

[59] *Dupont de Nemours v Dupont* [2006] 1 W.L.R. 2793 at [94], per May L.J.

[60] *Dupont de Nemours v Dupont* [2006] 1 W.L.R. 2793, described in *Zissis v Lukomski* [2006] 1 W.L.R. 2778 to be the leading case the distinction between reviews and rehearings.

[61] *Tanfern Ltd v Cameron-MacDonald* [2000] 1 W.L.R. 1311 at 1317, [31], per Brooke L.J.

In that context, Clarke L.J. (as he then was) has held that it is not appropriate to fetter the discretion allowed under r.52.11(1) to hold a rehearing rather than a review by laying down any general guidelines,[62] commenting that,

"a review of an exercise of a discretion is different in principle from a rehearing, at any rate if the rehearing is ... a rehearing in the fullest sense of the word, as occurred under the old RSC Order 58, rule 1. It seems to me that CPR Rule 52.11(1) empowers the appeal court to hold a rehearing of that kind if the justice of the particular case requires. It may be that the nature of the rehearing which is appropriate will itself depend upon the particular circumstances; so that there may be a difference between an appeal from a decision of this kind, involving an exercise of a discretion, and an appeal after a trial of an action. It is not, however, necessary to explore that possibility further in this case."

2–028   However, as Dyson L.J. said in the same case, there may be cases where it is difficult or impossible to decide an appeal justly without a rehearing; for example, if the judgment of the lower court is so inadequately reasoned that it is not possible for the appeal court to determine the appeal justly without a rehearing; or if there was a serious procedural irregularity in the court below so that, for example, the appellant was prevented from developing his case properly. But where the decision of the lower court is adequately reasoned and there has been no such procedural irregularity, it should usually be possible for the appeal court to determine the appeal by review and not rehearing.[63]

It has been suggested that where the decision of the lower court has been reached in the exercise of a discretion, there is a significant difference between an appeal by way of review and an appeal by way of rehearing in that whereas on a review the appeal court is limited to reviewing the decision to see whether it was wrong, a decision by the appeal court to proceed by way of rehearing frees it from such constraints and allows it to exercise the discretion afresh in circumstances where it would have been unable to do so had the appeal proceeded in the normal way, by way of review.[64] But it is suggested that first the appellant must convince the appellate court that the decision at first instance was wrong. The appellate court will then go on to consider what decision should have been made. That may require a "rehearing", in that it requires the appellate court to consider all relevant facts and matters. In this regard, May L.J. has explained that the attribution of the label "rehearing" is not, other than

[62] *Asiansky Television Plc v Bayer-Rosin* [2001] EWCA Civ 1792; [2002] C.P.L.R. 111 at [10], per Clarke L.J.
[63] *Asiansky Television Plc v Bayer-Rosin* [2001] EWCA Civ 1792; [2002] C.P.L.R. 111 at [82], per Dyson L.J.
[64] *Audergon v La Baguette Ltd* [2002] EWCA Civ 10; [2002] C.P. Rep. 27 at [85], per Jonathan Parker L.J.

exceptionally, necessary to enable the court upon a hearing by way of review to make the evaluative judgments necessary to determine whether the decision under appeal was or was not wrong.[65]

Appeals after trial

Where the appeal is in respect of judgment reached after a trial, then the distinction between review and rehearing is less significant.[66] The approach of the court is to consider the grounds of appeal by reference to general principle: for example, that the trial judge had the advantage of seeing and hearing the witnesses and assessing their credibility; the nature of the evaluation required, the standing and experience of the fact-finding judge or tribunal, and the extent to which the judge or tribunal had to assess the oral evidence. These issues are considered in more detail in Chapter 3.

2–029

---

[65] *Dupont de Nemours v Dupont* [2006] 1 W.L.R. 2793 at [97].
[66] *Assicurazioni Generali SpA v Arab Insurance Group* [2002] EWCA Civ 1642; [2003] 1 W.L.R. 577 at 583, [23], per Clarke L.J.

CHAPTER 3

Is the Decision Wrong?

INTRODUCTION

3–001   By CPR r.52.11(3), the appeal court will allow an appeal where the decision of the lower court was (a) wrong; or (b) unjust because of a serious
procedural or other irregularity in the proceedings in the lower court. The
second limb—where the decision was unjust by reason of some serious
irregularity—is addressed in Chapters 4 and 5. This chapter addresses the
first limb, which is used far more commonly used the second, pursuant to
which the appellant has to show that the decision of the lower court was
wrong.

Showing that a decision is wrong is not the same as showing that the
decision of the lower court is imperfect, or contains errors, or is difficult to
reconcile with some piece of evidence. Nor is it the same as showing that
the decision of the lower court might not be right.

What makes a decision wrong? That will depend upon the nature of the
decision.

(1) In theory, a decision about what the law is should admit only one
correct answer. It is either right or wrong.

(2) The application of a legal principle to facts, however, may be more
debatable; different judges may decide differently, without any of
those decisions necessarily being wrong.

(3) Where the decision is one of fact: what happened, when, how or
why, then it may not be possible to reach a decision which is in
some objective and verifiable sense the correct decision, because of
a lack of objective and verifiable evidence. In those circumstances,
it may be difficult to show that a decision is wrong, even though it
may not necessarily be right.

(4) Where the decision involves some exercise of judicial discretion,
then that decision will not be wrong unless the way in which the
judge exercised his discretion was itself wrong; either in some
identifiable manner, or because the result is so surprising that it
can only have arisen from an incorrect exercise of discretion.

Ascertaining whether the decision of the lower court was wrong accordingly depends upon correctly identifying the sort of decision the lower court was or perhaps should have been making. This chapter accordingly commences by attempting to define and distinguish decisions of law, decisions of fact and decisions which involve the exercise of judicial discretion.

DEFINITIONS AND DISTINCTIONS

What is a point of law?

Very often it is easy to identify a point of law. The necessary ingredients for   3–002
a tort; the legal consequences of a frustrated contract; whether a contract breaker is liable to account for profits he has made from his deliberate breach of contract; all these are legal questions. More difficult to identify are issues of application: how to decide whether particular facts satisfy a legal test. In some circumstances that may amount to a pure question of fact. In other circumstances, the manner in which the legal test is applied may be or include a question of law. In others—perhaps most—the decision will mix different questions of law and fact.

Although it may generally be easy to identify a point of law, there is no universally accepted definition of what makes a question of law. Lord Denning suggested in *British Launderers' Research Association v Borough of Hendon Rating Authority*[1] that a question of law could be identified by asking whether it required determination by a trained lawyer. If so, it was likely to be a question of law. If not, so that a layman could just as easily answer the question, it was likely to be a question of fact. This probably forms a useful, workable test. However, it has not been followed.[2]

It may also be possible to identify a question of law by working out what the answer is; if the law only allows one answer, then the question was one of law.[3] So, for example, a statutory provision should have one meaning, though the application of it may lead to different results in different factual situations. The meaning of the statutory provision is a question of law; but its application to the dispute will require the judge also to make findings of fact. It is not entirely satisfactory, however, to define a question by the nature of its answer, because the analysis may become circular.

---

[1] [1949] 1 K.B. 462 at 472.
[2] Timothy Endicott, "Questions of Law" (1998) L.Q.R. 292, 298–299.
[3] Timothy Endicott, "Questions of Law" (1998) L.Q.R. 292; *Ransom (Inspector of Taxes) v Higgs* [1974] 1 W.L.R. 1594 at 1618, per Lord Simon of Glaisdale; *Edwards v Bairstow* [1956] A.C. 14 at 36, per Lord Radcliffe.

What is a finding of fact?

3–003   The definition of a fact given in *Phipson on Evidence*[4] emphasises its cognitive or functional requirement: "Broadly it applies to whatever is the subject of perception or consciousness." A fact, for these purposes, is an act, action, event or happening or absence thereof, usually in the past but sometimes in the future, which the court must determine because it is relevant to the dispute before the court. Facts go beyond things or events. They include findings in relation to the quality or condition of a person or a thing. They include a person's state of mind. The fact may therefore be tangible or intangible. A fact may even be a negative: the absence of an act, action, condition or state of affairs.[5]

A finding of fact is usually a decision about an act, action, event, quality or condition: what happened; how it happened; when it happened; where it happened; what someone said; what they wrote; or whether it is likely or not something will happen in the future. Did the claimant and the defendant agree that the defendant should build the wall for £350? Did the defendant use his indicator before turning left? Did the claimant's agent explain to the defendant that she should obtain legal advice in relation to the mortgage? All these are questions of fact.

So, too, are the following, related questions: had the wall been built higher, would it have prevented the burglar from climbing into the garden? Did the failure of the defendant to use his indicator before turning left cause the accident, or did the pedestrian just step into the road without looking? If the defendant had obtained advice, would she have agreed to sign the mortgage deed in any event? They, however, require the judge to reach a conclusion about events which did not happen, by drawing inferences from the facts that did. These simple examples require a distinction to be drawn between findings of primary facts and findings of fact by inference.

The distinction between primary facts and inferences of fact

3–004   Primary facts are facts which are observed by witnesses and proved by oral testimony; or facts proved by the production of a thing itself, such as original documents.[6] Inferences of fact are decisions about historic or speculative facts which are not proven by direct evidence, but rather are made as a result of inferences from other facts. Identifying inferences of fact are important, because it may in some circumstances be as easy, or nearly as easy, for the appellate court to decide what inference should be drawn: see paras 3–043 to 3–045.

---

[4] 17th edn (2010), para.1–11.
[5] See the analysis of Finkelstein J. in *Jegatheeswaran v Minister for Immigration & Multicultural Affairs* [2001] FCA 865 at [55].
[6] *Metropolitan Borough of Battersea v The British Iron and Steel Research Association* [1949] 1 K.B. 434 at 471, per Denning L.J.

Distinguishing law and fact

Usually it is easy to distinguish a question of fact from a question of law.   3–005
Whether the engineer owed the building owner a duty to take reasonable
care and skill to avoid defects in the foundations of a building is a question
of law. Whether the building fell down is a question of fact. Whether it fell
down because the foundations were inadequate is a question of fact.
Whether it fell down because the foundations were not designed with the
care and skill to be expected of a reasonably competent engineer is also a
question of fact, although it requires the correct application of legal principles—that is to say, it requires the court correctly to identify and apply the
correct standard to what the engineer did.

Again, although it is usually relatively easy to distinguish law and fact,
the search for a defined distinction between a finding of fact and a finding of
law is a difficult one.

The traditional way to draw the distinction is the historical way: matters
of law are for the judge, and matters of fact are for the jury. Cross and
Harris said in *Precedent in English Law*[7] that the only definition of a
question of fact is whether or not it can be left to a jury; any other definition
is not possible, citing the decision in *Qualcast (Woverhampton) Ltd v
Haynes*.[8]

Most civil disputes have however now been decided without juries for
over a hundred years. Accordingly, any test which depends upon whether
something can be left to a jury is not a particularly useful test for modern
practitioners or judges.

Another distinction often relied upon is that a matter of fact is an issue of
fact raised on the pleadings; whereas a matter of law is some duty or
standard which it is the province of the court to apply and enforce.[9]
However, since the Civil Procedure Rules expressly allow parties to plead
issues of law as well as issues of fact,[10] it is in theory therefore no longer
sufficient for a party to rely upon the pleading of a particular issue as
determining that it is a matter of fact.

Mixed findings of fact and law

A mixed finding of fact and law is a decision which requires the judge to   3–006
apply a legal standard to the facts as he has determined them to be.[11] It may
involve the application of a not altogether precise legal standard to a
combination of features of varying importance. That falls within the class

---

[7] 4th edn (1990), p.224.
[8] [1959] A.C. 743.
[9] See *Phipson on Evidence*, 17th edn (2010), para.1–36.
[10] CPR PD 16 para.13.3. It is still quite uncommon expressly to plead law.
[11] *Designers Guild Ltd v Russell Williams (Textiles) Ltd* [2000] 1 W.L.R. 2416 at 2423, per
Lord Hoffmann. See also *Pro Sieben Media AG v Carlton UK Television Ltd* [1999] 1
W.L.R. 605; and *Norowzian v Arks Ltd (No.2)* [2000] F.S.R. 363 at 370.

of case in which an appellate court should not reverse a judge's decision unless he has erred "in principle".

The meaning of discretion

3–007   The word "discretion" is used in different ways by judges and even more widely by legal academics. If one is seeking to appeal a first instance decision, the precise meaning of the word "discretion" assumes some importance, because if a decision is properly categorised as one involving the exercise of a judge's discretion, then the appellate court is limited in its powers of review. As described in greater detail in paras 3–065 and 3–066, if a judge's decision should as a matter of law categorised as "discretionary", then the appellate court may interfere with it only in certain, circumscribed situations. In particular, it may not interfere with the decision solely on the basis that the appellate court would have exercised the discretion in a different way.

Discretion and judgment

3–008   Sometimes the word "discretion" is thought to be almost synonymous with "judgment".[12] However, the two concepts are distinct.[13]

The distinction was drawn by Swinton Thomas L.J. in *R. v Gloucestershire CC Ex p. Barry*.[14] Section 2(1) of the Chronically Sick and Disabled Persons Act 1970 requires a local authority to ascertain the "needs" of certain people before deciding the nature of the assistance with which they should be provided. The judge explained that the assessment of need was not a question of discretion, but a question of judgment. Once the needs of a particular person had been decided (by exercise of judgment), the provision of particular services was within the discretion of the local authority so that, for example, it could take into account other financial demands being made upon its services. However, that discretion as to what services should be provided was quite distinct from the first step, which was to judge the extent of the person's needs.

Discretion and findings of fact

3–009   Where the court at first instance is faced with a question of fact which is not capable of an objectively and verifiably correct answer, in that there is a

---

[12] For example, *Drury v Secretary of State for the Environment, Food and Rural Affairs* [2004] 2 All E.R. 1056 at 1068, per Ward L.J., criticised by Francis Bennion in "Judgment and discretion revisited: pedantry or substance?" [2005] P.L. 707.

[13] See the valuable article, upon which this section relies, by Francis Bennion, "Distinguishing judgment and discretion" [2000] P.L. 368.

[14] [1996] 4 All E.R. 421 at 438.

range of answers which are capable of being supported by the evidence, the first instance judge is obliged to choose between them. His decision may be described as discretionary, in that he is exercising a choice.

However, such a decision is not to be categorised as a discretionary decision but of making a finding of fact, by exercising judgment. Findings of fact are different from the exercise of judicial discretion and, as discussed further below, the tests to be applied are different. As Waller L.J. explained in *Manning v Stylianou*[15]:

> "I would like to add a few words on a point which has caused me a little concern. [Counsel for the appellant], in her skeleton seeking to direct attention as to the proper way we should approach the judge's findings of fact in this cases, has relied on a passage in the judgment of Brooke LJ in *Tanfern v Cameron-MacDonald*,[16] where Brooke LJ said:
>
> > '... the appellate court should only interfere when they consider that the judge of first instance has not merely preferred an imperfect solution which is different from an alternative imperfect solution which the Court of Appeal might or would have adopted, but has exceeded the generous ambit within which a reasonable disagreement is possible.'
>
> That judgment and the concept of 'exceeding generous ambit within which a reasonable disagreement is possible', is concerned with the exercise of discretion by the judge.... It is possible ... that practitioners are adopting 'the generous ambit' test as the proper approach the Court of Appeal should take to reviewing findings of fact, in reliance on the language used by Ward LJ in *Assicurazioni Generali SpA v Arab Insurance Group*.[17]
>
> The judgments of the court in that case, in particular the judgment of Clarke LJ ... [do] give guidance as to the role of the Court of Appeal when faced with appeals on fact. But the language of Ward LJ can sometimes be understood to equate the test applicable to the exercise of discretion with the approach of this court to findings of fact.
>
> I would emphasise that an appeal on fact is not concerned with reviewing the exercise of a judge's discretion. It is not because there is room for two views of the facts that the Court of Appeal is less inclined to interfere with the judge's conclusion as compared, for example, to his or her views on points of law. The finding of fact is a finding that, on the balance of probability, something actually existed or an event actually occurred. The deference that a court pays to a judge's findings of fact stems from the advantage that the judge may have had in the

---

[15] [2006] EWCA Civ 1655 at [19]–[20].
[16] [2000] 1 W.L.R. 1311 at [32], citing Lord Fraser of Tullybelton in *G v G (Minors: Custody Appeal)* [1985] 1 W.L.R. 647 at 652.
[17] [2003] 1 W.L.R. 577.

trial process, of seeing the witnesses, having a greater feel for the atmosphere of the trial and matters such as that. We have interfered in this case because we were in as good a position as the judge in relation to the photographs on which he founded his judgment. But what I urge practitioners to do is not to confuse the approach to reviewing an exercise of discretion with the approach to reviewing a judge's findings of fact. As I have said, I would allow the appeal for the reasons given by my Lord."

Where the question involves both facts and law, then the judge is required to exercise his judgment by applying the law to the facts as he has found them. Whilst, again, there may be more than one valid or acceptable answer, the process by which the answer is reached is not one of discretion, but judgment.

Case management, costs and discretion

3–010   Case management and costs decisions often involve the exercise of judicial discretion. When a judge decides how the case should proceed to trial, he chooses which of his powers to exercise, and in so doing exercises his discretion. When a party fails to comply with a rule of the court, the judge may have a range of different sanctions which he could reasonably impose. Selecting the sanction involves an exercise of judicial discretion. At the end of a hearing, the judge has open to him a wide range of possible and acceptable decisions about who should bear the costs of the legal fees incurred by the parties. The rules applying to appeals from case management decisions (including costs) accordingly involve similar criteria from those applying to appeals from exercises of judicial discretion which do not involve case management decisions.

Discretion and law

3–011   The word "discretion" is frequently used in jurisprudence to describe the element of flexibility that is apparent and almost certainly necessary in any system of law. Factual situations in which the law must be applied are so varied that no legislator could ever hope to foresee them all; so rules (or principles) must be sufficiently flexible to allow their application to be fair in unforeseen situations.[18]

Judicial discretion has been expressly equated with judicial rule-making; it has been said that the "discretion" enjoyed by the higher appellate courts—in particular the House of Lords and now, presumably, the Supreme Court—as to the outcome of the cases heard by it is far greater

---

[18] H.L.A. Hart, *The Concept of Law*, 2nd edn (1994), pp.124–154; see also *Lloyd's Introduction to* Jurisprudence, 8th edn (2008), pp.720–721.

than the language used to support the outcome would suggest; far from applying the law, the Law Lords had such wide discretion that they were in fact exercising political judgments and innovating new law.[19]

In the context of judicial hearings that meaning of discretion is not generally used, because, as a matter of legal theory, what is properly construed as a question of law will admit of only one correct answer. The use of the word "discretion" to describe that area of law which may be described as judge made law is one which is best reserved to jurisprudence and social science.

Discretionary judgment

Under the Human Rights Act 1998 the courts of England and Wales have what is sometimes called a "discretionary area of judgment", lying within the margin of appreciation permitted to local courts under the European Convention of Human Rights.[20] But that is probably best regarded as a particular phrase used in convention jurisprudence, which properly speaking describes the performance of the ordinary judicial task of weighing up the competing considerations on each side.[21] Under the definitions outlined above, it should not be considered a true exercise of judicial discretion.

3–012

APPEALING ON A POINT OF LAW

A decision of law will usually require the judge to interpret a statute, or to decide what the common law is, in relation to a particular dispute. A decision on a point of law may be wrong because the judge has misunderstood the statute, or a relevant statutory provision has been overlooked. Alternatively, the judge may have omitted to consider an authority which is relevant to the point he has to decide; or he may have misunderstood the meaning and effect of previous decisions. More unusually, there may be two or more apparently competing lines of authorities, which make it difficult to say what the law is. All these situations may give rise to an appeal on a point of law.

3–013

---

[19] This is the manner in which the word "discretion" is generally used in David Robertson, *Judicial Discretion in the House of Lords* (OUP, 1998). See, in particular, p.6, citing *Associated Newspapers v Wilson* [1995] 2 W.L.R. 354 as "an example of discretion because the result of manifestly could have been different—two of five Law Lords wanted a different result and had arguments that satisfied them to justify it".

[20] Lester and Pannick, *Human Rights Law and Practice*, 3rd edn (2009), para.3.19.

[21] *Huang v Secretary of State for the Home Department* [2007] 2 A.C. 167 at [16], Lord Bingham, giving the opinion of the judicial committee of the House of Lords.

A judge is presumed to know familiar law

3–014 Whilst generally a judge will make clear in his judgment the law that he is applying, if the point of law is a well known or commonly arising one, then the fact that he does not recite the law in detail does not give rise to an inference that he has misunderstood it. In the context of a *forum non conveniens* application, for example, made to a judge of the Commercial Court, it is reasonably to be expected that the judge knows the legal principles he has to apply, even if he has not spelt them out. Lawrence Collins L.J., as he was, said, in this regard[22]:

> "In such a familiar area the ex tempore judgment of an experienced commercial judge should not be expected to echo every nuance of Lord Goff's speech, nor should Lord Goff's speech be treated as a per-emptory statute. This is one of those cases where it can be assumed with some confidence that the judge was fully aware of the principles in *Spiliada*. The application of those principles is part of the regular diet of the judges in the Commercial Court. As Lord Hoffmann said in *Piglowska v Piglowski* [1999] 1 WLR 1360, at 1372 (in the context of the discretion under section 25(2) of the Matrimonial Causes Act 1973), where a judge gives an unreserved judgment, the judge's reasons should be read on the assumption that, unless he has demonstrated the contrary, the judge knew how he should perform his functions and which matters he should take into account. That was particularly true when the matters in question were well known, and an appellate court should resist the temptation to subvert the principle that it should not substitute its own discretion for that of the judge by a narrow textual analysis which enables it to claim that he misdirected himself. That is precisely what [counsel for the appellant] seeks to do in this appeal when he claims that the judge ignored crucial parts of Lord Goff's speech in *Spiliada*."

Precedent

3–015 English law favours certainty, and has developed strict rules that courts should be bound to decide issues in the same way that they have been decided in previous cases. A court is, generally speaking, bound to follow precedents of the higher courts, and is likely to follow decisions of judges sitting at the same level. The rule that precedents must be followed is known as stare decisis.

It is only the ratio decidendi which amounts to binding precedent. The ratio decidendi must be a proposition of law. Only propositions of law which the judge giving the judgment appears to consider are necessary for

---

[22] *Novus Aviation Ltd v Onur Air Tasimacilik AS* [2009] 1 Lloyd's Rep. 576 at [70], per Lawrence Collins L.J.

his decision form part of the ratio decidendi.[23] The ascertainment of the ratio decidendi must therefore depend upon an analysis of the language used by the judge whose decision is being examined; a subsequent judge is not entitled to derive a ratio decidendi by rationalising the decision in a different manner.

> "It is well established that if a judge gives two reasons for his decision, both are binding. It is not permissible to pick out one as being supposedly the better reason and ignore the other one; nor does it matter for this purpose which comes first and which comes second. But the practice of making judicial observations obiter is also well established. A judge may often give additional reasons for his decision without wishing to make them part of the ratio decidendi; he may not be sufficiently convinced of their cogency as to want them to have the full authority of precedent, and yet may wish to state them so that those who later may have the duty of investigating the same point will start with some guidance. This is a matter which the judge himself is alone capable of deciding, and any judge who comes after him must ascertain which course has been adopted from the language used and not by consulting his own preference."[24]

The ratio decidendi is to be evaluated in the context of the particular facts of the case, and in the light of the authorities referred to in it.

Because the ratio decidendi depends upon the reasoning of the decision, rather than the decision itself, whilst an assumed proposition may be part of the ratio, it does not have value as a precedent itself. A subsequent court is not bound by a proposition of law that was assumed by an earlier court; or that was not the subject of argument before or consideration by that court. It has been said that "to hold otherwise would be to come close to permitting the outcome of the case, rather than its reasoning, to dictate its status".[25] The scope of this exception to the rule that the ratio decidendi governs the precedential value of a decision is narrow. It must be shown that the point not only was not argued, but, further, that the court did not give it some further consideration so as to take it outside the parameters of mere assumption.[26]

The precise nature of the strict doctrine of the ratio decidendi may make its true identification quite challenging. It is therefore more usual for counsel and judges to analyse case law by reference to the precise words used by the particular judge. This is partly because the reasoning employed by the judge will make it easier to understand the decision.

---

[23] This sentence comes from Cross and Harris, *Precedent in English Law*, 4th edn (1991), p.72 and was approved in *R. (Kadhim) v Brent LBC Housing Benefit Review Board* [2001] Q.B. 955 at 961, per Buxton L.J.

[24] *Behrens v Bertram Mills Circus Ltd* [1957] 2 Q.B. 1 at 24, per Devlin J.

[25] *R. (Kadhim) v Brent LBC Housing Benefit Review Board* [2001] 1 Q.B. 955 at 965, per Buxton L.J.; *In Re Hetherington* [1990] Ch. 1.

[26] ibid.

3–016   If a passage is succinct, to the point and well expressed, then it may come to acquire great authority.[27] There are lots of examples of this, and, so long as it is remembered that the passage is not statute or akin to statute, it is unobjectionable. However, the striking phrase can lead to over-simplification or disguise unsafe assumptions. Professor Bennion has described the mischief that a striking judicial phrase may do to the effect or interpretation of statutes in the following way:

> "Acts ... faultily engendered pass in rapid succession before busy judges, assisted by busy advocates. Few of these have the time, or are equipped, for cool and deep analysis. Yet judges lean to the delivery of impromptu and pithy (and therefore doubly inaccurate) descriptions of the nature of statutes and the principles governing their interpretation. Often quotable, these get quoted...."[28]

If the ratio decidendi is difficult to identify, the decision has little or no precedent as authority. As Viscount Dunedin said[29]:

> "Now, when any tribunal is bound by the judgment of another Court, either superior or co-ordinate, it is, of course, bound by the judgment itself. And if from the opinions delivered it is clear—as is the case in most instances—what the ratio decidendi was which led to the judgment, then that ratio decidendi is also binding. But if it is not clear, then I do not think it is part of the tribunal's duty to spell out with great difficulty a ratio decidendi in order to be bound by it."

The lower courts are bound to follow the ratio of a decision of the higher courts, unless it can be distinguished, and all courts are likely to pay the ratio of any decided case significant respect even if it is not technically binding. Decisions of the Privy Council and courts of the commonwealth are of persuasive, but not binding authority.

The Supreme Court

3–017   The Supreme Court is a superior court of record to which an appeal lies (among other things) from any order or judgment of the Court of Appeal in England and Wales in civil proceedings. The Court has power to determine any question necessary to be determined for the purposes of doing justice in any appeal to it under any enactment.[30]

There is no indication that the transfer of powers from the House of Lords to the Supreme Court by the Constitutional Reform Act 2005 was

---

[27] Jolowicz, *On Civil Procedure* (CUP, 2000), p.286.
[28] *Bennion on Statutory Interpretation*, 5th edn (2008), p.10.
[29] *Great Western Ry v Owners of S.S. Mostyn* [1928] A.C. 57 at 73.
[30] Constitutional Reform Act 2005 s.40.

intended by Parliament to make any significant difference to the established principles of judicial precedent which had built up over time. It is therefore likely that the Supreme Court will follow or not follow previous decisions of the House of Lords in the same circumstances that the House of Lords would have followed them. This was confirmed by Lord Hope in *Austin v Mayor and Burgesses of the London Borough of Southwark*.[30a]

Decisions of the Supreme Court and the House of Lords bind all lower courts. Decisions of the Supreme Court and the House of Lords also bind the Supreme Court[31] save where the Supreme Court decides it is right to depart from a previous decision. It is likely that the Supreme Court will follow the text of or at least the principles of the 1966 Practice Direction, which applied in the House of Lords[32]:

> "Their Lordships regard the use of precedent as an indispensable foundation upon which to decide what is the law and its application to individual cases. It provides at least some degree of certainty upon which individuals can rely in the conduct of their affairs, as well as a basis for orderly development of legal rules.
>
> Their Lordships nevertheless recognise that too rigid adherence to precedent may lead to injustice in a particular case and also unduly restrict the proper development of the law. They propose, therefore, to modify their present practice and, while treating former decisions of this House as normally binding, to depart from a previous decision when it appears right to do so.
>
> In this connection they will bear in mind the danger of disturbing retrospectively the basis on which contracts, settlements of property and fiscal arrangements have been entered into and also the especial need for certainty as to the criminal law."

There are at least three reasons which have been given to explain why the House of Lords was entitled to depart from its previous decisions. The first is that the House of Lords, as part of Parliament, was never bound by its previous decisions; therefore whilst sitting judicially, although generally it was able to treat itself as being bound by previous decisions, it would exercise a discretion to decide a question differently.[33] That principle cannot apply to the Supreme Court, since the Supreme Court is not a part of Parliament. The second is that it is important that the appellate court of last resort is able to develop the law in a proper manner, which may on occasion require previous decisions to be departed from.[34] The third is that too rigid an adherence to the law rules of precedent may lead to injustice and if, in all the circumstances, it is right that the appellate court of last resort

3–018

[30a] [2010] UKSC 28 at [24]–[25].
[31] *London Tramways v London CC* [1898] A.C. 375.
[32] [1966] 1 W.L.R. 1234. See also paras 18–065 to 18–066.
[33] *Davis v Johnson* [1979] A.C. 264 at 336, per Viscount Dilhorne.
[34] *Davis v Johnson* [1979] A.C. 264 at 326, per Lord Diplock.

should depart from a previous decision, having taken into consideration the requirement that the law remains certain, as well as the perceived injustice of the previous decision, then it will duly exercise its discretion to do so.[35] These latter two reasons apply equally to the Supreme Court as they did to the House of Lords. Further, it seems most unlikely that the Supreme Court should decide that it had lesser powers than the House of Lords. Therefore it seems likely the Supreme Court will not consider itself bound for all time by its own decisions.

The requirement for certainty in the law means that it should only be in exceptional circumstances that the Supreme Court will depart from a previous decision. Where, for example, the correct interpretation of a statute was a matter of some doubt, it is not appropriate for the court to depart from a previous decision simply on the basis that the differently constituted court disagrees with the previous decision. Something more is required. On the other hand, if a previous decision is clearly wrong and is likely to produce injustice it may be overruled.[36] The fact that an unpopular decision has led to a multiplicity of decisions by lower courts that seek to distinguish the unpopular decision might similarly lead the court to be prepared to depart from that previous decision, for as Lord Reid held:

> "It is notorious that where an existing decision is disapproved but cannot be overruled courts tend to distinguish it on inadequate grounds. I do not think that they act wrongly in so doing: they are adopting the less bad of the only alternatives open to them. But this is bound to lead to uncertainty for no one can say in advance whether in a particular case the court will or will not feel bound to follow the old unsatisfactory decision. On balance it seems to me that overruling such a decision will promote and not impair the certainty of the law."[37]

3–019 The House of Lords was sometimes willing to use its power to depart from a previous decision if there had been a material change in factual circumstances itself rendering the previous decision unjust—for example, where the emergence of currency instability meant that it was unfair to require orders for the payment of money necessarily to be made in sterling[38]; or where the increase in dangerous uses of land created by developments in technology and increasing population density meant that it was appropriate to render landowners liable to take care to prevent children from injuring themselves.[39]

In every case, however, the requirement to avoid injustice, or to allow the proper development of the law must be balanced by the requirement to maintain certainty in the law, so that people may arrange their affairs with a reasonable expectation that they are properly advised as to what the law

---

[35] *Horton v Sadler* [2006] 2 W.L.R. 1346 at 1358.
[36] *Fitzleet Estates v Cherry* [1977] 1 W.L.R. 1345.
[37] *R. v National Insurance Comr Ex p. Hudson* [1972] A.C. 944 at 966, per Lord Reid.
[38] *Miliangos v George Frank (Textiles) Ltd* [1976] A.C. 443.
[39] *Herrington v British Railway Board* [1972] A.C. 877 at 929, per Lord Pearson.

is. For that reason, the exercise by the House of Lords of its power to depart from a previous decision was usually presaged by a number of factors. Lord Nicholls has described the way in which judicial development of the law takes place in the following terms[40]:

"Changes in the common law made by judges are usually described as 'development' of the common law. This is a helpful description, not a misleading euphemism. Judges do not have a free hand to change the common law. Judicial development of the common law comprises the reasoned application of established common law principles, of greater or less generality, in current social conditions. Development of the common law by the judges in any one case is usually marginal. Occasionally it is more far-reaching, as in *Donoghue v Stevenson* [1932] AC 562. In all cases development of the common law, as a response to changed conditions, does not come like a bolt out of a clear sky. Invariably the clouds gather first, often from different quarters, indicating with increasing obviousness what is coming. Cardozo J's colourful summary, in his *The Nature of the Judicial Process* (1921), p 141, merits repetition:

'The judge, even when he is free, is still not wholly free. He is not to innovate at pleasure. He is not a knight-errant, roaming at will in pursuit of his own ideal of beauty or of goodness. He is to draw his inspiration from consecrated principles. He is not to yield to spasmodic sentiment, to vague and unregulated benevolence. He is to exercise a discretion informed by tradition, methodized by analogy, disciplined by system, and subordinated to 'the primordial necessity of order in the social life'."

There was a further power of the House of Lords to decide cases in a different way, if it decided that changes in social thinking indicate that a previous decision should no longer hold sway. In *Rondel v Worsley*[40a] the House of Lords had confirmed that advocates had immunity in relation to the conduct of a case in court. In *Hall v Simons*[40b] the House of Lords held that the immunity should no long persist. They did not however invoke the 1966 Practice Direction to overrule *Rondel v Worsley*. Indeed, not one of the seven Lords of Appeal in Ordinary thought that *Rondel v Worsley* had been wrongly decided. They all agreed that the immunity had been based upon public policy; and that public policy considerations had now changed.

In *Fitzpatrick v Sterling Housing Association Ltd*[40c] the House of Lords   **3–020** held that a long term homosexual partner was a member of the original tenant's family for the purposes of Rent Act protection, although the phrase

---

[40] *In Re Spectrum Plus Ltd* [2005] 2 A.C. 680 at 697.
[40a] [1969] 1 A.C. 191.
[40b] [2002] 1 A.C. 615.
[40c] [2001] 1 A.C. 27.

would not have been interpreted in that way when it was first enacted in 1920. This again reflected a change in public policy considerations.

As indicated above, it is likely that the Supreme Court will follow the old practice of the House of Lords in relation to precedence. However, there must be at least a chance that since Parliament has expressed its view that the final court of appeal should be separate and distinct from Parliament with a greater degree of independence, their Lordships will consider it appropriate to reconsider the circumstances in which it will be just to develop the law, whilst maintaining the overriding importance of certainty.[41]

The Court of Appeal

3–021 From 1875, when the Court of Appeal was established, until 1944, it was unclear whether the Court of Appeal was bound by its own decisions.[42] However, since the judgment of Lord Greene M.R. in *Young v Bristol Aeroplane Co Ltd*,[42a] although some doubts have been expressed, the orthodox view has been that the Court of Appeal is bound to follow its previous decision as well as those of courts of co-ordinate jurisdiction save in the following circumstances:

(1) the court is entitled and bound to decide which of two conflicting decisions of its own it will follow;
(2) the court is bound to refuse to follow a decision of its own which, though not expressly overruled, cannot, in its opinion, stand with a decision of the House of Lords; and
(3) the court is not bound to follow a decision of its own if it is satisfied that the decision was given per incuriam.[43]

Per incuriam means "through lack of care". A decision which was given per incuriam does not bind a future court; however, the circumstances in which it is proper to describe a decision as per incuriam are exceptional. It is not sufficient that a past decision is wrong in the view of the subsequent court. It is only where a decision has been given in ignorance or forgetfulness of a particular statutory provision, or binding authority, that a decision may properly be described as per incuriam or where there is some other exceptional error. Only so restricted is the rule consistent with the doctrine of stare decisis.[44]

---

[41] In this regard, see para.1–047.
[42] The history is set out in Evans, "The Status of Rules of Precedent" [1982] C.L.J. 162, 170–171.
[42a] [1944] K.B. 718.
[43] Rule approved in *Davis v Johnson* [1979] A.C. 264
[44] *Morelle Ltd v Wakeling* [1955] 2 Q.B. 379 at 406.

The precedence of a decision of the Court of Appeal is generally the same whether the Court be constituted of two, three or five Lord or Lady Justices of Appeal.[45]

Applications for permission to appeal

Judicial decisions which decide only whether a party should have permission to appeal, or permission to apply for judicial review, do not generally have any significant value as precedents. Where the application is attended by one party only, or is an application for permission to appeal, or is a decision which decides only that an application is arguable:

3–022

(1) where the judgment was delivered before April 9, 2001, it may only be cited if there is an indication that it purports to establish a new principle or to extend the present law which is present in or clearly deducible from the language used in the judgment;
(2) where the judgment was delivered after April 9, 2001, it may only be cited if there is an express statement that it purports to establish a new principle or to extend the present law.[46]

High Court

A judge at first instance in the High Court is generally not bound to follow decisions of other judges sitting at first instance in the High Court.[47] However a first instance decision will of course be considered with care before an alternative view is taken. The freedom not to be bound by earlier decisions of equivalent ranked judges may be limited in certain circumstances. In particular, it may be that a point should be regarded as settled at first instance where a judge has fully considered an earlier case, and not followed it for reasons he has explained. The latter should be followed, except in the rare case where a third judge was convinced that the second was wrong, because, for example, some binding or persuasive authority had not been cited in either of the first two cases.[48]

3–023

---

[45] *Young v British Aeroplane Co Ltd* [1944] K.B. 718; *Limb v Union Jack Removals Ltd* [1998] 1 W.L.R. 1354. Decisions of constitutions of the Court of Appeal of two Lord or Lady Justices may not be binding on interlocutory issues: see *Boys v Chaplin* [1968] 2 Q.B. 1; *Langley v North West Water Authority* [1991] 1 W.L.R. 697; *Clark v University of Lincolnshire and Humberside* [2000] 1 W.L.R. 1988; *Cave v Rolf* [2001] EWCA Civ 245 and *Yacoubou v Secretary of State for the Home Department* [2005] EWCA Civ 1051. It should be noted that the Court of Appeal is duly constituted if it consists of one or more judges: Senior Courts Act 1981 s.54.
[46] *Practice Direction (Citation of Authorities)* [1999] 1 W.L.R. 1 at [6.1].
[47] *Forsikringaktieselskapet v Vesta v Butcher* [1986] 2 All E.R. 488, per Hobhouse J.; *In Re Saunders* [1997] Ch. 70, per Lindsay J.; *In Re Taylor* [2007] 2 W.L.R. 148, per Judge Kershaw QC.
[48] *Colchester Estates (Cardiff) v Carlton Industrial Plc* [1986] Ch. 80 at 85, per Nourse J.

Circuit judges are bound by decisions of a High Court judge.[49] However, where a recorder or a circuit judge is sitting as a judge of the High Court it may be arguable that he should be bound by precedent only in the same way that a High Court judge would be bound.

A master is bound by decisions of a High Court judge, though statements to this effect are limited, perhaps because traditionally it was thought that the masters had no authority to determine the law at all.[50] Now that masters are regularly required to make decisions on the law in (for example) summary judgment applications, that cannot remain the case.

The County Court

3–024 Whether judges of the County Court are bound by decisions of an individual High Court judge may be a matter of some doubt, though there is no doubt that they will differ only with great hesitation.[51]

Whether their decisions are of any weight as a matter of precedent has been clarified by the 2001 Practice Direction (Citation of Authorities)[52]:

(1) County Court decisions where the judgment was delivered before April 9, 2001 may only be cited if there is an indication that it purports to establish a new principle or to extend the present law which is present in or clearly deducible from the language used in the judgment.

(2) Where the judgment was delivered after April 9, 2001, it may only be cited if there is an express statement that it purports to establish a new principle or to extend the present law.

(3) The only exceptions are where cases are cited in order to illustrate the conventional measure of damages in a personal injury case or where they are cited in a County Court in order to demonstrate current authority at that level on an issue in respect of which no decision at a higher level of authority is available.[53]

European Court of Justice

3–025 Decisions of the European Court of Justice bind all national courts,[54] even when poorly reasoned or inconsistent with prior decisions.[55]

---

[49] *Gloucestershire CC v P* [2000] Fam. 1 at 12 G, per Butler-Sloss L.J.

[50] *Stumm v Dixon* (1889) 22 Q.B.D. 529 at 531, per Lord Esher M.R. This may in part rely upon the theory of delegated authority applying to Chancery Masters: see para.1–038.

[51] Allen, *Law in the Making*, 7th edn (1964), p.234.

[52] [2001] 1 W.L.R. 1001.

[53] *Practice Direction (Citation of Authorities)* [2001] 1 W.L.R. 1001 at 6.1–6.2.

[54] *National Navigation Co v Endesa Generacion (The Wadi Sudr)* [2009] EWHC 196 (Comm) at [83], overturned on appeal: [2009] EWCA Civ 1397; [2010] 1 Lloyd's Rep. 193.

[55] For example, *West Tankers Inc v RAS Riunione Adriatica di Sicurta SpA (The Front Comor)* [2009] 1 Lloyd's Rep. 413, for the reasons explained by Professor Adrian Briggs [2009] L.M.C.L.Q. 161 and Mr Edwin Peel (2009) 125 L.Q.R. 365.

Persuasive decisions

Decisions of the Privy Council, and decisions of other jurisdictions, are not   **3–026**
binding, but of persuasive effect. Decisions which are not binding may
nevertheless have persuasive effect.

The persuasive effect of a Privy Council decision may be so strong that in
the unusual situation that the Privy Council has considered a decision of the
Court of Appeal and decided that it was wrong, a High Court judge is not
bound by it.

> "The system of precedent would be shown in a most unfavourable
> light if a litigant in such a case were forced by the doctrine of binding
> precedent to go to the House of Lords (perhaps through a leap-frog
> appeal under the Administration of Justice Act 1969, section 12) in
> order to have the decision of the Privy Council affirmed. That would be
> particularly so where the decision of the Privy Council is recent, where
> it was a decision on the English common law, where the Board con-
> sisted mainly of serving Law Lords, and where the decision had been
> made after full argument on the correctness of the earlier decision."[56]

Decisions of foreign courts, especially common law jurisdictions, may be of
persuasive effect, in particular those of Australia and New Zealand, and
especially when considering the meaning or effect of international treaties
or conventions.

Any advocate who seeks to cite an authority from another jurisdiction
must:

(1) state the proposition of law that the authority demonstrates, and
    the parts of the judgment that support that proposition;
(2) indicate in respect of each authority what that authority adds that
    is not to be found in authority in this jurisdiction; or, if there is
    said to be justification for adding to domestic authority, what that
    justification is; and
(3) certify that there is no authority in this jurisdiction that precludes
    the acceptance by the court of the proposition that the foreign
    authority is said to establish.[57]

---

[56] *Daraydan Holdings Ltd v Solland International Ltd* [2005] Ch. 161 at [85], per Lawrence
Collins J. See also *Smith v Leech Brain & Co Ltd* [1962] 2 Q.B. 405 at 415, per Lord
Parker C.J. and *I Congreso del Partido* [1978] Q.B. 500 at 519, per Robert Goff J. Cf. *Att
Gen v Blake* [1996] 3 All E.R. 903 at 912, per Sir Richard Scott V.C. and *O'Kane v Jones*
[2003] EWHC 2518 (Comm) at [199], per Richard Siberry QC.
[57] *Practice Direction (Citation of Authorities)* [2001] 1 W.L.R. 1001 at 9.2.

Reputation of a particular judge

3–027 It is often said that the weight of particular reasoning is greater where it was given by a judge of high reputation.[58] The converse, that the reasoning of a judge of lower reputation will be afforded less weight, is generally left unsaid. In a trademark case Lord Diplock sought assistance from counsel on the reputation of Neville J. "Could you tell me this," he asked, "because I am not so familiar with the reputation of the Chancery judges. Where does Neville J rank in the hierarchy between Eve J and Kekewich J?" Counsel replied that he was bound to say at the Kekewich end of the scale, though Neville J. had in fact done quite a lot of trade mark work.[59] It is perhaps worth noting that in his decision Lord Diplock nevertheless referred to the particular judgment of Neville J. without comment, whilst disapproving a later judgment of Eve J.[60] Most advocates will steer clear of commenting on judicial reputations.

The effect of overruling

3–028 Where a decision has been overruled, or where it is departed from by the House of Lords (or now the Supreme Court) pursuant to the former's discretion as described in the 1966 Practice Direction,[61] the effect is, generally speaking, retrospective. At one stage this was thought to be because decisions of the courts do not properly speaking constitute the law, but are merely declaratory of the law; the task of the court is to expound, declare and publish the law. The judge declares what the law always has been. That, however, has long been derided: "the childish fiction employed by our judges, that judiciary or common law is not made by them, but is a miraculous something made by nobody existing, I suppose, from eternity, and merely declared from time to time by the judges"[62] and is now recognised as a fiction. The common law, like equity, is subject to development over time;

---

[58] *R. v G* [2004] A.C. 1034 at 1056, per Lord Bingham; *Antaios v Salen* [1985] A.C. 191 at 204, per Lord Diplock; *R. (Kadhim) v Brent Housing Board* [2001] Q.B. 955 at 964, per Buxton L.J. e.g. Fry L.J.: "a most exact and learned equity judge": *Barclays Bank Plc v Boulter* [1999] 1 W.L.R. 1919 at 1925, per Lord Hoffmann. Bucknill L.J.: "a good judge in Admiralty, who was also well versed in commercial matters" per Lord Denning M.R. in *Federal Commerce Ltd v Molena Alpha Inc* [1978] 1 Q.B. 927 at 976. Bowen L.J.: "the greatest of all the judges": *Imageview Management Ltd v Jack* [2009] EWCA Civ 63 at [65], per Mummery L.J. Farwill J.: "a judge peculiarly experienced and learned in real property law": *Ellenborough Park, Re* [1956] Ch. 131 at 160–161, per Evershed M.R. Kerr L.J.: "a master of international commercial law": *Societe Eram v Cie Internationale* [2004] 1 A.C. 260 at 284E, per Lord Hoffmann.

[59] *GE Trademark* [1973] R.P.C. 297 at 306.

[60] *Thorne & Sons v Pimms* (1909) 26 R.P.C. 221, per Neville J.; *Woodward Ltd v Boulton Macro Ltd* (1915) 32 R.P.C. 173. This example comes from Sir Gavin Lightman, "Civil Litigation in the 21st Century" [1998] C.J.Q. 373.

[61] [1966] 1 W.L.R. 1234

[62] J. Austin in R. Campbell (ed.), *Lectures on Jurisprudence* (London, 1885), p.634, cited in Evans "Precedent in the Nineteenth Century" in Goldstein L. (ed.), *Precedent in Law* (1987), p.67.

otherwise it would still be the same now as it was in the reign of King Henry II.

The retrospective nature of overruling is now understood as an inevitable consequence of the doctrine of precedence. The task of a judge is to decide a particular case on the basis of what he understands the law to be, from applicable statutes and, if there are any, from precedents drawn from reports of previous judicial decisions. He may derive assistance from academic writings in interpreting statutes or on the effect of reported cases; and he may have regard to decisions of judges of other jurisdictions. Where a judicial development is of a radical nature, constituting a departure from what was established principle, the effect of that development is of retrospective effect, because the judge must decide what is the outcome of a dispute which happened some time and probably some years before. It is, therefore, a necessary effect of judicial decision making that judicial decisions will have retrospective effect.[63]

In relation to a case about the compulsory acquisition of land Lord Reid described the retrospective effect of judicial pronouncements in this way:

> "We cannot say that the law was one thing yesterday but is to be something different tomorrow. If we decide that [the existing rule] is wrong we must decide that it always has been wrong, and that would mean that in many completed transactions owners have received too little compensation. But that often happens when an existing decision is reversed."[64]

The retrospective effect of a decision applies only to past disputes which have not already been decided by a court of law, unless an appeal is already pending or may still be brought. A case which has been decided under the law as previously understood which it is no longer possible to appeal may not be opened up solely upon the basis that the law has changed or developed.[65]

It appears to be the case that the House of Lords had the authority or discretion to decide that a change in the law should take effect prospectively, if the effect of the change would otherwise be gravely unfair.[66] However, that authority or discretion was never exercised, though it gave a prospective ruling as to what the law would require of individuals in particular situations.[67] Whether the Supreme Court will venture further is open to question. It has been suggested that the effect of a change in the law which depends upon changing public policy factors should take effect from

3–029

---

[63] *Kleinwort Benson Ltd v Lincoln CC* [1999] 2 A.C. 349 at 377, per Lord Goff.

[64] *West Midland Baptist (Trust) Association v Birmingham Corp* [1970] A.C. 874 at 898.

[65] *Kleinwort Benson Ltd v Lincoln CC* [1999] 2 A.C. 349 at 393, per Lord Lloyd.

[66] *In Re Spectrum Plus Ltd* [2005] 2 A.C. 680; Lord Rodger of Earlsferry, "A Time for Everything under the Law: some Reflections on Retrospectivity" (2005) 121 L.Q.R. 57.

[67] *Royal Bank of Scotland v Etridge Plc* [2002] 2 A.C. 773.

the date of pronouncement of judgment, rather than as at the date of the facts giving rise to the dispute.[68]

The European Court of Justice may limit the temporal effect of some of its rulings.[69] The European Court of Human Rights interprets the Convention in the light of present day conditions[70] and therefore what may constitute an acceptable derogation from a right under the Convention may change over time.[71]

APPEALING AGAINST A FINDING OF FACT

Introduction

3–030 Most cases turn on findings of fact. Whilst the advent of email has led to more communications being documented and, in theory, capable of objective ascertainment, a significant number of cases nevertheless require the trial judge to decide which of a number of competing recollections is more likely to be the correct one. Such a decision is a classic question of fact.

The process of deciding facts is difficult and important. It is difficult because the judge has to decide what happened on the basis of what is likely to be incomplete or faulty evidence. It is important because decisions of fact will probably decide the result; and decisions of fact are of supreme concern to the parties and the witnesses. A witness or party involved in litigation often knows or (perhaps more often) thinks that he knows the truth behind a factual dispute, and he comes to court expecting justice to be done. If the decision is against him, he will inevitably be disappointed. For the witness or party the decisions on disputes of fact are often those about which he is most interested.

All litigants should have been advised that all the judge can do is to decide the case on the evidence presented to him; and, indeed, as a matter of practical common sense, it is easy for anyone to understand that since the judge was not a witness himself to the relevant events, he might be led astray by misleading evidence. Nevertheless, if a judge makes a decision of fact that a litigant knows is wrong, he will inevitably wish to know if he can appeal against it.

An appeal against a decision of fact is difficult, but sometimes possible. Before considering the principles that the appellate court will apply in deciding whether or not a decision on a question of fact was wrong, it is important to understand the historical background to decisions on questions of fact.

---

[68] *Arthur JS Hall & Co v Simons* [2000] 3 All E.R. 673 at 725, per Lord Hope.
[69] *Defrenne v Sabena* [1976] I.C.R. 547; *R. (Bidar) v Ealing LBC* [2005] Q.B. 812.
[70] *Marckx v Belgium* (1979) 2 E.H.R.R. 330 at 353, [58].
[71] As described, for example, in *Goodwin v United Kingdom* (2002) 35 E.H.R.R. 18.

Fact finding: the historical role of the jury

Historically the common law left questions of fact to juries. The judge was responsible only for deciding questions of law. That still applies, of course, in criminal Crown Court cases. But the use of juries in civil disputes is now heavily circumscribed.

3–031

The Common Law Procedure Act 1854 first allowed judges to decide questions of fact if both parties consented. This proved popular. Judges were found to be more reliable finders of facts than a jury. Further, a decision, in particular about damages, was more predictable if given by a judge rather than a jury. By the end of the 19th century only half the civil trials in the High Court were heard with a jury. With unpopularity came suspicion: if a party did ask for a jury, that came to be seen as an indication that there was something suspicious about the case. In particular, a suspicion grew that a party requiring trial by jury might think that its best prospects of success lay in hoping for confusion.[72]

Eventually, the right to require a trial to be heard by jury was removed. The Administration of Justice (Miscellaneous Provisions) Act 1933 made the use of a jury in civil trials dependent upon obtaining the permission of the court.

It remains the case that the court may order civil disputes to be heard with a jury, but the discretion of the court in this regard is limited by statute. Juries are common only in actions in defamation, false imprisonment and malicious prosecution cases.

(a) In the High Court a civil action may now be tried with a jury only in the circumstances set out in s.69 of the Senior Courts Act 1981.

(b) In the County Courts the matter is dealt with by s.66 of the County Courts Act 1984.

Most common law countries have also circumscribed the use of juries in civil actions, save for the United States of America, where the right to trial by jury in civil actions for more than $20 is enshrined in art.3 of the United States Constitution.

It is nevertheless very important to remember the historical role of juries as finders of fact, because the use of juries to decide questions of fact still influences the way facts are found and the way questions of fact are approached by appellate courts.

3–032

In this regard, it has been common for judges to say that they address issues of fact in the same way that a jury would. Lord Asquith said that the Judge sitting alone who had to decide a question of causation "should

---

[72] J.H. Baker, *An Introduction to English Legal History*, 4th edn (2002), p.92; *Ward v James* [1966] 1 Q.B. 273 at 296, per Lord Denning M.R. See also "Law and Fact in Legal Development" (1967) in S.F.C. Milsom, *Studies in the History of Common Law* (1985), pp.171 et seq.

assume the mantle and the mentality of a jury".[73] That means, presumably, that the judge should decide what he thinks is more likely than not to have happened as if he were a sensible, pragmatic, reasonable member of the public—rather than a lawyer, or a philosopher, or a scientist.

The suggestion that the judge should consider a question in the manner of a juror may also imply that the judge's findings should not be subject to an inappropriately detailed investigation on appeal, perhaps because however elaborate the investigation the "true" answer will never be ascertained in an objectively verifiable manner. In other words, a judgment has to be made upon imperfect evidence, and there is no point agonising about it for too long.

However, there is another reason to recall the historic role of juries as finders of facts, because it explains the relatively recent development of the principles to be applied by appellate courts to reviews of findings of fact. There was historically no appeal from decisions of juries. Nor did juries give reasons for their decisions. Since the jury's decision could not really be analysed, it was not possible for the appellate court to review the jury's decisions of fact.

So long as there was evidence to support the jury's decision, and it was one at which a reasonable jury when properly directed might reasonably arrive, the decision would stand.[74] If there were not sufficient evidence, or the jury had been misdirected, then the dissatisfied litigant would bring a motion for a new trial.

Since judges have taken over the task of finding facts, the findings of fact have been encompassed within reasoned decisions and the reasons and the decision are amenable to appeal. In 1898 Lindley L.J. identified and explained the different approaches the appellate court would take to decisions of fact made on the one hand by juries and on the other hand by judges in the following way.[75]

> "The case was not tried with a jury, and the appeal from the judge is not governed by the rules applicable to new trials after a trial and verdict by a jury. Even where, as in this case, the appeal turns on a question of fact, the Court of Appeal has to bear in mind that its duty is to rehear the case, and the Court must reconsider the materials before the judge with such other materials as it may have decided to admit. The Court must then make up its own mind, not disregarding the judgment appealed from, but carefully weighing and considering it; and not shrinking from overruling it if on full consideration the Court comes to the conclusion that the judgment is wrong. When, as often happens, much turns on the relative credibility of witnesses who have been examined and cross-examined before the judge, the Court is sensible of the great advantage he has had in seeing and hearing them.

---

[73] *Stapley v Gypsum Mines Ltd* [1953] A.C. 663 at 687.
[74] *Watt v Thomas* [1947] A.C. 484 at 487, per Viscount Simon.
[75] *Coghlan v Cumberland* [1898] 1 Ch. 704 at 704–705.

It is often very difficult to estimate correctly the relative credibility of witnesses from written depositions; and when the question arises which witness is to be believed rather than another, and that question turns on manner and demeanour, the Court of Appeal always is, and must be, guided by the impression made on the judge who saw the witnesses. But there may obviously be other circumstances, quite apart from manner and demeanour, which may shew whether a statement is credible or not; and these circumstances may warrant the Court in differing from the judge, even on a question of fact turning on the credibility of witnesses whom the Court has not seen."

So appellate courts have had to develop means of distinguishing those findings of fact which should be left solely to the trial judge from those which should be reviewed. The old rules relating to directions given to the jury were no longer appropriate.   3–033

Further, the detailed rules of evidence became less important when the judge started to decide both facts and law, not only because a judge was less likely to give inappropriate weight to particular items of evidence, but also because his reasoned decision could be reviewed by the appellate court. The old rules based approach to evidence has been largely superseded by judicial discretion on admissibility and, more importantly, judgment about the weight to be attached to admitted evidence; whilst, as Lindley L.J. pointed out, respecting the advantage enjoyed by the trial judge of hearing the evidence and seeing the witnesses.

Presumption that the court below was correct

The principle is well settled that where there has been no misdirection on an   3–034
issue of fact by the trial judge the presumption is that his conclusion on issues of fact is correct. In this regard, "no misdirection" probably means that there is no reason when reading the judgment to think that the judge has approached his findings of fact in the wrong way.[76]

"The principle is well settled that where there has been no misdirection on an issue of fact by the trial judge the presumption is that his conclusion on issues of fact is correct. The Court of Appeal will only reverse the trial judge on an issue of fact when it is convinced that his view is wrong. In such a case, if the Court of Appeal is left in doubt as to the correctness of the conclusion, it will not disturb it. That is the first difficulty in the way of upholding the arguments of counsel for [the appellant]. But there is an additional obstacle. The Court of Appeal upheld the findings of fact of the trial judge on the actionability of the second and third representations. While the jurisdiction of the House is not in doubt, it is most reluctant to disturb concurrent

---

[76] *Smith New Court Securities Ltd v Citibank NA* [1997] A.C. 254 at 274, per Lord Steyn.

findings of fact. There are two reasons for this approach. First, the prime function of the House of Lords is to review questions of law of general public importance. That function it cannot properly discharge if it often has to hear appeals on pure fact. This point is underlined by the fact that, despite the economy of presentation of counsel, the hearing on liability lasted more than three days. Secondly, in the case of concurrent findings of fact, the House is confronted with the combined views of the first instance judge and the Court of Appeal. A suggestion that the House can be expected to take a different view on concurrent findings of fact generally gives rise to an initial sense of disbelief."

The advantage of seeing and hearing the witnesses

3–035 Where a judge has heard oral testimony from a witness, including under cross-examination, and has had the opportunity to judge his evidence against the other evidence in the case, then he has an advantage over the appellate court in deciding whether that witness's evidence is to be accepted. The appellate court can only read the transcript, and transcripts can give little of the atmosphere of the trial, or the appearance of the witness, which may have given the trial judge assistance in reaching his decision. Therefore the appellate court should be slow to overrule the judge's own judgment of a witness's credibility.

Lord Sumner expressed the view that is was much more difficult for the appellate court to judge matters of credibility equipped only with a note of the evidence since "a paper review of their words, [is] stripped of the material colour, which hesitation or promptitude, shiftiness or candour may well have given them".[77]

The underlying assumption is in part that a judge will rely upon his knowledge of people and behaviour when forming a judgment about the reliability of a particular witness based upon what they say and do when giving evidence. Lord Shaw of Dunfermline said in 1919 that:

"When a Judge hears and sees witnesses and makes a conclusion or inference with regard to what is the weight on balance of their evidence, that judgment is entitled to great respect, and that quite irrespective of whether the Judge makes any observation with regard to credibility or not. . . . [W]itnesses without any conscious bias towards a conclusion may have in their demeanour, in their manner, in their hesitation, in the nuance of their expressions, in even the turns of the eyelid, left an impression upon the man who saw and heard them which can never be reproduced in the printed page."[78]

---

[77] *Owners of S.S. Hontestroom v Owners of S.S. Sagaporack* [1927] A.C. 37 at 49.
[78] *Clarke v Edinburgh Tramways* [1919] S.C. (HL) 35 at 36.

Similarly, Lord Sumner said:

"... not to have seen the witnesses puts appellate judges in a permanent position of disadvantage as against the trial judge, and, unless it can be shown that he has failed to use or has palpably misused his advantage, the higher Court ought not to take the responsibility of reversing conclusions so arrived at, merely on the result of their own comparisons and criticisms of the witnesses and of their own view of the probabilities of the case."[79]

However, it is not sufficient for the judge simply to decide a case by relying on his judgment of the credibility of a witness in the witness box. The judge is obliged to test all the evidence by reference to the rest of the evidence, because liars are often good at lying, and those telling the truth are sometimes nervous when giving evidence. Judges have always recognised that, whilst it there is an advantage to being able to see the witness, it is more important to concentrate on weighing evidence with known facts.

In 1924 Atkin L.J. said this about the advantages enjoyed by the first instance judge[80]:

"There is no doubt that in dealing with a question of fact the Court of Appeal is in a less favourable position than the trial judge to the extent to which the trial judge derives advantage from actually seeing and hearing the witnesses and watching their demeanour. That advantage, to my mind, is capable of being exaggerated. As I have said on previous occasions, the existence of a lynx-eyed judge who is capable at a glance of ascertaining whether a witness is telling the truth or not is more common in works of fiction than in fact on the Bench, and, for my part, I think that an ounce of intrinsic merit or demerit in the evidence, that is to say, the value of the comparison of evidence with known facts, is worth pounds of demeanour. But, nevertheless, I agree that there is some advantage that the learned Judge derives on questions of fact from the fact that he sees the witnesses and the Court of Appeal do not."

Lord Greene M.R. said in *Yuill v Yuill* that:[81]   3–036

"Puisne judges would be the last persons to lay claim to infallibility, even in assessing the demeanour of a witness. The most experienced judge may, albeit rarely, be deceived by a clever liar, or led to form an unfavourable opinion of an honest witness, and may express his view that his demeanour was excellent or bad as the case may be. Most

---

[79] *Owners of S.S. Hontestroom v Owners of S.S. Sagaporack* [1927] A.C. 37 at 47. See also *Kinlock v Young* [1911] S.C. (HL) 1 at 4, per Lord Loreburn.
[80] *Societe d'Avances Commerciales v Merchants' Marine Insurance Co (The "Palitana")* (1924) 20 Lloyd's Rep. 74 at 152.
[81] [1945] P. 15 at 19.

experienced counsel can, I have no doubt, recall at least one case where this has happened to their knowledge. I may further point out that an impression as to the demeanour of a witness ought not to be adopted by a trial judge without testing it against the whole of the evidence of the witness in question. If it can be demonstrated to conviction that a witness whose demeanour has been praised by the trial judge has on some collateral matter deliberately given an untrue answer, the favourable view formed by the judge as to his demeanour must necessarily lose its value."

To similar effect, in *Att Gen of Hong Kong v Wong Muk Ping*,[82] Lord Bridge held:

"It is a commonplace of judicial experience that a witness who makes a poor impression in the witness box may be found at the end of the day, when his evidence is considered in the light of all the other evidence bearing upon the issue, to have been both truthful and accurate. Conversely, the evidence of a witness who at first seemed impressive and reliable may at the end of the day have to be rejected. Such experience suggests that it is dangerous to assess the credibility of the evidence given by any witness in isolation from other evidence in the case which is capable of throwing light on its reliability..."

Accordingly, the judge must test oral evidence by reference to the agreed issues[83] or to the documents.[84]

More recently, judges have been even more astute to recognise that it is dangerous to place too much emphasis on their ability to divine the truth from mere observation of oral testimony. There is a growing tendency for judges to be wary of explicitly relying on a witness's demeanour.

For example, in a case where witnesses had received witness training, a dispute arose about the extent to which the judge should rely on a witness's demeanour. The judge dealt with the dispute by emphasising the limited importance of demeanour in the process of deciding factual disputes:

"It is, of course, dangerous for a judge to play amateur psychologist and deliberately to look for clues to the question whether a witness is telling the truth. But everyone knows that when we watch and listen to people speaking a great deal is communicated non-verbally. It is impossible to disentangle the verbal from the non-verbal aspects of the

---

[82] [1987] A.C. 501 at 510.

[83] See, for example, *Yaqoob v Royal Insurance (UK) Ltd* [2006] EWCA Civ 885, a claim to be indemnified on an insurance policy against damage caused by fire, where the appellant successfully appealed against a decision of fact in which the judge failed to test the claimant's evidence against the facts in the agreed statement of the forensic engineers.

[84] See, for example, *Societe d'Avances Commerciales v Merchants' Marine Insurance Co (The "Palitana")* (1924) 20 Lloyd's Rep. 140, in which the Court of Appeal disagreed with the judge, and held instead that the Palitana had been scuttled, on the basis of (among other things) fraudulent invoices for cargo.

communication. I think that all that judges mean when they say that the "demeanour" of the witnesses has played a part in their assessment of the witnesses is that they have been influenced by non-verbal as well as verbal communication. I am sure that I have been."[85]

In *Compaq Computer Corp v Dell Computer Corp Ltd*[86] the dispute con-   3–037
cerned advertisements run by the defendant which sought to publicise the allegedly higher prices charged by the claimant for personal computers. The claimant said the advertisements were false in that (among other things) the prices for the defendant's computers in the adverts were only suggested retail prices. Aldous J. granted an interim injunction preventing any further advertisements which failed to clearly to state that the price shown was merely a suggested retail price. The defendant however published an advertisement in which the price shown for the claimant's computer had an asterisk next to it, which led to a notice in very small print at the bottom of the advertisement saying that the price was only a suggested one. The claimant brought a motion for sequestration for contempt.

The motion came before Harman J. who held that the defendant was in contempt of court. The judge formed an adverse view of the contemnor's managing director:

> "I regret that having carefully observed Mr Slagter's demeanour and tone of voice in the witness box I cannot accept that Mr Slagter genuinely believed what he swore to in his affidavit..."

The judge fined the defendant £250,000. The defendant appealed. The Court of Appeal upheld the finding of contempt, but disagreed that it merited any fine, because the defendant had taken significant steps to prevent the advertisement being published elsewhere. Steyn L.J. added this:

> "Finally, I turn to a matter that troubles me very much. The judge commented unfavourably on the evidence of Mr Slagter ... The judge based his findings on the demeanour and tone of voice of Mr Slagter. Here I take the liberty of quoting what I regard as wise words of McKenna J on an extra-judicial occasion. He said this:
>
> > 'I question whether the respect given to our findings of fact based on the demeanour of witnesses is always deserved. I doubt my own ability ... to discern from a witness's demeanour or the tone of his voice whether he is telling the truth. He speaks hesitantly. Is that the mark of a cautious man whose statements are for that reason to be respected, or is he taking time to fabricate? Is an emphatic witness

---

[85] *Ultraframe (UK) Ltd v Fielding* [2005] EWHC 1638 (Ch); [2006] F.S.R. 17 at [32], per Lewison J.
[86] Court of Appeal Unreported February 10, 1992, Dillon, Steyn L.JJ. and Sir Christopher Slade; transcript available on Lexis; cited in Drewry, Blom-Cooper and Blake, *The Court of Appeal* (2007), p.25.

putting on an act to deceive me, or is he speaking from the fullness of his heart, knowing that he is right? Is he likely to be more truthful if he looks me straight in the eye, than if he casts his eyes on the ground, perhaps in shyness or natural timidity? For my part, I rely on these considerations as little as I can.'[87]

I am very much of the same mind. I readily accept, of course, that Harman J cannot possibly be criticised for approaching the matter in a way which is supported by legal convention. But I do wish to record that I am nevertheless not persuaded that his comments on Mr Slagter's evidence were justified."

3–038 Other judges have also confessed that they have less confidence in being able to pinpoint the truth simply from their analysis of the witnesses giving evidence in the box. Extrajudicially Lord Bingham has pointed out that the difficulties in such a task are in truth obvious:

"the ability to tell a coherent, plausible and assured story, embellished with snippets of circumstantial detail and laced with occasional shots of life-like forgetfulness, is very likely to impress any tribunal of fact. But it is also the hallmark of the confidence trickster down the ages."[88]

The difficulty of judging a person's character on the basis of his demeanour in the witness box may be more difficult where the witness is from a different country or ethnic background or even class. Scrutton L.J. said that it was impossible to judge whether a witness was lying when the evidence was being translated.[89]

So whilst it remains the case that appellate courts will bear very well in mind that they, unlike the judge, have not had the benefit of hearing and seeing witnesses give evidence, it is of primary importance to judge oral evidence by reference to uncontested documents and any other incontrovertible or unchallenged evidence. The judgment of Robert Goff L.J., as he was, in *The Ocean Frost*[90] is now perhaps the leading guidance on judging the credibility of witnesses.

"Speaking from my own experience, I have found it essential in cases of fraud, when considering the credibility of witnesses, always to test their veracity by reference to the objective facts proved independently

---

[87] "Discretion", *The Irish Jurist*, Vol.IX (new series), 1, 10; see Tom Bingham, *The Business of Judging: Selected Essays and Speeches* (2000), p.9.

[88] Lord (Tom) Bingham, *The Business of Judging: Selected Essays and Speeches* (2000), p.10. See also *Fox v Percy* (2003) 214 C.L.R. 118 at 128–129, per Gleeson C.J., Gummow and Kirby JJ.

[89] *Compania Naviera Mariartu of Bilbao v Royal Exchange Assurance Corp* (1922) 13 Ll. L. Rep. 83 at 97.

[90] 1 Lloyd's Rep. 1 at 57; *Grace Shipping v CF Sharp* [1987] 1 Lloyd's Rep. 207 at 215; *Hurndell v Hozier* [2009] EWCA Civ 67 at [104], per Pill L.J. This passage is the main advice given in the JSB Civil Bench Book, para.5.6, which forms the section dealing with findings of fact in the chapter "Delivery of Judgments".

of their testimony, in particular by reference to the documents in the case, and also to pay particular regard to their motives and to the overall probabilities. It is frequently very difficult to tell whether a witness is telling the truth or not; and where there is a conflict of evidence such as there was in the present case, reference to the objective facts and documents, to the witnesses' motives, and to the overall probabilities, can be of very great assistance to a Judge in ascertaining the truth. I have been driven to the conclusion that the Judge did not pay sufficient regard to these matters in making his findings of act in the present case."

There undoubtedly remains a strong presumption that the judge hearing the evidence is in a better position to evaluate issues of credibility than the appellate court.[91] Nevertheless, appeals do lie on findings of fact, and it has been said that while fully recognising and respecting the advantages enjoyed by the trial judge, the Court of Appeal should not abdicate its duty of review.

"If the overwhelming weight of evidence on a point is to one effect, convincing grounds have to be shown for reaching a contrary conclusion. Where the trial judge has founded on a witness's oral evidence, the court will not uphold the finding if persuaded that it is not justified on a fair construction of what the witness actually said. The court will not support the dismissal of a witness's evidence where this rests on what is shown to be a misunderstanding, or a wrong impression."[92]

A convenient and often quoted summary of the principles may be found in   3–039
the speech of Lord Thankerton in *Watt v Thomas*[93]:

"I do not find it necessary to review the many decisions of this House, for it seems to me that the principle embodied therein is a simple one, and may be stated thus:

I. Where a question of fact has been tried by a judge without a jury, and there is no question of misdirection of himself by the judge, an appellate court which is disposed to come to a different conclusion on the printed evidence, should not do so unless it is satisfied that any advantage enjoyed by the trial judge by reason of having seen and heard the witnesses, could not be sufficient to explain or justify the trial judge's conclusion;

---

[91] *Watt v Thomas* [1947] A.C. 484; *Whitehouse v Jordan* [1981] 1 W.L.R. 246.
[92] *Eckersley v Binnie* (1988) 18 Con. L.R. 1 at 77, per Bingham L.J.
[93] [1947] A.C. 484 at 487; *Maynard v West Midland RHA* [1984] 1 W.L.R. 634 at 637, per Lord Scarman.

II. The appellate court may take the view that, without having seen or heard the witnesses, it is not in a position to come to any satisfactory conclusion on the printed evidence;

III. The appellate court, either because the reasons given by the trial judge are not satisfactory, or because it unmistakably so appears from the evidence, may be satisfied that he has not taken proper advantage of his having seen and heard the witnesses, and the matter will then become at large for the appellate court."

Other advantages enjoyed by the trial judge

3–040   The trial judge's advantage is not just in being able to assess the credibility of witnesses in part in the manner in which they gave evidence. The trial judge has sat through the evidence and argument, and has read the documents, and has reached his judgment based upon all of that material—not just that material to which he refers in his judgment.

In *Biogen v Medeva Plc*,[94] a trade mark case, one of the questions for the trial judge was whether an artificially constructed molecule of DNA was properly protected by a patent, or whether its development was (to a person appropriately skilled) "obvious", so that the patent should be revoked. The question of whether it was "obvious" is one of mixed law and fact, in that it requires the application of a legal standard to a factual situation. The relevant context made the factual situation particularly complicated, and in those circumstances the approach of the appellate court should be restrained, as Lord Hoffmann explained.[95]

"The question of whether an invention was obvious had been called "a kind of jury question" (see Jenkins L.J. in *Allmanna Svenska Elektriska A/B v. The Burntisland Shipbuilding Co. Ltd.* (1952) 69 R.P.C. 63, 70) and should be treated with appropriate respect by an appellate court. It is true that in *Benmax v. Austin Motor Co. Ltd.* [1955] A.C. 370 5 this House decided that, while the judge's findings of *primary* fact, particularly if founded upon an assessment of the credibility of witnesses, were virtually unassailable, an appellate court would be more ready to differ from the judge's evaluation of those facts by reference to some legal standard such as negligence or obviousness. In drawing this distinction, however, Viscount Simonds went on to observe, at page 374, that it was "subject only to the weight which should, as a matter of course, be given to the opinion of the learned judge".

---

[94] [1997] R.P.C. 1.
[95] [1997] R.P.C. 1 at 45, lines 20 to 45. See also *Grayan, Re* [1995] Ch. 241 at 245, per Hoffmann L.J. (as he then was) and *Designers Guild Ltd v Russell Williams (Textiles) Ltd* [2000] 1 W.L.R. 2416.

The need for appellate caution in reversing the judge's evaluation of the facts is based upon much more solid grounds than professional courtesy. It is because specific findings of fact, even by the most meticulous judge, are inherently an incomplete statement of the impression which was made upon him by the primary evidence. His expressed findings are always surrounded by a penumbra of imprecision as to emphasis, relative weight, minor qualification and nuance (as Renan said, la vérité est dans une nuance), of which time and language do not permit exact expression, but which may play an important part in the judge's overall evaluation. It would in my view be wrong to treat Benmax as authorising or requiring an appellate court to undertake a de novo evaluation of the facts in all cases in which no question of the credibility of witnesses is involved. Where the application of a legal standard such as negligence or obviousness involves no question of principle but is simply a matter of degree, an appellate court should be very cautious in differing from the judge's evaluation."

Importance of considering all the evidence

Lord Bingham has said, extra judicially, that the main tests needed to **3–041** determine whether a witness is lying (or, it may be added, whether a witness is telling the truth) are the following:

(a) the consistency of the witness's evidence with what is agreed, or clearly shown by other evidence, to have occurred;
(b) the internal consistency of the witness's evidence;
(c) consistency with what the witness has said or deposed on other occasions;
(d) the credit of the witness in relation to matters not germane to the litigation; and
(e) the demeanour of the witness.[96]

If a witness's evidence conflicts with what is clearly shown to have occurred, it may be regarded as suspect. If a witness's evidence conflicts with what he himself has said on the same or another occasion, then his evidence is suspect, although it may be difficult to decide which parts of his statements were accurate and which parts were inaccurate. In this regard, it will of course be vital to consider the reason why the particular statement was made.

---

[96] Lord (Tom) Bingham, *The Business of Judging: Selected Essays and Speeches* (2000), p.6. See also Brooke L.J. in *Laceys Footwear (Wholesale) Ltd v Bowler International Freight Ltd* [1997] 2 Lloyd's Rep. 369.

The judge must not reach his conclusion on a question of fact before surveying all the evidence relevant to the particular question of fact.[97] He must not prematurely give an indication that he has reached firm views about the credibility of a particular witness, particularly where the other side may call evidence relevant to credibility.[98]

The advantage to the judge over the appellate court of seeing and hearing the witnesses will vary with the subject matter of the case. A family case involving disputes of fact, with allegations and counter-allegations about past behaviour, will require careful consideration by the judge of the witnesses' demeanour, physique, temperament, education, use of language and personal interaction, and it will be difficult for the appellate court to conclude that the judge reached the wrong decision.[99] By contrast, in a case turning on issues of fact which largely appear from documents, the advantage of the trial judge will be less significant.

A finding of fact based upon photos

3–042   The appellate court is probably in just as a good position as the judge to interpret a photograph, at least where the photograph has not been explained by a witness. So, for example, in a run of the mill tripping case Steyn L.J. described as "unsupportable" the judge's view that a photograph of soft material surrounding a cracked paving brick bore the imprint of a lady's stiletto heel as opposed to, for example, a walking stick; and that the judge was wrong to say that a blob of mortar in another photograph looked like a botched attempt to repair the cracked paving brick.[100]

A finding of fact based upon inferences

3–043   The trial judge, as explained in paras 3–035 to 3–039, is in an advantageous position to evaluate the oral testimony of those who give evidence before him. There may also be a welter of unexplained inferences that he has drawn from the experience of being involved in the hearing which, though unexpressed in his judgment, properly led him to make the findings of fact that he made. With findings of fact of that nature, the appellate court will be slow to interfere.

However, where a finding of fact is, upon proper analysis, an inference drawn from primary findings of fact, the position of the appellate court is

---

[97] *Mibanga v Secretary of State for the Home Department* [2005] EWCA Civ 367 at [24], per Wilson J., approved in *Jakto Transport Ltd v Derek Hall* [2005] EWCA Civ 1327 at [29], per Smith L.J. and at [47], per Pill L.J.; reported in *The Times*, November 28, 2005.

[98] *Amjad v Steadman-Byrne* [2007] 1 W.L.R. 2484. It is possible that extreme examples of pre-judging a case will give rise to an appeal by reason of serious irregularity: see para.4–007.

[99] *Watt v Thomas* [1947] A.C. 484 at 488.

[100] *Mills v Barnsley MBC* Unreported February 6, 1992 CA, Lawtel No.AC0101337.

more akin to that of the trial judge, and therefore will be less reluctant to interfere with the trial judge's finding.

Lord Denning explained the distinction in the following way:

> "Primary facts are facts which are observed by witnesses and proved by oral testimony or facts proved by the production of a thing itself, such as original documents. Their determination is essentially a question of fact for the tribunal of fact, and the only question of law that can arise on them is whether there was any evidence to support the finding. The conclusions from primary facts are, however, inferences deduced by a process of reasoning from them. If, and in so far as, those conclusions can as well be drawn by a layman (properly instructed on the law) as by a lawyer, they are conclusions of fact for the tribunal of fact: and the only questions of law which can arise on them are whether there was a proper direction in point of law; and whether the conclusion is one which could reasonably be drawn from the primary facts: see *Bracegirdle v Oxley* [1947] KB 349.
>
> If, and in so far, however, as the correct conclusion to be drawn from primary facts requires, for its correctness, determination by a trained lawyer—as, for instance, because it involves the interpretation of documents or because the law and the facts cannot be separated, or because the law on the point cannot properly be understood or applied except by a trained lawyer—the conclusion is a conclusion of law on which an appellate tribunal is as competent to form an opinion as the tribunal of first instance."[101]

The leading case on the approach of the appellate courts to appeals from decisions involving inferences of fact is *Datec Electronics Holdings Ltd v UPS Ltd*.[102] In that case the claimant sought damages from the defendant carrier for lost packages. The House of Lords held that the contract pursuant to which the packages had been carried was governed by the Convention on the Contract for the International Carriage of Goods by Road (CMR).[103] By art.29(1) of the CMR the carrier may not limit its liability in respect of damage caused by its wilful misconduct or default or that of its agents or servants.   3–044

The trial judge made a number of findings of primary fact about what happened to the lost packages:

(a) they arrived at the defendant's hub in Amsterdam, surrounded by a 3m fence, destined for the consignee L&A;
(b) they were delivered into the defendant's secure warehouse;
(c) one of the defendant's employees had seen them stacked behind the relevant vehicle, to be driven by Mr K;

---

[101] *Battersea BC v The British Iron and Steel Research Association* [1949] 1 K.B. 434 at 471.
[102] [2007] UKHL 23; [2007] 1 W.L.R. 1325.
[103] Carriage of Goods by Road Act 1965.

(d) Mr K delivered one package to L&A, but not the three packages upon which the claim was brought;

(e) Mr K left work that evening and flew back to Morocco; he never returned to work for the defendant;

(f) when later returning to the Netherlands he voluntarily attended a police station where he said that other drivers had taken packages from his vehicle.

3–045 The trial judge held that the claimant had failed to prove that the packages had been lost by wilful misconduct. He said that the losses were probably accidental, which in the circumstances meant that they had been missorted, mislaid or damaged and then thrown away, or misdelivered.

Lord Mance held that the task for the Court of Appeal was to consider the inferences with regard to the causation of loss to be drawn from the primary facts. That was not a task which was analogous to an appeal against an evaluation or judgment or discretion; but was a task for which the appellate court was well placed. The appellate court, in other words, was entitled to re-consider for itself the judge's findings as to what should or should not be inferred regarding causation from the primary facts which he found.

In those circumstances, the House of Lords upheld the decision of the Court of Appeal to reverse the judge's finding that the losses had been accidental. On the balance of probabilities, the losses had been caused by wilful misconduct of servants or agents, and the defendant accordingly could not exclude or limit its liability.

Doubting the decision, Lord Walker said he was unsure that the Court of Appeal had had sufficient grounds for reversing the trial judge, who had the advantage of seeing and hearing the witnesses. Although there were in principle clear distinctions between findings of primary fact, factual inferences and the evaluations of factual matters, in practice they tended to run into each other; and so caution had to be exercised when differing any of the judge's findings, for the reasons explained by Lord Hoffmann in *Biogen Inc v Medeva Plc*,[104] referred to in para.3–040.

The facts in *Datec* were unusually amenable to distinctions between primary findings of fact—what was known about the movements of the parcel—and inferences drawn from those findings—why in fact it had never been properly delivered. Further, it appears that although the judge had rigorously considered the primary facts, and rigorously considered whether or not it was likely that the package had been stolen, he had failed so rigorously to consider whether the other reasons that the packages had been lost—the accidental reasons—were likely.

On a full analysis, such as that carried out by Richards L.J. in the Court of Appeal, they were not at all likely. To that extent, therefore, the appellate court was willing and, possibly, entitled only to overturn the judge's inference when it was supported by a proper and careful analysis of

---

[104] [1997] R.P.C. 1 at 45.

the primary facts. In other words, there has to be some reasoned and explicable reason to think that the judge's inference was wrongly drawn; but if there is, the appellate court may indeed decide that it was wrong.

Where an inference of fact is itself dependent upon seeing the witnesses, the appellate court should not overturn it. In *Thorner v Majors*,[105] the judge's decision required inferences to be drawn about what the deceased meant by what he said and did. Whilst that was one of inference, the judge's ability to draw the inference was based on other evidence, above all as to what the deceased had been like, which he had seen and the appellate court had not, and his decision was for that reason unassailable.

Experts

There is no clear distinction between the principles applied by appellate courts to decisions about conflicts of evidence between experts and conflicts of evidence between factual witnesses.

3–046

It has long been held that the appellate court should be slow to upset the judgement of the judge who both saw and heard the experts giving evidence.[106] Where expert witnesses are radically at issue about complex technical questions within their own field and are examined and cross examined at length about their conflicting theories, Lord Bridge has said that the judge's advantage in seeing them and hearing them is "scarcely less important" than when he has to resolve some conflict of primary fact between lay witnesses in respect of purely mundane matters.[107]

Where, on the other hand, expert evidence is less technical, and more factual, as may be the case with property valuation, for example, Nourse L.J. commented that it is rare for demeanour or reliability to affect findings of fact, so that "broadly speaking" the appellate court is in as good a position as the judge to assess the merits of the expert evidence.[108]

Because expert evidence is given primarily in written form and relates to matters of expertise, it is particularly important for the judge to resolve disputes of evidence between experts in a coherent and reasoned manner, rather than simply assuming that one is more likely to be right than another by reference to his qualifications or demeanour in the witness box.[108a] Whilst there must be an advantage of seeing and hearing experts, not least from being able to ask questions in relation to difficult issues, the appellate court is generally in a position to review the expert evidence if there is reason to think it is wrong with a good understanding of it,

---

[105] [2008] EWCA Civ 732, approved in this regard by the House of Lords [2009] UKHL 18; [2009] 1 W.L.R. 776.
[106] *Powell v Streatham Manner Nesting Home* [1935] A.C. 243 at 251, per Viscount Sankey L.C.; *Eckersley v Binnie* (1988) 18 Con. L.R. 1 at 54–57, per Russell L.J.; *Joyce v Yeomans* [1981] 1 W.L.R. 549 at 556, per Brandon L.J.
[107] *Wilsher v Essex AHA* [1988] A.C. 1074 at 1091, per Lord Bridge.
[108] *French v Commercial Union* [1993] 1 E.G.L.R. 113 at 114.
[108a] For the judicial duty to give reasons for preferring one expert witness over another, see para.5–011.

notwithstanding the fact it did not hear the oral testimony. Bingham L.J., as he then was, described the proper approach in the following terms:

> "In resolving conflict of expert evidence, the judge remains the judge; he is not obliged to accept evidence simply because it comes from an illustrious source; he can take account of demonstrated partisanship and lack of objectivity. But, save where an expert is guilty of a deliberate attempt to mislead (as happens only very rarely), a coherent reasoned opinion expressed by a suitably qualified expert should be the subject of a coherent reasoned rebuttal, unless it can be discounted for other good reason. The advantages enjoyed by the trial judge are great indeed, but they do not absolve the Court of Appeal from weighing, considering and comparing the evidence in the light of his findings, a task made longer but easier by possession of a verbatim transcript usually (as here) denied to the trial judge."[109]

Whilst it may be able to review the decision, the appellate court is not in a position to try the case on the transcripts[110] and so it may be difficult to substitute a new finding without remitting the case for reconsideration.

Foreign law[111]

3–047 Issues of foreign law are questions of fact, to be decided on expert evidence. It has been said that the question of foreign law is a question of fact of a peculiar kind.[112] It has, for example, long been a question for the judge and not for the jury. The same considerations do not apply in considering whether and to what extent an appellate court should interfere with the finding of a lower court, as in the case of ordinary questions of fact.[113]

Whilst issues of foreign law are questions of fact, the construction of a foreign law contract is for the judge, to be decided on such principles of construction, if any, as have been proven to apply as a matter of applicable foreign law.[114]

Because an issue of foreign law is one of fact, the approach of an appellate court to questions of foreign law is very different to its approach to questions about the law of England and Wales. In the context of a contract governed by foreign law, it circumscribes the ambit of appeals very significantly. The Bermuda form of reinsurance contract relies upon this principle to remove the right of appeal entirely, by providing that disputes must be decided by arbitrations under the Arbitration Act 1996 and New

---

[109] *Eckersley v Binnie* (1988) 18 Con. L.R. 1 at 77–78, per Bingham L.J.
[110] *Bull v Devon AHA* [1993] 4 Med. L.R. 117 at 142, per Mustill L.J.
[111] See Ch.9 of *Dicey & Morris on the Conflict of Laws*, 14th edn (2006).
[112] *Dicey & Morris on the Conflict of Laws*, 2006, para.9–010.
[113] *Parkasho v Singh* [1968] P. 233 at 250–254; *Macmillan Inc v Bishopsgate Investment Trust Plc (No.4), The Times*, December 7, 1998, CA.
[114] See the cases in fn.93 of *Dicey & Morris on the Conflict of Laws*, 2006, para.9–019.

York law. Because there is no appeal against findings of fact from arbitrations under the Arbitration Act 1996, this effectively removes any appeal on points of law at all.[115]

The rule that foreign law is treated as a question of fact is also capable of raising an anomaly in relation to cases which go to the House of Lords, or, now, the Supreme Court. Where a dispute is heard in a Court of England and Wales which includes consideration of the law of Scotland, the question of Scottish law will be a question of fact in the court of first instance and the Court of Appeal, but a question of law for the Supreme Court. This might, in turn, require the Supreme Court to decide the case differently to the lower courts; even in absolute contradiction to the evidence of Scottish law adduced below.[116]

It has been suggested that an appellate court may be in as good a position as the lower court to decide issues of foreign law.[117] The general position, however, is probably that the appellate court should still remember that it has not had the advantage of listening to the evidence.

Second appeals against concurrent findings of fact

Through long established rule of conduct, the Privy Council will not interfere with concurrent findings of judgments of two lower courts on a pure question of fact: that is to say, where a lower appellate court has reviewed a decision on a factual matter of a trial judge, and come to the same conclusion on that issue as the trial judge, the Privy Council will decline to review the evidence for a third time.[118]   3–048

The only exceptions to this rule of practice are if there are circumstances amounting to:

(a) some miscarriage of justice such as to make that which happened not in the proper sense of the word judicial procedure at all;
(b) violation of some principle of law which, if corrected, means that the finding cannot stand; or
(c) violation of some principle of procedure which, likewise, if corrected, means that the finding cannot stand.

There may also be a rule in the Court of Appeal and the Supreme Court, that only in exceptional circumstances will the second level appellate court

---

[115] See further, paras 21–016 and 21–017.
[116] *Cooper v Cooper* (1888) L.R. 13 App. Cas. 88 at 101, per Lord Halsbury L.C.
[117] *Al Jedda v Secretary of State for Defence* [2010] EWCA Civ 758 at [54], per Arden L.J., dissenting.
[118] *Robins v National Trust Co Ltd* [1927] A.C. 515 at 517–518; *Devi v Roy* [1946] A.C. 508 at 521; *Bekoe v Broomes* [2005] UKPC 39 at [11]–[12]. See further para.19–029.

will overturn a finding of fact where the first level appellate court agreed with the lower court.[119]

It is perhaps obvious that the second level appellate court will need considerable persuasion that both the first instance and the first level appellate court reached the wrong decisions.

However, it may be that there is another reason to support such a proposition. A fair and proportionate system of justice must favour some finality, and it may be thought that one go at overturning a decision on the facts is enough. In Australia the principle has been stated in this way:

> "[I]t is in the overall interests of ... the preservation of at least some vestige of practical equality before the law that, in the absence of special circumstances, there should be an end to the litigation of an issue of fact at least when the stage is reached that one party has succeeded upon it both on the hearing before the court of first instance and on a rehearing before the court of first appeal."[120]

Fraud

3–049 Where a party has been acquitted of fraud, the decision in his favour should not be displaced except on the clearest grounds.[121] But where, on analysis, the evidence indicates that there was, contrary to the finding of the judge, fraud, the appellate court must allow the appeal. A rare example may be found in the scuttling case *The Ikarian Reefer*.[122]

Appeals from decisions of Technology and Construction Court[123]

3–050 It is well established that it is difficult to appeal findings of fact made by the Technology and Construction Court. Indeed, it is difficult even to obtain permission to appeal.

Until 1988 it was not possible to appeal decisions from Official Referees on findings of fact. The policy behind that rule was to encourage finality in complicated cases.

---

[119] *Owners of the "P Caland" and Freight v Glamorgan S.S. Co Ltd* [1893] A.C. 207; *Smith New Court Securities Ltd v Citibank NA* [1997] A.C. 254 at 274, per Lord Steyn, quoted in para.3–034.

[120] *Waltons Stores (Interstate) Ltd v Maher* (1988) 164 C.L.R. 387 at 434–435; see also *Louth v Diprose* (1992) 175 C.L.R. 621 at 634; *Roads and Traffic Authority of NSW v Dederer* [2007] HCA 42.

[121] *Trka v Hulbert* [2007] EWCA Civ 1224.

[122] *National Justice Compania Naviera SA v Prudential Assurance Co Ltd (The Ikarian Reefer) (No.1)* [1995] 1 Lloyd's Rep. 455.

[123] See Michael Davis and Robert Akenhead QC (as he was) *Technology and Construction Court Practice and Procedure* (2006), pp.330–336. See also para.13–011.

"It was clearly felt that the factual minutiae with which official referees were required to deal were not suitable matters for reconsideration on appeal. It was better that, for better or worse, their decisions on such matters should stand, rather as if they were arbitrators."[124]

The lack of appeal on the facts was in itself a reason for certain cases not to be referred to the Official Referees: cases in which fraud[125] or professional negligence[126] was alleged were not, in the absence of an appeal against findings of fact, to be referred to the Official Referees.[127] In 1988 appeals were permitted by RSC Ord.58 r.4 on questions of fact with the leave of the court; and leave would be only granted in circumstances where the proposed appeal had reasonable prospects of success. But even in those circumstances appeals will be difficult.[128]

"Whether a ground will be regarded as having a reasonable prospect of success will of course depend on what the point is. A prospective appellant will have difficulty in showing that the test is satisfied if he is seeking to challenge:

(1) an official referee's findings of primary fact based on his evaluation of oral evidence, not because of any peculiar immunity enjoyed by official referees but because of the weight invariably given to the trial judge's factual conclusions unless and until they are shown to be wrong;

(2) the fine detail of an official referee's factual investigation: while the official referee's findings of this nature are no longer final, the Court of Appeal will not readily enter upon an enquiry of this kind;

(3) findings of fact falling within an official referee's area of specialised expertise, particularly if the official referee has had the advantage of inspecting the site or the subject matter of the dispute in question.

We do not suggest that these are no-go areas, only that the burden on a prospective appellant in these areas will be hard to discharge."

---

[124] *Virgin Management Ltd v De Morgan Group* (1994) 68 B.L.R. 26 at 33, per Bingham M.R., approving Waller L.J. in *Moody v Ellis* (1983) 26 B.L.R. 39 at 46.

[125] *Leigh v Brooks* (1877) 5 Ch. D. 592.

[126] *Osenton & Co v Johnston* [1942] A.C. 130.

[127] Appeals on findings of fact were permitted in professional negligence and fraud cases by RSC Ord.58 r.5, which meant that it was thereafter permissible for professional negligence cases to be decided by Official Referees: *Scarborough Rural DC v Moor* (1968) 112 Sol. Jo. 986, per Lord Denning M.R.

[128] *Virgin Management Ltd v De Morgan Group* (1994) 68 B.L.R. 26 at 35, per Bingham M.R., approved by May L.J. in *Yorkshire Water Services v Taylor Woodrow* [2005] B.L.R. 395 at 400.

Whilst appeals from the Technology and Construction Court are no longer governed by special rules, the same approach should be followed where a party seeks to appeal a finding of fact.[129]

Indeed, May L.J. has ventured that some questions of fact may be so complicated and technical that they should only be investigated in detail judicially once, provided that the resulting decision was not palpably incompetent; and that principle should not apply just to decisions of the Technology and Construction Court.[130] It is suggested that May L.J. did not mean to say that the courts should apply some test of "palpable incompetence" rather than the test laid down in CPR r.52.11(3) that appeals should be allowed where the decision below was wrong; but rather to underline the difficulty of establishing a real prospect of success under CPR r.52.3(6) that a complicated fact-finding decision was wrong.

Where the test for permission to appeal is met, the appellant is entitled to a review of the lower court's discretion, and the appellate court cannot excuse itself from the task of reviewing the decision below.[131]

Appeals from specialist tribunals

3–051 Although they lie outside the scope of this book, it should be noted that appeals against findings of fact of specialist tribunals, if they are allowed at all, will be difficult, because the tribunal has specialist knowledge to which it is likely that the appellate court should defer.[132]

QUESTIONS OF LAW AND FACT: SOME SPECIFIC EXAMPLES

The application of statutory tests to factual situations

3–052 The court will often have to apply a statutory test to a particular factual situation. In such circumstances, it may be difficult correctly to ascertain whether the question is one of fact or law. Whilst this is often described as a "mixed question of fact and law",[133] it may be more accurately described as a question of fact which might in some circumstances also include a question of law.

---

[129] *Yorkshire Water Services v Taylor Woodrow* [2005] B.L.R. 395; *Ove Arup & Partners v Mirant Asia-Pacific Construction* [2006] B.L.R. 187.
[130] *Yorkshire Water Services v Taylor Woodrow* [2005] B.L.R. 395 at 401, per May L.J.
[131] *The Glannibanta* (1876) 1 L.R. P.D. 283 at 287, per Baggallay J.A. See also the comments of Sir Christopher Staughton in *Assicurazioni Generali Spa v Arab Insurance* [2003] 1 W.L.R. 577 at 583.
[132] Competition Appeal Tribunal: *Hutchison 3G UK Ltd v The Office of Communications* [2009] EWCA Civ 683 at [107], per Etherton L.J. See further, para.13–011.
[133] *Smith (Inspector of Taxes v Abbott* [1994] 1 All E.R. 673.

In *Brutus v Cozens*[134] the appellant had interrupted a match at Wimbledon to protest against a South African playing in a doubles match. There was evidence that the interruption had been unpopular with the crowd; but magistrates decided that his behaviour was not "insulting" under s.5 of the Public Order Act 1936. The Divisional Court reversed the decision.

Allowing an appeal from the Divisional Court, the House of Lords held that the word "insulting" was intended to have its ordinary meaning; and in those circumstances it was for the tribunal deciding the case to decide whether the words of the statute covered or applied the facts which had been proved. On the facts, the tribunal had been entitled to decide that the appellant's behaviour had not been "insulting". Lord Reid held that "the meaning of an ordinary word of the English language is not a question of law".[135]

But words can mean different things in different circumstances. Parliament chooses particular words to frame particular tests and the ascertainment of the objective intention of Parliament when using particular words may raise questions of interpretation which are questions of law. "Even ordinary words can have more than one usual sense and be capable of differing applications depending upon the particular context in which they are found."[136]

In *R. v Barnet LBC Ex p. Nilish Shah*[137] the appellants were students who had entered into the United Kingdom at least three years earlier with the purpose of seeking an educational qualification by pursuing a course of study at a school or college, paying their own fees and relying on family resources for maintenance. Each then sought a mandatory grant to study for a university degree on the basis that he was "ordinarily resident" in a particular local authority area for the purposes of the Education Act 1962.

Lord Scarman held that the words "ordinarily resident" bore the same meaning as the House of Lords had given them in tax cases.[138] In those circumstances, there was no requirement on the students to have an intention of residing in the United Kingdom after completion of their degrees; all that was required was that they had been "ordinarily resident" for at least three years.

In so holding, Lord Scarman said that, "[t]hough the meaning of ordinary words is, as Lord Reid observed in *Brutus v Cozens*,[139] a question of fact, the meaning to be attributed to enacted words is a question of law, being a matter of statutory interpretation".[140]

The application of the statutory test to particular facts will often be given by Parliament to an agency, tribunal or other decision making entity. In

---

[134] *Brutus v Cozens* [1973] A.C. 854.
[135] *Brutus v Cozens* [1973] A.C. 854 at 861.
[136] *R. v Poplar Coroner Ex p. Thomas* [1993] Q.B. 610 at 630, per Simon Brown L.J.
[137] [1983] 2 A.C. 309.
[138] *Levene v Inland Revenue Commissioners* [1928] A.C. 217 and *Inland Revenue Commissioners v Lysaght* [1928] A.C. 234.
[139] [1973] A.C. 854.
[140] [1983] 2 A.C. 309 at 341.

those circumstances, the question arises as to the extent to which Courts may review that decision of fact. Alternatively, the application of the statutory test may be made by a first instance judge, where there is no statutory decision maker. In those circumstances, the question arises as to the extent to which the appellate court should interfere with the judge's decision. To distinguish questions of fact from questions of law in such cases may be difficult. It is suggested that the same analysis applies to reviews of statutory decision makers as to appeals from first instance judges, although the degree of enthusiasm on the part of the appellate court to interfere with the finding of fact may differ.

3–053   In *Edwards (Inspector of Taxes) v Bairstow*[141] the respondents purchased a complete spinning plant in 1946 for £12,000, agreeing between themselves to make a quick resale. By February 1948 they had sold the plant for over £18,000. The General Commissioners held that the adventure was not a "trade" such as to give rise to a tax liability under Case one of Sch.D of the Income Tax Act 1918.

The House of the Lords held that the Commissioners had erred in law. All the evidence was consistent with the sale and purchase being by way of "trade".

Lord Radcliffe held that the meaning of the word "trade" in D Income Tax Act was a question of law for the courts to interpret, having regard to the context in which it occurs and to the principles which they bring to bear upon the meaning of income. However, the definition of the word "trade" was not precise and there might be many combinations of circumstances in which it could not be said to be wrong to arrive at a conclusion one way or the other. If the Commissioners arrived at a decision which could not be said to be wrong, then that decision was not erroneous in point of law. On the contrary, such cases warranting a determination either way could be described as questions of degree and therefore as questions of fact.[142] However, if the facts found are such that no person acting judicially and properly instructed as to the relevant law could come to the determination under appeal, then the court has no option but to assume that there has been some misconception of the law and that this has been responsible for the determination.[143]

Under the provisions of the Unfair Contract Terms Act 1977 which depend on "the requirement of reasonableness," the decision of what is "fair and reasonable" is not an exercise of discretion, but of judgment. But just as exercises of discretion have different acceptable answers, so the exercise of judgment of what is "fair and reasonable" may, having regard to the various matters to which the court must consider, allow room for a legitimate difference of judicial opinion as to what the answer should be,

---

[141] [1956] A.C. 14.
[142] [1956] A.C. 14 at 33.
[143] [1956] A.C. 14 at 36.

where it will be impossible to say that one view is demonstrably wrong and the other demonstrably right.[144]

Accordingly, where a court or a statutory decision maker must apply a **3–054** statutory test to particular facts, that will always encompass a question of fact about whether or not the test has been satisfied. The meaning of the words in the statute may give rise to a question of law. However, if on the facts the court or the statutory decision maker could and does reach a reasonable decision then no question of law will arise.[145] If, on the other hand, the application of the statutory test to the particular facts requires one answer then a failure on the part of the court or the statutory decision maker to reach that answer will amount to an error of law.[146] Lord Hoffmann has commented that[147]:

> "It may seem rather odd to say that something is a question of fact when there is no dispute whatever over the facts and the question is whether they fall within some legal category. In his classic work on *Trial by Jury* (1956) Lord Devlin said, at p 61:
>
> > 'The questions of law which are for the judge fall into two categories: first, there are questions which cannot be correctly answered except by someone who is skilled in the law; secondly, there are questions of fact which lawyers have decided that judges can answer better than juries.'
>
> Likewise it may be said that there are two kinds of questions of fact: there are questions of fact; and there are questions of law as to which lawyers have decided that it would be inexpedient for an appellate tribunal to have to form an independent judgment. But the usage is well established and causes no difficulty as long as it is understood that the degree to which an appellate court will be willing to substitute its own judgment for that of the tribunal will vary with the nature of the question: see *In re Grayan Building Services Ltd* [1995] Ch 241, 254–255."

Whilst it might indeed seem odd that questions of application of statutory tests be considered questions of fact where the facts are not in dispute, that is probably because of the use of the word "question" rather than "fact". The court or statutory decision maker has to consider or judge whether a particular set of facts, either disputed or not, fulfil the requirements of the particular test. That is an exercise of judgment on the facts before him.

---

[144] *Geo Mitchell Ltd v Finney Lock* [1983] 2 A.C. 803 at 815–816.

[145] *Moyna v Secretary of State for Work and Pensions* [2003] 1 W.L.R. 1929 at 1935, [25], per Lord Hoffmann.

[146] Timothy Endicott, "Questions of Law" [1998] L.Q.R. 292, approved by Lord Woolf M.R. in *R. v Medicines Control Agency Ex p. Pharma Nord (UK) Ltd* [1998] 3 C.M.L.R. 109 at 122 and by Hidden J. in *R. v The Licensing Authority* Unreported March 30, 2000.

[147] *Moyna v Secretary of State for Work and Pensions* [2003] 1 W.L.R. 1929 at 1935–1936, [26]–[27].

Only if the test is difficult, or wrongly applied, may any question or judgment about what the law is arise.

Evidence

3–055   Generally speaking the question of whether there was sufficient evidence to warrant a judge's finding of fact will in itself be a question of fact; indeed, the very process of fact-finding requires the judge to weigh up different pieces of evidence. It has been held that if there was no evidence to support a finding of fact, that will amount to an error of law,[148] but since an absence of evidence will generally indicate that the finding was wrong, the significance of this point may be limited to the arena of judicial review.

The admissibility of evidence is a question of law. In trials with juries, it is for the judge to decide on whether or not evidence is admissible. Questions of credibility of witnesses, or weight to be attached to evidence are, on the other hand, questions of fact.

Contract[149]

3–056   Whether a contract has been agreed is a question of law, or perhaps a question of mixed fact and law.[150] Whether a document has contractual force is a question of law.[151]

What particular words in a contract mean is a question of fact. The question of what the contract means, however, is a question of law.[152] The interpretation of contracts is thus usually described as a mixed question of fact and law.

Lord Hoffmann has explained the reason for that approach in the following way.[153]

> "The difficulties which have arisen in this area are, I think, attributable to the historical origin of the distinction in trial by jury and the pragmatic way in which the courts have applied it. In his Hamlyn Lectures on *Trial by Jury* (1956), Lord Devlin said, at p. 61:
>
> > 'The questions of law which are for the judge fall into two categories: first, there are questions which cannot be correctly answered

---

[148] *R. v Warrnginton Crown Court Ex p. RBNB* [2001] 2 All E.R. 851.

[149] See also para.21–015.

[150] *Covington Marine Corp v Xiamen Shipbuilding Industry* [2006] 1 Lloyd's Rep. 745 at 756, per Langley J.

[151] *Covington Marine Corp v Xiamen Shipbuilding Industry Co Ltd* [2005] EWHC 2912 (Comm); [2006] 1 Lloyd's Rep. 745.

[152] *Pilgrim Shipping Co v The State Trading Co of India* [1975] 1 Lloyd's Rep. 356; *Andre et Cie v Cook Industries* [1986] 2 Lloyd's Rep. 200.

[153] *Carmichael v National Power Plc* [1999] 1 W.L.R. 2042 at 2048–2049, approved in *Thorner v Majors* [2009] UKHL 18; [2009] 1 W.L.R. 776 at [58] and [82].

except by someone who is skilled in the law; secondly, there are questions of fact which lawyers have decided that judges can answer better than juries.'

> Included in the second category is the construction of documents in their natural and ordinary meaning. An uninitiated person might have thought that, for example, the interpretation of a letter written by a layman, stating the terms upon which he offered work to someone else, should be a question of fact.... But the opposite is the case: see *Davies v. Presbyterian Church of Wales* [1986] 1 W.L.R. 323.... As Lord Devlin explains, at pp. 97-98, the rule was adopted in trials by jury for purely pragmatic reasons. In mediaeval times juries were illiterate and most of the documents which came before a jury were deeds drafted by lawyers. In the 18th and 19th centuries the rule was maintained because it was essential to the development of English commercial law. There could have been no precedent and no certainty in the construction of standard commercial documents if questions of construction had been left in each case to a jury which gave no reasons for its decision."

The existence or otherwise of certain terms in a contract is generally a question of fact.[154]

The question of whether a term is to be implied in a contract is a question of law not of fact. The primary facts, of course, and the surrounding circumstances have to be found by the tribunal of fact. But, that being done, the implication of a term is an implication of law.[155]

Whether a party is in breach of its obligations is a question of fact.[156]

Whether a contract has been repudiated is a question of mixed fact and law.[157]

Negligence

The existence of a duty of care is a question of law, but it is a question of fact whether the duty has been breached. It is a question of law whether,   3–057

---

[154] *Surefire Systems Ltd v Guardian ECL Ltd* [2005] EWHC 1860 (TCC); [2005] B.L.R. 534 (whether a contract was varied or not); *Plymouth City Council v DR Jones (Yeovil) Ltd* [2005] EWHC 2356 (TCC); *Chattan Developments Ltd v Reigill Civil Engineering Contractors Ltd* [2007] EWHC 305 (TCC).

[155] *O'Brien v Associated Fire Alarms Ltd* [1968] 1 W.L.R. 1916 at 1923, per Lord Denning M.R. and 1926, per Salmon L.J.

[156] *Portunus Navigation Co Inc v Avin Chartering SA* [1982] 1 Lloyd's Rep. 60 (short delivery); *Athenian Tankers Management SA v Pyrena Shipping Inc, The Arianna* [1987] 2 Lloyd's Rep. 376 (seaworthiness/suitability of a vessel); *Demco Investments & Commercial SA v SE Banken Forsakring Holding Aktiebolag* [2005] EWHC 1398 (Comm); [2005] 2 Lloyd's Rep. 650 (gross negligence).

[157] *The Aegean Dolphin* [1992] 2 Lloyd's Rep. 178 at 184.

from the given state of facts, negligence can be inferred, and a question of fact whether it ought to be.[158]

Defamation

3–058   In defamation it is a question of law whether the words used are capable of bearing a defamatory meaning and a question of fact whether they in fact bore that defamatory meaning.[159]

Causation

3–059   Whether X caused Y is a question of fact. So whether a breach of duty (contractual, statutory or tortious) has caused any loss is a question of fact.[160] Whether an insured peril has caused a loss against which insurers are obliged to indemnify is a question of fact: "I think the case turns on a pure question of fact to be determined by common-sense principles. What is the cause of the loss?"[161]

Common sense plays a significant part in judicial pronouncements on causation, perhaps because it avoids the need for articulating difficult judgments about legal policy, but more certainly because causation was traditionally a question for the jury, and the jury, one supposes, would approach it armed only with their common sense. Would the harm have occurred if the defendant had not driven negligently, or stored a dangerous substance on his land, or failed to provide a proper guard? Was the harm a consequence of the defendant's wrongful conduct or was something else the cause of the harm to the exclusion of the defendant's conduct?[162] All these are questions of fact.

However, it is important to note that there is always a very close connection between the scope of liability, which is a question of law, and the appropriate enquiry into causation. Professors Hart and Honoré explained that the problems of legal policy involved in determining the proper scope of statutory or common law rules, the type of damage for which the law provides a remedy, and the appropriate allocation of risks in different branches of the law raise questions of law, not fact.[163] More recently, Lord Hoffmann has explained the inter-relationship between rules of law and the factual enquiry in this way:

---

[158] *Metropolitan Railway v Jackson*, 3 App. Cas. 193 at 207.

[159] *Phipson on Evidence*, 2005, para.1–43.

[160] *Grant v Sun Shipping* [1948] A.C. 549 at 564; *Cork v Kirby Maclean Ltd* [1952] 2 All E.R. 402 at 406; *Stapley v Gypsum Mines Ltd* [1953] A.C. 663 at 681; *Alphacell Ltd v Woodward* [1972] A.C. 824 at 847; *Fairchild v Glenhaven Funeral Services Ltd* [2003] 1 A.C. 32 at 71.

[161] *Leyland Shipping Co v Norwich Union Fire Insurance Society* [1918] A.C. 350 at 363, per Lord Dunedin.

[162] Hart and Honoré, *Causation in the Law*, 2nd edn (1985), p.429.

[163] Hart and Honoré, *Causation in the Law*, 1985, p.429.

"The question of fact is whether the causal requirements which the law lays down for that particular liability have been satisfied. But those requirements exist by virtue of rules of law. Before one can answer the question of fact, one must first formulate the question. This involves deciding what, in the circumstances of the particular case, the law's requirements are. Unless one pays attention to the need to determine this preliminary question, the proposition that causation is a question of fact may be misleading. It may suggest that one somehow knows instinctively what the question is or that the question is always the same. As we shall see, this is not the case. The causal requirements for liability often vary, sometimes quite subtly, from case to case. And since the causal requirements for liability are always a matter of law, these variations represent legal differences, driven by the recognition that the just solution to different kinds of case may require different causal requirement rules."[164]

An alternative view, which may in effect be very similar, is that there are **3–060** two separate questions for the judge. The first is whether the wrongful conduct causally contributed to the loss; that is a question of fact. The second is whether the claimant's harm or loss should be within the scope of the defendant's liability, given the reasons why the law has recognised the cause of action in question. That is a question of law or a series of questions of law, involving the scope of the duty and remoteness.[165]

Once the correct causal test has been identified, the question of whether the claimant has satisfied it is one of fact.[166] This may require the claimant to show that the breach of duty caused something to happen in the way that it did. It may, for example, require the claimant to show that the injection of phenol into a patient's theca caused paralysis.[167]

Alternatively, it may require the judge to consider what would have happened if the breach of duty had not taken place. For example, if the surgeon had correctly advised the claimant that if she underwent a surgical procedure on her spine there was a small risk that the claimant would develop cauda equina syndrome, would she still have undergone that procedure?[168] The counter-factual consideration the judge is required to take will almost inevitably require the judge to draw inferences from the other facts in the case: what the claimant or other people would have done had

---

[164] *Fairchild v Glenhaven Funeral Services Ltd* [2003] 1 A.C. 32 at 72.
[165] *Kuwait Airways Corp v Iraqi Airways Co* [2002] 2 A.C. 883 at 1090.
[166] See fn.23.
[167] *Roe v Ministry of Health* [1954] 2 Q.B. 66; Hart and Honoré, *Causation in the Law*, 1985, p.409.
[168] *Chester v Afshar* [2005] 1 A.C. 134, although the House of Lords (Lord Bingham of Cornhill and Lord Hoffmann dissenting) held that even though she would still have had the operation, since the injury she sustained was within the scope of the defendant's duty to warn and was the result of the risk of which she was entitled to be warned when he obtained her consent to the operation in which it occurred, the injury was to be regarded as having been caused by the defendant's breach of that duty. As may be envisaged from the fact that Lord Bingham and Lord Hoffmann dissented, the decision is controversial.

the breach of duty not taken place; what would have happened to physical objects; what third parties would have done. The range of possibilities is probably endless, but the judge must reach a decision on what inferences should properly be drawn from the evidence. It would be wrong, however, to say that the appellate court is in as good a position as the judge to decide causation, because a decision in relation to causation is a multi-faceted one. In particular, where the question involves a complicated inter-relationship between evaluation of the claimant's character and the expert evidence, it may be very difficult for the appellate court to unpick the judge's decision to the extent that it can fairly be satisfied that the judge's decision was wrong.

Remoteness of damage

3–061   The question of whether damage is foreseeable is a question of fact.[169] The question of whether a given type of loss is one for which a party assumed contractual responsibility involves the interpretation of the contract as a whole against its commercial background, and is a question of law.[170]

Awards of damages[171]

3–062   The quantification of damages is a question of fact, although, since it often requires inferences to be drawn, the appellate court may be in a reasonable position to review the findings of fact at first instance, in line with the principles discussed in paras 3–043 to 3–045.

In accordance with the strict rules of precedence, there should in those circumstances be no recourse to authorities. However, in personal injuries that rule disappeared some time ago. It has been said that the "judicialisation" of the quantification of damages is in the interests of conformity and predictability.[172]

Contributory negligence

3–063   The question of whether there is jurisdiction on the part of the court to make a finding of contributory negligence is a question of law. If there is such jurisdiction, whether such a finding should be made and if so the

---

[169] *Monarch S.S. Co Ltd v Karlshamns Oljefabriker (A/B)* [1949] A.C. 196; *C Czarnikow Ltd v Koufos ("The Heron II")* [1969] 1 A.C. 350 at 397.

[170] *Transfield Shipping Inc v Mercator Shipping Inc ("The Achilleas")* [2009] 1 A.C. 61 at [25]. See also *Sylvia Shipping Co Ltd v Progress Bulk Carriers Ltd* [2010] EWHC 542 (Comm).

[171] See generally and in particular in relation to appeals against awards of damages made by juries, which are not considered in this book, *McGregor on Damages*, 18th edn (2010), Ch.46.

[172] J. Jolowicz, *On Civil Procedure* (CUP, 2000), p.282.

amount is a question of fact.[173] The lower court is likely to be in the best position to evaluate contributory negligence where a fact finding exercise has been undertaken at trial.

> "Involved in such an apportionment is a comparative examination of the whole conduct of each negligent party in relation to the circumstances of the accident and an evaluation of the comparative importance of the respective acts and omissions of the parties in causing the damage. Such decisions are evaluative and multi-factorial. Generally speaking, a trial judge, who has full knowledge of all of the evidence, will be in a better position to make such an apportionment correctly. An appellate court, even if it would have reached a different conclusion, will usually be hard pressed to identify an error that warrants disturbance of the primary judge's conclusion on such an issue. Tinkering with apportionments is to be discouraged."[174]

In the context of some issues of contributory negligence which are raised in different cases time and again, like the degree of fault to be attributed to the failure to wear a seat belt, there is a powerful public interest in the courts applying consistent reductions, and in avoiding enquiries into fine degrees of contributory negligence. This is in order to encourage the vast majority of such cases to be settled according to a well understood formula.[175]

APPEALING AGAINST THE EXERCISE OF JUDICIAL DISCRETION

Discretion and the rule of law

Many statutes grant to judges power or discretion to make decisions. In equity, a judge has discretion over the form of relief that he may grant. Such discretions give the judge the flexibility to tailor his decision to the particular facts of a case. However, it has long been recognised that an unfettered discretion may amount to a threat to the rule of law. Lord Camden, for example, trenchantly cautioned against the existence of judicial discretion in 1765:

3–064

---

[173] *Grant v Sun Shipping* [1948] 1 A.C. 549 at 565; *The MacGregor* [1943] A.C. 197; *Brown v Thompson* [1968] 1 W.L.R. 1003 at 1008–1011, per Winn L.J.; *Eagil Trust v Pigott-Brown* [1985] 3 All E.R. 119 at 121, per Griffiths L.J. See also *British Fame v Macgregor* [1943] A.C. 197 and *Ingram v United Automobile Service Ltd* [1943] K.B. 612.
[174] *Roads and Traffic Authority of NSW v Dederer* [2007] HCA 42 at [168], per Kirby J.
[175] *Froom v Butcher* [1976] Q.B. 286 at 296, per Lord Denning M.R.: "This question should not be prolonged by an expensive inquiry into the degree of blameworthiness on either side, which would be hotly disputed. Suffice it to assess a share of responsibility which will be just and equitable in the great majority of cases." *Stanton v Collinson* [2010] EWCA Civ 81 at [26], per Hughes L.J.

> "The discretion of a judge is the law of tyrants; it is always unknown; it is different in different men; it is casual and depends on constitution, temper and passion. In the best it is often caprice, in the worst it is every vice, folly and passion to which human nature is liable."[176]

It is necessary, therefore, that if a judge has a discretion, it must be exercised in a rational, just and equitable fashion. It has recently been said that,

> "the broader and more loosely-textured a discretion is, the greater the scope for subjectivity and hence for arbitrariness, which is the antithesis of the rule of law. The rule of law requires that discretion should ordinarily be narrowly defined and its exercise capable of reasoned justification."[177]

If discretion is within defined limits, and exercised in a manner which is capable of reasoned justification, then there is nothing objectionable about it. Lord Mansfield, perhaps replying to Lord Camden, said in 1768:

> "Discretion when applied to a court of justice means sound discretion guided by law. It must be guided by rule not humour; it must not be arbitrary, vague and fanciful; but legal and regular."[178]

The general approach

3–065   Decisions which properly speaking involve the exercise of judicial discretion fall into three main categories: equitable remedies; statutory discretions; and case management decisions. All may be approached from the same general starting point.

As explained in para.3–064, it is a necessary element of the rule of law that where a judge is given discretion whether or not to do something, that discretion must be exercised according to the rules of reason and justice, and not merely according to private opinion. The discretion must be exercised in a manner which is legal and regular, not arbitrary, vague or

---

[176] *Doe d. Hindson v Kersey* (1765), quoted in *"Judicial Discretion and its Exercise"* (The Holdsworth Club, 1962) Lord Hodson.

[177] "The Rule of Law": the sixth Sir David Williams Lecture delivered by Lord Bingham of Cornhill K.G., November 16, 2006, *http://cpl.law.cam.ac.uk/past_activities/the_rule_o-f_law_text_transcript.php*. Sir Edward Coke criticised the wide discretion given to Richard Empson and Edmund Dudley by 11 Hen.7 as leading to the "utter subversion of the common law", cautioning Parliament to leave "all causes to be measured by the golden and straight metwand of the law, and not to the incertain and crooked cord of discretion": Co.Inst. Vol. IV.

[178] *R. v Wilkes*, 4 Burr. 2527 at 2540. Though Burrow's report is dated 1770, this dictum appears to have been pronounced in 1768. In relation to the antagonism between Lord Camden and Lord Mansfield about the extent to which a judge might seek to uphold a will with technical defects, and, more widely, upon whether it was proper for a judge to seek to do justice, as opposed to decide a case upon decided law, see James Oldham, *English Common Law in the Age of Mansfield* (2004), pp.359–360.

fanciful; and exercised within the limits to which an honest man competent to discharge the duties of a judge ought to confine himself.[179]

Appellate courts have therefore, as a general rule, been reluctant to interfere with judicial exercises of discretion unless appropriate.[180] Those occasions when they are prepared to interfere are carefully circumscribed.

It has been suggested that the self-restraint exercised in relation to appeals against exercises of discretion is not because the appellate court is in as good a position to exercise the discretion as the first instance judge; but rather is predominantly to discourage appeals on the matters in question.[181] There may be in the circumstances of the particular case a number of different acceptable ways of exercising judicial discretion. Alternatively, there may be a number of different ways of exercising judicial discretion, none of which is particularly satisfactory, but one of which must be selected.[182] If an appeal were to be allowed frequently against exercise of judicial discretion then the result would be significantly to increase the expense of litigation[183] without necessarily improving the quality of the decisions made.

But there is another reason for the rule that appellate courts should overturn judicial exercises of discretion. The discretion given to the judge is given to him and not to anyone else. He has to make a choice between two or more decisions, and it is his choice to make. Whilst the appellate court has all the powers of the judge, it should not override the judge's choice without good reason.

The exercise of discretion is often multi-faceted. It may require consideration of several issues, some of which are obvious and some are not. It may be that the decision has to be exercised having listened to witnesses and having found a number of facts. Generally speaking, the case managing or trial judge is in the best position to understand the issues in the round as they appear at the particular point, and he exercises his discretion based upon that understanding. Accordingly, the appellate court does not, as a matter of principle, have the right to re-exercise that discretion unless it can be shown that the judge's exercise of it was wrong.[184]

CPR r.52.11(3) only permits an appeal to be granted where the decision **3–066** of the lower court was wrong or where it was unjust because of a serious procedural or other irregularity in the proceedings in the lower court.

The epithet "wrong" must be applied to the substance of the decision made by the lower court. Where the appeal is from the exercise of judicial discretion, the decision of the lower court is not "wrong" merely because the judge of first instance has preferred an imperfect solution which is

---

[179] *Sharp v Wakefield* [1891] A.C. 173 at 179, per Lord Halsbury L.C.; *Rooke's Case*, 5 Co. Rep 99b; 77 E.R. 209, per Walmsley J.; *Wilson v Rastall*, 4 T.R. 753; 100 E.R. 1283, per Lord Kenyon C.J.; *Ward v James* [1966] 1 Q.B. 273 at 294, per Lord Denning M.R.

[180] *Golding v Wharton Saltworks Co* (1876) 1 Q.B.D. 374 at 3705, per James L.J.

[181] J.A. Jolowicz, *On Civil Procedure*, 2000, p.278.

[182] *Clarke-Hunt v Newcombe* (1982) 4 F.L.R. 482 at 486, per Cumming-Bruce L.J.; *Kranidiotes v Paschali* [2001] EWCA Civ 357 at [25], per Aldous L.J.

[183] *Golding v Wharton Saltworks Co* (1876) 1 Q.B.D. 374 at 375, per James L.J.

[184] *Duport Steels Ltd v Sirs* [1980] 1 W.L.R. 142 at 160–161, per Lord Diplock.

different from an alternative imperfect solution which the appellate court might or would have adopted. It will only be "wrong" where, in the exercise of judicial discretion, the lower court has exceeded the generous ambit within which reasonable disagreement is possible.[185]

There are a number of ways in which the judicial exercise of discretion may be wrong so that it is outside the generous ambit within which reasonable disagreement is possible. The following list is not and cannot be exhaustive.

(1) First, the judge may have erred in law.

(2) Secondly, he may have taken into account some matter which he should not have taken into account.

(3) Thirdly, he may have left out of account some matter which he should have taken into account.

(4) Fourthly, he may have based the exercise of his discretion upon a misunderstanding of the evidence or upon an inference that particular facts existed or did not exist which was wrong.

(5) Finally, the fact that the result of the exercise of his discretion is wrong may in itself indicate that the decision must have been reached by a faulty assessment of the weights of the different factors which the judge should take into account.[186]

It is only if and after the appellate court has reached the conclusion that the lower court's exercise of discretion must be set aside for one of those reasons that the appellate court is itself entitled to exercise an original discretion of its own.[187] However, the fact that the appellate court considers what it would have decided had the discretion been its to decide before considering whether or not the lower court's decision was wrong does not in itself indicate that the appellate court has approached the question the wrong way around.[188]

Error of law

3–067 If the judicial exercise of discretion proceeds in relation to or is based upon an incorrect statement of the law then it is likely that the decision itself is

---

[185] *Tanfern Ltd v Cameron-MacDonald* [2000] 1 W.L.R. 1311 at 1317, per Brooke L.J.; *G v G* [1985] 1 W.L.R. 647 at 652, per Lord Fraser of Tullybelton; *Charles Osenton v Johnston* [1942] A.C. 130 at 138, per Viscount Simon L.C.

[186] *AEI Ltd v Phonographic Performance Ltd* [1999] 1 W.L.R. 1507 at 1523, per Lord Woolf M.R.; *Hadmor Productions Ltd v Hamilton* [1983] A.C. 191 at 220, per Lord Diplock; *Roache v News Group Newspapers Ltd* [1998] E.M.L.R. 161 at 172, per Stuart-Smith L.J.; *Alltrans Express Ltd v CVA Holdings Ltd* [1984] 1 W.L.R. 394 at 400, per Stevenson L.J., at 403, per Griffiths L.J.

[187] *Hadmor Productions Ltd v Hamilton* [1983] 1 A.C. 191 at 220, per Lord Diplock.

[188] *Awberry v Marley Building Materials Ltd* [2005] EWCA Civ 16 at [15], per Maurice Kay L.J.

wrong. However, it does not follow as a matter of course that incorrect legal reasoning will lead to a decision that is wrong.[189]

Whether or not the judge has proceeded on an incorrect understanding of the law is a question the appellate court will consider for itself by reference to the relevant substantive law.

In cases where the law is well established, the appellate court will presume that the first instance judge knew it and applied it correctly.[190]

In other cases, the judge's understanding of the law should appear clearly from his reasoned decision. If it does not, the dissatisfied party should in the first instance seek clarification from the judge.[191] If that is not forthcoming or not practicable, it may be necessary to infer what his understanding of the law was.

In some cases it may be possible to infer that the judge has misunderstood the correct legal principle from the decision he reached. In other circumstances, however, the mere coincidence of the fact that the judge did not spell out his understanding of the law and his decision was not one that the appellate court would have reached should not lead the appellate court into setting aside his decision.

Consideration of all relevant factors

The Court must consider all relevant factors, and not take into account a matter which is irrelevant, or fail to take into account a factor which is relevant.

3–068

The court may be able to consider criteria set down in guidelines; and if they exist, it may be obliged at least to consider them. Where a statute or statutory instrument lays out guidelines or principles which should guide the exercise of discretion, it is likely that a failure to follow those guidelines or principles will amount to an error of law, because the discretion may be trammelled by the guidelines or principles.

The courts sometimes draw up guidelines for factors which should be borne in mind in exercising a particular discretion, and factors which should be ignored. This helps to determine the way in which the discretion is exercised, and thus may encourage some measure of uniformity of judicial decision making.[192] Brennan J., sitting in the High Court of Australia, explained in *Norbis v Norbis*[193] held that the courts should be astute to ensure that such guidelines did not harden into legal principles that improperly fetter the judicial discretion; and nor should they be used to prevent judges from deciding cases on the basis of the range of permissible

---

[189] *Ross v Stonewood Securities Ltd* [2004] EWHC 2235 (Ch) at [41], per Lewison J.
[190] See the quotation from *Novus Aviation Ltd v Onur Air Tasimacilik AS* [2009] 1 Lloyd's Rep. 576 at [70], per Lawrence Collins L.J. (as he was) in para.3–014.
[191] See further paras 11–008 and 14–010.
[192] *Ward v James* [1966] 1 Q.B. 273 at 295, per Lord Denning M.R.
[193] (1986) 161 C.L.R. 513: a judgment praised by Lord Hoffmann in *Piglowska v Piglowski* [1999] 1 W.L.R. 1360 at 1373.

differences in standards and values which might be accepted as reasonable by the community over time. However, so long as the courts draw up guidelines only carefully and cautiously, they may be of great benefit:

> "It is inevitable that the wisdom gained in continually supervising the exercise of a statutory discretion will find expression in judicial guidelines. That is not to invest an appellate court with legislative power but rather to acknowledge that, in the way of the common law, a principle which can be seen to be common to a particular class of case will ultimately find judicial expression. The orderly administration of justice requires that decisions should be consistent one with another and decision-making should not be open to the reproach that it is adventitious."[194]

The House of Lords has held that in matters of practice and discretion if guidelines are needed they are better laid down by the Court of Appeal.[195]

Where guidelines exist, and a judge has failed to consider them, then the appellate court is likely to exercise the discretion again. The mere fact, however, that the judge has on the facts of a particular case declined to follow the guidelines cannot in itself amount to an exercise of discretion that is wrong, because that would elevate the guidelines to the status of legal rules.[196]

Discretion in equity

3–069   Equitable remedies are discretionary in nature. The proposition is easy to state but less easy to explain. It has been explained in the following terms:

> "All equitable remedies are, in an appropriate sense, discretionary. In the auxiliary jurisdiction of the court, for example, equitable discretions are exercised by taking into account all relevant matters that tend towards the justice or injustice of granting the remedy that is sought, such as hardship, laches, unfairness, the lack of clean hands, and so on, and by weighing them against each other in order to decide whether the particular relief that is in question should be granted in an absolute, partial or condition form or else refused."[197]

Many equitable remedies are discretionary in nature.

In relation to interlocutory injunctions, the proper approach for an appellate court was laid down by Lord Diplock in *Hadmor Productions v Hamilton*[198] in the following terms:

---

[194] *Norbis v Norbis* (1986) 161 C.L.R. 513 at 536.
[195] *Thompson v Brown* [1981] 1 W.L.R. 744 at 752, per Lord Diplock.
[196] See *Ward v James* [1966] 1 Q.B. 273 at 295, per Lord Denning M.R.
[197] Spry, *Equitable Remedies*, 6th edn (2001), p.4.
[198] [1983] A.C. 191 at 220.

"An interlocutory injunction is a discretionary relief and the discretion whether or not to grant it is vested in the High Court judge by whom the application for it is heard. Upon an appeal from the judge's grant or refusal of an interlocutory injunction the function of an appellate court, whether it be the Court of Appeal or your Lordships' House, is not to exercise an independent discretion of its own. It must defer to the judge's exercise of his discretion and must not interfere with it merely upon the ground that the members of the appellate court would have exercised the discretion differently. The function of the appellate court is initially one of review only. It may set aside the judge's exercise of his discretion on the ground that it was based upon a mis-understanding of the law or of the evidence before him or upon an inference that particular facts existed or did not exist, which, although it was one that might legitimately have been drawn upon the evidence that was before the judge, can be demonstrated to be wrong by further evidence that has become available by the time of the appeal; or upon the ground that there has been a change of circumstances after the judge made his order that would have justified his acceding to an application to vary it. Since reasons given by judges for granting or refusing interlocutory injunctions may sometimes be sketchy, there may also be occasional cases where even though no erroneous assumption of law or fact can be identified the judge's decision to grant or refuse the injunction is so aberrant that it must be set aside upon the ground that no reasonable judge regardful of his duty to act judicially could have reached it. It is only if and after the appellate court has reached the conclusion that the judge's exercise of his discretion must be set aside for one or other of these reasons, that it becomes entitled to exercise an original discretion of its own."

New evidence will only allow the appellate court to exercise the discretion afresh if it invalidates the reasons given by the judge for his decision.[199]

Statutory discretions

Appeals from exercises of judicial discretion are quite distinct from the judicial review of an exercise of administrative discretionary power. Whilst an appellate court will interfere with the judicial exercise of statutory discretion if is wrong, the court will not interfere with administrative discretion unless it is *Wednesbury* unreasonable.[200]   **3–070**

If the lower court was exercising a statutory discretion, the appellate court will not interfere with it unless it was wrong, in the *G v G* sense.[201]

---

[199] *Hadmor Productions v Hamilton* [1983] A.C. 191 at 220, per Lord Diplock.
[200] *Associated Provincial Picture Houses Ltd v Wednesbury Corp* [1948] 1 K.B. 223.
[201] *G v G* [1985] 1 W.L.R. 647 at 652, per Lord Fraser of Tullybelton; *Charles Osenton v Johnston* [1942] A.C. 130 at 138, per Viscount Simon L.C.; *Tanfern Ltd v Cameron-MacDonald* [2000] 1 W.L.R. 1311 at 1317, per Brooke L.J. See para.3–066.

"Courts of appeal exist to remedy mistakes in the first instance process. The Court of Appeal is not intended to be a forum in which unsuccessful litigants, where no error occurred at first instance, may have a second trial of the same issue by different judges under the guise of an appeal."

Case management decisions

3–071   Case management decisions usually amount to the exercise of judicial discretion. The appellate courts approach the review of case management decisions in the same way that they approach the review of other decisions involving discretion.

Paragraphs 4.4–4.5 of the Practice Direction to Pt 52 address appeals from case management decisions.

Paragraph 4.4 sets out an apparently non-exclusive list of decisions which are case management decisions: disclosure, filing of witness statements or experts' reports; directions about the timetable of the claim; adding a party to a claim; and security for costs. A more exhaustive list of case management powers appears in CPR r.3.1.

Paragraph 4.5 of PD 52 provides that, when considering whether or not to give permission to appeal, the court[202] may take into account whether:

(a) the issue is of insufficient significance to justify the costs of an appeal;

(b) the procedural consequences of an appeal outweigh the significance of the case management decision; and

(c) it would be more convenient to determine the issue at or after trial.

Considerations of proportionality and practical importance are likely to be important when considering whether to give permission to appeal against a case management decision, in order to allow the court to avoid the costs and delay associated with appeals which take place before trial.

Where a case is proceeding in the County Court case management decisions will probably be made by district judges, save where the case is in the Mercantile or Technology and Construction list, in which case they may be made by a circuit judge.

As described in more detail in Chapter 12, appeals against decisions of district judges lie to circuit judges; appeals against decisions of circuit judges lie to judges of the High Court.

In the Queen's Bench or Chancery Divisions of the High Court at the Royal Courts of Justice (but not one of the specialist courts of the Queen's Bench Division), it is likely that case management decisions will be made by

---

[202] CPR r.52.13. The court considering the application for permission to appeal could generally be either the lower court or the appellate court, unless it is a second appeal to the Court of Appeal, in which case it must be the Court of Appeal. See, for more detail, Ch.12.

masters, against whose decisions appeals lie to the judge. Outside the Royal Courts of Justice, decisions will be made by district judges sitting as registrars of the High Court.

In relation to first appeals from case management decisions of district judges and masters, the changes introduced by the Access to Justice Act 1999 in order to give effect to the recommendations of the Bowman Report are of great significance.

Under the old rules, echoes were still heard of the fact that Chancery masters had originally exercised powers delegated by judges; and litigants enjoyed a right to ask a judge to exercise his power personally, rather than through a master. Under that system, and in the Queen's Bench division, an "appeal" to a judge from a master was by way of rehearing and not review. Under the new rules, the position is quite different: the appeal will be allowed only if the decision of the lower court was wrong.

3–072

Under the new rules, the approach of appellate courts to case management directions is set out definitively in the judgment of Brooke L.J. in *Tanfern Ltd v Cameron-Macdonald*[203]:

> "30. As a general rule, every appeal will be limited to a review of the decision of the lower court. This general rule will be applied unless a practice direction makes different provision for a particular category of appeal, or the court considers that in the circumstances of an individual appeal it would be in the interests of justice to hold a rehearing: C.P.R., r. 52.11(1). The appeal court will only allow an appeal where the decision of the lower court was wrong, or where it was unjust because of a serious procedural or other irregularity in the proceedings in the lower court: C.P.R., r. 52.11(3).

> 31 This marks a significant change in practice, in relation to what used to be called 'interlocutory appeals' from district judges or masters. Under the old practice, the appeal to a judge was a rehearing in the fullest sense of the word, and the judge exercised his/her discretion afresh, while giving appropriate weight to the way the lower court had exercised its discretion in the matter. Under the new practice, the decision of the lower court will attract much greater significance. The appeal court's duty is now limited to a review of that decision, and it may only interfere in the quite limited circumstances set out in C.P.R., r. 52.11(3).

> 32 The first ground for interference speaks for itself. The epithet "wrong" is to be applied to the substance of the decision made by the lower court. If the appeal is against the exercise of a discretion by the lower court, the decision of the House of Lords in *G. v. G. (Minors: Custody Appeal)* [1985] 1 W.L.R. 647 warrants attention. In that case Lord Fraser of Tullybelton said, at p. 652:

---

[203] [2000] 1 W.L.R. 1311 at 1317.

'Certainly it would not be useful to inquire whether different shades of meaning are intended to be conveyed by words such as "blatant error" used by the President in the present case, and words such as "clearly wrong" "plainly wrong", or simply "wrong" used by other judges in other cases. All these various expressions were used in order to emphasise the point that the appellate court should only interfere when they consider that the judge of first instance has not merely preferred an imperfect solution which is different from an alternative imperfect solution which the Court of Appeal might or would have adopted, but has exceeded the generous ambit within which a reasonable disagreement is possible'."

The appeal exists against case management decisions to prevent serious injustice, rather than to tinker with discretionary decisions which are properly speaking in the judge's and not the appellate court's purview.

"...it is essential for the satisfactory operation of the new CPR regime that the authority of the judges in the lower case in case management issues should not be undermined by decisions of this court, unless this court considers that their decisions were clearly wrong, or that they have gone wrong in law, or there is some serious procedural mishap. This court of course performs an important function in ensuring that serious injustice does not occur and in drawing attention to the importance of compliance with rules in the practice direction."[204]

Case management in the specialist courts

3–073   The appellate courts are generally reluctant to conclude that decisions of specialist judges are wrong,[205] particularly in the context of case management decisions. Where, as with high cost cases in the Commercial Court and generally in the Technology and Construction Court, it is common for a case to be case managed by a particular judge, it will be particularly difficult for a party to appeal against a case management decision, because the judge at first instance has accumulated knowledge of the case and its background accumulated from a number of interlocutory hearings. In that context, the Court of Appeal will find it particularly difficult to say that the decision of the judge was wrong.[206]

---

[204] *Ahmed v Stanley A Coleman* [2002] EWCA Civ 935 at [46].
[205] See paras 3–050 to 3–051 and 13–011.
[206] *Morris v Bank of America* [2002] EWCA Civ 425 at [9], per Chadwick L.J.; *Law Debenture v Lexington* [2002] EWCA Civ 1673 at [5], per Clarke L.J. (although the appeal was in that case allowed).

Second appeals

In the majority of cases appeals against case management decisions will not be heard by the Court of Appeal, but by a single judge at a lower level. In those circumstances, it will be very difficult to bring an appeal to the Court of Appeal, because it will be a second appeal under CPR r.52.13, in respect of which only the Court of Appeal may give permission, and permission will be only given if the appeal raises an important point of principle, or there is some other compelling reason for the Court of Appeal to hear the appeal.[207]   **3–074**

In *Uphill v BRB (Residuary) Ltd*[208] the Court of Appeal emphasised that it was not sufficient for the decision to be wrong. In that case, the defendant sought to appeal a decision of a district judge to extend time to serve a claim form. The circuit judge dismissed the appeal. In the period of time between argument and handing down judgment on the first appeal to the circuit judge, the Court of Appeal gave guidance[209] which indicated that the district judge's decision was wrong. However, that authority was not drawn to the circuit judge's attention.

The Court of Appeal held that the mere fact that the circuit judge's decision was wrong was not sufficient to grant permission to appeal. In circumstances where the Court of Appeal had already given guidance, there was no important point of principle for the Court of Appeal to decide; nor was there any other compelling reason to allow the appeal. Accordingly, the Court of Appeal declined to grant permission to appeal.

Costs

Until October 1, 1993 s.18(1)(f) of the Senior Courts Act 1981, based upon s.49 of the Supreme Courts Act 1925 provided that no appeal would like to the Court of Appeal on a question of costs, from any order of the High Court or any other court or tribunal relating only to costs which are by law left to the discretion of the court or tribunal without the leave of the court or tribunal in question.   **3–075**

In *Scherer v Counting Instruments Ltd (Note)*[210] the Court of Appeal held that that ouster of jurisdiction did not apply if it was possible to say that the judge in the court below did not really exercise his discretion at all or based the exercise of his discretion upon an inadmissible reason. Section 18(1)(f) was deleted on October 1, 1993[211] by the Courts and Legal Services Act 1990 Sch.20, but decisions of the Court of Appeal pre-dating 1993 which

---

[207] Second appeals are addressed in more detail at para.12–025.
[208] [2005] 1 W.L.R. 2070.
[209] *Hashtroodi v Hancock* [2004] EWCA Civ 652; [2004] 1 W.L.R. 3206.
[210] [1986] 1 W.L.R. 615; approved in *BankAmerica Finance Ltd v Nock* [1988] A.C. 1002.
[211] Courts and Legal Services Act 1990 (Commencement No.9) Order 1993 (SI 1993/2132).

refer to a failure on the part of the judge to exercise his discretion need to be read with these factors in mind.

Appeals against costs orders are now subject to the same rules as those applying to other orders.

By s.51(1) of the Senior Courts Act 1981, the costs of and incidental to all proceedings in (a) the civil division of the Court of Appeal, (b) the High Court, and (c) any county court, shall be in the discretion of the court. As such, a decision about costs is treated in principle in the same way as any other discretionary decision: the appellate court will not interfere with it unless it is wrong; and in so doing, will interfere with the decision only when it considers that the judge of first instance has not merely preferred an imperfect solution which is different from an alternative imperfect solution which the appellate court might or would have adopted, but where the lower court has exceeded the generous ambit within which a reasonable disagreement is possible.[212]

This test requires the appellate court to consider whether or not, in a case involving the exercise of discretion, the judge has approached the matter applying the correct principles, has taken into account all relevant considerations and has not taken into account irrelevant considerations, and has reached a decision which is one which can properly be described as a decision which is within the ambit of reasonable decisions open to the judge on the facts of the case.[213]

3–076   CPR r.44.3 sets down principles that the court must consider when exercising its discretion about costs. Since r.44.3(4) provides that the court must have regard to all the circumstances when exercising its discretion, there is some scope for argument about whether or not the court has taken all relevant factors into consideration. However, appeals against orders for costs are notoriously difficult to sustain precisely because the trial judge has such a wide discretion, within which "there is usually much room for reasonable disagreement".[214]

Whilst it may be a useful reminder for a judge to state that he is applying the principles under CPR r.44, a judge should not be criticised for not expressly referring to it if it is obvious that he has applied the principles which are stated within that rule.[215]

It is suggested that in the context of costs appeals the appellate court will be particularly astute to remember that:

(a) the judge below will have had considerable experience of the litigation which will have informed his approach to costs; and

---

[212] *G v G (Minors: Custody Appeal)* [1985] 1 W.L.R. 647, per Lord Fraser, applied in *Tanfern Ltd v Cameron-Macdonald* [2000] 1 W.L.R. 1311 at 1317.
[213] *Solutia UK Ltd v Griffiths* [2001] C.P. Rep. 92 at [11], per Latham L.J.
[214] *Burchell and Bullard* [2005] EWCA Civ 358 at [25], per Ward L.J.
[215] *Olden v the Crown Prosecution Service* [2010] EWCA Civ 961 at [17], per Ward L.J. referring to *Grimes v the Crown Prosecution Service* [2003] EWCA Civ 1814 at [18], per Brooke L.J.

> (b) it is possible and perhaps even likely that the judge properly considered and relied upon factors which were not fully articulated in his decision.

The appellate court must, it has been said, exercise a degree of self-restraint and recognise the advantage which the trial judge enjoys as a result of his "feel" for the case which he has tried.[216]

It is more common for appeals against costs orders to go to the Court of Appeal than appeals against case management directions, because trials are heard by district judges only on the small claims and fast tracks (save with the consent of the parties) and cannot be heard by masters save with the consent of the parties. Accordingly, it is not uncommon for a party dissatisfied with a costs order made after trial to seek to appeal it to the Court of Appeal for the first time, so that the appeal is not limited by the provisions of CPR r.52.13 in relation to second appeals.

Appeals within detailed assessments

Where the appeal is against an order made by a costs judge in the context of a detailed assessment, it may be that the decision of the costs judge may be insufficiently reasoned to explain precisely why he has reached the decision he has reached. Although as discussed in Chapter 5, failure to give adequate reasons may sometimes by a ground of appeal in itself, in the context of costs assessments it will often be impossible and/or undesirable for the costs judge to spell out the exact process of reasoning which has led to the final figure, because it may be the result of a triangulation, based on the judge's expert "feel", between a variety of relatively unfixed possible positions.[217]   3–077

Wasted costs orders

Section 51 of the Senior Courts Act 1981 gives the court discretion to order legal representatives to pay wasted costs incurred by a party as a result of any improper, unreasonable or negligent act or omission on the part of that legal representative. This involves a two stage process: first, whether there is a prima facie case for an order; and secondly, the legal representative having been afforded the opportunity to make submissions, the decision about whether or not to make an order. It is very difficult to appeal from an order for wasted costs, because the judge below has the distinct advantage of being fully aware of the nature of the conduct, and any effect it has: it has been held that it will be rare for the court to interfere with a finding at first   3–078

---

[216] *Johnsey Estates (1990) Ltd v Secretary of State for the Environment* [2001] L. & T.R. 32 at [22], per Chadwick L.J.
[217] *Jemma Trust Co v Liptrott* [2004] EWHC 1404 (Ch); [2004] 4 Costs L.R. 610 at [26], per Hart J.

instance unless a "very strong" case for doing so is made out.[218] It is even more difficult to appeal against an order in relation to whether the applicant has established a prima facie case.[219]

---

[218] *Wall v Lefever* [1998] 1 F.C.R. 605 at 617F, per Lord Woolf M.R.
[219] *Fryer v Royal Institute of Chartered Surveyors* [2000] P.N.L.R. 649.

CHAPTER 4

Serious Irregularity

INTRODUCTION

By CPR r.52.11(3), the appeal court will allow an appeal where the deci- 4–001
sion of the lower court was (a) wrong; or (b) unjust because of a serious
procedural or other irregularity in the proceedings in the lower court. The
first ground—that the decision was wrong—is addressed in Chapter 3. This
chapter addresses the second ground: seeking to appeal because the decision
was unjust by reason of a serious procedural or other irregularity.

INJUSTICE BY REASON OF IRREGULARITY

The objective of the Civil Procedure Rules is, of course, to enable the court 4–002
to deal with cases justly.[1] Where a decision was unjust because of a serious
procedural or other irregularity in the proceedings below, the appellant
need not show that the decision was wrong. The irregularity refers to an
irregularity in the manner in which the decision was reached, rather than
the merits of the decision.[2]

However, the appellant must show that the irregularity was serious, and
that this caused the decision to be unjust.[3] This is an onerous task.[4] Whether
it was unjust will depend upon all the circumstances of the case.[5]

A FAIR TRIAL

Parties are entitled to a fair trial under art.6 of the European Convention on 4–003
Human Rights. The right to a fair trial in respect of civil rights encompasses

---

[1] CPR r.1.1(1).
[2] *Alder v First Choice Holidays & Flights Ltd* [2004] C.L.Y. 275.
[3] *Tanfern Ltd v Cameron-Macdonald* [2000] EWCA Civ 3023 at [33].
[4] *Keith Davy (Contractors) Ltd v Ibatex Ltd* [2001] EWCA Civ 740 at [20], per Tuckey L.J.
[5] *Hayes v Transco Plc* [2003] EWCA Civ 1261 at [14], per Clarke L.J.

the right to a fair and public hearing within a reasonable time by an independent and impartial tribunal established by law. Judgment should be pronounced publicly, though art.6 sets out circumstances in which the press and public may be excluded.

In considering whether there has been a fair trial for the purposes of art.6, the court must consider the trial as a whole, including the decision of the appellate court, whose procedure may be sufficient to remedy any unfairness caused at the trial.[6]

Article 6 does not compel the contracting states to set up courts of appeal. Nevertheless, a state which does institute such courts is required to ensure that persons amenable to the law enjoy before these courts the fundamental guarantees contained in art.6.[7] The right of access to such courts is not absolute, and the state is permitted to place limitations on the right to access. In this regard, although the state enjoys a margin of appreciation, any limitations must pursue a legitimate aim and there must be a reasonable relationship of proportionality between the means employed and the aim to be achieved.[8]

It cannot after 10 years of practice and experience seriously be contended that the essential elements of civil justice in England and Wales under the CPR, if properly implemented and followed, are incompatible with art.6. It is unlikely, therefore, that in the context of an appeal from the High Court or County Courts, the right to a fair trial under art.6 will materially add to or affect an allegation that there has been a serious procedural or other irregularity in the proceedings in the lower court. If the right to a fair trial has been impeded, there will almost certainly also have been a serious procedural or other irregularity.

EXAMPLES OF PROCEDURAL OR OTHER IRREGULARITIES

4–004   Bringing an appeal under CPR r.52.11(3)(b) requires the appellant to show first that there has been a procedural or other irregularity; secondly that it was serious; and thirdly that, as a result, the decision was unjust. The variety of possible irregularities is infinite, but serious irregularities are in practice rare. Whether an irregularity was serious or not will depend upon the nature of the irregularity, and it may depend upon the circumstances of the case in which it arose. Whether the decision was, as a result, unjust,

---

[6] *Edwards v United Kingdom* (1993) 15 E.H.R.R. 417 at [36]–[37]; a criminal case, but the principle is equally applicable to civil disputes.

[7] *Delcourt v Belguim* (1970) 1 E.H.R.R. 355 at [25]. *Delcourt* related to a criminal charge, but the principles apply to civil determinations too: *Nascimento v United Kingdom* (Application No.55331/00) Unreported January 31, 2002.

[8] *Brualla Gomez de la Torre v Spain* (2001) 33 E.H.R.R. 57 at [33]; *Nascimento v United Kingdom* (Application No.55331/00) Unreported January 31, 2002. See para.13–004 on the compatibility of the system requiring appellants to obtain permission to appeal with art.6.

requires the court to consider the effect of the irregularity. The following examples of irregularities appear from the case law.

BIAS

Where a judge is or appears to be biased, an appeal will lie for a serious procedural or other irregularity. If the judge is or appears to be biased, his decision will almost inevitably be unjust.   4–005

The test for bias is whether the fair-minded and informed observer, having considered the facts, would conclude that there was a real possibility that the tribunal was biased.[9] The fair-minded observer is "neither complacent nor unduly sensitive or suspicious".[10] The informed observer will understand the legal system.

If the test is satisfied, the judge must recuse himself. It is not a matter of discretion, but of judgment.[11] In most cases, the answer, one way or the other will be obvious. But if in any case there is real ground for doubt, that doubt should be resolved in favour of recusal.[12]

Useful guidance to what will and will not amount to bias was given by the Court of Appeal in *Locabail (UK) Ltd v Bayfield Properties Ltd*.[13] Whilst that case was decided under a slightly different test for bias, it remains reliable under the law as it presently stands.[14]

"It would be dangerous and futile to attempt to define or list the factors which may or may not give rise to a real danger of bias. Everything will depend on the facts, which may include the nature of the issue to be decided. We cannot, however, conceive of circumstances in which an objection could be soundly based on the religion, ethnic or national origin, gender, age, class, means or sexual orientation of the judge.

Nor, at any rate ordinarily, could an objection be soundly based on the judge's social or educational or service or employment background or history, nor that of any member of the judge's family; or previous political associations; or membership of social or sporting or charitable bodies; or Masonic associations; or previous judicial decisions; or extra-curricular utterances (whether in textbooks, lectures, speeches, articles, interviews, reports or responses to consultation papers); or

---

[9] *Porter v Magill* [2002] 2 A.C. 357 at 102, approving *In re Medicaments and Related Classes of Goods (No.2)* [2001] 1 W.L.R. 700 at 726–727.

[10] *Johnson v Johnson* (2000) 201 C.L.R. 488 at 509, [53], per Kirby J., cited with approval in *Gillies v Secretary of State for Work and Pensions* 2006 S.C. (HL) 71 at [17] and [39]; *Muscat v Health Professions Council* [2008] EWHC 2798 (Admin) at [59].

[11] *AWG Group v Morrison* [2006] 1 W.L.R. 1163 at [6].

[12] *Locabail (UK) Ltd v Bayfield Properties Ltd* [2000] Q.B. 451 at 480, [25].

[13] [2000] Q.B. 451 at 480, [25].

[14] *Porter v Magill* [2002] 2 A.C. 357 at [101]. See also *Lawal v Northern Spirit* [2003] I.C.R. 856.

previous receipt of instructions to act for or against any party, solicitor or advocate engaged in a case before him; or membership of the same Inn, circuit, local Law Society or chambers. . . .

By contrast, a real danger of bias might well be thought to arise if there were personal friendship or animosity between the judge and any member of the public involved in the case; or if the judge were closely acquainted with any member of the public involved in the case, particularly if the credibility of that individual could be significant in the decision of the case; or if, in a case where the credibility of any individual were an issue to be decided by the judge, he had in a previous case rejected the evidence of that person in such outspoken terms as to throw doubt on his ability to approach such person's evidence with an open mind on any later occasion; or if on any question at issue in the proceedings before him the judge had expressed views, particularly in the course of the hearing, in such extreme and unbalanced terms as to throw doubt on his ability to try the issue with an objective judicial mind (see *Vakauta v. Kelly* (1989) 167 C.L.R. 568); or if, for any other reason, there were real ground for doubting the ability of the judge to ignore extraneous considerations, prejudices and predilections and bring an objective judgment to bear on the issues before him.

The mere fact that a judge, earlier in the same case or in a previous case, had commented adversely on a party or witness, or found the evidence of a party or witness to be unreliable, would not without more found a sustainable objection. In most cases, we think, the answer, one way or the other, will be obvious. But if in any case there is real ground for doubt, that doubt should be resolved in favour of recusal. We repeat: every application must be decided on the facts and circumstances of the individual case. The greater the passage of time between the event relied on as showing a danger of bias and the case in which the objection is raised, the weaker (other things being equal) the objection will be."

It is obvious that a judge should recuse himself, if there is any fresh animosity between him and a party.[15]

As discussed in para.16-060, the suffering by a judge of a condition or symptom that was the subject of the case was no basis for recusal.[16]

In *Helow v Secretary of State for the Home Department*[17] it was held that a judge who was a member of the International Association of Jewish Lawyers and Jurists, whose magazine had carried a number of articles and pronouncements that were antipathetic to the Palestinian Liberation

---

[15] *Howell v Lees Millais* [2007] EWCA Civ 720, where the judge had recently been rejected for employment by a firm of solicitors, one of whose partners was a party to a dispute he had been listed to hear.

[16] *Baker v Quantum Clothing Group* [2009] EWCA Civ 566; [2009] C.P. Rep. 38 at [33]–[34].

[17] [2008] UKHL 62; [2008] 1 W.L.R. 2416.

Organisation, need not have recused himself from hearing an asylum appeal where the applicant was a sympathiser with the PLO and feared attack by Israeli agents.

Where in any particular case one or more members of a court which has partly heard proceedings are unable to continue the Master of Rolls has the power to give directions as to how the court is to continue hearing the case.[18]

THE JUDGE MAY NOT BE JUDGE IN HIS OWN CAUSE

A judge may not decide any matter in which he has a personal interest. So in *Dimes v Grand Junction Union Canal Co* an order of the Lord Chancellor was set aside because he had a substantial interest in the company.[19] More recently, an appeal was allowed where a member of the judicial committee of the House of Lords was a director of a charity intervening in the appeal.[20]   **4–006**

PRE-JUDGING THE DISPUTE

A judge is, of course, obliged to listen to the evidence, and make his decision on the basis of all the evidence. In the 1660s Hale C.J. wrote, "I suffer not myself to be prepossessed with any judgment at all, till the whole business and both parties be heard".[21]   **4–007**

That is not to say, of course, that a judge is not entitled to express provisional views during the hearing. Sir Thomas Bingham M.R., as he was, explained in *Arab Monetary Fund v Hashim*[22] that "the English forensic tradition sanctions and even encourages a measure of disclosure by the judge of his current thinking". It does not, however, sanction the premature expression of factual conclusions or anything prematurely indicating a closed mind. A judge may, in relation to some feature of a party's case which strikes him as inherently improbable, indicate the need for unusually compelling evidence to persuade him of the fact. An expression of scepticism is not suggestive of bias unless the judge conveys an unwillingness to be persuaded of a factual proposition whatever the evidence might be.[23]

Where a judge indicates that he has already made his mind up, before he has heard all the evidence, it is likely that his decision will have been reached irregularly. In one case, a judge said at the beginning of a case: "It

---

[18] Senior Courts Act 1981 s.54(4A).
[19] *Dimes v Grand Junction Canal Co* (1852) 3 H.L.C. 758.
[20] *R. v Bow Street Metropolitan Stipendiary Magistrate Ex p. Pinochet Ugarte (No.2)* [2000] 1 A.C. 119.
[21] Quoted in Lord Bingham, "Judicial Ethics", *The Business of Judging* (OUP, 2000), p.80.
[22] *The Times*, May 4, 1993.
[23] *Arab Monetary Fund v Hashim The Times*, May 4, 1993. See also *Johnson v Johnson* (2000) 201 C.L.R. 488.

seems to me that this case can be decided in a minute. There is no need for all this evidence." The Court of Appeal held that, were it not for an unanswerable point in the respondent's favour (which the judge had entirely ignored), a new trial would been ordered.[24]

An argument that the judge has decided the dispute prematurely may well overlap with an allegation that he is or appears to be biased. In *Ealing LBC v Jan*[25] the Court of Appeal held that a judge who had twice said about the respondent that he could not trust him further than he could throw him should not hear an application to commit the respondent for contempt.

In *Timmins v Gormley*[26] it was held that a recorder who had published articles in which he had expressed "pronounced pro-claimant anti-insurer views" should not decide a personal injuries case where the defendant was insured, though the Court of Appeal thought the issue very finely balanced, commenting that[27]:

> "It is not inappropriate for a judge to write in publications of the class to which the recorder contributed. The publications are of value to the profession and for a lawyer of the recorder's experience to contribute to those publications can further rather than hinder the administration of justice. There is a long established tradition that the writing of books and articles or the editing of legal textbooks is not incompatible with holding judicial office and the discharge of judicial functions. There is nothing improper in the recorder being engaged in his writing activities. It is the tone of the recorder's opinions and the trenchancy with which they were expressed which is challenged here. Anyone writing in an area in which he sits judicially has to exercise considerable care not to express himself in terms which indicate that he has preconceived views which are so firmly held that it may not be possible for him to try a case with an open mind. This is the position notwithstanding the fact that ..., there can be very real advantages in having a judge adjudicate in the area of law in which he specialises. But if this is to happen it must be recognised that his opinions as to particular features of the subject will become known. The specialist judge must therefore be circumspect in the language he uses and the tone in which he expresses himself. It is always inappropriate for a judge to use intemperate language about subjects on which he has adjudicated or will have to adjudicate."

---

[24] *Fitzkriston LLP v Panayi* [2008] EWCA Civ 283.
[25] [2002] EWCA Civ 329.
[26] Heard with the appeal in *Locabail (UK) Ltd v Bayfield Properties Ltd* [2000] Q.B. 451: see [71]–[89].
[27] *Locabail (UK) Ltd v Bayfield Properties Ltd* [2000] Q.B. 451 at [85].

JUDGE NOT AUTHORISED TO HEAR THE CASE

The fact that a judge was not authorised to hear the case probably amounts   **4–008**
to an irregularity, but it may not be serious, if the judge was qualified to
hear it. In a case where a circuit judge authorised to hear Technology and
Construction Court cases heard a Queen's Bench Division case in a district
registry, the decision was sound because it had been validly transferred to
the TCC; but even if it had not been, she would have had de facto authority
to hear the case at common law.[28]

The common law doctrine of de facto authority says that the acts of an
officer or judge may be held to be valid in law even though his own
appointment is invalid and in truth he has no legal power at all. The basis
for the rule has been said to be that once a court with competent jurisdiction is duly established, "a suitor who resorts to it for the administration of justice and the protection of private rights should not be defeated
or embarrassed by questions relating to the title of the judge, who presides
in the court, to his office".[29]

However, a judge who knows or should know that he does not have
authority to decide a case does not have de facto authority to decide it,
because the de facto doctrine cannot validate the acts nor ratify the
authority of a person who, though to all appearances a judge of the court in
which he sits, knows that he is not.[30]

It is suggested that if a judge was not authorised to hear the case and was
not qualified to hear it; or where he knew or should have known that he
was not authorised to hear it; or, perhaps, where he gave no proper thought
as to whether he was authorised to hear it, then there may be a serious
procedural irregularity sufficient to ground an appeal.

CASE MANAGEMENT DECISIONS

Some allegations of procedural irregularity arise in the context of com-   **4–009**
plaints about the judge's exercise of discretionary case management powers. It is difficult to conceive that a discretionary case management decision
could be unjust because of a serious procedural or other irregularity unless
the case management decision could also be characterised as wrong. In
other words, if the appellant is to show that the case management decision
was unjust because of some serious irregularity, the appellant will probably
in so doing have also to satisfy the appellate court that the judge's case
management decision has "exceeded the generous ambit within which a

---

[28] *Fawdry & Co v Murfitt* [2003] Q.B. 104.
[29] Sir Owen Dixon, later Chief Justice of Australia, "De Facto Officers" (first published in
Res Judicatae (Melbourne, 1938), reproduced in S. Woinarski (ed.), *Jesting Pilate* (1965)),
quoted by Hale L.J. (as she then was) in *Fawdry & Co v Murfitt* [2003] Q.B. 104 at [20].
[30] *Fawdry & Co v Murfitt* [2003] Q.B. 104 at [22] and [58]; *Coppard v Customs and Excise
Commissioners* [2003] Q.B. 1428 at [18]–[24]; *Baldock v Webster* [2006] Q.B. 315.

reasonable disagreement is possible".[31] It is perhaps possible that a case management decision could be "wrong" without also being unjust by reason of a serious procedural irregularity; but practically speaking, one would expect that, in the context of discretionary case management decisions, either the two tests in CPR r.52.11(3) will both be satisfied, or neither will be satisfied.

EFFECTIVE OPPORTUNITY TO MAKE REPRESENTATIONS

4–010   The common law rules of natural justice or procedural fairness are two-fold: first, the person affected has the right to prior notice and an effective opportunity to make representations before a decision is made; and secondly, the person affected has the right to an unbiased tribunal.[32] It follows that a party must be entitled to make representations on any issue relevant to the judge's decision, and a judge should allow submissions on any issue which is relevant to his decision. A failure to give the parties an effective opportunity to make representations is unusual in the context of litigation, though it is more often the source of complaints in arbitration, discussed in Part 5.

IRRELEVANT JUDICIAL COMMENTS

4–011   It has been held that irrelevant discussion and comment from the judge, for example in relation to whether a claim had been brought because the claimant had been "cold-called" by "ambulance chasing" solicitors, whilst unfortunate, was not sufficient to amount to a serious procedural or other irregularity.[33]

REFUSAL TO HEAR EVIDENCE

4–012   A refusal, or, perhaps, failure, to allow evidence on all relevant issues may give rise to a serious procedural or other irregularity. In a claim brought under the Sex Discrimination Act 1975, the appellant wished to adduce evidence to show that the membership rules of the Hackney Action for Racial Equality, whilst they appeared to allow anyone to join, were in fact a sham. Where she had not been permitted to do so, the Court of Appeal

---

[31] *Tanfern Ltd v Cameron-Macdonald* [2000] 1 W.L.R. 1311 at [32], per Brooke L.J.; see paras 3–071 and 3–072.

[32] *AMEC Capital Projects Ltd v Whitefriars City Estates Ltd* [2005] 1 All E.R. 723; [2005] B.L.R. 1 at [14], per Dyson L.J.

[33] *Ball v Plymouth City Council* [2004] EWHC 134 (QB).

allowed an appeal on the basis that there had been a serious procedural or other irregularity. Sir Christopher Staughton commented that whilst it seemed to him that in allowing the appeal they were "being a little indulgent ..., it is appropriate to do so".[34]

A refusal to allow evidence to be admitted may, of course, amount to an error of law: see para.3–055.

UNFAIR RESTRICTIONS ON CROSS-EXAMINATION

CPR r.32.1(3) gives the court a discretion to limit cross-examination. That discretion encompasses a range of acceptable restrictions which the judge may properly direct.[35] However, where a court decides to curtail cross-examination without notice or without the opportunity for submissions to be made in relation to the decision to curtail cross-examination, then it may amount to a serious procedural irregularity.[36] **4–013**

FAILING TO PAY PROPER ATTENTION DURING THE HEARING

It is occasionally alleged that a hearing was unfair by reason of the judge or a member of the tribunal failing or appearing to fail to pay proper attention to the hearing. **4–014**

In *Stansbury v Datapulse Plc*[37] the appellant had brought a claim in the Employment Tribunal for unfair dismissal. On appeal, he alleged that one of the lay members of an Employment Tribunal had fallen asleep, and was drunk. The Court of Appeal confirmed that it was the duty of the Tribunal to be alert during the whole of the hearing, and to appear to be so, by analogy with cases of bias.

> "A member of a tribunal who does not appear to be alert to what is being said in the course of a hearing may cause that hearing to be held to be unfair, because the hearing should be by a tribunal each member of which is concentrating on the case before him or her. That is the position, as I see it, under English law, quite apart from the European Convention on Human Rights. It is reinforced by article 6(1) of the Convention...."[38]

---

[34] *Sivanandan v Hackney Action For Racial Equality Executive Committee* [2002] EWCA Civ 111.
[35] *Watson v Chief Constable of Cleveland* [2001] EWCA Civ 1547 at [24], per Sir Murray Stuart-Smith.
[36] *Hayes v Transco Plc* [2003] EWCA Civ 1261.
[37] [2004] I.C.R. 523.
[38] [2004] I.C.R. 523 at [28].

If complaint is to be made about failure to pay proper attention, the complaint should be made at the time, and should be specific, so that it is clear what evidence was supposed to have been missed.[39] That should allow the difficulty to be remedied and for the hearing to continue effectively and fairly. In turn, that will save the expense and delay of an appeal. However, as the Court of Appeal also said in *Stansbury*[40]:

> "It is always desirable that a point on the behaviour of the employment tribunal be raised at the employment tribunal in the course of the hearing, but it is unrealistic not to recognise the difficulty, even for legal representatives, in raising with the employment tribunal a complaint about the behaviour of an employment tribunal member who, if the complaint is not upheld, may yet be part of the employment tribunal deciding the case."

How to prove that the judge was asleep may be a delicate issue. In *KD (Inattentive Judges) Afghanistan* the immigration judge vigorously denied having fallen asleep, saying he was "dumbfounded at the allegations" and that had there been any truth in the suggestion he had been asleep he would have taken "corrective measures". Counsel for the applicant, however, had noted contemporaneously on the backsheet of her brief that the "Judge appeared to be sleeping both on entering the court and at various times during the hearing". She provided a statement on appeal, which was supported by statements from her clients. No one else had been present throughout the hearing. In those circumstances, the Upper Tribunal found that there was sufficient evidence that the judge had given at least the appearance of not giving the hearing the attention it required.[41]

EXCESSIVE OR INAPPROPRIATE JUDICIAL QUESTIONING

4–015   It is possible that a judge's behaviour towards a witness was so poor that it gave rise to an appearance of bias; and if so, there will be a serious irregularity. But excessive or hostile questioning may amount to a serious irregularity even when short of bias or appearance of bias.

A judge should not examine or cross-examine a witness himself, because so doing may detract from his ability to decide the case fairly. Lord Greene M.R. explained in *Yuill v Yuill*[42] that:

---

[39]   *R. v Moringiello, The Times*, July 25, 1997. This was a criminal appeal. Different considerations may arise in criminal trials, because the judge does not decide disputes of fact: *Stansbury v Datapulse Plc* [2004] I.C.R. 523 at [21]–[24].

[40]   [2004] I.C.R. 523 at [23].

[41]   [2010] UKUT 261 (IAC); Nichol J. and Senior Immigration Judge Perkins.

[42]   [1945] All E.R. 183 at 189B. See also *Jones v National Coal Board* [1957] 2 Q.B. 55 at 63.

"A judge who observes the demeanour of the witnesses while they are being examined by counsel has from his detached position a much more favourable opportunity of forming a just appreciation than a judge who himself conducts the examination. If he takes the latter course he, so to speak, descends into the arena and is liable to have his vision clouded by the dust of the conflict. Unconsciously he deprives himself of the advantage of calm and dispassionate observation. It is further to be remarked, as everyone who has had experience of these matters knows, that the demeanour of a witness is apt to be very different when he is being questioned by the judge to what it is when he is being questioned by counsel, particularly when the judge's examination is, as it was in the present case, prolonged and covers practically the whole of the crucial matters which are in issue."

Whilst judges are entitled to be more proactive and interventionist than might have been the norm when *Yuill v Yuill* was decided, the Court of Appeal has emphasised that it remains the case that interventions by the judge in the course of oral evidence (as opposed to interventions during counsel's submissions) must inevitably carry the risk that the judge loses the benefit of "calm and dispassionate observation". The greater the frequency of the interventions, the greater the risk; and where the interventions take the form of lengthy interrogation of the witnesses, the risk becomes a serious one.[43]

In every case it will be necessary for the appellate court not just to consider whether, in retrospect, the judge had behaved in a manner that was seriously irregular, but also whether the decision was unjust. Merely asking a witness to clarify or amplify an answer previously given is not, of course unfair.[44] Even leading a witness or asking excessive questions may not amount to a serious irregularity.[45] On the other hand, where the judge asks questions to such an extent that the witness might feel that he is simultaneously facing two cross-examiners—counsel and the judge—then it may give rise to a serious irregularity.[46]

---

[43] *London Borough of Southwark v Kofi-Adu* [2006] EWCA Civ 281 at [144]–[145].
[44] *Cairnstores Ltd Generics (UK) Ltd v Aktiebolaget Hassle* [2002] EWCA Civ 1504; [2003] F.S.R. 23.
[45] *Uppal v Uppal* [2007] EWCA Civ 411; *Almeida v Opportunity Equity Partners* [2006] UKPC 44.
[46] *London Borough of Southwark v Kofi-Adu* [2006] EWCA Civ 281 at [57].

SITTING IN PRIVATE

4–016 Where a court should have sat in public but in fact sat in private, there is likely to have been a serious irregularity.[47] Whether a court or tribunal should sit in public is a matter of law: it should in general sit in public, though in certain circumstances the court has a discretion to sit in private.[48] Whether a court or tribunal was sitting in public or in private is a question of fact.[49] The irregularity is serious, because:

> "The need for public justice, which has now been statutorily recognised, is that it removes the possibility of arbitrariness in the administration of justice, so that in effect the public would have the opportunity of 'judging the judges:' by sitting in public, the judges are themselves accountable and on trial. This was powerfully expressed in the great aphorism that, 'It is not merely of some importance but is of fundamental importance that justice should not only be done but should manifestly and undoubtedly be seen to be done.' The opposite of public justice is of course the administration of justice in private and in secret, behind closed doors, hidden from the view of the public and the press and sheltered from public accountability."[50]

IMPROPER DISCLOSURE OF WITHOUT PREJUDICE OFFERS

4–017 A judge should not see without prejudice save as to costs or Pt 36 offers until after he has reached his decision, and he should not see without prejudice offers at all. But if he does, it does not necessarily follow that he may not hear the case. He must decide whether the disclosure of the offer makes a fair trial impossible and whether justice demands that he recuse himself. But judges should not be too ready to reach such a conclusion; the delay and extra cost occasioned by a recusal may be very considerable.[51]

---

[47] *Storer v British Gas Plc* [2000] 1 W.L.R. 1237.

[48] CPR r.39.2. The discretion to sit in private arises if one of the circumstances listed in r.39.2(3) occurs. See also CPR 39APD.1 and *R. v Bow County Court Ex p. Pelling (No.2)* [2001] U.K.H.R.R. 165.

[49] *Storer v British Gas Plc* [2000] 1 W.L.R. 1237 at [24]: "Whether a court is sitting in public may be, in any individual case, a question of fact and degree for the judge, a matter of discretion." It is respectfully suggested that it is a question of fact and, perhaps, degree, but not a matter of discretion in the sense that that phrase is usually used: see para.3–008.

[50] Sir Jack Jacob's Hamlyn Lecture, *The Fabric of English Civil Justice* (1987), pp.22–23, quoted by Lord Woolf M.R. in *Hodgson v Imperial Tobacco Ltd* [1998] 1 W.L.R. 1056 at 1069 and by Henry L.J. in *Storer v British Gas Plc* [2000] 1 W.L.R. 1237 at [32].

[51] *Berg v IML London Ltd* [2002] 1 W.L.R. 3271; *Garratt v Saxby* [2004] 1 W.L.R. 2152. Those cases indicate that the judge has a discretion whether to hear the case. It is submitted that the issue is in fact akin to deciding whether to recuse for bias or apparent bias, and as such, a question of judgment, not discretion. See para.4–016.

CONDUCT OF COUNSEL

It was held in an appeal from a professional conduct committee that the conduct of a hearing by an advocate who was palpably incompetent did not, on the facts, amount to a serious procedural or other irregularity.[52] In another case, the Court of Appeal adjourned an application for permission to appeal to allow a litigant in person to obtain a tape recording of proceedings in support of his allegation that the court had allowed counsel to consent to an order despite audible protestations from his client, on the basis that if that were true, it would be sufficiently irregular to found an appeal. The plea failed on the facts.[53]   4–018

Of course, where counsel has been obviously incompetent, it is likely that his client's recourse will lie in a professional negligence claim.

DELAY IN REACHING A DECISION

With the case management powers of the Civil Procedure Rules, and in particular the fact that case management should be reviewed by a judge on a regular basis, it is unlikely that a case could be subject to delays which could be said to amount to a serious procedural or other irregularity in the proceedings in the lower court.[54]   4–019

Where there has been a serious delay in the time taken for a case to come to hearing which was not occasioned by some default of the appellant, there may also have been a breach of art.6 of the European Convention. However, examples of sufficiently severe delays to breach art.6 are extremely rare in common law jurisdictions,[55] and there does not appear to have been a breach of art.6 by reason of delay under the Civil Procedure Rules.

There is some authority on when a decision will be irregular by reason of significant delay between the hearing and the handing down of judgment. In *Goose v Wilson*[56] a decision was handed down 20 months after the hearing. The judge had mislaid a chronology on which he had made manuscript notes of counsel's opening submissions; and also the written closing submissions prepared by plaintiff's counsel. Replacement documents were supplied, but the judge's own notes could not be replaced. The appellant argued that it should be inferred that the judge had forgotten large parts of the essential facts and evidence and that he had no clear recollection or impression of the demeanour of witnesses of fact or their credibility by the time he came to give judgment. The Court of Appeal ordered a new trial, holding that compelling parties to await judgment for an indefinitely

---

[52] *R. v Nursing & Midwifery Council* [2004] EWHC 2368 (Admin).
[53] *Melhuish v Waters* [2001] EWCA Civ 1174.
[54] See the comments made by the Court of Appeal in *Rocksteady Services Ltd, Re* [2001] B.C.C. 467.
[55] Lester and Pannick, *Human Rights Law and Practice*, 3rd edn (2009), para.4.6.46.
[56] (1998) 95(12) L.S.G. 27; *The Times*, February 19, 1998.

extended period prolonged, and probably increased, the stress and anxiety inevitably caused by litigation, and weakened public confidence in the whole judicial process. The delay had deprived the judge of the advantage of considering the evidence while having regard to the effect the witnesses made on him when they gave evidence.

That was an exceptional case. In general, where a judgment has been delayed, the Court of Appeal has said that it would be prudent for a judge to refer briefly to the reasons for the delay.[57] The fact that there has been excessive delay will not in itself cause the decision to be unjust by reason of serious procedural or other irregularity; it will always be necessary to consider what consequences, if any, the delay has caused.

> "Delay may have so adversely affected the quality of the decision that it cannot be allowed to stand. It may be established that the judge's ability to deal properly with the issues has been compromised by the passage of time, for example if his recollection of important matters is no longer sufficiently clear or notes have been mislaid."[58]

4–020 The following examples of delay indicate that it will always be necessary to investigate the reasons for the delay, and the consequences thereof, where an appeal is sought for delay in handing down judgment:

    (1) In *Keith Davy (Contractors) Ltd v Ibatex Ltd*, the judge forgot he was deciding only preliminary issues, and not the whole trial; then mislaid his first draft judgment; addressed the wrong issues in the second draft; and eventually handed down judgment in the form of a third draft. He frankly acknowledged that he had made a mess of preparing his judgment. The Court of Appeal held that whilst it could be characterised as a procedural or other irregularity, it had not caused any injustice.[59]

    (2) In a case where there was a delay of eight years, the delay, whilst deplorable, was partly the appellant's fault, and since it had not compromised the ability of the tribunal to decide the case in a fair manner, it did not found an appeal.[60]

    (3) A 12 month delay between the trial and the date of judgment had not caused any injustice, since the judge's notes were comprehensive and the minor errors contained in his judgment were irrelevant.[61]

    (4) A delay of 22 months between the conclusion of the hearing and delivery of the judgment had been caused by the pressures of work

---

[57] *Rolled Steel Ltd v British Steel Corp* [1986] Ch. 246 at 310.
[58] *Boodhoo v Att Gen of Trinidad and Tobago* [2004] 1 W.L.R. 1689 at 1694.
[59] *Keith Davy (Contractors) Ltd v Ibatex Ltd* [2001] EWCA Civ 740.
[60] *Wilston Campbell v Davida Hamlet* [2005] 3 All E.R. 1116 at [27]–[32].
[61] *Cobham v Frett* [2001] 1 W.L.R. 1775.

on the judge, who was engaged in establishing the Mercantile Court in Manchester, and had not caused any injustice.[62]

It is understood that such delays are now much less likely to occur, because the time taken to hand down judgment is monitored.[63]

FAILURE TO GIVE ADEQUATE REASONS FOR THE DECISION

Failure to give adequate reasons for a decision may amount to a serious irregularity. This issue, which is of some complexity, is dealt with separately in the next chapter.

4–021

---

[62] *Gardiner Fire Ltd v Jones* (1998) 95(44) L.S.G. 35; *The Times*, October 22, 1998.
[63] See *Gardiner Fire Ltd v Jones* (1998) 95(44) L.S.G. 35; *The Times*, October 22, 1998.

CHAPTER 5

Inadequacy of Reasons/Findings of Fact

INTRODUCTION

5-001   Historically, there was some doubt as to whether judges had a duty to give reasons for their decisions.[1] Recent decisions from the Court of Appeal have confirmed, however, that want of reasons can constitute a self-standing right of appeal.[2]

DUTY TO GIVE REASONS

5-002   At least since 1985, it has been accepted in English law that judges have a duty to give reasons for their decisions.[3] There are now a large number of Court of Appeal decisions that unequivocally confirm that the inadequacy of decisions can give rise to a valid ground of appeal. In *Coleman v Dunlop Ltd* Lord Justice Henry held that the common law had "evolved to the point that the judge, on the trial of the action, must give sufficient reasons to make clear his findings of primary fact".[4] This is despite the assumptions made in earlier cases, including in the House of Lords, that there is no such duty.[5] However, it is less clear precisely what is required to comply with that duty.

The common law duty to give reasons is now augmented by art.6 of the European Convention on Human Rights and the Human Rights Act 1998.

---

[1] See H.L. Ho, "The judicial duty to give reasons" (2000) *Legal Studies* 42 for historical cases on both sides of the divide.

[2] *Coleman v Dunlop Ltd* [1997] EWCA Civ 2828; *Flannery v Halifax Estate Agencies* [2000] 1 W.L.R. 377 CA at 378.

[3] *Eagil Trust v Pigott-Brown* [1985] 3 All E.R. 119 CA at 122; *Flannery v Halifax Estate Agencies* [2000] 1 W.L.R. 377 CA at 377; *English v Emery Reimbold & Strick Ltd* [2002] EWCA Civ 605; [2002] 1 W.L.R. 2409 from [15].

[4] *Coleman v Dunlop Ltd* [1997] EWCA Civ 2828.

[5] For example, *Jacobs v London CC* [1950] A.C. 361 at 363–364. See H.L. Ho, "The judicial duty to give reasons" (2000) *Legal Studies* 42.

In respect of the judge's decision on the merits of a case, the Convention has been held to require no more than is already required under domestic law.[6]

The duty to give reasons depends on the circumstances

The Court of Appeal has repeatedly stated that the duty to give reasons depends upon the circumstances of the case.[7] In cases involving irreconcilable difference between the evidence of witnesses of fact, for example, the judge may satisfy the duty to give reasons by summarising the evidence and indicating which of the witnesses is more credible.[8] It is sufficient if the judge "shows the parties and, if needs be, the Court of Appeal the basis on which he has acted".[9] On the other hand, as discussed further in para.5–011, where a judge is deciding between which expert he prefers, he should give his reasons.

5–003

Policy considerations

One of the early cases to recognise a duty to give reasons was *Coleman v Dunlop*.[10] Lord Justice Henry acknowledged that finding such a duty involved the "evolution" of the common law, but posited three policy considerations in support of recognising the duty:

5–004

(1) Giving reasons is a salutary discipline to all whose judgments may adversely affect their fellow citizens. The giving of reasons ensures that the parties' relevant submissions are confronted and not avoided.

(2) The necessity to give reasons is to ensure that when the parties leave the court, having had their day there, they know why they have won or why they have lost. This is particularly important where the losing party is a litigant in person.[11]

(3) The duty to give reasons ensures that the appellate court has the proper material to understand and do justice to the decisions taken at first instance,[12] remembering and respecting, as it always will, the advantages enjoyed by the court which heard the evidence.

---

[6] *English v Emery Reimbold & Strick Ltd* [2002] EWCA Civ 605; [2002] 1 W.L.R. 2409 at [12].

[7] See for example the decision of the Court of Appeal in *Cook v Consolidated Finance Ltd* [2010] EWCA Civ 369 at [23].

[8] *Flannery v Halifax Estate Agencies* [2000] 1 W.L.R. 377 CA at 382.

[9] *Eagil Trust v Pigott-Brown* [1985] 3 All E.R. 119 CA at 122, per Griffiths L.J., cited with approval in *Bassano v Battista* [2007] EWCA Civ 370 at [56].

[10] *Coleman v Dunlop* [1997] EWCA Civ 2828.

[11] *Alistair Greene v Half Moon Bay Hotel* [2009] UKPC 23 at [11].

[12] See, e.g. *Vernon v Spoudeas* [2010] EWCA Civ 666, where the Court of Appeal remitted for reconsideration a decision refusing relief from non-compliance with an unless order in circumstances where the judge at first instance had given no reasons for her decision, which was made on paper without an oral hearing.

Reasons for the decision will be required in order that the losing party can, if appropriate, avail itself of any right of appeal.

Inadequacy of reasons renders decision "unjust", not wrong

5–005 Where there are inadequate reasons for a decision, the rationale for the grant of appeal is that—by reason of the inadequacy of the reasoning—the court regards the decision as "unjust", not "wrong", under CPR r.52.11(3).[13]

Lord Justice Lawrence Collins, as he was, has explained the duty to give reasons in terms of the need for justice to be done:

> "The duty to give reasons is a function of due process and therefore justice, both at common law and under Article 6 of the Human Rights Convention. Justice will not be done if it is not apparent to the parties why one has lost and the other has won. Fairness requires that the parties, especially the losing party, should be left in no doubt why they have won or lost."[14]

The common law in other countries, however, has not universally evolved a duty to give reasons. Whilst Australian courts have accepted that such a duty arises, the courts in Canada and New Zealand have not done so.[15]

Costs considerations

5–006 The Court of Appeal has noted that the costs of appealing on the basis that no reasons were given can prove to be expensive. In particular, appeals that lead to a rehearing have been said to "involve a hideous waste of costs".[16] The Court of Appeal has indicated, therefore, that all action should be taken to avoid that eventuality. See paras 5–017 and 5–018.

The limit of this ground of appeal

5–007 In *Sibley & Co v Reachbyte Ltd* Mr Justice Peter Smith, on appeal from a deputy master, suggested that "tactical" appeals on the basis that no or inadequate reasons were given at first instance are to be deplored.[17] He

---

[13] The ground of appeal was said to be "unjust" under CPR r.52.11(3) in *Hicks Developments Ltd v Chaplin* [2007] EWHC 141 (Ch) at [24], per Briggs J.

[14] *Bassano v Battista* [2007] EWCA Civ 370 at [28].

[15] See H.L. Ho, "The judicial duty to give reasons" (2000) *Legal Studies* 42.

[16] *English v Emery Reimbold & Strick Ltd* [2002] EWCA Civ 605; [2002] 1 W.L.R. 2409 at [24].

[17] *Sibley & Co v Reachbyte Ltd, Kris Motor Spares Ltd* [2008] EWHC 2665 (Ch) at [37] and [38].

observed that an appellate court should only interfere with factual findings of a judge at first instance if it can be shown that no reasonable judge could have come to the conclusion he did based on the facts that were laid before him.[18] *Sibley* is perhaps an indication that—notwithstanding the now well-established acceptance of the duty to give reasons—appellate courts retain a discretion and will take a dim view of appellants who are acting "tactically".

THE CONTENT OF THE DUTY TO GIVE REASONS

There is no prescriptive formula stipulating what should be mentioned in the reasoning of a trial judge. The Court of Appeal has repeatedly quoted Lord Justice Griffiths who stated that a judge in giving his reasons need not deal with every argument presented by counsel in support of his case; it is sufficient if he shows the parties and, if needs be, the Court of Appeal, the basis on which he has acted.[19]   5–008

   This led the Court of Appeal in *English v Emery Reimbold & Strick Ltd*[20] to formulate the duty to give reasons in these terms:

> "[T]he judgment must enable the appellate court to understand why the judge reached his decision. This does not mean that every factor which weighed with the judge in his appraisal of the evidence has to be identified and explained. But the issues the resolution of which were vital to the judge's conclusion should be identified and the manner in which he resolved them explained. It is not possible to provide a template for this process. It need not involve a lengthy judgment. It does require the judge to identify and record those matters which were critical to his decision. If the critical issue was one of fact, it may be enough to say that one witness was preferred to another because the one manifestly had a clearer recollection of the material facts or the other gave answers which demonstrated that his recollection could not be relied upon."

Preferring the evidence of one witness

The quotation from *English v Emery*, above, makes it clear that in some circumstances the judge may be forced to determine the outcome of a case by deciding between the evidence given by two witnesses. Similarly, in *Flannery v Halifax Estate Agencies*, the Court stated that, where there is a   5–009

---

[18] *Sibley & Co v Reachbyte Ltd, Kris Motor Spares Ltd* [2008] EWHC 2665 (Ch) at [39].
[19] *Eagil Trust Co Ltd v Pigott-Brown* [1985] 2 All E.R. 119 CA at 122. Cited in *English v Emery Reimbold & Strick Ltd* [2002] EWCA Civ 605; [2002] 1 W.L.R. 2409 at [17] and in *Bassano v Battista* [2007] EWCA Civ 370 at [56].
[20] *English v Emery Reimbold & Strick Ltd* [2002] EWCA Civ 605; [2002] 1 W.L.R. 2409.

straightforward factual dispute whose resolution depends on which witness is telling the truth, it is likely to be enough for the judge—having summarised the evidence—to indicate that he believes one witness rather than the other.[21]

Where the case turns "on competing oral evidence, in relation to which no real assistance was to be obtained from documents, let alone from technical analysis" the trial judge may be excused from giving detailed reasons.[22] However, the number of cases in which reasons can be so simply put is likely to be small. The Court of Appeal has, on a number of occasions, ordered a retrial where the judge has preferred the evidence of one witness over others without giving sufficient reasons why that witness was to be believed.[23] In particular, there has been said to be a lack of reasons where the trial judge stated that he preferred one witness, but failed to address the evidence given by opposing witnesses, even though he found that the opposing witnesses were truthful.[24]

Generally the judge may not dispose of difficulties with opposing evidence by relying on the burden of proof and stating simply that the claimant has failed to prove its case.

A narrow exception: sensitivity to a witness

5–010   There may be one very narrow exception to the requirement for transparent reasons as to why a witness was not reliable. In *Bridges v P & NE Murray Ltd* the Court of Appeal accepted that the trial judge, faced with a claimant with psychiatric problems, had "spared the plaintiff a good deal of pain and humiliation" by failing to address head-on the trustworthiness of her evidence.[25] Even in this case, however, the tenor of the Court of Appeal's judgment suggested that a more direct approach would have been preferred.

Preferring one expert witness over another

5–011   Where the judge must decide which expert witness's evidence he accepts, the judge must give reasons. It has been held that, where the dispute involves "something in the nature of an intellectual exchange, with reasons and analysis advanced on either side", the judge must enter into the issues canvassed before him and explain why he prefers one case over the other.[26] This is likely to apply particularly in litigation where there is disputed expert evidence, but it is not necessarily limited to such cases.

---

[21] *Flannery v Halifax Estate Agencies* [2000] 1 W.L.R. 377 CA at 382.
[22] *Hicks Developments Ltd v Chaplin* [2007] EWHC 141 (Ch) at [25].
[23] *Gibbons (A Firm) v Pickard* [2002] EWCA Civ 1780 (Unreported).
[24] *Baird v Thurrock BC* [2005] EWCA Civ 1499.
[25] [1999] EWCA Civ 1461.
[26] *Flannery v Halifax Estate Agencies* [2000] 1 W.L.R. 377 CA at 382.

In *Flannery v Halifax Estate Agencies* the Court of Appeal was faced with such an "intellectual exchange" between expert witnesses, but the trial judge had done no more than say simply which expert witness he preferred. The Court of Appeal stated that judges in this kind of case should be able to engage in a "coherent reasoned rebuttal" of the expert with which he disagrees, and that the Court of Appeal would not infer the reasons relied upon if they were not apparent in the judgment.[27]

The case of *English v Emery Reimbold & Strick Ltd*[28] involved a number of appeals relating to expert witnesses. The court followed the rule in *Flannery v Halifax Estate Agencies* that the reasons for preferring one witness should be apparent, but it stressed that the "coherent reasoned rebuttal" does not require the judge to apply the same level of expertise possessed by the experts.[29] The reasoning will be adequate provided that the judge has identified the reason for his choice, for example by a finding that:

(1) the evidence of one expert accorded more satisfactorily with facts found by the judge;
(2) the explanation of one expert was more inherently credible than that of the other; and/or
(3) one expert was better qualified,[30] or manifestly more objective, than the other.[31]

A judge who could not decide between the evidence of opposing experts and relied merely on the burden of proof was said to be "abdicating his duty".[32]

In *Glicksman v Redbridge NHS Trust* Lord Justice Henry remitted a decision for retrial on the basis that the judge at first instance had failed to give any reasons for preferring one expert's opinion to another. In particular, Lord Justice Henry criticised the decision on the medical issues considered, because no reasoned rebuttal of any expert's view was attempted by the judge. He found that the judge had stated her conclusions baldly in circumstances which "called out for definition of the issues, for marshalling of the evidence, and for reasons to be given".[33] Lord Justice Henry observed that "those matters go to make up building blocks of the reasoned judicial process" and that the absence of those safeguards rendered the decision unjust. He expressed concern at the prospect of a finding of professional negligence being made in the absence of such safeguards, and allowed the appeal on liability.

---

[27] *Flannery v Halifax Estate Agencies* [2000] 1 W.L.R. 377 CA at 383.
[28] *English v Emery Reimbold & Strick Ltd* [2002] EWCA Civ 605; [2002] 1 W.L.R. 2409.
[29] *English v Emery Reimbold & Strick Ltd* [2002] EWCA Civ 605; [2002] 1 W.L.R. 2409 at [20].
[30] *Ludlow v National Power* Unreported November 17, 2000 CA (Case No.CCRTF 1999/1306).
[31] *English v Emery Reimbold & Strick Ltd* [2002] EWCA Civ 605; [2002] 1 W.L.R. 2409.
[32] *Sewell v Electrolux* [1997] EWCA Civ 2443. See [64].
[33] [2001] EWCA Civ 1097 at [10]–[11].

The degree to which reasons will be inferred

5–012   The Court of Appeal does not appear to be wholly consistent in its approach to the propriety of inferring reasons from the face of trial judges' judgments. On the one hand, in *Eagil Trust v Piggot Brown* Lord Justice Griffiths was happy to give the trial judge the benefit of the doubt as to the basis on which he had determined the issues. He found that, if the judge has not dealt with some particular argument but it can be seen that there are grounds on which he would have been entitled to reject it, the court should assume that he acted on those grounds unless the appellant can point to convincing reasons leading to a contrary conclusion.[34]

However, in *Flannery v Halifax Estate Agencies*[35] the Court of Appeal observed that, without express reasons, the trial judge's judgment would not be transparent, and the Court of Appeal could not know whether the judge had adequate or inadequate reasons for the conclusion he reached. In this case, in contrast to *Eagil Trust v Piggot Brown*, the Court of Appeal was unwilling to infer reasons from the judgment.

In *English v Emery Reimbold & Strick Ltd* the Court of Appeal took an active role in trying to decipher the judges' reasoning.[36] This case involved three appeals. In each of the appeals, the Court of Appeal examined in detail the evidence that had been available to the judge and heard submissions from counsel about that evidence. In one of the appeals, the trial judge had merely stated that he preferred the views of one of the experts "on the balance of probabilities", with no further explanation.[37] However, by examining the details of the case and hearing submissions from counsel the Court of Appeal was able to follow the judge's reasoning.

The proper degree of inference of a judge's reasoning is best explained by reference to the postscript to *English v Emery*, in which the Court of Appeal warned that an unsuccessful party should not seek to upset a judgment on the ground of inadequacy of reasons unless, despite the advantage of considering the judgment with knowledge of the evidence given and submissions made at the trial, that party is unable to understand why it is that the judge has reached an adverse decision.[38]

In other words, the Court was willing to consider those inferences that would have been evident to the parties in the case, bearing in mind all the circumstances known to those parties. Having done so, the Court asked

---

[34] *Eagil Trust v Pigott-Brown* [1985] 3 All E.R. 119 at 122.

[35] *Flannery v Halifax Estate Agencies* [2001] All E.R. 273.

[36] *English v Emery Reimbold & Strick Ltd* [2002] EWCA Civ 605; [2002] 1 W.L.R. 2409 at [57], [89] and [110].

[37] *English v Emery Reimbold & Strick Ltd* [2002] EWCA Civ 605; [2002] 1 W.L.R. 2409 at [50].

[38] *English v Emery Reimbold & Strick Ltd* [2002] EWCA Civ 605; [2002] 1 W.L.R. 2409 at [118]. This decision was followed in *Harris v CDMR Purfleet Ltd* [2009] EWCA Civ 1645 at [21] where it was held that, whilst it was "desirable" that a judgment be comprehensible to a first-time reader, this was not the test of adequacy, and the adequacy of the reasons given must be tested in the context of the knowledge and understanding of those who were present at the trial.

whether, objectively speaking, the real reason for the judgment was apparent. Given the court's oft-stated distaste for the costs involved in a retrial, the approach in *English v Emery* indicates that such appeals will only be granted where the reasoning is clearly inadequate.

An even stricter view is evident in the High Court decision of Mr Justice Peter Smith, hearing an appeal from a deputy master.[39] Mr Justice Peter Smith's judgment suggests that the test for allowing an appeal on the basis of inadequacy of reasoning should be in line with the test for overturning findings of fact. He held that an appellate court should only interfere with factual findings of a Judge at first instance if it can be shown that no reasonable judge could have come to the conclusion he did based on the facts that were laid before him. If a judge does not fully set out his reasoning, the appellate court should "consider the judgment as a whole in the light of the material before the judge" and should not be tempted into a detailed analysis of each and every reason or argument put forward by an appellant at first instance and allegedly not dealt with by the judge at first instance.

The appellate court may take into account any further reasons for the impugned decision volunteered by the first instance judge in a second judgment in that same matter, or any further reasons that could be inferred from that second judgment.[40]

The need to address all relevant issues

Though the Court of Appeal has repeatedly said that judges are not under a duty to address *all* the issues and arguments in the case,[41] it is equally clear that the reasoning should address all the *relevant* issues in a case.   5–013

In *Coleman v Dunlop*[42] the trial judge found that the claimant was not suffering from a particular ailment, though there was no dispute as to the symptoms displayed. On that basis, the judge had dismissed the case; but she had failed to consider the relevant issue of whether the symptoms were caused by the claimant's work, or whether the employer was in breach of duty. The Court of Appeal allowed the appeal.

Similarly, in *Baird v Thurrock BC* the trial judge had preferred the claimant's evidence, but had not addressed how it fitted with the other evidence in the case.[43] The appeal was allowed.

---

[39] *Sibley & Co v Reachbyte Limited, Kris Motor Spares Ltd* [2008] EWHC 2665 (Ch) at [39].
[40] *Roche v Chief Constable of Greater Manchester* [2005] EWCA Civ 1454 at [23]–[27].
[41] See para.5–008.
[42] *Coleman v Dunlop* [1997] EWCA Civ 2828.
[43] [2005] EWCA Civ 1499.

Cost orders

5–014   Whilst the Court of Appeal has recognised that judges have a duty to give reasons for their decisions, it was initially thought that costs decisions are an exception to the general rule, save that reasons were desirable, however, where the costs award is unusual.[44] However, the law on giving reasons for costs orders has now been brought in line with the general rule.

In *English v Emery* the Court of Appeal concluded that the Human Rights Act 1998 and European Human Rights jurisprudence apply equally to decisions on costs as they do to substantive decisions.[45] The practice whereby no reasons were given for costs orders was only acceptable as long as the reasons were "clearly implicit from the circumstances in which the award is made".[46] This obligation will normally be complied with where "costs follow the event", but where the trial judge applies some other formula, brief reasons should be given.

In effect, therefore, the rule for decisions as to costs is now identical to that for substantive decisions; where the judge's reasons are evident from the circumstances of the decision an appeal will not succeed. That the courts take the same approach to costs orders as to other decisions is made clear by the judgment in *English v Emery*: in that case one of the three appeals involved costs, and the Court of Appeal approached it in the same way as the other two appeals.

Exception for matters in the judge's discretion

5–015   In *Eagil Trust v Piggot Brown*, Lord Justice Griffiths alluded to "the field of discretion" where other exceptions to the general duty to give reasons might exist. Mr Justice Buckley has held that there are some sorts of interim applications "mainly of a purely procedural kind", upon which a judge exercising his discretion can properly make an order without giving reasons.[47] The examples given there included decisions as to whether a matter should be expedited or adjourned, or extra time should be allowed for a party to take some procedural step, or "possibly" whether relief by way of injunction should be granted or refused.

However, following the judgment in *English v Emery* it is less clear whether the exercise of judicial discretion in interim applications or procedural hearings may be excepted from the general duty to give reasons. The Court of Appeal in that case raised the spectre of a dual (conflicting) test depending on whether the case raises human rights issues. Focusing on

---

[44]   *Eagil Trust v Pigott-Brown* [1985] 3 All E.R. 119 at 122, per Griffiths L.J. Also *Flannery v Halifax Estate Agencies* [2000] 1 W.L.R. 377 CA at 381.

[45]   *English v Emery Reimbold & Strick Ltd* [2002] EWCA Civ 605; [2002] 1 W.L.R. 2409 at [14].

[46]   *English v Emery Reimbold & Strick Ltd* [2002] EWCA Civ 605; [2002] 1 W.L.R. 2409 at [14].

[47]   *Capital and Suburban Properties v Swycher* [1976] Ch. 319 at 325–326.

European Human Rights jurisprudence, the Court of Appeal characterised the duty to give reasons as limited to judicial decisions that affect the substantive rights of the parties:

(1) It observed that there are some judicial decisions where "fairness" does not demand that the parties should be informed of the reasoning underlying them; interim decisions in the course of case management provide an "obvious example".[48]

(2) However, with regard to the requirements of the common law, as opposed to the requirements of the European Convention on Human Rights, the Court did not consider that any similar limitation applies. The requirement for judges to set out their reasons, in sufficient detail to allow the appellate court to understand the principles upon which they acted, was stated to "apply to judgments of all descriptions".[49]

It is not clear from the judgment in *English v Emery* whether this general rule was intended to apply to all orders that a judge might make, within the field of discretion, which do not affect substantive rights. However, the fact that inadequate reasons are said to render a decision "unjust" rather than wrong[50] may suggest that some decisions can be so trivial as to fall outside the scope of the duty to give reasons.[51]

It is likely that a judge at first instance will be found to have a duty to give reasons for a decision on an interim application (as with costs) where that decision runs contrary to the prima facie assumption. See for example *Komtel v Totem LTL*[52] where a master's failure to give reasons for the dismissal of an application for security for costs taken together with a strong prima facie case for an order for security justified the setting aside of his order.

An exception: applications for leave to appeal to the court of last resort

It seems that judges are not bound to give reasons where they refuse leave to appeal to the court of last resort. For example, this is the position taken with regard to appeals to the House of Lords (now the Supreme Court).[53] The reason given for this approach is that the lack of another avenue of

5–016

---

[48] *English v Emery Reimbold & Strick Ltd* [2002] EWCA Civ 605; [2002] 1 W.L.R. 2409 at [13].

[49] *English v Emery Reimbold & Strick Ltd* [2002] EWCA Civ 605; [2002] 1 W.L.R. 2409 at [17] and [18].

[50] See para.5–005.

[51] See H.L. Ho, "The judicial duty to give reasons" (2000) *Legal Studies* 42, 53–55.

[52] Unreported April 3, 2006 (QBD, March 22, 2006).

[53] *Antaios Cia Naviera SA v Salen Rederierna AB (The Antaios)* [1985] A.C. 191 HL at 205–206 states that this is the practice of the House of Lords. See also *Mousaka Inc v Golden Seagull Maritime Inc* [2002] 1 W.L.R. 395 QB at [29].

appeal means that reasons serve no purpose other than satisfying the curiosity of the parties, and that there is a serious danger of undermining confidence in the original decision by adopting slightly different wording from that decision.[54]

PROCEDURE

5–017   In *English v Emery Reimbold & Strick Ltd*[55] Lord Phillips M.R. (handing down the judgment of the court) laid out the principles to be applied in applications for permission to appeal on the grounds of "no reasons". Despite disliking the idea of allowing trial judges "to have a second bite at the cherry" by giving them an opportunity to supplement their reasoning, Lord Phillips M.R. recognised that it would sometimes be necessary to order a retrial by the lower court.[56] In particular, a party that considers that it has grounds to appeal on the basis of insufficient reasoning should make the point clear to the trial judge when seeking leave to appeal. A judge who considers that the application has merit should set out to remedy the deficiency by giving additional reasons, refusing leave to appeal on that basis.[57] Indeed, the Court of Appeal has stressed that counsel has a positive duty at the handing down of a judgment to raise with the judge any apparent defect in the judge's reasoning or any genuine query or ambiguity in that judgment.[58] The appropriate time for that duty to be discharged is at the handing down of the judgment or promptly on receipt of the written judgment, not many months after judgment was handed down.[59]

Where a trial judge considers that they have given sufficient reasons, they will normally be expected to refuse leave to appeal, and the unsuccessful party can seek permission to appeal from the appellate court. Where the application for permission appears to be well founded, the appellate court should consider adjourning the application and remitting the case to the trial judge for the provision of additional reasons.[60]

5–018   In *English v Emery*, Lord Justice Sedley, giving permission to appeal, ordered the trial judge to edit and correct the original judgment, which his Lordship described as "a rambling and in places unintelligible document".[61]

Subsequent Court of Appeal judgments have reaffirmed this point, with Lord Justice Lawrence Collins telling would-be appellants that it should not

---

[54] *Mousaka Inc v Golden Seagull Maritime Inc* [2002] 1 W.L.R. 395 QB at [36].

[55] *English v Emery Reimbold & Strick Ltd* [2002] EWCA Civ 605; [2002] 1 W.L.R. 2409.

[56] *English v Emery Reimbold & Strick Ltd* [2002] EWCA Civ 605; [2002] 1 W.L.R. 2409 at [24].

[57] *English v Emery Reimbold & Strick Ltd* [2002] EWCA Civ 605; [2002] 1 W.L.R. 2409 at [25]. See also *T (A Child)* [2002] EWCA Civ 1736 at [49] and *In the matter of S (Children)* [2007] EWCA Civ 694 at [23]–[25].

[58] *In Re M(A Child) (Non Accidental Injury: Burden of Proof)* [2008] EWCA Civ 1261.

[59] *Michael Hyde Associates Ltd v JD Williams & Co Ltd* [2001] P.N.L.R. 233; *Aerospace Publishing Ltd v Thames Water Utilities Ltd* [2006] EWCA Civ 717.

[60] *English v Emery Reimbold & Strick Ltd* [2002] EWCA Civ 605; [2002] 1 W.L.R. 2409.

[61] [2002] EWCA Civ 605; [2002] 1 W.L.R. 2409 at [33].

be thought that an unsuccessful party faced with a decision which that party considers insufficiently reasoned should simply use the tactic of sitting back and taking its chances on an appeal. It should not be forgotten that a judge may be asked to give reasons after judgment.[62]

This approach of seeking extra reasons from the trial judge at the permission stage appears to have replaced suggestions made in *Flannery v Halifax Estate Agencies* by the Court of Appeal that potential respondents should consider inviting the judge to make an affidavit for use at the permission application and at any appeal hearing. The affidavit would allow the judge to give his reasons, and his explanation as to why they were not set out in the judgment.[63] The approach in *English v Emery* is likely to be preferred.

On an appeal on grounds of no or no adequate reasons, the appellate court will generally carry out a review of the decision impugned, not a re-hearing.[64] However, the appellate court may carry out a re-hearing if the lower court had refused, when requested, to give reasons; or if there was some other good reason for not asking the court below to give its reasons.[65]

Orders given upon a successful appeal for "no reasons"

Where the appellant is successful and demonstrates to the appellate court   5–019
that the reasons for the decision were not adequate, the appellate court will consider whether to proceed to a rehearing or to remit the case for a retrial.[66] In practice, it appears that successful appeals on the basis of inadequate reasons generally result in retrials.[67]

There is one exception to this general approach. Where the appeal is against an injunction, there is often no time for a retrial. The appellate court is likely to consider the evidence afresh and may discharge the injunction.[68]

---

[62] *Bassano v Battista* [2007] EWCA Civ 370 at [52].

[63] *Flannery v Halifax Estate Agencies* [2000] 1 W.L.R. 377 CA at 383.

[64] CPR r.52.11(1) provides that every appeal will be limited to a review of the decision of the lower court unless the court considers that in the circumstances of an individual appeal it would be in the interests of justice to hold a re-hearing. See, further paras 2–025 to 2–029.

[65] *Secretary of State for Trade and Industry v Lewis* [2001] 2 B.C.L.C. 597 at 600e–600g.

[66] *English v Emery Reimbold & Strick Ltd* [2002] EWCA Civ 605; [2002] 1 W.L.R. 2409 at [26].

[67] Retrials were ordered in *Coleman v Dunlop Ltd* [2007] EWCA Civ 2828; *Flannery v Halifax Estate Agencies* [2000] 1 W.L.R. 377 CA; *Gibbons (A Firm) v Pickard* [2002] EWCA Civ 1780; *Baird v Thurrock BC* [2005] EWCA Civ 1499. In *Cunliffe v Fielden* [2005] EWCA Civ 1508; [2006] Ch. 361 the Court of Appeal changed the sum awarded to a wife under the Inheritance (Provision for Family and Dependants) Act 1975—but the inadequacy of reasons was only one ground of complaint. In *Cooper v Floor Cleaning Machines Ltd* [2003] EWCA Civ 1649; [2003] All E.R. (D) 322 (Oct) no retrial was ordered in an "inadequacy of facts" case: see para.5–023.

[68] As happened in *Douglas v Hello! Ltd* [2001] Q.B. 967 at 973–974.

INADEQUATE FINDINGS OF FACT

5–020   Where a judge fails to make a finding of fact on an important issue there is a free-standing right of appeal. These cases are similar to those where the ground of appeal is the inadequacy of reasons, and will sometimes arise out of the same facts.[69–70]

There is no judicial authority on whether this ground of appeal falls within the "wrong" or the "unjust" category of CPR r.52.11(3). It may depend on the view taken by the appellate court; where a finding of fact was not made by the trial judge but the appellate court feels able to make such a finding, the original decision can be said to be wrong. Where the appellate court indicates that the trial judge failed to take account of some important piece of evidence, the result may be said to be unjust.

No finding of fact on an essential element of the case

5–021   The Court of Appeal has considered cases where the trial judge made a finding of fact, which they believed to make other findings unnecessary. On that basis the trial judge failed to make other findings of fact that would still have allowed that party to succeed.

For example, in *Coleman v Dunlop Ltd*[71] the trial judge made a finding that the claimant was not suffering from reflex sympathetic dystrophy. It was not in doubt, however, that the claimant's symptoms were real and that he had a bad back. By failing to consider the kind of work that the claimant was engaged in, or whether it caused the injury, the Court of Appeal held that the trial judge had failed to resolve the issues before her and had failed adequately to state her reasons.

Lord Justice Henry addressed this issue along with the duty to give reasons. He allowed the appeal on the basis that, if the judge has failed to give a judgment stating their findings of fact which form the basis of the order, then in subsequent proceedings the parties and the court may find it difficult to judge whether there has been a relevant change of circumstance which changes the basis of the judge's earlier order.[72]

Abdullah v Jalil was another case where the trial judge felt that he had done enough by dismissing one of the claimant's arguments, but failed to consider an alternative way in which the claimant's case had been put.[73] The case was remitted for a retrial.

[69–70] In *Baird v Thurrock BC* [2005] EWCA Civ 1499 at [18] one of the reasons for finding that the reasoning was inadequate was that the trial judge had failed to make findings of fact on crucial issues. Similarly, see *Coleman v Dunlop* [1997] EWCA Civ 2828.

[71] *Coleman v Dunlop* [1997] EWCA Civ 2828.

[72] *Coleman v Dunlop* [1997] EWCA Civ 2828.

[73] [2005] EWHC 1653 (Ch).

No findings of fact on evidence that should inform the overall decision

There is a further, different, category of cases, where the trial judge has failed to come to a finding of fact on a particular piece of evidence. An appeal will be successful if that evidence should have been considered by the judge in reaching their decision.[74]   5–022

It has been held that the trial judge should decide whether the issue is peripheral or critical to the case. Lord Justice Jonathan Parker has held that, where an issue of fact arises which is peripheral to the dispute which the court is required to resolve, and the evidence in relation to that issue is equivocal, the trial judge may well take the view that it is unnecessary to deal with that issue because it is "a trite proposition that a trial judge is not required to resolve every dispute of fact which may arise in the course of the trial". But where the issue is central to the issue which the court was required to resolve, the judge ought to tackle the issue head on and made a finding about it.[75]

The failure by the trial judge to address all relevant issues may be particularly stark where they accept the claimant's version of events without addressing the inconsistencies between that evidence and the evidence of other witnesses.[76] In some such situations the issue can be classified either as an inadequacy of reasoning or an inadequacy in fact-finding.

Reliance on the burden of proof to avoid a finding of fact

Where a trial judge addresses a question of fact, but cannot decide between two versions of events, they are expected to make findings of fact "so far as is practicable and so far as it is in accordance with their conscientious duty"[77] and should not simply fall back on the incidence of the burden of proof to determine the issues.   5–023

In some "exceptional" cases, however, appellate courts have accepted that the trial judge was acting properly where they were "wholly unable" to form a view as to which version of events was most likely to accord with the truth, and had "no alternative" but to rely on the burden of proof.[78] The appellate courts have stressed that such cases will be rare and that, generally, a judge should not take refuge behind the burden of proof to avoid taking difficult decisions.[79]

---

[74] *Lloyds TSB v Hayward* [2002] EWCA Civ 1813; *Baird v Thurrock BC* [2005] EWCA Civ 1499.

[75] *Lloyds TSB v Hayward* [2002] EWCA Civ 1813 at [66], per Jonathan Parker L.J. Similar sentiments are expressed by Butler-Sloss P. at [84].

[76] *Baird v Thurrock BC* [2005] EWCA Civ 1499.

[77] *Morris v London Iron and Steel Co Ltd* [1988] Q.B. 493 at 504, per May L.J.

[78] *Morris v London Iron and Steel Co Ltd* [1988] Q.B. 493; *Ashraf v Akram* [1999] EWCA Civ 640.

[79] *Morris v London Iron and Steel Co Ltd* [1988] Q.B. 493 at 504, per May L.J.

It was suggested by Lord Justice Thomas, in *Cooper v Floor Cleaning Machines*, that a judge who considers that a case is "exceptional", and that he may find that the burden of proof has not been discharged, should inform the parties and invite submissions.[80]

In *Cooper v Floor Cleaning Machines* it was said that it would be very rare for a traffic accident to fall within this "exceptional" category in which a judge may rely on the burden of proof, unless it is the kind of accident where no witness is alive or available to explain what happened.[81] In such a case, the judge should normally consider all the available evidence and decide which of the two versions of events is more likely. In *Cooper v Floor Cleaning Machines* the Court of Appeal looked at the evidence that had been available to the trial judge and not only concluded that the trial judge should have come to a decision, but also made a finding of fact as to who was at fault.

By contrast, in *Ashraf v Akram*[82] the trial judge had to decide between differing accounts of how a fight started. As in *Cooper v Floor Cleaning Machines* the judge had been faced with opposite accounts of the event in question, yet the Court of Appeal accepted that the trial judge could not have decided who was telling the truth.

Where the finding of fact relies on the truth of two opposing witnesses, therefore, it does appear that appellate courts will sometimes accept reliance on the burden of proof in disposing of the case. However, *Cooper v Floor Cleaning Machines* shows that where the surrounding circumstances make one version of events more inherently probable than the other, the judge will be expected to use those circumstances to make a finding of fact.

Where the issue is not the truthfulness of factual witnesses, but different analyses put forward by expert witnesses, appellate courts are hostile to reliance on the burden of proof. In *Sewell v Electrolux* the trial judge failed to make a finding of fact and this was said to have amounted to him "abdicating his duty".[83] This was so despite the difficulty in making a decision, in that "on the evidence before the recorder it was plainly open to him to accept or reject the plaintiff's case on causation".[84] It seems, therefore, that when confronted with expert evidence a judge has a duty to come down on one side of the line or the other, and that it is not permissible to rely on the burden of proof to avoid making the decision.

---

[80] *Cooper v Floor Cleaning Machines* [2003] EWCA Civ 1649 at [23]. This was done in *Ashraf v Akram* [1999] EWCA Civ 640.
[81] *Cooper v Floor Cleaning Machines* [2003] EWCA Civ 1649 at [19], per Scott Baker L.J. This is consistent with the earlier case of *Bray v Palmer* [1953] 1 W.L.R. 1455 CA.
[82] [1999] EWCA Civ 640.
[83] [1997] EWCA Civ 2443, per Hutchison L.J.
[84] ibid.

Appellate courts' approach to retrials

Unlike cases involving inadequate reasoning, appellate courts appear to be   5–024
more willing to make their own findings of fact where the trial judge has
failed to do so. For example, in *Abdullah v Jalil* Pumfrey J. expressed his
"deep regret" that he could not make findings of fact on the available
evidence and ordered a retrial.[85] In *Cooper v Floor Cleaning Machines* the
Court of Appeal did make determinative findings of fact.[86] However, following the trial judge's refusal to decide between expert evidence in *Sewell
v Electrolux* a retrial was ordered.[87]

---

[85] [2005] EWHC 1653 Ch.
[86] [2003] EWCA Civ 1649.
[87] [1997] EWCA Civ 2443.

CHAPTER 6

Admitting New Evidence

INTRODUCTION

6–001   Parties to litigation are expected to put before the court all the issues and evidence relevant to that litigation.[1] However, where fresh evidence comes to light after a judgment has been reached that puts that judgment in doubt, the unsuccessful party may—in limited circumstances—be permitted to invoke that fresh evidence in order to challenge the judgment by appeal to an appellate court.[2]

Where a party seeks to adduce new evidence in support of an appeal, the courts have traditionally taken a restrictive approach.

Where an appeal based on new evidence is allowed, the appellate court will only order a retrial if a retrial is "imperative in the interests of justice".[3] The first instance court may not reopen its judgment in order to take account of the fresh evidence, as that would offend the fundamental principle that the outcome of litigation should be final.[4]

POLICY CONSIDERATIONS

6–002   In considering whether to admit new evidence upon appeal, there is a balance to be struck between the courts' desire for truth and the courts' desire for finality. It has been recognised that courts may get a result wrong, and yet it still be in the interests of justice that the matter not be reopened. Lord Wilberforce acknowledged that sometimes fresh material may be

---

[1] *Henderson v Henderson* (1843) 3 Hare 100; *The Ampthill Peerage* [1977] A.C. 547.
[2] An exception to this is in cases where the fresh evidence shows that the judgment below was obtained by fraud: such cases are a special category of their own (see paras 6–024 to 6–025).
[3] *Transview Properties Ltd v City Site Properties Ltd* [2009] EWCA Civ 1255.
[4] This is the general rule: *In Re Barrell Enterprises* [1973] 1 W.L.R. 19 at 23–24; see also *Marchmont Investments Ltd v BFO SA* [2007] EWCA Civ 677. However, the Court of Appeal does have the power to reopen appeals where new evidence comes to light under CPR r.52.17, which codified the decision of the Court of Appeal in *Taylor v Lawrence* [2002] EWCA Civ 90; [2003] Q.B. 528 (see para.6–005 and Ch.8).

found, which might have led to a different result had it been available; but nevertheless "in the interest of peace, certainty and security" the law prevents further inquiry into this fresh material because "the law insists on finality".[5]

The longer the delay in the bringing of the new evidence, the less likely it is that it will be admitted. In *The Ampthill Peerage*,[6] the Committee for Privileges of the House of Lords had to consider evidence which would, in effect, have overturned a case decided 50 years earlier. Though the Committee was not formally a judicial committee, its decision was articulated by four Lords of Appeal in Ordinary. A prime reason for reaching the conclusion that the new evidence should not be considered was the fact that a person who has relied on a decision of the court, and lived his life accordingly, should not lightly have that decision overturned.

THE CIVIL PROCEDURE RULES

The admission of new evidence upon appeal is governed by CPR r.52.11(2): 6–003

"Unless it orders otherwise, the appellate court will not receive—

(a) oral evidence; or
(b) evidence which was not before the lower court."

There are no further provisions setting out the basis upon which an appellate court will consider whether to receive such further evidence. The only other provision of the CPR which applies is CPR r.1.1, the overriding objective, which requires that cases be dealt with justly.[7] The overriding objective in CPR r.1.1 provides the guide by which the appellate court will determine whether new evidence will, or will not, be admitted.[8]

There was a great deal of pre-CPR case-law on whether an appellate court will permit parties to an appeal to adduce new evidence.[9] The courts have stated that the pre-CPR cases will remain "powerful persuasive authority" because they illustrate the attempts of the courts to "strike a fair balance between the need for concluded litigation to be determinative of disputes and the desirability that the judicial process should achieve the right result".[10]

---

[5] *The Ampthill Peerage* [1977] A.C. 547 at 575, per Lord Wilberforce.
[6] *The Ampthill Peerage* [1977] A.C. 547 at 575, per Lord Wilberforce.
[7] *Hamilton v Al Fayed (No.2)* [2001] E.M.L.R. 15 at [11]; *Gillingham v Gillingham* [2001] C.P. Rep. 89 at [16], per Clarke L.J.
[8] *Hamilton v Al Fayed (No.2)* [2001] E.M.L.R. 15 at [11].
[9] Prior to the CPR coming into force in May 2000, under RSC Ord.59, r.10(2) the Court of Appeal would only receive further evidence "on special grounds" after there had been a trial on the merits. The "special grounds" were those set out in Lord Justice Denning's test in *Ladd v Marshall* [1954] 1 W.L.R. 1489 at 1491 (see para.6–004) subject to various exceptions.
[10] *Hamilton v Al Fayed (No.2)* [2001] E.M.L.R. 15 at [11].

This chapter, therefore, considers the pre-CPR law together with the case-law after 1999, but it should be noted that, where older cases are referred to, they are persuasive but no longer binding.

THE TEST IN LADD V MARSHALL

6–004   The leading pre-CPR decision on the admission of new evidence upon appeal was *Ladd v Marshall*. The appellant sought a retrial on the basis that a witness who had previously "lied" was now willing to "tell the truth". Lord Justice Denning's short judgment set out a three-pronged test:

> "first, it must be shown that the evidence could not have been obtained with reasonable diligence for use at the trial; secondly, the evidence must be such that, if given, it would probably have an important influence on the result of the case, though it need not be decisive; thirdly, the evidence must be such as is presumably to be believed, or in other words, it must be apparently credible, though it need not be incontrovertible."[11]

In spite of the introduction of the Civil Procedure Rules, the test in *Ladd v Marshall* remains good authority, and appellate courts continue to be guided by this test.

The test in *Ladd v Marshall* was further approved in *Hamilton v Al Fayed (No.2)* by the Court of Appeal, who confirmed that under the new, as under the old, procedure "special grounds must be shown to justify the introduction of fresh evidence on appeal".[12] In *Hertfordshire Investments Ltd v Bubb* the Court of Appeal noted that, whilst CPR r.52.11(2) did not retain the requirement for "special grounds", nevertheless the test outlined in *Ladd v Marshall* must be considered by the Court of Appeal when deciding whether to receive fresh evidence in the exercise of its discretion.[13]

However, in addition to applying the *Ladd v Marshall* test, the courts must now seek to give effect to the overriding objective of dealing with cases justly, enshrined in CPR r.1.1.[14] In *Hamilton v Al Fayed (No.2)* the Court of Appeal found that it was not bound by pre-CPR authority in determining what constitutes special grounds (although those cases remain

---

[11]   *Ladd v Marshall* [1954] 1 W.L.R. 1489 at 1491. A detailed discussion of the *Ladd v Marshall* test is set out in Vol.1 of the *Supreme Court Practice* (1999), pp.1063–1064.

[12]   [2001] E.M.L.R. 15. The continuing requirement for "special grounds"—such requirement to be applied in light of the overriding objective in CPR r.1.1—was confirmed by Elias L.J. in *Owens v Noble* [2010] EWCA Civ 224 at [34].

[13]   [2000] 1 W.L.R. 2318. An exception to this is in cases where the fresh evidence shows that the judgment below was obtained by fraud: such cases are a special category of their own (see para.6–024 and 6–025).

[14]   The importance of applying these wider principles, over and above the three-limbed *Ladd v Marshall* test, was emphasised by the Court of Appeal in *Muscat v Health Professions Council* [2009] EWCA Civ 1090 at [26] and *Sharab v Al-Saud* [2009] EWCA Civ 353 at [52].

"powerful persuasive authority"), and confirmed that in considering whether such special grounds are demonstrated regard must be had to the overriding objective in CPR r.1.1.[15]

Evidence available at trial

The first limb of Denning L.J.'s test in *Ladd v Marshall* provided that, in order to admit new evidence, that evidence could not have been available to the appellant, even acting with reasonable diligence, at the original trial. This continues to be a crucial factor in the application of the court's discretion. In *Taylor v Lawrence* Lord Woolf C.J. stated categorically (citing *Ladd v Marshall*) that it remains a "firm rule of practice" that appellate courts will not allow fresh evidence to be adduced in support of an appeal if that evidence was "readily accessible at the time of the original hearing".[16]   **6–005**

In *Taylor v Lawrence* the fresh evidence which the appellant sought to adduce in an appeal against an order for security for costs was evidence of the claimants' impecuniosity. Lord Woolf C.J. found that this evidence could and should have been put before the judge at the original hearing. Admitting this evidence at the appeal would, he considered, amount to a "new and very different" hearing from that at first instance.

However, even before the introduction of the CPR, it was clear that, even if evidence could and should have been obtained for the trial, that was not an absolute bar to its admission, particularly where the blame for the information not being before the court could be laid at the respondent's door.[17] Courts continue to take the approach that a failure to obtain available information for the trial will not automatically invalidate an application to adduce it, particularly in the situations set out below.

The diligence that is required of the appellant in relation to whether the evidence could have been adduced at first instance depends on the facts and circumstances of the case. It is clear, however, that an appellant will be required to demonstrate that he and his lawyers made sufficient enquiries, even if those enquiries relate to statements made by the other side.[18]

Where a party had no reason to suspect that the evidence might exist, the fact that enquiries might readily have brought the evidence to light will not necessarily mean that the first limb of the *Ladd v Marshall* test has not been satisfied[19]; it will depend on the circumstances.

In respect of appeals against orders made during interim hearings and, in particular, against successful applications for summary judgment, it would

---

[15] This decision was followed in *Riyad Bank v Ahli United Bank (UK) Plc* [2005] EWCA Civ 1419 and *Toth v Jarman* [2006] EWCA Civ 1028.

[16] *Ladd v Marshall* [1954] 1 W.L.R. 1489; *Taylor v Lawrence* [2002] EWCA Civ 90; [2003] Q.B. 528 at 534–535.

[17] *Skrzypkowski v Silvan Investments* [1963] 1 W.L.R. 525.

[18] As in *Toth v Jarman* [2006] EWCA Civ 1028; [2006] C.P. Rep. 44 at 89, relating to the experience of an expert instructed by the respondent.

[19] As where an appellant had no reason to suspect that a key witness had been demoted by the police force: *Meek v Fleming* [1961] 2 Q.B. 366.

appear that the *Ladd v Marshall* test applies in a modified form. It is recognised that defendants who are forced to prepare their evidence in opposition to an application for summary judgment are under pressure of time and may well find it difficult to produce the evidence that they would have obtained for trial.[20] Accordingly, in such circumstances, in demonstrating compliance with the first limb of the *Ladd v Marshall* test, appellants need only demonstrate a lower level of diligence in respect of material which could have been produced at the interim hearing.[21] However, parties are nevertheless expected to bring forward the full case at the interim hearing,[22] and where issues have been clear for some time prior to the decision in question the appellant will not be absolved from failures to make timely enquiries.[23]

Evidence must be influential

6–006 The second limb of the test in *Ladd v Marshall* requires that the new evidence produced for the appellate court must be such that it may have influenced the judgment of the court below. The new evidence must therefore relate to relevant and material issues. It must be shown that the new evidence would have altered, rather than reinforced, the judgment at first instance.[24] Where evidence is brought forward on matters that are essentially collateral, no retrial will be granted.[25]

Similarly, where evidence goes to a relevant issue but could not realistically have led to a different result, it will not be admitted. For example, additional evidence to undermine a party's credibility will not be admissible where the trial judge had already indicated that the party could not be trusted.[26] However, where evidence relates to the credibility of a crucial witness, and the appellate court is satisfied that the credibility of that witness was an important factor in the final outcome, it is more likely that a retrial will be ordered.[27]

Evidence must be apparently credible

6–007 The decision in *Ladd v Marshall* itself demonstrates that it is not sufficient to produce new evidence for the appellate court unless that evidence is apparently credible. Where a witness seeks to change their original evidence

---

[20] *Langdale v Danby* [1982] 1 W.L.R. 1123 at 1133, per Lord Bridge.
[21] *Langdale v Danby* [1982] 1 W.L.R. 1123; *Thune v London Properties Ltd* [1990] 1 W.L.R. 562; *Electra Private Equity v KPMG Peat Marwick* [1999] EWCA Civ 1247; [2000] B.C.C. 368; *Aylwen v Taylor Joynson Garrett* [2002] P.N.L.R. 1 at [47]–[49].
[22] *Thune v London Properties Ltd* [1990] 1 W.L.R. 562 at 571.
[23] *Al-Koronky v Time Life Entertainment Group* [2006] EWCA Civ 1123.
[24] *Dhami v Lloyds TSG General Insurance Ltd* [2009] EWCA Civ 1326.
[25] *Braddock v Tillotson's Newspapers* [1950] 1 K.B. 47.
[26] *Hamilton v Al Fayed (No.4)* [2001] E.M.L.R. 15.
[27] *Meek v Fleming* [1961] 2 Q.B. 366. Generally, see para.6–023.

on the basis that they had been coerced, but cannot convince the appellate court (even on paper) that there was any coercion, a retrial will not be granted.[28]

APPLICATION OF THE LADD V MARSHALL TEST: EXAMPLES

The *Ladd v Marshall* test applies equally to all types of new evidence which an appellant seeks to rely upon on appeal, whether that evidence is witness, expert, or documentary evidence. Each application is to be considered on its facts. There follows some examples of the application of the test to decided cases.
    6–008

Where a document was not disclosed by the respondent

The case of *Gillingham v Gillingham* suggests that appellate courts will be more willing to consider additional evidence where the respondent had, at one stage, possessed that same evidence. The Court of Appeal accepted that a letter could have been found if the appellant had exercised reasonable diligence. It held, however, that given the respondent must also have possessed a copy of the relevant letter, and had failed to disclose it, justice required the admission of the letter.[29]
    6–009

    The logic behind this decision appears to be that the respondent could not complain that the evidence was produced late where they should have disclosed it in the first place. However, the *Gillingham* decision did not include any finding that there had been a failure to disclose. Instead, Clarke L.J. held that even if the respondent's copy of the letter no longer existed, it should be admitted into evidence.[30]

Where the issue goes to admissibility of evidence originally heard at trial

In *Toth v Jarman*,[31] the Court of Appeal similarly held that the fact evidence could have been obtained before trial was not, on its own, decisive. In that case, the Court agreed that information could have been obtained at the time of trial about an expert witness's connections with the respondent, and yet still felt it necessary to consider the effect that evidence would have had. This was on the basis that the appellant had argued that the expert's
    6–010

---

[28] *Ladd v Marshall* [1954] 1 W.L.R. 1489.
[29] *Gillingham v Gillingham* [2001] C.P. Rep. 89. See also *Electra Private Equity Partners v KPMG Peat Marwick* [1999] EWCA Civ 1247; [2000] B.C.C. 368.
[30] *Gillingham v Gillingham* [2001] C.P. Rep. 89 at [30].
[31] *Toth v Jarman* [2006] EWCA Civ 1028 at [90] and [107].

connections would have disqualified him from giving evidence. On that basis, the Court considered whether it was "in the interests of justice to admit the new evidence",[32] though concluding finally that the evidence would not be admitted.

Evidence that amounts to further cross examination of a witness

6–011   In *Riyad v Ahli* the trial judge had made a finding at the end of the first part of a split trial, but the parties continued to correspond after the trial about the approach taken by an expert. Ultimately the appellant sought to adduce answers given in that communication to the appellate court.[33] The Court of Appeal described this correspondence as amounting to "further cross-examination" of the witness, and stated that the Court would be "particularly cautious" about admitting such evidence.[34]

However, the Court of Appeal did not address the question of whether this was evidence that could have been obtained for use at the trial, under the first limb of the *Ladd v Marshall* test. Although questions were put to the expert at trial, the Court did not comment on whether it was improper to seek to rely on answers to further questions posed after the hearing. Instead, the Court of Appeal considered the evidence contained in the correspondence and came to the conclusion, on the facts of that case, that the later answers given by the expert were of only marginal relevance. However, the facts of the case should be treated with care, as quantum had still not been assessed at first instance. This, coupled with the concession that the expert had not taken the approach set out in his report, meant that the credibility of the expert's figures could still be challenged in front of the trial judge.

Witnesses who seek to change their evidence

6–012   *Ladd v Marshall* itself was concerned with an application to recall a witness who had already given evidence at trial. She had originally said that she could not remember the relevant events, but was now willing to give an account in support of the appellants. In addition to setting out the tripartite test, Denning L.J. (as he then was) commented on the likelihood of an appeal succeeding on the basis that a witness has told a lie and now wishes to "tell the truth". He commented that "the fresh evidence of such a witness will not as a rule satisfy the third condition" because a "confessed liar cannot usually be accepted as being credible".[35] Denning L.J. stated,

---

[32] *Toth v Jarman* [2006] EWCA Civ 1028 at [107].
[33] *Riyad Bank v Ahli United Bank* [2005] EWCA Civ 1419.
[34] *Riyad Bank v Ahli United Bank* [2005] EWCA Civ 1419 at [28].
[35] At 1491.

however, that, if it was proved that the witness had been bribed or coerced into telling a lie at the trial, and was now anxious to tell the truth, that would be a ground for a new trial.[36]

Evidence going to the credibility of witnesses

There have been a number of cases where appellants have sought to adduce **6–013** new evidence which goes to the credibility of a witness at the original trial. Where the allegation amounts to fraud, in that the court at first instance was actively misled, the courts have ordered a retrial[37] or remitted the issue of fraud to the original trial judge.[38] In the absence of fraud, where the new evidence as to credibility was simply not before the court, it will "seldom, if ever" be sufficient to require a retrial.[39] In order to admit such evidence, it seems necessary that the evidence should be sufficiently serious that it would wholly undermine the witness's evidence such that the verdict could not stand.[40] Even if the evidence is particularly serious, it will not be admitted if it is clear that the witness's credibility had already been destroyed by other evidence and had not been relied upon.[41]

Generally, evidence undermining the credibility of one or two of a number of witnesses will not be sufficient in itself to show that the evidence is sufficiently influential as to be admitted.[42]

Evidence available through new techniques

There does not appear to be any authority suggesting that evidence which **6–014** becomes available through new technological advances should be admitted on appeal. The reason for this may be practical; any such evidence is only likely to arise after the passing of time, and that in itself appears to be a reason to refuse to accept the admission of additional evidence.[43]

Appeals against orders made otherwise than at trial

Appellate courts will generally be reluctant to admit fresh evidence in an **6–015** appeal against summary judgment under CPR r.24.2 or a striking out order under CPR r.3.4.[44] Where an appeal relates to a hearing which pre-dated

---

[36] At 1491–1492.
[37] *Meek v Fleming* [1961] 2 Q.B. 366.
[38] *Owens v Noble* [2010] EWCA Civ 284.
[39] *Hamilton v Al Fayed (No.4)* [2001] E.M.L.R. 15 at [34].
[40] *Braddock v Tillotson's Newspapers* [1950] 1 K.B. 47. Referred to with approval in *Hamilton v Al Fayed (No.4)* [2001] E.M.L.R. 15 at [34].
[41] *Hamilton v Al Fayed (No.4)* [2001] E.M.L.R. 15.
[42] *Ali v Ellmore* [1953] 1 W.L.R. 1300.
[43] See *The Ampthill Peerage* [1977] A.C. 547, where blood tests were not ordered.
[44] *Aylwen v Taylor Joynson Garrett* [2001] EWCA Civ 1171 at [47]–[49].

disclosure, and disclosure would have assisted the appellant in obtaining relevant evidence, there is authority pointing towards the admission of additional evidence.[45]

Where an appellate court does allow additional evidence on an appeal against an interim order, the correct approach is for the appellate court to consider whether the additional evidence invalidated the basis upon which the judge at first instance proceeded, and only if it does so should the court exercise its own discretion. It is insufficient for the appellate court to simply accept the new evidence and exercise its own discretion, without having considered whether it would have changed the judge at first instance's view.[46]

EVIDENCE OF EVENTS SUBSEQUENT TO ORIGINAL HEARING

6–016   Evidence of changed circumstances since the date of the hearing at first instance will only sparingly be admitted.[47]

Where events occur after judgment which, if they had occurred before the trial, would have led to an increased award the general rule is that the claimant cannot go back to court to seek greater damages. Similarly, a defendant cannot appeal on the basis that damages were too high, based upon subsequent events.[48]

Under the previous rules of procedure, there was an express, albeit exceptional, power to admit further evidence of events which occurred after the date of the trial or hearing in RSC Ord.59, r.10(2).[49] This rule carved out and distinguished "evidence as to matters which have occurred after the date of the trial or hearing" from the rule requiring special grounds for admitting new evidence.[50] Nevertheless, Ord.59, r.10(2) gave the courts discretion in determining whether to admit evidence of subsequent events, particularly in relation to awards for damages in personal injury claims.

There is no such express power in the CPR. CPR r.52.11 sets out the basic rule that evidence which had not been before the lower court (which, by definition, would include evidence of subsequent events) will not be admitted without an order of the appellate court. However, the Court of Appeal has reviewed the categories in which evidence of later events had

---

[45] *Electra Private Equity v KPMG Peat Marwick* [1999] EWCA Civ 1247; [2000] B.C.C. 368, although at 405 Clarke L.J. suggested that even without a relaxation of the test the evidence would have been admitted. In this case, disclosure was supposed to have taken place by the time of the original hearing, but did not occur until the day after the hearing at which the claim was struck out.

[46] *Hadmor Productions v Hamilton* [1983] A.C. 191.

[47] *R. (Iran) v SSHD* [2005] EWCA Civ 982 at [34].

[48] *Murphy v Stone-Wallwork (Charlton) Ltd* [1969] 1 W.L.R. 1023 at 1027, per Lord Pearce.

[49] See *Hughes v Singh, The Times*, April 21, 1989.

[50] RSC Ord.59, r.10(2).

been adduced under the pre-CPR regime[51] and, although the continued validity of those categories of event was not commented on specifically, by implication the Court of Appeal confirmed that those earlier authorities continue to be applicable. It can therefore be expected that, as with other categories of new evidence, the old cases will remain of persuasive authority.

Where appeals on other grounds are under consideration

In a number of cases, a party has appealed against the basis for an award of damages, and, during the course of that appeal, the claimant's situation has changed. In these circumstances, the appellate court has a discretion as to whether to reopen the assessment of damages in order to allow evidence of the subsequent events and reflect the change in circumstances. Despite reference for the need for "exceptional circumstances" before such a discretion will be exercised,[52] the cases show that subsequent events will often be taken into account.[53]

6–017

Where the subsequent events form the basis of the appeal

Where subsequent events emerge immediately after trial, and within the normal time period in which an appeal may be made, the courts have been sympathetic towards admitting evidence of those events.[54] The fact that the time for appeal had not expired appears to be a factor which points in favour of the subsequent event being taken into account.[55]

6–018

The factor which weighs most heavily in favour of accepting such additional evidence appears to be where the subsequent events falsify an assumption upon which the court below demonstrably relied in reaching its decision.[56]

However, where the time period for bringing an appeal has expired, it is more difficult to rely on subsequent events as grounds for challenging the original decision of the court. This is the cumulative effect of dicta which

---

[51] R. (Iran) v Home Secretary [2005] EWCA Civ 982 at [34].

[52] Mulholland v Mitchell [1971] A.C. 666 at 677, per Viscount Dilhorne and at 681, per Lord Pearson, who said that: "The normal rule in accident cases is that the sum of damages falls to be assessed once and for all at the time of the hearing. When the assessment is made, the court has to make the best assessment it can as to events which may happen in the future. If further evidence as to the new events were too easily admitted, there would be no finality in litigation". See also Owens v Noble [2010] EWCA Civ 224 at [14].

[53] Lim Poh Choo v Camden and Islington AHA [1980] AC 174. This category of cases was mentioned, without comment, as instances of the pre-CPR regime as to admission of new evidence: R. (Iran) v Home Secretary [2005] EWCA Civ 982 at [34].

[54] Murphy v Stone-Wallwork (Chartton) [1969] 1 W.L.R. 1023; Curwen v James [1963] 1 W.L.R. 748.

[55] Curwen v Jones [1963] 1 W.L.R. 748.

[56] Curwen v James [1963] 1 W.L.R. 748; Murphy v Stone-Wallwork (Charlton) Ltd [1969] 1 W.L.R. 1023; Mulholland v Mitchell [1971] A.C. 666.

suggest that, where the time period for an appeal has expired, subsequent events will only be taken into account in the most exceptional circumstances. For example, Lord Upjohn stated that where the time allowed for appeal has run out, whether it be to the Court of Appeal or to the House of Lord, the Court would apply "a very strict rule indeed".[57]

There is at least one authority in which an appeal out of time was allowed on the basis of events subsequent to the trial. "Exceptional circumstances" were said to exist,[58] but it has been doubted in subsequent cases.[59]

Examples

6–019 The admission of subsequent events has been said to depend upon discretion sensitive to the facts of the case.[60] It is therefore useful to summarise examples of cases in which such evidence has been allowed:

(1) Where a trial judge did not hear evidence of a widow's likelihood of re-marriage in assessing damages under the Fatal Accident Acts, the Court of Appeal heard evidence of the widow's remarriage on the very day on which the judgment was said to have been perfected. The appeal was originally based on other grounds, with this evidence adduced a few weeks later.[61]

(2) Where the court at first instance had awarded damages on the basis that the claimant would be offered a particular job by the defendant, but it later appearing that the defendant was not suited for that job, the Court of Appeal heard evidence of the wages actually received by that claimant. This is the one example of an appeal on the basis of evidence of subsequent events being made, and succeeding, out of time.[62]

(3) The House of Lords heard evidence of the claimant's dismissal by the defendant two weeks after the hearing of the appeal in the Court of Appeal. This was on the basis that both the court at first instance and the Court of Appeal proceeded on the assumption that the claimant would continue to be employed.[63]

---

[57] *Murphy v Stone-Wallwork (Charlton) Ltd* [1969] 1 W.L.R. 1023 at 1031. Reflected in the language of Lord Pearson in *Mulholland v Mitchell* [1971] A.C. 666 at 682.

[58] *Jenkins v Richard Thomas & Baldwins Ltd* [1966] 1 W.L.R. 476 at 479, per Salmon L.J.

[59] *Murphy v Stone-Wallwork (Charlton) Ltd* [1969] 1 W.L.R. 1023 at 1031, per Lord Upjohn.

[60] *Murphy v Stone-Wallwork (Charlton) Ltd* [1969] 1 W.L.R. 1023 at 1036, per Lord Pearson.

[61] *Curwen v James* [1963] 1 W.L.R. 748.

[62] *Jenkins v Richard Thomas & Baldwins Ltd* [1966] 1 W.L.R. 476.

[63] *Murphy v Stone-Wallwork (Charlton) Ltd* [1969] 1 W.L.R. 1023.

(4) Appeals have been allowed on the basis of admission of new evidence in relation to the claimant's care needs, where it had rapidly become obvious that greater care (and expense) was required.[64]

Injunctions

Under the former Rules of the Supreme Court, the appellate court would conduct a rehearing of the case. It was partly on this basis that evidence of subsequent events used to be accepted by the Court of Appeal in discharging an injunction, on the basis that the injunction was no longer needed.[65] It was accepted that even if the injunction had been correct at the time of the decision, it could be discharged on appeal.

6–020

It is not clear that subsequent events demonstrating that an injunction was *no longer* necessary could render the decision of the lower court "wrong" under the Civil Procedure Rules.[66] Nevertheless, recent Court of Appeal authority mentions without comment this type of case, as one in which evidence of subsequent events was admitted under the pre-CPR regime.[67]

PROCEDURE

Application to be made to the appellate court

Where a party seeks to rely on new evidence, the court at first instance does not have jurisdiction to reopen the case,[68] although a new claim will be entertained where the new evidence is aimed at proving that the case was tainted by fraud.[69] Application for permission to appeal on the basis of new evidence must be made to the appropriate appeal court.

6–021

It used to be thought that the Court of Appeal, likewise, does not have authority to reconsider an appeal on the basis of new evidence,[70] but more recent authority has held that it can do so, though such cases will be "exceptional".[71] The only case in which it has done so related to allegations of bias against a judge, and which therefore invoked the question of confidence in the administrations of justice.[72] The Court of Appeal further held

---

[64] *Mulholland v Mitchell* [1971] A.C. 666; *Lim Poh Choo v Camden and Islington AHA* [1980] A.C. 174.
[65] *Att Gen v Birmingham Tame and Rea District Drainage Board* [1912] A.C. 788.
[66] CPR r.52.11.
[67] *R. (Iran) v Home Secretary* [2005] EWCA Civ 982 at [34].
[68] *In re Barrell Enterprises* [1973] 1 W.L.R. 19.
[69] See paras 6–024 and 6–025.
[70] *In Re Barrell Enterprises* [1973] 1 W.L.R. 19 at 24, per Russell L.J.
[71] *Taylor v Lawrence* [2002] EWCA Civ 90; [2003] Q.B. 528 at [55]. This is now codified in CPR r.52.17 (see Ch.8).
[72] *Taylor v Lawrence* [2002] EWCA Civ 90; [2003] Q.B. 528 at [55].

that it would only reopen an appeal where it was satisfied that the Supreme Court would not give leave to appeal.[73]

De bene esse

6–022   On an application to adduce new evidence on appeal, the appellate court has to consider the evidence to decide whether it provides a proper basis for the appeal. Traditionally, the route taken was to admit the evidence, provisionally, for the purposes of ruling on its admissibility (on a *de bene esse* basis). It has been held that this approach is no longer appropriate, and that appellate courts should give permission for the evidence to be adduced, in order to consider whether the appeal should be granted.[74] However, courts continue to refer to reading evidence *de bene esse*.[75] It is not thought that the terminology used is of any great importance.

Subsequent orders

6–023   Depending on the circumstances, where an appeal based on new evidence is allowed, the appellate court may order a retrial if a retrial is "imperative in the interests of justice"[76]; or it may remit the relevant issue or decision to a different judge.[77] Alternatively, the appellate court may determine the matter itself on the basis of the fresh evidence.[78]

EVIDENCE OF FRAUD

New action or appeal

6–024   Where a disappointed party discovers evidence that the result at trial was procured by fraud, there are two possible courses of action:

(1) The fraud can form the basis of a new action seeking to set aside the judgment at first instance; or

---

[73] The House of Lords as it then was: *Taylor v Lawrence* [2002] EWCA Civ 90; [2003] Q.B. 528 at [55].

[74] *Hamilton v Al Fayed (No.4)* [2001] E.M.L.R. 15 at [67].

[75] *Aylwen v Garrett* [2002] P.N.L.R. 1 at [19].

[76] *Transview Properties Ltd v City Site Properties Ltd* [2009] EWCA Civ 1255.

[77] In *Clark v Thorpe* [2009] EWCA Civ 1000 the Court of Appeal remitted the assessment of damages to a different judge for rehearing because the fresh evidence went to quantum but not liability.

[78] For example, in *Mastercigars Direct Ltd v Withers LLP* [2009] EWHC 993 (Ch) the court held that it had jurisdiction to consider the fresh evidence that had not been adduced before the court at first instance and to determine the underlying dispute between the parties (which related to costs).

(2) An appeal can be brought, seeking remission or a retrial on the basis of the fraud proven by the subsequent documents.

Traditionally, it was thought that the proper course was to bring a new action.[79] However, recent authorities muddied the waters. In *Hamilton v Al Fayed (No.4)* the Court of Appeal said that an appeal seeking retrial on the basis of fraud is both the normal and the proper course of action.[80] However, the decision of the House of Lords, just two months later, in *Kuwait Airways v Iraqi Airways* stated that a new action is the proper approach.[81]

This "irreconcilable conflict" in the authorities has now been resolved by the Court of Appeal in *Owens v Noble*.[82] In that case the claimant was seriously injured in a traffic accident. Liability was admitted. At first instance the judge made a substantial award of damages on the basis that the claimant was seriously disabled by the accident. After judgment, the defendant obtained covert surveillance evidence which suggested that the claimant was not as seriously disabled as he had contended at trial. The defendant appealed, seeking (a) admission of the surveillance evidence, (b) an order setting aside the judgment at first instance, and (c) an order that the assessment of damages be re-tried. The Court of Appeal, allowing the appeal only in part, reviewed the conflicting line of authorities and concluded that, as a matter of jurisprudence, the House of Lords' decisions[83] (to the effect that the correct course of action is to commence a fresh action for fraud) are to be preferred. It was held that, where fresh evidence is adduced showing that the judge at first instance was deliberately misled, then—unless the fraud is either admitted or the evidence of fraud is incontrovertible—the disappointed party must plead and prove fraud before the established judgment can be set aside.

---

[79] *Flower v Lloyd* (1877) 6 Ch. D. 297; *Hip Foong Hong v H Neotia & Co* [1918] A.C. 888; *Jonesco v Beard* [1930] A.C. 298 at 300. In the latter case the rationale for the House of Lords' decision that the disappointed party should commence a fresh action for fraud was that the defendant should not lose his favourable judgment without clear evidence of fraud. The evidence of fraud in that case was not incontrovertible. The court should only order a retrial where the fraud was clearly established and/or undisputed.

[80] [2001] E.M.L.R. 15 at [21]. See also *Roe v Robert McGregor & Sons Ltd* [1968] 1 W.L.R. 925 where a retrial was ordered on appeal, although in that case *Jonesco v Beard* was not cited or considered. These judgments should be treated with caution following the decision of the Court of Appeal in *Owens v Noble* [2010] EWCA Civ 224.

[81] [2001] 1 Lloyd's Rep. 485. In that case, the fraud was not clearly established, and it was said that the allegations of fraud must be pleaded and properly proved in the fresh action. A later Privy Council decision, *Boodoosing v Ramnarace* [2004] UKPC 9, noting the earlier cases suggested that the appropriateness of either course will depend upon what is asked of the appellate court, so that an appeal is more appropriate where only one part of a judgment is impugned.

[82] [2010] EWCA Civ 224.

[83] *Jonesco v Beard* [1930] A.C. 298; *Kuwait Airways v Iraqi Airways* [2001] 1 Lloyd's Rep. 485. But note that the Court of Appeal in *Owens v Noble* [2010] EWCA Civ 224 distinguished divorce cases (in explanation of the House of Lords' decision to order a retrial on appeal in *Skone v Skone* [1971] 1 W.L.R. 812) on the basis that the strong public interest that a divorce petition should not be granted or refused on a wrong basis outweighed the public interest in the finality of litigation.

6–025   However, the Court of Appeal ordered that this be achieved, not by commencing a fresh action (as in *Jonesco v Beard*), but by remission of the fraud issue to a High Court judge for determination[84] pursuant to CPR r.52.10(2)(b).[85] Further, the Court of Appeal ordered in a separate judgment that remission of the fraud issue should be to the original trial judge.[86] It was held that the trial judge is the most appropriate person to determine the issue, being in a far better position to compare the new evidence with the evidence given at the original hearing.

This may lead to the question of whether there is any practical difference between, on the one hand, ordering on appeal a rehearing of the decision at first instance by the trial judge; and, on the other hand, remitting the fraud issue to the same trial judge for determination. The answer is that:

(1) in the former case (where a rehearing is ordered on appeal), the judgment at first instance will be set aside, and the issues determined by the court at first instance will be re-tried *de novo*;

(2) whereas, in the latter case (where the fraud issue is remitted to the trial judge), the judgment at first instance will stand unless or until the High Court judge finds that the allegations of fraud have been proved. So, if the High Court judge rejects the allegations of fraud, the original judgment or award of damages will stand; but if the High Court judge finds that fraud was proved, they should either set aside the judgment at first instance or (as the case may be) make a reassessment of the damages in light of those allegations.

Procedure

6–026   In light of the decision of the Court of Appeal in *Owens v Noble*,[87] the procedure that should therefore be adopted in cases where a party has obtained judgment by means of a fraud on the judge is as follows:

(1) If the fraud is admitted or the evidence of fraud is incontrovertible, the disappointed party should apply for permission to appeal the decision at first instance, seeking (a) admission of the fresh evidence; (b) an order setting aside that decision; and (c) a re-hearing.

(2) If the evidence of fraud is not incontrovertible, the disappointed party should apply for permission to appeal the decision at first instance, seeking (a) admission of the fresh evidence; and (b)

---

[84] The rationale for the Court of Appeal's decision was that it would be more cost effective and proportionate to remit the fraud issue to a High Court judge for determination than to require the disappointed party to issue a fresh claim in the High Court.

[85] CPR r.52.10(2)(b) provides that, in relation to an appeal, the appeal court has power to refer any claim or issue for determination by the lower court.

[86] [2010] EWCA Civ 224 at [29]. This was in spite of objections raised by the respondent: [2010] EWCA Civ 284 at [2]–[6].

[87] [2010] EWCA Civ 224; and [2010] EWCA Civ 284.

remission of the fraud issue to the original trial judge for determination.

The test for an appeal on the basis of fraud

As set out above, following *Owens v Noble*[88] the test now is that, where **6–027** fresh evidence is adduced showing that the judge at first instance was deliberately misled, the Court of Appeal will only order a retrial where the fraud is either admitted or the evidence of fraud is incontrovertible.

The *Ladd v Marshall* test[89] does not apply to evidence which points to fraud[90]: a less strict approach is applied. Whereas it is normally necessary to demonstrate that the new evidence would have had an important influence on the result, this is not necessary where there is prima facie evidence of fraud. It is not clear whether this is based upon a lesser test[91] or an assumption that the presence of fraud will almost certainly have undermined the fraudster's case.[92]

However, it must nevertheless be demonstrated that the original trial judge was actively deceived on a material matter. This can be contrasted with evidence which merely goes to the credit of a witness.[93] New evidence will not be admitted where fraud is alleged but the appellate court concludes that, even with full knowledge of the fraud, the court at first instance would have reached the same result. So, where the alleged fraud goes to an issue on quantum, but the appellate court is satisfied that the fraud would not have affected the decision on liability, the judgment as a whole cannot be reopened.[94]

The appellant must generally demonstrate that the evidence of fraud could not have been obtained prior to the trial with reasonable diligence.[95]

---

[88] [2010] EWCA Civ 224.
[89] See para.6–004.
[90] *Owens v Noble* [2010] EWCA Civ 224 at [39].
[91] Which might be inferred from *Hamilton v Al Fayed (No.4)* [2001] E.M.L.R. 15 at [15].
[92] Suggested by Taylor J. in the High Court of Australia in *McDonald v McDonald* (1965) 113 C.L.R. 529 at 537.
[93] See para.6–013.
[94] *Boodoosingh v Ramnarace* [2005] UKPC 9.
[95] *Skone v Skone* [1971] 1 W.L.R. 812.

CHAPTER 7

The Effect of Settlement, Consent and Concessions

DISMISSAL OF APPLICATIONS OR APPEALS BY CONSENT

7–001   Applications for permission to appeal, and appeals, may be dismissed on the request of the appellant or by consent between the parties, subject to paras 12 and 13.2 respectively of the Practice Direction to Pt 52.

Appellant no longer wishes to pursue appeal

7–002   Where the appellant no longer wishes to pursue an application for permission to appeal or (in circumstances where permission has already been granted) an appeal, the appellant may request from the appeal court an order that the application or appeal be dismissed,[1] unless any party to the proceedings is a child[2] or protected party,[3] or the appeal or application is to the Court of Appeal from a decision of the Court of Protection.[4] The appellant's request must contain a statement confirming that no party to the

---

[1] CPR PD 52 para.12.2. Under the pre-CPR law, the appellant could apply for permission to withdraw an appeal. Withdrawal of the appeal (unlike dismissal) left the door open for the appeal to be renewed, albeit an application for extension of time would have to be made: *Buckbod Investments Ltd v Nana-Otchere* [1985] 1 All E.R. 283. However, under the CPR the appellant may not apply for permission to withdraw the appeal; where the appellant no longer wishes to pursue the appeal then he must apply for an order dismissing the appeal. This change in procedure reflects the greater emphasis on the finality of litigation in the CPR.

[2] CPR PD 52 para.12.4 provides that "child" is to have the same meaning as in CPR r.21.1(2), which defines a child as "a person under 18".

[3] CPR PD 52 para.12.4 provides that "protected party" is to have the same meaning as in CPR r.21.1(2), which defines a protected party as "a party, or an intended party, who lacks capacity to conduct the proceedings".

[4] CPR PD 52 para.12.1.

proceedings is a child or protected party, and that the appeal or application is not from a decision of the Court of Protection.[5]

The appeal court may (and usually will) grant the appellant's request, usually without a hearing. If the request is granted, the court will usually order that the appeal or application be dismissed on the basis that the appellant pays the costs of the application or appeal.[6] That will be an end to the appeal proceedings. If the appellant wishes to have the application or appeal dismissed without costs, the appellant's request must be accompanied by a consent order signed by the respondent or their legal representative stating that:

(1) the respondent is not a child or protected party and the appeal or application is not from a decision of the Court of Protection; and

(2) the respondent consents to the dismissal of the application or appeal without costs.[7]

Appeal dismissed by consent

On the other hand, where the parties have agreed settlement terms disposing of the application or appeal, a request to the appeal court for dismissal of the application or appeal must be a joint request from all parties (accompanied by a consent order for approval) stating that[8]:

7–003

(1) none of the parties is a child or protected party;

(2) the appeal or application is not from a decision of the Court of Protection; and

(3) requesting that the application or appeal be dismissed by consent.

The request should make clear whether any order is sought as to the costs of the application or appeal. The appeal court may (and usually will) grant the parties' request, usually without a hearing. If the request is granted, the application or appeal will be dismissed and that will be an end to the appeal proceedings.[9]

---

[5] CPR PD 52 para.12.2.
[6] CPR PD 52 para.12.2.
[7] CPR PD 52 para.12.3.
[8] CPR PD 52 para.12.4.
[9] CPR PD 52 para.12.4(2).

Tomlin form of consent order

7–004 The consent order accompanying the request may be in the form of a Tomlin order.[10] A Tomlin order usually provides that all further proceedings in the claim be stayed except for the purpose of carrying the settlement terms into effect, with liberty to apply as to carrying such terms into effect.[11] Ordinarily the parties to a Tomlin order would apply to the court that made the order in the event of any breach of the order. However, a Tomlin order accompanying a request to dispose of appeal proceedings should provide that any application for carrying the terms of the order into effect be made to the lower court.

Where appeal court's approval is required

7–005 However, if a party to the proceedings is a child or protected party, or the appeal or application is from a decision of the Court of Protection, the approval of the court is required before an application or appeal can be dismissed, even where the parties consent to dismissal or the appellant wishes to withdraw its application or appeal. In those circumstances, the appeal court's approval is required for[12]:

(1) a settlement relating to the appeal or application;
(2) an agreement reached at appeal stage to pay periodical payments in a personal injury claim for damages for future pecuniary loss; or
(3) a request by an appellant for an order that their application or appeal be dismissed (whether with or without the consent of the respondent).

APPEAL COURT WILL NOT NORMALLY ALLOW AN APPEAL BY CONSENT

7–006 Different principles apply in the more unusual circumstances where the parties seek to have an appeal allowed (rather than dismissed) by consent, or where the respondent does not oppose the appeal. The general rule is that an appeal court will not normally allow an appeal, or resolve an issue of law, by consent between the parties, unless it has satisfied itself that the decision of the lower court was wrong, or the decision suffered from a serious procedural or other irregularity. The policy underlying this general

---

[10] As suggested by Tomlin J. in *Practice Note* [1927] W.N. 290, following the decision in *Dashwood v Dashwood* (1927) 71 S.J. 911. The settlement terms are set out in a schedule to the order.

[11] Per the guidance in the *White Book* notes to CPR r.40.6 at para.40.6.2.

[12] CPR PD 52 para.13.2. The procedure to be followed where para.13.2 applies is set out in paras 13.3–13.5.

rule is that an appeal court will not reverse a judgment of a court below without hearing the appeal[13]: the law cannot be stated by agreement between the parties.[14] By contrast, an appeal court will be prepared to dismiss an application or appeal by consent (as set out above at paras 7–001 to 7–004), because the appellant thereby merely gives up their right of appeal, and the decision of the court or tribunal below is left standing.[15]

The position is now governed by para.13.1 of the Practice Direction to Pt 52, which provides that, notwithstanding the general rule, the appeal court can nevertheless set aside or vary the order of the court below where the parties have reached agreement or the respondent does not oppose the appeal:

> "The appeal court will not normally make an order allowing an appeal unless satisfied that the decision of the lower court was wrong, but the appeal court may set aside or vary the order of the lower court with consent and without determining the merits of the appeal, if it is satisfied that there are good and sufficient reasons for doing so."

Nevertheless, para.13.1 of the Practice Direction to Pt 52 does not affect the general principle that an appeal court will not find that the decision of a lower court was wrong merely because the parties have agreed that it was wrong. The leading pre-CPR authority which states the general rule is *Slaney (Inspector of Taxes) v Kean*,[16] and that remains good law. That case involved an appeal by the Crown from a decision of the general commissioners that a particular deduction by a taxpayer was proper. Counsel for the Crown appeared at the appeal hearing alone (the taxpayer did not attend) and produced a document stating that the parties had agreed that the appeal should be allowed, and the decision of the general commissioners reversed. Megarry J. refused to reverse the decision, and held that the appeal court would not allow an appeal by consent:

> "An appeal may, of course, be dismissed by consent; for the appellant thereby merely gives up his right of appeal, and the decision of the court or tribunal below is left standing. But certainly under the general law, an appeal court will not allow an appeal by consent. If it were to do so, it would be making an order holding that the decision below was wrong; and it would be doing this merely on the agreement of the

---

[13] *Slaney (Inspector of Taxes) v Kean* [1970] Ch. 243 at 246. See also *Lees v Motor Insurers' Bureau* [1953] 1 W.L.R. 620 CA and *Lloyd v Rossleigh Ltd* [1961] R.V.R. 448 CA.

[14] *Lloyd v Rossleigh Ltd* [1961] R.V.R. 448 CA, per Sellers L.J. This was a rating appeal from the Lands Tribunal. Counsel for the valuation officer informed the Court of Appeal that the successful ratepayers had agreed with the valuation officer that the appeal should be allowed. Sellers L.J. said: "They cannot do that. They can agree different figures, but they cannot allow the appeal. We alone can do that. You will either have to withdraw or dismiss it. I am sorry, but we never allow an appeal unless we have heard it. It has the same effect; but I do not think it is fair to the Lands Tribunal or anybody else to allow an appeal by consent. It has never been done in the Court of Appeal, so far as I am aware...".

[15] *Slaney (Inspector of Taxes) v Kean* [1970] Ch. 243 at 246.

[16] [1970] Ch. 243.

parties and without hearing the case. Indeed, the appeal court might be reversing a decision based upon propositions of law which, if argued, would be held to be entirely correct. The law is a matter for decision by the court after considering the case, and not for agreement between John Doe and Richard Roe, with the court blindly giving its authority to whatever they have agreed."[17]

7–007 Megarry J. found support for the general proposition that an appeal court would not allow appeals by consent in two earlier cases, *Lees v Motor Insurers' Bureau*[18] and *Lloyd v Rossleigh Ltd*.[19] In the latter case, Devlin L.J. held that the Court of Appeal had no power to make the order allowing the appeal which was sought by Counsel for the valuation officer because "... you are asking us to straighten the law without satisfying us that it has gone crooked, merely because you say two members of the Bar have agreed that it has gone crooked. Plainly we cannot do that." Instead, the Court of Appeal ordered that the appeal be withdrawn.

In refusing to reverse the decision of the court below, Megarry J. in *Slaney (Inspector of Taxes) v Kean*[20] relied in particular on the fact that (as in *Lloyd v Rossleigh Ltd*) the appeal lay only on a point of law, and the relief in question concerned the alteration of an official document, rather than payment of a sum of money.

The effect of para.13.1 of the Practice Direction to Pt 52 is that, in appropriate cases, the appeal court will instead set aside or vary the order of the court below to reflect the practical consequences of the agreement reached between the parties, without the need to determine the underlying merits of the decision of the court below. So, for example, the appeal court may order that a different sum of money be paid, or may change the terms on which an injunction was granted. However, it remains the case that an appeal court cannot allow an appeal on a point of law, or resolve an issue of law, merely by consent between the parties, unless it has satisfied itself that the decision of the lower court was wrong, or the decision suffered from a serious procedural or other irregularity.

Procedure

7–008 Where the parties seek an order setting aside or varying the order of the court below, the parties should make a request to the appeal court (signed by all the parties to the appeal) setting out the following:

---

[17] [1970] Ch. 243 at 246.
[18] [1953] 1 W.L.R. 620 CA. In that case the Court of Appeal refused to reverse the judgment of Lord Goddard C.J. in the court below. Denning L.J. said that "an appeal could not be allowed by consent, for that would be reversing the judgment of Lord Goddard C.J. without hearing the appeal" (at 621).
[19] [1961] R.V.R. 448 CA.
[20] [1970] Ch. 243.

(1) the relevant history of the proceedings;

(2) the matters relied on as justifying the proposed order;

(3) a copy of the proposed order; and

(4) a statement that none of the parties is a child or protected party and that the application or appeal is not from a decision of the Court of Protection.[21]

APPEALING AN ORDER MADE BY CONSENT

An appeal court will not normally permit a party to appeal against an order that was made by the court pursuant to a consent order[22] or pursuant to an agreement between the parties. The general rule is that the court will uphold agreements freely entered into at arm's length, and there is a public policy that there should be finality in litigation.[23] However, in exceptional circumstances, a court order made pursuant to a consent order or agreement may (in the exercise of the court's discretion) be set aside or varied, either under CPR r.3.1(7)[24] or on appeal,[25] where it is just and appropriate to do so. A consent order reflects an agreement made between the parties and the court will be very careful in exercising this discretion in favour of setting aside or varying a consent order.[26]   7–009

Many of the authorities relating to appeals against consent orders are appeals from ancillary relief proceedings. The principles applicable to ancillary relief appeals are different from those applicable to appeals in other branches of the law because a consent order in ancillary relief proceedings derives authority from the court, whereas a consent order in other proceedings derives its authority from the agreement between the parties and hence contractual doctrines apply.[27] However, the ancillary relief authorities can be applied to other cases provided that difference of authority is borne in mind.

A court order made pursuant to a consent order or agreement may be set aside or varied where, for example:

---

[21] CPR PD 52 para.13.1.

[22] CPR r.40.6 provides that, where all the parties agree the terms in which a judgment should be given or an order should be made, a court officer may enter and seal an agreed judgment or order provided that none of the parties is a litigant in person and the approval of the court is not required (approval is required where, e.g. one of the parties is a child or patient). Otherwise, the court will approve the consent order and enter judgment or make an order in the terms agreed (CPR r.40.6(5)).

[23] *S v S (Ancillary Relief: Consent Order)* [2002] 3 W.L.R. 1372 at [23].

[24] CPR r.3.1(7) gives the court power to vary or revoke an order it has made.

[25] See para.7–010 for discussion as to where an application under CPR r.3.1(7), or an application for permission to appeal, is the appropriate means of setting aside the consent order.

[26] *Weston v Dayman* [2006] EWCA Civ 1165 CA.

[27] *S v S (Ancillary Relief: Consent Order)* [2002] 3 W.L.R. 1372 at [30].

(1) A party to the consent order lacked capacity to contract at the time the consent order was agreed.[28]

(2) The consent order was vitiated by misrepresentation[29]; mistake as to facts or law[30] (including where the parties were mistaken as to the applicable law,[31] save in ancillary relief proceedings[32]); breach of the duty of full, frank and clear disclosure[33]; fraud; or undue influence.[34]

(3) The parties to the consent order may be relieved of their obligations under the consent order as a result of an unforeseen or unforeseeable supervening event under the doctrine of frustration.[35] A subsequent and significant change in the law may constitute a supervening event, provided that the parties to the consent order could not with reasonable diligence have known that a change in the law was imminent.[36]

On the other hand, an order made by consent will not be set aside or varied because one of the parties agreed to the consent order on the basis of bad or negligent legal advice,[37] or due to a mistaken appreciation of the commercial effects of the agreement.[38]

The interests of justice in setting aside a consent order will be weighed against the principle of finality in litigation.[39] In deciding whether to exercise its discretion, the appeal court will take into account the

---

[28] In *B v L* [2009] EWCA Civ 1263, a wife sought permission to appeal against an order entered by consent in ancillary relief proceedings, on the grounds that she lacked capacity at the time the consent order was entered due to mental health problems. The Court of Appeal refused permission to appeal against the order, on the basis that the medical evidence on which she relied did not establish that she lacked capacity at the material time.

[29] *Jenkins v Livesey (Formerly Jenkins)* [1985] A.C. 424.

[30] *De Lasala (Ernest Ferdinand Perez) v de Lasala (Hannelore)* [1980] A.C. 546; *Cornick v Cornick* [1994] 2 F.L.R. 530.

[31] *Kleinwort Benson Ltd v Lincoln City Council* [1999] 2 A.C. 349.

[32] *S v S (Ancillary Relief: Consent Order)* [2002] 3 W.L.R. 1372 at [70].

[33] *Raja v Hoogstraten* [2005] EWHC 2668 Ch (a freezing order made by consent was varied to include assets not disclosed at the time the consent order was entered).

[34] *Walkden v Walkden* [2009] EWCA Civ 627 at [47].

[35] *Walkden v Walkden* [2009] EWCA Civ 627 at [47]. In ancillary relief cases, *Barder v Barder* [1988] A.C. 20 will apply. In that case it was held that an appeal may be made against a lump sum settlement in ancillary relief cases where "new events have occurred since the making of the order which invalidates the basis or fundamental assumption on which the order was made". Hale J. (as she then was) held that this principle was akin to the doctrine of frustration in *Cornick v Cornick* [1994] 2 F.L.R. 530 at 533.

[36] *S v S (Ancillary Relief: Consent Order)* [2002] 3 W.L.R. 1372 at [38] and [51]–[54].

[37] *Tibbs v Dick* [1998] 2 F.L.R. 1118; *Harris (Formerly Manahan) v Manahan* [1996] 4 All E.R. 454. The remedy in that case is an action against the legal advisor.

[38] *WL Gore & Associates GmbH v Geox SpA* [2008] EWHC 462. In that case Lewison J. refused the claimants' application under CPR r.3.1(7) to vary a consent order, holding that the claimants' changed appreciation of the commercial effects of the agreement did not amount to a material change of circumstances.

[39] *S v S (Ancillary Relief: Consent Order)* [2002] 3 W.L.R. 1372.

promptness of the application for permission[40] and any prejudice to the respondent(s).[41]

Appeal, or application to set aside/vary

The question arises whether the order of the court below should be set aside   7–010
on appeal to the appeal court, or on application to the first instance court
under CPR r.3.1(7). The power of the court to vary or set aside an order
under CPR r.3.1(7) cannot be used as an equivalent to an appeal against
that order, or to circumvent an appeal.[42] If the applicant is able to place
new material before the court, whether in the form of evidence or argument, that was not placed before the court that made the order, then the
applicant should make an application to set aside or vary the order under
CPR r.3.1(7).[43] In all other cases, the applicant must bring an application
for permission to appeal if they wish to have the order set aside or varied.[44]

THE EFFECT OF CONCESSIONS

A judge (either at first instance or on appeal) has a discretion to allow a   7–011
party to rely on a claim or argument that had previously been abandoned or
conceded.[45] Even abandonment in the face of the court at trial may not be
finally irrevocable.[46] In *Worldwide Corp Ltd v Marconi Communications
Ltd* the claimant, through leading counsel, unequivocally abandoned its
original primary claim in the course of oral applications seeking permission
to amend its pleadings at the beginning of the first instance trial of the
matter before Moore-Bick J. (as he then was). Permission to amend was
refused. At a later hearing of the adjourned first instance trial, the claimant
(now acting through a different leading counsel) sought permission to

---

[40] *Barder v Barder* [1988] A.C. 20; *S v S (Ancillary Relief: Consent Order)* [2002] 3 W.L.R. 1372 at [57] to [62]; *Greig Middleton & Co Ltd v Denderowicz* [1998] 1 W.L.R. 1164 at 1172–1173.

[41] *Greig Middleton & Co Ltd v Denderowicz* [1998] 1 W.L.R. 1164 at 1179.

[42] *Collier v Williams* [2006] EWCA Civ 20; *Edwards v Golding* [2007] EWCA Civ 416 at [24].

[43] *Collier v Williams* [2006] EWCA Civ 20. The judge said that "for the High Court to revisit one of its earlier orders, the Applicant must either show some material change of cir-cumstances or that the judge who made the order was misled in some way, whether innocently or otherwise, as to the correct factual position before him". *Edwards v Golding* [2007] EWCA Civ 416 at [24] held that the case before the court before which CPR r.3.1(7) is moved must be "essentially different from one of simple error that could be righted on appeal".

[44] *Collier v Williams* [2006] EWCA Civ 20. The judge said that "[i]f all that is sought is a reconsideration of the order on the basis of the same material, then that can only be done, in my judgment, in the context of an appeal".

[45] *Worldwide Corp Ltd v Marconi Communications Ltd, Times Law Reports,* June 22, 1999; *Kuwait Airways Corp v Iraqi Airways Corp* [2002] EWCA Civ 515.

[46] *Worldwide Corp Ltd v Marconi Communications Ltd, Times Law Reports,* June 22, 1999; *Kuwait Airways Corp v Iraqi Airways Corp* [2002] EWCA Civ 515 at [15].

resuscitate that original primary claim. Moore-Bick J. refused permission. The Court of Appeal refused the claimant's application for permission to appeal against Moore-Bick J.'s ruling, finding that it was "impossible to mount an attack" on his exercise of his discretion.

Waller L.J. held that the balancing exercise carried out by Moore-Bick J. in the exercise of his discretion whether to allow the claimant to rely on the abandoned claim or not, was "impeccable". The factors taken into account by Moore-Bick J. were cited by Waller L.J. in his judgment and were as follows:

(1) Whether the abandoned claim or argument has real prospects of success.

(2) Was the decision to abandon the claim or argument taken deliberately or by mistake.

(3) Was the decision to abandon the claim or argument taken with the benefit of legal advice. If so, the prospects of successfully resuscitating the claim or argument will be reduced, regardless of whether it might be said this advice was negligent; in his judgment on appeal, Mance L.J. held that the court will not conduct an investigation into whether the legal advice was negligent or not.

(4) The prejudice to the other party or parties to the proceedings resulting from the delay to the proceedings.

(5) Whether an award of costs would adequately compensate the other party or parties to the proceedings for any prejudice caused.

(6) The reason for the change of heart or change in circumstances. Moore-Bick J. held that "it is incumbent on a party who wishes to change his mind to provide a good explanation for it and to demonstrate that it would be in the overall interest of justice to allow him to do so". If there were new developments or a change in circumstances this might justify reversing the abandonment; but having "second thoughts about their decision to abandon the major part of their existing case" was not considered by Moore-Bick J. to be a factor militating in favour of resuscitating the claim.

(7) The stage of the proceedings at which the claim or argument was abandoned. Moore-Bick J. held that "when the action has reached trial the time has come for final decisions to be made on which the court and other parties to the litigation can rely".

7–012   If a party is permitted to rely on a claim or argument that had earlier been abandoned, such permission will be conditional on that party providing security for costs.[47]

In *Kuwait Airways Corp v Iraqi Airways Corp* the Court of Appeal followed *Worldwide v Marconi* and emphasised that abandonment is a matter which goes "very much" to the judge's discretion.[48] In that case the

---

[47] *Worldwide Corp Ltd v Marconi Communications Ltd, Times Law Reports*, June 22, 1999.
[48] [2002] EWCA Civ 515 at [15].

judge at first instance found that the claimant's abandonment of certain claims was deliberate in one case but inadvertent in other cases. The Court of Appeal nevertheless dismissed the claimant's application for permission to appeal against the judge's decision that the claimant was not entitled to resuscitate any of the abandoned claims, on the basis that the judge had not misdirected himself in law.[49]

---

[49] *G v G* [1985] 1 W.L.R. 647 at 652; *Tanfern Ltd v Cameron-MacDonald* [2000] 1 W.L.R. 1311 at 1317.

CHAPTER 8

Reopening Appeals

INTRODUCTION

8–001 The general rule is that the appeal court's decision on an appeal is final and conclusive; once that decision is handed down, the court has no further jurisdiction.[1] However, in truly exceptional circumstances, the Court of Appeal and the High Court have the power to reopen an appeal, where the restrictive requirements of CPR r.52.17 are met. This power has only very rarely been exercised.

POLICY CONSIDERATIONS: JUSTICE VS FINALITY

8–002 The power of the Court of Appeal and the High Court to reopen appeals was codified in CPR r.52.17, following the unanimous decision of a five-judge[2] Court of Appeal in *Taylor v Lawrence*.[3] The Court of Appeal held that it had a residual jurisdiction to reopen an appeal after its conclusion, in exceptional circumstances, in order to avoid significant injustice. The power to reopen appeals, it was held, was implicit in order that the Court of Appeal could achieve its objectives of correcting wrong decisions, clarifying and developing the law, and setting precedents.[4] However, the Court of Appeal acknowledged that those objectives had to be balanced against the fundamental principle that the outcome of litigation should be final.[5] To that end, the Lord Chief Justice, giving the judgment, emphasised that the jurisdiction to reopen an appeal after its conclusion would seldom be exercised.

After the decision in *Taylor v Lawrence*, the Court of Appeal in *Seray-Wurie v Hackney LBC* held that the High Court had the same jurisdiction

---

[1] *Flower v Lloyd* (1877) 6 Ch. D. 297 at 300–301.
[2] Namely, Lord Woolf C.J., Lord Phillips M.R., Ward L.J., Brooke L.J. and Chadwick L.J.
[3] [2002] EWCA Civ 90; [2003] Q.B. 528.
[4] *Taylor v Lawrence* [2002] EWCA Civ 90; [2003] Q.B. 528 at 540.
[5] *The Ampthill Peerage* [1977] A.C. 547 at 569; *Taylor v Lawrence* [2002] EWCA Civ 90; [2003] Q.B. 528 at 535.

to reopen an appeal following its conclusion, subject to the same restrictions.[6] Brooke L.J. held that the High Court possessed an inherent jurisdiction to "do what it needs must have power to do in order to maintain its character as a court of justice".[7]

THE CIVIL PROCEDURE RULES

CPR r.52.17(1) provides that the Court of Appeal or the High Court will not reopen either a final determination of any appeal, or an application for permission to appeal,[8] unless each of the following requirements is met: 8–003

(1) it is necessary to do so in order to avoid real injustice;
(2) the circumstances are exceptional and make it appropriate to reopen the appeal; and
(3) there is no alternative effective remedy.

These highly restrictive requirements are applied narrowly and it will only be in very rare cases that those requirements will be found to have been met.

The power to reopen an appeal was not originally included in CPR Pt 52. This power was added[9] in order to codify the decisions of the Court of Appeal in *Taylor v Lawrence*[10] and *Seray-Wurie v Hackney LBC*[11] and regulate the exercise of this jurisdiction.[12]

The principles outlined in *Taylor v Lawrence* and the cases underlying and proceeding it will continue to be considered and analysed by the appeal court considering an application for permission to reopen an appeal notwithstanding the codification of those principles in CPR r.52.17.[13]

---

[6] *Seray-Wurie v Hackney LBC* [2002] EWCA Civ 909; [2003] 1 W.L.R. 257. In that case the Court of Appeal refused the application for permission to reopen the appeal.

[7] Brooke L.J. was referring to Lord Diplock's comments on the High Court's inherent jurisdiction to control its own procedure in *Bremer Vulkan Schiffbau und Maschinenfabrik v South India Shipping Corp Ltd* [1981] A.C. 909 at 977 (which were cited by Lord Woolf CJ in *Taylor v Lawrence* [2002] EWCA Civ 90; [2003] Q.B. 528 at 546).

[8] CPR r.52.17(2) provides that the references to "appeal" in CPR r.52.17(1), (3), (4) and (6) include an application for permission to appeal. To this limited extent, this is an exception to the rule outlined by the House of Lords in *Lane v Esdaile* [1891] A.C. 210 that a decision of a court refusing permission to appeal is final. This exception includes circumstances where permission to appeal has been granted in relation to some issues but not others, and the appellant wishes to reopen the decision to refuse permission to appeal those remaining issues: see *Indicii Salus Ltd v Chandrasekaran* [2008] EWCA Civ 67.

[9] Introduced by r.14 of the Civil Procedure (Amendment No.4) Rules 2003 (SI 2003/2113) with effect from October 6, 2003, and amended by the Civil Procedure (Amendment No.2) Rules 2009 (SI 2009/3390).

[10] *Taylor v Lawrence* [2002] EWCA Civ 90; [2003] Q.B. 528.

[11] *Seray-Wurie v Hackney LBC* [2002] EWCA Civ 909; [2003] 1 W.L.R. 257.

[12] *In Re Uddin (A Child)* [2005] 1 W.L.R. 2398 at [5]; *Jaffray v The Society of Lloyds* [2007] EWCA Civ 586 at [8].

[13] On the basis that the CPR does not contain or extend the court's jurisdiction but only gives directions as to how that jurisdiction is to be exercised: *Jaffray v The Society of Lloyds* [2007] EWCA Civ 586 at [8].

The County Court does not have jurisdiction, in relation to its own appellate jurisdiction, to reopen an appeal that has been concluded: CPR r.52.17(3).[14] However, the Supreme Court has long-established inherent jurisdiction, in exceptional cases, to reopen an appeal which had been concluded.[15] This jurisdiction is premised on its status as a final appellate court.

OVERLAP WITH THE LADD V MARSHALL TEST

8-004   The starting point is that permission to reopen an appeal will not be granted on the grounds of an argument that was open to the applicant at the time of the original hearing or evidence that could with reasonable diligence have been brought forward at the original hearing.[16] The application must be founded on fresh evidence. Hence permission to reopen an appeal will not be granted unless it is established[17] that there is a real prospect of the appeal court admitting the fresh evidence alleged to form the grounds of the application for permission to reopen the appeal under CPR r.52.11(2) pursuant to the principles outlined in *Ladd v Marshall*.[18]

However, the emergence of fresh evidence suggesting that the decision below was wrong does not, without more, count as an exceptional circumstance justifying the reopening of an appeal. In *In Re Uddin (A Child)*,[19] the Court of Appeal refused to grant permission to reopen an appeal on grounds of fresh evidence, observing that the test for reopening an appeal under CPR r.52.17(1) is far more stringent than the test for admitting fresh evidence on appeal under CPR r.52.11(2) and the *Ladd v Marshall* test. Dame Elizabeth Butler-Sloss observed that the *Taylor v Lawrence* jurisdiction is not concerned with the case where the earlier process has produced a wrong result: this is the scope of applications to admit fresh evidence and is "the stuff of first-time-round appeals". In addition to satisfying the *Ladd v Marshall* test, the three restrictive requirements outlined in CPR r.52.17(1) must also be met.

---

[14] See also *Gregory v Turner* [2003] 1 W.L.R. 1149, and para.8–010.

[15] *R. v Bow Street Metropolitan Stipendiary Magistrate Ex p. Pinochet Ugarte* [2000] 1 A.C. 119.

[16] *Jaffray v The Society of Lloyds* [2007] EWCA Civ 586 at [62]; *Bassi v Anas* [2007] EWCA Civ 903 at [43]. See Ch.18, para.18–067.

[17] *Couwenbergh v Valkova* [2004] EWCA Civ 676 at [26]–[27]; *In re Uddin (A Child)* [2005] 1 W.L.R. 2398; *Jaffray v The Society of Lloyds* [2007] EWCA Civ 586 at [27] and [34]; *Bassi v Anas* [2007] EWCA Civ 903 at [25].

[18] [1954] 1 W.L.R. 1489 at 1491. See para.6–004.

[19] [2005] 1 W.L.R. 2398 at [18] to [21].

THE RESTRICTIVE REQUIREMENTS

Necessary in order to avoid real injustice

It must be clearly established that the integrity of the first instance decision 8–005
and/or the appeal itself has been critically undermined, with the result that
a "significant injustice" has probably been perpetrated and "the process
itself has been corrupted".[20] In addition, a causal connection must be
demonstrated: it must also be established that there is a strong possibility
that such injustice or corruption affected the result of the case.[21] Further, it
is necessary to prove that, had the court known the true position at the
original hearing (at first instance or on appeal), it is highly likely that it
would have reached a different conclusion[22]; and that there is a powerful
probability that (by reason of the injustice or corruption) an erroneous
result was arrived at in these earlier proceedings.[23]

In *In Re Uddin (A Child)* the Court of Appeal observed that there may be
circumstances where reopening an appeal would be appropriate in the
absence of corrupted process, namely if the injustice that would be perpetrated if the appeal were not reopened would be so grave as to overbear the
pressing claims of finality in litigation.[24] However, the Court of Appeal
emphasised that the case where the process has been corrupted was the
"paradigm" case.

This requirement for real injustice may be found to have been met, for
example, where:

(1) The decision was made by a court which was biased: in those
circumstances the appeal may be reopened in order to maintain
confidence in the administration of justice.[25]
(2) The judge at first instance or in the appeal had read the wrong
papers.[26]
(3) The court was not competent to hear the case[27] (for example,
because it was wrongly constituted).

---

[20] *Taylor v Lawrence* [2002] EWCA Civ 90; [2003] Q.B. 528 at [55]; *In Re Uddin (A Child)* [2005] 1 W.L.R. 2398 at [18]; *Richmond upon Thames LBC v Secretary of State for Transport* [2006] EWCA Civ 193.
[21] *First Discount Ltd v Guinness* [2007] EWCA Civ 378 at [15]; *Jaffray v The Society of Lloyds* [2007] EWCA Civ 586 at [26]; *Bassi v Anas* [2007] EWCA Civ 903 at [41].
[22] *Feakins v DEFRA* [2006] EWCA Civ 699.
[23] *In Re Uddin (A Child)* [2005] 1 W.L.R. 2398 at [22]; *Richmond upon Thames LBC v Secretary of State for Transport* [2006] EWCA Civ 193.
[24] *In Re Uddin (A Child)* [2005] 1 W.L.R. 2398 at [21].
[25] *Taylor v Lawrence* [2002] EWCA Civ 90; [2003] Q.B. 528 at [55].
[26] *Taylor v Lawrence* [2002] EWCA Civ 90; [2003] Q.B. 528 at [40] to [41] referring to the earlier judgment in *In Re J (A Child)* Unreported February 7, 2000 at [8] and [19]; *In Re Uddin (A Child)* [2005] 1 W.L.R. 2398 at [18].
[27] *Taylor v Lawrence* [2002] EWCA Civ 90, [2003] Q.B. 528 at [40] referring to the earlier judgment in *In Re J (A Child)* Unreported February 7, 2000 at [8]. It may be that some decisions can be saved by the de facto jurisdiction referred to in para.4–008.

The requirement for real injustice may, in very limited circumstances, be found to have been met where the decision was obtained by fraud, provided that it is appropriate that fraud be relied upon to reopen a concluded appeal rather than to found a fresh cause of action.[28] However, the circumstances in which this proviso will be satisfied have been drastically reduced as a consequence of the decision in *Owens v Noble*.[29] This is discussed further at para.8–007.

The requirement for real injustice will not be found to have been met where the complaint is simply that the court reached conclusions on an issue on which it did not have proper evidence: that is a matter for a first-time-round appeal, not for a *Taylor v Lawrence* application.[30]

In assessing whether the reopening of an appeal is necessary to avoid real injustice, the appeal court must have regard to the principle of finality of judgments, "a cardinal principle of justice".[31] To that end the appeal court will take into account the effect that the reopening of the appeal would have on others and the extent to which the applicant has been the author of their own misfortune.[32] Further, the longer the delay in bringing the application, the less likely it is that permission to reopen the appeal will be granted.[33] In *First Discount Ltd v Guinness* an application for permission to reopen an appeal was dismissed where the original judgment had stood for nearly 10 years and the defendants to the original proceedings were now bankrupt.[34]

Exceptional circumstances

8–006 There is some overlap between the requirement for exceptional circumstances and the requirement that reopening of the appeal be necessary in order to avoid real injustice. In *In Re Uddin (A Child)*,[35] the Court of Appeal held that it is the "corruption of justice" that, as a matter of policy, warrants an exceptional recourse which "relegates the high importance of finality in litigation to second place".

The exceptional nature of this jurisdiction has been much misunderstood. In the year after the Court of Appeal's decision in *Taylor v Lawrence*, over 200 applications for permission to reopen appeals were made to the Court of Appeal. All these applications were unmeritorious and were dismissed;

---

[28] As was the case in *Couwenbergh v Valkova* [2004] EWCA Civ 676; see also the discussion in *In Re Uddin (A Child)* [2005] 1 W.L.R. 2398 at [18].

[29] [2010] EWCA Civ 224; and [2010] EWCA Civ 284.

[30] [2002] EWCA Civ 90; [2003] Q.B. 528 at [56].

[31] *Couwenbergh v Valkova* [2004] EWCA Civ 676 at [48].

[32] *Taylor v Lawrence* [2002] EWCA Civ 90, [2003] Q.B. 528 at [55]; *Butland v Powys CC* [2009] EWHC 151.

[33] *Couwenbergh v Valkova* [2004] EWCA Civ 676 at [48].

[34] [2007] EWCA Civ 378 at [11].

[35] [2005] 1 W.L.R. 2398 at [18].

the Court of Appeal was critical of the misunderstanding (often by litigants in person) of this jurisdiction.[36]

The first successful application for permission to reopen an appeal was in *Couwenbergh v Valkova*.[37] That case concerned a dispute over the capacity of a testator to make a will and whether witnesses had attested the will. An application for permission to appeal was brought (unsuccessfully) on grounds of error of law. After the appeal, fresh evidence came to light following a police investigation into the death of the testator, namely, new statements from the supposed witnesses to the will which were materially inconsistent with the statements of those witnesses which had been put before the court at first instance. The appellant applied to renew his application for permission to appeal on the grounds that the decision at first instance had been obtained by fraud. It appears that the circumstances were considered as exceptional in that case because, if the new statements were true, it would follow that the initial statements were fraudulent and the will was invalid. Ward L.J. held that "if ever there is a reason for the Court of Appeal to reconsider the correctness of a decision of the court below, then it is when a deceit has been practised on that court".[38] It now appears that this case is probably best considered as a decision on its own facts: see para.8–007.

No alternative effective remedy

Reopening an appeal is a last resort; permission to reopen the appeal will only be granted where the applicant has no alternative effective remedy.   8–007

Where the alternative remedy is an appeal to the Supreme Court, permission to reopen an appeal will only be given in circumstances where the Supreme Court would not give permission to appeal.

The appeal court will have regard both to the existence of an alternative effective remedy against the party or parties to the original proceedings, and also of any alternative effective remedy against a third party.[39]

Decisions obtained by fraud are a special case; this has been subject of some debate in recent authorities. However, following the decision of the Court of Appeal in *Owens v Noble*,[40] it is now unlikely that permission to reopen an appeal will be granted where the grounds of the application are that the decision was obtained by fraud:

---

[36] See the discussions in *Matlasek v Bloom Camillin* [2003] EWCA Civ 154 at [30]; *Gregory v Turner* [2003] 1 W.L.R. 1149 at [28]; and *Bhamjee v Forsdick (No.1)* [2003] EWCA Civ 799 at [26] and [30].

[37] [2004] EWCA Civ 676. See further para.8–007. The reopened appeal was successful: [2005] EWCA Civ 145.

[38] *Couwenbergh v Valkova* [2004] EWCA Civ 676 at [47].

[39] *First Discount Ltd v Guinness* [2007] EWCA Civ 378 at [15].

[40] [2010] EWCA Civ 224; and [2010] EWCA Civ 284.

(1) It had been assumed in earlier cases (without the issue being argued or determined) that the *Taylor v Lawrence* jurisdiction extended to cases of fraud as well as to cases of bias,[41] notwithstanding *Taylor v Lawrence* distinguished fraud cases. Citing the authority of *Flower v Lloyd*,[42] the Court of Appeal in *Taylor v Lawrence* had noted that, in cases of fraud, there is an alternative effective remedy (namely, a new action to set aside the judgment at first instance or the appeal on grounds that it was obtained by fraud).

(2) *Flower v Lloyd* had established that, where it was discovered that a decision at first instance was obtained by fraud, the appropriate course of action was to bring a new action to set aside that judgment, rather than seeking to appeal on the basis of the fresh evidence. That decision was followed in a number of cases,[43] although (as set out at para.6–024) some authorities muddied the waters,[44] suggesting that instead of bringing a new action, the disappointed party should bring an appeal seeking remission or a retrial on the basis of the fraud.

(3) It was in the context of this conflict in the authorities that the Court of Appeal gave permission to reopen an appeal on grounds of fraud in *Couwenbergh v Valkova*.[45] The Court of Appeal referred to *Flower v Lloyd* and related authorities, but concluded that a retrial would be more cost effective and would bring benefits which would be unobtainable in a fresh action, in particular the power to deal effectively with a fair allocation of the costs of the original action. Hence the Court of Appeal concluded that a fresh action was not an effective remedy in that case.

(4) However, in *Jaffray v The Society of Lloyds*[46] the Court of Appeal held obiter that *Flower v Lloyd*[47] and *Jonesco v Beard*[48] preclude the reopening of an appeal on grounds of fraud because the proper recourse is to bring a new action to set aside the original judgment or appeal. *Couwenbergh v Valkova*[49] was distinguished,[50] and described as a case decided on its own facts, because in that case

---

[41] *Couwenbergh v Valkova* [2004] EWCA Civ 676; *In Re Uddin (A Child)* [2005] 1 W.L.R. 2398; *Pell v Express Newspapers* [2005] EWCA Civ 46; and *First Discount Ltd v Guinness* [2007] EWCA Civ 378. See the discussion at *Jaffray v The Society of Lloyds* [2007] EWCA Civ 586 at [11] and [22].

[42] (1877) 6 Ch. D. 297.

[43] *Hip Foong Hong v H Neotia & Co* [1918] A.C. 888; *Jonesco v Beard* [1930] A.C. 298 at 300; *Kuwait Airways v Iraqi Airways* [2001] 1 Lloyd's Rep. 485.

[44] *Hamilton v Al Fayed (No.2)* [2001] E.M.L.R. 15 at [21].

[45] [2004] EWCA Civ 676. The reopened appeal was successful: [2005] EWCA Civ 145.

[46] [2007] EWCA Civ 586 at [22]. This point had not been taken by the respondent in that case so the Court of Appeal could not finally determine the issue, and its comments are obiter.

[47] (1877) 6 Ch. D. 297.

[48] [1930] A.C. 298.

[49] [2004] EWCA Civ 676.

[50] The discussion of *Couwenbergh v Valkova* is at [2007] EWCA Civ 586 at [30]–[32].

the issue (namely, whether the witnesses had attested the will) was self-contained and a retrial would be a short and simple matter with no need for fresh pleadings. Further, it was noted that the costs issue was of central importance in *Couwenbergh v Valkova* and was a powerful consideration militating in favour of reopening the appeal.

(5) The Court of Appeal also rejected an application for permission to reopen an appeal on grounds of fraud in *Bassi v Anas*.[51] It held obiter that it would be wrong to fetter the *Taylor v Lawrence* jurisdiction by ruling that there were no circumstances in which it could be invoked where the decision was obtained by fraud; but that in every case it was necessary to ask whether the circumstances were such that the more sensible way forward is an appeal leading to a retrial or "whether it is better simply allow the allegations of fraud to be properly pleaded and to form the subject matter of a separate action in which those issues are properly defined".[52] It was clear from this decision that the Court of Appeal preferred the latter approach to the former approach.

(6) The "irreconcilable conflict" in the authorities identified at para.8–007(3) has now been resolved by the Court of Appeal in *Owens v Noble*,[53] as set out at para.6–024. It is now clear that, where fresh evidence is adduced showing that the judge at first instance was deliberately misled, the Court of Appeal will only order a retrial on appeal where the fraud is either admitted or the evidence of fraud is incontrovertible.

Hence, in light of *Owens v Noble*,[54] if fraud is disputed and the fresh evidence of fraud is not incontrovertible, an application for permission to reopen an appeal will be refused on the basis that the applicant has an alternative effective remedy, namely a fresh action to set aside the judgment on grounds of fraud.

---

[51] [2007] EWCA Civ 903. The Court of Appeal found in that case at [44] that the *Ladd v Marshall* test was not satisfied and that none of the three requirements in CPR r.52.17(1) had been met; hence the decision on alternative remedy is obiter.

[52] [2007] EWCA Civ 903 at [45].

[53] [2010] EWCA Civ 224.

[54] [2010] EWCA Civ 224.

PROCEDURE

Permission to appeal is required

8–008   Permission is needed to make an application for the reopening of a final determination of an appeal under CPR r.52.17[55]:

(1) The requirement for permission applies even where no permission was required for the previous appeal under CPR r.52.3(1).

(2) There is no right to an oral hearing of an application for permission to reopen the final determination of an appeal.[56]

(3) However, the judge may, exceptionally, direct that there be an oral hearing of the application for permission to reopen the final determination of an appeal.

(4) The appellant should make the application for permission to reopen the final determination of an appeal on notice to the respondent.[57] The judge will not grant permission without directing that the application be served on the other party to the original appeal. The court will give the other party an opportunity to make representations.[58]

(5) The judge's decision on the application for permission is final. There is no right of appeal or review from the judge's decision on that application.[59]

The application for permission must be made in accordance with the procedure set out in para.25 of s.IV of the Practice Direction to CPR Pt 52. This provides that:

(1) Permission must be sought from the court whose decision the applicant wishes to reopen.[60]

(2) The application for permission to reopen the appeal must be made by application notice, supported by written evidence verified by a statement of truth.[61]

(3) Where the court has directed that the application for permission is to be served on another party, that party may (within 14 days of

---

[55] CPR r.52.17 reflects the per curiam comments made in *Taylor v Lawrence* [2002] EWCA Civ 90; [2003] Q.B. 528 at [56] regarding the appropriate procedure where permission to reopen an appeal was sought.

[56] CPR r.52.17(5).

[57] But a copy of the application should not be served on any other party, unless the Court so directs: CPR PD 52 para.25.5.

[58] CPR r.52.17(6); CPR PD 52 para.25.6.

[59] CPR r.52.17(7).

[60] CPR PD 52 para.25.3.

[61] CPR PD 52 para.25.4.

service of the application) file and serve a written statement either supporting or opposing the application.[62]

The application for permission to reopen the appeal (and any written statements in support or in opposition) will be considered on paper by a single judge. The application will only be allowed to proceed (to either an oral hearing of the application or the reopening of the appeal) if the single judge so directs.[63] Applications for permission to reopen an appeal will normally be discharged by this summary process without any oral hearing.[64]

Subsequent orders

If permission to reopen the appeal is granted, the matter will proceed to a full hearing of the appeal. If, exceptionally, an oral hearing of the application for permission to reopen the final determination of an appeal is directed, the hearing of the application should be listed together with the appeal hearing itself, in case permission to reopen is granted.[65] This practice will result in a saving of costs and court resources. 8–009

If permission to reopen the appeal is granted, the court hearing the reopened appeal will be entitled to exercise the same powers as an appeal court hearing a first appeal under CPR r.52.10.

COUNTY COURT HAS NO JURISDICTION TO REOPEN AN APPEAL

Notwithstanding the County Court has an appellate jurisdiction, CPR r.52.17 does not apply to appeals to the County Court,[66] and the County Court has no inherent jurisdiction to reopen appeals.[67] 8–010

In part, this appears to reflect policy considerations. In *Gregory v Turner*, Brooke L.J. observed that it was obvious "given the tendency of a significant number of unsuccessful litigants in person to refuse to take 'No' for an answer" that the work of circuit judges in the county courts would be very badly disrupted if there were an inherent jurisdiction to reopen appeals.[68]

---

[62] CPR PD 52 para.25.6.
[63] CPR PD 52 para.25.7.
[64] *Jaffray v The Society of Lloyds* [2007] EWCA Civ 586 at [4].
[65] In *Couwenbergh v Valkova* [2004] EWCA Civ 676 at [52] Ward L.J. noted that it was unfortunate that the matter had been listed for the grant of permission only and that the Court had not been able to deal with the appeal itself if that permission were granted.
[66] CPR r.52.17(3).
[67] *Gregory v Turner* [2003] 1 W.L.R. 1149.
[68] *Gregory v Turner* [2003] 1 W.L.R. 1149 at [28].

CHAPTER 9

Interested Parties, Interveners and Appeals

APPEALS BROUGHT BY INTERESTED PARTIES

Introduction

9–001   In the vast majority of appeals the appellant will be one of the parties to the original action who is dissatisfied with a decision that has been made in the course of that same action. However, judicial decisions made in the course of litigation may affect those other than the parties to that litigation. There is therefore jurisdiction for the appellate court to allow an appeal to be brought by a non-party (an "interested party") in limited circumstances.[1]

Jurisdiction to allow a non-party appeal

9–002   The jurisdiction of the appellate court to allow a non-party to bring an appeal is longstanding, although its origin is obscure. Paragraph 59/3/3 of The Supreme Court Practice 1999 stated that, in accordance with Old Chancery Practice, any person could appeal by leave[2] if "he could by any possibility have been made a party to the action by service". That paragraph was approved by Lord Evershed M.R. in *In Re B (An Infant)*.[3] So, before the Civil Procedure Rules, a non-party could apply for leave to appeal if they might properly have been made a party to the proceedings below. Leave would not be granted to a person who could not have been a party to the proceedings below.[4]

Since the Civil Procedure Rules came into effect, the rules governing who may appeal a decision of a lower court are now less restrictive. However,

---

[1] See also paras 2–021 and 2–022.
[2] Leave was obtained on an ex parte application to the Court of Appeal.
[3] [1958] 1 Q.B. 12 at 17.
[4] *Crawcour v Salter* (1882) 30 W.R. 329 CA; *Youngs, Doggett v Revett, Re* (1885) 30 Ch. D. 421 CA; *The Millwall* [1905] P. 155 at 163.

the discretion of the appellate court to allow a non-party to bring an appeal will seldom be exercised.

CPR r.52.1(3)(d) defines an appellant widely as "a person who brings or seeks to bring an appeal". This provision neither expressly contemplates nor precludes the bringing of an appeal by a person who was not a party to the proceedings below.

By contrast, a respondent is defined more narrowly in CPR r.52.1(3)(e) as:

> "(i) a person other than the appellant who was a party to the pro-
> ceedings in the lower court and who is affected by the appeal;
> and
>
> (ii) a person who is permitted by the Appeal Court to be a party to
> the appeal."

The definition of an appellant therefore includes no limitation on who can be an appellant by reference to the parties to the proceedings in the lower court, in contrast to the definition of a respondent. The Court of Appeal held in *MA Holdings v Tewkesbury BC*[5] (the first authority on this issue post-CPR) that there is no limitation in the Civil Procedure Rules upon the jurisdiction of the appellate court to allow, in its discretion, a non-party to bring an appeal against a particular decision.

The Court of Appeal in *MA Holdings v Tewkesbury BC*[6] considered CPR r.52.1(3)(d), and decided that the court had jurisdiction under that provision to allow a non-party to appeal.[7] The Court of Appeal observed that, before the introduction of Pt 52 of the CPR, the appeal court had the power to grant leave to appeal to non-parties in certain circumstances, and reasoned that it was unlikely that the CPR was intended to restrict appellate standing, because the overriding object of the CPR was to allow courts to deal with cases justly. The Court held that a rule prohibiting non-parties from bringing an appeal might lead to unjust results where the non-party had a real interest in the outcome of proceedings and the losing party did not wish to appeal.

High Court vs County Court

It may be that as a result of the difference between the wording of s.16 of the Senior Courts Act 1981 and s.77 of the County Court Act 1984 there is no statutory entitlement for a non-party to appeal against a decision of a County Court. Section 16 of the Senior Courts Act 1981 provides that the Court of Appeal may hear and determine appeals from any judgment or

9–003

---

[5] [2008] 1 W.L.R. 1649.
[6] [2008] 1 W.L.R. 1649 CA.
[7] The Court of Appeal therefore concluded at [23] that it was not necessary to decide whether it had a similar power as part of its inherent jurisdiction.

order of the High Court; whereas s.77 of the County Court Act 1984 expressly provides that "if any party to the proceedings in the county court" is dissatisfied with the determination, then the dissatisfied party may appeal from it to the Court of Appeal. The question of whether Pt 52 gives the Court of Appeal jurisdiction to allow non-parties to make appeals against County Court decisions has not been decided post-CPR.

Test for exercise of the jurisdiction

9–004   It will only be in rare cases that the discretion of the appellate court to allow a non-party to bring an appeal will be exercised. The need to seek the exercise of this jurisdiction will only arise where the aggrieved party to the litigation does not itself seek to apply for permission to appeal.

It appears from the decision of the Court of Appeal in *MA Holdings v Tewkesbury BC*[8] that there are broadly two requirements which must be met before the appellate court will exercise its discretion in favour of giving a non-party permission to appeal (over and above the usual requirements for the grant of permission to appeal[9]):

(1)   First, the would-be appellant must have a real and "sufficient" interest in the outcome of the proceedings, rather than being "a mere busybody". A sufficient interest appears to be one that would lead to a "real injustice" to the non-party were the right to appeal to be denied.

(2)   Secondly, there must be no other party who would represent those interests by bringing an appeal. If another party is willing and able to bring the appeal then that is likely to militate against allowing the non-party to make the appeal, although the non-party may be allowed to make submissions as an interested party.

Significance of pre-CPR case-law

9–005   It is clear from *MA Holdings v Tewkesbury BC* that it is not necessary that the non-party would have been allowed to join the proceedings below had it (or another party) so applied.[10] However, the Court of Appeal indicated that the pre-CPR principle (that a non-party could apply for permission to appeal if they might properly have been made a party to the proceedings below) would at least influence practice under the CPR.

In considering whether to exercise its discretion in the non-party's favour, therefore, it may be that the appellate court will require the non-

---

[8] [2008] 1 W.L.R. 1649 CA.
[9] i.e. there must be a real prospect of success or other compelling reason to hear the appeal.
[10] The Court of Appeal held at [28] that it was highly likely that an application by MA Holdings to be a party to the proceedings in the court below would have failed.

party to show good reason why it was not a party to the original proceedings if it could have been joined. If the non-party should have been a
party to the original proceedings (because it would always have been
interested in the outcome and it could have been joined), then the appellate
court may refuse to allow it permission to appeal. However, if the non-
party could not have been a party to the proceedings, but has nevertheless
been affected by the decision, then that may militate in favour of permission
being granted.

Procedure: timing of the application for permission

The non-party's application for permission to appeal should be made as   9–006
soon as possible (and within the usual time limits for the bringing of an
application for permission to appeal) but it is reasonable for the non-party
to wait until it has seen the draft judgment, and until the losing party in the
court below has indicated that it does not intend to appeal.[11]

Should the non-party bring a parallel application for joinder

Where a non-party is given permission to bring an appeal against a decision   9–007
in proceedings to which he is not a party, the rules do not appear to require
them to be joined as a party to the proceedings. Nevertheless, it is suggested
that as a matter of good practice the non-party should be joined as a party
to the proceedings, both so that the non-party would be bound by the result
of the appeal and so that the non-party can more effectively enforce the
outcome of that appeal.

Joinder of additional parties

The Court of Appeal has power to join additional parties to an appeal, even   9–008
after the court's order has been sealed, if this is necessary for the purpose of
dealing with ancillary orders.[12]

---

[11] *MA Holdings v Tewkesbury BC* [2008] 1 W.L.R. 1649 CA at [25].
[12] *KR v Bryn Alyn Community (Holdings) Ltd (In Liquidation)* [2003] EWCA Civ 783.

INTERVENTION BY NON-PARTIES IN STATUTORY APPEALS

Introduction

9-009 The appellate court also has jurisdiction to allow a person who was not a party to the proceedings below to make representations in a statutory appeal if they are affected by the appeal or have a legitimate interest in the appeal. A statutory appeal is an appeal under any enactment (other than by way of case stated) from a decision of a Minister of State, government department, tribunal or other person[13] who makes a decision under statute.[14] The non-party is often referred to as an intervener.

Jurisdiction to allow a non-party to file evidence and make representations on a statutory appeal

9-010 Intervention in appeals by non-parties is governed by CPR r.52.12A, which provides that:

"(1) In a statutory appeal, any person may apply for permission—

(a)   to file evidence; or
(b)   to make representations at the appeal hearing.

(2) An application under paragraph (1) must be made promptly."

CPR r.52.12A is drafted in very broad terms. Any person may apply for permission to appeal: the appeal court's power to join non-parties to an appeal or to permit non-parties to intervene is not restricted to the Minister of State, government department, tribunal or other person who made the decision which is under appeal.

Where the appeal is from an order of decision of a Minister of State or government department, the Minister or department is entitled as of right to attend the appeal hearing and to make representations to the appeal court.[15]

There are many and varied circumstances in which non-parties other than the statutory decision-maker may be permitted to intervene in appeals, and the appeal court will consider applications under CPR r.52.12A on a case-by-case basis. For example, permission to intervene may be granted to

---

[13] This would include an ombudsman: see, e.g. *Moore's (Wallisdown) Ltd v Pensions Ombudsman* [2002] 1 W.L.R. 1649.
[14] CPR PD 52 para.17.1(1).
[15] CPR PD 52 para.17.6.

a charitable organisation that campaigns on issues germane to the appeal[16]; or to an organisation representing persons whose profession or business is affected by the decision under appeal.[17] Permission to intervene is not restricted to public law litigation,[18] although the prospects of obtaining permission to intervene are increased where the litigation has wider implications of public importance.[19]

The appeal court's power to join non-parties to an appeal or to permit non-parties to intervene extends to the period even after the appeal court's order has been sealed, where it is necessary for the purpose of dealing with ancillary orders.[20]

9–011

Where the statutory decision-maker's representations on the appeal are unsuccessful and the decision is reversed, the court may exercise its discretion to award costs against the statutory decision-maker under CPR r.44.3.[21]

In matters of public law,[22] or matters of private law which concern public duties and are of public importance,[23] the Supreme Court has a discretion to hear an appeal, and to hear the interveners' representations, even if a compromise has taken place between the parties to that appeal. This is an

---

[16] See, e.g. *R. v Bow Street Metropolitan Stipendiary Magistrate Ex p. Pinochet Ugarte* [1998] 3 W.L.R. 1456 where permission to intervene in the appeal against the quashing of the arrest warrant of the Chilean head of state was given to Amnesty International, the Medical Foundation for the Care of Victims of Torture, the Redress Trust, and several individuals. Additionally, an order was made permitting Human Rights Watch and Nicole François Drouilly, a representative member of the Association of the Relatives of the Disappeared Detainees, and Marco Antonio Enriquez Espinoza, to intervene to the extent of making available to solicitors and counsel for Amnesty International the arguments and material which they wished to lay before the House of Lords. All of the interveners had campaigned for Pinochet Ugarte to be extradited to Spain to stand trial on charges of genocide.

[17] See, e.g. *Bowman v Fells* [2005] EWCA Civ 226; [2005] 1 W.L.R. 3083 where the Bar Council, the Law Society, and the National Criminal Intelligence Service (NCIS) were given permission to intervene in an appeal relating to the conduct of litigation in light of s.328 of the Proceeds of Crime Act 2002.

[18] For example, property developers are often granted permission to intervene in appeals by individuals against the Secretary of State's refusal on judicial review to quash the grant of planning permission to that developer.

[19] The Court of Appeal granted permission to a number of bodies to intervene in private law litigation in *Callery v Gray* [2001] 1 W.L.R. 2112; affirmed [2002] 1 W.L.R. 2000. This case concerned an order for costs in a personal injury claim arising out of a road traffic accident; the particular issue was the recoverability of a success fee under a conditional fee agreement, so the issue (albeit one relating to private rights and obligations) nevertheless had wider implications of public importance.

[20] *KR v Bryn Alyn Community (Holdings) Ltd (In Liquidation)* [2003] EWCA Civ 783.

[21] *Moore's (Wallisdown) Ltd v Pensions Ombudsman* [2002] 1 W.L.R. 1649 at [7].

[22] *R. v Secretary of State for the Home Department Ex p. Salem* [1999] 1 A.C. 450 at 456.

[23] *Bowman v Fels* [2005] EWCA Civ 226; [2005] 1 W.L.R. 3083 at [13].

exception to the general rule that an appeal court will not rule on academic or hypothetical issues[24]; this exception is justified by the public importance of the issue. However, the appeal court's jurisdiction to hear disputes that have been compromised, even in the area of public law, should be exercised with caution, and appeals which are academic between the parties should not be heard unless there is a good reason in the public interest for doing so. A good reason might be found where a discrete point of statutory construction arose which did not involve detailed consideration of facts, and where a large number of similar cases exists, so that the issue would most likely need to be resolved in the near future in any event.[25]

Procedure

9–012   In the case of statutory appeals, the appellant must serve its notice on the Minister of State, government department, chairman of the tribunal or other person from whose decision the appeal is brought.[26] This enables the decision-maker to decide promptly whether to intervene in the appeal.

Guidance as to applications to intervene in statutory appeals is provided in the Practice Direction to Pt 52 at paras 17.7 to 17.11:

(1) An application for permission to intervene must be made by letter to the relevant court office, identifying the appeal, explaining who the applicant is and indicating why and in what form the applicant wants to participate in the hearing.[27]

(2) If the applicant is seeking a prospective order as to costs, the letter must say what kind of order and on what grounds.[28]

(3) The application may be determined without a hearing provided that all the parties to the appeal so consent,[29] and in most cases the application is determined without a hearing.

(4) Permission to intervene may be given on conditions, such as conditions as to costs, or conditions restricting the intervener to

---

[24] The decisions in *Sun Life Assurance Co of Canada v Jervis* [1944] A.C. 111 at 113–114 and *Ainsbury v Millington (Note)* [1987] 1 W.L.R. 379 at 381 are authority for the proposition that the appeal court will only entertain live issues and will not rule on theoretical or academic questions which have no immediate consequence to the parties' rights. In *R. v Secretary of State for the Home Department Ex p. Salem* [1999] 1 A.C. 450 at 456 and *Bowman v Fels* [2005] EWCA Civ 226; [2005] 1 W.L.R. 3083 at [11]–[13] it was held that these decisions are limited to disputes concerning private law rights between the parties to the case which have no general public importance.
[25] *R. v Secretary of State for the Home Department Ex p. Salem* [1999] 1 A.C. 450 at 456; *Bowman v Fels* [2005] EWCA Civ 226; [2005] 1 W.L.R. 3083 at [12]–[13].
[26] CPR PD 52 para.17.5(1).
[27] CPR PD 52 para.17.9.
[28] CPR PD 52 para.17.10.
[29] CPR PD 52 para.17.7.

making written submissions only[30]; the appeal court may make case management directions consequent on granting permission to intervene.[31]

Whilst the requirement for making an application under CPR r.52.12A is that it is made "promptly", para.17.11 of the Practice Direction to Pt 52 provides that applications to intervene must be made at the earliest reasonable opportunity. There is no material or practical difference between these requirements, in spite of the inconsistency in terminology.

Interveners in the Supreme Court

Rule 15(1) of the Supreme Court Rules provides that "any person" may make written submissions to the Supreme Court in support of an application for permission to appeal, and request that the Supreme Court take them into account. Any person is said to include, in particular, any official body or non-governmental organisation seeking to make submissions in the public interest, or any person with an interest in proceedings by way of judicial review. Any submissions made by an intervener in the Supreme Court will be taken into account on the application for permission to appeal and on the appeal itself.[32] The Crown has the right to intervene in any appeal where the Supreme Court is considering whether to declare that a provision of primary or subordinate legislation is incompatible with a Convention right under r.40.[33]

9–013

---

[30] See, e.g. *R. v Bow Street Metropolitan Stipendiary Magistrate Ex p. Pinochet Ugarte* [1998] 3 W.L.R. 1456 where some of the interveners were given permission to make oral submissions, but some were given permission to intervene on the condition that they made only written submissions.

[31] CPR PD 52 para.17.8.

[32] See further para.18–032.

[33] The relevant procedure is set out in PD 9.

CHAPTER 10

Judicial Review of County Court Decisions

INTRODUCTION

10–001 Under CPR r.52.3, and as provided in the Practice Direction to CPR Pt 52, an appellant requires permission from a circuit judge to appeal against the decision of a district judge in a county court; and requires permission from the High Court to appeal against the decision of a circuit judge in a county court. Section 54(4) of the Access to Justice Act 1999 provides that there is no appeal against refusal of permission in these circumstances.[1] This is confirmed at para.4.8 of the Practice Direction to CPR Pt 52. Therefore the effect of s.54(4) of the Access to Justice Act 1999 is that refusal of such permission is the "end of the road".[2] If both the lower court and the appeal court refuse permission to appeal, it is not possible to appeal to a higher court.

However, in certain very rare and exceptional circumstances, an applicant may apply to the Administrative Court seeking permission for judicial review of a decision of a county court (which could include an interlocutory decision, or a final decision, or indeed a decision refusing permission to appeal).[3] A county court is an inferior court created by statute, and the High Court has always asserted jurisdiction (principally by the judicial review mechanism governed by CPR Pt 54) to review the question of whether a county court has acted within its jurisdiction.[4] This jurisdiction is, however, rarely exercised, and does not provide an appeal of the decision "by the back door": the jurisdiction permits only exceptionally a review of

---

[1] s.54(4) of the Access to Justice Act 1999 provides that: "No appeal may be made against a decision of a court under this section to give or refuse permission (but this subsection does not affect any right under rules of court to make a further application for permission to the same or another court)."

[2] *Moyse v Regal Partnerships Ltd* [2004] EWCA Civ 1269 at [31].

[3] *R. (Mahon) v Taunton County Court* [2001] EWHC Admin 1078; *R. (Messer) v Cambridge County Court* [2002] EWCA Civ 1355; *Sivasubramaniam v Wandsworth County Court* [2002] EWCA Civ 1738.

[4] *R. v Worthington-Evans Ex p. Madan* [1959] 2 Q.B. 145 at 152.

the legality of the decision in the following limited (and unusual) circumstances.

EXCEPTIONAL CIRCUMSTANCES

In *Sivasubramaniam v Wandsworth County Court* the Court of Appeal made clear that, whilst s.54(4) of the Access to Justice Act 1999 did not impliedly oust the High Court's judicial review jurisdiction in respect of decisions of judges in county courts, permission to proceed to judicial review of a county court decision would normally be refused because the Civil Procedure Rules had introduced a coherent and sensible statutory scheme governing appeals from county court decisions which was a suitable alternative remedy. The Court of Appeal held that an applicant ought not to be permitted to bypass this statutory scheme by pursuing a "collateral" claim for judicial review, unless there were exceptional circumstances, because otherwise the object of this statutory scheme would be defeated.

10–002

The Court of Appeal further considered the position where the applicant sought permission to proceed to judicial review of a decision in respect of which the applicant had already been refused permission to appeal. The Court held that, even where all avenues of appeal have been exhausted (and permission to appeal had been refused), applications for permission to proceed to judicial review of circuit judges' decisions should still be summarily dismissed by the Administrative Court, save in "very rare" and exceptional circumstances where there has been either a "jurisdictional error in the narrow, pre-*Anisminic* sense"[5] or "procedural irregularity of such a kind as to constitute a denial of the applicant's right to a fair hearing".[6]

Lord Philips giving the judgment in *Sivasubramaniam v Wandsworth County Court* considered it unlikely that a county court judge might exceed their jurisdiction where that jurisdiction was the statutory power to determine an application for permission to appeal from the decision of a district judge.

The scope of the exceptional circumstances referred to in *Sivasubramaniam v Wandsworth County Court* was elucidated by the Court of Appeal in *Gregory v Turner*.[7] A mere error of law or irregularity in procedure is not sufficient. What is required to found an application for judicial review is a complete disregard by the county court of its duties, i.e. some

---

[5] i.e. a clear want of jurisdiction of the type required to found judicial review before the House of Lords' decision in *Anisminic Ltd v Foreign Compensation Commission* [1969] 2 A.C. 147.

[6] *Sivasubramaniam v Wandsworth County Court* [2002] EWCA Civ 1738 at [54]–[56].

[7] *Gregory v Turner* [2003] 1 W.L.R. 1149 at [38]–[45]. In this case the Court of Appeal observed that it had recently become the practice of litigants in person to seek orders from the Administrative Court for permission to apply for judicial review to quash the decision of a circuit judge to refuse permission to appeal against the decision of a district judge.

fundamental departure from the correct procedures. The court stressed that such cases will be very rare.

In *R. (oao Strickson) v Preston County Court* the Court of Appeal upheld the decision of the judge hearing the judicial review application, who considered that the district judge and the circuit judge had reached wrong conclusions, but nevertheless declined to grant relief by way of judicial review.[8] In identifying the exceptional circumstances that might justify judicial review, the Court of Appeal drew a distinction between a case where the judge gets the decision wrong, or even extremely wrong (on law or on the facts or both); and a case where "the judicial process itself has been frustrated or corrupted". The former case would not warrant judicial review; the latter case may. The Court of Appeal observed that one example of the latter case might include the court's refusal to go into a point of law in a particular area which, against a background of conflicting decisions of a lower tribunal, the public interest obviously required to be decided.[9]

In all these cases the court has been at pains to stress that it will only be in very rare cases that the court will grant judicial review of refusal of permission to appeal against the decision of the County Court.

PROCEDURE

Permission is required

10–003   Under CPR r.54.4 the court's permission is required in a claim for judicial review. The procedure is the standard procedure for applying for permission for judicial review: i.e. an application for permission to proceed to judicial review, together with the claim form, should be made by the applicant to the Administrative Court. The claim form should be filed promptly and, in any event, no later than three months after the decision the applicant seeks to impugn (CPR r.54.5(1)) and it should comply with the requirements set out in CPR r.54.6 and the Practice Direction to CPR Pt 54.

The Treasury Solicitor on behalf of the defendant (i.e. the relevant county court) must file an acknowledgment of service (in accordance with CPR r.54.8) and issue a detailed document setting out the grounds on which it resists the application for permission (which will usually include the bundle of authorities relied upon by the respondent) pursuant to CPR r.54.14.

The party or parties to the original County Court proceedings (other than the applicant in the judicial review proceedings) will be classed as an interested party in the application for permission to proceed to judicial review. The interested party must serve an acknowledgment of service if it

---

[8] *R. (oao Strickson) v Preston County Court* [2007] EWCA Civ 1132.

[9] As in *R. (oao Sinclair Investments (Kensington) Ltd) v The Lands Tribunal* [2005] EWCA Civ 1305.

wishes to contest the claim (CPR r.54.8) and may serve its grounds for resistance or write to the court adopting the defendant's grounds for resistance.

In the first instance the Administrative Court will consider the application on paper. If the application for permission for judicial review is refused on paper, the applicant "may not appeal" (CPR r.54.12(3)) and the applicant does not have any right to have the decision reconsidered at an oral hearing: para.8.4 of the Practice Direction to CPR Pt 54. However, the applicant does have the right to *request* an oral hearing (CPR r.54.12(3)). The court therefore has a discretion whether to reconsider the refusal of the application for judicial review at an oral hearing or not.

If the court orders that there be an oral hearing, neither the defendant nor the interested party need attend, but either or both may attend. However, if they attend they will not recover their costs of attending. The costs order that the court may grant is limited to the costs of the Acknowledgement of Service only, and does not include the costs of attendance at any hearing.

Appeal against refusal of permission for judicial review

Where the Administrative Court has refused permission for judicial review 10–004 at an oral hearing, the applicant may apply to the Court of Appeal for permission to appeal against the refusal of the application for permission for judicial review (CPR r.52.15(1)). The time limit for the appeal to the Court of Appeal is seven days from the date of the High Court's decision to refuse permission (CPR r.52.15).

In considering the application for permission to appeal, the Court of Appeal has a discretion (CPR r.52.15(4)) and may either dismiss the application; grant the applicant permission to appeal (in which case an oral hearing of the substantive appeal in the Court of Appeal would follow); or grant the applicant permission to apply for judicial review (in which case the matter would proceed straight to a hearing of the substantive judicial review in the High Court).

PART 3

Practice and Procedure for Appeals under the CPR

CHAPTER 11

The Judgment and Order

This chapter addresses matters relating to the source of the appeal, the judgment and the order and issues arising with the content of both. **11–001**

WHAT IS THE APPEAL AGAINST?

The first matter to identify is what the appeal is in respect of. While the focus of an appeal will involve an analysis and consideration of the lower court's judgment the jurisdiction of the Court of Appeal is limited to hearing and determining appeals from the order of the lower court. **11–002**

> "Subject as otherwise provided by this or any other Act ... the Court of Appeal shall have jurisdiction to hear and determine appeals from any judgment or order of the High Court."[1]

Although there is reference to "judgment" in the phrase "judgment or order", the phrase does not seek to draw a distinction between the judgment of the court and the court order subsequently sealed on the basis of that judgment. Both refer to the decision of the court as recorded in the sealed order of the court.

The phrase "judgment or order" reflects the historical distinction between on the one hand an "action" which was commenced by a writ and resulted in a "judgment", and on the other hand a "matter" that was commenced by an "originating process (summons or application)" and resulted in an "order".[2]

The distinction between actions and matters does not appear in the Civil Procedure Rules, though both the terms "judgment" and "order" have been copied, "apparently unthinkingly",[3] into the new rules.

---

[1] s.16 of the Senior Courts Act 1981. This reflects in material part the language of s.27(1) of the Supreme Court of Judicature (Consolidation) Act 1925.

[2] A full explanation of the historical differences and their repeated use in differing contexts in the CPR can be found in the *White Book*, 2010, para.40.1.1.

[3] Per the editors of the *White Book*, 2010, para.40.1.1

Colloquially, "judgment" usually refers to the judge's reasoned decision, whereas "order" refers to the document sealed by the court giving effect to the decision.

What is important in the context of appeals, is that the meaning of the words used in s.16 of the Senior Courts Act 1981 is that the appeal is against the order representing the conclusion of the Court and not the judgment containing the reasoning and rationale in reaching that conclusion.

The jurisdiction to hear an appeal is limited to the decision of the court as recorded in the order sealed by the court.[4] Where there is no formal order, an appeal can only be against that part of the decision which would have been recorded in a formal order had one been drawn up.[5] The only exception to this is where the statutory jurisdiction to hear the particular appeal provides for a broader jurisdiction. This only arises usually in specific statutory appeals which are beyond the scope of this work.

Appeal against the lower court's order

11–003   While the grounds of appeal may involve challenges to the findings of fact of the lower court or the reasons given or omitted in the underlying judgment, the appeal itself is against the order of the lower court. This means that the appeal cannot be made against a discrete part of the lower court's judgment (in its broad sense) such as the findings of fact made or the reasons given by the lower court in the course of reaching its judgment, without a challenge to the overall conclusion of the lower court as recorded in the order.[6]

Findings of fact

11–004   A party cannot therefore appeal against a finding of fact on its own unless it is formally recorded by way of a declaration in the order.[7] Particularly in the context of preliminary issues, parties should consider the appropriateness of requesting the court to make a declaration in respect of key findings of fact. Otherwise it may not be possible to challenge on appeal an unfavourable finding of fact in the judgment.

---

[4] *Lake v Lake* [1955] P. 336. Referred to with approval in the dissenting judgment (although not on this point) of Lord Hope in *HM Treasury v Ajmed* [2010] UKSC 5 at 16. See too the reference in the Access to Justice Act 1999 (Destination of Appeals) Order 2000 where "decision" is defined as being "any judgment, order or direction" of the lower court.

[5] *Lake v Lake* [1955] P. 336 as explained in *Compagnie Noga D'Importation Et D'Exportation SA v Australia and New Zealand Banking Group Ltd* [2002] EWCA Civ 1142; [2003] 1 W.L.R. 307 at [27], per Tuckey L.J. and at [53], per Hale L.J.

[6] *Kynaston v Carroll* [2004] EWCA Civ 1434 at [10] and [22], per Neuberger L.J.

[7] The extent to which a lower court should take in to account matters relating to the appellate process are helpfully explored and explained in the Court of Appeal decision of *Compagnie Noga D'Importation Et D'Exportation SA v Australia and New Zealand Banking Group Ltd* [2002] EWCA Civ 1142.

Similarly (and leaving on one side the realm of statutory appeals with different appellate jurisdiction provisions[8]) a party successful at first instance cannot challenge adverse findings of fact made by the lower court judge.[9] Such an appeal would not be against the lower court's order.

The only way that a challenge could be made would be by either challenging the order in the successful party's favour or, in response to an appeal by the unsuccessful party, in seeking to uphold the decision of the lower court on the basis of different reasons and where the controversial fact is linked to those reasons. The former route is unattractive to a party successful in the lower court and the latter is outside the control of that party.

A possible exception in the Court of Appeal

The Court of Appeal may have jurisdiction to overturn or remove specific findings of fact in a judgment of a lower court in exceptional circumstances. 11–005

Lord Justice Neuberger, as he then was, was prepared to assume that there was such a jurisdiction, without reaching any positive conclusion to that effect, when delivering judgment on an application for permission to appeal in *Kynaston v Carroll*.[10]

In that case the lower court judge had made various statements about the applicant's credibility which she wished to challenge on appeal. On appeal she sought to rely on American jurisprudence which recognised an inherent jurisdiction in the appeal court to expunge from the judgment of the lower court various "outrageous observations".

Lord Justice Neuberger, as he then was, said: "We do not need to decide whether such an exceptional jurisdiction exists in this country." However, he said, he would assume that it did, since he could see "much to be said for it if it were regrettably necessary to invoke it".[11]

However, it does not appear that the Court of Appeal has ever decided either that there is such a jurisdiction, or that it was appropriate to use it in a particular case.

---

[8] The statute may provide for wider powers for the appeal court to interfere with the lower court's decision. One example is s.15 of the Social Security Act 1998 which permits the Court of Appeal to hear appeals on a question of law which relates to "any decision" and therefore permits an appeal of the lower court's decision even by a successful party. *Morina v Secretary of State for Work and Pensions* [2007] EWCA Civ 749; [2007] 1 W.L.R. 3033. The Secretary of State for Work and Pensions had argued two grounds: the first disputing the jurisdiction of the court and the second disputing the claim on the merits. The Secretary of State's arguments on the merits were accepted, but not those on jurisdiction. Accordingly the Secretary of State had succeeded, but was left with an unhelpful (to him) decision on jurisdiction. The Court of Appeal held that the breadth of the jurisdiction given by s.15 of the Social Security Act 1998 to consider any question of law relating to "any decision" permitted even the successful first instance Secretary of State to bring an appeal relating to the point of law.

[9] This has long been the position. *Lake v Lake* [1955] P. 336.

[10] *Kynaston v Carroll* [2004] EWCA Civ 1434 at [22], per Neuberger L.J.

[11] *Kynaston v Carroll* [2004] EWCA Civ 1434 at [22], per Neuberger L.J.

It is difficult to see why a jurisdiction should not exist if it were necessary to remedy an injustice. It is suggested, however, that an appellant would need to show not only that the decision of the lower court was wrong and/or unjust by reason of some serious procedural or other irregularity, but also that, if left undisturbed, the decision would cause the appellant a serious injustice which was not capable of being remedied by any other means.

THE IMPORTANCE OF RECORDING THE JUDGMENT OR ORDER OF THE LOWER COURT ACCURATELY

11–006   Given that the appeal is against the order of the lower court as opposed to the judgment, it is of paramount importance that the order accurately reflects the judgment (in its narrower sense) of the lower court. Inadequate drafting can lead to many problems flowing from the fact that it will not reflect the lower court's decision. These include, in no particular order:

(1) This creates injustice as between the parties: it does not reflect accurately the resolution of the dispute between them.

(2) It undermines the confidence of the public in the court process: it is the order that represents the recorded conclusion of the lower court and it is that which will be first considered. If it is inaccurate then the public will be precluded from knowing the true conclusion of the court.

(3) It is a matter of professional embarrassment to those responsible for recording the judgment: the inability to translate the court's order reflects an inability to understand the judgment or an implicit criticism of the lower court judge in failing to present accurately his or her conclusion in the judgment.

From the perspective of the appeals process leaving aside the obvious point that an appeal may be misconceived if the order does not reflect the actual judgment of the lower court it can cause jurisdictional issues in terms of the appeal being pursued before the wrong court.

As considered in greater detail in Chapter 12 the nature of the decision of the lower court and in particular whether it is a "final decision" will determine the particular appeal court with jurisdiction. A mistake in the order can mean that an appeal is pursued before a court with no jurisdiction to hear the appeal and the problem only being discovered during the hearing of the appeal proper, by which time much time and expense will have been wasted. The party to blame, most often the appellant, is likely to face criticism and adverse costs orders.[12]

---

[12] In *Graham v Chorley BC* [2006] EWCA Civ 92 the appeal was really in respect of the Court's decision to accept the defendant's submission of no case to answer. That should have been heard by the High Court (paras 19–20). Since the order recorded only the judgment, and this formed the basis of the appeal (paras 20–22) the Court of Appeal determined it held jurisdiction.

Understanding the judgment of the lower court

Usually there should be no dispute as to the judgment of the lower court   **11–007**
and what should be included in the order. This should be clear from the
judgment.

Given the pressures on the time of judges it is perhaps not unsurprising
that on occasions a judgment may not be entirely clear in all aspects to the
parties and the parties thereby seek assistance from the lower court before
settling the order. However, such disputes usually arise not from a deficiency in the judgment, but where one party seeks to stretch the judgment
of the lower court in to a more favourable order than that in fact included
in or intended by the judgment.

Referring the matter back to the judge of the lower court

Where a genuine issue arises the matter will need to be referred back to the   **11–008**
relevant judge.

Before any reference back is made each party should explain in writing to
the other the reasons for their draft by reference to the judgment and
provide a copy of the relevant excerpts of the judgment. Normally this
process reveals the absurdity of one party's position.

Where there is true ambiguity in the judgment or real grounds for seeking
clarification this process will provide a helpful basis for the judge to consider the matter when it is returned to him.

As a point of practice, it will be obvious that unless the judgment is truly
ambiguous then wasting judicial time on spurious applications to clarify a
judgment is likely to result in at best displeasure with the party who is
perceived as having been unreasonable or wrong in its construction of the
judgment or order.

There are other instances where the parties may refer the matter back to
the lower court judge for clarification and correction which are addressed in
paras 11–015 et seq.

SETTLING THE ORDER FOLLOWING JUDGMENT

The responsibility for drawing up the order of the lower court depends on   **11–009**
the court in which the judgment is given, the practice of that court and any
specific requests of the judge.

CPR r.40.3(1) provides guidance as to the drawing up and filing of
judgments and orders.

CPR r.40.3(2) provides that the court may direct that a judgment or
order drawn by a party is checked by the court before it is sealed; or that
before a judgment or order is drawn up by the court the parties must file an
agreed statement of its terms.

The usual position will be that the court will draw up the order unless:

(1) the court orders a party to draw it up;
(2) a party, with the permission of the court, agrees to draw it up;
(3) the court dispenses with the need to draw it up; or
(4) it is a consent order made under CPR r.40.6.

The particular practice depends on the court, the particular judge and the manner in which judgment is handed down:

(1) In County Courts the order is usually drawn up and issued by the court. Regrettably, it is far from unusual for such orders to contain mistakes, and in those circumstances, the parties should write a letter, agreed if possible, asking for the errors to be corrected under the slip rule.[13] This is discussed further at para.11–013.

(2) In proceedings in the Queen's Bench Division other than pro-ceedings in the Administrative Court the parties must draw up the order of the court.[14] This includes the Commercial Court and the Technology and Construction Court.

   (a) The almost invariable practice is that the advocates are asked to agree the form of Order and the claimant's or applicant's counsel's clerk arranges for it to be sealed.

   (b) Any disagreement about the terms of the order is usually dealt with by email to the judge's clerk.

(3) In the Chancery Division, including the Companies and the Bankruptcy Courts, it is usual for the Court to draw up and issue the Order. If the judge or master directs that a statement of the terms of an order be agreed and signed, the agreed statement should be filed in Room TM5.04 in accordance with the Chancery Guide. The practice for agreeing an order follows that described in respect of the Queen's Bench Division above.

(4) In the Court of Appeal the parties are usually requested to agree a draft order.

   (a) When completed this should be faxed or e-mailed to the clerk to the relevant judge or Presiding Judge (together with any pro-posed corrections or amendments to the draft judgment about which see para.17–078.

   (b) Four copies (with completed back-sheets) should be filed in the relevant court office by 12.00 pm on the working day before the day prescribed for handing down of the judgment.

---

[13] In particular if they are issued by London County Courts, where staff recruitment and retention face considerable difficulties, as noted in successive annual court reports.

[14] CPR r.40.3(4). This applies in the specialist divisions of the Queen's Bench Division including the Commercial (CPR r.58.15) and Mercantile Courts (CPR r.59.12) and the TCC (CPR r.60.7 (1).

Where the lower court delivers an ex tempore judgment the judge will **11–010** usually indicate how the order is to be drawn up. If this is not made clear then it is good practice for the advocates to confirm the court's preference.

Where a draft judgment is provided in advance of handing down, Practice Direction E to Pt 40 para.4.1 requires the parties to seek to agree orders consequential upon the judgment.

In this situation the claimant's advocate should prepare and attempt to agree a draft of the Order with the other parties in advance of the date for handing down the judgment.

Once agreed a draft should be provided to the judge in advance of handing down the judgment.

Time for drawing up the order

CPR r.40.3 (3) provides that: **11–011**

(1) where the judgment or order is to be drawn up by a party, that party must file it no later than seven days after the date on which the court ordered or permitted him to draw it up so that it can be sealed by the court; and
(2) if that party fails to file it within that period, any other party may draw it up and file it.

Form of Order

There are specific provisions governing the manner in which orders are to **11–012** be drawn up. From the perspective of appeals and ensuring that the order is correctly drawn it is most important that the decision of the court should be clear on the face of the order. In this regard the order should not cross refer to paragraphs of the judgment.[15]

There are other important formal requirements of the order prescribed by the CPR:

(1) CPR r.40.2 (1) requires that every "judgment or order" must record the name and status of the judge making the order unless the order is made by a court officer such as a default judgment, judgment on admission, a consent order or similar.
(2) CPR r.40.2(2) requires every "judgment or order" to bear the date on which it is given or made and to be sealed by the court.
(3) CPR r.40.2(3)–(4) provides that if a party applies for permission to appeal at the hearing at which judgment is handed down the "judgment or order" must also state:

---

[15] *Richardson Roofing Co Ltd v The Colman Partnership Ltd* [2009] EWCA Civ 839 at [22], per Jacob L.J.

(a) whether or not the judgment or order is final;

(b) whether an appeal lies from the judgment or order and, if so, to which appeal court;

(c) whether the court gives permission to appeal; and

(d) if not, the appropriate appeal court to which any further application for permission to appeal may be made, if any.

(4) Practice Direction E to Pt 40 provides that a draft order prepared by the parties must bear the case reference, the date of handing down and the name of the judge or the presiding judge.

CORRECTING THE ORDER OF THE LOWER COURT UNDER THE "SLIP RULE"

11–013 While it is hoped that the order will be drawn accurately and correctly, inevitably there are occasions when the language of the order is ambiguous or does not reflect accurately the decision of the lower court.

Although on sealing the order the lower court is *functus officio*, the lower court still retains the jurisdiction to correct an accidental slip or omission in its order or judgment.

The "slip rule", as it is commonly known, is set out at CPR r.40.12 and provides:

"40.12

(1) The court may at any time correct an accidental slip or omission in a judgment or order.

(2) A party may apply for a correction without notice."

Where the order as drawn does not reflect the judgment or order of the lower court the parties should ask the lower court to amend the order under the slip rule so that the decision(s) which the judge made are accurately and clearly recorded.[16]

Although the application may be done without notice, it is generally good practice to notify the other parties of the application. The slip rule is only for errors in the court's order where there has been an accidental slip or omission. It cannot be used as a vehicle for correcting a consent order that is ambiguous.[17]

---

[16] *Scribes West Ltd v Relsa Anstalt* [2004] EWCA Civ 965 at [29]; *Graham v Chorley BC* [2005] EWCA Civ 92 at [21]–[22].

[17] *Richardson Roofing Co Ltd v The Colman Partnership Ltd* [2009] EWCA Civ 839 at [12]–[13] and [30], per Jacob L.J.

DATE OF EFFECT OF "JUDGMENT OR ORDER" OF LOWER COURT

A judgment or order of the court takes effect from the day when it is given **11–014** or made unless the court specifies that it is only to take effect from a later date under CPR r.40.7.

By contrast to the jurisdictional approach to "judgment or order" addressed above, in this context the reference to "judgment or order" relates to the date judgment is delivered orally or, if in writing, the date when it is formally handed down. This date is important because among other things this is the date from which time starts to run for the filing of an appeal notice.[18] This is addressed further in Chapter 14.

REVISITING THE JUDGMENT BEFORE THE ORDER IS SEALED

The following paragraphs consider the court's jurisdiction to revisit its judg- **11–015** ment before the order is sealed. This can in certain circumstances avoid the costs of an appeal and where appropriate (such as a need for amplification of the reasons) the parties are obliged to raise such matters before the lower court.

Jurisdiction for revisiting the judgment

The appeal is against the order of the court and not the judgment. The order **11–016** of the court is perfected by being sealed.[19] Prior to the sealing of the order the lower court judge has jurisdiction to alter, amend, update and even reverse his or her decision, at any time.

Previously the court's jurisdiction to revisit a judgment before the order was sealed was unrestricted.[20]

That jurisdiction has now been narrowed. In summary a court should only revisit its judgment in the "most exceptional circumstances"[21] or where there are "strong reasons" for doing so.[22]

---

[18] *Sayers v Clarke Walker* [2002] EWCA Civ 645 and *Owusu v Jackson* [2002] EWCA Civ 877.

[19] *In Re Suffield and Watts* (1888) 20 Q.B.D. 693; *Paulin v Paulin and Cativo Ltd* [2009] EWCA Civ 221 at [30(b)], per Wilson L.J.

[20] *In Re Harrison's Shared under a Settlement* [1955] Ch. 260 at 275–276.

[21] *In Re Barrell Enterprises* [1973] 1 W.L.R. 19 at 23H–24B; *Stewart v Engel* [2000] 1 W.L.R. 2268 at 2275H–2276D, per Sir Christopher Slade; *Taylor v Lawrence* [2002] EWCA Civ 90; [2003] Q.B. 528 at [13]; *Robinson v Fernsby and Scott-Kilvert* [2003] EWCA Civ 1820 at [96]. See too the discussion in *Paulin v Paulin and Cativo Ltd* [2009] EWCA Civ 221 at [30(c)–(g)], per Wilson L.J.

[22] *Compagnie Noga d'Importation et D'Exportation SA v Abacha* [2001] 3 All E.R. 513 at [42]–[43], per Rix L.J. and *Robinson v Fernsby and Scott-Kilvert* [2003] EWCA Civ 1820 at [96], per May L.J.

While examples from previous cases are instructive, because of the narrowing of the court's jurisdiction in 1972, care needs to be taken when considering pre-1972 cases in this regard. However some earlier cases have recently been implicitly approved as correctly decided under the law as it presently stands. In *Paulin v Paulin* the Court of Appeal referred to the following four previous cases as being instructive of when the jurisdiction may be exercised:

(1) *Miller's Case* (1876) 3 Ch. D. 166: the Articles of Association of the company compelled a conclusion opposite to that which had been reached. It had been appropriate to draw the court's attention to those Articles of Association.
(2) In *Millensted v Grosvenor House (Park Lane) Ltd* [1937] 1 K.B. 717 the judge on his initiative decided to reduce the value of damages awarded to the claimant from £50 to £35 the day following judgment on the basis he considered them excessive.
(3) In *Harrison's Shares under a Settlement, Re* [1955] 2 Ch. 260 the judge changed his decision 10 days after reaching it, in light of a relevant decision of the House of Lords in another case.
(4) In *Dietz v Lennig Chemicals Ltd* [1969] 1 A.C. 170 the master changed his approval of a settlement of a widow and child's proceedings where it was discovered that three weeks prior to his decision the widow had remarried.

The first and fourth cases are examples of corrections involving indisputable matters of fact which undermined the reasoning of the court's decision. The alteration of the judgment did not arise from a matter of fact determined during the hearing.

The third case is an example of the law being "clarified" following judgment.

The second case demonstrates a court revising its underlying judgment in respect of matters already considered and determined by it. It is therefore a change based not on any external events, but reflects a change in the judge's own view. It is therefore a change of greater controversy. This case demonstrates the obligation on a judge to alter his or her decision if he or she concludes that the draft judgment is wrong and there is therefore a judicial obligation to correct the judgment before the order is sealed.[23]

11–017 The amenability of a court to reconsider its judgment will depend to a certain extent on the manner in which the judgment to be altered, amended, updated or reversed has been presented to the parties.

A draft written judgment is more open to reversal prior to its formal handing down than a judgment that has been handed down and thus finally delivered.[24]

---

[23] *Robinson v Fernsby and Scott-Kilvert* [2003] EWCA Civ 1820 at [98] and [120].
[24] *Robinson v Fernsby* [2003] EWCA Civ 1820 at [98], per May L.J. and at [113], per Mance L.J.

Equally a written reserved judgment is less amenable to reversal than an ex tempore judgment.[25]

However the underlying principles as to the need for "exceptional" or "strong reasons" apply to all judgments: after all the draft judgment is intended to be precisely what it says. The reasoning for finality in respect of judgments delivered also applies in respect of draft judgments:

> "When oral[26] judgments have been given, either in a court of first instance or on appeal, the successful party ought save in most exceptional circumstances to be able to assume that the judgment is a valid and effective one. The cases to which we were referred in which judgments in civil courts have been varied after delivery (apart from the correction of slips) were all cases in which some most unusual element was present."[27]

As the heading on draft judgments makes clear, the primary purpose of circulating a draft judgment is to enable any typographical or similar error in the judgment to be notified to the court; to enable the parties to prepare drafts of consequential orders to be made on handing down; and to prepare submissions on costs and, if appropriate, for permission to appeal.

The draft judgment is not intended to provide an opportunity for a party to reopen or reargue the case.[28] Attempts to reargue the case by repeating submissions or even raising new ones are not appropriate[29] and may well amount to an abuse of process.[30]

Such a practice is frowned upon:

11–018

> "4 The primary purpose of this practice is to enable any typographical or similar errors in the judgments to be notified to the court. The circulation of the draft judgment in this way is not intended to provide an opportunity to any party (and in particular the unsuccessful party) to reopen or reargue the case, or to repeat submissions made at the hearing, or to deploy fresh ones. However on rare occasions, and in exceptional circumstances, the court may properly be invited to reconsider part of the terms of its draft. (see for example *Robinson v Fearsby* [2003] EWCA Civ 1820 and *R (Edwards) v The Environment Agency* [2008] 1 WLR 1587). For example, a judgment may contain detrimental observations about an individual or indeed his lawyers, which on the face of it are not necessary to the judgment of the court

---

[25] *Stewart v Engel* [2000] 1 W.L.R. 2268 at 2276A, per Sir Christopher Slade.

[26] The reference to "oral judgments" is in contradistinction not to written, reserved judgments but to written, sealed orders. *Paulin v Paulin and Cativo Ltd* [2009] EWCA Civ 221 at [30(d)], per Wilson L.J.

[27] *In Re Barrell Enterprises* [1973] 1 W.L.R. 19 at 23H–24B.

[28] *R. (on the application of Edwards) v The Environment Agency* [2008] UKHL 22 at [66].

[29] *Robinson v Fernsby and Scott-Kilvert* [2003] EWCA Civ 1820 at [96].

[30] *R. (on the application of Edwards) v The Environment Agency* [2008] UKHL 22 at [66].

and appear to be based on a misunderstanding of the evidence, or a concession, or indeed a submission. As we emphasise, an invitation to go beyond the correction of typographical errors and the like, is always exceptional, and when such a course is proposed it is a fundamental requirement that the other party or parties should immediately be informed, so as to enable them to make objections to the proposal if there are any."

Draft judgments—as their standard heading makes clear—are confidential to the parties and their legal advisers. They may not be shown or discussed with anyone else. The definition of "legal advisers" is narrow. It may be shown to counsel and solicitors directly involved in the case, but not other people. Equally it may only be shown to those individuals within the client necessary for taking instructions.[31] It may not, for example, be sent around the solicitors' firm or other organisations. Other people interested in the outcome—for example, insurers, shareholders, funders—may not see the judgment or learn of its substance without the permission of the court. If there is any doubt at all about whether it is appropriate to let somebody know of or see the draft judgment, the proper course is to ask the court for permission.

Examples of grounds for revisiting the draft or final judgment

11–019   The following paragraphs address some of the different reasons for seeking the lower court to revisit its judgment.

(1) *Typographical and factual corrections*: Where the proposed changes fall within those specifically requested by the court, such as in respect of typographical or factual corrections on circulation of a draft judgment, then it will, of course, be proper to suggest them. They do not seek to alter the rationale or basis of the draft judgment; they are rather in the nature of editorial comments. Accordingly as such these are not formal changes to the substance of the judgment.

(2) *Amplifying the judgment: providing further reasons for the decision*: Where one party (normally the unsuccessful party) considers the judgment to contain inadequate reasons[32] for the decision

---

[31] *DPP v P* [2008] 1 W.L.R. 1024.

[32] In this regard the advocate will recall, as set out in more detail in Ch.5, that extensive reasons are not essential in all decisions. Where the issue is a simple one such as whether or not to extend time, the absence of clear and cogent reasons will not of itself justify a full rehearing on appeal particularly where the reasoning can be determined elsewhere in the judgment: *Robert v Momentum Services Ltd* [2003] EWCA Civ 299 at [28]. By contrast where the issue is complex the Court should justify its decision by reasons. See further Ch.5.

reached or requires clarification of aspects of the judgment which are unclear then this should be raised with the lower court judge at or before the handing down of the judgment.

(a) The court has "an untrammelled jurisdiction to amplify them at any time prior to the sealing of the order".[33]

(b) Raising it at this stage allows the lower court judge the opportunity to deal with the point(s) raised without the expense of the appeal process.[34]

(c) There is a positive duty on the advocate to bring such matters to the court's attention.[35]

(d) If this does not happen and the point is first raised on an application for permission to appeal before the appellate court, then the appellate court may well adjourn the permission hearing and remit the matter to the lower court judge in order to give the lower court judge the opportunity to deal with the point(s) raised.[36]

(e) Unless there is a good reason why the matter was not brought to the lower court's attention at the handing down of judgment there are likely to be negative costs implications and criticism of the appellate's advocate if the point is held back until the appeal stage.[37] This is considered further in Chapter 14.

(3) *Palpable error in the judgment*: It is proper to invite the court to reconsider part of the terms of its draft where the judgment contains a palpable error which, if altered, would save the parties the expense of an appeal.[38]

(4) *Development in the law*: Where there has been a new development in the law with the result that the draft judgment or judgment would be wrong in law, the parties should bring it to the court's attention as soon as possible. A failure to do so may mean that permission to appeal may be refused, at least on a second appeal basis.[39]

---

[33] *Paulin v Paulin and Cativo Ltd* [2009] EWCA Civ 221 at [30(a)], per Wilson L.J.

[34] *T (Contact: Alienation: Permission to Appeal), Re* [2002] EWCA Civ 1736 at [41], per Arden L.J.; *In the matter of S (Children)* [2007] EWCA Civ 694 at [23]–[25]; *Paulin v Paulin and Cativo Ltd* [2009] EWCA Civ 221 at [30(a)], per Wilson L.J.

[35] *In the matter of M (A Child)* [2008] EWCA Civ 1261 at [36]–[38].

[36] *English v Emery Reimbold & Strick Ltd* [2002] EWCA Civ 605 at [25].

[37] *In the matter of M (A Child)* [2008] EWCA Civ 1261 at [40], per Wall L.J.

[38] *Robinson v Fernsby and Scott-Kilvert* [2003] EWCA Civ 1820 at [94].

[39] This happened in *Uphill v BRB (Residuary) Ltd* [2005] EWCA Civ 60. Following judgment, in another case the Court of Appeal decided a point which was inconsistent with the lower appeal court's decision. The prospective appellant's legal advisers were aware of the decision after receipt of the draft judgment, but did not appreciate its significance to their client's case before agreeing to seal the Order recording the lower appeal court's decision. That was a significant factor in not permitting permission for a second appeal. This is addressed further at para.13–033.

(5) *Opportunity to address points not raised during the hearing*: It may be appropriate to raise submissions where the advocate believes that the judge has decided the case on a point which was not properly argued; or has relied on an authority which was not considered.[40] The court may allow further submissions on a point of wider legal significance referred to in obiter comments of the court in a draft judgment on which legal submissions were not developed.[41]

(6) *Removal of findings immaterial to judgment*: It may be appropriate to remove a paragraph in a judgment dealing with a matter that was not the subject of the case and to alter the judgment where the judgment contains detrimental observations about an individual or indeed his lawyers which on the face of it are not necessary to the judgment of the court and appear to be based on a misunderstanding of the position.[42]

Procedure for revisiting draft judgments

11–020   A party seeking to revisit a judgment must act rapidly:

(1) A party proposing to apply to the lower court to revise or alter the judgment should let the other parties know immediately.

"As we emphasise, an invitation to go beyond the correction of typographical errors and the like, is always exceptional, and when such a course is proposed it is a fundamental requirement that the other party or parties should immediately be informed, so as to enable them to make objections to the proposal if there are any."[43]

(2) The lower court judge should first decide whether to entertain any submissions.

(3) If they are to be permitted then all parties must be given an equal opportunity to make submissions. This may be by way of written submissions or following a further oral hearing.[44]

(4) If following such submissions the lower court judge considers that the judgment is defective the judgment can be supplemented or withdrawn and a new judgment issued.

(5) It is open to the court to adjourn for this purpose if needed.

(6) The question of permission to appeal can then be addressed as against the supplemented or replacement judgment.

[40] *Egan v Motor Services (Bath) Ltd* [2007] EWCA Civ 1002; [2008] 1 W.L.R. 1589, per Smith L.J. giving the judgment of the Court at [49]–[51].

[41] *Director of Public Prosecutions v P (No.2) (Note)* [2007] EWHC 1144.

[42] *R. (on the application of Mohamed) v The Secretary of State for Foreign and Commonwealth Affairs* [2010] EWCA Civ 158; February 26, 2010 at [5].

[43] *R. (on the application of Mohamed) v The Secretary of State for Foreign and Commonwealth Affairs* [2010] EWCA Civ 158 at [4] and see too [6].

[44] *Zeital v Kaye* [2010] EWCA Civ 159 at [57].

(7) If such submissions are not permitted and the judge does not consider it appropriate to revise the draft judgment then the judge should direct that the order be drawn up in accordance with the judgment.

CHAPTER 12

Identifying the correct Appeal Court

INTRODUCTION

12–001   Identification of the correct appeal court is thanks to considerable guidance from the courts and the Court Service now usually straightforward. This chapter addresses the jurisdiction for appeals and the application of relevant rules. A summary and a flow chart are contained at the end of the chapter.

HISTORICAL CONTEXT

12–002   As discussed in more detail in Chapter 2, for non-statutory claims, the original jurisdiction to entertain an appeal is found in the County Courts Act 1984 (for County Courts) and the Senior Courts Act 1981 (for the High Court and the Court of Appeal).

This broad appellate jurisdiction has been significantly modified particularly by the Access to Justice Act 1999 (Destination of Appeals) Order 2000[1] ("the Destination Order").

For statutory appeals the relevant appeal court is usually found in the statute giving rise to the underlying action.

ORIGINAL COUNTY COURT JURISDICTION

12–003   The County Courts Act 1984 s.77(1)–(1A) provides that, subject to rules to the contrary, the Court of Appeal has jurisdiction to hear an appeal from decisions in the County Court and for appeals from decisions of district judges or equivalent to be heard by a judge of the county court:

---

[1] In force from May 2, 2000.

"(1) Subject to the provisions of this section and the following provisions of this Part of this Act and to any order made by the Lord Chancellor under section 56(1) of the Access to Justice Act 1999, if any party to any proceedings in a county court is dissatisfied with the determination of the judge or jury, he may appeal from it to the Court of Appeal in such manner and subject to such conditions as may be provided by Civil Procedure Rules.

(1A) Without prejudice to the generality of the power to make rules of court under section 75, such rules may make provision for any appeal from the exercise by a district judge, assistant judge or deputy district judge of any power given to him by virtue of any enactment to be to a judge of a county court."

Thus prior to the Destination Order (about which see paras 12–009 et seq.) an appeal from a decision lay as of right to the Court of Appeal, or where rules provided to a judge of the county court. The destination of appeals (and the requirement for permission) has been significantly altered by the Destination Order.

It is also worth noting that there are other statutory limits on appeals from decisions in the County Court:

(1) Section 77(6) of the County Courts Act 1984 limits the jurisdiction to hear appeals on questions of fact relating to possession proceedings.
(2) Section 77(7)(b) provides that the s.77 does not create any right of appeal on a question of fact.

In addition the parties can agree to exclude an appellate jurisdiction in the County Court. The County Courts Act 1984 s.79(1) provides:

"(1) No appeal shall lie from any judgment, direction, decision or order of a judge of county courts if, before the judgment, direction, decision or order is given or made, the parties agree, in writing signed by themselves or their legal representatives or agents, that it shall be final."[2]

---

[2] County Courts Act 1984 s.79(1) as amended by the Courts and Legal Services Act 1990 s.125(3), Sch.18 para.49(3).

APPEALS IN THE HIGH COURT AND THE COURT OF APPEAL

12–004 The Senior Courts Act 1981[3] provides jurisdiction for the Court of Appeal and the High Court in respect of appeals from lower courts.

Original jurisdiction for appeals in the High Court

12–005 The High Court has jurisdiction to hear and determine appeals from inferior courts by virtue of any Act or from decisions that it historically was entitled to hear prior to the coming into force of the Senior Courts Act 1981.[4]

Original jurisdiction for the Court of Appeal to hear appeals

12–006 The Court of Appeal has jurisdiction to hear appeals from those decisions that it had jurisdiction to hear immediately prior to the coming in to force of the Senior Courts Act 1981 and those specified by the Senior Courts Act 1981 or by any other statute.[5]

The jurisdiction for most appeals is derived from s.16(1) of the Senior Courts Act 1981 which provides:

> "(1) Subject as otherwise provided by this or any other Act ... or as provided by any order made by the Lord Chancellor under section 56 (1) of the Access to Justice Act 1999, the Court of Appeal shall have jurisdiction to hear and determine appeals from any judgment or order of the High Court."[6]

Court of Appeal jurisdiction for a new trial

12–007 In this context it is worth noting that analogous to an appeal, the Court of Appeal also has jurisdiction to hear applications for a new trial.[7]

---

[3] Previously the Supreme Court Act and renamed in 2009 to avoid confusion with the introduction of the Supreme Court in place of the House of Lords from October 1, 2009.

[4] Senior Courts Act 1981 s.28(3).

[5] Senior Courts Act 1981 s.15(2).

[6] This is subject to a leap-frog appeal to the Supreme Court under s.13(2)(a)) of the Administration of Justice Act 1969 and the seldom instituted Prize Acts 1864 to 1944 disputes where the appeal is to Her Majesty in Council—s.16 (2) of the Senior Courts Act 1981.

[7] Senior Courts Act 1981 s.17(1). Although rules of court may provide that where the trial is by judge alone and where no error of court is alleged then the application can be heard and determined by the High Court. Senior Courts Act 1981 s.17(2).

MODIFICATIONS TO THE ORIGINAL JURISDICTION

As mentioned above the destination of the appeal and the jurisdiction of   **12–008**
the appeal courts to hear appeals have been substantially affected by the
Destination Order. This is addressed immediately below. It is also important to stress that the jurisdiction of the Court of Appeal derives from
statute and therefore can be limited by statute. This is addressed further at
para.12–032.

THE DESTINATION ORDER

The Access to Justice Act 1999 s.56 empowered the Lord Chancellor to   **12–009**
alter the destination of civil appeals:

> "(1) The Lord Chancellor may by order provide that appeals which
> would otherwise lie to—
>
> (a) a county court,
> (b) the High Court, or
> (c) the Court of Appeal,
>
> shall lie instead to another of those courts, as specified in the order."

The Lord Chancellor made such modifications through the Access to Justice
Act 1999 (Destination of Appeals) Order 2000.[8] The overall effect of the
Destination Order is that many of the appeals that would have gone direct
to the Court of Appeal no longer do so and the appeals are now heard by
the next level in the judicial hierarchy.

JURISDICTION FOR APPEALS FOLLOWING THE
DESTINATION ORDER

The appropriate appellate court following the Destination Order now   **12–010**
depends on the nature of the decision and the decision maker. The possibilities are multiple. The helpful tables in the *White Book* identify the
possible[9] routes of appeal. These stretch over nearly six pages.[10]

---

[8] In force from May 2, 2000.
[9] As the notes to the 2010 edition of the *White Book* identify, the tables in para.2A.1 do not
identify recorders sitting in county courts. Appeals from such decisions are the same as
from circuit judges subject to CPR PD 52 para.8.13(1) which provides that an appeal or
permission to appeal from the decision of a recorder may be heard by a designated civil
judge who is authorised to act as a judge of the High Court.
[10] 2010 edition of the *White Book*, pp.1527–1532. There is an interactive guide on the Court
of Appeal's website: *http://www.hmcourts-service.gov.uk/infoabout/coa_civil/routes_app/
index.htm.*

The general position is as follows:

(1) The first appeal will be to the next level of judicial hierarchy or to the Court of Appeal in certain limited cases.
(2) A second appeal, if it is within the jurisdiction of the Senior Courts, will almost without exception lie to the Court of Appeal.
(3) If the first appeal was to the Court of Appeal, a second appeal may proceed, with permission, to the Supreme Court. Any unsuccessful party to an appeal in the Court of Appeal may apply for permission to the Supreme Court, but, as discussed in Chapter 18, obtaining permission to appeal is subject to narrow rules.

The effect of the new system is that, whilst it used to be said that the Court of Appeal was, for practical purposes, almost always the final court of appeal, it is now the case that for most civil disputes decided in the county courts, the final court of appeal will be either a recorder, a circuit judge or a High Court judge.

APPEAL FROM A DECISION IN THE COUNTY COURT

12–011 The default position is that appeals from district or deputy district judges are to a judge of the county court (i.e. either a circuit judge or a recorder) and from a judge of the county court to the High Court.

Decisions on the small claims track

12–012 Small claims track cases are likely to be heard by a district judge and therefore the appeal will usually be heard by a circuit judge within the County Court.

(1) The designated civil judge in consultation with his presiding judges has responsibility for allocating appeals from decisions of district judges to circuit judges.[11]
(2) Where, unusually, a circuit judge hears a small claims track claim then the appeal is to a High Court judge.
(3) Second appeals are to the Court of Appeal.

Decisions on the fast track

12–013 For fast track cases the same approach applies: decisions are usually made by district judges, and more rarely by circuit judges or recorders.

---

[11] CPR PD 52 para.8A.1.

(1) If the decision being appealed was made by a district judge then the appeal is to a circuit judge.

(2) Where the decision being appealed was made by a circuit judge or a recorder then the appeal is to a High Court judge.

(3) Second appeals are again to the Court of Appeal.

Part 8 Claims

Where the decision on a Pt 8 Claim being appealed was made by a district judge then the appeal is to a circuit judge and where made by a circuit judge then to a High Court judge. This is the case even though Pt 8 claims are treated as having been allocated to the multi-track. Second appeals are to the Court of Appeal.   **12–014**

APPEAL FROM A DECISION IN THE HIGH COURT

Appeals from masters and district judges

In the High Court, if the judge hearing the matter is a judge of lower rank in the judicial hierarchy to a High Court judge such as a master, then unless the case falls in to one of the exceptions addressed at para.12–017 and following (such as a final decision on a multi-track claim or in specialist proceedings) the appeal will be to a High Court judge rather than the Court of Appeal. So an appeal from a decision of a district judge in the District Registry is usually to a High Court judge.   **12–015**

In practice, appeals from district judges in District Registries are often heard by a circuit judge, usually the designated civil judge, who has s.9 jurisdiction to sit as a High Court judge. Thus, whilst sitting in a different court, there may, outside London, be little difference in terms of the identity of the judge hearing the appeal between an appeal from a district judge in the County Court and a district judge sitting in the High Court.

Appeals from High Court judge

An appeal from a decision of a High Court judge is to the Court of Appeal unless a leap-frog procedure to the Supreme Court is justified. This is considered at para.18–006.   **12–016**

EXCEPTIONS TO THE GENERAL POSITION

An appeal remains direct to the Court of Appeal in three categories of case: **12–017**

(1) where the decision is a final decision on a multi-track claim[12];

(2) where the decision is a final decision in specialist proceedings[13];

(3) where the decision itself was made on appeal.[14]

12–018 The preservation of an appeal direct to the Court of Appeal in respect of the first two categories (multi-track claims and specialist proceedings) is provided for by art.4 of the Destination Order which provides:

> "An appeal shall lie to the Court of Appeal where the decision to be appealed is a final decision—
>
> (a) in a claim made under Part 7 of the Civil Procedure Rules 1998 and allocated to the multi-track under those Rules; or
>
> (b) made in proceedings under the Companies Act 1985 or the Companies Act 1989 or to which Sections I, II or III of Part 57 or any of Parts 58 to 63 of the Civil Procedure Rules 1998 apply."

With the exception of identifying what constitutes a "final decision" the analysis of these preconditions for an appeal direct to the Court of Appeal is relatively straightforward.

Criteria for an appeal under article 4(a) of the Destination Order to the Court of Appeal

The claim must be a Part 7 Claim

12–019 Part 8 Claims, although treated as multi-track claims under Pt 8.9 (c), do not fall within this paragraph of the Destination of the Order, nor do claims allocated to the multi-track under any other provision.[15-16]

The claim must have been allocated to the multi-track

12–020 A case has to have been allocated to the multi-track.[17] Allocation must have preceded the decision to be appealed. It is not sufficient that the case would

---

[12] The Destination Order art.4(a).

[13] Proceedings under the Companies Act 1985, the Companies Act 1989 or to which ss.I, II or III of Pt 57 or any of Pts 58 to 63 of the Civil Procedure Rules 1998 apply. The Destination Order art.4(b).

[14] The Destination Order art.4(b).

[15-16] See art.4(a) of the Destination Order and para.16 of *Tanfern Ltd v Cameron–MacDonald (Practice Note)*. *Sherrington v Berwin Leighton Paisner* [2006] EWCA Civ 1319 at [2], per Lloyd L.J. was a decision referred up under CPR r.52.14 and is *not* an exception to the rule.

[17] CPR PD 7 para.3.3 provides that unless the claimant states in his claim form that the claim is to proceed under Pt 8, the claim will proceed under Pt 7.

or should have been allocated to the multi-track[18] or was allocated between the decision and the date the appeal is heard.[19]

Criteria for an appeal under article 4(b) of the Destination Order to the Court of Appeal

The claim must have been made in specialist proceedings as defined. These are: 12–021

(1) Proceedings under the Companies Act 1985 and 1989.
(2) Contentious probate proceedings under CPR Pt 57.
(3) Commercial Court proceedings under CPR Pt 58.
(4) Mercantile Court proceedings under CPR Pt 59.
(5) Technology and Construction Court proceedings under CPR Pt 60.
(6) Admiralty proceedings under CPR Pt 61.
(7) Arbitration proceedings under CPR Pt 62.
(8) Patents and other intellectual property proceedings under CPR Pt 63.

WHAT IS A FINAL DECISION?

This potentially complicated question arises in determining whether the decision being appealed amounts to a "final decision" within the meaning of the Destination Order. 12–022

A "final decision" is defined at art.1 of the Destination Order as follows:

"(2) (c) 'final decision' means a decision of a court that would finally determine (subject to any possible appeal or detailed assessment of costs) the entire proceedings whichever way the court decided the issues before it.

(3) A decision of a court shall be treated as a final decision where it—

(a) is made at the conclusion of part of a hearing or trial which has been split into parts; and
(b) would, if made at the conclusion of that hearing or trial be a final decision under paragraph 2 (c)."

There are therefore two types of "final decisions":

---

[18] *Clark (Inspector of Taxes) v Perks* [2001] 1 W.L.R. 17 at [7] and [54]; *7E Communications Ltd v Vertex Antennentechnik GmbH* [2007] EWCA Civ 140 at [15]; [2007] 1 W.L.R. 2175.
[19] *Milward v Three Rivers DC*, October 25, 2000 at [6] and [7].

(1) Category A: decisions that meet the definition under art.1(2)(c).

(2) Category B: decisions that are deemed to be within the definition of "final decision" by virtue of art.1(3).

For the purposes of Category B decisions (art.1(3) of the Destination Order) it is not necessary for the court to have made a specific order splitting the trial in to distinct parts.[20] For example, a decision on an application of a submission for no case to answer[21] may amount to a decision made at a hearing split in to parts.

12–023   The Practice Direction to Pt 52 paras 2A.2–2A.4 set out art.1 of the Destination Order and provide further guidance as to what amounts to a "final decision":

> 2A.2 ... Decisions made on an application to strike-out or for summary judgment are not final decisions for the purpose of determining the appropriate route of appeal ... Accordingly
>
> (1) a case management decision;
> (2) the grant or refusal of interim relief;
> (3) a summary judgment;
> (4) a striking out
>
> are not final decisions for this purpose.
>
> 2A.4 An order made:
>
> (1) on a summary or detailed assessment of costs; or
> (2) on an application to enforce a final decision,
>
> is not a 'final decision' ..."

A decision at the end of a trial on liability and quantum is obviously a "final decision". Decisions on costs at the end of a trial[22] including determinations of applications for wasted costs orders[23] also form part of a "final decision".

Some applications can cause confusion. A submission of no case to answer is one. In *Graham v Chorley*[24] the judge heard a submission and made two decisions:

---

[20] *Persaud v Dulovic* [2002] EWHC 889, per Silber J.; [2002] C.P. Rep. 56.

[21] *Graham v Chorley BC* [2006] EWCA Civ 92.

[22] *Dooley v Parker* [2002] EWCA Civ 96 at [6]–[7] in which the Court of Appeal clarified the end of para.17 of *Tanfern Ltd v Cameron-MacDonald (Practice Note)*.

[23] *Persaud v Dulovic* [2002] EWHC 889; [2002] C.P. Rep. 56. This is the position even if the decision on an application is made some days after the final decision on substance. However, it is because the costs form part of the order being made. If the substantive decision is not final or the decision is made independent of a final decision then the ordinary rules will apply. *Gray v Going Places Leisure Travel Ltd* [2005] EWCA Civ 189 at [18]–[19], per Neuberger L.J.

[24] *Graham v Chorley BC* [2006] EWCA Civ 92.

(1) He accepted the defendant's submission that there was no case to answer (Decision 1).

(2) He entered judgment in favour of the defendants (Decision 2).

The judge could have made a third decision. If the claimant had submitted **12–024** that the judge should not have heard a submission of no case to answer without first putting the defendants to their election as to whether to call evidence (Decision 3).

In this context Decisions 1 and 3 would not have amounted to "final decisions" because neither would have been finally determinative of the entire proceedings.

However Decision 2 would be a "final decision": it was finally determinative of the entire proceedings and therefore a final decision.[25]

Although decisions on strike out and summary judgment applications could potentially determine the proceedings if found in favour of the applicant, they do not amount to final decisions because they would not dispose of the proceedings if the respondent were to succeed.[26] The same analysis applies to an application to amend a statement of case.

By contrast a decision on limitation or other preliminary issue if determined at a separate hearing or part of the trial is a final decision. Although the decision relating to a limitation defence or other preliminary issue would not necessarily determine the "entire" proceedings "whatever way the court decided it", such a decision is deemed under art.3 to be a "final decision".[27] The reasoning is that the particular issue is decided finally and the defendants cannot re-open it at a later trial.[28]

In this regard a "final decision" under the Destination Order is not to be confused with a decision deemed by a statute to be a final decision and therefore not subject to an appeal. This is addressed at para.12–029.

The problems should be addressed before the lower court at the time of the order. CPR r.40.2(4) requires the lower court on an application for permission to appeal to state in the order whether the decision is final and the correct appeal . However this is sometimes overlooked and despite the authorities generated to date, problems can still arise and practitioners are advised to raise genuine issues of concern with the Civil Appeals Office.

---

[25] *Graham v Chorley BC* [2006] EWCA Civ 92 at [23]. However if the decision appealed was that there was no case to answer without having put the defendant to his election then that would not have been a final decision—see para.20 of the same judgment.

[26] *Tanfern Ltd v Cameron–MacDonald (Practice Note)* at [18].

[27] *Tanfern Ltd v Cameron–MacDonald (Practice Note)* at [17]; *Scribes West Ltd v Relsa Anstalt (Practice Note)* [2004] EWCA Civ 965 at [24]; [2005] 1 W.L.R. 1839.

[28] *Tanfern Ltd v Cameron–MacDonald (Practice Note)* at [17] and *Lloyd Jones v T Mobile (UK) Ltd* [2003] EWCA Civ 1162 at [25]; [2004] C.P. Rep. 10.

SECOND APPEALS

12–025 A second appeal from a lower court will always be to the Court of Appeal,[29] whether the decision to be appealed from is a decision on an appeal in the County Court or High Court.[30]

A second appeal is—as its name suggests—a further appeal from the first appeal court's decision in respect of the original decision of the lower court. Such an appeal may be made either by the successful party in the lower court who is unsuccessful on appeal or the unsuccessful party in the lower party who is also unsuccessful on appeal.

Deemed first appeals

12–026 There are a number of decisions referred to the County Court and the High Court from Tribunals or other decision making bodies. The courts have held that these are for the most part[31] encompassed by s.55 of the Access to Justice Act 1999. The effect of s.55 of the Access to Justice Act 1999 is to impose a more stringent test for permission to appeal because the unfettered right of access to the courts has been implicitly repealed.[32] The result is that any subsequent challenge to the decision of the County Court or High Court will be a "second appeal".[33] Such decisions include:

(1) an appeal to the High Court on a point of law pursuant to s.11 of the Tribunals and Inquiries Act 1992 from a tribunal;

(2) any application to the High Court which can be categorised as an appeal by way of case stated[34];

(3) an appeal to a county court on a point of law from a decision of a local housing authority under s.204(1) or s.204A of the Housing Act 1996[35];

(4) any other appeal to the High Court or the county court from any other tribunal or other body or person.

---

[29] art.5 of the Destination Order.

[30] art.5 of the Destination Order.

[31] This does not apply to challenges to decisions where the statutory framework has not been implicitly repealed by s.55 of the Access to Justice Act 1999 such as appeals under s.97(3) of the Patents Act 1977. *Smith International Inc v Specialised Petroleum Services Group Ltd* [2005] EWCA Civ 1357; [2006] 1 W.L.R. 252 at [13]–[15], per Mummery L.J.

[32] *McNicholas Construction Ltd v Customs and Excise Comrs* and *Clark v Perks* [2001] 1 W.L.R. 17 at [13], per Brooke L.J.

[33] *McNicholas Construction Ltd v Customs and Excise Comrs* and *Clark v Perks* [2001] 1 W.L.R. 17 at [13], per Brooke L.J.

[34] A list of statutes then existing which created "case stated" procedures can be found in Annex 2 to the Law Commission's consultation paper on Judicial Review and Statutory Appeal (1993) (Law Com No.126). Examples include s.137 of the Water Industry Act 1991; s.65(1) of the Planning (Listed Buildings and Conservation Areas) Act 1990; s.289(1) of the Town and Country Planning Act 1990; s.42(3) of the Building Act 1984; and s.146 of the Representation of the People Act 1983.

[35] *Cramp v Hastings BC* [2005] EWCA Civ 439 at [12].

Appeals from many Tribunals will now usually fall under the new regime of the Tribunal, Courts and Enforcement Act 2007. This introduces a two-tier tribunal structure whereby the Upper Tribunal (a superior court of record) for the most part hears appeals from the Lower Tribunal. An appeal from the Upper Tribunal lies to the Court of Appeal. This is subject to a restricted test of permission for second appeals whereby the appeal must raise some important point of principle or practice or that there is some other compelling reason for the appellate court to hear the appeal.[36]

Distinguishing appeals of decisions of the appeal court ancillary to the appeal

A distinction needs to be drawn between a decision of the appeal court in respect of the decision of the lower court and a decision of the appeal court made as part of the appeal process and ancillary to the appeal. An appeal of the former is a "second appeal" whereas an appeal of the latter is considered a "first appeal."   12–027

This has practical consequences of some significance. As addressed further in Chapter 13 there is no appeal from a refusal to grant permission to appeal.[37] However, if in the process of refusing permission to appeal the appeal court makes a decision ancillary to that refusal of permission to appeal that may provide an opportunity for a further appeal. A refusal to grant an extension of time may give rise to a further appeal.[38] An appeal against an order for costs in respect of the appeal will be treated as a first appeal.[39]

The Court of Appeal has emphasised that the lower appeal courts should be sensitive to this:

> "judges in lower appeal courts should be vigilant to take steps by which [the Court of Appeal] can know whether they consider that an application for an adjournment in a case like this was in their opinion a sham, designed to lead to the possibility of a further appeal to this court, in circumstances where this court would have no jurisdiction to entertain an appeal against an order refusing permission to appeal."[40]

The order of the lower appeal court should be drawn in such a way as to set out the reasons for an order clearly so that the Court of Appeal can discern

---

[36] The Appeals from the Upper Tribunal to the Court of Appeal Order 2008 (SI 2008/2834).
[37] Access to Justice Act 1999 s.54(4) and CPR PD 52 para.4.8.
[38] However an order imposing conditions on the appeal would not give rise to a second appeal. *Foenander v Bond Lewis & Co* [2001] EWCA Civ 759; [2002] 1 W.L.R. 525; *Jolly v Jay* [2002] EWCA Civ 277.
[39] *Jolly v Jay* [2002] EWCA Civ 277, per Brooke L.J. giving the judgment of the Court at [51]–[52].
[40] *Paulson v Bandegani* [2001] EWCA Civ 1274 at [24], per Brooke L.J.

them readily.[41] Where the order is drawn by the court the court staff should consult with the judge in cases of any doubt.[42]

OTHER LIMITS TO THE APPEAL COURT'S JURISDICTION

12–028 As set out above the jurisdiction to hear appeals is a creature of statute and therefore the court's appellate jurisdiction can be limited by other statutes. Where a statute other than the original founding jurisdiction under the Senior Courts Act 1981 or the County Courts Act 1984 provides that there should be no appeal or that an appeal is direct to a certain court then that statute will prevail.

Final decisions

12–029 Where a statute provides that a decision of a court or tribunal is to be final, the appellate court will have no power to hear an appeal even on a point of law.

Section 18 of the Senior Courts Act 1981 limits the jurisdiction to hear appeals from certain decisions of the High Court. No appeal shall lie to the Court of Appeal in the following categories of case:

(1) A decision of the High Court in any criminal case except as provided for by the Administration of Justice Act 1960.[43]

(2) A decision providing an extension of time for appealing a judgment or order.

(3) A decision which is stated to be final by virtue of any statute.

(4) A decree absolute of divorce or nullity of marriage where the prospective appellant had the time and opportunity to appeal from the underlying decree nisi and had not done so.

(5) A dissolution order, nullity order or presumption of death order under Chapter 2 of Pt 2 of the Civil Partnership Act 2004 where the prospective appellant had the time and opportunity to appeal from the underlying conditional order and had not done so.

(6) A decision under Pt I of the Arbitration Act 1996 except as provided for in that Act.

---

[41] *Tanfern Ltd v Cameron-Macdonald* [2000] 1 W.L.R. 1311 at [46], per Brooke L.J; *Paulson v Bandegani* [2001] EWCA Civ 1274 at [22], per Brooke L.J.

[42] *Paulson v Bandegani* [2001] EWCA Civ 1274 at [22] and [24], per Brooke L.J.

[43] An appeal is to the Supreme Court under s.1(1) of the Administration of Justice Act 1960. However this does not apply to an application for judicial review of a decision in a criminal cause or matter. *Ewing v Director of Public Prosecutions* [2010] EWCA Civ 70 at [16]–[17], per Laws L.J.

These are considered in greater detail at paras 2–007 to 2–009.

ALTERNATIVE JURISDICTION AND PROCEDURES FOR APPEALS

Article 1(4) of the Destination Order recognises that for certain appeals   **12–030**
other procedures and jurisdictions for appeals will prevail.

"1. (4) Articles 2 to 6—

(a) do not apply to an appeal in family proceedings; and
(b) are subject to—

(i) any enactment that provides a different route of appeal (other than section 16(1) of the Senior Courts Act 1981 or section 77(1) of the County Courts Act 1984); and
(ii) any requirement to obtain permission to appeal."

Family proceedings

Appeals in family disputes are outside the scope of this book and reference   **12–031**
should be made to the specialist texts. However in terms of jurisdiction
appeals in family proceedings are governed by the Family Proceedings Rules
1991[44] in the county courts and the High Court.

- An appeal from a district judge in the county court is to a circuit judge.
- An appeal from a district judge sitting in the Principal Registry of the Family Division is to a High Court judge of the Family Division.
- An appeal from a decision of a circuit judge sitting in a county court or as a judge of the Family Division of the High Court is to the Court of Appeal.
- Similarly an appeal from a High Court judge is to the Court of Appeal.
- A second appeal is to the Court of Appeal.

Other enactments etc.

The Destination Order is subject to any enactment which provides a dif-   **12–032**
ferent route of appeal.[45] Thus if the particular proceedings are already

---

[44] Family Proceedings Rules (SI 1991/1247).
[45] The Destination Order art.1(4)(b)(i).

governed by a statutory scheme which provides for the destination of the appeal then that statute will prevail.

Insolvency proceedings

12–033 The detail of appeals in insolvency proceedings is also beyond the scope of this work. However they are an example of an alternative statutory scheme for appeals.

Section 375 of the Insolvency Act 1986 provides that an appeal from a decision in exercise of a bankruptcy or insolvency jurisdiction of a district judge or circuit judge in a county court or a registrar in bankruptcy of the High Court is to a High Court judge.

An appeal of a decision made by a High Court judge in exercise of a bankruptcy or insolvency jurisdiction is to the Court of Appeal as is a decision on an appeal.[46]

Committal and applications for contempt of court

12–034 Appeals from committal orders are treated differently both in terms of the need for permission and the destination of the appeal.

An appeal against a committal order (including a suspended order for committal) made by a district judge is to a circuit judge in the County Court whereas an appeal of a committal order made by a circuit judge or recorder is to the Court of Appeal under s.13(2) of the Administration of Justice Act 1960.

Where the order appealed against is not a committal order, but is an order punishing contempt of court made under the jurisdiction under s.13 of the Administration of Justice Act 1960, then the destination of the appeal is the same, the only difference being that permission to appeal is required.[47]

This jurisdiction extends to any order made by the lower court when exercising that jurisdiction even if it only concerns a decision not to make an order or the grant of an adjournment.[48]

DESTINATION OF APPEALS IN SUMMARY

12–035 (1) **A first appeal** is to the next level of the judicial hierarchy. An appeal from a district judge will be to a circuit judge[49]; from a

---

[46] Again there is no requirement for permission to appeal.
[47] *Hampshire CC v Gillingham*, June 22, 2000. *Barnet LBC v Hurst* [2002] EWCA Civ 1009; [2003] 1 W.L.R. 722; [2002] C.P. Rep. 74.
[48] *Barnet LBC v Hurst* [2002] EWCA Civ 1009 at [26]; [2003] 1 W.L.R. 722; [2002] C.P. Rep. 74.
[49] The default position under Destination Order art.3(2).

circuit judge to a High Court judge[50] (who also hears appeals from High Court masters[51]); and from a High Court judge to the Court of Appeal[52];

(2) **Unless** the appeal is from a "**final decision**" in a specialist[53] or Pt 7 multi-track claims[54] in which case the appeal is to the Court of Appeal irrespective of the rank of the lower court judge.

(3) **A second appeal** is always to the Court of Appeal (unless the first appeal is to the Court of Appeal).

ASSIGNMENT OF APPEALS DIRECT TO THE COURT OF APPEAL

Where the appeal raises an important point of principle or practice or there is some other compelling reason for the Court of Appeal to hear it then the appeal may be assigned direct to the Court of Appeal under CPR r.52.14.[55]   **12–036**

An application for transfer of the appeal to the Court of Appeal instead of the designated appeal court can be made to the lower court that made the decision to be appealed, unless the lower court has already refused permission to appeal,[56] or to the higher court from where permission to appeal is sought.[57]

This is a power that should be used sparingly and if there is any doubt the matter should be referred to the Master of the Rolls for consideration.

Where an appeal is transferred to the Court of Appeal under CPR r.52.14 the Court of Appeal may give such additional directions as are appropriate for the resolution of the case.[58]

The Master of the Rolls also has the power to direct that such an appeal be heard by the Court of Appeal under s.57 of the Access to Justice Act 1999.

The Master of the Rolls or the Court of Appeal can remit an appeal back to the court in which it was or would have been brought if it is not suitable for the Court of Appeal.

---

[50] The default position under Destination Order art.3(1).

[51] The individuals listed in Pt II of Sch.2 to the Senior Courts Act 1981 include High Court registrars, a district judge of the High Court or a deputy appointee to such office. Destination Order art.2(a)–(c).

[52] *Tanfern Ltd v Cameron-MacDonald (Practice Note)* [2000] 1 W.L.R. 1311 at [15].

[53] art.4(b) of the Destination Order provides for an appeal to the Court of Appeal from a final decision in proceedings under the Companies Act 1985 or Companies Act 1989 or to which ss.I, II or III of CPR Pt 57 or any of Pts 58–63 of the Civil Procedure Rules 1998 apply.

[54] art.4(a) of the Destination Order.

[55] CPR r.52.14 (1).

[56] *7E Communications Ltd v Vertex Antennentechnik GmbH* [2007] EWCA Civ 140; [2007] 1 W.L.R. 2175.

[57] CPR r.52.14 (1).

[58] CPR PD 52 para.10.1.

PRACTICAL CONSEQUENCES OF FILING AN APPEAL IN THE WRONG COURT

12–037   Although the correct appeal court should be readily identifiable, mistakes do occur. The solution will depend on when the problem is identified and the jurisdiction of the court to address the situation:

(1) Where an appellant makes a mistake about the identity of the correct appeal court, the problem may be identified by the Court office, and the parties notified. Paragraph 2A.5 of the Practice Direction to Pt 52 provides that a court officer may, after discussion with a judge of the relevant appeal court or, in the Court of Appeal with a specified court officer,[59] notify the applicant that that court does not have jurisdiction in respect of the notice.

(2) However, the court officer's position on the issue of jurisdiction may not be accepted by one of the parties. In those circumstances the jurisdiction of the relevant appeal court will need to be determined.[60]

(3) If the problem is not resolved at that stage then there may be a practical solution available through the appeal court. In an appeal wrongly filed in the Court of Appeal instead of the High Court, the parties can, with the agreement of the Court, agree that a Court of Appeal judge can hear the appeal sitting as a High Court judge under the discretion which lies with the Master of Rolls under CPR r52.14.[61] However this requires the goodwill and co-operation of the court which is less likely to be forthcoming where the appellant has been the cause of the problem or is on notice of the problem and does not resolve it before the hearing.[61a]

It goes almost without saying that while a solution may exist the problem is best avoided by identifying the correct appeal court in the first place.

---

[59] CPR r.52.16 provides for barrister or solicitor court officers in the Civil Appeals Office to carry out certain administrative and non contentious functions with the consent of the Master of the Rolls.

[60] In *Tanfern Ltd v Cameron-MacDonald (Practice Note)* [2000] 1 W.L.R. 1311 the circuit judge took a different view albeit under the old rules and in *Dooley v Parker* [2002] EWCA Civ 96 the circuit judge and the parties took a different view leading to a jurisdictional hearing before a three judge Court of Appeal.

[61] This procedure was adopted by Henry L.J. in *Milward v Three Rivers DC*, October 25, 2000 where the point was drawn to the attention of the Court of Appeal once the appeal was in place—see para.7. In *Scribes West Ltd v Relsa Anstalt* [2004] EWCA Civ 965 at [34], Brooke L.J. proposed this having concluded that the appeal should have been to a High Court judge rather than the Court of Appeal.

[61a] *Chadwick v Hollingsworth* [2010] EWCA Civ 1210.

FLOWCHART OF DETERMINING NEXT LEVEL OF APPEAL JUDGE

12–038

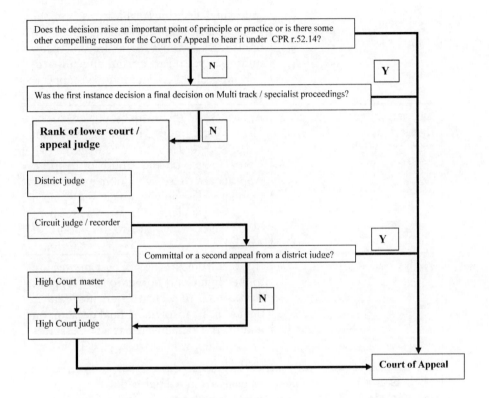

TABLE SHOWING APPEAL JUDGES

Level of first instance judge	Level of appeal judge
District judge / deputy district judge	Appeals are to the circuit judge other than in respect of appeals from final decisions on multi-track claims or specialist proceedings[62] which are to the Court of Appeal.

---

[62] Identified as proceedings under the Companies Act 1985 or the Companies Act 1989 or to which ss.I, II, or III of Pt 57 or any of Pts 58–63 of the Civil Procedure Rules 1998 apply.

Circuit judges / recorders	Appeals from circuit judges and recorders are generally to the High Court or the Court of Appeal.[63] Appeals are to a High Court judge other than appeals from the following decisions which are to the Court of Appeal: (i) final decisions on multi-track claims; (ii) a decision committing a person to prison; and (iii) second appeals, i.e. decisions on appeals from a district judge.
District judge sitting as a district judge of the Registry of a High Court	Appeals from the district judge are to the High Court judge, including a circuit judge or recorder sitting as a deputy High Court judge, or the Court of Appeal. Appeals are to a High Court judge other than appeals involving a final decision on a multi-track claim such as an assessment of damages which are to the Court of Appeal.
High Court master	Appeals from the High Court master are to the High Court or the Court of Appeal. Appeals are to a High Court judge other than appeals involving a final decision on a multi-track claim such as an assessment of damages which are to the Court of Appeal.
High Court judge (including a circuit judge or recorder sitting as a deputy High Court judge)	Appeals from a High Court judge go to the Court of Appeal.

---

[63] A designated civil judge who is authorised to sit as a deputy High Court judge may hear an appeal from a recorder sitting in the county court— CPR PD 52 para.8.13(1A).

CHAPTER 13

Permission to Appeal

PERMISSION TO APPEAL IS A RELATIVELY NEW REQUIREMENT

With the exception of appeals, as they then were, to the House of Lords, until relatively recently a party did not need to obtain permission to appeal. Nowadays obtaining permission to appeal is a mandatory requirement for almost all types of appeal.[1] **13–001**

Lord Woolf's final report on "Access to Justice" in July 1996 recommended that all interim appeals should require permission. In October 1996 Sir Jeffery Bowman was asked to conduct a full review of the civil division of the Court of Appeal. **13–002**

The review team, which included Lord Woolf, published its report, known as the Bowman Report, in September 1997. That review said that appeals should be dealt with in ways that were proportionate to the grounds of complaint and the subject matter of dispute. More than one level of appeal was not justifiable unless the case involved an important point of principle or practice.

The Bowman Report's proposals were introduced through the Access to Justice Act 1999 and the Access to Justice Act 1999 (Destination of Appeals) Order 2000 made under s.56 of the Access to Justice Act 1999.

---

[1] See paras 1–033 et seq. for the background. Additional background to this change is set out in the notes to the *White Book* paras 52.0.2–52.0.5. Initially the restriction was in respect of certain appeals to the Court of Appeal—Courts and Legal Services Act 1990 s.7 which resulted in Ord.59 r.1B of the Rules of the Supreme Court added by SI 1993/2133. For further details of the more recent legislative history see the judgment of the Vice-Chancellor in *Colley v Council for Licensed Conveyancers* [2001] EWCA Civ 1137; [2002] 1 W.L.R. 160 at [27].

THE STATUTORY REQUIREMENT FOR PERMISSION TO APPEAL

13–003 The current requirement for permission to appeal finds its statutory source in s.54 of the Access to Justice Act 1999 which provides:

"54(1) Rules of court may provide that any right of appeal to—(a) a county court, (b) the High Court, or (c) the Court of Appeal, may be exercised only with permission."

The relevant rule of court is CPR r.52.3(1) which provides that, with limited exceptions, permission is required for most appeals:

"52.3(1) An appellant or respondent requires permission to appeal

(a)   where the appeal is from a decision of a judge in a county court or the High Court, except where the appeal is against—

(i)   a committal order;
(ii)   a refusal to grant habeas corpus; or
(iii)   a secure accommodation order made under section 25 of the Children Act 1989; or

(b)   as provided by Practice Direction 52.

(Other enactments may provide that permission is required for particular appeals.)"

Part 52 is subject to "any rule, enactment or practice direction which sets out special provisions with regard to any particular category of appeal".[2] Thus in addition to those categories of appeal identified in CPR r.52.3(1)(a), the requirement for permission does not apply to various proceedings where another statutory regime prevails such as in family proceedings and insolvency proceedings[3] or Pt 52 does not apply such as an appeal in detailed assessment proceedings against a decision of an authorised costs officer.[4]

---

[2]   CPR r.52.1(4). An appeal is to a costs judge or a district judge of the High Court. The appeal does not require permission and is a complete rehearing. A second appeal is to a High Court judge. It is not a second appeal under the Destination Order and is not subject to CPR r.52.1(2).

[3]   See paras 12–032 to 12–034. Family proceedings are governed by the Family Proceedings Rules 1991 and insolvency proceedings by the Insolvency Act 1986[3] and Insolvency Practice Direction. In neither case is permission required for an appeal from the lower courts. Arbitration proceedings are subject to ss.69(2) and (3) of the Arbitration Act 1996. This is addressed in Ch.21 (Arbitration Appeals). The County Courts Act 1984 prohibits appeals in possession proceedings on question of fact in certain instances: County Courts Act 1984 s.77(6).

[4]   CPR r.52.1(2).

Similarly where a statute precludes the right of appeal in certain proceedings because the decision is "final" then that is the end of the matter and the question of permission does not arise.[5]

PERMISSION TO APPEAL AND ARTICLE 6

It is unlikely that, correctly applied, the limitation of appeals to those who have first obtained permission infringes art.6 of the European Convention on Human Rights.   **13–004**

Article 6 does not compel the contracting states to set up courts of appeal. Nevertheless, a state which does institute such courts is required to ensure that persons amenable to the law enjoy before these courts the fundamental guarantees contained in art.6.[6]

In civil proceedings the right of access to such courts is not absolute, and the state is permitted to place limitations on the right to access. In this regard, although the state enjoys a margin of appreciation, any limitations must pursue a legitimate aim and there must be a reasonable relationship of proportionality between the means employed and the aim to be achieved.[7]

In *Nascimento v United Kingdom*[8] the district judge had debarred the claimant from pleading particulars of the injury he had suffered in a bicycle, because he had failed to file medical evidence in accordance with an unless order, and the recorder had dismissed his appeal.   **13–005**

The European Court of Human Rights held that the requirement that an appellant must obtain permission from the Court of Appeal to bring a second appeal, which would only be given if (among other things) the case raised a point of principle, did not infringe art.6, because it was a reasonable and proportionate measure taken in pursuit of the fair and efficient administration of justice.

That case was decided under the consolidated Court of Appeal practice direction of April 26, 1999, but it is suggested that the rules relating to permission to appeal presently existing are likewise reasonable and proportionate.

At the time Mr Nascimento had been declined permission to appeal to the Court of Appeal, the proviso that the point of practice had to be "important" had been deleted from the test for whether permission should be granted, which the Strasbourg Court commented was a "significant" change.

Section 55(1)(a) of the Access to Justice Act 1999 and CPR r.52.13(2)(a) reinstated the word "important". It is not thought that the difference

---

[5] Senior Courts Court Act 1981 s.18(1)(c). *Westminster City Council v O'Reilly* [2003] EWCA Civ 1007; [2004] 1 W.L.R. 195. See paras 2–007 to 2–009 and 12–029.

[6] *Delcourt v Belguim* (1970) 1 E.H.R.R. 355 at [25]. Delcourt related to a criminal charge, but the principles apply to civil determinations too: *Nascimento v United Kingdom* (Application No.55331/00) Unreported January 31, 2002.

[7] *Brualla Gomez de la Torre v Spain* (2001) 33 E.H.R.R. 57 at [33].

[8] Application No.55331/00 Unreported January 31, 2002.

between points of practice and important points of practice is of significance in considering whether or not the requirements for permission to appeal are compatible with art.6, because it relates to whether the point of practice is important for the civil justice system as a whole, rather than whether it is important for the result of the particular dispute.

If that is right, it probably follows that the availability of a second appeal where it would be useful for the civil justice system as whole for the Court of Appeal to consider a point of practice has a very limited impact on an individual's rights under art.6.

THE TEST FOR OBTAINING PERMISSION TO APPEAL

13–006 The requirements that must be met to obtain permission to appeal are set out in CPR r.52.3(6):

"(6) Permission to appeal may be given only where—

(a) the court considers that the appeal would have a real prospect of success; or

(b) there is some other compelling reason why the appeal should be heard."

The tests are alternative

13–007 Under the new regime the test is alternative. If either of the two limbs (a) or (b) is satisfied, the court "may" grant permission to appeal.

Permission remains subject to the court's discretion

13–008 Before the coming in to force of the CPR the court would invariably grant permission if the appellant had a real prospect of success.[9] Now the discretionary nature of the decision to grant permission may lead to permission to appeal being refused even where either limb (a) or (b) of the test is satisfied. However in practice this is unlikely to occur frequently. A first appeal with real prospects of success would only be denied permission for a good reason.[10]

---

[9] *Smith v Cosworth Casting Ltd (Practice Note)* [1997] 1 W.L.R. 1538 at [1]: "The Court will only refuse leave if satisfied that the applicant has no realistic prospect of succeeding on the appeal."

[10] CPR para.1.2.

The first limb of the test: a real prospect of success

The word "real" in the phrase "a real prospect of success" has the same   13–009
meaning as it has in the phrase "real prospect of succeeding" under CPR
r.24.2.[11] This means a realistic, as opposed to a fanciful, prospect of
success.[12]

Although the test is reasonably easy to describe its application without
hearing the appeal in full can be difficult. For this reason in many cases the
issue of permission to appeal is directed to be determined with the appeal to
follow immediately thereafter.[13] The practical effect of the direction is that
the appeal court usually hears the appeal in full and then determines the
issue of permission. While wholly understandable in terms of the appeal
court's desire to understand the issues for consideration on the appeal
process it does undermine the two stage test and the intended costs savings
associated with the pre-condition of obtaining permission first.

The second limb: some other compelling reason

The second limb reflects the jurisdiction the Court of Appeal had before the   13–010
CPR came in to force to hear an appeal where it might not have acceptable
prospects of success.[14] The need for this jurisdiction was explained by Lord
Woolf in a practice note[15] as follows:

> "There can be many reasons for granting leave even if the court is not
> satisfied that the appeal has any prospect of success. For example, the
> issue may be one which the court considers should in the public interest
> be examined by this court or, to be more specific, this court may take
> the view that the case raises an issue where the law requires clarifying."

As this limb is an alternative to the test under the first limb a judge can give
permission irrespective of whether or not the appeal has a real prospect of
success.[16]

Examples of where permission has been granted under the second limb
where the appeal had no real prospects of success include:

(1) Where binding authority on the Court of Appeal rendered the case
hopeless at that level, but the point was potentially arguable in the

---

[11] *Tanfern v Cameron-McDonald* [2000] 1 W.L.R. 1311 at [21].
[12] *Swain v Hillman* [2001] 1 All E.R. 91, and see also on the pre-CPR test *Smith v Cosworth (Practice Note)* [1997] 1 W.L.R. 1538 at [1]: the word "realistic" makes it clear that a fanciful prospect or an unrealistic argument is not sufficient.
[13] *Society of Lloyd's v Sir William Jaffray* [2001] EWCA Civ 1485 at [11]; *Morris v Bank of India* [2004] EWCA Civ 1286 at [21].
[14] See the Bowman Report Ch.3, para.37–38.
[15] *Smith v Cosworth Practice Note* [1997] 1 W.L.R. 1538.
[16] *Morris v Bank of India* [2004] EWCA Civ 1286 at [9]–[10].

Supreme Court. In such a case the Court of Appeal may well grant permission but dismiss the appeal, so that the appellant is not precluded from appealing to the Supreme Court.[17]

(2) Where a proposed appeal raised a question of public importance which the Court of Appeal thinks should be finally decided after full argument.[18]

By contrast matters discrete to the parties will not amount to a compelling reason even though the matter is financially significant[19] or has significant personal or professional implications for one party.[20]

The second limb uses the same language of the under the second limb of CPR r.52.13. However, caution must be exercised in considering the authorities in context because what is a compelling reason for granting permission to appeal for a first appeal may not amount to a compelling reason for granting permission for a second appeal.

PERMISSION TO APPEAL FROM SPECIALIST COURTS AND TRIBUNALS—A HIGHER HURDLE?

13–011 The courts have long shown a deference to decisions taken by some specialist courts and tribunals.[21] This can sometimes give the impression that a higher test for permission to appeal is being applied, even though the test is the same.

In *Cooke v Secretary of State of Social Security*,[22] an appeal from the Social Security Commissioners, the Court of Appeal considered applications for permission to appeal from specialist tribunals.

The test for permission to appeal was confirmed to be the same whether or not the appeal was from a specialist court or tribunal. However the court would take into account various matters in assessing whether there was a real prospect of success including:

(1) the decision had been taken by a specialist tribunal;
(2) the decision may already have been through an independent appellate system before it reached that specialist tribunal; and

---

[17] *Beedell v West Ferry Printers Ltd* [2001] EWCA Civ 400; [2001] C.P. Rep. 83; *Family Housing Association v Donnellan* [2001] EWCA Civ 1840.

[18] *R. v The Prime Minister Ex p. Gentle* [2006] EWCA Civ 1078.

[19] *Morris v Bank of India* [2004] EWCA Civ 1286 at [19].

[20] *Hickey v Marks*, July 6, 2000 at [41], per May L.J.; *Morris v Bank of India* [2004] EWCA Civ 1286 at [19].

[21] *R. v Preston Supplementary Benefits Appeal Tribunal* [1975] 1 W.L.R. 624 at 631–632, per Lord Denning M.R., where he urged the courts "to leave the tribunals to interpret the Act in a broad and reasonable way according to the spirit and not the letter ... The courts should only interfere when the decision of the tribunal is unreasonable in the sense that no tribunal acquainted with the ordinary use of language could reasonably reach that decision."

[22] [2001] EWCA Civ 734; [2002] 3 All E.R. 279.

(3) the decision may have been taken by legally qualified practitioners experienced in the area.

Accordingly the courts "should approach such cases with an appropriate degree of caution"[23] when considering an appeal.

This approach was endorsed by the House of Lords in *Hinchy v Secretary of State for Work and Pensions*.[24]

A similar "respectful" stance is given to decisions from the predecessor to the Immigration and Asylum Chamber of the Upper Tribunal,[25] the Competition Appeal Tribunal[26] and the predecessor to the Lands Chamber of the Upper Tribunal[27] as well as statutory appeals from a decision of a professional committee or panels in respect of disciplinary matters.[28]

This approach also applies in respect of decisions from specialist courts such as the Technology and Construction Court. The Court of Appeal has endorsed the pre-CPR approach[29] of affording special regard to decisions on questions of fact by the judges or official referees on the basis of their experience of hearing multiple claims of a technical nature.[30]

By contrast in patent cases the Court of Appeal's guidance is that where permission to appeal is sought the trial judge should grant permission to appeal unless the case is very clear[31] or the application for permission to appeal can be understood sufficiently readily in an hour or so.[32] This is limited to patent cases, perhaps because of the specific treaty obligations[33] relating to formal reviews of patent decisions.

However the level of "caution" to be applied will necessarily depend on the basis of the appeal.

(1) Where the issue on the appeal is a question of law such as the interpretation of relevant statutes or where the conduct of the process is in issue the level of persuasion will be no different to the

---

[23] At [15]–[17], per Hale L.J. who gave the leading judgment.

[24] [2005] UKHL 16: "[The Commissioners] have practical experience of the day-to-day working of the benefit system and I think that the principles they have devised to give effect to the legislative scheme dealing with overpayments are entitled to great respect."

[25] *SSHD v Akaeke* [2005] EWCA Civ 947 at [28]–[30] and *R. (Iran) v SSHD* [2005] EWCA Civ 982 at [92]–[93]. Cf. the previous approach in *Koller v Secretary of State for the Home Department* [2001] EWCA Civ 1267.

[26] *Napp Pharmaceutical Holdings Ltd v Director General of Fair Trading* [2002] EWCA Civ 976; [2002] 4 All E.R. 376 at [34].

[27] *Cawsand v Fort Management Co Ltd v Stafford* [2007] EWCA Civ 231 at [12].

[28] The stated rationale is because their principal purpose is the preservation and maintenance of public confidence in the profession—*Fatnani and Raschid v General Medical Council* [2007] EWCA Civ 46 at [19], [16] and [26], per Laws L.J.

[29] Which was on a point of law or with permission on a question of fact—as explained by Lord Bingham M.R. in *Virgin Management Ltd v De Morgan Group*, 68 B.L.R. 26 at 33.

[30] *Skanska Construction UK Ltd v Egger (Barony) Ltd* [2002] EWCA Civ 1914 at [7] and *Yorkshire Water Services v Taylor Woodrow Construction Northern Ltd* [2005] EWCA Civ 894; [2005] B.L.R. 395 at [27].

[31] Presumably that there is no real prospect of success.

[32] *Pozzoli SPA v BDMO SA* [2007] EWCA Civ 588 at [10].

[33] art.32 of the TRIPS Agreement (Annex 1(C)) to the Treaty establishing the World Trade Organisation made at the Uruguay Round of the GATT talks in April 1994.

ordinary case[34] and there is no basis for any such caution or deference.[35]

(2) However where the appeal relates to matters that were determined by the committee or panel using their professional judgment then more caution or deference may be appropriate.[36]

PERMISSION TO APPEAL FROM CASE MANAGEMENT DECISIONS

13–012 As many case management decisions tend to be based on an exercise of discretion an appeal from a case management decision is usually difficult as addressed in greater detail in paras 3–071 et seq.

The Court of Appeal has long recognised the authority of the judge managing the relevant case and on appeal the relevant designated civil judge to determine matters of case management:

> "the authority of the designated civil judge in raising local standards and correcting sloppy practice is a very important feature of the new CPR dispensation, and this court should not lightly override it."[37]

Paragraph 4.4 of the Practice Direction to Pt 52 identifies a number of case management decisions where particular care is required:

(1) decisions made under CPR r.3.1(2);
(2) decisions about disclosure;
(3) decisions about the timetable for filing of witness statements or experts' reports;
(4) directions about the timetable of the claim;
(5) decisions about whether to add a party to a claim; and
(6) decisions on security for costs matters.

Paragraph 4.5 of the Practice Direction to Pt 52 provides:

> "Where the application is for permission to appeal from a case management decision, the court dealing with the application may take into account whether:
>
> > (1) the issue is of insufficient significance to justify the costs of an appeal;

---

[34] *MA v Merck Sharp & Dohme Ltd* [2008] EWCA Civ 1246 at [18].

[35] *Cawsand Fort Management Co Ltd v Stafford* [2007] EWCA Civ 1187; [2008] 1 W.L.R. 371.

[36] *Meadow v General Medical Council* [2006] EWCA Civ 1390 at [69] and [82] and *Cheatle v General Medical Council* [2009] EWHC 645 at [15].

[37] *Calden v Dr Nunn and Partners* [2003] EWCA Civ 200 at [47], per Brooke L.J.

(2) the procedural consequences of an appeal (e.g. loss of trial date) outweigh the significance of the case management decision;

(3) it would be more convenient to determine the issue at or after trial."

The factors under para.4.5 are not dissimilar to the considerations that the court would need to consider in any event under the overriding objective when exercising its discretion.

Nonetheless the appellate court's jurisdiction to determine appeals is not fettered by these provisions where the lower court has taken matters in to account it should not have or overlooked matters it should have considered or where the decision of the lower court is plainly wrong.[38]

RESPONDENT'S APPLICATION FOR PERMISSION TO APPEAL—A LOWER HURDLE FOR PERMISSION?

The rule requiring permission to appeal applies to any respondent who wishes to uphold the lower court's decision on different reasons or to challenge another part of the order. The criteria for granting permission to appeal are the same for appellant and respondent. However the editors of the *White Book*[39] correctly point out that where a respondent's prospective appeal is linked to that of the application for permission to appeal it may be illogical to refuse permission on the cross-appeal where it has already been granted on the appeal. For example, on an appeal against the finding of liability by the defendant it may be logical also to consider a cross-appeal on the appropriate level of contributory negligence. Thus a respondent may find permission to appeal more readily forthcoming on issues linked to those for which the appellant has already obtained permission to appeal.

13–013

LIMITED PERMISSION

CPR r.52.3(7) provides that an order giving permission to appeal may limit the issues for which permission to appeal is granted.

13–014

The Practice Direction to Pt 52 paras 4.18–4.21 explains the process. If the court decides to limit the scope of permission to appeal to specified issues it can either refuse permission on certain issues or reserve the question of permission to appeal on any remaining issues to the court hearing the appeal.

The rules permit the lower court to grant limited permission to appeal only, and that happens relatively frequently in practice.

---

[38] *Royal & Sun Alliance Insurance Plc v T&N Ltd (In Administration)* [2002] EWCA Civ 1964; [2003] P.I.Q.R. 26.

[39] Commentary on CPR r.52.5, 2010 edn, para.52.5.4.

If the lower court grants permission to appeal on restricted issues, and if the appellant wishes to apply for permission to appeal on further issues, the appellant must then file an appellant's notice seeking wider permission from the appellate court.

The order granting permission to appeal should in all circumstances make clear what has been ordered:

(1) Whether the court has refused permission to appeal on certain issues; or, alternatively,

(2) that it has not granted permission but has left the issue of whether permission should be granted to be determined by the appeal court at the appeal hearing.

In the former position, the appellant is precluded from seeking to appeal the further issues; in the latter, the appellant has a final chance to persuade the appellate court that it should be entitled to seek to appeal those further issues.

13–015   Although the rules do not expressly make it clear, it must be the case that only the appellate court and not the lower court may reserve the issue of whether permission to appeal should be granted to the hearing of the appeal itself, for otherwise the lower court would be trespassing upon the appellate court's jurisdiction to grant permission to appeal on paper.

If the question of permission to appeal on the additional issues is to be left to the appeal court then the appellant needs to obtain permission from the appellate court before the issues can be raised in the appeal hearing.[40-41]

To do so the appellant must notify the appeal court and the respondent in writing within 14 days of service of the court's order in accordance with para.4.19 of the Practice Direction to Pt 52.

The purpose of requiring written notice to be given is to alert the court and the other parties to the fact that the application for permission to appeal will be renewed and has not been abandoned.

There is no particular form of writing that must be used; a letter to the appellate court copied to the respondents clarifying the position will suffice.

If the appellant seeks to renew its application for permission to appeal on a more restricted basis than would be suggested by the appellant's notice and/or skeleton argument, the written notice should, it is suggested, make that clear.

It may also be appropriate to file a supplemental skeleton argument under para.5.11A of the Practice Direction to Pt 52 which clarifies or limits the particular point the appellant wishes to pursue; though whenever an appellant seeks to rely on a supplemental skeleton argument, he should bear in mind the guidance given by Buxton L.J. in *The "Kriti Palm"* that it should not be abused to raise a completely revised and expanded case.[42]

[40-41] *Tanfern Ltd v Cameron-MacDonald* [2000] 1 W.L.R. 1311 at [22].

[42] *AIC Ltd v ITS Testing Services (UK) Ltd (the "Kriti Palm")* [2007] 1 Lloyd's Rep. 555 at [393].

If, on the other hand, the appeal court refuses permission to appeal on the remaining issues without a hearing, the appellant may, in the usual way, renew its application orally.

If the appellant wishes to do so, it must file a request within seven days of notification of the refusal of permission in accordance with CPR r.52.3(5).

If permission to appeal is refused after an oral hearing then the application for permission to appeal cannot subsequently be renewed on the appeal hearing.[43]

EXCEPTIONAL JURISDICTION UNDER CPR R.52.17

There is an exceptional jurisdiction to renew applications for permission to appeal which have only been partially successful under the *Taylor v Lawrence* jurisdiction embodied in CPR r.52.17,[44] discussed further in Chapter 8. Such a jurisdiction will only be exercised if it is necessary to do so in order to avoid real injustice; the circumstances are exceptional and make it appropriate to reopen the appeal; and there is no alternative effective remedy.[45]   **13–016**

THE SMALL CATEGORY OF APPEALS IN WHICH PERMISSION IS NOT REQUIRED

There are exceptions to the general rule that permission to appeal is required. CPR r.52.3 identifies those exceptions: **13–017**

> "52.3 (1) An appellant or respondent requires permission to appeal
>
> (a) where the appeal is from a decision of a judge in a county court or the High Court, except where the appeal is against...
>
> (i)   a committal order;
> (ii) a refusal to grant habeas corpus; or
> (iii) a secure accommodation order made under section 25 of the Children Act 1989; or
>
> (b) as provided by the relevant practice direction.
>
> (Other enactments may provide that permission is required for particular appeals)."

---

[43] See CPR PD 52 para.4.21 and s.54(4) of the Access to Justice Act 1999. *Fieldman v Markovic* [2001] C.P. Rep. 119; *James v Baily Gibson & Co* [2002] EWCA Civ 1690 at [6]–[8]; [2003] C.P. Rep. 24.
[44] *Indicii Salus Ltd v Chandrasekaran* [2008] EWCA Civ 67 at [28]–[29].
[45] CPR r.52.17(1).

High Court judge sitting under a different jurisdiction

13–018 Limb (a) of the CPR r.52.3(1) refers to "a judge in a county court or the High Court". The requirement for permission does not apply in the unusual circumstances that a High Court judge is sitting not as a judge of the High Court but under a different jurisdiction, even though he sits under that jurisdiction by virtue of being a High Court judge.[46]

The three specified exceptions to the requirement for permission in CPR r.52.3(1)(a)

13–019 The common feature of these three exceptions under limb (a) of CPR r.52.3(1) is that the liberty of the prospective appellant is at stake.

Committal orders

13–020 Section 13(1) of the Administration of Justice Act 1960 provides that an appeal lies to the Court of Appeal "from any order or decision of a court in the exercise of jurisdiction to punish for contempt of court". CPR r.52.3(1)(a) reflects this.

The key point is that the appeal must lie "in the exercise of the jurisdiction" to punish for contempt of court.

No permission to appeal is required by the contemnor who is committed or made subject to a suspended sentence of imprisonment[47] or a refusal to reduce the period of imprisonment.[48]

However if the lower court makes any other order then the ordinary rules requiring permission to appeal apply.[49]

An unsuccessful applicant for a committal order requires permission to appeal against the refusal of the lower court to make a committal order[50]

---

[46] *In Re B (A Patient) (Court of Protection: Appeal)* [2006] 1 W.L.R. 278. A nominated judge exercising jurisdiction under the Mental Health Act 1983 Pt VII (before its repeal by the Mental Capacity Act 2005) was for historical reasons not sitting as a judge of the High Court. The historical background to the separate jurisdictions are set out in *MB (A Patient)*, *Re* [2005] EWCA Civ 1293; [2006] 1 W.L.R. 287 at [22]–[38]. This particular problem has been resolved by the provision in Pt 2 of the Mental Capacity Act 2005 s.53 for the Court of Protection to make rules requiring permission before an appeal can be commenced. At the time the Court of Appeal expressed the view that this was an accidental lacuna in the rules. Other lacunae that appear are likely to be closed by subsequent legislation to achieve uniformity.

[47] *Wilkinson v The Lord Chancellor's Department* [2003] EWCA Civ 95 at [57].

[48] *CJ v Flintshire BC* [2010] EWCA Civ 393 at [4], per Wilson L.J.—although the point was not argued before the Court.

[49] *Government of Sierra Leone v Davenport* [2002] EWCA Civ 230 at [7] and [8], per Jonathan Parker L.J. and at [33], per Laws L.J.

[50] *Government of Sierra Leone v Davenport* [2002] EWCA Civ 230 at [34]; *Kynaston v Carroll* [2004] EWCA Civ 1434 at [14] and [37].

and an appeal against an order to pay costs on such an application would require permission.[51]

A refusal to grant habeas corpus

An appeal against a refusal to grant habeas corpus does not require permission.

13–021

A secure accommodation order made under section 25 of the Children Act 1989

An appeal against a secure accommodation order made under s.25 of the Children Act 1989 does not require permission. An appeal against a refusal to grant such an order would require permission.

13–022

Permission "as required by the relevant practice direction"

At present there are no further exceptions provided by practice directions.[52] The generic references to permission to appeal and the application of Pt 52 to appeals in the Practice Direction to Pt 52 do not count for this purpose despite attempts in the past to argue the same.[53]

13–023

PERMISSION TO RAISE A NEW ARGUMENT ON APPEAL

There is sometimes a temptation for an unsuccessful party to seek raise on appeal an argument not previously argued in the lower court. In order to do so, a party requires permission to raise the new argument.

13–024

Permission will be given only in exceptional circumstances.[54] The reasons for restricting a party from raising a new argument were helpfully summarised in the Court of Appeal decision of *Jones v MBNA* as follows:

> "52. Civil trials are conducted on the basis that the court decides the factual and legal issues which the parties bring before the court.

---

[51] *London Borough of Barnet v Hurst* [2002] EWCA Civ 1009; [2003] 1 W.L.R. 722 at [25]–[27]; *Kynaston v Carroll* [2004] EWCA Civ 1434 at [12]–[19], [35]–[37]; *Poole BC v Hambridge* [2007] EWCA Civ 990 at [6] and [22].

[52] *White Book*, 2010 edn, para.52.3.1. The jurisdictional question of whether a practice direction can limit such matters was considered in *Colley v Council for Licensed Conveyancers* [2002] 1 W.L.R. 160. It was held that para.6 of Sch.I to the 1997 Act provided the necessary jurisdiction—see paras 40–44.

[53] *Colley v Council for Licensed Conveyancers* [2002] 1 W.L.R. 160 at [49] (in respect of the earlier Practice Direction in materially similar language) and see *In Re B (A Patient)* [2005] EWCA Civ 1293; [2006] 1 W.L.R. 278 at [44]–[46].

[54] Permission is even less likely in the House of Lords: "Only rarely and with extreme caution will the House permit counsel to withdraw from a concession which has formed the basis of argument and judgement in the Court of Appeal." *Grobbelaar v New Group Newspapers Ltd* [2002] UKHL 40 at [21], per Lord Bingham.

Normally each party should bring before the court the whole relevant case that he wishes to advance. He may choose to confine his claim or defence to some only of the theoretical ways in which the case might be put. If he does so, the court will decide the issues which are raised and normally will not decide issues which are not raised. Normally a party cannot raise in subsequent proceedings claims or issues which could and should have been raised in the first proceedings. Equally, a party cannot, in my judgment, normally seek to appeal a trial judge's decision on the basis that a claim which could have been brought before the trial judge would have succeeded if it had been so brought. The justice of this as a general principle is, in my view, obvious. It is not merely a matter of efficiency, expediency and cost, but of substantial justice. Parties to litigation are entitled to know where they stand. The parties are entitled, and the court requires, to know what the issues are. Upon this depends a variety of decisions, including, by the parties, what evidence to call, how much effort and money it is appropriate to invest in the case, and generally how to conduct the case; and, by the court, what case management and administrative decisions and directions to make and give, and the substantive decisions in the case itself. Litigation should be resolved once and for all, and it is not, generally speaking, just if a party who successfully contested a case advanced on one basis should be expected to face on appeal, not a challenge to the original decision, but a new case advanced on a different basis. There may be exceptional cases in which the court would not apply the general principle which I have expressed. But in my view this is not such a case."[55]

Other than in exceptional cases[56] the test for obtaining permission to raise a new matter on appeal is that:

(1) The appeal court must have before it all the facts bearing upon the new issue or argument as if it had been raised at trial.[57]

(2) There is no possibility that had the matter been raised at trial that:

(a) a witness could have explained the matter[58]; or

(b) further evidence could have been produced at trial on it[59]; or

[55] *Jones v MBNA*, June 30, 2000, at [32], per May L.J. See too the judgment of Peter Gibson L.J. at [38].

[56] *Niblett v Confectioners' Materials Co* [1921] 3 K.B. 387 at 397, per Scrutton L.J.; *Rogers v Parish Ltd* [1987] 1 Q.B. 933 at 945, per Mustill L.J.

[57] *The Owners of the Ship "The Tasmania" v The Owners of the Ship "City of Corinth"— The Tasmania* (1890) 15 App. Cas. 223 at 225, per Lord Herschell. Cited by Lord Nicholls of Birkenhead and Lord Walker of Gestingthorpe at [64] in their opinion in *Paramount Export Ltd (In Liquidation) v New Zealand Meat Board* [2004] UKPC 45—dissenting in the result but agreeing on the legal principle. See a similar line taken in New Zealand in *Otago Station Estates Ltd v Par* [2005] NZSC 16.

[58] *The Owners of the Ship "The Tasmania" v The Owners of the Ship "City of Corinth"— The Tasmania* (1890) 15 App. Cas. 223 at 225, per Lord Herschell.

[59] *Jones v MBNA* at [38], per Peter Gibson L.J.

   (c)   the trial would have been conducted differently by the other
         side.[60]

The following are examples of where new points may be permitted to be   **13–025**
run on appeal where not argued at first instance:

   (1)   *Party has reserved his position expressly on the point:* Where a
         party has reserved its position on a point of law because of a
         binding authority then while the point may on one view be new in
         the sense that it was not argued at first instance, since the point
         was identified and the party's position reserved then it should not
         fall foul of the above criteria. The opposing party has been alerted
         to it and has had the opportunity to adduce evidence in relation to
         it at first instance. Whether permission to appeal will be granted
         will depend on whether there is a real prospect of the appeal court
         distinguishing or overturning the previous authority or a higher
         appeal court on a second appeal overturning or distinguishing the
         previous authority.
   (2)   *Developments in the law:* Where a party seeks to raise on appeal a
         new point because of the development in the law in other litigation
         which could not fairly have been anticipated at the time of the
         trial, then the court is likely to look sympathetically at an appli-
         cation to raise the new point on appeal. Whether the development
         could and should have been anticipated will be an area for argu-
         ment on any application.
   (3)   *Submissions not fact sensitive:* Where the facts underlying the
         submission are not in issue, an attempt to raise a new argument on
         appeal is more likely to succeed.[61] For instance a new argument on
         the construction or interpretation of a contract where the under-
         lying factual matrix had been fully investigated at first instance
         may well be permitted on appeal.[62]
   (4)   *Public interest:* Where the point is of importance to the public
         interest in that it might leave open a precedent causing a public
         body to pay significant sums which it should not properly do then
         the court may well allow the new point to be run on appeal.[62a]

---

[60]   *Crane v Sky In-Home Ltd* [2008] EWCA Civ 978 at [21]; *In the matter of Southill Finance
       Ltd* [2009] EWCA Civ 2 at [35] in respect of a litigant in person.
[61]   *Pittalis v Grant* [1989] 1 Q.B. 605 at 611; *In the matter of Southill Finance Ltd* [2009]
       EWCA Civ 2 at [49].
[62]   *Paramount Export Ltd (In Liquidation) v New Zealand Meat Board* [2004] UKPC 45 at
       [47].
[62a] *Paramount Export Ltd (In liquidation) v New Zealand Meat Board* [2004] UKPC 45 at
       [47].

Prejudice to the respondent

13–026   In assessing whether to give permission to raise a new point on appeal the appeal court will assess the prejudice it may cause the respondent. Respondents tend to argue that additional disclosure or evidence would have been required and/or adduced. However unless the respondent is specific as to the type of disclosure or evidence that would have been called or, the manner in which the trial would have been conducted differently and can identify the prejudice that will be suffered if permission to raise the new issue is granted, the court is unlikely to be impressed by the submission.

Consequences of permission to appeal where a new ground of appeal is raised

13–027   Where an appellant obtains permission to appeal it does not amount to a grant of permission binding on both parties to rely on a new case on appeal. It only permits the appellant the right to argue in favour of this at a full hearing.[63]

Possible costs orders

13–028   Additionally where permission is granted to introduce a new argument on appeal and the point succeeds the losing party may well be protected by a special order as to costs.[64]

SECOND APPEALS: THE TEST FOR PERMISSION TO APPEAL ON SECOND APPEALS

13–029   All second appeals are made to the Court of Appeal unless it was the first appeal court. Thus other than second appeals to the Supreme Court, which are considered in Chapter 18, the test is that set out in CPR r.52.13.

Only the Court of Appeal can give permission for a second appeal.[65] The granting of permission to appeal to the Court of Appeal by a junior appeal court is a nullity.[66]

The test for permission to appeal on second appeals is intentionally stringent. The recommendation of the Bowman Report was that one level of appeal was appropriate and reflects the need for certainty, reasonable

---

[63] *In the matter of Southill Finance Ltd* [2009] EWCA Civ 2 at [29].
[64] *Crane v Sky In-Home Ltd* [2008] EWCA Civ 978 at [22].
[65] Access to Justice Act 1999 s.55.
[66] *Clark (Inspector of Taxes) v Perks* [2001] 1 W.L.R. 17 at [16].

expense and proportionality. Parliament "has made it clear that it is only in an exceptional case that a second appeal may be sanctioned".[67] A second appeal should only be necessary in special circumstances.[68]

The jurisdiction and the threshold for granting permission on a second appeal is set out in s.55 of the Access to Justice Act 1999:

> "(1) Where an appeal is made to a county court or the High Court in relation to any matter, and on hearing the appeal the court makes a decision in relation to that matter, no appeal may be made to the Court of Appeal from that decision unless the Court of Appeal considers that—
>
> (a) the appeal would raise an important point of principle or practice, or
> (b) there is some other compelling reason for the Court of Appeal to hear it."

CPR r.52.13 tracks the language of limbs (a) and (b) of s.55(1) of the Access to Justice Act 1999.

It is no longer possible to pursue a second appeal merely because the appeal is properly arguable or has a real prospect of success. While the appeal court on a second appeal may well consider that it would have reached a different decision that of itself is not sufficient. The philosophy of the Civil Procedure Rules is to confirm and bolster the authority of the judges in the lower courts rather than to replace its decision with that of the appeal court's preferred resolution of the issue.[69]

A trap: is the appeal really a second appeal?

In the ordinary course of civil litigation through the courts there will be no doubt as to when an appeal is a first or second appeal. However as set out in Chapter 12 care needs to be taken in determining whether a decision made at an appeal hearing is a decision on an appeal or a first decision. An appeal will not be a second appeal if it is an appeal in respect of an ancillary matter to the appeal such as the costs of an adjourned hearing.[70]

13–030

From a practical perspective it may therefore be that parts of the decision being appealed give rise to a "second appeal" whereas others are only on proper analysis a "first appeal". As addressed in Chapter 12 this may mean that the destination of the appeal may be different for particular aspects of the decision. This also affects the test for permission to appeal and can give

---

[67] *Tanfern v Cameron-Macdonald* [2000] 1 W.L.R. 1311 at [41], per Lord Justice Brooke.
[68] The Bowman Report Chs 2 and 4. See too *Tanfern Ltd v Cameron-McDonald Practice Note* [2000] 1 W.L.R. 1311 at [44]–[46], per Brooke L.J. and *Uphill v BRB (Residuary) Ltd* [2005] 1 W.L.R. 2070 at [17], relying on *Tanfern* (ibid.) at [41]–[46].
[69] *Iftakhar Ahmed v Stanley A Coleman & Hill* [2002] EWCA Civ 935 at [2].
[70] *Foenander v Bond Lewis & Co* [2001] EWCA Civ 59; [2002] 1 W.L.R. 525; *Jolly v Jay* [2002] EWCA Civ 2777.

rise to curious anomalies where there is an overlap in the exercise of the lower court and the appeal court in the decisions made.

This happened in the case of *Convergence Group Plc v Chantrey Vellacott (A Firm)*.[71] The claimant applied to amend its pleadings before the master. The application was refused. On appeal to the High Court judge the claimant sought to introduce further amendments. The High Court upheld the master's decision and refused the new amendments. On a further appeal to the Court of Appeal the issue arose as to which test should apply for determining permission to appeal. The claimant contended that it should be that applying to first appeals whereas the defendant said it should be that applying to second appeals. There was a middle ground that different tests should apply depending on whether the amendment was one first raised before the master or not. Somewhat pragmatically the Court of Appeal held that it should be the test under CPR r.52.3(6), but, if it was wrong, and the court had determined that the appeal should be allowed then that would be a "compelling reason" for the purposes of CPR r.52.13.

The first limb of the second-appeal hurdle: appeal would raise an important point of principle or practice: CPR r.52.13(2)(a)

13–031 An important point of principle or practice means an important point of principle or practice that has not yet been established.[72]

It is therefore essential to distinguish between:

(1) establishing a principle or practice; and
(2) applying an established principle or practice correctly.

Where the application of the point of principle has yet to be determined and it is of sufficient importance then it will satisfy the first limb of the test under CPR r.52.13(2)(a).

By contrast where an appeal concerns the correct application of a principle or practice whose meaning and scope has already been determined by a higher court, then it does not satisfy CPR r.52.13(2)(a).[73]

---

[71] [2005] EWCA Civ 290.

[72] *Uphill v BRB Residuary Ltd* [2005] EWCA Civ 60; [2005] 1 W.L.R. 2070 at [18].

[73] *Uphill v BRB Residuary Ltd* [2005] EWCA Civ 60; [2005] 1 W.L.R. 2070 at [18]. In *Clark v Perks* [2001] 1 W.L.R. 17 at [34]–[35] permission was given where the decision reached on the point of practice was different to that previously applied by tax commissioners and there were consequential multiple challenges.

The second limb of the second-appeal hurdle: some other compelling reason: CPR r.52.13(2)(b)

The Court of Appeal, with the approval of the Master of the Rolls and Vice-President of the CA, has given guidance as to the meaning of "other compelling reason" as it arises in respect of second appeals[74]:

> "(1) A good starting point will almost always be a consideration of the prospects of success. It is unlikely that the court will find that there is a compelling reason to give permission for a second appeal unless it forms the view that the prospects of success are very high, for instance where the judge in the first appeal made a decision which is perverse or otherwise plainly wrong. It may be clear that the decision is wrong because it is inconsistent with authority of a higher court which demonstrates that the decision was plainly wrong. Subject to what we say at (3) below, anything less than very good prospects of success on an appeal will rarely suffice. In view of the exceptional nature of the jurisdiction conferred by CPR r 52.13(2), it is important not to assimilate the criteria for giving permission for a first appeal with those which apply in relation to second appeals.
>
> (2) Although the necessary condition which we have mentioned at (1) is satisfied, the fact that the prospects of success are very high will not necessarily be sufficient to provide a compelling reason. An examination of all the circumstances of the case may lead the court to conclude that, despite the existence of very good prospects of success, there is no compelling reason for giving permission to appeal. For example, if it is the appellant's fault that the first appeal was dismissed, because he failed to refer to a relevant authority, the court may conclude that justice does not require the opportunity of a second appeal ... On the other hand, if the authority of a higher court which shows that the decision on the first appeal was wrong post-dated that decision, then there might be a compelling reason for giving permission for a second appeal.
>
> (3) There may be circumstances where there is a compelling reason to grant permission to appeal even where the prospects of success are not very high, for instance that the hearing was tainted by some procedural irregularity so as to render the first appeal unfair. In such a situation the court might conclude that there was a compelling reason to give permission for a second appeal, even though the appellant had no more than a real, as opposed to fanciful, prospect of success. It would be plainly unjust to deny an appellant a second appeal in such a case, since to do so might, in effect, deny him a right of appeal altogether."

13–032

---

[74] *Uphill v BRB Residuary Ltd* [2005] EWCA Civ 60; [2005] 1 W.L.R. 2070 at [24].

13-033   On the facts in *Uphill* the Court found that the second appeal had very strong prospects of success, but declined to give permission to appeal.

Following judgment the Court of Appeal in another case had decided a point which suggested that the lower appeal court's decision was wrong and that a second appeal had very strong prospects of success.

The prospective appellant's legal advisers were aware of the decision after receipt of the draft judgment, but did not appreciate its significance to their client's case before agreeing to seal the Order recording the initial appeal decision.

The failure to raise the new decision with the lower appeal court judge between the handing down of his judgment in draft and agreeing to seal the order was a significant factor in the Court's conclusion that on the facts of the case there was no compelling reason to permit the defendant "a third bite at the cherry".[75]

The principles in *Uphill* are not exhaustive. There may be other factors that amount to a compelling reason under CPR r.52.13(2)(b).[76] Those identified by the courts include:

(1) An appeal judge addressing the wrong test on an appeal from an administrative decision. In *Cramp v Hastings BC*[77] permission was given for a second appeal where the appeal judge had relied on his own view as to what administrative enquires should have been made by the local authority rather than assessing whether the view taken by the local authority was reasonable.

(2) Where the decision involves real complexity. Complexity was found to be a compelling reason within the meaning of CPR r.52.3(6) and CPR r.52.13 in *esure Insurance Ltd v Direct Line Insurance Plc*.[78]

(3) An inappropriate exercise of appeal court's powers. A real prospect of showing that the lower appeal court judge had exercised his appellate powers incorrectly could on its own amount to a compelling reason for granting permission for a second appeal.

Relevance of the test under the first limb of CPR r.52.3(6) to the test under CPR r.52.13(2)

13-034   There is no link between the test under CPR r.52.13(2) for second appeals and the test under the first limb of CPR r.52.3(6) that the appeal has a real prospect of success. That the second limb of CPR r.52.13 is identical to the second limb of CPR r.52.3(6)(b) suggests that the tests are exclusive.

---

[75] *Uphill v BRB (Residuary) Ltd* [2005] EWCA Civ 60 at [29]–[31].
[76] *Cramp v Hastings BC* [2005] EWCA Civ 439 at [18] and [19].
[77] [2005] EWCA Civ 1005.
[78] *esure Insurance Ltd v Direct Line Insurance Plc* [2008] EWCA Civ 842 at [65]; [2009] Bus. L.R. 438.

However it would seem strange if the first limb of the test under CPR r.52.3 (a real prospect of success) was not also a pre-condition to a second appeal:

(1) In *Uphill*[79] the Court of Appeal emphasised that care should be taken not to assimilate the tests under CPR r.52.3(6) and CPR r.52.13.

(2) As set out above the analysis in *Uphill* was that the issue of whether an appeal has a real prospect of success may be relevant to determining whether there is a compelling reason under the second limb of CPR r.52.13.

(3) In *Thenga v Quinn*[80] the tests were described as being "complementary". Whether an appeal had a real prospect of success was relevant to whether the appeal was of sufficient "importance". By contrast if the resolution of the point of practice or principle is so obvious that the appeal has no real prospect of success then the point is not one of sufficient importance.[81]

PERMISSION TO APPEAL FROM DECISIONS FROM TRIBUNALS

Appeals from many Tribunals will now usually fall under the new regime of the Tribunal, Courts and Enforcement Act 2007 with a two-tier structure whereby the Upper Tribunal (a superior court of record) for the most part hears appeals from the Lower Tribunal from where an appeal lies to the Court of Appeal. This is subject to the same strictures of a second appeal. For permission to appeal, the appeal must raise some important point of principle or practice or that there is some other compelling reason for the appellate court to hear the appeal.[82]   **13–035**

EFFECT OF REFUSAL OF PERMISSION TO APPEAL

No appeal against a refusal of permission to appeal is permitted.   **13–036**
    Section 54(4) of the Access to Justice Act 1999 provides:

"54(4) No appeal may be made against a decision of a court under this section to give or refuse permission (but this subsection does not affect any right under rules of court to make a further application for permission to the same or another court).

---

[79] *Uphill v BRB Residuary Ltd* [2005] EWCA Civ 60; [2005] 1 W.L.R. 2070 at [24].
[80] *Thenga v Quinn* [2009] EWCA Civ 151 at [19].
[81] *Thenga v Quinn* [2009] EWCA Civ 151 at [19].
[82] The Appeals from the Upper Tribunal to the Court of Appeal Order 2008 (SI 2008/2834).

This is reiterated in para.4.8 of the Practice Direction to Pt 52:

"There is no appeal from a decision of the appeal court, made at an oral hearing, to allow or refuse permission to appeal to that court."

This reflects the position that applied immediately before the introduction of the CPR whereby a provision requiring the leave or permission of a court to appeal was considered necessarily to exclude an appeal against the grant or refusal of permission, despite the general language of a statutory right of appeal.[83]

While a prospective appellant can renew an application for permission to appeal refused by the lower court to the appeal court, if permission to appeal is refused by the appeal court then at the subsequent hearing of the appeal the appellate court has no jurisdiction to reconsider whether or not to grant permission to appeal. This has been confirmed by the Court of Appeal on several occasions.[84]

JUDICIAL REVIEW OF THE GRANT OR REFUSAL OF PERMISSION TO APPEAL

13–037   The jurisdiction of the High Court to review decisions of lower courts to determine whether they have acted within or outside of their jurisdiction survives the introduction of s.54(4) of the Access to Justice Act 1999.[85]

Thus the grant or refusal of permission to appeal by a judge of the county court is technically capable of being challenged by way of an application for judicial review if there is no other way of challenging it.[86]

However as discussed further in Chapter 10 for the most part any such application is likely to be dismissed summarily because the system of appeals in place is considered an adequate and sufficient method of review

---

[83] See the principle in *Lane v Esdaile* [1891] A.C. 210 as described by Lord Hoffmann in *Kemper Reinsurance Co v Minister of Finance* [2000] 1 A.C. 1 at [13].

[84] *Fieldman v Markovitch*, July 4, 2001; [2001] C.P. Rep. 119; *The Times*, July 31, 2001; *Riniker v University College London* [2001] 1 W.L.R. 13; *Hyams v Plender* [2001] 1 W.L.R. 32; *Jolly v Jay* [2002] EWCA Civ 277 at [16]–[18] rejecting an attempt to rely on CPR r.52.13(1); *James v Baily Gibson & Co* [2002] EWCA Civ 1690 at [5]–[8]; [2003] C.P. Rep. 24; *Moyse v Regal Mortgages Ltd Partnership* [2004] EWCA Civ 1269 at [21]–[31]; [2005] C.P. Rep. 9; *7E Communications Ltd v Vertex Antennentechnik GmbH* [2007] EWCA Civ 140; [2007] 1 W.L.R. 2175.

[85] *The Queen on the application of Sivasubramaniam v Wandsworth County Court* [2002] EWCA Civ 1738; [2003] 1 W.L.R. 475; [2003] C.P. Rep. 27 at [44], per Lord Phillips M.R.

[86] *The Queen on the application of Sivasubramaniam v Wandsworth County Court* [2002] EWCA Civ 1738; [2003] 1 W.L.R. 475; [2003] C.P. Rep. 27 at [47]–[48], per Lord Phillips M.R.

for decisions made and a further review by the High Court is not necessary.[87]

Exceptional cases may be where the applicant challenges the jurisdiction of the appeal court judge who has given or refused permission to appeal on the basis of a clear want of jurisdiction or there has been such a substantial procedural irregularity as to have denied the applicant a fair hearing.[88] The threshold for the latter would require a fundamental departure from the correct procedures or a complete disregard by the lower court judge of his duties.[89]

By contrast the Court of Appeal has no inherent jurisdiction to hear an appeal of a junior appeal court refusing permission to appeal.[90]

DIFFERENT PROVISION RELATING TO APPEALS ON APPLICATIONS FOR JUDICIAL REVIEW

The position is slightly different with applications for judicial review. The applicant may apply to the Court of Appeal for permission to appeal against the High Court's refusal of an application for permission to apply for judicial review.   13–038

CPR r.52.15 provides:

"52.15 (1) Where permission to apply for judicial review has been refused at a hearing in the High Court, the person seeking that permission may apply to the Court of Appeal for permission to appeal."

The application must be made within seven days of the decision of the High Court refusing to give permission to apply for judicial review.

The Court of Appeal can instead of giving permission to appeal simply give permission to apply for judicial review in which case the judicial review will proceed in the High Court unless the Court of Appeal orders otherwise.[91]

Further reference should be made to the specialist textbooks as judicial review appeals are beyond the scope of this work.

---

[87] *The Queen on the application of Mahon v Taunton County Court* [2001] EWHC Admin 1078; [2002] A.C.D. 192; *The Queen on the application of Messer v Cambridge County Court* [2002] EWCA Civ 1355.

[88] *The Queen on the application of Sivasubramaniam v Wandsworth County Court* [2002] EWCA Civ 1738; [2003] 1 W.L.R. 475; [2003] C.P. Rep. 27 at [49]–[56], per Lord Phillips M.R.

[89] *Gregory v Turner* [2003] EWCA Civ 183; [2003] 1 W.L.R. 1149 at [38]–[45].

[90] *Riniker v University College London* [2001] 1 W.L.R. 13; *Clark (Inspector of Taxes) v Perks* [2001] 1 W.L.R. 17 at [20].

[91] CPR r.52.15(2)–(4).

LEAPFROG APPEALS

13–039   For those cases where the normal route of appeal would be to an appellate court lower in the hierarchy than the Court of Appeal and there is an important point of principle or of practice or some other compelling reason to go to the Court of Appeal the appeal may be assigned direct to the Court of Appeal. For appeals direct from the High Court to the Supreme Court, see paras 18–006 to 18–010.

Section 57 of the Access to Justice Act 1999 provides:

> "57(1) Where in any proceedings in a county court or the High Court a person appeals, or seeks permission to appeal, to a court other than the Court of Appeal or the House of Lords—
>
> (a) the Master of the Rolls, or
> (b) the court from which or to which the appeal is made, or from which permission to appeal is sought, may direct that the appeal shall be heard instead by the Court of Appeal.
>
> (2) The power conferred by subsection (1)(b) shall be subject to rules of court."

CPR r.52.14 provides:

> "52.14(1) Where the court from or to which an appeal is made or from which permission to appeal is sought ('the relevant court') considers that—
>
> (a) an appeal which is to be heard by a county court or the High Court would raise an important point of principle or practice; or
> (b) there is some other compelling reason for the Court of Appeal to hear it,
>
> the relevant court may order the appeal to be transferred to the Court of Appeal.
>
> . . .
>
> (2) The Master of the Rolls or the Court of Appeal may remit an appeal to the court in which the original appeal was or would have been brought."

The test

13–040   It will immediately be seen that CPR r.52.14 provides the exact same test for transfer of an appeal to the Court of Appeal on the basis of a leap-frog as that for a second appeal to the Court of Appeal under CPR r.52.13.

Rare exercise of jurisdiction

The guidance from the Court of Appeal is that this power should be   13–041
exercised only in clear circumstances by the lower court.

If there is any uncertainty the matter should be referred to the Master of
the Rolls for consideration.[92]

The Court of Appeal has granted permission where the same point arises
in a number of cases and its resolution will assist in concluding those other
cases.[93]

The Manual of Civil Appeals[94] identifies the following as criteria established by Lord Woolf when Master of the Rolls for considering whether to
make a direction:

(1) where there appear to be conflicting authorities requiring resolution by the Court of Appeal;
(2) in relation to points of practice or procedure where there is no
guidance at present and the point is of significant importance for
the practice or procedure of the courts;
(3) where the issue is one of general principle and importance in the
development of the substantive law; or
(4) the issue is one where there are a number of appeals on similar
points so as to suggest that a theme or trend is developing which
the Court of Appeal needs to consider.

Paragraph 10.1 of the Practice Direction to Pt 52 provides that where an
appeal is transferred to the Court of Appeal under CPR r.52.14, the Court
of Appeal may give such additional directions as are appropriate.

Requirement for permission

However the right to transfer the appeal direct to the Court of Appeal only   13–042
arises in respect of the issue of transfer. The question of permission to
appeal remains a matter for the original lower court or appellate court.[95–98]

REOPENING OF FINAL APPEALS

There is a very limited jurisdiction of the High Court and the Court of   13–043
Appeal to reopen a decision under CPR r.52.17. This is considered in detail
in Chapter 8.

---

[92] *Clark (Inspector of Taxes) v Perks* [2001] 1 W.L.R. 17 at [9] and [57].
[93] *Tankard v John Fredericks Plastics Ltd* [2008] EWCA Civ 1375 at [2] on construction of
the Conditional Fee Agreement Regulations 2000.
[94] 2nd edn, para.3.38.
[95–98] *In the Matter of Claims Direct Test Cases* [2002] EWCA Civ 428 at [23]; [2002] P.I.Q.R.
Q11; *Moyse v Regal Mortgages Ltd Partnership* [2004] EWCA Civ 1269 at [27]. [2005]
C.P. Rep. 9; *7E Communications Ltd v Vertex Antennentechnik GmbH* [2007] EWCA Civ
140 at [13] and [14]; [2007] 1 W.L.R. 2175.

CPR r.52.17 confirms the jurisdiction of the Court of Appeal and the High Court's jurisdiction[99] to reopen a final determination of an appeal in exceptional circumstances.

This jurisdiction had been recognised by a five judge Court of Appeal in *Taylor v Lawrence*[100] and as applying to the High Court in *Seray-Wurie v Hackney LBC.*[101]

The CPR were amended with effect from October 6, 2003 to reflect this jurisdiction by the introduction of CPR r.52.17.

The test

13–044　The test set out in CPR r.52.17(1) is as follows:

> "52.17(1) The Court of Appeal or the High Court will not reopen a final determination of any appeal unless—
>
> (a)　it is necessary to do so in order to avoid real injustice;
> (b)　the circumstances are exceptional and make it appropriate to reopen the appeal; and
> (c)　there is no alternative effective remedy."

In *Taylor v Lawrence* the Court of Appeal held that the jurisdiction could only be exercised to avoid "real injustice in exceptional circumstances".[102] The Court of Appeal has since described it as only exercisable "in extraordinary circumstances"[103] and "only very rarely".[104]

The jurisdiction can only be properly invoked where it is demonstrated that the integrity of the earlier litigation process, whether at trial or at the first appeal, has been critically undermined.[105]

Where fresh evidence is the basis for the application to reopen the appeal it must at least be shown that:

(1)　the fresh evidence demonstrates a real possibility that an erroneous result was arrived at in the earlier proceedings; and

---

[99]　CPR r.52.17 does not apply to appeals in a county court. The power of a county court judge to order a hearing under CCR Ord.37 r.1 has been revoked in relation to civil proceedings to which the CPR apply, but is still available in family proceedings. *H (Children) (Application for Rehearing)* [2003] EWCA Civ 345 at [7]–[8], per Thorpe L.J.
[100]　*Taylor v Lawrence* [2003] Q.B. 528 at 54 in a five judge division of the Court of Appeal. This has sine been codified by CPR r.52.17.
[101]　*In Seray-Wurie v Hackney LBC* [2002] EWCA Civ 909; [2003] 1 W.L.R. 257 at [17], [21] and [22], per Brooke L.J.
[102]　*Taylor v Lawrence* [2002] EWCA Civ 90; [2003] Q.B. 528 at [54], per Lord Woolf.
[103]　*Bloom Camillin v Matlaszek*, February 5, 2003; [2003] EWCA Civ 154.
[104]　*Malski v St Albans City and DC* [2003] EWCA Civ 61.
[105]　*In Re Uddin (A Child)* [2005] EWCA Civ 52; [2005] 1 W.L.R. 2398 at [18], per Dame Elizabeth Butler-Sloss P.

(2) there exists a powerful probability that such a result has in fact been perpetrated[106]; and

(3) the injustice which would be perpetrated if the appeal was not re-opened must be "so grave as to overbear the pressing claims of finality in litigation".[107]

Where it was "highly likely" that if the court had known the true position at the original hearing as to the evidence it would have reached a different decision then permission to appeal on this basis is likely to be given.[108]

There is strong judicial guidance not to make frivolous applications under this jurisdiction:

"The fact that the jurisdiction has been identified for the purposes of [avoiding][109] significant injustice in extraordinary circumstances must not be shown as giving any form of green light to the kind of applications that we have received today, unless those making it are completely satisfied that it does indeed fall within this particular rubric."[110]

Preliminary review on paper

Before an application is made under this rule permission is required even in the rare cases where permission was not required for the original appeal.[110a] The application should be made to the court whose decision the applicant wishes to reopen.[110b] The application must be made by way of formal application notice and supported by written evidence verified by a statement of truth.[110c] The application for permission, and any written statements supporting or opposing it will be considered on paper by a single judge and will be allowed to proceed only if the judge so directs. **13–045**

No service of application unless directed

The application must *not* be served on any other party to the original appeal unless the court so directs.[111] This is to avoid the risk of the **13–046**

---

[106] *In Re Uddin (A Child)* [2005] EWCA Civ 52; [2005] 1 W.L.R. 2398 at [22], per Dame Elizabeth Butler-Sloss P.

[107] *In Re Uddin (A Child)* [2005] EWCA Civ 52; [2005] 1 W.L.R. 2398 at [21], per Dame Elizabeth Butler-Sloss P.

[108] *Feakins v DEFRA* [2006] EWCA Civ 699 at [38]. The initial source of the misleading evidence was Counsel for the successful party. This was compounded by a statement from that party purporting to clarify matters, but was subsequently discovered to contain serious inaccuracies as to the operation of the repayment system under consideration.

[109] The word "awarding" in the judgment must be a typographical mistake for "avoiding".

[110] *Matlaszek v Bloom Camillin* [2003] EWCA Civ 154 at [30], per Brooke L.J.

[110a] CPR r.52.17(4).

[110b] CPR PD 52 para.25.3.

[110c] CPR PD 52 para.25.4.

[111] CPR PD 52 para.25.5.

respondent expending money on responding to the application for permission to appeal.

Respondent's response

13–047   Where the appeal court directs that the application is to be served on the other parties to the appeal, the respondent is permitted to file and serve a written statement either supporting or opposing the application. That response must be filed within 14 days of the service on him of the copy of the application.[112] The application for permission to appeal itself is considered in more detail in the next chapter.

---

[112] CPR PD 52 para.25.6.

CHAPTER 14

Applications for Permission to Appeal

This chapter addresses the process facing a prospective appellant in seeking   **14–001**
permission to appeal, and the steps required of the respondent.

INTRODUCTION

As addressed in Chapter 12, it is a pre-condition to nearly all appeals that   **14–002**
the appellant obtains permission to appeal. Save for second appeals to the
Court of Appeal, and all appeals to the Supreme Court, permission may be
granted either by the court that made the Order the appellant wishes to
appeal, or by the appellate court.

(1) Where the lower court refuses permission, the appellant may apply
    to the appellate court.
(2) Initially the application to the appellate court will be considered
    on paper.
(3) If it is refused on paper, the appellant has the right, save in limited
    circumstances discussed in paras 14–023 et seq., to renew the
    application orally.
(4) If permission is refused by the appellate court, then that is the end
    of the prospective appeal, and there is no appeal against the refusal
    of permission to appeal.

GENERAL DUTIES FOR PROSPECTIVE APPELLANT ON APPLICATION FOR PERMISSION TO APPEAL

Applications for permission to appeal are often made without the presence   **14–003**
of the prospective respondent particularly when made to the appeal court.
The party seeking permission to appeal must comply with a number of
duties before, during and after the application for permission to appeal. A

failure to do so may well result in any grant of permission being overturned, adverse costs orders and professional embarrassment.

Duty to put the matter fairly

14–004   There is a duty on the appellant to draw to the court's attention all relevant matters relating to whether or not to grant permission to appeal. This is particularly important when the application for permission to appeal is made to the appeal court, since it will be unfamiliar with the issues in the case.

The Court of Appeal has emphasised the importance of presenting the application fairly, particularly in complex commercial cases. Where the outcome of an appeal is likely to depend on the court's application of a key authority it should be referred to by the proposed appellants in their skeleton argument and not, for example, alluded to by way of a document annexed to the skeleton.[1]

Whilst it is important to comply with the duty to present the application fairly, and it is no doubt prudent, as well as good advocacy, to raise and address the points the respondent would take if it were making submissions on whether permission should be granted, the duty is probably not as extensive or onerous as the duty of full and frank disclosure on an ex parte application for an injunction, because the granting of permission to appeal does not of itself interfere with the respondent's rights, liabilities, liberty or property.

Duty to inform the court of any material change to application

14–005   There is a duty on an applicant for permission to appeal both before and after the grant of permission to inform the relevant appeal court in writing if there has been any material change which would affect the question of whether permission should be given or should have been given.[2] Examples might include:

(1) the fact that a relevant judgment has been handed down or has been discovered by one of the parties in the interim between the judgment or order and the determination of the application for permission;

(2) that a relevant issue has been resolved that will affect the utility or effect of the order or the appeal;

(3) the fact that one of the parties or a relevant entity has entered some form of insolvency; or

(4) the death of a party.

---

[1] *Mamidoil-Jetoil Greek Petroleum Co SA v Okta Crude Oil Refinery AD* [2003] EWCA Civ 617; [2003] 2 L.L.R. 645 at [26].

[2] *Walbrook Trustee (Jersey) Ltd v Fattal* [2008] EWCA Civ 427 at [49], per Collins L.J.

Duty to correct any mistaken assumption of the appeal court in giving permission

If it appears from the reasons given on an application for permission to appeal that permission has been granted on the basis of a misapprehension on the court's part, the appellant should write to the appropriate appeal court to explain the position and seek appropriate directions.[3]

14–006

No reference to Part 36 Offers and payments

CPR r.52.12 provides that no Pt 36 Offer or payment into court should be disclosed to any judge of the appeal court who is to hear or determine the application for permission to appeal or an appeal until all questions (other than costs) have been determined unless the Pt 36 Offer or payment into court is relevant to the substance of the appeal or is properly relevant to the matter to be decided.[4]

14–007

Although by CPR r.36.3 a Pt 36 Offer made in the proceedings at first instance will not have consequences in the appeal proceedings and a fresh Pt 36 Offer needs to be made for it to have any effect, no mention should be made of any Pt 36 Offer at either the permission or appeal stage of an appeal—unless, of course, the appeal is against a costs decision, and the Pt 36 offer was or should arguably have been considered by the judge when deciding the incidence of costs.

If there is an inadvertent reference to a Pt 36 Offer this will not lead to the automatic recusal of the appeal judge. The editors of the *White Book* suggest[5] that the same test should apply to the appeal court as to the lower court as summarised by Lord Justice Dyson, as he then was, in his judgment in *Garratt v Saxby*[6]:

> "It is for the judge to decide in each case whether the disclosure of a Part 36 offer or payment makes a fair trial impossible and whether justice demands that he recuse himself. But judges should not be too ready to reach such a conclusion; the delay and extra costs occasioned by a recusal may be very considerable. Moreover, when exercising their discretion, judges should remind themselves that they ought to have little difficulty in analysing and deciding the issues in the case on their merits without being influenced by their knowledge of the amount of the Part 36 offer or payment."

---

[3] *Walbrook Trustee (Jersey) Ltd v Fattal* [2008] EWCA Civ 427 at [49], per Collins L.J.
[4] CPR r.52.12.
[5] *White Book* (2010), para.52.12.1.
[6] [2004] EWCA Civ 341 at [20]–[21]; [2004] 1 W.L.R. 2152.

APPLICATIONS FOR PERMISSION TO APPEAL

14–008 A prospective appellant has more than one attempt at applying for permission to appeal. In almost all cases the prospective appellant will have two opportunities to apply for permission to appeal and in some instances there may be up to four attempts.

(1) The first opportunity is at the hearing at which the decision to be appealed is made.

(2) If the lower court refuses the application for permission to appeal, the application can be renewed to the appeal court in an appellant's notice.[7]

(3) If the application to the appeal court is considered on paper and rejected the prospective appellant is usually[8] entitled to renew the application at an oral hearing, thus giving a possible third attempt at obtaining permission.

(4) If the appeal court on the oral hearing decides to leave over the question of permission to appeal on certain grounds of appeal to the appeal court hearing the full appeal, then the prospective appellant will again have an opportunity to renew his application to renew his application for permission to appeal potentially for the fourth time.

Application to the lower court

14–009 The rules provide that the application for permission to appeal may be made either to the lower court[9] or to the appeal court.[10] Despite this apparent flexibility the first application should usually be made to the lower court.

The Practice Direction to Pt 52 directs that the first application should be made to the lower court.[11] The reasoning for this set out in the commentary in the *White Book* (and has been endorsed by the Court of Appeal[12]) is:

(1) The judge below is fully seised of the matter and so the application will take minimal time. The judge may have already decided that the case raises questions fit for appeal.

---

[7] CPR r.52.3(3).

[8] Subject to the exception where the single Lord Justice considers the application to be totally without merit where a renewed hearing is not available. CPR r.52.3(4A). See paras 14–023 et seq.

[9] An application made other than "at the hearing" will be a nullity. *Jones v T Mobile (UK) Ltd* [2004] EWCA Civ 1162 and *Jackson v Marina Homes* [2007] EWCA Civ 1404.

[10] CPR r.52.3(2).

[11] The "may" in CPR r.52.3 is replaced with "should" in CPR PD 52 para.4.6.

[12] *T (A Child)* [2002] EWCA Civ 1736 at [12]–[13].

(2) An application at that stage involves neither party in any material additional costs.
(3) No harm is done if the application fails because the party may make a further application to the appeal court.
(4) If the application succeeds and the party then decides to appeal he avoids the expensive and time-consuming permission stage in the appeal court.
(5) If the application succeeds and the party then decides not to appeal no harm is done.

For this reason, if there is any possibility that the client will wish to appeal the decision, an advocate should generally obtain in advance instructions to seek permission to appeal assuming the grounds are present and, unless there is good reason not to do so, apply orally for permission to appeal when the judgment is given or handed down.

Generally, it will, for obvious reasons, be easier to persuade the lower court to give permission to appeal on questions of law than on questions of fact or discretionary decisions. The judge may be happy to accept, on difficult points of law, that an appellate court will take a different view. It is much more difficult to persuade a judge that his decision on a question of fact is arguably wrong, or that he has exercised his discretion wrongly.

A further reason: inadequate reasons and clarification of the judgment

As addressed in Chapter 10, a court has the jurisdiction to alter its judg-   **14–010**
ment at any time before the order is sealed.[13]

A further reason for making the first application for permission to appeal to the lower court is that the lower court may in response to the application for permission to appeal respond by amplifying its judgment and obviating the need for an appeal.

This particularly arises where the lower court's judgment might be said to contain inadequate reasons, did not deal with an argument raised by a party or did not take in to account relevant matters.

First, it is a matter of professional duty[13a] to bring such matters to the court's attention at the handing down of judgment. Secondly, there is unlikely to be any tactical advantage in not raising the point at the time because the appeal court may well return the matter to the lower court before determining the permission application. This has been the result in most cases where an appellant has succeeded in asserting that the lower

---

[13] Where a party asks the court to amplify its reasons that jurisdiction is "untrammelled": *Paulin v Paulin* [2009] EWCA Civ 221 at [30(a)].
[13a] *In the matter of S (Children)* [2007] EWCA Civ 694 at [23]–[25]; *In Re T (Contact: Alienation Permission to Appeal)* [2002] EWCA Civ 1736; [2003] 1 F.L.R. 531 at [50]; *In Re M (A Child) (Non Accidental Injury: Burden of Proof)* [2008] EWCA Civ 1261 at [37].

court's judgment did not contain sufficient reasons[14] even after significant delay.[15-19]

14-011   Indeed that may not be the end of the lower court's involvement. The appeal court can on a renewed application for permission to appeal adjourn the application for permission before it and remit the case to the trial judge with an invitation to provide additional reasons for the decision or, where appropriate, the reasons for a specific finding or findings. The source of this jurisdiction has not been determined.

Initially it appeared on one reading of a judgment[20] to derive from CPR r.52.10(2)(b) which includes among the powers of the appeal court the power to refer any claim or issue for determination by the lower court.

However it is perhaps better considered as deriving from the inherent power of the Court of Appeal.[21]

There may be an inherent jurisdiction within the Court of Appeal to refer a decision to the lower court judge for further reasons even after permission to appeal has been granted.[22] If the appeal court holds that the lower court has not made findings on particular issues it may take into consideration a supplementary judgment by the lower court dealing with those issues to the extent that such a judgment would not alter the perfected order.[23]

Where the appeal court is in doubt as to whether the reasons are adequate, it may direct that the renewed application for permission be adjourned to an oral hearing, on notice to the respondent.[24]

Whether or not it is appropriate to refer the matter back to the lower court will inevitably depend on the facts of the case. There is no "normal or default procedure".[24a] Requesting a judge to supplement his judgment a year after it was handed down was criticised in one case, despite the recognised pragmatic benefits in terms of cost savings of so proceeding.[24b] Similarly where permission to appeal has been granted on additional grounds and a judge has already been asked to provide further reasons and declined to do so referring the matter back to the lower court judge may give rise to a risk of ex post facto rationalisation.[24c]

---

[14]   *English v Emery Reimbold & Strick Ltd* [2002] EWCA Civ 605. This is also the position in other areas: on statutory appeals: *Adami v Ethical Standards Officer of the Standards Board for England* [2005] EWCA Civ 1754 at [24]–[25]; in judicial review proceedings: *R. v Higher Education Funding Council Ex p. Institute of Dental Surgery* [1994] 1 W.L.R. 242.

[15-19]   The case was remitted after 18 months in *Adami v Ethical Standards Officer of the Standards Board for England* [2005] EWCA Civ 1754 at [32]–[33].

[20]   *Adami v Ethical Standards Officer of the Standards Board for England* [2005] EWCA Civ 1754 at [20].

[21]   *Aerospace Publishing Ltd v Thames Water Utilities Ltd* [2006] EWCA Civ 717 at [11].

[22]   *Aerospace Publishing Ltd v Thames Water Utilities Ltd* [2006] EWCA Civ 717 at [11], per Rix L.J.

[23]   *Roche v Chief Constable of Greater Manchester Police* [2005] EWCA Civ 1454 at [25]–[27], per Buxton L.J.

[24]   *English v Emery Reimbold & Strick Ltd* [2002] EWCA Civ 605 at [25].

[24a]   *Aerospace Publishing Ltd v Thames Water Utilities Ltd* [2006] EWCA Civ 717 at [17].

[24b]   *Michael Hyde Associates Ltd v JD Williams & Co Ltd* [2001] P.N.L.R. 8 at [20].

[24c]   *Aerospace Publishing Ltd v Thames Water Utilities Ltd* [2006] EWCA Civ 717 at [12] and [13].

TIMING OF THE APPLICATION FOR PERMISSION TO APPEAL TO THE LOWER COURT

The application should be made at the hearing at which the judgment is handed down.[25] The lower court does not have jurisdiction to entertain an application for permission at a new hearing.[26]   **14–012**

Although it is generally prudent to ask for permission to appeal, after an ex tempore judgment it is possible that an advocate may make what in hindsight may not have been the appropriate application for permission to appeal. Equally in the absence of instructions an advocate may not be able to make such submissions. Similar difficulties may arise after the handing down of a reserved judgment.

A solution has been provided by an amendment to the CPR. Paragraph 4.3B of the Practice Direction to Pt 52 permits a party to request the trial judge to adjourn the hearing to give the party an opportunity to apply for permission at a later date.

If no such adjournment is sought because at the time of hearing an appeal was not anticipated then the prospective appellant must make his application to the appeal court unless it is possible to persuade the lower court to order an adjournment of the hearing at which the appeal is handed down retrospectively. There are two conflicting decisions as to whether the court has jurisdiction to do this. This is ripe for determination at appeal level.[27]

Preparation for an application for permission to appeal to the lower court

There is no getting away from the difficulty of formulating grounds of appeal immediately following judgment particularly if attention has been focussed on contentious disputes on costs. A party is well advised to consider in advance of the hearing its intentions in the event that the lower court's decision goes against it and to identify its likely grounds of appeal.   **14–013**

The preparation that a prospective appellant can take before an application for permission to appeal to the lower court will depend on the nature of the issues before the court.

If the substance of the hearing turns on a point of law on which there is no authority from a higher court or two different and apparently conflicting lines of higher authority then this preparation should be relatively straightforward. However where findings of fact or other "judge sensitive" issues arise then the preparation will be more difficult.

An advocate can seek a short adjournment of the hearing in which to take instructions on whether to make an application for permission to appeal. However in reality there is often no available court time. In those

---

[25] CPR r.52.3(2).

[26] *Jackson v Marina Homes* [2007] EWCA Civ 1404; [2008] C.P. Rep. 17 at [4], per Sir Henry Brooke.

[27] *Balmoral Group Ltd v Borealis (UK) Ltd* [2006] EWHC 2228 at [14] where the Court held that it did not have jurisdiction. *Multiplex Construction (UK) Ltd v Honeywell Control Systems Ltd* [2007] EWHC 236; [2007] Bus. L.R. D13 at [19]–[25], per Jackson J.

circumstances unless the advocate is able to formulate his application for permission to appeal with appropriate instructions he should apply for the hearing to be adjourned to a later date to consider the issue of permission to appeal. However, inappropriate applications for such adjournments are likely to be met with subsequent costs sanctions.

At an adjourned hearing to consider the question of permission to appeal the prospective appellant should have had sufficient time to prepare the following documents:

(1) as formal a note of the judgment as possible;
(2) draft grounds of appeal; and
(3) a skeleton argument addressing the grounds of appeal.

Unless the parties have made arrangements for their own transcript it may be that a formal transcript from the official court transcriber may not be available for the restored hearing.

In such cases the appellant should prepare a typed note of the judgment from his own notes of the hearing. The appellant should consider providing a copy of this note to the respondent in advance of the adjourned hearing to invite its agreement. This can avoid subsequent disputes over whether permission was given on the basis of a misleading record of the lower court's judgment.

Where the court reserves its judgment it is likely to circulate a draft in advance of the formal handing down of the judgment some days in advance of the actual handing down of the judgment.

Accordingly the parties should have sufficient time to prepare the same documents for an application for permission to appeal as they would do for an adjourned hearing following an ex-tempore judgment. The prospective appellant should prepare a skeleton argument, grounds of appeal and a note of judgment.

It is a matter for the advocate as to whether or not to provide a copy of the written grounds of appeal to the other side in advance of the formal handing down of the judgment. There are different views. Unless there is a perceived risk that prior submission of the grounds to the judge might adversely affect your client's position on costs arguments then it is appropriate to provide a copy of the same in advance to the court and the other party. This ensures that the court can be addressed properly at the hearing as to whether permission to appeal should be granted. If the decision on costs gives rise to a further ground of appeal then this can be added to the draft grounds of appeal at the hearing.

Form of order on permission to appeal from the lower court

14–014 If an application for permission to appeal is made to the lower court then the judge must specify certain matters in the order.

These are identified in the Practice Direction to Pt 52 para.4.3A as:

(1) whether or not the judgment or order is final;
(2) whether an appeal lies from the judgment or order and, if so, to which appeal court;
(3) whether the court gives permission to appeal; and
(4) if not, the appropriate appeal court to which any further application for permission to appeal may be made.

Where permission to appeal is not required from the lower court, it may give an indication of its opinion as to whether permission should be given.[28]

Application for permission to appeal to the appeal court

There is no appeal from a decision refusing permission to appeal. However a prospective appellant can apply to the appeal court. An application to the appeal court must be in an appellant's notice[29] which must be filed with the correct appeal court. The identification of the correct appeal court is addressed in Chapter 11.

14–015

The party which might wish to appeal

It is not unheard of that both parties are dissatisfied with the lower court's decision. Whether both parties seek permission to appeal from the lower court may depend on the objectives of each party.

14–016

If party B thinks that it might wish to appeal, or to cross-appeal in the event that party A obtains permission to appeal, it can either make its application for permission at the same time as A, or it can leave its application for permission to appeal to a respondent's notice, which must be filed and served within 14 days of (if permission was granted by the lower court) the date of service of A's appellant's notice or (if permission was granted by the appellate court) the date of service of notification of permission to appeal by the appellate court.[30]

Whether B should apply at the same time as A will depend upon whether B wants to seek to appeal in any event, or whether it wants to seek to appeal only if A obtains permission to appeal. For example, B may be happy with the decision, but if the appeal court decides that it was wrong, B would want to persuade the appeal court to enter some different order, or reach the same order but for different reasons. In that case, B's appeal is properly speaking a cross-appeal, and it can be made by way of respondent's notice. If, on the other hand, B is dissatisfied with the decision in any event, then he should apply to the lower court and, if necessary, the appellate court by way of appellant's notice at the same time as A.

---

[28] CPR PD 52 para.4.3.
[29] CPR r.52.3(2)(b) and (3) and CPR PD 52 para.4.7, CPR r.52.4(2).
[30] CPR r.52.5.

Time for application for permission to appeal to appeal court on non-statutory appeals

14–017　There are strict time limits for filing an appellant's notice.
CPR r.52.4(2) provides:

> "(2) The appellant must file the appellant's notice at the appeal court within—
>
> (a) such period as may be directed by the lower court (which may be longer or shorter than the period referred to in sub-paragraph (b)); or
>
> (b) where the court makes no such direction, 21 days after the date of the decision of the lower court that the appellant wishes to appeal."

An appellant's notice must be filed within 21[31] days of the date of the decision of the lower court that the appellant wishes to appeal.[32]

As noted in Chapter 10, time does not run from the date of the Order against which the appellant wishes to appeal, but the date of the judgment. Indeed, if the lower court and/or the parties are dilatory in drawing up or issuing the order following the relevant decision, it is possible for the prospective appellant to find that he must file his appellant's notice before the order against which he wishes to appeal has been issued.

Where the court hands down its judgment but decides to revisit it before the order is perfected or sealed[33] time runs from the date the revised judgment is handed down. As the application for permission to appeal to the appeal court must be contained in the appellant's notice it is this document which must be filed by that time.[34] The contents of the appellant's notice are addressed below.

---

[31] The time was originally 14 days under the CPR and some of the court service leaflets have not updated this information.

[32] A historical summary of the time periods for appeals can be found in the judgment of Brooke L.J. at paras 12–16 of *Sayers v Clarke Walker* [2002] EWCA Civ 645; [2002] 1 W.L.R. 3095. In summary until October 1982 there was a six-week time limit for appealing to the Court of Appeal against final orders and two-week time limit for appeals against interlocutory orders. This was then changed by an amendment to RSC Ord.59 r.4(1) which introduced a standard time limit of four weeks for appealing against all orders unless otherwise provided. The Bowman report considered four weeks was too short and proposed extending it to six weeks for appeals other than appeals against procedural decisions which should be reduced to seven days. The Civil Procedure Rule Committee decided to have a single set of rules and provided initially for 14 days; that was later extended to 21 days.

[33] *Robinson v Fernsby* [2003] EWCA 1820. The same considerations identified in the pre-CPR authority in *Barrell Enterprises, Re* [1973] 1 W.L.R. 19 still apply. "Serious" or "exceptional" reasons are needed before a Court should alter an oral judgment, a draft written judgment or a judgment once handed down. However where the judge unprompted has considered that his decision was wrong before the order is sealed. See "Correcting draft of undelivered judgment" [2004] C.J.Q. 93–96. See paras 11–015 et seq.

[34] CPR r.52.4(1).

If the sealed order is not available at the date the appellant's notice must be filed, the appellant should still file the appellant's notice and explain why the sealed order is not available; give a reasonable estimate of when it can be filed; and file it as soon as reasonably practicable.[35]

The lower court has the power to alter the date the appellant's notice must be filed to a shorter or longer period and so consideration should be given as to whether a longer period of time is required at the time of any refusal of permission to appeal. This is perhaps an obvious point, but it can easily be overlooked at the hearing at which judgment is handed down and permission to appeal from the lower court is refused.

Potential timing difficulties with an application to the appeal court

As set out above, CPR r.52.4(2) provides that an appellant's notice must be filed within 21 days of the date of the decision. The date of the decision is the date of an oral judgment, or where judgment is reserved, the date the judgment is handed down.[36] If the judge in the lower court adjourns the hearing at which the decision is handed down so that permission can be determined at a later date and then refuses permission to appeal, time will still have been running in the intervening period for the purposes of CPR r.52.4(2). Thus the potential appellant may find that by the time his application for permission to appeal is declined by the lower court the time for filing an appellant's notice has also expired.

14–018

This difficulty can be avoided by requesting the lower court to extend the time for filing an appeal notice with the appeal court pursuant to its powers under CPR r.52.4(2)(a) which provides that the lower court may extend the 21 day period.[37] If this is overlooked then that may not be the end of the road. The prospective appellant can do one of two things.

(1) it can file the appellant's notice within time with an undertaking to provide such documents as are not yet drawn up (such as the sealed Order) in due course; or

(2) it can seek an extension of time from the appeal court in its appellant's notice.

---

[35] CPR PD 52 para.5.7.

[36] *Sayers v Clarke Walker* [2002] EWCA Civ 645 at [8]–[9]; *Owusu v Jackson* [2002] EWCA Civ 877 at [24]–[27]. See too CPR r.40.7: (1) A judgment or order takes effect from the day when it is given or made, or such later date as the court may specify; (2) This rule applies to all judgments and orders except those to which r.40.10 (judgment against a State applies). However this does not apply when a draft judgment is provided to the parties in accordance with *Practice Statement (Supreme Court: Judgments) (No.2)* [1999] 1 W.L.R. 1; *Prudential Assurance Co Ltd v McBains Cooper* [2000] 1 W.L.R. 2000.

[37] For example in the case of a reserved judgment where the attendance of the parties is to be excused and one party indicated its intention to seek permission to appeal then after handing down the judgment the judge should have formally adjourned the hearing to give that party the opportunity to apply for permission to appeal and extended the period for filing the notice of appeal for a further three weeks from the date of his refusal of permission. *Jackson v Marina Homes Ltd* [2007] EWCA Civ 1404 at [8].

The first is preferable and avoids the risk that no extension of time will be granted. The difficulty with the second is justifying an extension of time. In this regard the Bowman Report considered that the time limits should not be extended save in exceptional circumstances when a longer time for filing an appeal notice than now exists was envisaged.[38]

The lower court should not normally extend time for filing the appellant's notice by more than 35 days.[39] It is suggested that a good reason will be required to extend time by more than 35 days. The lower court should always bear in mind the importance for case management and the administration of justice generally and requiring the appellant's notice to be issued and filed timeously, whilst all the relevant facts are fresh in the parties' and their representatives' minds.

Lower court's power to retrospectively extend the time for filing an appellant's notice

14–019　It was initially thought that unless the lower court granted an extension of time at the date of handing down judgment then it could not do so subsequently as it had no jurisdiction.[40] However that decision was made without reference to the Court of Appeal decision of *Aujla v Songhera*.[41] That provides that it is open for the trial judge to extend time for filing a notice of appeal even though he has made no such order at the time when he gave his decision as was made clear by Mr Justice Clarke in *Dalkia Utilities Services Plc v Celtech International Ltd (No.2)*.[42]

Applications to the appeal court

14–020　The appeal court is likely to consider the application for permission to appeal on paper based on the contents of the appellant's notice and appeal bundle unless it is considered that the prospective appellant would exercise his right to an oral hearing in any event.

If the appeal court grants permission to appeal on paper then the normal procedures for preparing for the appeal proper apply. These are addressed in Chapter 14 and the time for the respondent to file any respondent's notice commences.

The appeal court may instead direct an oral hearing of the application for permission to appeal which the prospective appellant will be required to attend.

---

[38] paras 56–57: "...There should be realistic time limits. There should be a strong presumption that time limits should not be extended save in exceptional circumstances. A similar view should be taken about all the rules of the Court of Appeal. If they are not complied with, the applicant or appellant should be at risk of having his or her case dismissed or at least being penalised in costs."

[39] CPR 52 PD para.5.19.

[40] *Yorkshire Water Services v Taylor Woodrow* [2004] B.L.R. 409.

[41] [2004] EWCA Civ 121.

[42] [2006] EWHC 63 (Comm).

Where the appeal court refuses permission to appeal it must provide adequate reasons, to comply with art.6 of the ECHR.[43] However, it is not necessary for the reasons to be extensive, and usually they amount to no more than a short paragraph.

Renewing the application to the appeal court for an oral hearing

Assuming that the appeal court refuses the application for permission to appeal on paper in part or in its entirety then, subject to an exception in the Court of Appeal for certain cases, the prospective appellant can request the appeal court to reconsider the application for permission to appeal at an oral hearing.

14–021

The oral hearing may be before the same judge who declined the application for permission to appeal on paper.[44] However in the Court of Appeal, oral applications are generally heard before a constitution of the court without the single Lord Justice who refused permission on paper.[45]

Appellant's additional statement before renewed oral hearing Where permission to appeal has been refused on paper and the prospective appellant seeks to renew his application for permission to appeal at an oral hearing, the appellant must address the reasons given for refusing permission to appeal on paper.

14–022

CPR PD 52.4.14A provides:

"4.14 A(1) This paragraph applies where an appellant, who is represented, makes a request for a decision to be reconsidered at an oral hearing.

(2) The appellant's advocate must, at least 4 days before the hearing, in a brief written statement—

(a) inform the court and the respondent of the points which he proposes to raise at the hearing;

(b) set out his reasons why permission should be granted notwithstanding the reasons given for the refusal of permission; and

(c) confirm where applicable, that the requirements of paragraph 4.17 have been complied with (appellant in receipt of services funded by the Legal Services Commission)."

At least four days before the hearing the prospective appellant is required to file a written statement setting out why permission to appeal should be

---

[43] *Hyams v Plender* [2001] 1 W.L.R. 32 at [17], per Peter Gibson L.J.

[44] *Sengupta v Holmes* [2002] EWCA Civ 1104 at [35]–[40], per Laws L.J. and at [48], per Keene L.J. *Dwr Cymru Cyfyngedig v Albion Water* [2008] EWCA Civ 97 at [9]–[11], per Sir Anthony Clarke M.R.

[45] *White Book*, para.52.3.18.

granted despite the reasons for rejection on paper. This will supplement the skeleton argument which is already likely to have been lodged.

The importance of this has been emphasised by the courts:

> "[the right to renew the application for permission at an oral hearing] is a right which is important but it must not be abused. Obviously, if a judge of this court in his reasoning for provisional refusal has overlooked a relevant consideration or taken account of an irrelevant consideration or otherwise fallen into error, then it is the right and duty of the bar to correct him at the oral hearing. If the member of the bar has nothing new to say that has not been encompassed in his first skeleton argument and considered by the member of the court in his reasoned refusal, there is no discernible purpose in the renewed hearing."[46]

While the respondent is not required to attend the oral hearing, unless directed to, the prospective appellant is still required to provide copies of these documents to him.

At the application itself the appellant's advocate will need to concentrate on making his best points quickly and succinctly, whilst presenting the application fairly, and addressing why the appeal should be permitted despite the reasons given for rejecting permission on paper.

14–023 **The Court of Appeal exception: appeals totally without merit** Although normally an order made on the court's own initiative can be challenged by a party not present under CPR r.3.3(5), CPR r.52.3(4B) disapplies this section and provides that if the Court of Appeal refuses permission on paper and considers the application to be totally without merit it may make an order that the person seeking permission may not request an oral hearing.[47] That order cannot be challenged.

Time for applying to renew application orally

14–024 CPR r.52.3(5) provides that if a party requests an oral hearing, that request must be filed within seven days after service of the notice that permission has been refused. This is amplified in the Practice Direction to Pt 52:

> "4.13 If permission is refused without a hearing the parties will be notified of that decision with the reasons for it. The decision is subject to the appellant's right to have it reconsidered at an oral hearing. This may be before the same judge.
>
> 4.14 A request for the decision to be reconsidered at an oral hearing must be filed at the appeal court within 7 days after service of the

---

[46] *J (A Child), Re* [2001] EWCA Civ 1813 at [4], per Thorpe L.J.
[47] CPR r.52.3(4A).

notice that permission has been refused. A copy of the request must be served by the appellant on the respondent at the same time."

The appeal court has the power to extend this period under CPR r.3.1(2)(a),[48] but applications are likely to be treated with considerable circumspection unless there are strong extenuating circumstances.

Appellant in receipt of LSC funding

Where the application for permission to appeal is refused on paper and the appellant is in receipt of services funded by the Legal Services Commission the appellant must send a copy of the reasons the appeal court gave for refusing permission to the relevant office of the Legal Services Commission as soon as it has been received from the court. The appeal court will require confirmation of this before allowing an oral hearing of the permission application.[49]   **14–025**

Appellant receiving only limited permission to appeal on paper

As discussed in para.13–014, where the court only permits the appellant limited permission to appeal it will either refuse permission on the remaining issues or leave the question of permission to appeal on those issues to the court hearing the appeal.   **14–026**

If permission to appeal is refused without a hearing on certain issues then the appellant must renew his application for an oral hearing within seven days after service of notice of the decision refusing permission to appeal on those issues.

The Practice Direction to Pt 52 para.4.20 makes clear that any application for an extension of time needs to be made promptly and not left over to the appeal hearing proper:

> "The court hearing the appeal on the issues for which permission has been granted will not normally grant, at the appeal hearing, an application to extend the time limit in rule 52.3(5) for the remaining issues."

If the issue of permission to appeal on the remaining issues is leftover to the appeal court then the appellant must within 14 days after service of the court's order inform the appeal court and the respondent in writing whether he intends to pursue the reserved issues at the appeal. If that is the case the time estimate for the appeal must include a time estimate for the reserved issues.[50]

---

[48] *Slot v Isaac* [2002] EWCA Civ 481 at [15].
[49] CPR PD 52 para.4.17.
[50] CPR PD 52 para.4.19.

If the appeal court refuses permission to appeal at an oral hearing then those issues cannot be raised at the appeal hearing.[51]

Failure to attend hearing

14–027   If the appellant fails to attend the oral hearing of his renewed application for permission to appeal he does not have a right to a further hearing. It is a matter for the discretion of the court as to whether to reinstate the application under CPR r.23.11 taking in to account the reasons for the non-appearance, any delay in making the application and the underlying merits of the application.[52]

ROLE OF THE RESPONDENT ON APPELLANT'S APPLICATION FOR PERMISSION TO APPEAL

14–028   Where the appellant files an appellant's notice with the appeal court then the respondent is not formally required, or indeed entitled, to take any steps.

Paragraph 5.22 of the Practice Direction to Pt 52 provides:

"Unless the court otherwise directs a respondent need not take any action when served with an appellant's notice until such time as notification is given to him that permission to appeal has been given."

The role of a prospective respondent will depend on a number of factors, particularly whether he is present at the hearing at which the application for permission to appeal is made and whether he is making an application for permission to appeal as well. However as the Practice Direction to Pt 52 para.4.22 makes clear attendance will be rare:

"4.22 in most cases, applications for permission to appeal will be determined without the court requesting—

(1) submissions from, or
(2) if there is an oral hearing, attendance by the respondent."

---

[51] Access to Justice Act 1999 s.54(4); CPR PD 52 para.4.21.
[52] R. (on the application of Idubo) v Secretary of State for the Home Department [2003] EWCA Civ 1203 at [7], per Pumfrey J.

Submissions or attendance of the respondent at the application for permission to appeal

Where the appellant's application for permission to appeal to the appeal court is refused on paper and the appellant requests an oral hearing then the respondent will be given notice of that hearing.

The respondent is not required to attend that hearing unless the court so directs.[53]

The appeal court may request submissions and/or the attendance of the respondent at the oral hearing of the application for permission to appeal.

Even where not requested by the appeal court the respondent is permitted to file written submissions on whether permission to appeal should be granted and to attend the oral hearing where he may be granted permission to address the court.

The Court of Appeal has provided the following guidance as to such submissions:

> "submissions should be limited to whether the appeal would meet the relevant threshold test or tests i.e. that it has a real prospect of success or there is some other reason for the appeal to be heard for first appeals and whether the appeal raises an important point of principle or practice or there is some other compelling reason for the Court of Appeal to hear it for second appeals.
>
> — if there is a material inaccuracy in the papers placed before the court which might reasonably be expected to lead the court to grant permission when it would not have done so, the respondent should bring this to the Court's attention.
> — such submissions should be in writing where the application is being determined on paper and consideration should be given to written submissions even where there is an oral hearing for permission."[54]

As a matter of practice an advocate for a respondent who makes such submissions can expect to receive a letter from the Court of Appeal asking him to confirm in writing whether or not the submissions comply with this guidance.

A respondent should file any written submissions or skeleton argument as soon as reasonably possible and in good time for the application for permission hearing.[55] A respondent who attends the application for permission

14–029

---

[53] CPR PD 52 para.4.15.
[54] *Jolly v Jay* [2002] EWCA Civ 277 at [44] and [47].
[55] *Philosophy Inc v Ferretti Studio SRL* [2002] EWCA Civ 921; [2003] E.T.M.R. 8 at 40, per Brooke L.J.

to appeal without having first filed a skeleton argument is unlikely to be heard by the court.[56]

The court will not normally allow the respondent his costs if permission is refused unless submissions or attendance were requested by the court. In that case, where permission is refused then the appeal court will normally allow the respondent his costs of preparation.[57]

If the court directs the attendance of the respondent then the appellant must supply the respondent with a copy of the appeal bundle within seven days of being notified of the request unless the court orders a different period. The appellant is required to prepare a copy of the bundle at his own costs, but those costs can subsequently form part of the costs of the permission application.[58]

Application for permission to appeal and appeal heard together

14–030   A respondent may also find that he is present on the application for permission to appeal where the appeal court lists the hearing for permission to appeal with the appeal to follow or that the permission hearing should be on notice to the prospective respondent. In such circumstances the respondent will need to address both the question of permission and the substantive basis of the appeal.

RESPONDENT'S APPLICATION FOR PERMISSION TO APPEAL

14–031   As with the appellant the respondent (as he may later become) may seek permission to appeal either from the lower court and/or the appeal court. As addressed in para.14–016 this will depend on the tactics being deployed.

APPLICATION TO THE LOWER COURT IMMEDIATELY FOLLOWING THE GRANT OF PERMISSION OF APPEAL

14–032   A respondent should make an application to the lower court for permission to appeal. CPR r.52.3 provides:

"52.3 (1) An appellant or respondent requires permission to appeal . . .

---

[56] *Robert Horne Group Plc v Ablett and Ablett* [2003] EWCA Civ 1310 at [14]–[16], per Brooke L.J.
[57] CPR PD 52 paras 4.23–4.24.
[58] CPR PD 52 para.4.16.

(2) An application for permission to appeal may be made—

(a) to the lower court at the hearing at which the decision to be appealed was made; or

(b) to the appeal court in an appeal notice."

CPR r.52.3(2) does not distinguish between an appellant and a respondent in terms of making an application to the lower court and none of the other rules under CPR r.52.3 distinguish between appellant and respondent.

As a matter of proportionality there is no obvious reason why an application for permission to appeal by a respondent should not be made to the lower court immediately following the grant of permission to appeal: the lower court is seised of the matter, knows the issues and is able to make a decision. Indeed all of the reasons that apply to the appropriateness of making the first application to the lower court for an appellant referred to above apply equally to the respondent.

Application to appeal court in respondent's notice

CPR r.52.5(3) requires an application by a respondent for permission to appeal to be contained in a respondent's .   **14–033**

CPR 52.5 provides:

"52.5 (1) A respondent may file and serve a respondent's notice.

(2) A respondent who—

(a) is seeking permission to appeal from the appeal court; or

(b) wishes to ask the appeal court to uphold the order of the lower court for reasons different form or additional to those given by the lower court.

must file a respondent's notice.

(3) Where the respondent seeks permission from the appeal court it must be requested in the respondent's notice."

A respondent who seeks permission to appeal from the appeal court must file a respondent's notice and seek permission to appeal by way of that notice. The contents of a respondent's notice are addressed in Chapter 15. They are very much the same as those required in an appellant's notice.

Test for permission to appeal

As set out in Chapter 12 the criteria for granting permission to appeal are   **14–034**
the same for appellant and respondent although in practice the respondent

may find it easier to obtain permission to appeal on a linked cross-appeal. See para.13–013.

Timetable for filing a respondent's notice

14–035 CPR r.52.5 provides a strict timetable for filing a respondent's notice.

> "52.5(4) A respondent's notice must be filed within—
>
> (a) such period as may be directed by the lower court; or
> (b) where the lower court makes no such direction, 14 days after the date in paragraph (5).
>
> (5) The date referred to in paragraph (4) is
>
> (a) the date the respondent is served with the appellant's notice where—
>
> (i) permission to appeal was given by the lower court; or
> (ii) permission to appeal is not required;
>
> (b) the date the respondent is served with notification that the appeal court has given the appellant permission to appeal; or
> (c) the date the respondent is served with notification that the application for permission to appeal and the appeal itself are to be heard together."

Thus the time for filing a respondent's notice depends on whether permission to appeal was necessary or was granted by the lower court.

If no permission was required or the lower court gave permission to appeal then the respondent must file the respondent's notice within 14 days of service of the appellant's notice.[59]

Where permission to appeal is given by the appellate court, the respondent must file his notice within 14 days of service of the notification from the appellate court that permission to appeal has been granted or that the hearing for permission and the appeal are to be heard together.[60]

There can in practice be quite a delay between the decision to grant permission and receipt of the notice by the respondent. Often, particularly towards the end of term there can be a backlog of orders to be sent out. Once the orders are physically put in the post then another two days will be counted for postal service before the 14 day clock starts counting down.

The lower court has the power to provide a specified period of time for filing the respondent's notice. Where permission to appeal is granted by the lower court a respondent who is likely to require longer than 14 days is well advised to make an application at that stage for additional time. If the

---

[59] CPR rr.52.5(4) and 52.5(5)(a).
[60] CPR rr.52.5(4) and 52.5(5)(b)–(c).

lower court does not provide any direction as to the period in which a respondent's notice must be filed then the default provisions set out above apply.

A respondent can also apply for an extension of time for service of the respondent's notice. This should be done in the respondent's notice. If the time extension is reasonably short and comes with an agreement from the appellant it is likely to be granted. However an application for longer periods such as six weeks would be unlikely to be acceded to unless there was a good reason. The same reasoning as for filing an appellant's notice timeously applies. See para.14–018.

14–036

Subject to any contrary order by the appeal court, the respondent must serve the respondent's notice on the appellant and any other respondent as soon as practicable and in any event not later than seven days after it is filed.[61]

On filing the respondent's notice with the appeal court, the respondent must file two additional copies for the appeal court and further copies for the appellant and any additional respondent(s).[62]

Together with or within 14 days after service of the respondent's notice the respondent must file a skeleton argument addressing the reasons why it is said the appeal court should uphold the lower court's decision on additional and/or different reasons. If, however, the respondent does not wish to do anything other than uphold the decision for the reasons the judge gave, his skeleton argument does not need to be filed until seven days before the appeal.[63]

Respondent's additional duty in the Court of Appeal

The Practice Direction to Pt 52 para.15.6 provides:

14–036A

"15.6 A respondent must, no later than 21 days after the date he is served with notification that—

(1) permission to appeal has been granted; or
(2) the application for permission to appeal and the appeal are to be heard together,
   inform the Civil Appeals Office and the appellant in writing whether—

(a) he proposes to file a respondent's notice appealing the order or seeking to uphold the order for reasons different from, or additional to, those given by the lower court; or
(b) he proposes to rely on the reasons given by the lower court for its decision."

---

[61] CPR r.52.5(6).
[62] CPR PD 52 para.7.10(1).
[63] CPR PD 52 para.7.7(2).

A respondent must notify his intentions in respect of the appeal in writing to the court and to the appellant within 21 days of receipt of notification of permission to appeal or notice that the permission hearing is to be heard at the same time as an appeal. The purpose of this provision is to allow the Court of Appeal to manage the time required for the appeal, and if the respondent does not comply with it, it can cause the Court of Appeal significant difficulties.[64]

PROCEDURAL MATTERS FOLLOWING GRANT OF PERMISSION TO APPEAL

14–037 Where permission to appeal is given by the appeal court and the respondent has not attended then the appeal bundle must be served on each respondent within seven days of receiving the order giving permission to appeal.

APPEALS TOTALLY WITHOUT MERIT

14–038 CPR r.52.10(5)–(6) provides for the court to take certain steps if it considers the appeal totally without merit:

"52.10 (5) If the appeal court—

(a) refuses an application for permission to appeal;
(b) strikes out an appellant's notice;
(c) dismisses an appeal,

and it considers that the application, the appellant's notice or the appeal is totally without merit, the provisions of paragraph (6) must be complied with.

(6) Where paragraph (5) applies—

(a) the court's order must record the fact that it considers the application, the appellant's notice or the appeal to be totally without merit; and
(b) the court must at the same time consider whether it is appropriate to make a civil restraint order."

Essentially there are three types of civil restraint order:

(1) a limited civil restraint order,
(2) an extended civil restraint order; and
(3) a general civil restraint order.

---

[64] *Mlauzi v SSHD* [2005] EWCA Civ 128 at [30]–[31].

A limited restraint order may be made by a judge of any court where a party has made two or more applications which are totally without merit.

An extended civil restraint order may be made by a designated civil judge or his appointed deputy in a county court; a High Court judge; and a Court of Appeal judge where the party has persistently issued claims or made applications which are totally without merit.

A general civil restraint order made be made by the same judges as have the power to make an extended civil restraint order where the party persists in issuing claims or making applications which are totally without merit in circumstances where an extended civil restraint order would not be sufficient or appropriate.

The test of whether or not to make a civil restraint order under CPR r.3.11 is beyond the scope of this work, but the reader is referred to the Practice Direction on Civil Restraint Orders made pursuant to CPR r.3.11 and the commentary in the *White Book*.

GENERAL PROVISIONS RELATING TO STATUTORY APPEALS AND APPEALS BY WAY OF CASE STATED

The Practice Direction to Pt 52 provides general guidance as to these appeals and then specific procedural guidance in respect of particular appeals under statutes to the County Court, High Court and Court of Appeal. While the detail of the procedure relating to such appeals is beyond the scope of this work the following represents a summary of the general procedure set out in the Practice Direction to Pt 52. Further reference should be made to the relevant section of the Practice Direction for more details and the relevant textbooks.   14–039

Time for filing an appellant's notice in statutory appeals

The time for filing an appellant's notice on a statutory appeal is normally 28 days after the date of the decision of the lower court being appealed unless a statement of the reasons for the decision is given later than the notice of the decision in which case the 28 days only starts to run from the date on which the statement of reasons is received by the appellant.[65]   14–040

Where the appeal is against a decision of the Administrative Appeals Chamber of the Upper Tribunal the time for filing the appellant's notice to be filed is 42 days from the date on which the Upper Tribunal's decision on permission to appeal to the Court of Appeal was given. An appeal of a decision of any other Chamber of the Upper Tribunal must be filed within 28 days of the Upper Tribunal's decision on permission to appeal.[66]

---

[65] CPR PD 52 paras 17.3–17.4.
[66] CPR PD 52 para.17.4A.

Service of the appellant's notice in statutory appeals

14–041   The appellant must serve the appellant's notice on the respondent to the appeal and also on the chairman of the tribunal, Minister of State, government department or other person from whose decision the appeal is brought other than when an appeal is against a decision of the Upper Tribunal. Where there is no chairman, the appellant's notice must be served on the member or members of the Tribunal.[67]

Application for additional parties to be heard on statutory appeal

14–042   There is provision for non parties to the appeal to apply to make submissions at the hearing.
  CPR r.52.12A provides:

  "(1) In a statutory appeal, any person may apply for permission—

  (a)   to file evidence; or
  (b)   to make representations at the appeal hearing.

  (2) An application must be made promptly."

The procedures for making such an application are set out at paras 17.7–17.11 of the Practice Direction to Pt 52:

  (1)   An application for permission must be made by letter to the relevant court office, identifying the appeal, explaining who the applicant is and indicating why and in what form the appellant wants to participate in the hearing.
  (2)   If the applicant is seeking a prospective order as to costs, the letter must say what kind of order and on what grounds.
  (3)   Applications to intervene must be made at the earliest reasonable opportunity.
  (4)   Where all the existing parties to the appeal consent to the new party making submissions then the court can deal on paper with the application to file evidence or to make representations at the hearing. Otherwise the application may be dealt with by an oral hearing.
  (5)   Where the court gives permission for a person to file evidence or to make representations at the appeal hearing, it may do so on conditions and may give case management directions.

---

[67] CPR PD 52 para.17.5.

Right of Minister to be heard

Where the appeal is from an order or decision of a Minister of State or government department, the Minister or department is entitled to make representations to the court at the hearing of the appeal.[68]

14–043

Appeals by way of case stated from the Crown Court or Magistrates Court

The procedure for filing to have a case stated for the opinion of the High Court is set out in the Crown Court Rules 1982 and the Magistrates' Courts Rules 1981.

14–044

- Once the stated case is received, the appellant's notice must be filed at the appeal court within 10 days.[69]
- The appellant must file the following documents with his appellant's notice:

(1) the stated case;
(2) a copy of the judgment, order or decision in respect of which the case has been stated; and
(3) where the judgment, order or decision in respect of which the case has been stated was itself given or made on appeal, a copy of the judgment, order or decision appealed from.[70]

- The appellant must serve the appellant's notice and accompanying documents on all respondents within four days after they are filed or lodged with the appeal court.[71]

Appeals by way of case stated by Minister, government department, tribunal or other person

The procedure for stating a case will be set out in the relevant enactment or any rules of procedure relating to the process.

14–045

The party who requested the case to be stated and on whom the stated case was served must file the appellant's notice and the stated case at the appeal court and serve copies of the notice and stated case on the Minister, tribunal etc. who stated the case and every party to the proceedings to which the stated case relates within 14 days of service of the stated case.[72]

---

[68] CPR PD 52 para.17.6.
[69] CPR PD 52 para.18.4.
[70] CPR PD 52 para.18.5.
[71] CPR PD 52 para.18.6.
[72] CPR PD 52 para.18.11.

If this is not done then any other person served by the Minister, tribunal, etc as an interested party may file an appellant's notice with the stated case within 14 days from the last day on which the party on whom the stated case was served should have filed an appellant's notice.

Where the Minister or tribunal is permitted to state a case or refer a question of law without a request then it must file an appellant's notice and serve copies on all interested parties within 14 days of stating the case.[73]

---

[73] CPR PD 52 para.18.12.

CHAPTER 15

Preparation for an Appeal

This chapter addresses the various steps in the preparation for an appeal   **15–001**
hearing. These are addressed in the following order:

(1) Preparation of the appellant's notice.
(2) The respondent's role before permission to appeal is given.
(3) The respondent's duties following the grant of permission to appeal and preparation of the respondent's notice.
(4) General guidance on document preparation.
(5) General provisions about statutory appeals and appeals by way of case stated.
(6) Preparing for oral submissions to the appeal court.

There is a table setting out the key procedural steps at the end of this chapter.

THE JUDGMENT

Unless seeking to appeal a judgment handed down in writing, the first step   **15–002**
for the appellant will be to obtain a transcript or other note of the judgment.

Transcript of judgment

The parties will need to obtain a copy of the judgment for the purposes of   **15–003**
the appeal.

The Practice Direction to Pt 52 provides that where the judgment has been officially recorded by the court, an approved transcript of that record should be used and that it should be an original approved transcript.

"Suitable record of the judgment

5.12 Where the judgment to be appealed has been officially recorded by the court, an approved transcript of that record should accompany the appellant's notice. Photocopies will not be accepted for this purpose ..."

For judgments delivered in the Royal Courts of Justice, the appellant should ask the Mechanical Recording Office to prepare the transcript. In other courts, the appellant should make enquiries of the court staff as to how to obtain a copy.

The appellant should request a copy of the transcript as quickly as possible, because the time taken for preparation of a transcript can take a significant time.

Options where no transcript available

15–004   Where there is no officially recorded judgment there are a number of options, which are identified as being acceptable by the practice direction to Pt 52.[1]

Written judgment

15–005   The preferred option in the absence of the availability of a transcript is a copy of the written judgment endorsed with the judge's signature. This is quite unusual in the Royal Courts of Justice, but more usual in County Courts and District Registries.

Note of judgment

15–006   If there is no written judgment, then a note of the judgment needs to be prepared and put before the lower court judge for approval. If one or more of the parties are represented the Practice Direction to Pt 52 para.5.14 provides that the advocates' brief or, where appropriate, refresher includes remuneration for taking a note of the judgment and taking steps[2] to have it approved by the judge.

Judge's note

15–007   If no note has been taken by either party (which would be surprising) then in the County Court a party may apply to the judge to prepare a "judge's

---

[1] CPR PD 52 para.5.12.
[2] These are identified in the practice direction as including having the note transcribed accurately; attempting to agree the note with the other parties (if represented); submitting the note to the judge for approval where appropriate; revising it if so requested by the judge; providing copies to the appeal court, instructing solicitors and lay client; and providing a copy of the note to an unrepresented opposing party.

note on appeal" pursuant to s.80 of the County Courts Act 1984 which provides:

"Judge's note on appeal

80(1) At the hearing of any proceedings in a county court in which there is a right of appeal or from which an appeal may be brought with leave, the judge shall, at the request of any party, make a note—

    (a) of any question of law raised at the hearing; and
    (b) of the facts in evidence in relation to any such question; and
    (c) of his decision on any such question and of his determination of the proceedings.

(2) Where such a note has been taken, the judge shall (whether notice of appeal has been served or not), on the application of any party to the proceedings, and on payment by that party of such fee as may be prescribed by an order under section 92 of the Courts Act 2003 (fees), furnish him with a copy of the note, and shall sign the copy, and the copy so signed shall be used at the hearing of the appeal."

As at October, 2010 the relevant Fees Order is the Civil Proceedings Fees Order 2008 (SI 2008/1053), as amended, which provides fees for both High Court and County Court processes. This is likely to be updated on a regular basis and reference should be made to the current statutory instrument for guidance as to applicable fees.

SEALED COPY OF THE ORDER BEING APPEALED AND ORDER GIVING/REFUSING PERMISSION TO APPEAL

The appellant must include with his appeal notice a sealed copy of the relevant orders: **15–008**

    (1) A copy of the order being appealed must be included.
    (2) If permission to appeal has been granted or refused a copy of that order together with a copy of the judge's reasons for allowing or refusing permission to appeal should also be included.[3]
    (3) Where the decision being appealed was itself made on appeal in addition to the above documents, the following will need to be included:

        (a) the original order of the lower court;
        (b) the reasons given; and
        (c) the appellant's notice used to appeal from that order.[4]

---

[3] CPR PD 52 para.5.6(2)(d)–(e).
[4] CPR PD 52 para.5.6A(1)(i).

(4) For judicial review and statutory appeals the original decision which was the subject of the application to the lower court must be included in the appeal bundle.[5]

(5) Where the appeal is from a tribunal, the appeal bundle should contain:

(a) a copy of the tribunal's reasons for the decision;
(b) a copy of the decision reviewed by the tribunal;
(c) the reasons for the original decision; and
(d) any document filed with the tribunal setting out the grounds of appeal from that decision.

TRANSCRIPTS OF EVIDENCE IF RELEVANT

15–009 Where the evidence is relevant[5a] to the appeal an official transcript of the relevant evidence is required.

The Practice Direction to Pt 52 provides:

> "5.15 When the evidence is relevant to the appeal an official transcript of the relevant evidence must be obtained. Transcripts or notes of evidence are generally not needed for the purpose of determining an application for permission to appeal."

Where a transcript cannot be obtained notes of the evidence are permissible. However notes of evidence are not those of the parties, but a typed version of the judge's notes as made clear by the Practice Direction:

> "5.16 If evidence relevant to the appeal was not officially recorded, a typed version of the judge's notes of evidence must be obtained."

As with the transcript of the judgment early application for the transcripts of evidence to the relevant bodies referred to in para.15–003 should be made because of the problems associated with delay in their preparation.

---

[5] CPR PD 52 para.5.6A(1)(j).

[5a] Care should be taken to consider whether a transcript is necessary. A transcript of an interlocutory hearing will only be justifiable for the purposes of an appeal in exceptional cases such as to show that an argument which is said to have been taken was not raised, to establish that some concession was or was not made, or to show some misconduct or misunderstanding on the part of somebody at the hearing and then only when the relevant facts could not be agreed and only that part of the transcript as required. *Matthew Fiddes v Channel Four Television Corp, Studio Lambert Ltd and Preston* [2010] EWCA Civ 730 at [13] and [14], per Lord Neuberger.

Obtaining copies of the transcript at public expense

It is open to the lower court or appeal court to certify for those that cannot meet the costs of a transcript that one copy should be provided at public expense.   **15–010**

The Practice Direction to Pt 52 sets out the criteria:

> "**Transcripts at public expense**
>
> 5.17 Where the lower court or the appeal court is satisfied that—
>
> (1) an unrepresented appellant; or
> (2) an appellant whose legal representation is provided free of charge to the appellant and not funded by the Community Legal Service;
>
> is in such poor financial circumstances that the cost of a transcript would be an excessive burden the court may certify that the cost of obtaining one official transcript should be borne at public expenses.
>
> 5.18 In the case of a request for an official transcript of evidence or proceeding to be paid for at public expense, the court must also be satisfied that there are reasonable grounds for appeal. Whenever possible a request for a transcript at public expenses should be made to the lower court when asking for permission to appeal."

These narrow criteria are therefore:

(1) the party must be a litigant in person or if represented then on a pro bono basis;
(2) the prospective appellant must have reasonable grounds for his appeal; and
(3) the cost of obtaining a transcript would pose an excessive burden on the prospective appellant.

An application for the transcript should be made to the lower court when asking for permission to appeal. This means that in proving that there are reasonable grounds of appeal the prospective appellant must articulate his or her grounds without a transcript of the judgment or where appropriate the evidence. The possible unfairness of this position was raised by the prospective appellant in *Perotti v Westminster City Council*[6] without success. The lower court judge rejected the argument on the basis that the main complaint against the lower court's decision was an alleged violation of the prospective appellant's right to a fair and impartial hearing and that he did

---

[6] [2005] EWCA Civ 581; [2005] C.P. Rep. 38.

not need the transcript in order to settle grounds of appeal on this basis. The Court of Appeal upheld the order.[7]

THE APPELLANT'S NOTICE

15–011 The appellant's notice is the originating document for both an application for permission to appeal to the appeal court and the appeal.

The appellant's notice is on a standard form, Form N161 for all appeals other than appeals in the small claims track which use Form N164.

Form N161 contains guidance as to its completion. Additional guidance leaflets are available on the Courts Service website and should also be available at no charge from any county court and from the Clerk of the Lists General Office/Appeals Office, Royal Courts of Justice, Strand WC2A 2LL. Practitioners will find a copy on the Forms CD-Rom which comes with the *White Book*.

Completing the appellant's notice is for the most part relatively straightforward; although one practical problem that often arises is that the Form N161 does not provide sufficient space for the details relevant to the appeal particularly where there are multiple parties.

The guidance makes clear that any additional information can be provided on a separate sheet of paper.

If this is done then it is very important that each additional sheet is securely attached to the appeal notice and marked with sufficient details of the claim—including in particular the claim number—so that if the additional sheet(s) get separated from the appellant's notice there is at least some means of them being reunited.

There are strict time limits for filing the appellant's notice. These are addressed in Chapter 13. For almost all non-statutory appeals the appellant's notice must be filed within 21 days of the decision of the lower court or such later date as the court may order. For statutory appeals the time can be longer and reference should be made to the relevant statute or rules.

The sealed appellant's notice must be served on all respondents as soon as practicable and in any event within seven days of filing.[8] A draft notice is not sufficient. There is a material difference between notice of an intimated appeal and the fact that an appeal is pending.[9] If there has been a failure to

---

[7] The facts of that case were somewhat unique in that the grounds of appeal for Mr Perotti's challenge were not a challenge to a finding of fact or law, but rather a challenge to the procedure, by the time of the appeal Mr Perotti was the subject of a civil restraint order, appeared to have been permitted to use his own tape recorder at the hearing, had not sought a copy of the judgment from counsel instructed by Westminster City Council and the decision was made after the Court of Appeal had in fact ordered that a transcript be prepared at public expense.

[8] CPR r.52.4.

[9] *Regional Court in Konin, Poland (A Polish Judicial Authority) v Walerianczyk* [2010] EWHC 2149 (Admin) August 12, 2010 at [13], per Stanley Burnton L.J. and at [44] and [46], per Nicol J. in the context of an extradition appeal where the time limits for an appeal are limited under s.28 of the Extradition Act 2003.

apply the court stamp then that may be a deficiency curable under CPR r.3.10.[10]

The appellant's notice must contain and/or be accompanied by a number of additional documents which are addressed below.

GROUNDS OF APPEAL

A document containing the grounds of appeal is mandatory in every appeal. **15–012** They are an essential part of the appellant's notice[11] and a respondent's notice where the respondent wishes the appeal court to vary the order of the lower court in any way.[12]

The Practice Direction to Pt 52 provides the following guidance to the contents of grounds of appeal:

> "3.1 Rule 52.11(3)(a) and (b) sets out the circumstances in which the appeal court will allow an appeal.
>
> 3.2 The grounds of appeal should—
>
> (1) set out clearly the reasons why rule 52.11(3)(a) or (b) is said to apply; and
> (2) specify, in respect of each ground, whether the ground raises an appeal on a point of law or is an appeal against a finding of fact."

The grounds of appeal should set the basis for and the extent of the appeal. They should identify succinctly and precisely why the appeal court can and should interfere with the decision of the lower court. They must set out why the appellant or, in the case of a cross-appeal, the respondent:

(1) has grounds for asking the appeal court to review the decision of the lower court, and
(2) identify whether it is the appellant's case that the decision of the lower court was "wrong" and/or was unjust because of a serious procedural or other irregularity.

As addressed in Chapter 2, a decision is "wrong" if the lower court erred in law, erred in fact or erred (to the appropriate extent) in the exercise of its discretion. Accordingly if the ground of appeal is that part of the decision is

---

[10] *Regional Court in Konin, Poland (A Polish Judicial Authority) v Walerianczyk* [2010] EWHC 2149 (Admin); August 12, 2010 at [33], per Stanley Burnton L.J. and at [44], per Nicol J.

[11] s.6 of Form N161 provides that the appellant must set out on a separate sheet in numbered paragraphs the Grounds of Appeal.

[12] CPR PD 52 para.7.1 emphasises that the respondent in such circumstances must obtain permission and prepare grounds of appeal as the appellant does.

"wrong" the grounds of appeal must address the part of the decision said to be wrong and identify:

(1) in what way it is said to be wrong—i.e. an error of law, an error of fact and/or an error in the exercise of discretion; and

(2) why it is wrong.

As also addressed in Chapter 2, a decision is "unjust" because of a serious procedural or other irregularity if it has caused the decision of the lower court to be unjust. If the ground of appeal is that part of the decision arose out of a serious procedural or other irregularity then:

(1) the nature of the irregularity; and

(2) how that irregularity caused the decision of the lower court to be unjust,

must be set out.

Importance of the grounds of appeal

15–013   The grounds of appeal are likely to be the first document considered by the appeal court and consequently well settled grounds of appeal are likely to enhance the prospects of succeeding on the appeal.

Drafting grounds of appeal

15–014   The structure and length of the grounds of appeal will depend on the decision of the lower court.

The emphasis will always be on keeping them succinct. A failure to do so is likely to meet with criticism and is unlikely to assist the appellant's case. The appeal courts are not averse to expressing criticism where the grounds of appeal are unnecessarily long:

> "...this was then followed by professionally drafted grounds of appeal, of inordinate length (28 pages) and a skeleton argument of about the same length, both settled by Counsel ... These took a variety of points, but their length and complication was such as to make it more likely to confuse than to enlighten the reader as to what were the real issues in the case."[13]

However in the desire for succinctness it is important not to omit an issue upon which the appeal is to be put. The appellant will need to obtain the permission of the appeal court to rely on additional points not included in the grounds of appeal.

---

[13] *In the matter of Southill Finance Ltd* [2009] EWCA Civ 2 at [18].

The inclusion of additional points in the skeleton argument accompanying the grounds of appeal is not an appropriate way of including additional points.[14]

Distinguishing between errors of fact and the exercise of discretion

As discussed in more detail in Chapter 3, one common problem arising in settling grounds of appeal is the distinction between an error of fact and an exercise of discretion.   15–015

This problem arises because many decisions of fact require a judge to assess and balance a large number of factors which may be perceived to be an exercise of discretion.

Distinguishing between a true error of fact and an exercise of discretion is critical: the test applied by the appeal court is different as considered in Chapter 3.

The distinction was emphasised by Lord Justice Waller in *Manning v Stylianou*[15] where he sought to correct what he feared was then a growing tendency among practitioners to equate "the generous ambit" test used in respect of challenges to exercises of discretion to the test to be used in respect of challenges on appeals of fact based possibly on a misunderstanding of a judgment in an earlier Court of Appeal case.[16]

An area where this problem has arisen is in appeals involving decisions on applications to strike out for abuse of process. In such cases the lower court is required to take in to account a number of factors in considering whether the claim amounts to an abuse of process. However the actual decision as to whether an abuse of process has occurred is a decision of fact.[17] Accordingly an appeal court will apply the test on appeal as to whether the decision was wrong as a matter of fact and interfere with the decision of the lower court where the judge has taken in to account immaterial factors, omitted to take account of material factors, erred in principle or come to a conclusion that was impermissible or not open to him or her rather than approaching it as a matter of discretion.[18]

---

[14] *Levicom International Holdings BV & Levicom Investments Curacao NV v Linklaters* [2010] EWCA Civ 494 at [278]–[281], per Lloyd L.J.
[15] *Manning v Stylianou* [2007] EWCA Civ 1655 at [19].
[16] The judgment of Ward L.J. in *Assicurazioni Generali SpA v Arab Insurance Group* [2002] EWCA Civ 1642.
[17] *Aldi Stores Ltd v WSP Group Plc* [2008] 1 W.L.R. 748 at [16].
[18] *Aldi Stores Ltd v WSP Group Plc* [2008] 1 W.L.R. 748 at [16].

SKELETON ARGUMENT

15–016   Skeleton arguments are required from all represented appellants and almost[19] all respondents who wish to address the appeal court. While unrepresented appellants and respondents are not required to, they are encouraged to.[19a]

Section 6 of Form N161 provides room for a skeleton argument. The form notes that where there is insufficient space that a skeleton argument in support of the grounds of appeal should be provided on a separate sheet. In fact, almost always the skeleton argument will be set out in a separate document. There is a standard court form for a skeleton argument (Form N163) however usually an advocate prepares the skeleton argument from scratch, bearing the full court heading and "applicant's skeleton argument" in tramlines.

The purpose of the skeleton argument

15–017   The skeleton argument is intended to identify those points which are, and those that are not, in issue, and in relation to those points which are in issue the nature of the argument.

Contents of the skeleton argument

15–018   The importance of the skeleton argument cannot be overstated. It will have been read by each appellate judge before the hearing, and it is the appellant's first and best chance to convince the appellate court of the merits of the appeal or application for permission to appeal. The skeleton should identify concisely the nature of the case generally and those background facts relevant to the appeal, the propositions of law relied on with reference to the relevant authorities, and the submissions to be made with reference to the appeal. The CPR does provide some guidance. The Practice Direction to Pt 52 addresses skeleton arguments at paras 5.9–5.11.

Point by point approach

15–019   Paragraph 5.10 of the Practice Direction to Pt 52 provides:

> "5.10(1) A skeleton argument must contain a numbered list of the points which the party wishes to make. These should both define and confine the areas of controversy. Each point should be stated as concisely as the nature of the case allows."

---

[19] The exception is a respondent to an appeal from a claim allocated to the small claims track which is to be heard in a county court or the High Court—CPR PD 52 para.7.7A(1).
[19a] CPR PD 52 paras 5.9(3) (appellant) and 7.7A(2) (respondent).

So the skeleton argument should attempt to make one point in each paragraph and to ensure a coherent structure that allows the reader to tie in the skeleton to the grounds of appeal. The use of headings as signposts can assist in achieving this objective. The skeleton argument must be in numbered paragraphs.

Use of abbreviations

The use of abbreviations such as "C" for claimant or "A" for appellant and abbreviated references to bundles and dates is sensible so long as they are clear from the skeleton. Reference should be made to the particular practice guides for the court in which the appeal is to be heard for the preferences of the court.

15–020

References to documents

References to documents relied on by a party should, if possible, be included in the body of the skeleton. The Practice Direction to Pt 52 provides:

15–021

> "5.10(2) A numbered point must be followed by a reference to any document on which the party wishes to rely."

This gives rise to a practical point: the skeleton argument will probably not be capable of being finalised until the appeal bundle has been put together and given page numbers. Therefore, when preparing an appeal, consideration needs to be given at an early stage to what documents need to go into the appeal bundle, so that it can be prepared as soon as possible. There is, as discussed in para.15–027, an extra 14 days allowed to file the skeleton argument, so if necessary page numbers can be inserted at this stage.

Time estimates and pre-reading

It is a requirement for skeleton arguments filed in the Court of Appeal that the appellant identifies in the first paragraph of the skeleton the advocate's time estimate for the hearing of the appeal.[20] In appeals to other courts the advocate should also consider including this information. In addition all courts are grateful for assistance in essential pre-reading, particularly if there are important documents that the court might otherwise not consider and particularly if the documents are voluminous.

15–022

Reference to authorities

The Practice Direction to Pt 52 para.5.10(3) provides the following guidance:

15–023

---

[20] CPR PD 52 para.5.10(7).

"(3) A skeleton argument must state, in respect of each authority cited—

    (a) the proposition of law that the authority demonstrates; and

    (b) the parts of the authority (identified by page or paragraph references) that support the proposition.

(4) If more than one authority is cited in support of a given proposition, the skeleton argument must briefly state the reason for taking that course.

(5) The statement referred to in sub-paragraph (4) should not materially add to the length of the skeleton argument but should be sufficient to demonstrate, in the context of the argument—

    (a) the relevance of the authority or authorities to that argument; and

    (b) that the citation is necessary for a proper presentation of that argument."

This reflects the Practice Direction on the Citation of Authorities introduced by the Lord Chief Justice on April 9, 2001. Its purpose was to reduce the burden on the courts of over citation of inappropriate and unnecessary authorities. The practice direction provides further guidance and identifies authorities that should not be cited or only cited in limited circumstances:

    (1) Unless the judgment clearly indicates that it purports to establish a new principle or to extend the present law and (for judgments following the practice direction) the judgment provides an express statement to that effect, the following judgments should not be cited as authorities:

        (a) judgments on applications attended by one party only;

        (b) applications for permission to appeal;

        (c) decisions on applications that only decide that the issue is arguable;

        (d) county court cases (unless to demonstrate the conventional measure of damages in a personal injury case or cited in a county court to demonstrate current authority at that level on an issue in respect of which no decision at a higher level of authority is available).

    (2) Where a judgment contents any indication that the court was only applying decided law to the facts of the particular case or otherwise as not extending or adding to the existing law the advocate seeking to cite such a case must justify the decision to cite it.

This does not in any way dilute the duty of an advocate to draw the attention of the court to any authority not cited by an opponent which is adverse to the case being advanced.

Hierarchy of reported cases

If a case is reported in the official Law Reports published by the Incorpo-   **15–024**
rated Council of Law Reporting for England and Wales that report should
be cited in preference to others. Where a decision of the Court of Appeal
given after January 10, 2001 is to be cited the system of neutral citation
numbers should be used.[21]

Length of skeleton arguments

The length of the skeleton will inevitably depend on the nature of the issues   **15–025**
in dispute. However it is important to remember that the skeleton argument
is not intended as a replacement for oral advocacy and the document should
be concise.

The Chancery Guide provides that a skeleton argument for any matter
including a trial should "be as brief as the nature of the issues allows—it
should not normally exceed 20 pages of double-spaced A4 paper and in
many cases it should be much shorter than this".[22]

The skeleton argument for an appeal should in most cases be considerably less long. Cases where the skeleton arguments have stretched
beyond 50 and even 100 pages have received strong criticism.[23] The following extract from the judgment of the Court of Appeal is an important
indication of what is—and is not—expected:

> "125. Practitioners who ignore practice directions on skeleton argu-
> ments (see CPR PD 52 para.5.10: "Each point should be stated as
> concisely as the nature of the case allows") and do so without the
> imposition of any formal penalty are well advised to note the risk of
> the court's negative reaction to unnecessarily long written submissions.
> The skeleton argument procedure was introduced to assist the court, as
> well as the parties, by improving preparations for, and the efficiency of,
> adversarial oral hearings, which remain central to this court's public
> role.
>
> 126. We remind practitioners that skeleton arguments should not be
> prepared as verbatim scripts to be read out in public or as footnoted
> theses to be read in private. Good skeleton arguments are tools with

---

[21] *Practice Direction (Judgments: Neutral Citations)* [2002] 1 W.L.R. 346.
[22] Chancery Guide App.7.
[23] *Tombstone Ltd v Raja* [2008] EWCA Civ 1444 in response to a 110 page skeleton
argument with a further 64 pages of appendices. *Midgulf International Ltd v Groupe
Chimique Tunisien* [2010] EWCA Civ 66; *The Times*, March 3, 2010 where the first
skeleton argument of 132 pages was supplemented by a further 30 page skeleton argument,
the appellant already having been directed by the supervising Lord Justice to produce a
proper summary of its argument. Criticism has also been meted out in *Leicester Circuits
Ltd v Coates Brothers Plc* [2002] EWCA Civ 474 at [5] in respect of a 64 page skeleton
argument and in *Speymill Contracts Ltd v Baskind* [2010] EWCA Civ 120 (albeit sotto
voce) at [26] and [27] of Lord Justice Jackson's judgment.

practical uses: an agenda for the hearing, a summary of the main points, propositions and arguments to be developed orally, a useful way of noting citations and references, a convenient place for making cross references, a time-saving means of avoiding unnecessary dictation to the court and laborious and pointless note taking by the court.

127. Skeleton arguments are aids to oral advocacy. They are not written briefs which are used in some jurisdictions as substitutes for oral advocacy. An unintended and unfortunate side effect of the growth in written advocacy (written opening and closing submissions and "speaking notes", as well as skeleton arguments) has been that too many practitioners at increased cost to their clients and diminishing assistance to the court, burden their opponents and the court with written briefs. They are anything but brief. The result is that there is no real saving of legal costs, or of precious hearing, reading and writing time. As has happened in this case, the opponent's skeleton argument becomes longer and the judgment reflecting written submissions tends to be longer than is really necessary to explain to the parties why they have won or lost an appeal.

128. The skeletal nature of written advocacy is in danger of being overlooked. In some cases we are weighed down by the skeleton arguments and when we dare to complain about the time they take up, we are sometimes told that we can read them "in our own time" after the hearing. In our judgment, this is not what appellate advocacy is about, or ought to be about, in this court."[24]

A well crafted skeleton is likely to be of significant use by a judge in preparing the court's judgment. Thus care must be given that the drive for conciseness does not lead to the omission of material and useful matters in the skeleton that may provide a useful template for the court in its judgment. Determining the appropriate contents will be a matter of judgment based on the particular needs and features of the case and the advocate's own experience.

Costs sanctions

15–026 Unless an advocate complies with the requirements set out in the Practice Direction to Pt 52 (i.e. in respect of numbered paragraphs, cross referencing and proper citation of authorities) then the default position is that the costs of preparing the skeleton will not be recoverable.

The Practice Direction to Pt 52 para.5.10(6) provides:

"(6) The cost of preparing a skeleton argument which—

---

[24] *Tombstone Ltd v Raja* [2008] EWCA Civ 1444 at [125]–[128]; [2009] 1 W.L.R. 1143 and [2009] C.R. Rep. 18.

(a) does not comply with the requirements set out in this paragraph; or

(b) was not filed within the time limits provided by this Practice Direction (or any further time granted by the court),

will not be allowed on assessment except to the extent that the court otherwise directs."

An advocate who has filed a skeleton late or recognises that it does not comply with para.5.10 is well advised if successful at appeal to seek a direction that notwithstanding para.5.10(6) of the Practice Direction to Pt 52 his or her client should still be entitled to recover the costs of preparing the skeleton should there be good reasons for making such an application.

Filing the skeleton argument

The appellant's skeleton argument must be filed with the appellant's notice or, where it is impracticable to do so, within 14 days of filing the appellant's notice.[25] Like the appellant's notice, it must be served on all respondents.[26]   15–027

CHRONOLOGY, DRAMATIS PERSONAE AND GLOSSARY OF TERMS

Paragraph 5.11 of the Practice Direction to Pt 52 makes it the appellant   15–028
advocate's responsibility to consider what other information the appeal court will need including whether a list of persons featuring in the case (the successor to the dramatis personae) and a chronology of relevant events will assist. The preparation of the chronology may well avoid interruptions of the advocate during oral submissions thus allowing the appellant to develop the submissions in accordance with his intended plan. Even if there are judicial interruptions then it allows for an easy response by reference to the relevant document. Glossaries of complicated terms and a dramatis personae have similar benefits. If such documents are to be prepared the advocate needs to be careful in the preparation of these as they should be neutral documents.

THE APPEAL BUNDLE

The appellant needs to give careful thought to preparation of the appeal   15–029
bundle. An untidy or disorganised bundle or a bundle containing duplicated

---

[25] CPR PD 52 para.5.9.
[26] CPR PD 52 para.5.9.

documents or omitting important documents may be rejected by the court; even if it is not rejected, it will undoubtedly irritate the appellate court before it has even started reading the papers. By contrast, a tidy, well ordered, sensibly arranged bundle will be easier to read and welcomed.

The contents of the appeal bundle will depend on the appeal. There are certain mandatory documents identified by para.5.6A of the Practice Direction to Pt 52 (the preparation of which has already been addressed above): the sealed appellant's notice; the skeleton argument (unless it is coming within the next 14 days, in which case space must be left for it); a sealed copy of the order being appealed; a copy of any order giving or refusing permission to appeal together with the judge's reasons; a transcript or note of judgment; and any relevant transcript or note of evidence.

15–030   There are detailed requirements in para.15.4 of the Practice Direction to Pt 52 which apply to preparation of appeal bundles filed for the Court of Appeal, but they set out good practice to follow for other courts too.

The bundle needs to have dividers and an index. Careful thought needs to be given to the index and dividers. If permission to appeal is granted, then the appellant will need to update the bundle with a copy of the order giving permission to appeal, any respondents' notices, and the respondents' skeleton arguments. It is worth thinking about where they will go at the outset. While the precise order of documents specific to the appeal will depend on the nature of the appeal, the core documents will normally be placed in the appeal bundle in the following order:

(1) The appellant's grounds of appeal and skeleton argument and if contained outside of the appeal notice, then the appeal notice as well.

(2) The respondent's grounds of appeal (if any) and skeleton argument and respondent's notice where appropriate.[27]

(3) Any agreed documents necessary for the appeal such as a chronology, dramatis personae and glossary of essential terms.

(4) The order granting permission to appeal and if at an oral hearing the transcript or note of the judgment giving permission to appeal.[28]

(5) If necessary the relevant parts of the transcript of evidence from the lower court.

(6) Statements of case. Where relevant to the appeal the appeal bundle should also include the claim form, statements of case and any application notice or case management documentation that is relevant to the appeal[29]:

(a) It is important that only pleadings or other documents relevant to the appeal should be included; it is not necessary to copy the whole of the solicitor's pleading bundles, or the case

---

[27] CPR PD 52 para.6.3A(1).
[28] CPR PD 52 para.6.3A(1).
[29] CPR PD 52 para.5.6A(1)(g)–(h).

management bundle, and unnecessary inclusion of pleadings or orders will give rise to criticism.

(b) Pleadings should be assembled in "chapter" form with the claim form followed by the particulars of claim, further information, defence etc. Any overtaken or unnecessary documents should be omitted.[30]

(7) Relevant directions. The appellant must include a copy of the order allocating a case to a track if any.[31]

(8) Contract(s) if necessary or relevant to the appeal.

(9) Other relevant documents: The appeal bundle should only include affidavits, witness statements, summaries, experts' reports and exhibits relevant to the lower court decision where these are directly relevant to the subject matter of the appeal.[32]

(10) Affidavits/witness statements in support of applications: The appellant should include with his appeal notice and in the appeal bundle any affidavit or witness statement filed in support of any application included in the appeal notice.[33] Applications are discussed further in chapter 16.

(11) Party to party correspondence is unlikely to be required. If any is to be included then only those letters that will need to be referred to should be copied.[34] It may be sensible to have available in the Court copies of potentially relevant inter-solicitor correspondence in the event that unexpectedly it becomes necessary to refer to parts of the correspondence.

(12) Original documents should not be placed in the bundles of documents other than the transcript of the court's decision and, where appropriate, of the evidence. The bundles lodged with the court may well end up being destroyed after the hearing. Originals of essential documents should be brought to the hearing. If they are handed up during the course of the hearing, they must be retrieved at the end of the hearing.[35]   **15–031**

(13) No documents within the bundle should be stapled.

(14) Documents should not be printed on both sides (unlike in the Supreme Court).

(15) The bundle needs to be paginated.

(16) The bundle needs to have a spine which identifies, correctly but concisely, the name of the case, its claim number and, if possible, the appeal number. It is preferable for the bundle to be labelled on the front cover too; and for it to have a sticker or other label on the

---

[30] CPR PD 52 para.15.4(9). So earlier versions of the particulars of claim can be omitted unless relevant to the appeal. Equally where a response to a request for further information contains or makes clear the nature of the original request, the request can be omitted.

[31] CPR PD 52 para.5.6(2)(g).

[32] CPR PD 52 para.5.6A(2).

[33] CPR PD 52 para.5.6(2)(f).

[34] CPR PD 52 para.15.4(11).

[35] CPR PD 52 para.15.11C(2).

inside front left hand side of the bundle, so that the judge can see what bundle he is reading when it is open.

(17) Finally, and importantly, the bundles should not be over-filled. The Commercial Court Guide suggests that no bundle should contain more than 300 pages[36] and it is suggested that this guidance should be followed for appeal bundles too. A bundle which has too many pages is likely to fall apart, and the most inauspicious start for an application for permission to appeal is to require a Lord or Lady Justice of Appeal first to reconstruct his or her bundle.

Failure to prepare bundles in accordance with Court of Appeal guidelines

15–032 The consequences of failing to comply with rules about appeal bundles may lead to unfavourable cost orders[37] and possible public censure in a judgment. This may occur even if the parties compromise the underlying appeal.[38]

Further, the Practice Direction to Pt 52 is explicit in identifying the consequences for failing to prepare and provide the bundles in accordance with the specified guidance. The Practice Direction to Pt 52 provides:

"**Rejection of bundles**

15.4(1) Where documents are copied unnecessarily or bundled incompletely, costs may be disallowed. Where the provisions of this Practice Direction as to the preparation or delivery of the bundles are not followed the bundle may be rejected by the court or be made the subject of a special costs order.

. . .

Sanctions for non-compliance

15.4(12) If the appellant fails to comply with the requirements as to the provision of bundles of documents, the application or appeal will be referred for consideration to be given as to why it should not be dismissed for failure to so comply."

While these provisions apply to the Court of Appeal, all levels of appeal courts have powers under CPR r.52.9 to impose sanctions and impose

---

[36] The Admiralty and Commercial Court Guide, App.10, para.2(vii).
[37] CPR PD 52 para.15.4(1) provides that where documents are copied unnecessarily or bundled incompletely then costs may be disallowed and where the other provisions are not complied with this may lead to the rejection of the bundles and the making of a special costs order.
[38] R. (on the application of Jeyapragash) v Immigration Appeal Tribunal [2004] EWCA Civ 1260.

conditions on appeals. Accordingly the parties should comply with any specific directions applicable to the particular appeal or in default those set out by the Court of Appeal to avoid facing sanctions or unwanted conditions.

Certificate as to the contents of the appeal bundle in the Court of Appeal

Where the appellant is represented then a certificate must be signed by his solicitor, counsel or other representative to the effect that he has read and understood para.5.6A(2) of the Practice Direction to Pt 52 requiring all documents extraneous to an appeal to be excluded from the appeal bundle and that the appeal bundle complies with that requirement.[39]

15–033

NEW HUMAN RIGHTS POINT ON APPEAL

If the appellant seeks permission to raise for the first time on an appeal an issue under the Human Rights Act 1998 or a remedy available under that Act, the appeal notice must include the information required by para.15.1 of the practice direction supplementing Pt 16.[40]

15–034

The appeal notice must state that the issue or remedy is sought under the Human Rights Act 1998.

The appeal notice must also provide the following details:

(1) it must give precise details of the Convention right which it is alleged has been infringed and details of the alleged infringement;
(2) it must specify the relief sought;
(3) it must state if the relief sought includes a declaration of incompatibility in accordance with s.4 of that Act, and, if so, give precise details of the legislative provision alleged to be incompatible and details of the alleged incompatibility, and where the claim is founded on a finding of unlawfulness by another court or tribunal, give details of the finding; or
(4) state if the relief sought includes damages in respect of a judicial act to which s.9(3) of that Act applies and provide details of the judicial act complained of and the court or tribunal which is alleged to have made it.[41]

Where a declaration is sought under s.4 of the Human Rights Act 1998 or a claim is based on s.9(3) of the Act the appellant must give at least 21 days

---

[39] CPR PD 52 para.5.6A(3).
[40] CPR PD 52 para.5.1A.
[41] CPR r.19.4A(3). CPR PD 16 para.15.1.

notice to the Crown before any such declaration or award of damages is to be made.[42] The court will normally consider giving notice to the Crown at the application for permission to appeal.[43]

COURT IN WHICH THE APPELLANT'S NOTICE SHOULD BE FILED

15-035 The particular court in which the appellant's notice should be filed will depend on the appropriate appeal court for the appeal. Identifying the correct destination of the appeal is addressed in Chapter 11.

If the destination of the appeal is to a circuit judge in the County Court, the appellant's notice should be filed in the office of the County Court where the case was being handled for the lower court proceedings.

Where the appeal is to the High Court the appeal notice should be filed at the appropriate appeal centre for the lower court:

> (a) On the South Eastern Circuit such appeals should be filed at the Royal Courts Justice. High Court procedure is addressed further in Chapter 16.
>
> (b) An appeal to the Court of Appeal will take place in the Royal Courts of Justice and the appeal should be filed in the Civil Appeals Office, Room E307, Royal Courts of Justice, Strand, London WC2A 2LL.

It often seems to be the case that documents are filed on the last day for filing them; if so, representatives must take care that they know when the relevant court office will close for the afternoon.

PAYMENT OF FEE ON FILING OF APPELLANT'S NOTICE

15-036 Usually a prospective appellant will have to pay a fee on filing an appellant's notice.[44] However there are circumstances where the fee or part of it may be waived where, for example, the prospective appellant is receiving State benefits. Details can be found in the booklet and application form EX160A Court Fees available from the court office; the courts service web-

---

[42] CPR r.19.4A. Further details of service on the Crown are provided in CPR PD 19 paras 6.1–6.6.

[43] CPR PD 19 para.6.2 as applicable to appeal notice by reason of CPR PD 52 para.5.1B.

[44] In October 2010 the fee on filing an appellant's notice or respondent's notice was £100 for appeals from small claims track in the County Court, £120 for all other appeals in the County Court and £200 for appeals to the High Court. In the Court of Appeal the fee for filing an application for permission to appeal is £200; there are various other fees payable at later stages. See s.10 of the *White Book*.

site; and the *White Book*. It is important if filing on the last day that a solicitor remembers to give the person filing the documents a cheque as otherwise the court may refuse to accept it.

SERVICE OF DOCUMENTS ON THE RESPONDENT

The appellant's notice

Normally the court where the appeal is filed will issue the appeal and serve copies of the filed documents on any respondent by first class post. A prospective appellant can request that he or she takes responsibility for service and if so the court will provide the prospective appellant with sealed copies of the appellant's notice for service. CPR r.52.4 provides that where service is to be carried out by the appellant it must be effected as soon as practicable and at the latest by seven days thereafter. **15–037**

> "52.4(3) Unless the appeal court orders otherwise, an appellant's notice must be served on each respondent—
>
> (a) as soon as is practicable; and
> (b) in any event not later than 7 days, after it is filed."

The skeleton argument

The skeleton argument must be served, with the appellant's notice or, where it is impracticable to do so, within 14 days of filing the notice.[45] **15–038**

Certificate of service

The appellant must then file a certificate of service of the appellant's notice and the skeleton argument on each respondent. Form N215 provides a generic certificate of service which may be adapted for this purpose. **15–039**

---

[45] CPR PD 52 para.5.9.

STEPS FOLLOWING GRANT OF PERMISSION TO APPEAL

Service of the appeal bundle on the respondent following permission to appeal

15–040   If the appeal court gives permission to appeal, the appellant must serve the appeal bundle on each of the respondents within seven days of receiving the order giving permission to appeal.[46]

Listing of the appeal

15–041   At the same time as notifying the parties that permission to appeal has been granted and the appeal is to proceed the appeal court should send the parties notification of the date of the hearing or the period of time (the "listing window") during which the appeal is likely to be heard and in the Court of Appeal, the date by which the appeal will be heard (the "hear by date").[47] The Court of Appeal will also send the appellant a listing questionnaire which requires the appellant's counsel to give a time estimate for the appeal. The appeal court should at the same time as serving notice of the date of the appeal hearing or listing window also send a copy of the order giving permission to appeal and any other directions for the appeal.[48] This is important because most of the later time limits—including the date by which the respondent's notice must be filed—commence from the date of notification of the grant of permission to appeal.

Updating the appeal bundle

15–042   Subject to any directions the court may give the appellant must add the following additional documents to the appeal bundle:

(1) the respondent's notice and skeleton argument (if any);
(2) those parts of the transcript of evidence which are directly relevant to any question at issue on the appeal;
(3) the order granting permission to appeal and, where permission was granted at an oral hearing, the transcript (or note) of any judgment which was given; and
(4) any document which the appellant and respondent have agreed to add to the appeal bundle in accordance with para.7.11 of the Practice Direction to Pt 52.

---

[46] CPR PD 52 para.6.2.
[47] CPR PD 52 para.6.3(1).
[48] CPR PD 52 para.6.3(2)–(3).

If permission to appeal has been granted on a limited basis then the appellant must remove from the appeal bundle all documents relevant only to the issue(s) on which permission to appeal has not been allowed.[49]

PREPARING FOR AN APPEAL AS A RESPONDENT

The preparation to be taken by a respondent to an appeal depends greatly on the nature of that party's stance in an appeal. Broadly speaking there are three stances a respondent can take: **15–043**

(1) The respondent can seek to appeal part of the decision of the lower court.
(2) The respondent can seek to uphold the decision of the lower court for different and/or additional reasons given by the lower court.
(3) The respondent can seek to uphold the decision of the lower court for the reasons given by the lower court.

Respondent seeking to appeal part of the decision of the lower court

If a respondent wishes to appeal part of the decision of the lower court then he requires permission to do so under CPR r.52.3. The process for seeking permission to appeal is addressed in Chapter 13.   **15–044**

Respondent seeking to uphold the decision of the lower court for different and/or additional reasons

A respondent who wishes to uphold the decision of the lower court for different and/or additional reasons given by the lower court does not require permission to appeal, but is required to file a respondent's notice and a skeleton argument. The respondent is required to meet the same strict time limits for filing a respondent's notice as a respondent seeking permission to appeal.   **15–045**

---

[49] CPR PD 52 para.6.3A(2).

Respondent who is seeking to uphold the decision of the lower court for the same reasons given

15–046   A respondent seeking to uphold the decision of the lower court for the reasons given by the lower court is not required to file a respondent's notice, but may file a respondent's notice. Other than in the Court of Appeal[50] such a respondent need only file a skeleton argument seven days before the appeal hearing. This date can of course be altered by a court officer or judge of the Court of Appeal. It is likely to be shortened in the case of an expedited appeal or an appeal assigned to the short-warned list.[51]

CONSEQUENCES OF NOT FILING A RESPONDENT'S NOTICE

15–047   In the event that no respondent's notice is filed, the respondent risks losing the right to do anything other than support the decision of the lower court. Paragraph 7.3(2) of the Practice Direction to Pt 52 provides that:

> "if the respondent does not file a respondent's notice he will not be entitled, except with the permission of the court, to rely on any reason not relied on in the lower court."[52]

On one reading this might leave open an argument that the respondent might rely on reasons advanced by it in the lower court, but not relied on by the lower court in reaching the decision, and possibly even rejected by the lower court.

This cannot have been the intention of the draughtsman because it would be inconsistent with and defeat the purpose of the requirement to file a notice as explained in the immediately preceding paragraph:

> "7.3(1) A respondent who wishes to appeal or who wishes to ask the appeal court to uphold the order of the lower court for reasons different from or additional to those given by the lower court must file a respondent's notice."

It is respectfully suggested that a court is likely to find that the word "in" at the end of para.7.3(2) should be read as "by".

---

[50] Where the respondent is required to write to the Civil Appeals Office confirming his intention on the appeal within 21 days—CPR PD 52 para.15.6. See Ch.13.
[51] See para.17–054.
[52] CPR PD 52 para.7.3(2).

RESPONDENT IN APPEAL TO THE COURT OF APPEAL

There is an additional requirement for a respondent in an appeal to the Court of Appeal.   15–048

The Practice Direction to Pt 52 para.15.6 provides:

"15.6 A respondent must, no later than 21 days after the date he is served with notification that—

(1) permission to appeal has been granted; or
(2) the application for permission to appeal and the appeal are to be heard together,
    inform the Civil Appeals Office and the appellant in writing whether—

(a) he proposes to file a respondent's notice appealing the order or seeking to uphold the order for reasons different from, or additional to, those given by the lower court; or
(b) he proposes to rely on the reasons given by the lower court for its decision."

THE RESPONDENT'S NOTICE

As set out above, a respondent's notice is required in all appeals other than   15–049
those where the respondent seeks to rely solely on the reasons given by the lower court. A respondent's notice is currently contained in a standard Form N162. Again, the form may be obtained from the court, or downloaded from the Court Service website; or a version is included in the Forms CD with the *White Book*.

Contents of the respondent's notice

The respondent's notice is divided in to ten sections over eight pages.   15–050

(1) Sections 1 and 2 are informational sections identifying the claim and the respondent's details.
(2) Section 3 requires the respondent to provide a time estimate and details of representation.
(3) Sections 4 and 5 relate to appeals where the respondent also seeks to appeal part of the decision of the lower court. The respondent is required to identify the order or parts of the order he wishes to appeal from.
(4) Section 6 is the key section where the respondent identifies its grounds for appeal or upholding the order.

(5) Section 7 provides for arguments in support of the grounds in section 6 if not to be contained in a separate skeleton argument.

(6) Section 8 requires the respondent to identify the order it seeks.

(7) Section 9 is for any additional applications that are needed.

(8) Section 10 identifies the required supporting documents.

As with the appellant's notice there is guidance available on completing the notice from the county court or the Clerk of the List General Office/Appeals Office at the Royal Courts of Justice.

Time for filing the respondent's notice

15–051   The respondent has 14 days to file the respondent's notice from the date on which he is served with notice either that the appeal is to proceed or that the appellant has been granted permission to appeal.[53] Where no permission is required this will be the date of filing the appellant's notice. As most appeals require permission, normally this time will run from service of the order granting permission to appeal or notice that the application for permission to appeal will be heard together with the appeal which will follow if permission is granted.

Service of respondent's notice on the appellant and other parties

15–052   Subject to any other direction by the appeal court, the respondent must serve the respondent's notice on the appellant and any other respondent as soon as practicable and in any event no later than seven days after it has been filed.[54] As noted in para.15–042, it is the appellant's obligation to update the appeal bundle to include the respondent's notice.

RESPONDENT'S SKELETON ARGUMENT

15–053   Respondents' skeleton arguments are expected in almost all appeals:

(1) Where a respondent is legally represented and wishes to address the appeal court a skeleton argument must be filed and served[55] unless the appeal is from a small claims track claim and is heard in the county court or the High Court.[56]

---

[53] CPR r.52.5(4)–(5).
[54] CPR r.52.5(6).
[55] CPR PD 52 para.7.6.
[56] CPR PD 52 para.7.7A(1).

(2) While an unrepresented respondent is not required to file a skeleton argument, he or she is encouraged to do so in order to assist the court.[57]

A respondent can use the standard form Form N163 for a skeleton argument but the general practice is to use a new document in similar form to the appellant's skeleton argument, discussed in para.15–016.

Purpose of the respondent's skeleton

The editors of the *White Book* identify[58] three important functions of the respondent's skeleton argument as follows:

    15–054

(1) Case management: the respondent's skeleton argument will assist the appeal court in case management.
(2) Focussing the oral argument: the respondent's skeleton argument may inspire some of the court's questions to the appellant's advocate.
(3) Summary of the respondent's position: if the respondent is called upon the respondent's skeleton argument will represent the summary of its submissions.

The primary focus of the respondent's skeleton argument where no separate cross-appeal is brought is to respond to the appellant's skeleton argument. This is emphasised by the Practice Direction to Pt 52.[59]

Importance of skeleton argument

The respondent's skeleton argument is the most important document the respondent is likely to prepare as it will set out the basis of its stance in relation to the appeal. As the respondent does not file any grounds of appeal (unless there is a separate ground of appeal being pursued), the appeal court will be wholly reliant on the respondent's skeleton to understand the basis upon which the respondent puts its case.

    15–055

Contents of the skeleton argument

The respondent's skeleton argument must conform to the same strictures of the appellant's skeleton argument set out in paras 5.10 and 5.11 of the

    15–056

---

[57] para.7.7A(2).
[58] *White Book*, 2010, para.52.5.6.
[59] CPR PD 52 para.7.8.

Practice Direction to Pt 52 as appropriate for a respondent.[60] These are addressed at paras 15–018 et seq.

Where the respondent is seeking permission to appeal or to support the decision of the lower court on different or additional grounds then the advocate will need to consider whether to address these matters first before addressing the appellant's grounds of appeal or to attempt to address both at the same time.

Filing of respondent's skeleton argument

15–057 Where the respondent is required to serve a respondent's notice then he must file his skeleton argument at the same time as filing his respondent's notice or within 14[61] days of receiving the appellant's skeleton arguments.[62]

If the respondent files a skeleton argument with his respondent's notice he must file two additional copies for the appeal court.[63]

Where the appellant was granted permission to appeal by the lower court, and a respondent is seeking permission to appeal, at the time for filing his respondent's notice he may not yet have received the appellant's skeleton argument. In those circumstances, he should still file and serve his skeleton within 14 days of filing the respondent's notice, rather than waiting for the appellant's skeleton to arrive.

Any additional arguments in response to the appellant's skeleton can be raised by way of a supplemental skeleton from the respondent. The Court of Appeal has emphasised the importance of the respondent filing its skeleton argument at this early stage to assist in case management decisions for the appeal.[64]

Where no respondent's notice is to be filed the respondent is required to file and serve a skeleton argument seven days before the hearing.[65]

Service of respondent's skeleton argument

15–058 The respondent is required to serve his skeleton argument on the appellant and any other respondent at the same time as he files it at the court. He must also file a certificate of service.[66]

[60] CPR PD 52 para.7.8.
[61] This has been reduced from the proposed 28 days in the Bowman Report and the 21 days when the CPR was first introduced to its current 14 days.
[62] The skeleton can be served at the time of filing the respondent's notice. See CPR PD 52 paras 7.6 and 7.7(1).
[63] CPR PD 52 para.7.10(2).
[64] *Philosophy Inc v Ferretti Studios SRL* [2002] EWCA Civ 921 at [30] and [37]–[40].
[65] CPR PD 52 para.7.7(2).
[66] CPR PD 52 para.7.7B.

AGREEING CHRONOLOGY, DRAMATIS PERSONAE AND OTHER DOCUMENTS

The appellant may well have prepared a chronology and dramatis personae   **15–059**
and other documents at the same time as filing his skeleton argument in
accordance with the guidance in the Practice Direction to Pt 52 para.5.11.
Such documents should be uncontroversial and may be capable of agreement by the respondents. Where however there are areas of disagreement
the parties should take steps to prepare an agreed chronology or dramatis
personae. The courts are likely to take a dim view of parties who are unable
to reach agreement on what should be an uncontroversial document.

AGREEING AND UPDATING THE CONTENTS OF THE APPEAL BUNDLE OR PREPARING A RESPONDENT'S BUNDLE

The stance taken by the respondent in the appeal will determine what, if   **15–060**
any, additional documents are required to be added to the appeal bundle.
The respondent is under a duty to make "every effort" to agree amendments to the appeal bundle.[67] Normally this can be achieved satisfactorily.
Where agreement cannot be reached in terms of updating the appellant's
bundle, the respondent should prepare a supplemental respondent's bundle.
However the need to do so may well signal unreasonable conduct on one or
other party which may be investigated by the appeal court.

READING LIST

The appeal court will welcome an agreed reading list which should be   **15–061**
appropriate balanced and fair, together with a time estimate for reading the
documents identified in the reading list.

ADDITIONAL DOCUMENTS

Where the bundles have already been delivered to the court, additional   **15–062**
documents should be unstapled, hole-punched and properly paginated with
the appropriate bundle/page number so that they can be added to the court
documents easily.[68] Where there are likely to be a substantial number of
new documents produced the parties should prepare an additional file for

---

[67] CPR PD 52 para.7.11.
[68] CPR PD 52 para.15.4(10)(a).

this purpose with dividers or tabs in place and an updated index showing the addition of the new documents.[69-71]

PROVISION OF APPEAL BUNDLES FOR THE APPEAL HEARING IN THE COURT OF APPEAL

15–063   In the Court of Appeal all the documents which are needed for the appeal hearing must be filed at least seven days before the hearing. Where a document has not been filed 10 days before the hearing it is the practice of the Civil Appeals Office to send out a reminder. If a party fails to comply then he may be required to attend before the presiding Lord Justice to seek permission to proceed with, or to oppose, the appeal.

PREPARATION OF SUPPLEMENTAL SKELETON ARGUMENT

15–064   As skeleton arguments will have been filed often long in advance[72] of the appeal hearing it may be necessary for one or more parties to the appeal to file a supplemental skeleton argument. As before the supplemental skeleton arguments are required to comply with the provisions of para.5.10 of the Practice Direction to Pt 52.[73]

Time for filing supplemental skeleton argument

15–065   There are strict time limits:

(1) If the appellant wishes to file a supplemental skeleton argument it *must* be filed at least 14 days before the hearing.[74]
(2) If the respondent wishes to file a supplemental skeleton argument it *must* be filed at least seven days before the hearing.[75]

There is a practical reason for these cut-off dates. The papers are usually provided to the judges in the Court of Appeal seven days in advance of the appeal. If a supplemental skeleton is not with the Civil Appeals Office by then it may not reach the judges in time. Even if it does so, it may mean that some of a judge's pre-reading becomes wasted by focussing on aspects of the appeal that are no longer pursued or put a different way.

[69-71] CPR PD 52 para.15.4(10)(b).
[72] The appellant's skeleton argument will have been filed with the appellant's notice or shortly thereafter in accordance with CPR PD 52 para.5.9.
[73] CPR PD 52 para.15.11A(3).
[74] CPR PD 52 para.15.11A(1).
[75] CPR PD 52 para.15.11A(2).

The consequences of a failure to file a supplemental skeleton argument within these time limits may lead to the appeal court refusing to hear the argument[76] and/or to unfavourable costs sanctions.

CORE BUNDLE

The appellant is required to prepare the core bundle in consultation with the respondent's solicitors and taking in to account the same considerations as set out above.

15–066

In document heavy appeals, a core bundle will almost always be appropriate. The guidance provides that where the appeal bundles contain more than 500 pages excluding transcripts then the appellant's solicitors must file a core bundle.[77]

The core bundle should not exceed 150 pages and must contain the key documents.

In certain appeals, there may be a number of documents competing for inclusion and it is not unheard of for an appeal court to identify as key a document that neither party considered as such. Sensible co-operation between the advocates and solicitors for the parties should be able to identify these core documents although disputes are not unknown.

The timing for filing the core bundle depends on whether permission was required and, if so, which court provided it:

(a) If no permission was required or permission to appeal was given by the lower court, then the core bundle must be filed within 28 days of service of the appellant's notice on the respondent.
(b) Where permission to appeal is obtained from the appeal court then the core bundle must be filed within 28 days of receipt of the order giving permission to appeal.[78]

BUNDLE OF AUTHORITIES

The appellant's advocate is responsible for lodging a bundle containing copies of the authorities relied on once the date fixed for the hearing has been notified to the parties. He must consult his opponent before lodging the bundle which is intended to contain copies of the authorities upon which each side relies.[79]

15–067

The time required to put together a bundle of authorities should not be under-estimated. If the respondent has not filed a respondent's notice, then

---

[76] CPR PD 52 para.15.11A(4).
[77] CPR PD 52 para.15.2.
[78] CPR PD 52 para.15.3(1).
[79] CPR PD 52 para.15.11(1).

he need not file a skeleton argument until seven days before the hearing. That is the same deadline by which the bundle of authorities must be filed. The appellant's advocate must be alive to the fact that he may have to ask his opponent what authorities he wishes to refer to in advance, because he may not have a skeleton argument to take them from. The respondent's advocate must be prepared to identify the authorities upon which he wishes to rely before the date for filing his skeleton argument.

It is not expected that the Bundle of Authorities will contain more than 10 authorities although this will inevitably depend on the number and complexity of the issues on appeal.

Each advocate must certify that the bundle of authorities complies with the requirements of sub-paras (3) to (5) of para.5.10 of the Practice Direction to Pt 52 have been complied with in respect of each authority included in the bundle.

15–068   The Practice Direction to Pt 52 makes clear[80] that the bundle should not include authorities for propositions that are not in dispute. Inclusion of excessive authorities will be marked with disapproval by the court.[81]

The relevant passages of the authorities relied on should be marked[82] by the advocate seeking to rely on the authority. The usual way is to place a line beside the passage(s) relied on in the margin. While there may be a temptation to highlight specific parts of the text experience suggests that judges prefer to carry out their own highlighting of the text and in any event highlighting either does not photocopy at all, or may obscure the text once it has been photocopied.

Where the law report contains two columns then the line should be placed in the appropriate margin. Otherwise the mark is placed on the right hand side. It is good practice where more than one party relies on an authority to distinguish the relevant passage(s) relied on by each party by a suitable and consistent reference such as A for appellant and R for respondent directly above the line. This is preferable to using different colours to distinguish the parties—these often get lost in the photocopying process. Where the authority is lengthy it may be appropriate to flag up the relevant page with a sticker to assist the court.

15–069   It is important that the person putting together the bundle uses copies of the printed paper copy of the relevant law report. Most electronic case law providers now permit users to download pdf copies of the printed reports. Downloaded texts which do not mimic printed reports should only be used if it is not possible to obtain a copy of the printed reports.

As set out in para.15–024, cases should always be cited from the Law Reports (i.e. A.C., Ch., Q.B., Fam., Bus. L.R. or W.L.R.) in preference to any other. Transcripts or authorised copies of judgments should only be used if the judgment has not been reported anywhere.

---

[80] CPR PD 52 para.15.11(2).

[81] See by way of example *Midgulf International Ltd v Groupe Chimique Tunisien* [2010] EWCA Civ 66; February 10, 2010; *The Times*, March 3, 2010 at [71]–[73]. In that case there were five volumes of authorities totalling well over 100 authorities.

[82] CPR PD 52 para.15.11(2).

Time for filing of authorities bundles

The bundle of authorities *must* be filed at least seven days before the   15–070
hearing or if there is less time available *immediately*.[83] If the appeal is in the
short-warned list and is listed for hearing then the parties must do their best
to provide an agreed bundle "as rapidly as possible".[84]

Supplementing the authorities bundle

The parties may agree a further authorities bundle. Again the responsibility   15–071
for filing this bundle is on the appellant's advocate. The cut-off date for
filing this additional bundle is *at least 48 hours*[85] before the hearing commences. If this cut-off date is not met it will be a matter for the appeal court
as to whether to allow the party to rely on the additional authority. In the
absence of good explanation for the delayed identification of the authority
the appeal court may well refuse to admit it although if it is a binding
authority then the appeal court may be unlikely to proceed without taking
it in to account. A possible consequence will be the adjournment of the
appeal hearing to allow the other side sufficient time to consider the
authority and to adduce a supplemental skeleton probably at the expense of
the party seeking to rely on the authority at late notice or a provision that
further written submissions on the additional authority be provided after
the hearing again with the defaulting party liable to meet the additional
costs of such submissions in any event.

PREPARING FOR ORAL SUBMISSIONS

Each advocate has their own style of advocacy and will adapt it to fit the   15–072
needs of the case. The purpose of the balance of this chapter is not to
attempt to provide instruction in advocacy, but to identify some to the tips
and techniques that may assist in presenting an appeal.

The symbiosis of oral and written advocacy is at the fore in appeals.
Much of what will need to be said by way of oral submission will be
influenced by what has already been submitted by way of the written
documents, particularly the skeleton argument. However care needs to be
taken in preparation of both with the emphasis on succinctness. The
advocate must therefore identify when preparing his written skeleton and
long before his oral submissions precisely what each will cover and what is
appropriate to include for the permission hearing. The *White Book* guidance in this regard is apposite[86]:

[83] CPR PD 52 para.15.11(3).
[84] *Scribes West Ltd v Relsa Anstalt* [2004] EWCA Civ 835; [2005] C.P. Rep. 2 at 29.
[85] CPR PD 52 para.15.11(4).
[86] *White Book*, 2010 edn, para.52.3.16 for such guidance.

"The rules governing permission to appeal have the potential to protect litigants from enormous cost and delay. If they are to achieve this objective without causing injustice, there must be both careful preparation by the court and high standards of preparation and presentation by the advocates."

At the permission stage

15–073 At the permission stage the objective is not to satisfy the judge hearing the application for permission that the appeal will succeed, but that it meets one of the two criteria under CPR r.52.3(6), considered in Chapter 2. Forgetting this can lead the advocate in to the trap of overstating his case at the permission stage, leading to a possible subsequent application to set aside permission under CPR r.52.9. In this regard it is essential that the advocate considers his duty to draw attention to any adverse authorities or factors that might be taken in to account given that in all likelihood at the permission stage no other party will be represented.

The oral hearing of an application for permission is likely to be of a limited duration. It is therefore imperative that the advocate appearing focuses on the best points of the appeal and addresses them succinctly.

The advocate must anticipate in advance the extent and level of background detail the appeal court may require and, as with all advocacy, be as well prepared as can be to respond to judicial questions.

The judge hearing the application for permission to appeal is unlikely to have had the time or opportunity to consider more than the basic documents for the appeal. Usually the judge will have considered the grounds of appeal, the order of the lower court and the skeleton argument. It is however unlikely that there will have been sufficient court time for the judge to have read the relevant part of the judgment or any other documents.

While many judges appear blessed with perception that allows them to glean from these documents and, where appropriate, the relevant parts of the judgment, sufficient information relating to the matter to allow them to understand the issues on the appeal, this is not always the case. Care needs to be taken to ensure that essential information is presented to the appeal court. An inadequate skeleton argument or omitted essential document may well damage the client's prospects of obtaining permission to appeal. Failure to address this in oral submissions will only compound the problem.

In respect of the underlying facts of the case it may be appropriate for a paragraph of the skeleton to set out the nature of the underlying claim, the issue that was determined and the basis of the appeal. To the extent appropriate that can then be developed, albeit briefly, in oral submissions.

Where the decision relates to an appeal of a case management decision then the skeleton will need to focus more on the procedural background. A chronology will often be an essential aide.

As set out above the advocate on an application for a renewed applica- 15–074
tion for permission to appeal following a refusal on paper is required to file
a written statement before the oral hearing setting out among other things
why permission to appeal should be given notwithstanding the reasons for
the refusal of permission on paper. In preparing for oral submissions the
advocate will need to address these matters at the outset as they are likely to
be the focus of the appeal court. This is often a difficult task. The advocate
will need to explain tactfully quite why the judge was wrong to reject the
application on paper. It is possible that the judge who initially refused
permission on paper will be the judge who reconsiders the application at an
oral hearing as CPR PD 52 para.4.13 reminds the advocate:

> "If permission is refused without a hearing the parties will be notified
> of the decision with the reasons for it. The decision is subject to the
> appellant's right to have it reconsidered at an oral hearing. This may be
> before the same judge."

The same judge may ultimately be sitting as a member of the appeal court
on the hearing of the appeal.[87]

On the appeal hearing

The following were given as key tips for appellate advocacy by Lord 15–075
Bingham in a seminar delivered at the Inner Temple on May 10, 2008:

(1) The advocate must try to interest the court in the case.
(2) The advocate should not read out his presentation—this is a quick
    way of losing the court's attention.
(3) The advocate should rely on principles of law, rather than seeking
    to develop analogies from the facts of earlier authorities to the
    present case.
(4) Brevity is encouraged and appreciated. If the point is good then the
    advocate should be able to explain it succinctly.
(5) Numbered propositions assist the court in following oral
    submissions.
(6) The advocate should not assume that matters covered in skeleton
    arguments have been read as carefully as the advocate might like.

---

[87] *Sengupta v Holmes* [2002] EWCA Civ 1104. There may be cases where the judge has so
expressed himself or reached such a settled conclusion of the facts that he is unable to take
a fair view of the case—see paras 32–34, per Laws L.J. However this is likely to arise more
in respect of the trial judge hearing an appeal than an appeal judge rejecting an application
for permission to appeal on paper. In the Court of Appeal the practice generally is that a
judge who refused an application for permission to appeal on paper will not be part of the
constitution of the court hearing the renewed oral application for permission to appeal.

Capturing the court's interest

15–076   In attempting to interest the court the advocate should place considerable importance on the first minute or so of the submissions when the court is less likely to interrupt the advocate:

  (1) At the very outset the advocate should try to encapsulate the issues. The first five or so sentences of the submissions are particularly important.[88]
  (2) By defining the issues at the beginning the advocate focuses the court's attention and, with luck, interest on the central aspects of the appeal.
  (3) By contrast, to open with some matter of housekeeping, or an inquiry about whether the judges have the relevant papers will lose the interest of the court, particularly in the Court of Appeal.[89]

The advocate needs to have at the forefront of his mind a clear idea of what he is asking the appellate court to do. It is useful as an aide memoire to have prepared a draft order to have as a reference point in the oral submissions.

Holding the court's attention

15–077   If the attention of the court can be obtained from the outset, by encapsulating the issues that arise, the next most important point is not to lose it:
    Reading from a script or, even worse, the skeleton argument, or constant reference to notes or delays in taking instructions may risk losing that attention. These can only be avoided by comprehensive preparation.

Addressing the specialist member of the court

15–078   It is worth bearing in mind that the Court of Appeal sits in its civil division with at least one member who is likely to be a specialist in the area of law that arises on the appeal. That member of the court is likely to write the lead judgment in relation to the case. Once the constitution of the court is known the advocate should identify which member of the court is the specialist and then tailor the style and pace of the submissions in particular to suit that member. However the submissions should be addressed to the entire court so as not to alienate the other members of the court.

---

[88] Advice given by May L.J. at the same seminar on May 10, 2008.
[89] The Court of Appeal has excellent support staff and if the bundles had not been received the advocates would undoubtedly have been told of this.

Responding to questions from the court

In answering questions posed by the court the advocate should answer them   15–079
directly. If answering the question completely will require a lengthy
diversion from the point then being addressed the advocate should answer
the question as succinctly as possible and indicate that the point can either
be developed further at that point or subsequently depending on the court's
preference. This inevitably requires flexibility on the part of the advocate in
re-ordering his or her submissions.

Unarguable and arguable points

An advocate should not argue a point that he does not consider to be   15–080
properly arguable. However if it is properly arguable he should argue it
without reservation.[90] If there are bad or difficult points for the advocate's
case, these should be dealt with head on. If they are not grappled with upfront then one's opponent and the court are likely to make them look far
worse.

Timing

An advocate must stick to the time allotted to the case. A court will readily   15–081
remind an advocate of any estimates given and if not the opposing party
may well make the point.

Costs

The Practice Direction to Pt 52[91] provides that costs are likely to be assessed   15–082
by way of summary assessment at the following hearings which include
appeals:

(1) contested directions hearings;
(2) applications for permission to appeal at which the respondent is
    present;
(3) dismissal list hearings in the Court of Appeal at which the
    respondent is present;
(4) appeals from case management decisions;
(5) appeals listed for one day or less.

---

[90] Bar Code of Conduct, para.708(f) and cf. para.704(b) in respect of written submissions.
See too *Richard Buxton Solicitors v Mills-Owen* [2010] EWCA Civ 122 at [43], per Dyson
L.J. and the implication of CPR r.1.3 on solicitors.
[91] CPR PD 52 para.14.1.

Parties attending any of these hearings should be prepared to deal with the summary assessment of costs immediately following the hearing[92] and this should always be included in the advocate's checklist for preparation for oral advocacy at the appeal stage as it is at the lower court stage.

TIMETABLE FOR APPEALS

15–083   The following is an overview of the key steps that need to be taken in an appeal. This timeline is intended as a general guide. It is not comprehensive and is of course subject to variation by court order and changes to the CPR or particular court practice. Reference should be made to the earlier chapters in this book and the relevant rules and guidance.

Date	Step	Rule
Handing down of judgment	Application for permission to appeal and any application for an alteration of time for serving appellant's notice	CPR r.52.3(2)(a)
Appellant's notice		
Subject to other direction by the court, 21 days following handing down of judgment	Appellant's notice to be filed with any application for permission to appeal from the appeal court	CPR r.52.4(2)
As soon as practicable after filing appellant's notice and not later than 7 days later	Service of appellant's notice on each respondent	CPR r.52.4(3)
Within 14 days of filing appellant's notice	Skeleton argument to be filed (if impractical to include with appellant's notice)	CPR PD 52.5.9(2)
As soon as skeleton argument is filed	Service of skeleton argument on each respondent if filed separately to appellant's notice	CPR PD 52.5.21(1)
Renewed oral hearing for permission to appeal		
Within 7 days of receipt of notice that permission to appeal has been refused on paper	Appellant must file a request for reconsideration by the appeal court at a hearing of the issue of permission to appeal	CPR r.52.3(4) and (5)

---

[92] CPR PD 52 para.14.2.

At least 4 days before hearing	Appellant must file a brief written statement identifying points to be raised at hearing, addressing issue of permission in light of reasons given for refusing on paper and other necessary matters	CPR PD 52.4.14A(2)
Service of appeal bundle(s)		
Within 7 days of receipt of order giving permission to appeal	Appellant must serve the appeal bundle as updated in accordance with CPR PD 52 6.3A on each respondent	CPR PD 52.6.2
Within 28 days of receipt of order giving permission to appeal or where granted by the lower court within 28 days of service of the appellant's notice	Appellant must file core bundle where appropriate	CPR PD 52.15.3(1)
Respondent's notice		
Subject to other direction by the court: (a) 14 days following service of the appellant's notice where permission granted or not required; and (b) otherwise 14 days following notification that either permission granted by the appeal court or permission and appeal to be heard together	Respondent's notice to be filed where necessary	CPR r.52.5(4) and (5)
As soon as practicable and not later than 7 days later	Service of respondent's notice on the appellant and any other respondent	CPR r.52.5(6)
Within 14 days of filing respondent's notice	Skeleton argument to be filed (if not included with respondent's notice). If no respondent's notice required and respondent wishes to address appeal court then the skeleton to be served at least 7 days before the hearing (see below)	CPR PD 52.7.7(1)(b)
At the same time as skeleton argument is filed	Service of skeleton argument on the appellant and any other respondent	CPR PD 52.7.7B(1)
Following service of skeleton	Respondent to file certificate of service	CPR PD 52.7.7B(2)

No later than 21 days after notification that permission to appeal granted or permission and appeal to be heard together	In CofA respondent must inform the Civil Appeals Office whether a respondent's notice is to be filed or he proposes to rely on the lower court's reasons	CPR PD 52.15.6
Appeal questionnaire in CoA		
Within 14 days of letter notifying hear by date of appeal	Appellant to file the appeal questionnaire and serve a copy on each respondent	CPR PD 52.6.5
Within 7 days of receipt of appeal questionnaire	Any respondent who disagrees with the appellant's time estimate must notify the Civil Appeals Office	CPR PD 52.6.6
Pre-hearing		
At least 14 days before the hearing	In CofA appellant must file any supplementary skeleton to be relied on	CPR PD 52.15.11(1)(a)
At least 7 days before the hearing	In CofA respondent must file any supplementary skeleton	CPR PD 52.15.11(2)(a)
At least 7 days before the hearing	Generally if respondent has not filed a skeleton argument because relying only on reasons of the lower court then he must file skeleton if he wishes to address the appeal court	CPR PD 52.7.7(2)
At least 7 days before the hearing or if less than 7 days notice immediately	In CofA agreed bundle of authorities to be filed	CPR PD 52.15.11(3)
At least 7 days before the appeal hearing	In CofA all documents which are needed for the appeal hearing to have been filed	CPR PD 52.15.11B(1)
At least 48 hours before the hearing	In CofA if essential a second agreed bundle of authorities	CPR PD 52.15.11(4)
Post-hearing		
Within 21 days of decision if attended or date of notification of decision	Collect all papers from the Civil Appeals Office which will otherwise be destroyed	CPR PD 52.15.11C

CHAPTER 16

Case Management of Appeals

This chapter addresses the lower court and appeal court's powers to attach **16–001** conditions and make other directions in respect of appeals. These are addressed in the following order:

(1) Sources of case management power.
(2) The general application process.
(3) Application for extension of time for filing appellant's or respondent's notice of appeal.
(4) Application to amend appeal notice.
(5) Application under CPR r.52.7 for a stay of execution of the order of the lower court pending the appeal.
(6) Imposing conditions on the grant of permission to appeal under CPR r.52.3(7).
(7) Application for security for the costs of an appeal under CPR r.25.15.
(8) Protective cost orders on appeals.
(9) The appeal court's powers under CPR r.52.9(7) to strike out an appeal notice, vary conditions and/or impose new conditions.
(10) Application for a non-party to be joined as a party for the purposes of the appeal.
(11) Application for recusal of an appeal court judge.
(12) Settlement and discontinuance of appeals and children and court of protection considerations.

SOURCES OF POWERS OF THE LOWER AND APPEAL COURT

The jurisdiction for the case management powers discussed in this chapter **16–002** is found in a number of different sources including:

(1) The court's general case management powers set out in CPR r.3.1.

(2) The power under CPR r.52.3(7) to make the grant of permission to appeal subject to conditions.

(3) The power to stay the execution of the lower court's order pending an appeal under CPR r.52.7.

(4) The power of the appeal court under CPR r.52.9 to:

    (a) strike out the appeal notice;

    (b) to impose conditions on the appeal and/or to vary conditions imposed on the appeal by the lower court; and

    (c) to set aside permission to appeal.

(5) The power to make an order for security for costs of the appeal under CPR r.25.15.

(6) The Court of Appeal and High Court can also call upon their inherent jurisdiction in the appeal process to make such orders and directions as appropriate to ensure the due and proper conduct of appeals.

THE GENERAL APPLICATION PROCESS

16–003   The process for making applications depends on whether the application is made to the lower or appeal court and the nature of the application.

Application to the lower court

16–004   While formally applications are required to be made to the lower court by way of a Pt 23 application notice, it is unusual to file an application notice for an application for permission to appeal or an application in relation to an application for permission to appeal if it is made to the lower court at the handing down of judgment. There are good reasons for this:

(1) the judge is already fully seised of the matter, so the application will take minimal time; and

(2) on an application for permission to appeal at least there is no reason to give the other parties any notice of the grounds of appeal, because it is for the judge to decide whether or not to grant permission to appeal without necessarily hearing from the other parties.

Accordingly, the overriding objective is best furthered by allowing an oral application under para.3 of the Practice Direction to Pt 23.

If, however, a party wishes to ask for an unusual order which the other parties should be given notice of, so that instructions can be taken or evidence adduced, then a Pt 23 notice should be filed.

Application to the appeal court

An application to the appeal court for it to exercise its powers ancillary to   16–005
appeals can be made in one of two ways.

- (1) It can be made in the appellant's/respondent's notice, which contains specific space for such applications.
- (2) Alternatively it can be made by way of a standard Pt 23 application notice. In either case the provisions of Pt 23 apply.[1]

Additional copies of application to be filed

The applicant must file additional copies of the application notice: one   16–006
additional copy of the application notice for the appeal court and one copy
for each of the respondents. In addition the applicant must file a sealed copy
of the order which is the subject of the appeal.

Bundle preparation

For the hearing of the application the applicant must file a bundle of   16–007
documents which should include the Pt 23 application notice; and any
witness statements and affidavits filed in support of the application notice.[2]

EXTENSIONS OF TIME FOR FILING APPELLANT OR RESPONDENT'S NOTICE

As addressed in Chapter 13, CPR r.52.4 provides that for non-statutory   16–008
appeals the period for filing an appellant's notice will be that directed by the
lower court or if there is no such direction then 21 days after the date of the
decision of the lower court that the appellant wishes to appeal. Thus an
appellant who anticipates requiring a longer period for filing an appellant's
notice should seek the same from the lower court. However there may still
be occasions when an application for an extension of time needs to be made
to the appeal court.

CPR r.52.6 provides:

"(1) An application to vary the time limit for filing an appeal notice
must be made to the appeal court.

---

[1] CPR PD 52 para.11.1.
[2] CPR PD 52 para.11.2.

(2) The parties may not agree to extend any date or time limit set by (a) these Rules; (b) Practice Direction 52; or (c) an order of the appeal court or the lower court.

(Rule 3.1(2)(a) provides that the court may extend or shorten the time for compliance with any rule, practice direction or court order (even if an application for extension is made after the time for compliance has expired).) (Rule 3.1(2)(b) provides that the court may adjourn or bring forward a hearing.)"

Application to appeal court

16–009 An application for an extension of time for filing an appellant's or a respondent's notice can be made to the appellate court.[3] This applies even where the lower court has ordered that appeal notices should be filed by a particular time.[4]

Application in appeal notice

16–010 The application must be contained in the appeal notice.

Paragraph 5.2 of the Practice Direction to Pt 52 provides for the appeal notice:

"5.2 Where the time for filing an appellant's notice has expired, the appellant must—

(a) file the appellant's notice; and
(b) include in that appellant's notice an application for an extension of time.

The appellant's notice should state the reason for the delay and the steps taken prior to the application being made."

Paragraph 7.5 of the Practice Direction to Pt 52 provides for the respondent's notice:

"7.5 Where an extension of time is required the extension must be requested in the respondent's notice and the reasons why the respondent failed to act within the specified time must be included."

---

[3] For the difference between CPR rr.52.4 and 52.6 see *Aujla v Sanghera* [2004] EWCA Civ 121; [2004] C.P. Rep. 31 at [14]–[21], per Arden L.J.
[4] *Aujla v Sanghera* [2004] EWCA Civ 121; [2004] C.P. Rep. 31 at [14]–[21], per Arden L.J.

Factors relevant to application

Clearly each appeal will have its own factual sensitivities which will **16–011** influence whether or not to grant an extension of time.[5] The approach will depend on whether the application is made before or after the deadline has expired.

If the application is made before the deadline and the extension sought is modest then the appeal court is likely to grant it.

The factors for extending the period where the application is made after, and particularly long after, the deadline were considered by a specially convened three-judge division of the Court of Appeal in the case of *Sayers v Clarke Walker*.[6] Lord Justice Brooke (with whom the other Lord Justices of Appeal agreed) provided the following guidance as to how the court should approach an application for an extension of time made after the deadline:

(1) As with the exercise of the court's general power to extend time for compliance under CPR r.3.1(2)(a) the court will take into account the overriding objective in CPR r.1.1.[7]

(2) The court will consider the reason for the delay and the steps taken prior to the application being made required by the relevant paragraphs in the practice direction. In ordinary cases this should be sufficient to resolve the matter.[8]

(3) If the answer is not clear the court will consider the application against the check-list in CPR r.3.9.[9]

    (a) While the factor relating to the interests of the administration of justice is unlikely to be significant unless the delay is more than about two months,[10] for applications where the delay is longer

---

[5] Specific factors apply in respect of an appeal from the former Asylum and Immigration Tribunal (now the Immigration and Asylum Chamber of the Upper Tribunal) by the person seeking asylum and where permission to appeal had been granted by the Tribunal. *BR (Iran) v Secretary of State for the Home Department* [2007] EWCA Civ 198; [2007] 1 W.L.R. 2278 at [23]. Such considerations did not apply to an appeal to the Secretary of State: *Omar v Secretary of State for the Home Department* [2009] EWCA Civ 383; [2009] 1 W.L.R. 2265 at [8].

[6] *Sayers v Clarke Walker* [2002] EWCA Civ 645; [2002] 1 W.L.R. 3095. In that case the appeal was against two orders made in the High Court in a professional negligence action on October 12 and 17, 2001. The orders were not sealed until November 16, 2001 and in the meantime the lawyers for the appellant had been given the mistaken impression by the Civil Appeals Office that the 14 day period for filing an appellant's notice ran from the date the order was sealed rather than the date of the decision being challenged. The notice of appeal was not effectively lodged until December 20, 2001.

[7] *Sayers v Clarke Walker* at [18].

[8] *Sayers v Clarke Walker* at [19].

[9] This is because the party seeking the extension has failed to comply with the relevant rule or practice direction and will therefore be unable to participate in the appeal process unless an extension is granted: *Sayers v Clarke Walker* [2002] EWCA Civ 645; [2002] 1 W.L.R. 3095 at [21].

[10] Contrast *Sayers v Clarke Walker* at [25] (a delay of about two months) and *Smith v Brough* [2005] EWCA Civ 261 refusing to extend time by 39 months. See too *Woodpecker v Revenue & Customs Commissioners* [2009] EWHC 3442 (Ch).

the court should consider the principles set out by Lord Woolf in *Taylor v Lawrence (Appeal: Jurisdiction to Reopen)* [2002] EWCA Civ 90 when deciding where the interests of justice truly lie.[11]

(b) In assessing the impact of delay and finality the court will take in to account whether the respondent to the appeal has been apprised of the appeal such that the expectation of finality of litigation from its part is reduced.[12]

(4) Where the other factors are evenly balanced the court will need to consider the merits of the proposed appeal in order to form a judgment on what the defaulting party will be losing if no extension of time is granted.[13]

Respondent's role

16–012 The respondent has the right to make submissions on an appellant's application for an extension of time if it is objected to. Where the matter is controversial and the respondent wishes to address the appeal court in respect of the appellant's application for an extension of time the appellant must serve a copy of the appeal bundle on the respondent. However respondents who oppose an application for an extension of time unreasonably are likely to face an order for costs. Paragraph 5.3 of the Practice Direction to Pt 52 is explicit in this regard. The same can be expected of an appellant who unreasonably opposes a respondent's application for an extension of time.

Position of other parties

16–013 While the parties may not agree an extension, their stance may be of significance. The practice in the Court of Appeal is to advise the appellant to obtain the respondent's views on the application for an extension of time.[14] The appeal court is likely to be more ready to grant an extension of time if it is unopposed by the respondent. However the matter will always be for the appeal court rather than the parties.

---

[11] *Smith v Brough* [2005] EWCA Civ 261 at [34] and [35], per Arden L.J. and at [54] and [55], per Brooke L.J.

[12] *Jackson v Marina Homes* [2007] EWCA Civ 1404; [2008] C.P. Rep. 17 at [20]–[21], per Sir Henry Brooke. Where the delay is significant then the importance of the finality in litigation will militate against an extension of time. See *Smith v Brough* [2005] EWCA Civ 261 refusing to extend time by 39 months.

[13] *Sayers v Clarke Walker* [2002] EWCA Civ 645; [2002] 1 W.L.R. 3095 at [34].

[14] *Manual of Civil Appeals*, 2nd edn, para.4.41.

Notice

Certain appeals require that notice of an application to extend time for filing an appeal notice must be served on third parties.[15]　　16–014

Limit on jurisdiction to extend time for filing appellant's notice

However it should be noted that for certain appeals there is a set time for filing the appellant's notice and the lower court has no power to extend the time.[16]　　16–015

APPLICATION TO AMEND APPELLANT'S OR RESPONDENT'S NOTICE

Occasionally issues arise requiring a party to amend its appeal notice. This requires the permission of the court under CPR r.52.8:　　16–016

> "52.8 An appeal notice may not be amended without the permission of the appeal court."

This applies as much to proposed amendments to the grounds of appeal as to any other aspect of the relevant appeal notice.[17]

Application to appeal court

The application must be made to the appeal court where the appeal is to be heard. It cannot be made to the lower court.　　16–017

Factors

The court will apply the general principles on amendments as would apply under CPR Pt 17.　　16–018

If the amendment is made soon after filing the appellant's notice and relates to a point raised at first instance then subject to any issues of

---

[15] This arises particularly in statutory and specialist appeals such as family proceedings, e.g. CPR PD 52 para.21.1(5) provides that where the appellant is seeking an extension of time for service of the appeal notice on an appeal against decree nisi of divorce or nullity of marriage, etc. he must serve notice on the appropriate district judge.

[16] For instance CPR PD 52 para.21.1(4) provides that the lower court is not permitted to extend the 28 day time limit for filing an appeal against a decree nisi of divorce or nullity of marriage or a conditional dissolution or a nullity order in relation to a civil partnership.

[17] *Shire v Secretary of State for Work and Pensions* [2003] EWCA Civ 1465.

prejudice and costs it is likely to be permitted, particularly if it is made before the grant of permission to appeal.

If the amendment seeks to raise a new point not made previously in the lower court or to attempt to withdraw a concession made previously then the court is likely to be far more circumspect in considering whether to grant permission.

Adding new ground of appeal

16–019   An application to amend the appeal notice will usually arise when the appellant wants to raise an additional argument on the appeal not identified in the original appeal notice. This will normally entail an extension of the basis upon which permission to appeal was granted particularly if the matter is a new issue not previously raised.[18]

Procedure

16–020   The procedure to be followed will depend on the timing and nature of the proposed amendment. The following represents good practice:

(1) The appellant or respondent, as the case may be, should write to the appeal court and the other party indicating the proposed nature of the changed case. The appeal court may well require the appellant to confirm that it has served a copy on the respondents.

(2) The proposed amendment should be readily identifiable. It should be underlined or the change indicated in a different coloured ink as applicable to an amended pleading under para.2 of the Practice Direction to Pt 17.

(3) The other parties should then set out their views on whether the amendments should be allowed.

(4) The appeal court can then consider whether the amendments should be allowed or not; whether it should be permitted by consent or whether the proposed change needs to be determined at an oral hearing.

(5) If it is to be considered at an oral hearing, the appellate court will need to consider whether that should take place in advance of the hearing of the appeal proper.

(6) As a matter of practice if the application is delayed until the appeal then it is unlikely to be permitted if it will cause any prejudice to the other parties to the appeal or an adjournment is required.

---

[18] *Jones v MBNA International Bank*, June 30, 2000.

Costs

As in proceedings at first instance, the party seeking to amend will bear the   **16–021**
costs of and occasioned by the amendments, unless there is some good
reason for another order.

CPR R.52.7: APPLICATIONS FOR A STAY OF EXECUTION OF THE ORDER OR DECISION OF THE LOWER COURT

Both the appeal court and the lower court have the power to order a stay of   **16–022**
execution of the order or decision of the lower court. The purpose of a stay
of execution of the judgment is to alleviate any serious risk of injustice
caused by the enforcement of the judgment pending hearing of the appeal or
the application for permission to appeal.

The default position is that the grant of permission to appeal does not
give rise to a stay of execution of the order of the lower court.

CPR r.52.7 provides:

> "52.7 Unless—
>
> (a) the appeal court or the lower court orders otherwise; or
> (b) the appeal is from the Asylum and Immigration Tribunal
>
> an appeal shall not operate as a stay of any order or decision of the
> lower court."

This reflects the position before the introduction of the CPR. Under RSC
Ord.59 the courts had developed the principle that unless there was a good
reason not to permit it, the successful party should be able to benefit from
the lower court's decision in its favour.

Discretion of court

The court has an unfettered discretion to grant a stay in the interests of   **16–023**
justice:

> "The proper approach is to make the order which best accords with
> the interests of justice. Where there is a risk of harm to one party or
> another, whichever order is made, the court has to balance the alter-
> natives to decide which is less likely to cause injustice. The normal rule
> is for no stay, but where the justice of that approach is in doubt, the
> answer may well depend on the perceived strength of the appeal."[19]

---

[19] *Leicester Circuits Ltd v Coates Brothers Plc* [2002] EWCA Civ 474 at [13]. See in similar
terms *Gater Assets Ltd v Nak Naftogaz Ukrainiy* [2008] EWCA Civ 1051 at [3].

An applicant should show "solid grounds" for the grant of a stay of execution. These should demonstrate the risk of "some form of irremediable harm if no stay is granted".[20] In making an application the appellant must produce cogent evidence to show "that there is a real risk of injustice if enforcement is allowed to take place pending appeal".[21]

16–024 In relation to money judgments, the factors that may be important in considering whether or not to order a stay of execution include:

(1) the ability of the paying party/appellant to recover the sum paid under the order from the receiving party/respondent in the event the appellant succeeds on the appeal:

  (a) the appellant needs to establish more than just a risk that the monies to be paid might not be returned[22];
  (b) the evidence must be sufficient to persuade the court that the respondent would not be in a position to discharge his obligations to the appellant if the appeal were successful.

(2) the risk that further delay pending the appeal may make recovery of the sum due under the order more difficult to recover from the paying party/appellant.

(3) the risk that the appeal will be stifled if the paying party/appellant is required to satisfy the judgment.[23]

When considering this aspect, the court may take in to account not only the means of the appellant but also those resources to which he or she has access. This includes:

(1) in the case of a company, the company's directors, shareholders, other backers and interested persons[24];

(2) in the case of private individuals support from close family members and backers such as those whom might become subject to a third party costs order.

However the potential loss of the growth in the value of an asset[25] or the fact that enforcement is unlikely actually to take place before the hearing of the appeal are not relevant considerations for these purposes.[26]

---

[20] *DEFRA v Downs* [2009] EWCA Civ 257 at [8] and [9], per Sullivan L.J.
[21] *Hammond Suddards v Agrichem International Holdings Ltd* [2001] EWCA Civ 2065 at [18]. Contract *Facilities Ltd v Estate of Rees (Deceased)* [2003] EWCA Civ 465 at [10]–[12].
[22] *Leicester Circuits Ltd v Coates Brothers Plc* [2002] EWCA Civ 474 at [19].
[23] *Hammond Suddards Solicitors v Agrichem International Holdings Ltd* [2001] EWCA Civ 2065 at [22], per Clarke L.J. giving the judgment of the Court.
[24] *Contract Facilities Ltd v Estates of Rees (Deceased)* [2003] EWCA Civ 465 at [10].
[25] *Dumford Trading AG v OAO Atlantrybflot* [2004] EWCA Civ 1265 at [43].
[26] *Dumford Trading AG v OAO Atlantrybflot* [2004] EWCA Civ 1265 at [43].

In relation to non-money judgments, the court will consider the level of prejudice caused to the respective parties by enforcing the order prior to the appeal hearing. This will be fact sensitive. Examples include: **16–025**

(1) in asylum cases involving an order for deportation it may well be appropriate to stay an order, for obvious reasons[27];
(2) similarly in a case where a party is ordered to remove a building or structure allegedly trespassing on someone else's land, it may well be appropriate to stay execution pending the appeal.

Timing of application

The application should be made at the handing down of judgment in the lower court, at the same time as the application for permission to appeal. If permission to appeal is refused and no stay granted then the appellant can reapply to the appeal court for a stay of execution of the order of the lower court in the appellant's notice when renewing the application for permission to appeal. **16–026**

Alternative powers

The court may decide instead of staying enforcement to select an alternative power or condition such as imposing a partial stay, such as a stay of the costs order,[28] or to impose a condition on the appeal, such as ordering the appellant to pay the judgment sum in to court pending the outcome of the appeal. **16–027**

Appeals

A party can appeal against the lower court's order imposing a stay.[29] **16–028**

CPR R.52.3(7): IMPOSING CONDITIONS ON THE GRANT OF PERMISSION TO APPEAL

CPR r.52.3(7) provides: **16–029**

"52.3(7) An order giving permission may—

---

[27] *YD (Turkey) v Secretary of State for the Home Department* [2006] EWCA Civ 52; [2006] 1 W.L.R. 1646.
[28] *Contract Facilities Ltd v Estates of Rees (Deceased)* [2003] EWCA Civ 465 at [13]–[15].
[29] *Aoun v Bahri* [2002] EWCA Civ 1141; [2003] C.P. 6 at [23].

...

(b) be made subject to conditions.

(Rule 3.1 (3) also provides that the court may make an order subject to conditions.)

(Rule 25.15 provides for the court to order security for costs of an appeal.)"

Breadth of powers

16–030   CPR r.52.3(7) does not identify the nature or extent of the conditions that the court can impose. The absence of any restriction and the cross-reference to the court's other powers suggests that the nature or type of condition the court may impose is uninhibited, so long as it is consistent with the overriding objective. This accords with the view taken by the editors of the *White Book* and is consistent with the breadth of directions applied by the courts under this power.[30]

Exercise of discretion

16–031   In deciding whether or not to impose a condition under CPR r.52.3(7)(b) the court should apply the same principles as it would do under its ordinary case management powers under CPR r.3.1, taking in to account that the factual and procedural landscape for an appeal will be different to that applying prior to judgment.[31]

The court will look to the conduct of the party against whom the order is sought to determine whether there is a sufficient (or perhaps a "compelling") basis to justify imposing a condition:

(1) Conduct including a party's failure to comply with previous court orders is relevant.

(2) Similarly a deliberate failure to pay the judgment sum in the absence of any financial difficulty may well be a sufficient basis for making an order.[32]

(3) Evidence that the appellant has sought to dissipate its assets in order to avoid paying the judgment may also be considered a sufficient reason.[33] By contrast the disposition of assets in the ordinary course of business would not be.

---

[30] *White Book*, 2010 edn, para.52.3.15.

[31] *CIBC Mellon Trust Co v Stolzenberg* [2004] EWCA Civ 117 at [12], per Sir Swinton Thomas.

[32] These three reasons were identified in *Bell Electric Ltd v Aweco Appliance Systems GmbH & Co KG* [2003] 1 All E.R. 34 at [22], per Potter L.J. *Day's Medical Aids Ltd v Pihsiang Machinery Manufacturing Co Ltd* [2004] EWCA Civ 993 at [25].

[33] *Dumford Trading AG v OAO Atlantrybflot* [2004] EWCA Civ 1265 at [13].

The Court of Appeal has indicated that it will adopt a cautious approach[34] in assessing such applications and that "it will be an unusual, and perhaps rare, case in which it will be appropriate to make such an order, especially an order imposing as a condition the payment of the whole judgment sum into court".[35]

The court will be slow to impose a condition that might stifle the appeal. The appellant will need to ensure that sufficient evidence is before the court to support any argument that a condition will stifle the appeal. A company may have funding available to it through related companies and this is relevant in assessing whether the appeal will be stifled.[36]

Possible requirement for compelling reason

CPR r.52.3(7) appears to provide a very broad discretion subject only to the overriding objective. This is to be contrasted to the requirement for a "compelling reason" required for the appeal court to impose a condition under CPR r.52.9(1)(c) (see below at paras 16–045 et seq.). Although the courts have recognised this distinction[37] and the Court of Appeal has consistently proceeded on the basis that a compelling reason needs to be shown to justify imposing a condition[38] there is no clear authority as to whether something less than a "compelling reason" will justify the imposition of a condition under CPR r.52.3(7). 16–032

Examples of conditions on grant of permission to appeal

The following are some of the common conditions made on the grant of permission to appeal in appropriate circumstances. 16–033

[34] *Hammond Suddards v Agrichem* [2001] EWCA Civ 2065 at [48].
[35] *Dumford Trading AG v OAO Atlantrybflot* [2004] EWCA Civ 1265 at [9].
[36] *Dumford Trading AG v OAO Atlantrybflot* [2004] EWCA Civ 1265 at [16].
[37] *Komercni Bank AS v Stone and Rolls Ltd* [2003] EWCA Civ 311; [2003] C.P. Rep. 58 at [13], per Potter L.J.: "However, it seems to me that CPR r.52.9(1) is intended to be directed to the position where permission has already been granted, whereas the general discretion under 52.3(7)(b), relating to permission to appeal, is the one which is in fact applicable. The discretion contained in that provision is completely general in its terms and does not speak to a 'compelling reason' being required in order for a condition to be imposed. Nonetheless, I am quite prepared to proceed on the basis that it is, because I am satisfied that such compelling reason exists in this case."
[38] *CIBC Mellon Trust Co v Stolzenberg* [2004] EWCA Civ 117 at [33], per Sir Swinton Thomas. *Day's Medical Aids Ltd v Pihsiang Machinery Manufacturing Co Ltd* [2004] EWCA Civ 993 at [5], per Dyson L.J.: "The argument before me has proceeded on the basis that it is immaterial under which of these two rules the issue is to be considered. Either way the court should only impose conditions where there is a compelling reason for doing so. I am content to proceed on that basis." It is not clear that the second sentence amounts to judicial endorsement of the position. However this approach was again followed by the Court of Appeal in *Radmacher v Granatino* [2008] EWCA Civ 1304; [2009] 1 F.L.R. 1566 at [10] and [11], per Wilson L.J.

Payment of the judgment sum and/or costs in to court as a condition of the appeal

16–034 A common order sought is that the appellant is required to pay the judgment sum and the costs in to court as a condition for granting permission to appeal. As set out above there is no general rule that permission to appeal should be subject to such a condition.[39]

Limited recovery of appeal costs even if successful

16–035 The court may make it a condition of permission that the appellant is unable to recover some or all of his costs even if successful on the appeal. Such an order may be appropriate where the appellant wishes to appeal in order to obtain clarification of the law, in particular where the appeal will be disproportionate to the particular factual dispute in relation to which the point of law arises.[40] See, further, para.16–044 on protective costs orders.

Equally where a party has failed to comply with the court rules or previous orders the court may make the grant of permission to appeal subject to a condition that the appellant should not recover the costs of the appeal even if successful. Such a condition was imposed where a large corporation sought to appeal a decision on a preliminary issue where the trial was yet to take place and the application for permission to appeal was made significantly out of time.[41]

New issue on appeal not reserved at first instance

16–036 As addressed in Chapter 13 the court has the power to give permission in exceptional circumstances for a party to raise a new point on appeal. Where this happens the court giving permission to appeal on this basis may order that irrespective of the outcome of the appeal, as a condition of permission to appeal the costs order at first instance should remain undisturbed and the appellant should pay the costs of the respondent on the appeal.[42]

CPR R.25.15 AND APPLICATIONS FOR SECURITY FOR COSTS OF AN APPEAL

16–037 As with cases in the lower court, so the appeal court has the jurisdiction to order an appellant to provide security for the costs of the appeal.

---

[39] *Day's Medical Aids Ltd v Pihsiang Machinery Manufacturing Co Ltd* [2004] EWCA Civ 993 at [24]–[25].

[40] *Morris v Wrexham CBC and the National Assembly for Wales* [2001] EWHC Admin 697 where the National Assembly for Wales wished to clarify the law.

[41] *Lloyd Jones v T Mobile (UK) Ltd* [2004] C.P. Rep. 10.

[42] *Ungi v Liverpool City Council* [2004] EWCA Civ 1617 at [12]. See too *Southern & District Finance Plc v Turner* [2003] EWCA Civ 1574. This order was not made, but the Court of Appeal identified that it was open to the judge in considering whether to grant an appeal.

CPR r.25.15 provides jurisdiction to the court to make an order for the security of the costs of an appeal:

"25.15 (1) The court may order security for costs of an appeal against—

    (a) an appellant;

    (b) a respondent who also appeals,

on the same grounds as it may order security for costs against a claimant under this Part.

(2) The court may also make an order under paragraph (1) where the appellant, or the respondent who also appeals, is a limited company and there is reason to believe it will be unable to pay the costs of the other parties to the appeal should its appeal by unsuccessful."

There is a two stage process:

(1) First the applicant for an order for security of costs of an appeal needs to establish that one of the grounds set out in CPR r.25.13(2) applies to the prospective appellant.

(2) Then the court must be persuaded that it is just to make an order having regard to all the circumstances of the case.

The threshold grounds

The grounds under CPR r.25.13(2) as applicable for CPR r.25.15 are: 16–038

(1) The appellant is resident out of the jurisdiction but not resident in a Brussels Contracting State, a state bound by the Lugano Convention[43] or a Regulation State, as defined in s.1(3) of the Civil Jurisdiction and Judgments Act 1982 (CPR r.25.13(2)(a)). The purpose of this rule is not designed to provide a defendant with security for costs against a claimant who lacks funds.[44]

(2) The appellant is a company or other body (whether incorporated inside or outside Great Britain) and there is reason to believe that it will be unable to pay the defendant's costs if ordered to do so (CPR r.25.13(2)(c)). This is not on the basis of the company's nationality but to reflect the additional burden of enforcement abroad. An

---

[43] Amended with effect from January 1, 2010 to reflect the coming in to force of the Lugano Convention which is defined in CPR r.6.31 as the Convention on jurisdiction and the recognition and enforcement of judgments in civil and commercial matters, between the European Community and the Republic of Ireland, the Kingdom of Norway, the Swiss Confederation and the Kingdom of Denmark and signed by the European Community on October 30, 2007.

[44] *Porzelack v Porzelack* [1987] 1 All E.R. 1074.

order for security for costs should only follow where enforcement would be more difficult.[45]

(3) The appellant has changed his address since the claim was commenced with a view to evading the consequences of the litigation (CPR r.25.13(2)(d)).

(4) The appellant failed to give his address in the claim form, or gave an incorrect address in that form (CPR r.25.13(2)(e)).

(5) The appellant is acting as a nominal claimant, other than as a representative claimant under Pt 19, and there is reason to believe that he will be unable to pay the respondent's costs if ordered to do so (CPR r.25.13(2)(f)).

(6) The appellant has taken steps in relation to his assets that would make it difficult to enforce an order for costs against him (CPR r.25.13(2)(g)).

Factors as to whether it is just to make an order

16–039   The starting point is to consider whether the appellant should be permitted to pursue an appeal without securing the costs in case the appeal is unsuccessful. The fact that the appellant has been given permission to appeal does not mean that security should not be ordered.[46]

No order that will stifle an appeal

16–040   As with an order staying execution of the lower court's order, an application for security of costs of an appeal will not generally be granted where it would stifle the appeal.

Historically, less weight was given to this consideration at the appeal stage than at the lower court hearing stage. The reasons for this are not clear. The editors of the *White Book* suggest that one justification was that a respondent to an appeal deserved additional protection at the appeal stage because of the fact that he had already succeeded in the lower court. However the authors of the Bowman review considered that this operated unfairly against appellants of limited means and that the approach at the appeal stage should be analogous to that applied at the lower court level.[47]

The burden of satisfying the court that the appeal will be stifled if an order for security for costs was to be made is the person seeking to resist the order.

As with applications for a stay of execution where a party's means is relevant discussed at para.16–024 the court is entitled to take in to account

---

[45] *Nasser v United Bank of Kuwait* [2001] EWCA Civ 556; [2002] 1 W.L.R. 1868 at [59]–[67] in considering the apparent discriminatory nature of this rule under the ECHR.

[46] *Nasser v United Bank of Kuwait* [2001] EWCA Civ 556; [2002] 1 W.L.R. 1868.

[47] See notes to the *White Book*, 2009 edn, para.25.15.1.

not just the means of the person against whom the order is sought, but those from whom support might be given.[48]

Where the liberty of the appellant is at stake—such as in respect of an appeal against an order for committal—the court will not normally make an order for payment of security.[49]

Time for payment

Where a sum is ordered to be paid in to court by a certain date, unless **16–041** expressly provided for in the order, then that date refers to the receipt by the Court Funds Office of the relevant cheque.[50]

Security for costs in period before permission to appeal is granted

There is some uncertainty as to whether CPR r.25.15 provides jurisdiction **16–042** to make an order in the period before permission to appeal is granted.[51] The point is somewhat moot, because if CPR r.25.15 does not apply, then the court would have power to make an order for security of costs under its general case management powers under CPR r.3.1.[52]

Such an order might be appropriate where the application for permission is adjourned to an oral hearing with the appeal to immediately follow.

The respondent will be required to attend and may incur substantial costs in attending the hearing whether permission is granted or not.

Again the overriding consideration is that the condition or order should not stifle the appeal.[53]

---

[48] *Hammond Suddards Solicitors v Agrichem International Holdings Ltd* [2001] EWCA Civ 1915 at [27], per Clarke L.J. giving the judgment of the Court applying the factors set out in the judgment of Peter Gibson L.J. in *Keary Developments Ltd v Tarmac Construction Ltd* [1995] 3 All E.R. 534 at 539h to 542j which are applicable to post-CPR applications. *Dumford Trading AG v OAO Atlantrybflot* [2004] EWCA Civ 1265 at [38]; *Contract Facilities Ltd v The Estate of Rees* [2003] EWCA Civ 1105 at [10]; *Great Future International Ltd v Sealand Housing Corp* [2003] EWCA Civ 682 at [12], per Waller L.J.

[49] *Hoods Barrs v Heriot* [1896] 2 Q.B. 375 applied by *Gulf Azov Shipping Co Ltd v Chief Idsi (Security for Costs)*, December 19, 2000 at [13] and [14].

[50] *Petroleo Basilieiro SA v ENE Kos 1 Ltd* [2009] EWCA Civ 1127 at [25]–[27] and [39].

[51] In *Gulf Azov Shipping Co Ltd v Chief Idisi (Security for Costs)*, December 19, 2000, the Court of Appeal considered that CPR r.25.15 extended to the period before permission to appeal. See the judgment of Mance L.J. However in *Great Future International Ltd v Sealand Housing Corp* [2003] EWCA Civ 682, Waller L.J. accepted the position of the parties that CPR r.25.15 did not so apply. The point was not argued in either case.

[52] *Great Future International Ltd v Sealand Housing Corp* [2003] EWCA Civ 682 at [3] and [8], per Waller L.J.

[53] *Great Future International Ltd v Sealand Housing Corp* [2003] EWCA Civ 682 at [12], per Waller L.J.

Costs of lower court proceedings

16–043   The court has the power to make it a condition of the appeal that the appellant gives security in respect of the costs of the proceedings below.[54] However this is truly an exercise of its discretion in imposing a condition on the appeal rather than under CPR r.25.15 and the factors under CPR r.52.9 as addressed above will apply.

PROTECTIVE COSTS ORDERS

16–044   A party can apply for a protective costs order on an appeal. The guidance in *R. (Corner House Research) v Secretary of State for Trade and Industry*[55] applicable in the lower court also applies to the procedure on appeals.[56]

Where the recipient of a protective costs order was successful at first instance the appellate court is likely to continue the protective costs order.[57]

The position is likely to be less straightforward where the recipient of a protective costs order in the lower court wishes to appeal, as there may no longer be an issue of general public importance or a public interest in appealing the case.

The application for a protective costs order should presumably first be made to the lower court with the application for permission to appeal.

If application for permission to appeal is sought from the appellate court, it should be made with the application for permission to appeal, because both applications will involve some consideration of the merits of the appeal.[58]

The respondent to the application will have an opportunity of providing written reasons why the continuation of a protective costs order would be inappropriate.

The decision will be taken on paper by a single Lord Justice. If that application is refused the applicant can apply orally. If granted then the respondent can only set it aside on the basis of compelling reasons.

Appeals from the refusal to grant or refuse an application for a protective costs order should also be dealt with first on paper and in the ordinary course of events there will be no order for costs.

Only in exceptional circumstances such as where the application is held to have been an abuse of process will costs be permitted.[59]

---

[54]   *Dar International FEF Co v Aon Ltd* [2003] EWCA Civ 1833.

[55]   [2005] EWCA Civ 192; [20005] 1 W.L.R. 2600.

[56]   *R. (Compton) v Wiltshire Primary Care Trust* [2008] EWCA Civ 749 at [47]; *R. (Buglife) v Thurrock Thames Gateway Development Corp and Rosemound Developments Ltd* [2008] EWCA Civ 1209 at [32].

[57]   *R. (Compton) v Wiltshire Primary Care Trust* [2008] EWCA Civ 749 at [47]–[49] and [95].

[58]   *R. (Buglife) v Thurrock Thames Gateway Development Corp and Rosemound Developments Ltd* [2008] EWCA Civ 1209 at [33]–[35].

[59]   *R. (Compton) v Wiltshire Primary Care Trust* [2008] EWCA Civ 749 at [32]–[36].

CPR R.52.9: STRIKING OUT THE APPEAL NOTICE, SETTING ASIDE PERMISSION TO APPEAL, VARYING CONDITIONS TO APPEAL

The appeal court has the power to alter the grant of permission to appeal   **16–045**
and attendant conditions under CPR r.52.9 where there is a compelling
reason to do so as well as the power to strike out the appeal notice.
CPR r.52.9 provides:

"(1) The appeal court may—

(a)   strike out the whole or part of an appeal notice
(b)   set aside permission to appeal in whole or in part;
(c)   impose or vary conditions upon which an appeal may be
      brought;

(2) The appeal court will only exercise its powers under paragraph (1)
where there is a compelling reason for doing so.

(3) Where a party was present at the hearing at which permission was
given he may not subsequently apply for an order that the court."

Timing of application

An application under CPR r.52.9 should be made promptly and as soon as   **16–046**
possible after the order granting permission has been drawn up and the
grounds for making it are apparent. It should not be delayed until the
appeal hearing.[60]

Caution before application

The courts have repeatedly emphasised that the powers under CPR r.52.9   **16–047**
should not be used by a party to attempt to obtain tactical advantage.
Criticism and negative costs consequences are likely to follow inappropriate
applications.[61] An application should only be made if properly formulated
and should not be allowed to proceed on a contradictory basis.[62]

---

[60] *Tradigrain SA v Intertek Testing Services (ITS) Canada Ltd* [2007] EWCA Civ 154; [2007]
      1 C.L.C. 188 at [12], per Moore-Bick L.J.
[61] *Barings Bank Plc (In Liquidation) v Coopers & Lybrand* [2002] EWCA Civ 1155 at [43],
      per Laws L.J.
[62] *Mamidoil-Jetoil Greek Petroleum Co SA v Okta Crude Oil Refinery Ltd* [2003] EWCA
      Civ 617; [2003] 2 L.L.R. 645 at [9]–[11], per Clarke L.J.

CPR r.52.9(1)(a): striking out an appeal notice

16–048   CPR r.52.9 provides an exhaustive statement of the court's jurisdiction to strike out a notice of appeal. A compelling reason must be made out.[63]

Abuse of process

16–049   Striking out the appeal notice on the basis of an abuse of process would be appropriate if an abuse of the court's procedure by the appellant has prevented a fair hearing of the appeal.[64]

No real prospect of success

16–050   Theoretically an application could be made to strike out the appeal notice on the basis that it is frivolous or vexatious or has no real prospect of success. However such appeals should have been weeded out at the permission stage.[65]

Breach of rule, practice direction or court order

16–051   An application to strike out an appeal notice is most likely to arise where the appellant has either failed to comply with the rules and practice directions in terms of the preparation and filing of the appeal notice or where it has persistently failed to comply with the appeal court's directions.

So where the appellant is in deliberate breach of an underlying order to pay a judgment sum; or has applied for and been refused a stay; and still has not paid despite no financial difficulty then a "compelling reason" is likely to be established.[66]

However the threshold for strike out is a high one. For instance a breach of disclosure obligations in the underlying proceedings may not be a compelling reason where it does not affect the conduct of the appeal.[67]

An order under CPR r.52.9(1)(a) can be given prospectively on an "unless basis" when coupled with conditions imposed on the appeal especially in the context of an order directing security for payment of costs.[68]

---

[63] *Dadourian Group International Inc v Simms* [2009] EWCA Civ 169; [2009] 1 L.L.R. 601 at 229 and 234.

[64] *Dadourian Group International Inc v Simms* [2009] EWCA Civ 169; [2009] 1 L.L.R. 601 at 232.

[65] *Turner v Haworth Associates* [2001] EWCA Civ 370 at [26], per Chadwick L.J. In that case there was no requirement for permission to appeal and the circuit judge had struck out the appeal notice on the basis that it was an abuse of the court's process.

[66] *Bell Electric Ltd v Aweco Appliance Systems GmbH & Co* [2002] EWCA Civ 1501; [2003] C.P. Rep. 18 at [22], per Potter L.J.

[67] *Dadourian Group International Inc v Simms* [2009] EWCA Civ 160; [2009] 1 L.L.R. 601 at 232.

[68] *Carr v Bower Cotton* [2002] EWCA Civ 789; [2002] C.P. Rep. 60 at [36], per Chadwick L.J.; *Moses-Taiga v Taiga* [2004] EWCA Civ 1399 at [18]–[19], per Potter L.J.

CPR r.52.9(1)(b): setting aside permission to appeal

To set aside permission to appeal the respondent needs to show that the appeal would have no prospect of success.   16–052

A respondent present at the application for permission to appeal may not subsequently apply to set it aside under CPR r.52.9. Accordingly, if there is an oral hearing for permission to appeal, the respondents should raise any relevant arguments at that stage.

Where either the lower or the appellate court has granted permission to appeal, the Court of Appeal has discouraged applications to set aside permission on the basis that the appeal has no real prospects of success, unless there has been something improper in the application for permission: after all, the respondent can argue against the appeal on the same basis at the appeal hearing itself, which will avoid the risk of satellite litigation.

There is a high hurdle to overcome in making a successful application to set aside permission.[69] There must be a compelling reason to set aside permission to appeal and in this context this means that there must have been something "which is sufficiently serious to be in the nature of an irregularity in the grant of permission".[70]

If the respondent seeks to show that there was something improper in the application for permission, it must show that:

(1) the materials put before the judge who gave permission to appeal were inaccurate or incomplete;

(2) these deficiencies had a bearing upon the grounds on which permission to appeal was given;

(3) but for the misleading factors, permission to appeal would not have been given.[71]

The following may amount to compelling reasons sufficient to set aside the grant of permission to appeal: 16–053

(1) Where the court granting permission had overlooked or not been shown a decisive authority or statutory provision.

(2) Where the court has been materially misled in the presentation of the application.[72]

(3) Where the appellant has obtained permission to appeal following the grant of an extension of time which should not have been given.[73]

---

[69] *Nathan v Smilovitch* [2002] EWCA Civ 759 at [39], per Longmore L.J.; *Barings Plc (In Liquidation) v Coopers & Lybrand* [2002] EWCA Civ 1155 at [43], per Laws L.J.

[70] *Barings Plc (In Liquidation) v Coopers & Lybrand* [2002] EWCA Civ 1155 at [34] citing with approval Longmore L.J. in *Nathan v Smilovitch* [2002] EWCA Civ 759 at [34], [37] and [39].

[71] *Hertsmere BC v Harty* [2001] EWCA Civ 1238 at [2], per Sedley L.J.

[72] *Nathan v Smilovitch* [2002] EWCA Civ 759 at [34], per Longmore L.J. as qualified by Laws L.J. in *Barings Plc (In Liquidation) v Coopers & Lybrand* [2002] EWCA Civ 1155 at [43].

[73] *Jackson v Marina Homes Ltd* [2007] EWCA Civ 1404 at [17], per Sir Henry Brooke obiter and at [25], per Sedley L.J.

(4) Where the judge granting permission lacked jurisdiction to do so.[74]

Where the judgment below has been set aside because of fraud,[75] the permission to appeal will fall away without any need for a review of the decision granting permission to appeal.[76]

The courts have rejected applications to set aside permission where the reasons relied upon were relevant to costs,[77] or where considerable indulgence had been shown to the appellant in granting permission.[78]

If an application is to be made it should be made promptly.[79]

CPR r.52.9(1)(c): imposing or varying conditions on appeal

16–054　The power to impose or vary conditions on an appeal is a standalone power. The appeal court is not limited to a supervisory review of the lower court's case management decision as it would be on an appeal from that condition.[80] Conditions may include a requirement that the appellant or a third party provides security or a guarantee in respect of the judgment, or pays particular sums.[81]

Compelling reason to impose or vary conditions against the appellant

16–055　As with the other powers under CPR r.52.9 an application to impose or vary conditions will only succeed where there is a compelling reason.

Applications are commonly made under this limb of CPR r.52.9 to make it a condition of the appeal that the appellant pays the judgment sum in to court. The Court of Appeal has given guidance to the effect that it would be an unusual case in which it would be appropriate to make such an order.[82]

A compelling reason sufficient to trigger the power under CPR r.52.9(1)(c) to vary or impose conditions at the respondent's request is

---

[74] *Athletic Union of Constantinople v National Basketball Association (No.2)* [2002] EWCA Civ 830; [2002] 1 W.L.R. 2863.

[75] *Dadourian Group International Inc v Simms* [2009] EWCA Civ 169; [2009] 1 L.L.R. 601 at 232, per Arden L.J. giving the judgment of the Court.

[76] *Morris v Bank of India* [2004] EWCA Civ 1286 at [14], per Clarke L.J.

[77] *Barings Plc (In Liquidation) v Coopers & Lybrand* [2002] EWCA Civ 1155 at [36], per Laws L.J.

[78] *Tradigrain SA v Intertek Testing Services (ITS) Canada Ltd* [2007] EWCA Civ 154; [2007] 1 C.L.C. 188 at [12], per Moore-Bick L.J.

[79] *Okta Crude Oil Refinery AD v Moil-Coal Trading Co Ltd* [2003] EWCA Civ 617; [2003] 2 Lloyd's Rep. 645 at [10], per Clarke L.J.

[80] *King v Daltry* [2003] EWCA Civ 808; June 12, 2003 at [15], per Sedley L.J.

[81] *Hammond Suddard Solicitors v Agrichem International Holdings Ltd* [2001] EWCA Civ 1915 at [41], per Clarke L.J. giving the judgment of the Court; *Okta Crude Oil Refinery AD v Moil-Coal Trading Co Ltd* [2003] EWCA Civ 617 at [41]–[42]. The security/guarantee was not ordered, but sums were required to be paid and a freezing order would have been made were it not for an undertaking. It will sometimes be appropriate to impose such conditions and sometimes it will not. See by contrast *CIBC Mellon Trust Co v Mora Hotel Corp NV* [2002] EWCA Civ 1688; [2003] 1 All E.R. 564.

[82] *Dumford Trading AG v OAO Atlantrybflot* [2004] EWCA Civ 1265 at [9], per Clarke L.J.

likely to arise in the same circumstances as an application under CPR r.52.9(1)(a), considered in para.16–051.

The conduct of the appellant is likely to be highly relevant. The following may give rise to a compelling reason:

(1) a deliberate failure to comply with an order of the lower court, particularly a failure to pay the judgment sum, even after an application for a stay of execution was refused[83];

(2) where there is reason to suspect a lack of frankness in the application for permission[84];

(3) where there is evidence that an appellant has dissipated or sought to dissipate its assets in order to avoid paying a judgment.[85]

As with an application to set aside permission to appeal under CPR r.52.9(1)(b) a respondent who was present at the permission hearing is precluded from making an application to impose or vary conditions on an appeal. However the appellant is not under such a constraint.[86]

Varying the conditions in favour of the appellant

Respondents have attempted to argue that CPR r.52.9(3) prevents an appellant applying to vary or impose conditions because it was present at the application for permission hearing. **16–056**

CPR r.52.9(3) provides:

> "52.9 (3) Where a party was present at the hearing at which permission was given he may not subsequently apply for an order that the court exercise its powers under sub-paragraphs (1)(b) or (1)(c)."

However the courts have consistently held that the appeal court has jurisdiction to hear appellants' applications. The reasoning has varied.

In *Société Eram Shipping Co Ltd v Compagnie Internationale de Navigation*[87] Rix L.J. suggested that CPR r.52.9(3) did not apply where permission to appeal had been granted by the lower court, because although the parties are likely all to have been present at the hearing, there is no reason to think that it is necessary in every case for the parties to be in a position to ask for conditions to be imposed at the same time. Accordingly, he suggested, it may only apply where an application for permission had been made to the appeal court and considered at an oral hearing.

---

[83] *Bell Electric Ltd v Aweco Appliance Systems GmbH & Co* [2002] EWCA Civ 1501; [2003] C.P. Rep. 18 at [22], per Potter L.J.

[84] *Hammond Suddard Solicitors v Agrichem International Holdings Ltd* [2001] EWCA Civ 1915 at [41]–[42], per Clarke L.J. giving the judgment of the Court.

[85] *Dumford Trading AG v OAO Atlantrybflot* [2004] EWCA Civ 1265.

[86] *Kuwait Airways Corp v Iraqi Airways Co (Application for Permission to Appeal)* [2005] EWCA Civ 934 at [73]–[75].

[87] [2001] EWCA Civ 568 at [18].

The position was left open in *Contract Facilities Ltd v Estate of Rees (deceased)*[88] and it was pointed out that the appellate court can achieve the same result through its case management powers under CPR r.3.1 in any event. There may be on one view be some tension between the view that the Court can rely on its other case management powers when it approaches CPR r.52.9(1)(b)–(c) and the conclusion that that in respect of CPR r.52.9(1)(a), the appeal court's exclusive jurisdiction is provided by that section.[89]

Where there is convincing evidence that a consequence of maintaining the condition will be that the appeal is stifled the appeal court is likely to vary the condition to permit the appeal to proceed.[90]

Timing of applications

16–057   Applications under CPR r.52.9 should be made promptly. A party should not be permitted to amend its grounds for making the application at the hearing,[91] unless, presumably, there is good reason to do so.

APPEAL BY A NON-PARTY

16–058   As discussed in Chapter 9, it is possible for someone who was not a party to the proceedings below who is adversely affected by the decision to apply for permission to appeal and to be joined as a party to the proceedings for the purposes of the appeal.[92]

The new party must show that he has a real interest as opposed to being a "mere intermeddling busybody"[93] and an application for permission to appeal where there is no such interest will be refused even if the appeal has a real prospect of success.[94]

While it is relevant to the exercise of the discretion whether to grant that new party permission to appeal as to whether or not that party had applied to be added as a party to the proceedings in the lower court, a refusal by the

---

[88] [2003] EWCA Civ 1105 at [19].

[89] *Dadourian Group International Inc v Simms* [2009] EWCA Civ 160; [2009] 1 L.L.R. 601 at 229 and 234.

[90] *Kuwait Airways Corp v Iraqi Airways Co (Application for Permission to Appeal)* [2005] EWCA Civ 934 at [73]–[75].

[91] *Okta Crude Oil Refinery AD v Moil-Coal Trading Co Ltd* [2003] EWCA Civ 617 at [9]–[11], per Clarke L.J.

[92] *MA Holdings Ltd v George Wimpey UK Ltd and Tewkesbury BC* [2008] EWCA Civ 12; [2008] 1 W.L.R. 1649. Wimpey had succeeded in quashing the local authority's decision to adopt the local plan thereby directly affecting the property interests of MA Holdings Ltd. There is a possible distinction between appeals from the High Court and appeals from the County Court in this regard: see para.9–003.

[93] *MA Holdings Ltd v George Wimpey UK Ltd and Tewkesbury BC* [2008] EWCA Civ 12; [2008] 1 W.L.R. 1649 at [26], per Dyson L.J.

[94] *MA Holdings Ltd v George Wimpey UK Ltd and Tewkesbury BC* [2008] EWCA Civ 12; [2008] 1 W.L.R. 1649 at [24], per Dyson L.J.

lower court to add a party to those proceedings is not determinative of the exercise of the discretion on the appeal.[95]

Application by non-party to file evidence and make representations on a statutory appeal

CPR r.52.12A provides: 16–059

"(1) In a statutory appeal, any person may apply for permission—

(a) to file evidence; or
(b) to make representations at the appeal hearing.

(2) An application under paragraph (1) must be made promptly."

Further guidance as to applications in respect of statutory appeals is provided in the Practice Direction to Pt 52. The procedure is set out in paras 17.7 to 17.11 of the Practice Direction.

An application for permission must be made by letter to the relevant court office, identifying the appeal, explaining who the applicant is and indicating why and in what form the applicant wants to participate in the hearing.[96] If the applicant is seeking a prospective order as to costs, the letter must say what kind of order and on what grounds.[97]

Although the requirement for making an application under CPR r.52.12A is that it is made "promptly", para.17.11 of the Practice Direction to Pt 52 provides that applications to intervene must be made at the earliest reasonable opportunity.

In the context of statutory appeals any person who may apply for permission to appeal to the Court of Appeal has the power to join additional parties to an appeal. This power extends to the period even after the court's order has been sealed where it is necessary for the purpose of dealing with ancillary orders.[98]

APPLICATION FOR RECUSAL OF APPEAL COURT JUDGE

The test for recusal is the same as in the lower court, namely whether a fair-   16–060
minded and informed observer, having considered the relevant facts, would

---

[95] *MA Holdings Ltd v George Wimpey UK Ltd and Tewkesbury BC* [2008] EWCA Civ 12; [2008] 1 W.L.R. 1649 at [28] and [29], per Dyson L.J.
[96] CPR PD 52 para.17.9.
[97] CPR PD 52 para.17.10.
[98] *DK v Bryn Alyn Community (Holdings) Ltd (In Liquidation)* [2003] EWCA Civ 783.

conclude that there existed a real possibility that the judge was biased.[99] In this regard the fair-minded observer is "neither complacent nor unduly sensitive or suspicious".[100]

The question is one of law to be answered in light of the relevant facts which may include a statement from the judge as to what he or she knew at the time although the court is not bound to accept any such statement at face value.[101] The judge will not be cross-examined and any statement as to the impact of particular knowledge on his or her mind is to be disregarded.[102]

A tenuous connection between a judge and a firm of solicitors could not ever be regarded by the reasonable well informed observer as giving rise to a possibility of bias. The previous receipt of instructions by a judge to act for or against any party, solicitor or advocate engaged in the trial before him or her would not normally give rise to a need for recusal.[103] Similarly the suffering by a judge of a condition or symptom that was the subject of the case was no basis for recusal.[104]

Where in any particular case one or more members of a court which has partly heard proceedings are unable to continue the Master of Rolls has the power to give directions as to how the court is to continue hearing the case.[105]

CONSENT ORDERS INVOLVING CHILDREN, PROTECTED PARTIES OR APPEALS FROM THE COURT OF PROTECTION

16–061   Special provisions arise in respect of these categories of appeals, particularly in the context of settlement or discontinuance.

Where one of the parties is a child or a protected party or the application or appeal is to the Court of Appeal from a decision of the Court of Protection the following require the court's approval:

---

[99] *Porter v Magill* [2002] 2 A.C. 357, cited in *Helow v Secretary of State for the Home Department* [2008] UKHL 62; [2008] 1 W.L.R. 2416 at [39], per Lord Hope.

[100] per Kirby J. in *Johnson v Johnson* (2000) 201 C.L.R. 488 at [53] as approved in *Gillies v Secretary of State for Work and Pensions* [2006] 1 W.L.R. 781 at [17] and [39] and in *Helow v Secretary of State for the Home Department* [2008] UKHL 62; [2008] 1 W.L.R. 2416 at [39], per Lord Hope.

[101] *Helow v Secretary of State for the Home Department* [2008] UKHL 62; [2008] 1 W.L.R. 2416 at [39], per Lord Hope.

[102] *Locabail (UK) Ltd v Bayfield Properties* [2000] Q.B. 451 at [19], per Lord Bingham.

[103] *Locabail (UK) Ltd v Bayfield Properties* [2000] Q.B. 451.

[104] *Baker v Quantum Clothing Group* [2009] EWCA Civ 566; [2009] C.P. Rep. 38 at [33]–[34]. See too *Helow v Secretary of State for the Home Department* [2008] UKHL 62; [2008] 1 W.L.R. 2416, where a judge who was a member of the International Association of Jewish Lawyers and Jurists whose magazine had carried a number of articles and pronouncements that were antipathetic to the Palestinian Liberation Organisation should not have recused himself from hearing an asylum appeal where the applicant was a sympathiser with the PLO and feared attack by Israeli agents.

[105] Senior Courts Act 1981 s.54(4A).

(1) a settlement relating to an appeal or application;
(2) an agreement at the appeal stage in a personal injury action for damages for future pecuniary loss that such losses be paid by periodical payments; and
(3) a request by an appellant for an order that the party's application or appeal be dismissed with or without the consent of the respondent.[106]

In cases involving a child or a protected party a copy of the proposed order signed by the parties' solicitors should be sent to the appeal court together with a supportive opinion from the advocate acting on behalf of the child or protected party.[107] In addition for a protected party the request should also be accompanied by any relevant reports prepared for the Court of Protection.[108]

Where periodical payments for future pecuniary loss have been negotiated in a personal injury action under appeal, the request should also be accompanied by those documents which would be required in the case of a personal injury claim for damages for future pecuniary loss dealt with at first instance and set out in the Practice Direction to Pt 21.

DISCONTINUANCE AND COMPROMISE OF APPEALS

Where a claim is discontinued in the lower court (or struck out) then any appeal will be vacated. An order dismissing an appeal will normally be accompanied by an order that the appellant pays the costs of the application or appeal.[109] See further Chapter 7.

16–062

There are standard forms in the Court of Appeal for making an application for dismissal of the appeal or application: Forms 253, 254A and 254B.

The requirements relating to children and the Court of Protection apply in respect of the discontinuance and compromise of appeals. If an appellant chooses to discontinue an appeal then unless the party is a child or protected party or the appeal or application is from a decision of the Court of Protection then the appellant can request the appeal court to make an order that the appeal be dismissed.

Where the appellant seeks a different order in respect of costs then he must have the respondent's written signed consent which must state that the respondent is not a child or protected party and that the appeal or application is not from a decision of the Court of Protection; and that the party consents to the dismissal of the application or appeal without costs.[110]

---

[106] CPR PD 52 para.13.2.
[107] CPR PD 52 para.13.3–4.
[108] CPR PD 52 para.13.4.
[109] CPR PD 52 para.12.1–2.
[110] CPR PD 52 para.12.3.

Similarly if a settlement is reached between the parties which disposes of the appeal, the parties may make a joint request to the court requesting that the appeal be dismissed. Such a request from the parties must, as with the other requests, include a statement that none of the parties is a child or a protected party and the appeal or application is not from a decision of the Court of Protection, and asking that the application or appeal be dismissed by consent.[111] If a Tomlin order is submitted for approval then it should provide that any permission to apply for further directions is made to the lower court.

Where the respondent to an appeal does not oppose it, the situation is more complicated because to allow the appeal the appeal court must exercise its jurisdiction to alter the lower court's order. The appeal court will not normally make an order allowing an appeal unless satisfied that the decision of the lower court was wrong, but the appeal court may set aside or vary the order of the lower court with consent and without determining the merits of the appeal if it is satisfied that there are good and sufficient reasons for doing so. In such cases, a request should be made by all parties to the appeal and should contain the following:

(1) the relevant history of the proceedings;
(2) the matters relied on as justifying the proposed order;
(3) a copy of the proposed order; and
(4) a statement that none of the parties is a child or protected party and that the application or appeal is not from a decision of the Court of Protection.[112]

The appeal court may consider an application by all parties to allow the application or appeal on the papers without an oral hearing.

---

[111] CPR PD 52 para.12.4.
[112] CPR PD 52 para.13.1.

CHAPTER 17

Practice Points in Different Courts

This chapter addresses particular points of practice in the different courts. **17–001**
They are addressed in the following order:

(1) Appeals in the County Court.
(2) Appeals to the High Court, including particular matters relating to
    appeals in the Chancery Division and the Queens' Bench Division
    and particular provisions relating to statutory appeals.
(3) Appeals to the Court of Appeal including certain statutory
    appeals.

PRACTICE POINTS ON APPEALS IN THE COUNTY COURT

Small claims track appeals

Initially Pt 52 did not apply to appeals from the small claims track. **17–002**
However following the repeal of CPR r.27.12 and 27.13, Pt 52 now applies
to appeals from decisions from claims allocated to the small claims track.
   However there are some slightly less onerous requirements in terms of
preparation of documents:

(1) Whilst the appellant must still file an appeal notice, it is on a
    different form (Form N164).
(2) The appeal notice should include a sealed copy of the order being
    appealed and any order giving or refusing permission to appeal.
(3) The appellant need only file a record of the reasons for judgment of
    the lower court where the court has so directed to enable it to
    decide if permission should be granted or to determine the appeal.[1]
(4) The appellant has the option of filing any of the other documents
    that may be filed with an appeal notice that are relevant to the

---

[1] CPR PD 52 para.5.8.

issues to be determined on an appeal. In this regard the appellant should consider whether copies of the pleadings, application notices, witness statements, contracts or photographs are necessary for determination of the application for permission to appeal or the appeal proper.

The appellant must comply with the provisions of service of the appeal notice and accompanying documents as discussed in Chapters 14 and 15.

Hearing of appeals in the County Court

17–003 Paragraph 8A.1 of the Practice Direction to Pt 52 provides that the designated civil judge in consultation with his presiding judge has responsibility for allocating appeals from decisions of district judges to circuit judges.

- Appeals from district judges are often heard by the designated circuit judge at the trial centre for which the county court is the feeder court.[2]
- There are certain restrictions as to which judges may hear appeals in the County Courts. For instance a district judge may not hear appeals under s.204 or s.204A of the Housing Act 1996.[3]

Statutory appeals in the County Court

17–004 The following statutory appeals are to be determined by the County Court rather than the High Court:

(1) appeals under ss.21, 23 or 35 of the Local Government (Miscellaneous Provisions) Act 1976;
(2) appeals under ss.204 and 204A of the Housing Act 1996;
(3) an appeal under Pt II of the Immigration and Asylum Act 1999;
(4) an appeal of a decision referred to in s.56(1) of the Representation of the People Act 1983; and
(5) an appeal under s.11 of the UK Borders Act 2007.

Specific guidance as to which parties are to be joined to such statutory appeals and the specific procedures relevant to such appears are set out at paras 24.1 to 24.7 of the Practice Direction to Pt 52 which are self-explanatory and are not repeated here.

---

[2] *The Civil Court Practice* (2010) Vol.1, CPR r.52.5, p.1311.
[3] CPR PD 2B para.9.

PRACTICE POINTS ON APPEALS TO THE HIGH COURT

Introduction

The Practice Direction to Pt 52 provides general guidance in respect of **17–005** appeals to a High Court judge from decisions of a County Court or a district judge of the High Court. The guides of the relevant divisions of the High Court provide further guidance as to such appeals as well as appeals within the High Court.

Appeal court judge in the High Court

Where the lower court is a County Court then the appeal can be heard **17–006** before a High Court judge, or, where requested by the Lord Chief Justice or, in his absence, the Master of the Rolls, a judge of the Court of Appeal or a person who has been a puisne judge of the High Court.

An appeal or application for permission to appeal from the decision of a recorder in the county court may also be heard by such judges and in addition any designated civil judge who is authorised under para.(5) of the table in s.9(1) of the Senior Courts Act 1981 to act as a judge of the High Court.[4]

For other applications anyone authorised under s.9 of the Senior Courts Act 1981 to sit as a judge of the High Court may hear the application including those appointed as deputy judges.[5]

Appeal centre for appeal to High Court

Where an appeal is from the decision of a county court or a district judge of **17–007** the High Court it is necessary to determine the appropriate appeal centre where the appeal is to be filed. This depends on the circuit on which the lower court from whose decision the appeal is to be brought is situated.

Appeals from decisions on the South Eastern Circuit

On an appeal from a decision of a lower court on the South Eastern Circuit **17–008** the appeal must be filed at one of the following appeal centres on the South Eastern Circuit:

(1) The Royal Courts of Justice;
(2) Chelmsford;
(3) Lewes;
(4) Luton;

---

[4] CPR PD 52 para.8.13(1) and (1A).
[5] CPR PD 52 para.8.13(2).

(5) Maidstone;

(6) Norwich;

(7) Oxford;

(8) Reading; and

(9) St Albans.

Unless the appeal court orders otherwise, the appeal will be managed by the Royal Courts of Justice.

An order that the appeal is to be managed or heard at an appeal centre other than the Royal Courts of Justice can only be made with the consent of the presiding judge of the circuit in charge of civil matters.[6] The circumstances when this is likely to take place are limited, but may arise where there are a number of appeals on the same or similar points arising from decisions on different cases or similar case management reasons.

A respondent's notice must be filed at the Royal Courts of Justice unless the appeal has been transferred to another appeal centre, in which case it must be filed at that appeal centre.[7]

Appeals on circuits other than the South Eastern Circuit

17–009   Appeals from lower courts on circuits other than the South Eastern Circuit must be filed at one of the applicable appeal centres on the relevant circuit. These are:

(1) Midland Circuit: Birmingham and Nottingham.

(2) North Eastern Circuit: Leeds, Newcastle and Sheffield.

(3) Northern Circuit: Manchester, Liverpool, Preston and Chester.

(4) Wales Circuit: Cardiff, Swansea and Mold.

(5) Western Circuit: Bristol, Exeter and Winchester.

The appeal will be managed and heard at the appeal centre where the appellant's notice is filed unless the appeal court orders otherwise.

The respondent should file any respondent's notice at the appeal centre where the appellant's notice was filed unless the appeal has been transferred to another appeal centre.

Applications

17–010   Unless the management of the appeal has been directed to be heard at another appeal centre then any applications should be made to the appeal centre where the appeal is being managed.[8]

---

[6] CPR PD 52 para.8.7.

[7] CPR PD 52 para.8.8.

[8] CPR PD 52 para.8.11.

Transfer to another appeal centre and/or hearing only centre

The appeal court may transfer an appeal to another appeal centre on the same or another circuit for management and hearing or for the hearing of the appeal only.   **17–011**

In deciding whether to order a transfer the appeal court will apply the same criteria set out in CPR r.30.3.

However a transfer of an appeal to another circuit for management or hearing can only be ordered with the consent of the Presiding Judge of that circuit in charge of civil matters.[9]

A transfer may be ordered on the court's own initiative or on the application of a party.

If an appeal is transferred, then notice of the transfer must be given to every person on whom the appellant's notice was served.[10] Although the practice direction does not specify who is responsible for so doing it is implicit that it is for the appellant to do so.

Procedures specific to the Chancery and Queens Bench Divisions

The relevant guides for the divisions of the High Court provide further guidance as to matters relating to appeals such as the preparation of papers and listing of appeals as well as matters specific to statutory appeals. These complement the sections of Pt 52 and the Practice Direction to Pt 52 which address statutory appeals and are addressed below.   **17–012**

The Chancery Division

Within the Chancery Division there are four main categories of appeals: **17–013**

(1) Appeals within the ordinary work of the Chancery Division at the Royal Courts of Justice, from masters to High Court judges.

(2) Insolvency appeals from High Court registrars and from county courts to High Court judges.[11]

(3) Appeals to High Court judges in the Chancery Division from orders in claims proceeding in a county court.

(4) Statutory appeals from tribunals and other decision maker to the Chancery Division.

---

[9] CPR PD 52 para.8.9.
[10] CPR PD 52 para.8.9.
[11] This does not include appeals from a final decision of the registrar of the Companies Court. These appeals are direct to the Court of Appeal because proceedings under the Companies Acts are specialist proceedings.

Permission to Appeal

17–014   It is the usual practice of the Chancery Division that notice of a hearing for permission to appeal is given to the respondent.

The respondent may submit written submissions on the issue of whether permission to appeal should be granted and/or attend the hearing. The respondent will not necessarily be awarded any costs of so doing even if permission to appeal is refused.[12] The submissions should be limited to the issue of whether permission to appeal should be granted.

Documents unavailable for filing with appellant's notice

17–015   The Chancery Guide para.10.9 provides that the High Court Appeals Office is able to allow further time by way of an extension for the filing of documents.

Any further extension will require an application to a judge who will consider the application on paper.

The guidance recommends that where a transcript of the underlying judgment is unavailable the appellant should file a note of the judgment as an interim measure.

If the required documents for an application for permission to appeal are not filed within the relevant time period or extension thereof then the case may be listed for an oral hearing in the Dismissal List where the appellant will be required to show cause as to why the application should not be dismissed. The respondent would not normally be notified of such a hearing.[13]

Appeals from masters in cases proceeding in the Chancery Division

17–016   An appeal from a master in a case proceeding in the Chancery Division usually lies to a High Court judge of the Chancery Division. However an appeal from a final decision of a master on a multi-track case will be to the Court of Appeal.

The Chancery Guide provides that the appeal will be limited to a review of the decision of the lower court "unless the court considers that, in the circumstances of the individual appeal, it would be in the interests of justice to hold a re-hearing".[14] This picks up the provision in CPR r.52.11(1)(b) and the guidance that applies to that provision.

An application for permission to appeal from a decision of a master must be lodged in the Clerk of the Lists' Offices in Room WG7. The application must be stamped with the appropriate fee having been paid within 21 days from the decision of the master. The application for permission to appeal will be listed for hearing in the Interim Hearings List.[15]

---

[12] Chancery Guide para.10.7.
[13] Chancery Guide para.10.10.
[14] Chancery Guide para.10.14.
[15] Chancery Guide para.6.19.

Where permission to appeal has been granted by the master then the appellant must file the appeal with the Clerk of the Lists' Office in Room WG7 stamped with the appropriate fee having been paid within such time as directed by the master or where none has been specified within 21 days.

Insolvency appeals

An appeal lies from a County Court (circuit or district judge) or a High Court registrar in bankruptcy or company insolvency matters to a High Court judge of the Chancery Division, for which permission is not required. This includes appeals under the Company Directors Disqualification Act 1986.　　　　　　　　　　　　　　　　　　　　　　　　　**17–017**

The time limit for filing an appellant's notice is the same as for ordinary Chancery appeals (i.e. 21 days).[16]

As with appeals from masters, the notice of appeal from the decision of a registrar or of a county court must be lodged in the Clerk of the Lists' Office in Room WG7 with the appropriate fee having been paid.

An appeal will be limited to a review of the decision of the lower court.[17]

Appeals from orders made in County Court claims to the Chancery Division of the High Court

Appeals from county court claims that would be suitable for the Chancery Division in terms of the subject matter will be heard by a High Court judge where the appeal is destined for the High Court.　　　　　**17–018**

As set out in Chapter 12 an appeal against a decision of a circuit judge in a claim proceeding in a county court lies to the High Court, unless either the decision is a final decision in a multi-track claim or in specialist proceedings to which CPR r.49(2) applies, or the decision is itself an appeal.

Listing of appeals in the Chancery Division

Appeals from masters are heard in the Interim Hearings List whereas other appeals such as revenue, bankruptcy and pension appeals are heard in the general list. An appeal from a master will appear in the Appeals Warned List. On confirmation that the case has been placed in the Warned List the solicitors acting for the parties must "forthwith" inform the Chancery Judge's Listing Officer whether they intend to instruct counsel and, if so, the name or names of counsel.[18] Insolvency and Revenue appeals will also be entered in the Appeals Warned List, usually with a fixed date. The date of a hearing with a fixed date will be fixed by appointment with the Chancery Judge's Listing Officer.　　　　　　　　　　　　　　　**17–019**

---

[16] Chancery Guide paras 10.11 and 10.17.
[17] *Vadiher v Wesigard* [1997] B.C.C. 219.
[18] Chancery Guide para.6.18.

Listing appointments

17–020 The Chancery Judge's Listing Officer will seek to have the appeal heard without undue delay while taking into account insofar as it is practical to do so any difficulties the parties may have as to the availability of counsel and the convenience of the parties.[19] For revenue appeals the Chancery Listing Officer will, if requested and convenient for counsel and/or solicitors, endeavour to fix two or more revenue appeals so that they will come on consecutively.[20]

Communications with the court

17–021 The central point of contact for appeals for hearing by High Court judges in the Chancery Division is the Clerk of the Lists, High Court Appeals Office (Room WG8) in the Royal Courts of Justice.[21]

Dismissal of appeals by consent

17–022 Where parties wish for an appeal to be dismissed by consent, the Chancery Division adopts the practice set out in para.12 of the Practice Direction to Pt 52 addressed in Chapter 16.

A document signed by all parties must be lodged with the High Court Appeals Office (Room WG7), Royal Courts of Justice, London WC21 2LL, requesting dismissal of the appeal.

The appeal can be dismissed without any hearing by an order made in the name of the Chancellor. Any orders with directions as to costs will be drawn by the Chancery Associates.

In the case of a first appeal in an insolvency matter, reference should be made to para.17.22(8) of the Practice Direction for Insolvency Proceedings which provides:

> "where an appeal has been settled or where an appellant does not wish to continue with the appeal, the appeal may be disposed of on paper without a hearing. It may be dismissed by consent but the appeal court will not make an order allowing an appeal unless it is satisfied that the decision of the lower court was wrong. Any consent order signed by each party or letters of consent from each party must be lodged not later than 24 hours before the date fixed for the hearing of the appeal at the address of the appropriate venue as set out in sub-paragraph 17.22(2) above and will be dealt with by the Judge of the appeal court. Attention is drawn to paragraph 4.4(4) of the Practice Direction to CPR Part 44 regarding costs where an order is made by consent without attendance."

---

[19] This is the guidance for fixing a trial within a trial window and there is no reason to doubt that such an approach would also apply for the listing of an appeal.

[20] Chancery Guide para.6.25.

[21] Chancery Guide para.6.16.

Queen's Bench Division in the Royal Courts of Justice

There is slightly less specific guidance in the Queen's Bench Guide and specialist guides on particular aspects of appeals. The focus is on the listing of appeals.

17–023

Listing of Appeals in the Queen's Bench Division

Appeals in the Queen's Bench Division are listed in the Interim Hearings List.[22]

17–024

Appeals will initially be listed for hearing in Room E101 before the Interim Applications judge. If the appeal cannot be dealt with within one hour it will not be taken on the date given for the listed hearing.

(a) If the parties agree in advance that the matter cannot be dealt with in less than an hour the appellant may on filing the notice of appeal seek to have the matter placed directly into the Interim Hearings Warned List.

(b) If this is not done then the appellant must as soon as is practicable and, in any event not later than 24 hours before the hearing date, apply to transfer the matter into the Interim Hearings List.

(c) If the parties are unable to agree that the matter can be disposed of within an hour or agree less than 24 hours before the hearing date the parties must attend on the date.[23]

Appeals in the Interim Hearings List will be listed by the Clerk of the Lists in Room WG3 and the parties will be notified by the Listing Office (Room WG5) of the date on which the matter will enter the Warned List. Matters in the Warned List may be listed for hearing at any time on or after that date.[24]

The Clerk of the Lists publishes each week, usually on a Thursday, the "Warned List" for the following week. This shows the matters in the Interim Hearings List that are liable to be heard in the following week.[25]

Fixtures are only given in exceptional circumstances.

The parties may by agreement "offer" preferred dates for their matter to be heard, to be taken from the List on designated days, within the week following entry into the Warned List in accordance with Listing Office practice:

(a) Matters lasting less than a day are usually offered for two pre-ferred consecutive days.

---

[22] Queen's Bench Guide para.9.5.1.
[23] Queen's Bench Guide para.9.7.2.
[24] Queen's Bench Guide para.9.7.3.
[25] Queen's Bench Guide para.9.5.2.

(b) Matters lasting more than a day are usually offered for three preferred consecutive days.[26]

Where no date has been fixed then the matter will be liable to appear in the List for hearing with no warning other than the "Cause List" for the following day which is posted each afternoon outside room WG5.[27]

Where an appeal is listed on the Daily Cause List as "unassigned" then it will be assigned to a judge who is able to hear the case because a case in his or her list is ineffective. Usually, but not always, the appeal will be heard on the specified day. The procedure is for the parties to attend outside the court where the matter is listed and the Clerk of the Lists will notify them as soon as possible which judge is to hear the matter.[28]

Appeals in August and September

17–025   In August appeals can only be made with the permission of the judge unless they are appeals in respect of orders:

(1) to set aside a claim form, or service of a claim form;
(2) to set aside a judgment;
(3) for a stay of execution;
(4) for any order by consent;
(5) for permission to enter judgment;
(6) for approval of settlements or for an interim payment;
(7) for relief from forfeiture;
(8) for a third party debt order;
(9) for a garnishee order;
(10) for relief by way of a High Court Enforcement Officer's interpleader;
(11) for relief by way of sheriff's interpleader;
(12) for transfer to a county court or for trial by master; or
(13) for time where time is running in the month of August.

Preparation of papers

17–026   The parties must prepare a complete set of papers in proper order for the judge to read before the hearing. Further details as to the preparation of appeal bundles are set out in Chapter 15.

The bundle should contain copies of all the relevant documents including the notice of appeal and the statements of case. In appeals from a district judge a copy of the order together with the notes (if any) of reasons given by the district judge, prepared by the district judge, counsel or solicitors should be lodged.

The bundle should be properly paginated and indexed.

---

[26] Queen's Bench Guide para.9.5.3.
[27] Queen's Bench Guide para.9.5.2.
[28] Queen's Bench Guide para.9.6.1.

When ready the bundle should be lodged in room WG4:

(1) Where a date for the hearing has been arranged the bundle must be lodged not later than three clear days before the fixed date.
(2) For appeals where there is no fixed date for hearing, the bundle must be lodged not later than 48 hours after the parties have been notified that the matter is to appear in the warned list.[29]

Except with the permission of the judge no document may be used in evidence or relied on unless a copy of it has been included in the bundles. If a party intends to rely on written evidence which has not been included in the bundle, that party should lodge the original (with copy exhibits) in Room WG5 in advance of the hearing, or otherwise with the court associate before the hearing commences.

Statutory appeals and appeals by way of case stated in the High Court

Statutory appeals and appeals by way of case stated are beyond the scope of this work. They are addressed in part in CPR Pt 52, the Practice Direction to Pt 52 and in the Guides to the Chancery Division and Queens' Bench Division. Accordingly a summary of the main guidance provided therein is set out below.   **17–027**

General

CPR Pt 52 identifies certain statutory rights of appeal to the High Court as follows: **17–028**

(1) CPR r.52.18 provides that an appeal lies to the High Court against a decision of the Secretary of State under para.16 of Sch.15 to the Law of Property Act 1922. Such an appeal is to the Chancery Division as set out in the Practice Direction to Pt 52 para.23.2.
(2) CPR r.52.19 provides for a party to proceedings before a tribunal referred to in s.11(1) of the Tribunals and Inquiries Act 1992 who is dissatisfied in point of law with the decision of the tribunal to appeal to the High Court. Additionally a tribunal may of its own initiative or at the request of a party to the proceedings before it, state, in the form of a special case for the decision of the High Court, a question of law arising in the course of the proceedings.
(3) CPR r.52.20 provides that where the Secretary of State has given a decision in proceedings on an appeal under Pt VII of the Town and Country Planning Act 1990 against an enforcement notice; under Pt VIII of that act against notice under s.207 of that Act; or under

---

[29] Queen's Bench Guide para.9.7.6.

s.39 of the Planning (Listed Buildings and Conservation Areas) Act 1990 against a listed building enforcement notice the appellant, local planning authority or any other person interest may appeal to the High Court against the decision on a point of law.

The Practice Direction to Pt 52 provides further specific guidance as to statutory appeals in the Chancery Division and the Queen's Bench Division and this is supplemented by the relevant practice guides.

Statutory appeals in the Chancery Division

17–029   The Chancery Division is the appropriate court for a variety of appeals and cases stated under various statutes. Paragraph 23.2 of the Practice Direction to Pt 52 provides that any appeal to the High Court and any case stated or question referred to the opinion of that court under the following enactments be heard in the Chancery Division and in respect of some of them provides further procedural steps as indicated.

Statute giving rise to appeal to Chancery Division	Part 52/Part 52 Practice Direction paragraph
Para.16 of Sch.15 to the Law of Property Act 1922	CPR r.52.18
The Industrial Assurance Act 1923	Para.23.6
The Land Registration Act 1925	—
S.205(4) of the Water Resources Act 1991	—
S.38(3) of the Clergy Pensions Measure 1961	—
The Industrial and Provident Societies Act 1965	Para.23.7
S.151 of the Pension Schemes Act 1993	—
S.173 of the Pension Schemes Act 1993	—
S.97 of the Pensions Act 1995	—
The Charities Act 1993	Para.23.8A
Ss.13 and 13B of the Stamp Act 1891	—
S.705A of the Income and Corporation Taxes Act 1988	Para.23.8
Reg.22 of the General Commissioners (Jurisdiction and Procedure) Regulations 1994	Para.23.8
Ss.53, 56A or 100C(4) of the Taxes Management Act 1970	Paras 23.4–23.5
Ss.222(3), 225, 249(3) or 251 of the Inheritance Tax Act 1984	Paras 23.3–23.5

Regs 8(3) or 10 of the Stamp Duty Reserve Tax Regulations 1986	Para.23.5
The Land Registration Act 2002	Para.23.8B
Reg.74 of the European Public Limited Liability Company Regulations 2004	Para.23.8C

This list is said to be "non-exhaustive". The Chancery Division is also the   **17–030** appropriate venue for appeals from:

(1) the Pensions Ombudsman and the Occupational Pensions Regulatory Authority,
(2) the Comptroller General of Patents, Designs and Trade Marks,
(3) the Chief Land registrar,
(4) the Commons Commissioners, and
(5) the Charity Commissioners under the Charities Act 1993.

Chapters 23 and 25 of the Chancery Guide provide specific guidance to appeals in patent, design and trade mark matters and to Tax and VAT appeals.

The Practice Direction to Pt 52 para.23.9 also provides procedural steps for appeals by way of case stated to the Chancery Division under the Commons Registration Act 1965.

Statutory Appeals in the Queen's Bench Division

The Queen's Bench Division is the appropriate court for a variety of appeals   **17–031** and cases stated under various statutes. Paragraph 22.1 of the Practice Direction to Pt 52 provides that the following categories of appeal to the High Court are to be heard in the Queen's Bench Division and provides certain specific procedural guidance:

Statute giving rise to appeal to Queen's Bench Division	Part 52 Practice Direction paragraph reference
Appeals under the Merchant Shipping Act 1995	Para.22.2
Appeals against decisions affecting the registration of architects under s.22 of the Architects Act 1997	Para.22.3
Appeals against the registration of healthcare professionals under:	Para.22.3

(i) ss.82(3) or 83(2) of the Medicines Act 1968; (ii) s.12 of the Nurses, Midwives and Health Visitors Act 1997; (iii) art.38 of the Nursing and Midwifery Order 2001; (iv) s.10 of the Pharmacy Act 1954; (v) s.40 of the Medical Act 1983; (vi) s.29 or s.44 of the Dentists Act 1984; (vii) s.23 of the Opticians Act 1989; (viii) s.31 of the Osteopaths Act 1993; and (ix) s.31 of the Chiropractors Act 1994.	
Appeal under s.41 of the Consumer Credit Act 1974 from a determination of the Office of Fair Trading	Para.22.4
Appeal under ss.18 or 58(8) of the Social Security Administration Act 1992	Para.22.6
Appeals under ss.26 or 28 of the Extradition Act 2003	Para.22.6A
Appeals under s.49 of the Solicitors Act 1974	Para.22.6B
Appeals under s.289(6) of the Town and Country Planning Act 1990 and s.26(5) of the Planning (Listed Buildings and Conservation Areas) Act 1990	Para.22.6C
Appeal from a tribunal constituted under s.46 of the National Health Service Act 1977	Para.22.6D
Appeal from a tribunal constituted under s.1 of the Employment Tribunals Act 1996	Para.22.6E

17–032   The Practice Direction to Pt 52 paras 22.7–22.8A provide procedural steps for appeals by way of case stated to the Queen's Bench Division under the following statutory provisions:

(1) s.6 of the Agriculture (Miscellaneous Provisions) Act 1954 from the Agricultural Land Tribunal;
(2) s.78(8) of the Mental Health Act 1983 from a Mental Health Review Tribunal;
(3) s.289 of the Town and Country Planning Act 1990; and
(4) s.65 of the Planning (Listed Buildings and Conservation Areas) Act 1990.

PRACTICE POINTS IN THE COURT OF APPEAL

17–033   In this part of the chapter matters specific to practice in the Court of Appeal are considered. There is inevitably some overlap with earlier chapters, in particular Chapters 14, 15 and 16 in respect of applications for permission to appeal, preparation for appeals and case management of appeals.

Statutory jurisdiction

As discussed in Chapters 2 and 11, the Court of Appeal's power to hear appeals from the High Court is derived from ss.15–18 of the Senior Courts Act 1981 and from the County Court under ss.77–81 of the County Courts Act 1984. Where a statute provides that any order, judgment or decision of a court or tribunal is final the Court of Appeal has no power to hear an appeal in respect of that order, judgment or decision.[30]   **17–034**

> "The Court of Appeal is a statutory creation with the boundaries of its jurisdiction identified by, and subject to, restrictions imposed by statute."[31]

Composition of the Court of Appeal

The Court of Appeal has jurisdiction to hear cases with one or more single Lord Justice of Appeal.[32]   **17–035**

Normally the Court of Appeal sits with two or three judges. The Master of the Rolls may with the agreement of the Lord Chancellor provide directions about the minimum number of judges of which a court must consist of to be duly constituted for the purposes of "any description of proceedings"[33] and for particular cases the Master of the Rolls or any Lord Justice of Appeal designated for the purpose may determine the number of judges for the purpose of any particular proceedings.[34]

The obvious risk of having an even number of judges determining a case in the Court of Appeal is that the members of the Court are equally divided. In the event that happens then any party to the appeal can apply for the appeal to be re-argued before and determined by an uneven number of judges being no fewer than three.[35]

---

[30] Senior Courts Act 1981 s.18(1)(c). *Westminster City Council v O'Reilly* [2003] EWCA Civ 1007; [2004] 1 W.L.R. 195. In *Farley v Child Support Agency* [2005] EWCA Civ 869 where the Court of Appeal had handed down a judgment where it had no jurisdiction to do so (none of the parties having identified the problem) it arranged for an expedited judicial review hearing.

[31] *Westminster City Council v O'Reilly* [2003] EWCA Civ 1007; [2004] 1 W.L.R. 194 at [6].

[32] Senior Courts Act 1981 s.54(2). This means that there is no longer an appeal to the full court from an order made by a single Lord Justice. *Paragon Finance Plc v Noueiri* [2001] EWCA Civ 1114; [2002] C.P. Rep. 141.

[33] Senior Courts Act 1981 s.54(3). Description presumably means "type".

[34] Senior Courts Act 1981 s.54(4).

[35] Senior Courts Act 1981 s.54(5).

Delegation of jurisdiction over non-contentious and certain procedural matters in the Court of Appeal

17–036   CPR r.52.16 provides for the jurisdiction of the Court of Appeal to be exercised by certain individuals in respect of uncontroversial or incidental matters relating to appeals.

The purpose of this is to allow the less onerous tasks of the Court of Appeal to be performed by persons other than the Court of Appeal judges whose time is already occupied by the appeals themselves such as where standard directions are made following the transfer of an appeal to the Court of Appeal under CPR r.52.14.[36]

The individuals permitted to act in this way must be a court officer assigned to the Civil Appeals Office who is a barrister or solicitor and has the consent of the Master of the Rolls to act in such capacity[37]:

(1) When the Head of the Civil Appeals Office exercises a judicial capacity in this way he is described as the master.

(2) Other designated individuals when exercising such judicial capacity are described as deputy masters.[38]

The master and deputy masters can determine a broad range of matters. They are entitled to make these decisions without a hearing.[39]

The breadth of this jurisdiction is set out in CPR r.52.16(2) which provides that they can consider any matter incidental to any proceedings in the Court of Appeal; any other matter where there is no substantial dispute between the parties; and the dismissal of an appeal or application where a party has failed to comply with any order, rule or practice direction.

The decisions are made under the direction of the appropriate supervising Lord Justice. The prefix of the court appeal reference number indicates the relevant section handling the appeal within the Civil Appeals Office.

However the court officers are not permitted to decide the following applications[40]:

(1) an application for permission to appeal;

(2) an application for bail pending an appeal;

(3) an application for an injunction;

(4) an application for a stay of any proceedings, other than a temporary stay of any order or decision of the lower court over a period when the Court of Appeal is not sitting or cannot conveniently be convened.

---

[36] CPR PD 52 para.10.1.
[37] CPR r.52.16(1).
[38] CPR PD 52 para.15.5.
[39] CPR r.52.16(4).
[40] These are set out at CPR r.52.16(3).

Where a party is dissatisfied with a decision made in this way, the party can ask that the decision of the court officer is reviewed by the Court of Appeal:

(1) Where the decision was made without a hearing, a party may request that a hearing be held to reconsider the decision.[41]
(2) However there are strict time limits for requesting a review of a court officer's decision or to apply for an oral hearing. The request must be filed within seven days after the party is served with notice of the decision.[42]
(3) Similar provisions apply in respect of the decision of a single lord justice of appeal made without a hearing.

Confirming jurisdiction of the Court of Appeal

While the Court of Appeal will readily recognise jurisdiction on appeals from High Court judges, because its jurisdiction is limited in respect of appeals from the county court it will need to be satisfied that the decision being appealed was a final decision from a case allocated to the multi-track:

17–037

(1) Whether or not the decision was a "final decision" should be apparent from the order of the lower court being appealed if properly drawn.
(2) However whether the case has been allocated to the multi-track prior to the decision may not be clear.
(3) Accordingly an applicant for permission to appeal to the Court of Appeal from the county court should file with his appeal documents the order allocating the case to the multi-track.

Powers of the Court of Appeal

The powers of the Court of Appeal are considered in more detail in Chapter 2. The Court of Appeal has wide powers under CPR r.3.1 to make orders and directions in respect of appeals as well as its more specific powers under CPR Pt 52. In addition the Court of Appeal can call upon its inherent jurisdiction in the appeal process to make such orders and directions as appropriate to ensure the due and proper conduct of appeals.[43] This may involve listing of appeals to be heard together and granting the necessary

17–038

---

[41] CPR r.52.16(6).
[42] CPR r.52.16(6A).
[43] In *YD (Turkey) v Secretary of State for the Home Department* [2006] EWCA Civ 52; [2006] 1 W.L.R. 1646 the Court of Appeal held that it could prevent the Home Secretary from removing an applicant between the time when an out-of-time application for an extension of time for filing an application for permission to appeal was filed at the Civil Appeals Office and the time such an application was determined where such an order was preserving the status quo.

extensions of time and other directions to effectively case manage the appeals.[44]

Obtaining permission to appeal in the Court of Appeal

17–039 Aside from very limited cases permission is required for all appeals to the Court of Appeal. Where permission is sought from the Court of Appeal then the appellant will have to file an appeal notice in accordance with the rules as described in Chapter 14. In the Court of Appeal the application for permission is likely to be considered first on paper by a single Lord Justice of appeal.

Where permission is refused, the options for the prospective appellant depend on the decision of the single Lord Justice and his analysis of the prospects of the appeal:

(1) If the judge reviewing the application for permission to appeal considers that the application is totally without merit the single lord justice may debar the prospective appellant from requesting an oral hearing.[45] In those circumstances the prospective appellant can take his appeal no further: the order cannot be challenged. Although normally an order made on the court's own initiative can be challenged by a party not present under CPR r.3.3(5), CPR r.52.3(4B) disapplies this section.

(2) Otherwise the prospective appellant can renew his application for permission to appeal at an oral hearing. Such an application must be made within seven days of notification of the decision refusing permission to appeal. There are specific provisions requiring the prospective appellant to address why despite the reasons given by the single lord justice for rejecting the application for permission to appeal, such permission should nonetheless be granted.[46]

(3) Normally the single Lord Justice who refused application for permission to appeal in writing will not be part of the constitution of the court for hearing the renewed oral application for permission to paper.[47]

---

[44] In R. (On the application of Shiner) v Revenue & Customs Commissioners [2010] EWCA Civ 558 the Court of Appeal granted permission to the appellant to apply for judicial review rather than granting permission to appeal in order that the proceedings could be could be heard at the same time as another appeal in relation to a direct attack on the retrospectivity of the Finance Act s.58. The rationale was that both cases raised related issues that would ultimately fall to be determined by the Court of Appeal.

[45] CPR r.52.3(4A).

[46] CPR r.52.3(3).

[47] White Book, 2010, para.52.3.18.

Procedure following grant of permission to appeal in the Court of Appeal

As with other appeals, following on the grant of permission to appeal or a decision that the issue of permission to appeal and the appeal hearing will be heard one after the other, there are certain procedural steps the parties must comply with. These are addressed in Chapter 15.   **17–040**

The appellant is required to serve the appeal bundle on the respondent within seven days of receiving the order giving permission to appeal.[48]

Appeal questionnaire

The Court of Appeal will send the parties the date of the hearing or the period of time during which the appeal is likely to be heard as well as the date by which the appeal will be heard.[49] At the same time it will send an appeal questionnaire to the appellant.   **17–041**

The appellant must complete this within 14 days of the date of the letter of notification and return it to the Civil Appeals Office with:

(1) the appellant's time estimate of the appeal;
(2) confirmation that any outstanding transcriptions have been ordered;
(3) confirmation that appeal bundles are being prepared and will be held ready for the use of the Court of Appeal and an undertaking that they will be supplied to the court on request; and
(4) confirmation that copies of the appeal questionnaire and the appeal bundle have been served on the respondent, and the date of that service.

These requirements are set out in para.6.5 of the Practice Direction to Pt 52.

Time estimates

Paragraph 6.6 of the Practice Direction to Pt 52 provides that the advocate who will argue the appeal must provide the time estimate for the appeal. The time estimate should exclude the time required by the court to give judgment. Where the respondent's counsel disagrees with the time estimate the respondent must inform the court within seven days of receipt of the appeal questionnaire from the appellant. If the respondent does not do so he will be taken to have accepted the appellant's time estimate.   **17–042**

---

[48] CPR PD 52 para.6.2.
[49] CPR PD 52 para.6.3.

Respondent's duty to notify the appellant and the Civil Appeals Office of intention relating to the appeal

17–043   The respondent must notify the Civil Appeals Office and the appellant in writing as to:

(1) whether he intends to file a respondent's notice appealing the lower court's order;

(2) to seek to uphold it on different or additional grounds; or

(3) whether he intends to rely only on the reasons given by the lower court for its decision.[50]

The time for doing this is no later than 21 days after notification that the appellant has received permission to appeal or that the application for permission to appeal and the appeal are to be heard together.

Filing documents in the Court of Appeal

17–044   Documents relevant to appeal proceedings in the Civil Division of the Court of Appeal must be filed in the Civil Appeals Office Registry, Room E307, Royal Courts of Justice, Strand, London WC2A 2LL. Where a party is required to serve a document on another party then that party must effect service. The Civil Appeals Office will not serve documents.[51]

Filing by email

17–045   If a party is represented by a firm of solicitors the Court of Appeal allows certain documents to be filed by email using the email account specified in the "Guidelines for filing by Email" on the Court of Appeal website.[52] The documents that solicitors representing a party can file in this way are:

(1) an appeal notice,

(2) a respondent's notice,

(3) an application notice.[53]

17–046   The Court of Appeal guidelines[54] provide:

"**Guidelines for filing Appellants' Notices, Respondents' Notices and Application Notices by e-mail**

---

[50] CPR PD 52 para.15.6. See *Mlauzi v SSHD* [2005] EWCA Civ 128 where this was not done.

[51] CPR PD 52 para.15.1.

[52] *http://www.hmcourts-service.gov.uk/cms/7735.htm*

[53] CPR PD 52 para.15.1A(1).

[54] As at August 2010.

1. These are the guidelines referred to in paragraph 15.1A(2) of the Practice Direction to Part 52 of the Civil Procedure Rules.

2. This service is only available to a party who is represented by a firm of solicitors.

3. A party seeking to file an appellant's notice, a respondent's notice or an Application Notice (severally, a "Notice") by e-mail may do so (subject to the limitations contained in these guidelines) by e-mailing the documents to the Civil Appeals Office registry, using this address: *civilappeals.registry@hmcourts-service.gsi.gov.uk*.

   The inbox for this address will be checked twice daily. E-mails received before 10:00 am will not be dealt with until the Civil Appeals Office registry opens for business that day. E-mails received after 4:30 pm will not be dealt with until the next working day.

4. Where a party files a Notice by e-mail the e-mail must contain:

   (a) the sender's name, together with confirmation that the sender is authorised to give undertakings on behalf of the firm of solicitors concerned; and

   (b) an undertaking by the firm of solicitors representing that party to pay the requisite fee as soon as practicable, and in any event no later than 7 days from the date on which the email is sent.

   Failure to comply with the undertaking will render the application liable to automatic dismissal. The Court may also direct that a breach of undertaking be reported to the Law Society.

5. A Notice filed by e-mail will not be accepted if:
   (a) the requirements set out in paragraphs 2 to 4 above are not complied with;
   (b) any attachment is in a format other than Microsoft Word or Adobe Acrobat (.pdf); or
   (c) the document exceeds 20 pages in length, 2 megabytes in file size or contains material colour content.

6. A Notice filed by e-mail:
   (a) will be accepted as having been filed on the date of receipt if it is received by 4:30 pm;
   (b) will be treated as having been filed on the next working day if received after 4:30 pm.

7. E-mail correspondence will not be given priority over postal or fax receipts."

The Court Service website also advises that where the matter is urgent the party applying to file by e-mail should do so as early as possible during the course of the day on which filing will take place. The party should telephone the Registry of the Civil Appeals Office to inform them of its intention to file electronically.[55]

Where documents are filed with the Court of Appeal by this method the Civil Appeals Office will normally notify the party if there are any defects found in the documents. However it remains the party's responsibility to ensure that the documents filed are in order and comply with the prescribed time limits.

Electronic documents and statements of truth

17–047   Where a party files a document electronically and the document requires the party to sign a statement of truth, the party should file with the court a version of the document on which the name of the person who has signed the statement of truth is typed underneath the statement. The party should retain the original containing the original signature.[56]

Deadline for filing of documents

17–048   All documents must be filed with the Court of Appeal at least seven days before an appeal is due to be heard. Where this is impossible the Court of Appeal must be told why there has been such a default.[57] If there is a delay in filing a skeleton argument then the Court of Appeal and the other parties must be advised of this.[58]

Communications and the Civil Appeals Office

17–049   All communications with the Court of Appeal should be with the Civil Appeals Office and not the supervising Lord Justice or his or her clerk. This includes requests for directions or rulings. The reason for this is explained by the Practice Direction to Pt 52[59] to be so that all requests for directions or rulings (whether relating to listing or any other matters) are centrally monitored and correctly allocated.

Use of video and telephone conferencing in the Court of Appeal Civil Division

17–050   The Court of Appeal has mobile cameras and screens which can be set up in most courtrooms. It is the parties' duty to consider in each case whether the

---

[55] The number given is 020 7947 6409.
[56] CPR PD 52 para.15.1A(1).
[57] *Mlauzi v SSHD* [2005] EWCA Civ 128 at [39].
[58] *Mlauzi v SSHD* [2005] EWCA Civ 128 at [37]–[38].
[59] CPR PD 52 para.15.10.

use of video and/or telephone conference facilities would be appropriate particularly in the context of reducing the cost of proceedings.[60]

Guidance relating to the Court of Appeal's video conferencing facilities is available on the court service website.[61] This guidance recommends video-conferencing where savings in costs can be achieved. Where the hearing of an application is likely to last half an hour or less then the parties should consider using the Court of Appeal video conferencing facilities particularly where legal representation is based outside of London.[62] Video conferencing is also recommended to avoid public disruption; to facilitate an early listing; in cases involving vulnerable parties, overseas parties, prisoners and emergency cases in which the parties cannot readily attend court.

However the convenience of video conferencing will not always be appropriate and a judgment must be made in each case as to whether its use will be likely to be beneficial to the efficient, fair and economic disposal of the litigation.[63]

Permission is required for the use of video conferencing[64]:

(1) A party must apply to the Civil Appeals Listing office to determine the availability of video conferencing equipment for the day or days of their hearing which should be followed by a written application to the Listing office.

(2) The application will be referred to the presiding judge due to hear the case or to the supervising Lord/Lady Justice for the case if no hearing has yet been allocated.

(3) If all parties agree to video conferencing then the written application will usually mean that no oral hearing is necessary.

If the Court of Appeal approves the application for video conferencing it is incumbent on the party who applied for it to organise it. The costs of arranging it, including costs of transmission, hire of equipment and operators at remote sites, will initially be the responsibility of the party who requested the video facilities.[65] Those costs will then become costs of the proceedings and it will be for the court to determine who should ultimately pay for them. Further details about the technical arrangements are available on the court service website. **17–051**

The procedure at a video conference will be determined by the presiding judge. A decision will be made in advance as to whether formal court dress is required. Parties are required to arrive at the video conference venues 20

---

[60] CPR r.1.1 and 1.3. *Black v Pastouna* [2005] EWCA Civ 1389; [2006] C.P. Rep. 11 at [13]–[14], per Brooke L.J.

[61] *http://www.hmcourts-service.gov.uk/cms/1270.htm*

[62] *Black v Pastouna* [2005] EWCA Civ 1389; [2006] C.P. Rep. 11 at [12]–[15], per Brooke L.J.

[63] CPR PD 32 Annex 3 para.2.

[64] CPR PD 32 Annex 3 para.8.

[65] CPR PD 32 Annex 3 para.9. The costs of using facilities at local courts were stated to be £21.60 per half hour plus any specific "remote" court charges as at October 2010: *http://www.hmcourts-service.gov.uk/cms/1270.htm*

minutes before the hearing is due to start.[66] The judges will not normally enter court until both sites are online.[67]

The video conference constitutes court proceedings and no recording of them other than the official version may be made.[68] The person organising them must ensure that there is sufficient space at the local site for members of the public to attend[69] and where possible for the royal coat of arms to be placed above the judges' seat, although generally the Lord Justices of Appeal will be sitting in a court with video conferencing facilities in any event.[70-71]

Where a party is unrepresented then he or she will normally be required to use a remote video conferencing centre based at their local court. Solicitors may make use of their own video conferencing facilities.

For telephone conferencing it is possible to have the call at a person's home or at a court with available telephone conferencing facilities. If the call is to take place at a person's home then a "responsible person" is required to be present during the hearing. A "responsible person" may be a barrister, solicitor, legal executive, doctor, clergyman, police officer, prison officer or other person of comparable status. The identity of the "responsible person" must be disclosed to the Court of Appeal at least seven days prior to the hearing date. Unless exempt from the hearing costs a party requesting telephone conference facilities will be liable for the costs of the same. Further details are available on the Courts Service website.

LISTING OF THE APPEAL

17-052 The Court of Appeal has a Civil Appeals list divided into seven lists as follows:

List	
The Applications List	The list for applications for permission to appeal and other applications.
The Appeals List	The list for appeals where permission to appeal has been given or is unnecessary where a hearing date is fixed in advance unless requiring special listing arrangements (see Special Fixtures List).
The Expedited List	The list for appeals or applications where the Court of Appeal has directed an expedited hearing.

---

[66] CPR PD 32 Annex 3 para.11.
[67] CPR PD 32 Annex 3 para.19.
[68] CPR PD 32 Annex 3 para.15.
[69] CPR PD 32 Annex 3 para.13.
[70-71] CPR PD 32 Annex 3 para.14.

The Stand-Out List	The list for appeals or applications which are not ready to proceed and have been stood out by judicial direction.
The Special Fixtures List	The list for appeals requiring special listing arrangements in terms of listing with other appeals, before the same constitution of the court, in a particular order, or at a particular location.
The Second Fixtures List	The list for appeals listed where the list is already fully booked in the period but where the case may be called on to be heard if a suitable gap occurs in the list.
The Short-Warned List	The list for appeals deemed suitable for being called on at short notice because alternative counsel to instructed counsel should if needed be able to master the appeal within a short period of half a day.

The applications list and the appeals list

These lists are the two principle lists and need no further explanation.　17–053

The expedited list

The expedited list is, as its name suggests, the list for urgent appeals that　17–054
should take priority over other appeals.

While there are certain appeals where such urgency is self-evident, there has been a temptation in less obvious cases of urgency for the affected parties to see a case as suitable for expediting which is not subsequently shared by the court. This is particularly so given the ever increasing demands on the finite resources of the Court of Appeal.

This is not a new problem and the Court of Appeal's current practice stems from a practice note from a 1994 case, *Unilever Plc v Chefaro Proprietaries Ltd (Practice Note).*[72] The Practice Direction to Pt 52 para.15.8 makes clear that this remains the current practice.

There are two broad categories of appeals for the expedited list: those obviously suitable for the expedited list and those potentially suitable.

Appeals that would usually be suitable for the expedited list include the following:

(1) Appeals against committal orders, particularly if the adverse finding is challenged or the sentence is short.

---

[72] [1995] 1 W.L.R. 243.

(2) Cases where children might suffer extraordinary prejudice (that is prejudice beyond that almost inevitably consequent on involvement in proceedings) if a decision is delayed.

(3) Cases under the 1980 Hague Convention on the Civil Aspects of International Child Abduction.

(4) Asylum appeals concerning return to third countries where the right to return might be jeopardised by delay.

(5) Cases in which a possession order is about to be executed and which appear to have some merit.

(6) Cases in which an irrevocable decision was about to be implemented or will confer rights on third parties.

(7) Cases in which allegedly unlawful material was about to be published.

(8) Appeals against decisions in the course of continuing proceedings.

17–055 Appeals that are potentially suitable for the expedited list include the following:

(1) Where a party might lose its livelihood or home or suffer irreparable loss or extraordinary hardship through delay.

(2) Where unless heard swiftly the appeal would become futile.

(3) Where the resolution of numerous cases, turning on the outcome of the case under appeal, will be unreasonably delayed, or the orderly management of class or multi-party litigation in a lower court will be disrupted.

(4) Where widespread divergences of practice are likely to continue, with the prospect of multiple appeals until the correct practice is laid down.

(5) Where there would be a risk of serious detriment to good public administration or to the interests of members of the public not concerned in the appeal.

17–056 A factor always present in determining whether a case should be put on the expedited list is the impact and consequential delay it will have on the hearing of other appeals either in requiring an already fixed appeal to be vacated or for other appeals to wait longer.[73]

If an appeal is accepted on to the expedited list, the court will in fixing the date for an expedited appeal give weight to the interests of the parties adversely affected by the underlying order. However the court will be less amenable to accommodating counsel's availability in listing the expedited appeal than it might in other appeals.

The court may impose conditions on assignment of the appeal to the expedited list such as placing strict predetermined limits on the time allowed for oral argument on the appeal.[74]

---

[73] *Unilever Plc v Chefaro Proprietaries Ltd (Practice Note)* [1995] 1 W.L.R. 243.
[74] The Review of the Legal Year 1993 to 1994.

An application for an expedited hearing should be made to the Civil Appeals Listing Office by letter. The letter should set out the reasons why expedition is needed and be accompanied by a bundle of documents relied on in support[75] together with a transcript (or note) of the judgment being appealed.[76]

Applications for an expedited appeal will be determined by a single Lord Justice or master. The principles to be applied are set out below in respect of expedited hearings.

The stand out list

The stand out list is for appeals or applications which for good reason are not at present ready to proceed and have been stood out by judicial direction.   **17–057**

The special fixtures list

The Civil Appeals Office has a "special fixtures" list for appeals requiring special listing arrangements.   **17–058**

The Practice Direction to Pt 52 para.15.9A(1) provides examples of categories of appeals that would be considered suitable for the special fixtures list. These include:

(1) Appeals which need to be listed before a certain constitution of the Court of Appeal.
(2) Appeals that need to be heard in a particular order.
(3) Appeals that need to be heard during a particular time period.
(4) Appeals that need to be heard in a specific location.

The Civil Appeals Office will notify the parties through their legal representatives or directly, if acting in person, of the particular arrangements that are to apply and in particular the details of the specific period during which a case is scheduled to be heard and where appropriate directions for the filing of any outstanding documents.[77]

The second fixtures list

The second fixtures list are for those appeals that have a degree of urgency, but are not sufficient to justify an expedited hearing. By being placed in the   **17–059**

---

[75] *Unilever Plc v Chefaro Proprietaries Ltd (Practice Note)* [1995] 1 W.L.R. 243.
[76] *Hertsmere BC v Harty* [2001] EWCA Civ 1238 at [5], per Sedley L.J. and at [20]–[21], per Stuart-Smith L.J.
[77] CPR PD 52 para.15.9A(2).

second fixtures list the appeal has a good chance of getting on earlier as some appeals do not in the end proceed or occupy less of the court's time than anticipated. Where an appeal listed in the second fixtures list is not heard because space does not become available then the appeal will be granted a first fixture on the earliest convenient date thereafter.

The short warned list

17–060   The short warned list exists to allow certain appeals to be called on at short notice where there is available court time for the appeal. Not all cases are suitable for the short warned list. The test used to be that a case was suitable for the short warned list if the appellate brief was capable of being mastered in half a day.[78] If a case is assigned to the short warned list the Civil Appeals Listing Officer will in due course place the appeal in the short warned list "on call" from a given date and will inform the parties' advocates.[79] The minimum notice period for an appeal being heard is half-a-day. The court can provide a longer period.[80] The consequences of an appeal being assigned to the short warned list places a burden on all involved because of the need to act swiftly from the moment of notification.

Notifying the client and advocate on the short warned list

17–061   The solicitors acting for the parties are required to notify their advocate and their client that this has happened "as soon as"[81] the Civil Appeals Office notifies them that the appeal has been assigned to the short warned list. A letter might not be sufficient to meet the urgency required by the Practice Direction. A telephone call followed up in writing by email and/or fax would be appropriate.

Applying to have the case taken out of the short warned list

17–062   Solicitors and the advocate will need to give prompt consideration as to whether an application should be made for the case to be taken out of the short-warned list if it is inappropriate for it.

There are strict time limits. An application in writing must be made within 14 days of notification of the appeal's assignment to the short warned list.

Such applications are strongly discouraged. As the Practice Direction makes clear, these applications will only be granted "for the most compelling reasons".[82]

What would amount to "most compelling reasons" is not obvious given that the decision to list the matter to the short-warned list will only have

---

[78] Practice Direction (Court of Appeal: Civil Division: Short Warned List) 1992.
[79] CPR PD 52 para.15.9(4).
[80] CPR PD 52 para.15.9(5).
[81] CPR PD 52 para.15.9(2).
[82] CPR PD 52 para.15.9(3).

been made after consideration of the appeal. That the preparation by replacement counsel may take longer than half a day would not of itself be a reason to take the case out of the short-warned list given that the Civil Appeals Office can provide a longer notice period.[83]

If made the application will be decided by a Lord Justice, or the master.[84]

Preparing and filing appeal documents on a shortened timetable

The time for filing any remaining documents for the appeal is likely to be abridged.[85] This means that particularly in the case of a respondent who is yet to file a skeleton argument that this is likely to be required within a very short time period.[86]

17–063

Linked appeals

Any party (or advocate instructed in the case) that becomes aware that an application or an appeal is linked with another case, or raises similar issues to those in another application or appeal should inform the Civil Appeals Office by letter as soon as practicable in order that consideration can be given to listing the appeals to be heard together.[87]

17–064

Hear by dates

The *Practice Note (Court of Appeal: Listing Windows) No.2*[88] provides the following periods for a listing window and hear-by dates.

17–065

Type of appeal		Listing window	
		Start window for appeal	Hear-by date, end window for appeal
Family	Child cases	3 months	4 months
	Financial and other	5 months	9 months
Administrative Court	Immigration appeals, interlocutory and education appeals	4 months	6 months
	Other Administrative Court final orders	5 months	8 months
High Court	CPR Pt 24	4 months	6 months

---

[83] CPR PD 52 para.15.9(5).
[84] CPR PD 52 para.15.9(3).
[85] CPR PD 52 para.15.9(1).
[86] *Scribes West Ltd v Relsa Anstalt* [2004] EWCA Civ 835; [2005] C.P. Rep. 2 at [24].
[87] *Manual of Civil Appeals*, 2nd edn, para.4.108.
[88] [2003] 1 W.L.R. 838.

	Other interlocutory orders	4 months	8 months
	Bankruptcy and directors' dis-qualification cases	4 months	6 months
	Preliminary issues	4 months	6 months
	Final orders	5 months	9 months
	Possession	4 months	6 months
County Court	Interlocutory orders	4 months	8 months
	Possession	4 months	6 months
	Preliminary issues	4 months	6 months
	Final orders	5 months	9 months
Tribunals	Other than immigration and social security appeals	5 months	9 months
	Social security appeals	5 months	9 months
	Immigration appeals	4 months	6 months

If a party wishes for the appeal to take place after the hear-by date then he must demonstrate compelling reasons[89] and make a formal application which will be considered by a single Lord Justice or master.

Listing and convenience of counsel

17–066   The Court of Appeal will make efforts to accommodate the availability of counsel and can on application sometimes sit earlier than the usual court times in order to permit counsel with another court commitment to attend the hearing.[90]

However the convenience of counsel is only one of a number of factors to be taken in to account in listing. This applies as much for appeals on the special fixtures list[91] as for other appeals.

In terms of appeals heard in the Royal Courts of Justice in London, it is the practice of the Civil Appeals Office to consult with counsel's clerks in terms of availability and listing.

Where the Court of Appeal is sitting on circuit, the same flexibility is not available. The Court of Appeal will only be sitting in one of the few centres for one or two separate weeks in each year. There is often a public interest in the court sitting locally to resolve local appeals and therefore justifying the appeal being heard by the Court of Appeal sitting outside of London.

---

[89]   para.2 of the *Practice Note (Court of Appeal: Listing Windows)*.
[90]   *White Book*, para.52.12.6 citing the case of *In the matter of N and N (Children)* [2006] EWCA Civ 1562.
[91]   CPR PD 52 para.15.9A(3).

Therefore counsel's availability will be secondary to the importance of the appeal being heard in the relevant weeks.

Unavailability of counsel for appeal

In those circumstances if the first choice of counsel is unavailable then **17–067** alternative counsel will have to be instructed. An adjournment of the appeal is unlikely to be granted where alternative appropriate counsel could properly and effectively be instructed for a hearing on the listed date and prejudice would be caused to the other side in granting an adjournment.[92]

If an advocate instructed on the appeal is unable to appear his "immediate professional duty" is to take "all practicable measures" to ensure that his lay client is represented at the hearing by an advocate who is fully instructed and able to argue the appeal.[93]

Whilst these provisions are, in the CPR, specifically directed at appeals in the Court of Appeal, it is thought they must apply equally to other appeals.

What precisely an advocate should do is not spelled out. Guidance can be found from the pre-CPR Practice Direction which provides that once a case was assigned to the list (now "on call") it was the duty of instructed counsel to ensure his lay client was represented by fully instructed counsel who could argue the appeal. This means returning the brief and assisting his instructing solicitor to brief a substitute counsel who might or might not be a member of the same chambers, the choice being that of his professional and lay client.

The full extent of what this requires will depend on the circumstances of the case, the period of notice, and the time available to the original appellate advocate and thus it is restricted to "all practicable measures".

Counsel who is unavailable must first take steps to assist his instructing solicitor in finding a suitable available alternative advocate. This may include making enquiries through his clerks of availability within and outside of chambers of available suitable counsel.

Next counsel must take all practicable steps to ensure that the replacement advocate is fully instructed. This is an "immediate professional duty".[94]

At short notice one would expect the first advocate to explain to the replacement advocate the central issues in the case and the manner in which the appeal was to be presented, the perceived strengths and weaknesses of the different grounds of appeal and other salient points. Where more time is available then one might expect the instructing solicitor to be responsible for some of these tasks, though no doubt the advocate will always remain responsible for explaining how and why the appeal has been brought, and the way in which he or she would have argued it.

---

[92] See *Newport City Council v Charles* [2008] EWCA Civ 893 at [5].
[93] CPR PD 52 para.15.9(6).
[94] CPR PD 52 para.15.9(6).

Under the pre-CPR Practice Direction breaches of the duty were specified as giving grounds for wasted costs order and possible reference of counsel's conduct to the Bar Council and there is no reason to think that anything has changed in this regard.[95]

When these situations are examined with the benefit of hindsight the standard expected of advocates tends to be high.

PREPARATION IN ADVANCE OF THE APPEAL HEARING

17–068 The preparation for the appeal hearing is addressed in detail in Chapter 15. The filing of supplement skeleton arguments and of bundles of authorities can give rise to problems and the key points are set out below. Further reference should be made to Chapter 15.

Filing of supplemental skeleton arguments

17–069 Paragraph 15.11A of the Practice Direction to Pt 52 provides:

> "15.11A (1) A supplementary skeleton argument on which the appellant wishes to rely must be filed at least 14 days before the hearing.
>
> (2) A supplementary skeleton argument on which the respondent wishes to rely must be filed at least 7 days before the hearing.
> (3) All supplementary skeleton arguments must comply with the requirements set out in paragraph 5.10.[96-97]
>
> (4) At the hearing the court may refuse to hear argument from a party not contained in a skeleton argument filed within the relevant time limit set out in this paragraph."

The purpose of this provision is not to permit a party to submit a completely revised case on the appeal at great length. While it may be that a different counsel is instructed on the appeal after the filing of the original skeleton this provision does not permit the new counsel to file a substantial skeleton argument in place of the original one.

> "The rule is designed to provide for lately decided or, within limits, discovered authority; changes of underlying factual circumstances; or

---

[95] Practice Direction (Court of Appeal: Civil Division: Short Warned List) 1992.

[96-97] These are the requirements relating to skeleton arguments including the provision that the argument must contain a numbered list of points which the party wishes to make; in respect of each authority cited a requirement that the proposition of law is cited and the parts that demonstrate the proposition are referred to.

the brief answering of points in the other side's argument that genuinely do not arise out of the original grounds of appeal."[98]

If a party finds that it wishes to submit an expanded case or to alter the time estimate for the hearing it must provide the court with full details at the earliest date on which it becomes apparent in order that the matter can be placed before the master or a deputy master or, if appropriate, Lord Justice to resolve the issue and avoid jeopardising the appeal hearing itself.[99]

As the papers are likely to be sent to the relevant Lord Justices hearing the appeal seven days before the hearing, a respondent should not delay filing any respondent's supplemental skeleton beyond the seven day deadline even if the appellant has not complied with the 14 day deadline as otherwise it may well not be received in time and he or she may not be able to rely on the new points identified.

Authorities bundles

Authorities bundles must be agreed and lodged, suitably marked up, at least seven days before the appeal is to be heard. Where appeals are listed on an expedited basis, the advocates are required to "do their best" to provide an agreed bundle of authorities as rapidly as possible.[100]   **17–070**

NOTIFICATION OF SETTLEMENT OR NARROWING OF ISSUES

The provisions relating to the settlement or dismissal of appeals by consent and particularly where children and vulnerable persons are involved are addressed in detail Chapter 16.   **17–071**

In accordance with the parties' duty under CPR r.1.3 to help the court to achieve the overriding objective the parties are under an obligation to inform the court as soon as it is known that a matter listed for hearing will not be effective or is likely to take less time than set out in the time estimate on the appeal questionnaire.[101]

---

[98] *AIC Ltd v ITS Testing Services (UK) Ltd* [2006] EWCA Civ 1601; [2007] 1 L.L.R. 555 at [393], per Buxton L.J. In the *AIC Ltd* case the appellant sought to file a substitute skeleton consisting of 168 pages and an increased time estimate for the appeal of five to six days (from the original three days). Buxton L.J. made clear that it was principally because the appellants stood convicted of fraud that the substitute skeleton was permitted to be relied upon.

[99] *AIC Ltd v ITS Testing Services (UK) Ltd* [2006] EWCA Civ 1601; [2007] 1 L.L.R. 555 at [394], per Buxton L.J.

[100] *Scribes West Ltd v Relsa Anstalt* [2004] EWCA Civ 835; [2005] C.P. Rep. 2 at [29].

[101] *Tasyurdu v The Secretary of State for the Home Department* [2003] EWCA Civ 447; [2003] C.P. Rep. 61 at [13], per Lord Phillips; *Red River UK Ltd v Sheikh* [2009] EWCA Civ 643; [2009] C.P. Rep. 41 at [34]–[37], per Arden L.J.

Once meaningful negotiations are underway the parties should as soon as possible notify the Civil Appeals Office. If the settlement looks likely to occur or happens when the judges are likely to be preparing for the appeal and the Civil Appeals Office is closed, the parties should contact the 24 hour switchboard at the Royal Courts of Justice to obtain the telephone number of the clerk of the senior presiding judge in order that the relevant judges can be advised of the developments. If all that remains is the determination of costs the Civil Appeals Office should be notified by a letter so that the Court of Appeal can give consideration to an appropriate order to make.[102]

There are standard forms available (Forms 253, 254A and 254B) for notifying a settlement of an appeal. Deputy masters in the Court of Appeal can approve consent orders pursuant to CPR r.52.16. An application for dismissal of an appeal will be considered by the master or a deputy master in the Court of Appeal and can be made without a hearing. This can be reconsidered at an oral hearing under CPR r.51.16(6).

Settlement after the hearing and before judgment

17–072 If the parties to an appeal compromise their dispute after the hearing or argument, but before the judgment has been distributed in draft then the Appellate Court has a discretion to continue to draft and publish the judgment.[103–104]

The circumstances in which it will do so will depend on what is just and fair in the circumstances. Once the draft judgment is prepared and distributed, as with courts at first instance the Appellate Court has a discretion whether to hand down its judgment even in the face of objections from all the parties. Where substantial costs have been incurred by the parties and the judgment has already been prepared and the judgment is required for determination of the costs the Court of Appeal may well decide that the fair and pragmatic approach is to deliver the judgment.[105]

Costs sanctions

17–073 If an appeal is settled and the requirements of the Practice Direction have not been complied with the Court of Appeal may well insist on the parties attending to explain their breach of the Practice Direction. Where costs could have been avoided and reduced if one of the parties had contacted the

---

[102] *Red River UK Ltd v Sheikh* [2009] EWCA Civ 643; [2009] C.P. Rep. 41 at [35], per Arden L.J.

[103–104] *Prudential Assurance Co Ltd v McBains Cooper* [2000] EWCA Civ 172; [2000] W.L.R. 2000 at [31], per Brooke L.J. In the House of Lords see *Grovit v Doctor* [1997] 1 W.L.R. 640.

[105] *R. (on the application of Lodhi) v Secretary of State for the Home Department*, March 11, 2010.

court to inform them of relevant matters and the court could of its own volition have made an appropriate order disposing of the case the costs order is likely to be directed against that party and there may well be public criticism.[106]

OTHER ISSUES THAT CAN ARISE ON APPEALS

The following are examples of the many procedural and other issues that can arise on appeals.

17–074

Bankruptcy of appellant

On the bankruptcy of an individual then the cause of action no longer rests with the individual unless it is personal to an individual as in the case of divorce or defamation proceedings. Thus any further steps in the appeal process are not for the individual, but for his trustee in bankruptcy.[107] This can lead to delays in the appeal process. The courts tend to be sympathetic to such delays. The position can be complicated where the cause of action includes both types of cause of action such as in a claim for personal injuries where although the cause of action vests in the trustee he will hold the right to recover personal damages such as right to damages for pain and suffering on constructive trust for the bankrupt.[108] Careful consideration needs to be given to which part(s) of the appeal the individual is entitled to still proceed with and, inevitably, how such proceedings are to be funded.

17–075

Academic appeals

In a number of cases, by the time the appeal is to be heard, the underlying issue has become academic. The question may arise as to whether it is appropriate for the appeal to proceed. This is addressed in detail in Chapter 2. The position is summarised below:

17–076

(1) An extant dispute is normally considered a prerequisite for an appeal: "There should exist between the parties a matter in actual controversy."[109]

---

[106] *Tasyrudu v The Secretary of State for the Home Department* [2003] EWCA Civ 447; *Kutchouk v The Secretary of State for the Home Department* [2003] EWCA Civ 804; *Yell Ltd v Garton* [2004] EWCA Civ 87; and *Red-River UK Ltd v Sheikh* [2009] EWCA Civ 643.

[107] Insolvency Act 1986 s.306. *Heath v Tang* [1993] 1 W.L.R. 1421; [1993] 4 All E.R. 694.

[108] *Ord v Upton* [2000] Ch 352; [2000] 1 All E.R. 193; *Khan v Trident Safeguards Ltd* [2004] EWCA Civ 624 where the bankrupt was permitted to continue with only the personal part of a "hybrid" claim.

[109] *Sun Life Assurance Co of Canada v Jervis* [1944] A.C. 111 at 113–114.

(2) Where there is no purpose in the appeal continuing the Court of Appeal is likely to decline jurisdiction. Different considerations will apply where the case is a test case, a "friendly action"[110] or involves issues of public importance.

(3) Where the case involves issues of public importance the Court of Appeal can with the consent[111] of all parties entertain an appeal even though the dispute between the parties has been compromised at the time of the hearing. This is likely to take place where third parties have intervened on discrete issues such as points of statutory construction.[112]

Non-attendance of a party

17–077   The appeal court can proceed in the absence of a party to an appeal to determine the appeal. In appeals relating to serious procedural irregularity, where a party has a track record of non-attendance at hearings then the appeal court may determine the appeal on the basis of the findings of fact made by the lower court rather than refer it back for a re-trial.[113]

Draft judgments

17–078   In many cases the Court of Appeal will circulate its judgment in draft and request that lists of typographical errors and other corrections be provided.

Any proposed correction to the draft judgment should be sent to the clerk to the judge who prepared the draft with a copy to any other party.[114]

As with other courts the draft judgment is circulated on a confidential basis and its contents are not to be disseminated. Communications relating to draft judgments are subject to the same level of confidentiality as the draft judgment even where submissions and discussions about draft judgments take place in open court.[115]

As addressed in Chapter 11 the temptation for the unsuccessful party to reopen or reargue the case or to repeat submissions made at the hearing or

---

[110] *Ainsbury v Millington* [1987] 1 W.L.R. 379 at 380A–380G, 381C–381D.

[111] By contrast in matters of public law the House of Lords has a discretion to hear the appeal even if a compromise has taken place: *Bowman v Fells* [2005] EWCA Civ 226; [2005] 1 W.L.R. 3083.

[112] *Bowman v Fells* [2005] EWCA Civ 226; [2005] 1 W.L.R. 3083.

[113] *Launahurst Ltd v Nigel Larner* [2010] EWCA Civ 334.

[114] CPR PD 40E para.3.1.

[115] *R. (on the application of Mohamed) v Secretary of State for Foreign and Commonwealth Affairs* [2010] EWCA Civ 158; February 26, 2010 at [12]. In this regard CPR r.31.22 does not apply to such submissions.

to deploy fresh ones often arises at this stage. This has been strongly discouraged[116] and may well amount to an abuse of process.[117]

There are however instances where it is perfectly proper to invite the court to reconsider part of the terms of its draft and if a judge concludes that the draft judgment is wrong then he is obliged to alter the judgment.[118]

(a) If the judgment contains a palpable error the alteration of which would save the parties the expense of an appeal then it may be appropriate to correct the judgment.[119]

(b) Where the judgment contains detrimental observations about an individual or indeed his lawyers which on the face of it are not necessary to the judgment of the court and/or appear to be based on a misunderstanding of the evidence, or misunderstanding of a concession or a submission then it may be appropriate to request the court to amend its draft judgment so that it reflects the true position.[120]

(c) It may be appropriate to remove a paragraph in a judgment dealing with a matter that was not the subject of an appeal.

Any such changes will however be exceptional.[121]

If a party is to make submissions it is imperative that he notifies the other parties by copy of his letter simultaneously or immediately.[122]

Publication of judgments

All substantive decisions of the Court of Appeal are published on the website of the British and Irish Legal Information Institute: *www.bailii.org*.   **17–079**

Collection of bundles following an appeal

Unless collected the Civil Appeals Office will destroy all bundles other than one set retained for the official transcriber. The Practice Direction to Pt 52 para.15.11C explains what will happen in the Court of Appeal: **17–080**

---

[116] *The Royal Brompton Hospital National Health Service Trust v Hammond* [2001] EWCA Civ 778 at [11], [12]–[19]; *Watchtower Investments Ltd v Payne* [2001] EWCA Civ 1261 at [4], per Peter Gibson L.J.; *Robinson v Fernsby and Scott-Kilvert* [2003] EWCA Civ 1820 at [94]; *R. (on the application of Mohamed) v Secretary of State for Foreign and Commonwealth Affairs* [2010] EWCA Civ 158; February 26, 2010.

[117] *R. (on the application of Edwards) v The Environment Agency* [2008] UKHL 22 at [66].

[118] *Robinson v Fernsby and Scott-Kilvert* [2003] EWCA Civ 1820 at [98] and [120].

[119] *Robinson v Fernsby and Scott-Kilvert* [2003] EWCA Civ 1820 at [94].

[120] *R. (on the application of Mohamed) v Secretary of State for Foreign and Commonwealth Affairs* [2010] EWCA Civ 158; February 26, 2010 at [5].

[121] *Robinson v Fernsby and Scott-Kilvert* [2003] EWCA Civ 1820 at [96].

[122] *R. (on the application of Mohamed) v Secretary of State for Foreign and Commonwealth Affairs* [2010] EWCA Civ 158; February 26, 2010 at [7].

(1) If an application for permission to appeal is rejected on paper by a single Lord Justice of Appeal the bundles will not be destroyed until after the time limit for seeking a hearing has expired.[123] It is implicit in this that if an application is made for an oral hearing then the bundles will not be destroyed, but will be preserved for the renewed oral application. However there is no harm in requesting that the bundles be preserved at the same time as making the application for an oral hearing.

(2) If permission to appeal is refused at an oral hearing, the Civil Appeals Office will destroy the Court bundles other than one for the official transcriber unless collected within 21 days of the hearing.

(3) If permission to appeal is granted either by a single Lord Justice of Appeal on paper or at a separate permission hearing, the court will retain the application bundles.[124]

(4) After the appeal proper, the Civil Appeals Office will make arrangements to destroy all court bundles (other than the official transciber's set) unless collected within 21 days of the date of the hearing when the court's decision or of notification of the court's decision if the hearing was unattended.[125]

Enforcement of an appeal order

17–081 The lower court may enforce an order of the Court of Appeal and it should be to the lower court that enforcement proceedings should be addressed.[126]

SPECIFIC PROVISIONS RELATING TO CERTAIN STATUTORY APPEALS IN THE COURT OF APPEAL

17–082 The balance of this chapter addresses the prescribed procedural matters of certain statutory appeals set out in the CPR. Reference should be made to the specialist textbooks for further guidance in respect of such appeals.

---

[123] CPR PD 52 para.15.11C(4).
[124] CPR PD 52 para.15.11C(3).
[125] CPR PD 52 para.15.11C(1).
[126] *Ager v Ager* [1998] 1 W.L.R. 1074; [1998] 1 All E.R. 703.

Appeal against decree nisi of divorce or nullity of marriage or conditional dissolution or nullity order in relation to civil partnership

Specific guidance for appeals against decree nisi of divorce or nullity of   17–083
marriage or conditional dissolution or nullity order in relation to civil
partnership is provided at para.21.1 of the Practice Direction to Pt 52.

The appeal notice must be filed at the Court of Appeal within 28 days
after the date on which the decree was pronounced or conditional order
made. The lower court has no power to extend this.

The appellant must file the decree or conditional order and a certificate of
service of the appeal notice with the appeal notice and serve a copy on the
appropriate district judge.

Where a party has had the opportunity of appealing from the decree nisi
and has not so appealed then there is no appeal from the subsequent decree
absolute of divorce or nullity of marriage.[127]

Appeal against order for revocation of patent

Specific guidance for an appeal against revocation of a patent is provided at   17–084
para.21.2 of the Practice Direction to Pt 52.

The appellant is required to serve an additional copy of the appeal notice
on the Comptroller-General of Patents, Designs and Trade Marks.

If the respondent chooses not to oppose the appeal or not to attend the
hearing he must immediately serve notice of that decision on the appellant
and the Comptroller.

The respondent must also serve copies of the original petition, any
statements of claim and any written evidence filed in the claim on the
Comptroller.

The Comptroller must then indicate within 14 days whether or not he
intends to attend the appeal hearing.

The Court of Appeal may also permit the Comptroller to attend and
oppose the appeal, particularly where the respondent decides to withdraw
his opposition during the hearing of the appeal itself.

Appeal from Patents Court on appeal from Comptroller

Paragraph 21.3 of the Practice Direction to Pt 52 provides: 17–085

(a) Where the appeal is from a decision of the Patents Court which
was itself made on an appeal from a decision of the Comptroller-
General of Patents, Designs and Trade Marks, the appellant must

---

[127] Senior Courts Act 1981 s.18(1) and *Lomas v Lomas* [2001] EWCA Civ 1891.

serve the appeal notice on the Comptroller in addition to the persons to be served under CPR r.52.4(3).

(b) If there are related proceedings before the European Patent Office, the parties must co-ordinate with each other, the European Patent Office and the Civil Appeals Listing Office in relation to listing.[128]

Appeals in cases of contempt of court

17–086   In an appeal under s.13 of the Administration of Justice Act 1960 against any order or decision of a court in the exercise of jurisdiction to punish for contempt of court (including criminal contempt), the appellant must serve the appeal notice on the court or the Upper Tribunal from whose order or decision the appeal is brought, as well as the persons to be served under CPR r.52.4(3).[129]

Although the High Court and the Court of Appeal have the power under RSC Ord.109 r.3 to release an appellant on bail, such applications are rare in the Court of Appeal.

Where the appellant is in custody the Court of Appeal will attempt to hear the appeal as quickly as possible at an expedited hearing.[130]

The powers of the Court of Appeal on an appeal from a contempt hearing are wide ranging. It can order the committal proceedings to be heard before a different judge,[131] and in exceptional circumstances it can increase or impose a sentence where none was given by the lower court.[132]

Appeals direct to the Court of Appeal involving a point of law relating wholly or mainly to the construction of an enactment or statutory instrument from the Value Added Tax and Duties Tribunal or the Special Commissioners

17–087   The Practice Direction to Pt 52 paras 21.6 and 21.8 provide guidance as to the procedure to be followed where the relevant tribunal has certified that its decision involves a point of law relating wholly or mainly to the construction of an enactment or a statutory instrument or in certain cases any of the EC treaties or instruments.

For appeals direct to the Court of Appeal from the Value Added Tax and Duties Tribunals and from the Special Commissioners under s.56A of the Taxes Management Act 1970 and an appeal from the Value Added Tax and Duties Tribunal of (i) a statutory instrument; (ii) any of the Community

---

[128] *Eli Lilly & Co v Human Genome Sciences* [2009] EWCA Civ 168.
[129] CPR PD 52 para.21.4.
[130] *Manual of Civil Appeals*, 2nd edn, p.162.
[131] *Duo v Duo* [1992] 3 All E.R. 121; [1992] 1 W.L.R. 611.
[132] *Wilson v Webster* [1998] 2 FCR 575; [1998] 1 F.L.R. 1097.

Treaties; or (iii) any Community Instrument[133] the application for permission to appeal must be made within 28 days after the date on which the tribunal certifies that its decision involves a point of law which has been fully argued before and fully considered by it relating wholly or mainly to the construction of an enactment.[134]

In each case the parties must jointly file the application for permission to appeal in an appeal notice which contains a statement of the grounds for the application and is accompanied by a copy of the decision to be appealed endorsed with the certificate of the tribunal.[135]

Where the Court of Appeal gives permission to appeal the appellant must serve the appeal notice on the chairman of the tribunal or the Clerk to the Special Commissioners (as the case may be) as well as the persons to be served under CPR r.52.4(3) within 14 days of being notified of the Court of Appeal's decision to grant permission to appeal.[136]

If the Court of Appeal refuses permission to appeal direct to it, the period for the appellant to renew an appeal to the High Court is to be calculated from the date of the notification of the refusal.[137]

Appeals from the application for permission to appeal must also be made within 28 days after the date on which the Special Commissioners certify that their decision involves a point of law relating wholly or mainly to the construction of an enactment which has been fully argued before and fully considered before them.

Asylum and Immigration Appeals to the Court of Appeal

The Practice Direction to Pt 52, at para.21.7, provides special procedural steps for appeals to the Court of Appeal from the Immigration and Asylum Chamber of the Upper Tribunal under s.13 of the Tribunals, Courts and Enforcement Act 2007.   17–088

The appeal notice must be filed within 14 days after the appellant is served with written notice of the decision of the Tribunal to grant or refuse permission to appeal and it must be served on the Immigration and Asylum Chamber of the Upper Tribunal as well as the persons to be served under CPR r.52.4(3).

---

[133] CPR PD 52 para.21.6(1).
[134] CPR PD 52 paras 21.6(1) and 21.8(1).
[135] CPR PD 52 paras 21.6(2) and 21.8(2).
[136] CPR PD 52 paras 21.6(3)(a) and 21.8(3)(a).
[137] CPR PD 52 paras 21.6(3)(b) and 21.8(3)(b).

The appellant is not required to file an appeal bundle, but must file the documents specified in paras 5.6(2)(a)–(f) of the Practice Direction to Pt 52[138] together with a copy of the Tribunal's determination.

On service of the appeal notice the Immigration and Asylum Chamber of the Upper Tribunal must then send to the Court of Appeal copies of the documents that were before the relevant Tribunal when it considered the appeal.

The Practice Direction to Pt 52 para.21.7 provides further procedural guidance in respect of appeals from the Immigration and Asylum Chamber of the Upper Tribunal which would otherwise be treated as abandoned under s.104(4A) of the Nationality, Immigration and Asylum Act 2002, but meet the conditions set out in s.104(4b) or s.104(4c) of that Act.

Appeals from the Lands Tribunal

17–089   An appellant must file an appeal notice at the Court of Appeal within 28 days after the date of the decision of the Tribunal.[139]

Appeals from the Competition Appeal Tribunal

17–090   The time for filing an appeal notice on an appeal from the Competition Appeal Tribunal is 14 days from the date of the decision where the appellant has applied for permission to appeal at the hearing at which the decision is delivered by the tribunal or where the appellant has applied in writing to the registrar of the tribunal whether or not the application for permission to appeal is granted by the tribunal.[140] Where no such application is made the appeal notice seeking permission to appeal must be filed within 14 days after the end of the period within which the appellant could have made a written application to the registrar of the tribunal.[141]

---

[138] Two additional copies of the appeal notices for the appeal court; and one copy of the appeal notice for each of the respondents; one copy of the appellant's skeleton for each copy of the appeal notice that is filed; a sealed copy of the order being appealed; a copy of any order giving or refusing permission to appeal, together with a copy of the judge's reasons for allowing or refusing permission to appeal; and any witness statements or affidavits in support of any application included in the appeal notice.

[139] CPR PD 52 para.21.9.

[140] CPR PD 52 paras 21.10(1) and 21.10(2).

[141] CPR PD 52 para.21.10(3).

Appeals relating to the application of articles 81 and 82 of the EC Treaty and Chapters I and II of Part I of the Competition Act 1998

Paragraph 21.10A of the Practice Direction to Pt 52 provides guidance for an appeal which raises an issue relating to the application of art.81 or 82 of the Treaty establishing the European Community or Chapter I or II of Pt I of the Competition Act 1998.

17–091

The appeal notice must state that the appeal raises such an issue and serve a copy of the appeal notice on the Office of Fair Trading at the same time as it is served on the other party to the appeal.[142]

Paragraphs 21.10A(4) and (5) of the Practice Direction to Pt 52 draw attention to the provisions of art.15.3 of the Council Regulation (EC) No.1/2003 of December 16, 2002 on the implementation of the rules on competition and the entitlement of the competition authorities and the European Commission to submit written observations to national courts on issues relating to the application of arts 81 and 82 and, with the permission of the court in question, to submit oral observations to the court and that this practice applies to the Court of Appeal.

If a national competition authority or the European Commission wishes to make written observations to the Court of Appeal it must give notice of its intention to do so by letter to the Civil Appeals Office "at the earliest opportunity".

An application for permission to make oral representations must be made by letter again "at the earliest opportunity" and the letter must identify the appeal and indicate why the applicant wishes to make oral representations.[143]

If the national competition authority or European Commission wishes to request documents relating to the appeal it should do so at the same time as giving notice to make written observations or applying to make oral representations.[144] A copy of the notice or application must be served on every party to the appeal.[145]

Every party to an appeal raising an issue relating to the application of art.81 or 82 and any national competition authority which has been served with a copy of a party's appeal notice, is under a duty to notify the Court of Appeal at any stage of the appeal if they are aware that the Commission has adopted or is contemplating adopting a decision in relation to proceedings which it has initiated and the decision has or would have legal effects in relation to the particular agreement, decision or practice in issue before the court.[146]

---

[142] CPR PD 52 para.21.10A(3). The Practice Direction requires the copy to be addressed to the Director of Competition Policy Co-ordination, Office of Fair Trading, Fleetbank House, 2–6 Salisbury Square, London EC4Y 8JX.

[143] CPR PD 52 para.21.10A(6)–(7).

[144] CPR PD 52 para.21.10A(9).

[145] CPR PD 52 para.21.10A(8).

[146] CPR PD 52 para.21.10A(12).

Where the Court of Appeal becomes aware that the Commission is contemplating adopting a decision relevant to the appeal it shall consider whether to stay the appeal pending the decision.[147]

Where any judgment is given which involves a decision on the application of art.81 or 82, the court shall direct that a copy of the transcript of the judgment shall be sent to the Commission.[148]

Appeal from the Proscribed Organisations Appeal Commission

17–092   The time for filing an appeal notice for an appeal from the Proscribed Organisations Appeal Commission is 14 days after the date when permission to appeal was granted or, where s.6(2)(b) of the Terrorism Act 2000 applies, refused permission to appeal.[149]

Appeal from the Court of Protection

17–093   Where proceedings involve a person who lacks or who is alleged to lack capacity within the meaning of the Mental Capacity Act 2005 to make a decision or decisions in relation to any matter that is subject to an order of the Court of Protection there are special procedural rules relating to appeals set out at para.21.12 of the Practice Direction to Pt 52.

In such an appeal where the person who lacks or is alleged to lack capacity is not a party to the appeal and unless the Court of Appeal orders otherwise, the appellant, his agent or such other person as the Court of Protection may direct must notify him in language appropriate to his circumstances[150] of various steps in the appeal process as directed by the Court of Appeal[151] and in particular:

(1)   the fact that an appeal notice has been filed with the Court of Appeal and who the appellant is;
(2)   what final order the appellant is seeking;
(3)   what will happen if the Court of Appeal makes the final order sought by the appellant; and
(4)   that he may apply under CPR r.52.12A by letter for permission to file evidence or make representations at the appeal hearing.

The time for doing this is within 14 days of the date on which the appeal notice was filed.[152]

---

[147] CPR PD 52 para.21.10A(13).
[148] CPR PD 52 para.21.10A(13). This can be done electronically to compamicus@cec.eu.int or by post to the European Commission—DG Competition, B-1049 Brussels.
[149] CPR PD 52 para.21.11(1).
[150] CPR PD 52 para.21.12(4).
[151] CPR PD 52 para.21.12(2)(c).
[152] CPR PD 52 paras 21.12(2)(a) and 21.12(3)(a).

Similarly the same process must be followed in respect of the final order. The appellant, his agent or such other person as the Court of Protection may direct must notify the person who lacks or is alleged to lack capacity of the fact of the final order, its effect and what steps he can take in relation to it. The notification must be in language appropriate to the individual's circumstances. The time for doing this is also within 14 days of the date on which the final order is made.[153]

In notifying the person who lacks or who is alleged to lack capacity, an explanation of a document must include what the document is and what effect, if any, it has or in the case of an event, what the event is and its relevance to him.[154]

A Form N165 must be filed within seven days of the notification stating the date of notification and that the notification took place in accordance with para.21.12 of the Practice Direction to Pt 52.[155] Where no notification has taken place, a Form N165 must be filed stating the reason why no notification has been effected within 21 days of the appeal notice being filed with the Court of Appeal or the final order being made or as the Court of Appeal may direct.[156]

A person may apply to the Court of Appeal for an order dispensing with the provisions of para.21.12 of the Practice Direction to Pt 52 or requiring some other person to comply with them. The application should be made in the appeal notice or by way of a Pt 23 application notice.[157]

Appeals in relation to serious crime prevention orders

In an appeal in relation to a serious crime prevention order made under   **17–094**
s.23(1) of the Serious Crime Act 2007 or s.16 of the Senior Courts Act 1981, the appellant must serve the appeal notice on any person who made representations in the proceedings by virtue of s.9(1), (2) or (3) of the Serious Crime Act 2007 in addition to the person to be served under CPR r.52.4(3).[158]

---

[153] CPR PD 52 paras 21.12(2)(b) and 21.12(3)(b).
[154] CPR PD 52 para.21.12(5).
[155] CPR PD 52 para.21.12(6).
[156] CPR PD 52 para.21.12(7)–(8).
[157] CPR PD 52 para.21.12(9)–(10).
[158] CPR PD 52 para.21.13.

PART 4

The Higher Appellate Courts

CHAPTER 18

Practice in the Supreme Court

"A thousand years of judgment stretch behind—
The weight of rights and freedoms balancing
   With fairness and with duty to the world:
The clarity time-honoured thinking brings."

From "Lines for the Supreme Court",
Andrew Motion, 2009[1]

INTRODUCTION

The Supreme Court of the United Kingdom ("the Supreme Court") is the   **18–001**
final court of appeal for all civil cases in all United Kingdom courts, and for
criminal cases in England, Wales and Northern Ireland.[2] The Supreme
Court hears appeals on arguable points of law of general public importance. The Supreme Court also plays an important role in the development
of the law in the United Kingdom.

As discussed in Chapter 1, until October 1, 2009, the House of Lords was
the final court of appeal and the highest court in the United Kingdom. The
judicial function of the House of Lords was exercised by 12 Lords of
Appeal in Ordinary (known as "Law Lords") sitting in the Appellate
Committee of the House of Lords. Since October 1, 2009, this function has
been carried out by the new Supreme Court.[3] The 12 Law Lords became

---

[1] Andrew Motion, poet laureate from 1999 to 2009, was commissioned by the Justices of
the Supreme Court to write a poem commemorating the establishment of a Supreme Court
for the United Kingdom. The poem has also been engraved onto stone benches outside the
front entrance of the Supreme Court building by artist Richard Kindersley.
[2] Criminal appeals are outside the scope of this book.
[3] Following the establishment of the Supreme Court of the United Kingdom, the former
Supreme Court of England and Wales (which comprised the Court of Appeal, the High
Court, and the Crown Court) was renamed the Senior Courts of England and Wales (under
s.59 of the Constitutional Reform Act 2005).

Supreme Court Justices,[4] and the court moved across Parliament Square from the Palace of Westminster to the newly renovated Middlesex Guildhall.[5] The Supreme Court Registry ("the Registry") also took over the functions of the Judicial Office in the House of Lords.

The replacement of the House of Lords Appellate Committee with the Supreme Court has been heralded as a landmark in constitutional and legal development in the United Kingdom. It has introduced a clear separation of powers between the legislature, the judiciary and the executive.[6] Lord Phillips of Worth Matravers, the first President of the Supreme Court, has said that this separation of powers "emphasises the independence of the judiciary, clearly separating those who make the law from those who administer it".[7]

The Supreme Court was established, and its jurisdiction was defined, by Pt 3 of the Constitutional Reform Act 2005 and Schs 9 to 11 thereto.[8]

THE PURPOSE OF THE SUPREME COURT

18-002   In his wide-ranging review of the Civil Division of the Court of Appeal,[9] Sir Jeffery Bowman concluded that the purpose and rationale of an appeals

---

[4] s.23 of the Constitutional Reform Act 2005 provided that the Supreme Court would comprise 12 judges to be known as Justices of the Supreme Court, appointed by the Queen by letters patent. S.24 of the Constitutional Reform Act 2005 provided that the first 12 Justices would be the 12 Lords of Appeal in Ordinary in office when s.23 came into effect. Thereafter those Lords are disqualified from sitting and voting in the House of Lords while they remain Justices (s.137 of the Constitutional Reform Act 2005). New judges appointed to the Supreme Court will not become Members of the House of Lords.

[5] The Queen officially opened the Supreme Court at Middlesex Guildhall on October 16, 2009. Middlesex Guildhall houses the Judicial Committee of the Privy Council as well as the Supreme Court.

[6] As further discussed in para.1–047, the establishment of the Supreme Court was not universally welcomed. In the Law Lords' response to the Government's consultation paper on "Constitutional Reform: a Supreme Court for the United Kingdom" (CP 11/ July 3, 2003), divided views emerged. Several of the Law Lords recorded their view that the change in arrangements was "unnecessary and will be harmful". Other Law Lords, on the contrary, stated that the functional separation of the judiciary from the legislature and executive was an important step as a matter of constitutional principle.

[7] Press Notice of the Supreme Court No.01/09 dated October 1, 2009 (*www.supremecourt.gov.uk*).

[8] The jurisdiction of the Supreme Court corresponds to that of the House of Lords in its judicial capacity under the Appellate Jurisdiction Acts 1876 and 1888 (which Acts were repealed). In addition, the Supreme Court took over the devolution jurisdiction of the Judicial Committee of the Privy Council under the Scotland Act 1998, the Northern Ireland Act 1998, and the Government of Wales Act 2006. Devolution matters raise issues of constitutional importance as to the purported or proposed exercise of a function by a member of the Scottish Executive, a Minister in Northern Ireland or a Northern Ireland department or the Welsh Ministers or as to the legislative competence of the Scottish Parliament under the Scotland Act 1998, the Northern Ireland Assembly under the Northern Ireland Act 1998, and the Welsh Assembly under the Government of Wales Act 2006. The devolution functions of the Supreme Court (which are addressed in the Supreme Court Rules 2009 r.41 and the Supreme Court PD 10) are outside the scope of this book.

[9] Sir Jeffery Bowman, *Report to the Lord Chancellor by the Review of the Court of Appeal (Civil Division)*, November 6, 2007 ("the Bowman Report").

system is two-fold. First, the private purpose is to correct an error, unfairness or wrong in the exercise of discretion which has led to an unjust result in the court below. Secondly, the public purpose is to ensure public confidence in the administration of justice and, in appropriate cases, to clarify and develop the law, practice and procedure; and to help maintain the standards of first instance courts and tribunals. This duality of purpose applies similarly to the work of the Supreme Court[10]; however, the public purpose takes precedence in the Supreme Court,[11] not least due to the limited resources available to the Supreme Court as compared with the Court of Appeal, and the desirability of avoiding duplication by the Supreme Court of review of decisions by the Court of Appeal. This was reiterated by Lord Bingham in *R. v Secretary of State for Trade and Industry Ex p. Eastaway*. Applying the decision in *Lane v Esdaile*,[12] he observed that:

> "In its role as a supreme court the House [of Lords] must necessarily concentrate its attention on a relatively small number of cases recognised as raising legal questions of general public importance. It cannot seek to correct errors in the application of settled law, even where such are shown to exist."[13]

As a consequence, the decision as to whether the Supreme Court will entertain an appeal is almost always left to the Supreme Court itself (see para.18–024).

THE SUPREME COURT JUSTICES

Up to 12 Supreme Court Justices are appointed to hear appeals which raise   **18–003** arguable points of law of general public importance which ought to be considered by the Supreme Court.

The Supreme Court panel hearing an appeal must consist of an uneven number of Justices (at least three), of whom more than half are permanent

---

[10] In their valedictory for the House of Lords, *The Judicial House of Lords 1876–2009* (OUP, 2009) Louis Blom-Cooper, Brice Dickson and Gavin Drewry characterised this private purpose as a form of "quality control"; and the public purpose as a form of supervision: i.e. the process of laying down fresh precedents and statutory interpretations, and resolving legal problems of a particularly high order (both in terms of complexity and also in respect of public importance).

[11] The extent to which the public purpose takes precedence over the private purpose is illustrated by the decision of the House of Lords to grant leave to appeal in *Scandinavian Trading Tanker Co AB v Flota Petrolera Ecuatoriana* [1983] 2 A.C. 694 (a case concerning relief from forfeiture in the context of a charterparty) not because there was any need to give fuller consideration to the decision of the Court of Appeal, but "in order that a matter of such practical importance to the shipping world should, by a decision of the highest appellate court, but put beyond reach of future challenge" (at 700).

[12] [1891] A.C. 210.

[13] [2000] 1 W.L.R. 2222 at 2228B.

Justices.[14] The Supreme Court usually sits in panels of five, but sometimes sits in panels of seven or nine for appeals of particular difficulty or importance. It appears that, when the Court is at full strength, the practice will be more often to sit in panels of seven than was the case for the House of Lords.

The Constitutional Reform Act 2005 made provision for a new appointments process for Justices of the Supreme Court.[15] The selection commission is composed of the President and Deputy President of the Supreme Court and members of the appointment bodies for England, Wales, Scotland and Northern Ireland. New Justices will not be made peers as of right. A Justice who is not a peer should be referred to in Court as (for example) "my lord, Sir John Dyson" and in writing as "Sir John Dyson SC"; whereas a Justice who is a peer should be referred to in Court as (for example) "my Lord" or "my Lady" and in writing as "Lord Phillips" or "Lady Hale".

THE JURISDICTION OF THE SUPREME COURT

18–004   The jurisdiction of the Supreme Court is defined by s.40 of, and Sch.9 to, the Constitutional Reform Act 2005.[16] By s.40(5), the Supreme Court has power to determine any question necessary to be determined for the purposes of doing justice in an appeal to it under any enactment.[17]

Subject to statutory restrictions in respect of specific matters (see para.18–005), an appeal lies to the Supreme Court from:

> (1) any order or judgment of the Court of Appeal in England and Wales,[18] or in Northern Ireland,[19] with the permission of that court or, if refused, by permission of the Supreme Court[20];

---

[14] Constitutional Reform Act 2005 s.42(1).

[15] Constitutional Reform Act 2005 ss.25–31 and Sch.8. S.25 (the statutory qualifications for appointment) has been amended by ss.50–52 of the Tribunals and Enforcement Act 2007.

[16] The Supreme Court's jurisdiction, as defined by s.40 of, and Sch.9 to, the Constitutional Reform Act 2005 is summarised at Practice Direction 1, paras 1.2.1 to 1.2.5. See also para.2–002.

[17] This provision has the effect of re-enacting s.4 of the Appellate Jurisdiction Act 1876 (repealed).

[18] sub-s.40(2) of the Constitutional Reform Act 2005. The principal provisions relating to civil appeals from Northern Ireland are set out in s.42 of the Judicature (Northern Ireland) Act 1978 as amended by the Constitutional Reform Act 2005.

[19] The principal provisions relating to civil appeals from Northern Ireland are in s.42 of the Judicature (Northern Ireland) Act 1978 as amended by the Act. The law relating to civil appeals in Northern Ireland is outside the scope of this book.

[20] sub-s.40(6) of the Constitutional Reform Act 2005 provides that an appeal under sub-s.40(2) lies only with the permission of the Court of Appeal or the Supreme Court; but this is subject to provision under any other enactment restricting such an appeal.

(2) any order or judgment of a court in Scotland if an appeal lay from that court to the House of Lords immediately before the commencement of the Constitutional Reform Act 2005[21]; and

(3) exceptionally, an appeal lies to the Supreme Court direct from a decision of the High Court of Justice in England and Wales by permission of the Supreme Court (known as a "leapfrog" appeal: see para.18–006).

The statutory restrictions on the Supreme Court's jurisdiction[22]

There is no right of appeal to the Supreme Court from: 18–005

(1) an order of the Court of Appeal refusing permission for an appeal to the Court of Appeal from a lower court (s.54(4) of the Access to Justice Act 1999)[23];

(2) incidental decisions of the Court of Appeal which may be called into question by rules of court (s.58 of the Senior Courts Act 1981, as amended by s.60 of the Access to Justice Act 1999);

(3) a decision of the Court of Appeal on any appeal from a county court in any probate proceedings (s.82 of the County Courts Act 1984);

(4) a decision of the Court of Appeal on an appeal from the decision of the High Court on a question of law under Pt III of the Representation of the People Act 1983;

(5) the refusal by the Court of Appeal of permission to appeal against the Administrative Court's refusal of permission to apply for judicial review[24]; or

(6) the refusal by the Court of Appeal to reopen a previously concluded appeal or application for permission to appeal under the *Taylor v Lawrence* jurisdiction[25] (CPR r.52.17): see Chapter 8.

---

[21] sub-s.40(3) of the Constitutional Reform Act 2005. The principal provisions relating to civil appeals from courts in Scotland are set out in s.40 of the Court of Session Act 1988 as amended by the Constitutional Reform Act 2005. The law relating to civil appeals in Scotland is outside the scope of this book.

[22] These statutory restrictions are summarised at PD 1 para 1.2.7.

[23] s.54(4) of the Access to Justice Act 1999 enacts the ratio to the same effect in the decision of the House of Lords in *Lane v Esdaile* [1891] A.C. 210 (expounded in *Kemper Reinsurance Co v Minister of Finance* [2000] 1 A.C. 1). In *Final Appeal: a Study of the House of Lords in its Judicial Capacity* (OUP, 1972), Louis Blom-Cooper and Gavin Drewry commented that, whilst this rule enabled the House of Lords to dispose summarily of a high proportion of unmeritorious petitions for leave, it has not deterred aspiring appellants (often litigants in person) from bringing such applications.

[24] *R. v Secretary of State for Trade and Industry Ex p. Eastaway* [2000] 1 W.L.R. 2222 applying the decision in *Lane v Esdaile* [1891] A.C. 210; PD 1 para.1.2.21. However, if the Court of Appeal grants permission to appeal to it against the Administrative Court's refusal of permission to apply for judicial review, but then refuses permission to apply for judicial review, the Supreme Court does have jurisdiction to hear an appeal against that refusal: *R v Hammersmith and Fulham LBC Ex p. Burkett* [2002] 1 W.L.R. 1593.

[25] *Taylor v Lawrence* [2002] EWCA Civ 90; [2003] Q.B. 528 at 540.

Further, the Supreme Court has no jurisdiction to hear applications for permission to appeal by a person in respect of whom the High Court has made an order under s.42 of the Senior Courts Act 1981 (restriction of vexatious legal proceedings).

APPEALS DIRECT FROM THE HIGH COURT: LEAPFROG APPEALS

18–006   An appeal may exceptionally (and subject to certain conditions) be permitted to be made direct to the Supreme Court from the High Court[26] if it involves a point of general public importance: (a) relating wholly or mainly to the construction of an enactment or of a statutory instrument, or (b) in respect of which the judge is bound by a decision of the Court of Appeal or of the Supreme Court in previous proceedings. These appeals are referred to as "leapfrog appeals" and are governed by ss.12 to 16 of the Administration of Justice Act 1969.[27] The purpose of the leapfrog procedure is to save time and expense by cutting out an intermediate tier of appeal and providing that the matter in question is resolved in one forum only.[28] However, the procedure is seldom used.[29]

A leapfrog appeal will only be permitted if: (a) the judge hearing the matter in the High Court grants a certificate under s.12 of the Administration of Justice Act 1969, and (b) the Supreme Court grants permission for the appeal.[30] Permission is rarely granted.

The leapfrog certificate

18–007   The prospective appellant cannot apply to the Supreme Court for permission to bring a leapfrog appeal unless or until the judge in the High Court has granted a certificate certifying that he or she is satisfied that:

---

[26] The leapfrog procedure applies to any civil proceedings in the High Court which are either proceedings before a single judge of the High Court or proceedings before a Divisional Court: s.12(2) of the Administration of Justice Act 1969. The procedure for applying for permission to make a leapfrog appeal is outlined in PD 3 paras 3.6.1–3.6.16. See also para.18–009.

[27] This procedure was introduced on the recommendation of the Evershed Committee in *Final Report of the Committee on Supreme Court Practice and Procedure*, Cmnd.8878 (1953), paras 483–530.

[28] *R. (Jones) v Ceredigion CC* [2007] 1 W.L.R. 1400 at [19].

[29] For example, from 1967 to 1996, only 54 leapfrog appeals were heard by the House of Lords: Bruce Dickson, "The Lords of Appeal and their Work 1967–96" published in B. Dickson and P. Carmichael (eds), *The House of Lords: Its Parliamentary and Judicial Roles* (Oxford: Hart, 1999), pp.127–54, at p.146.

[30] The requirements and procedure relating to leapfrog appeals is summarised in PD 1 paras 1.2.17–1.2.19.

(1) the "relevant conditions" in s.12(3) of the Administration of Justice Act 1969 are satisfied;
(2) a sufficient case has been made out to justify an application for permission to appeal to the Supreme Court; and
(3) that all parties to the proceedings consent.[31]

The "relevant conditions" are set out in s.12(3) of the Administration of Justice Act 1969. They require that the High Court judge be satisfied that:

(1) the appeal involves a point of law of general public importance; and
(2) either:

   (a) the point of law relates wholly or mainly to the construction of an enactment or of a statutory instrument and has been fully argued in the proceedings and fully considered in the judgment of the judge in the proceedings (s.12(3)(a) of the Administration of Justice Act 1969). This condition will be interpreted narrowly: the judge will look at how much of the argument and judgment turned on the point of statutory construction[32]; or
   (b) the point of law is one in respect of which the judge is bound by a decision of the Court of Appeal or of the Supreme Court in previous proceedings, and that point of law was fully considered in the judgments given by the Court of Appeal or the Supreme Court (as the case may be) in those previous proceedings (s.12(3)(b) of the Administration of Justice Act 1969).

Even if the relevant conditions are met, and the other requirements of   **18–008**
s.12(1) of Administration of Justice Act 1969 are satisfied, the High Court judge is not compelled to grant the leapfrog certificate. The judge has a judicial discretion whether or not to grant the certificate.[33] There may be circumstances where the judge considers it desirable that the Supreme Court should have the benefit of the decision and judgments of the Court of Appeal. In *IRC v Church Commissioners of England*, Megarry J. commented that this may be the case where the High Court proceedings centred on disputed questions of fact, because the case would have been argued by both sides before the facts were found. Therefore the parties' advocates may not have argued the point "with the full range of authorities and arguments which are appropriate to the facts as ultimately found".[34] Further, he observed, the High Court judge may decline to grant a certificate where the case is within the letter, but not the spirit, of s.12 of Administration of Justice Act 1969.

---

[31] Administration of Justice Act 1969 s.12(1).
[32] *IRC v Church Commissioners for England* [1975] 1 W.L.R. 251 at 272.
[33] *R. (Jones) v Ceredigion CC* [2007] 1 W.L.R. 1400 at [6]; *IRC v Church Commissioners for England* [1975] 1 W.L.R. 251 at 272.
[34] [1975] 1 W.L.R. 251 at 272.

The prospective appellant must apply for a certificate immediately after judgment is handed down, or make an application within 14 days of the judgment.[35] There is no right of appeal against the refusal by a judge to grant a leapfrog certificate under s.12 of the Administration of Justice Act 1969.[36]

Permission of the Supreme Court

18–009   If a leapfrog certificate is granted, the Supreme Court may grant permission to bring the leapfrog appeal if it appears to the Supreme Court that it is "expedient" to do so.[37] The prospective appellant must make an application for permission to appeal to the Supreme Court within one month from the date on which the High Court judge granted the certificate.[38] The application will be determined on paper, without a hearing.[39]

Permission to bring a leapfrog appeal will not be granted where the case concerns contempt of court,[40] or if the case is one in which an appeal to the Court of Appeal either: (a) would not have lain even with permission,[41] or (b) would not have had permission granted for it.[42]

In other cases the Supreme Court has a discretion whether or not to grant permission. Guidance as to how that discretion is likely to be exercised is found in the Supreme Court Practice Direction 3 para.3.6.12, which states that the Appeal Panel will only grant permission to appeal where:

(1)   there is an urgent need to obtain an authoritative interpretation by the Supreme Court; or

(2)   the case is one in which permission to appeal to the Supreme Court would have been granted if it had not been brought direct to the Supreme Court and the judgment had been that of the Court of Appeal; and

(3)   it does not appear likely that any additional assistance could be derived from a judgment of the Court of Appeal.

---

[35]   Administration of Justice Act 1969 s.12(4).

[36]   Administration of Justice Act 1969 s.12(5).

[37]   Administration of Justice Act 1969 s.13(2).

[38]   Administration of Justice Act 1969 s.13(1). The applicant must file one copy of the High Court judge's certificate with the application, and the application should indicate whether the certificate was granted under s.12(3)(a) or s.12(3)(b) of the Administration of Justice Act 1969 (PD 3 para.3.6.9). Within seven days of filing the application, the applicant should file four additional copies of the application, four copies of the order of the High Court, four additional copies of the High Court judge's certificate (if not contained in the order) and four copies of the transcript of the High Court judgment (PD 3 para.3.6.10). These documents must be presented in the form required by PD 5 para.5.1.2 (i.e. legible and bound on A4 printed on both sides).

[39]   Administration of Justice Act 1969 s.13(3); PD 3 para.3.6.11.

[40]   Administration of Justice Act 1969 s.15(4).

[41]   Administration of Justice Act 1969 s.15(1) and (2).

[42]   Administration of Justice Act 1969 s.15(3).

Loss of the right to appeal to the Court of Appeal

If the Supreme Court grants permission for a direct leapfrog appeal against **18–010** a decision of the High Court, no appeal against the High Court's decision shall lie to the Court of Appeal.[43] Once permission to bring a leapfrog appeal is granted, therefore, the appellant loses any right to apply for permission to appeal to the Court of Appeal, and any permission to appeal to the Court of Appeal that might already have been granted is overridden. If, however, a leapfrog certificate is granted but no application for permission is made to the Supreme Court within one month of the granting of that certificate, the appellant's right to appeal to the Court of Appeal is reinstated.[44] If, as must be very unusual, the appellant declines to pursue his leapfrog appeal, it is suggested that he must still file his appellant's notice for the Court of Appeal within the usual period allowed under CPR r.52.4[45] or otherwise seek an extension of time from the Court of Appeal.[46]

If the Supreme Court grants permission to make a leapfrog appeal subject to any conditions, and the appellant does not accept those conditions, then any right of appeal to the Court of Appeal is reinstated.[47] If there are two or more grounds of appeal, and the Supreme Court grants permission to appeal on only one of those grounds, then the appellant's right to appeal to the Court of Appeal on the other ground(s) is also reinstated.[48]

PROCEDURE IN THE SUPREME COURT

Procedure in the Supreme Court is governed by the Supreme Court Rules **18–011** 2009 ("the Rules")[49] and by Practice Directions issued by the President of

---

[43] Administration of Justice Act 1969 s.13(2)(a).

[44] Administration of Justice Act 1969 s.13(5)(a).

[45] See para.15–011.

[46] See para.16–008.

[47] *R. (Jones) v Ceredigion CC* [2007] 1 W.L.R. 1400 at [18]–[25]. The appellant in that case sought permission to appeal against the decision of the High Court on two grounds. The High Court judge certified a leapfrog appeal on both grounds, and also gave contingent permission to appeal to the Court of Appeal in the event that the House of Lords did not grant permission for a leapfrog appeal. The House of Lords refused permission to appeal on the first ground, but granted permission to appeal on the second ground, subject to a condition relating to costs. The appellant did not accept the condition. It withdrew its appeal to the House of Lords, and instead sought to appeal to the Court of Appeal on the first ground. The respondent challenged its right to do so. The House of Lords (upholding the Court of Appeal's decision that it had jurisdiction to hear the appeal on the first ground) held that, if a prospective appellant is granted leave to appeal subject to terms which he is unwilling to accept, he has the option of declining to pursue his appeal without losing his full rights of appeal in the Court of Appeal.

[48] Further, in *R. (Jones) v Ceredigion CC* [2007] 1 W.L.R. 1400 (obiter) at [25] the House of Lords held that the Court of Appeal also had jurisdiction to hear the appeal on the second ground.

[49] SI 2009/1603 (pursuant to s.45 of the Constitutional Reform Act 2005). The Rules apply to the whole of the United Kingdom, to both civil and criminal appeals, and to appeals and references under the Supreme Court's devolution jurisdiction (r.2(1)). The Rules can be downloaded from the Supreme Court's website at *www.supremecourt.gov.uk/procedures/rules-of-the-court* and are in s.4A of Vol.2 of the *White Book*.

the Supreme Court under r.3(3) of the Rules ("the Practice Directions").[50] The Rules and the Practice Directions largely follow the Directions that formerly regulated procedure in the House of Lords. There is a great deal of (often unnecessary) repetition and paraphrasing of the Rules in the Practice Directions (often without cross-reference), and there is a lot of repetition between Practice Directions, but the Practice Directions do supplement the Rules in many ways so both must be read together.

By way of summary, the facts and issues relevant to the appeal are recited in an agreed statement of facts and issues. Documents relevant to the appeal—again, which must be agreed—appear in the appendix to the statement. The parties then file and exchange written cases, equivalent to skeleton arguments, well in advance of the hearing. The appellant's solicitors must then ensure that all documents, including authorities, are filed in preparation for the hearing. The general practice is for all documents and authorities to be filed in A4 sized comb bound volumes, printed on both sides and no more than approximately one inch thick; lever arch files are not, generally, acceptable. The time taken to prepare and reproduce the bundles for an appeal to the Supreme Court should not be underestimated. Generally, documents must be signed (in hand) by counsel, rather than, as has become the practice in the lower courts of England and Wales, simply bearing counsel's printed name.

The staff in the Registry are accustomed to the fact that lawyers representing the parties may not have much or indeed any experience of preparing cases for the Supreme Court, and are happy to answer questions: if in doubt, ring them up. The Supreme Court has a useful website, at *www.supremecourt.gov.uk* from which rules, practice directions and forms may be downloaded.

Overriding objective

18–012   The overriding objective of the Rules is to secure that the Supreme Court is "accessible, fair and efficient".[51] The Rules are to be interpreted and applied in such a way as to discourage "unnecessary disputes over procedural matters".[52] This reflects the practical approach taken by the registrar and the Supreme Court to procedural matters given that the caseload of the Court is such that it is unlikely that a large body of case-law on the application or interpretation of the Rules and Practice Directions will develop. The Rules and Practice Directions are nevertheless highly prescriptive in many respects, and sanctions for non-compliance may be imposed where appropriate.

---

[50] The Practice Directions replaced the Civil, Criminal and Taxation Practice Directions and standing orders of the Appellate Committee of the House of Lords. They can be downloaded from the Supreme Court's website at *www.supremecourt.gov.uk/procedures/practice-directions* and are in s.4A of Vol.2 of the *White Book*.

[51] r.2(2); PD 1 para.1.1.3.

[52] r.2(3).

Compliance with the Rules

Failure to comply with the Rules or any relevant practice direction will not **18–013** "invalidate" the proceedings.[53] However, in the case of non-compliance, the Supreme Court may give whatever directions appear appropriate, depending on the seriousness of the breach and the circumstances of the case.[54] Those directions may include severe sanctions such as summarily dismissing an appeal or debarring a respondent from resisting an appeal.[55] In particular, the registrar may refuse to accept a document if it does not comply with the Rules or a relevant Practice Direction.[56]

Transitional arrangements

The Rules apply, with any necessary modification, to appeals which were **18–014** proceeding and petitions for leave that were lodged before the establishment of the Supreme Court on October 1, 2009, unless the Supreme Court or the registrar of the Supreme Court ("the registrar") directs otherwise. The Supreme Court or the registrar may give special directions regarding petitions for leave and ongoing appeals lodged before October 1, 2009.[57]

Listing

The listing officer manages the Supreme Court list under the direction of the **18–015** registrar. Enquiries about the listing of appeals should be addressed to the listing officer in the first instance.[58]

The Registry of the Supreme Court[59]

Enquiries about fees and the filing of documents, papers and volumes **18–016** should be addressed to the Registry. Enquiries about the assessment of costs

---

[53] r.8(1).
[54] r.8(2). A direction made by the Supreme Court under r.8(2) is a procedural decision within r.9 and therefore (subject to r.9(2)) may be made by a single Justice or the registrar without an oral hearing.
[55] r.8(4).
[56] r.8(3).
[57] r.55; PD 1 para.1.1.4.
[58] PD 2 para.2.1.4.
[59] The Registry's postal address is: The Registry, The Supreme Court of the United Kingdom, Parliament Square, London SW1P 3BD (DX 157230 Parliament Square 4). Its telephone numbers are 020 7960 1991 and 020 7960 1992. The email address for the Registry is registry@supremecourt.gsi.gov.uk. The Registry is open from 10.00 am to 4.30 pm on Mondays to Thursdays during the law terms and from 10.00 am to 4 pm on Fridays and outside law terms. During August, the Registry is open from 10.00 am to 2.00 pm: PD 2 paras 2.1.2–2.1.3. When the Registry is closed, the registrar can be contacted regarding urgent business via the Supreme Court switchboard on 020 7960 1900.

should be addressed to the registrar or the costs clerk.[60] The registrar has a wide range of powers, as set out in the sections below. The registrar may also refer the matter to a single Justice or to a panel of three Justices for decision.[61] A party who is dissatisfied with a decision of the registrar may apply for that decision to be reviewed by a single Justice.[62]

Forms

18–017   Parties should use the prescribed forms, which are set out in Annex 1 to Practice Direction 7.[63] Rule 4(2) requires that these forms shall be used in the cases to which they apply, and in the circumstances for which they are provided by the relevant Practice Directions, but a form may be varied by the Supreme Court or a party if the variation is required by the circumstances of a particular case.[64] The prescribed forms are:

(1) Form 1: Application for permission/notice of appeal.
(2) Form 2: Application form.
(3) Form 3: Notice of objection/acknowledgment by respondent.
(4) Form 4: Passes for appearing before the court.

Where no particular form is prescribed for a document (e.g. in the case of a statement of facts and issues, or the appellant's and respondent's written cases) parties may follow the former practice in the House of Lords but are not required to do so. If there is any doubt about how a document should be presented or a form completed, the parties are encouraged by the Practice Directions to consult the registrar and discuss the appropriate practice,[65] and (in the case of an application for permission to appeal or a notice of appeal) even to send documents in draft.[66] However, the various provisions relating to the presentation and filing of documents are highly prescriptive and detailed.

Regardless of whether a document is to be in a prescribed form or not, all formal documents produced for the Supreme Court or the Registry must comply with the requirements of Practice Direction 5 para.5.1.2,[67] i.e. they must be printed or reproduced (both as to font size and otherwise) so as to be easily legible; reproduced on paper of A4 size, printed on both sides; and

---

[60] PD 1 para.2.1.4.
[61] PD 1 para.1.3.5.
[62] PD 1 para.1.3.6. Any application must be made in Form 2 in accordance with PD 7 (Applications) and must be filed within 14 days of the registrar's decision: r.9(5). A fee is payable as set out at Annex 2 to PD 7.
[63] The forms can be downloaded from the Supreme Court website at *www.supreme-court.gov.uk/court-forms*. They are also available on the CD-Rom of forms which accompanies the *White Book*.
[64] PD 1 para.1.1.5. R.4(2) reflects CPR r.4(2).
[65] PD 5 para.5.1.1 and PD 6 para.6.1.1.
[66] PD 3 para.3.1.2; PD 4 para.4.2.1.
[67] This requirement is repeated throughout the Practice Directions, e.g. in PD 3 para.3.1.3; PD 4 para 4.2.1; and PD 7 para.7.2.1.

(unless this causes great difficulty) presented in bound form, properly labelled and indexed. Documents must be presented in a form which is robust, manageable and not excessively heavy. Duplication of material must be avoided particularly where two or more appeals are heard together. Documents may be filed by electronic means[68] in accordance with Practice Direction 14, with the consent of the registrar. Documents which are not legible or which are not produced in the authorised form or which are unsatisfactory for some other similar reason are not accepted by the Registry.

Time limits

The Supreme Court has the power to extend or shorten any of the time limits set out in the Rules or Practice Directions (unless to do so would be contrary to any enactment).[69] The Supreme Court may exercise these powers either of its own motion or on an application by one or more parties,[70] and may do so even if the time limit has already expired.[71] If the Supreme Court varies a time limit, the registrar must notify the parties of that variation.[72]

18–018

If an appellant has applied for public funding, the registrar must be informed in writing within the original time limit (28 days for an application for permission under r.11; 42 days for a notice of appeal under r.19) that public funding has been applied for. The relevant time limit will then be extended to 28 days after the final determination of the application for funding, including any appeals.[73] Notification to the registrar is a precondition for the extension of time, and a copy of the order from which an appeal is sought must be included with the notice.[74] A party to an appeal who has obtained a public funding or legal aid certificate must file a copy of that certificate (including an emergency certificate or amendment to a certificate) at the Registry as soon as possible after it is granted.[75]

If the time limit specified by the Rules or Practice Directions, or by any judgment or court order, for doing any act at the Registry ends on a day on which the Registry is closed, that act shall be in time if it is done on the next day on which the Registry is open.[76]

---

[68] "Electronic means" is defined at r.3(2) as meaning CD Roms, memory sticks, email, fax or other means of electronic communication of the contents of documents.

[69] r.5(1). A decision made by the Supreme Court under r.5(1) is a procedural decision within r.9 and therefore (subject to r.9(2)) may be made by a single Justice or the registrar without an oral hearing.

[70] r.5(2).

[71] r.5(4).

[72] r.5(3).

[73] r.5(5).

[74] PD 8 para.8.12.4.

[75] PD 8 para.8.12.2.

[76] r.5(6).

Service

18–019   Documents such as applications for permission to appeal and notices of appeal must be served on the respondents (or their solicitors), in accordance with r.6 or with any relevant statutory provisions, before they are filed.[77] Where a Rule or Practice Direction provides that a document should be served, supplied, submitted or notified by one party to another,[78] this may be achieved by any of the following methods[79]:

(1) personal delivery;

(2) first class post (or an alternative service which provides for delivery on the next working day);

(3) (with the consent of the party to be served[80]) through a document exchange; or

(4) (with the consent of the party to be served[81] or at the direction of the registrar) by electronic means[82] in accordance with Practice Direction 14.

If the address of the person on whom the document is to be served is unknown, the registrar may direct that service is to be effected by an alternative method of service.[83] "Alternative method" has the same meaning as "other service" in CPR r.6.3(1)(b) and para.3 of Practice Direction A to CPR Pt 6, i.e. leaving a document with or delivering the document to a service provider or having a document collected by a service provider.

A document served by first-class post or through a document exchange will be taken to have been served on the second day after it was posted or left at the document exchange, as the case may be (not including days which are not business days[84]).[85] The date of service may be important because some time limits imposed by the Rules are calculated from the date on which a document was served.

After service, when the document is filed, it must be filed together with a certificate of service giving details of the persons served, the method of

---

[77] PD 2 para.2.1.23.

[78] In accordance with the definition of "service and related expressions" at r.3(2).

[79] r.6(1).

[80] Consent will be deemed where the writing paper of a party or its solicitor includes a fax number or a numbered box at a document exchange, unless they have indicated in writing that they are not willing to accept service by that method: PD 2 para.2.1.23.

[81] Consent will be deemed where the writing paper of a party or its solicitor includes a fax number or a numbered box at a document exchange, unless they have indicated in writing that they are not willing to accept service by that method: PD 2 para.2.1.23.

[82] "Electronic means" is defined at r.3(2) as meaning CD Roms, memory sticks, email, fax or other means of electronic communication of the contents of documents.

[83] r.6(2).

[84] Business days are defined at r.3(2) and mean any day other than a Saturday, Sunday, Christmas Day, Good Friday or a bank holiday under the Banking and Financial Dealings Act 1971, in England and Wales.

[85] r.7(2); PD 2 para.2.1.8.

service used, and the date on which the document was served.[86] The certificate of service must be included either in the original document and signed, or a separate certificate of service must be provided.[87]

Filing and issue of documents

Where a Rule or Practice Direction provides that a document should be filed, it should be filed in the Registry in accordance with r.7. In line with the provisions relating to service, documents may be filed by any of the following methods[88]:   **18–020**

(1) personal delivery;
(2) first class post (or an alternative service which provides for delivery on the next working day);
(3) through a document exchange; or
(4) (with the consent of the registrar) by electronic means[89] in accordance with Practice Direction 14.

A document filed by first-class post or through a document exchange will be taken to have been filed on the second day after it was posted or left at the document exchange, as the case may be (not including days which are not business days[90]).[91] Where a document is received on a business day at a time when the Registry is closed, the document will be taken to have been filed in time and the registrar may give whatever consequential directions appear appropriate. The date of filing may be important because some time limits imposed by the Rules are calculated from the date on which a document was filed.

Except with the consent of the registrar, the contents of documents filed in hard copy must also be provided to the Registry by electronic means, and documents filed by electronic means[92] must also be provided to the Registry in hard copy in accordance with the relevant practice direction.[93]

When either an application for permission to appeal, a notice of appeal, a notice of objection, an acknowledgement by a respondent or an application is filed, it must be sealed by a court officer (i.e. a member of staff in the Registry).[94]

---

[86] r.6(4).
[87] PD 2 para.2.1.24.
[88] r.7(1); PD 2 para 2.1.7.
[89] "Electronic means" is defined at r.3(2) as meaning CD Roms, memory sticks, email, fax or other means of electronic communication of the contents of documents.
[90] Business days are defined at r.3(2) and mean any day other than a Saturday, Sunday, Christmas Day, Good Friday or a bank holiday under the Banking and Financial Dealings Act 1971, in England and Wales.
[91] r.7(2); PD 2 para.2.1.8.
[92] In accordance with PD 14.
[93] r.7(3); PD 2 para.2.1.9.
[94] r.7(4); PD 2 para.2.1.7.

The registrar may refuse to accept any document which is illegible or does not comply with any provision in the Rules or a relevant practice direction. On refusing to accept a document, the registrar will give whatever directions are appropriate,[95] including sanctions such as dismissing an appeal or debarring a respondent from resisting an appeal.[96]

18–021 The Registry will not issue an application for permission to appeal or other document unless[97]:

(1) it has been properly served on the respondent(s) in accordance with r.6;

(2) all the required documents are supplied in accordance with r.7(3); and

(3) where a fee is payable, the prescribed fee is paid (or a request for fee remission from court fees is made). Rule 45 gives the registrar power to refuse to accept a document or to allow a party to take any step unless the relevant fee is paid. The amount of the relevant fees is prescribed by the Supreme Court Fees Order 2009[98] under s.52 of the Constitutional Reform Act 2005, and those fees are set out in Annex 2 to Practice Direction 7.

Exercise of the Supreme Court's jurisdiction

18–022 Some of the powers of the Supreme Court may be exercised by a single Justice and by the registrar without an oral hearing under r.9(1),[99] unless the matter relates to a contested application: (a) alleging contempt of court, or (b) for a direction under r.8 dismissing an appeal or debarring a respondent from resisting an appeal, or (c) for security for costs.[100] In those excepted cases, the contested application shall be referred to a panel of Justices.[101] A contested application alleging contempt of court must be heard at an oral hearing; in the other cases, the panel of Justices may hold an oral hearing.

Where the Supreme Court's powers are exercised by a single Justice or the registrar under r.9(1), they may decide the matter on paper, direct an oral hearing, or refer the matter to a panel of Justices to be decided with or without an oral hearing.[102] In addition, the registrar may refer the matter to

---

[95] r.8(3); PD 2 para.2.1.10.

[96] r.8(4).

[97] PD 2 para.2.1.11.

[98] SI 2009/2031.

[99] r.9(1); PD 1 paras 1.3.1–1.3.2. Those powers are r.5 (time limits), r.8 (non-compliance with rules), r.11 (rejection of applications), r.33 (change of interest), r.34 (withdrawal of appeal), r.35 (advocate to the court and assessors), r.36 (security for costs), r.37 (stay of execution) and r.41 (devolution jurisdiction).

[100] r.9(2); PD 1 para.1.3.4.

[101] A panel of Justices comprises at least three Justices: r.3(2).

[102] The powers of the single Justice are set out at r.9(3); the powers of the registrar are set out at r.9(4).

a single Justice. The registrar will normally make decisions under r.9(1) without an oral hearing.[103] Oral hearings on procedural matters must be heard in open court or in a place to which the public are admitted,[104] subject to r.27. Rule 27 provides that an appeal (or in the case of r.9(1), a procedural application) may be heard in private if it is necessary in the interests of justice or in the public interest. It is only in exceptional cases that an appeal will be heard in private: see para.18–058.

Where the matter has been determined by the registrar (with or without an oral hearing), a party may apply for that decision to be reviewed by a single Justice. An application for review must be made on notice in Form 2 within 14 days of the registrar's decision[105] in accordance with r.30 (which sets out the requirements for procedural applications).

Rule 9(7) provides that, if any procedural question arises which is not dealt with by the Rules, the court or the registrar may adopt any procedure that is consistent with the overriding objective, the Constitutional Reform Act and the Rules.[106] This is an important provision which enacts the Supreme Court's inherent power to regulate its own processes. It is not qualified by nor does it qualify other Rules.

APPLICATION FOR PERMISSION TO APPEAL

When permission is required

The previous requirements for permission for appeal to the House of Lords have been maintained in the Rules. The provisions relating to applications for permission to appeal are in Pt 2 of the Rules, rr.10–17. They apply equally to applications for permission to cross-appeal.[107] Permission to appeal is required for every civil appeal from England, Wales and Northern Ireland, either from the court appealed from or (more usually) from the Supreme Court itself. Conversely, most civil appeals from Scottish courts to the Supreme Court do not require permission.

18–023

The Court of Appeal and permission

It remains the case that an application for permission to appeal to the Supreme Court must first be made to the court below (i.e. at the conclusion of the hearing in the court below). A renewed application for permission to appeal may only be made to the Supreme Court (on application) after the

18–024

---

[103] PD 1 para.1.3.5.
[104] r.9(6).
[105] r.9(5).
[106] r.9(7); PD 1 para.1.3.1.
[107] r.25(3). See para.18–053.

court below has refused to grant permission.[108] In practice, for some time it has been, and remains, extremely rare for the Court of Appeal to grant permission to appeal to the House of Lords (formerly) or the Supreme Court (latterly).[109] This trend is a reflection of the House of Lords', and now the Supreme Court's, focus on a small number of cases which raise legal questions of general public importance. The Court of Appeal's highly restrictive approach to applications for permission to appeal enables the Supreme Court to retain control over the number and nature of appeals it entertains. The Court of Appeal outlined this principle in *Taylor v Lawrence*[110]:

> "In the case of an appeal to the House of Lords it is not enough to show a sufficient prospect of the appeal succeeding. The would-be appellant has to show in addition that the case is of such importance that it justifies the attention of the House of Lords. It is the House of Lords which is the best judge of whether a particular case meets this test. It is the House of Lords which is the best judge of whether its limited judicial resources are properly deployed in hearing a particular appeal. That is why this court rarely exercises its jurisdiction to give permission to appeal to the House of Lords."

The test

18–025   Permission to appeal may be granted if the appeal concerns an arguable point of law of general public importance which ought to be considered by the Supreme Court at that time, bearing in mind that the matter will have already been the subject of judicial decision and may have already been reviewed on appeal.[111] The Supreme Court has a high degree of discretion as to whether or not to grant permission to appeal, which reflects the importance of its role in developing the law.

Permission may be refused if the point of law is hypothetical[112] or academic.[113] Further, permission may be refused or revoked if, after the application is made, an event occurs which deprives the appeal of practical

---

[108] r.10(2).

[109] For example, in the first half of 2001, applications for leave to petition the House of Lords were made in 147 cases out of the 398 appeals heard by the Court of Appeal; but of those only two applications (1.3%) were granted. By way of comparison, in 1952 to 1968 78% of the civil appeals held by the House of Lords had been granted leave to appeal by the court below. Source: Blom-Cooper, Dickson and Drewry, *The Judicial House of Lords 1876–2009* (OUP, 2009).

[110] [2002] 3 W.L.R. 640 at [46]–[47].

[111] PD 3 para.3.3.3.

[112] *R. (oao Bushell) v Newcastle upon Tyne Licensing Justices* [2006] UKHL 7; [2006] 1 W.L.R. 496.

[113] *Sun Life Assurance Co of Canada v Jarvis* [1944] A.C. 111; *Ainsbury v Millington* [1987] 1 W.L.R. 379.

significance to the parties.[114] It is only in exceptional cases that the Supreme Court will entertain appeals relating to procedural issues,[115] or costs.[116]

Applications for permission to appeal are considered by a panel of at least three Justices, sometimes referred to as an Appeal Panel.[117] Applications are generally decided on paper, without a hearing.[118]

The registrar has wide powers in relation to applications for permission to appeal. The registrar may refuse to accept an application for permission on the ground that the Supreme Court does not have jurisdiction under s.40 of the Constitutional Reform Act 2005,[119] it contains no reasonable grounds, or it is an abuse of process.[120] In that case the registrar may give whatever directions appear appropriate. The applicant would have the right to seek a review of the registrar's decision by a single Justice pursuant to r.9(5), on application notice (in Form 2) within 14 days of the date of that decision.

Form of application for permission

An application to the Supreme Court for permission to appeal must be made in Form 1,[121] and must be signed by the applicant or their agent.[122] The application should set out briefly the facts and points of law, and include a summary of the reasons why permission should be granted.[123] Whilst there is space in the form for those reasons, it is more normal for them to be set out in an accompanying document. The reasons must seek to convince the panel of Justices that permission should be granted, and so must explain the point clearly, fairly and succinctly, ensuring that it explains why the test for permission is satisfied.

The application should include (in s.9 of Form 1) the neutral citation of the judgment appealed against, the references of any law report in the

18–026

---

[114] This is likely to be the effect of r.33(d).

[115] *Birkett v James* [1978] A.C. 297 at 317.

[116] In *Callery v Gray (Nos 1 & 2)* [2002] 1 W.L.R. 2000 at 2005, Lord Bingham held that "the responsibility for monitoring and controlling the developing practice in a field such as [personal injury costs] this lies with the Court of Appeal and not the House [of Lords], which should ordinarily be slow to intervene. The House cannot respond to changes in practice with the speed and sensitivity of the Court of Appeal, before which a number of cases are likely over time to come. Although this is a final and not an interlocutory appeal, there is in my view some analogy between appeals on matters of practice and interlocutory appeals, of which Lord Diplock in *Birkett v James* [1978] A.C. 297 at 317 observed that only very exceptionally are appeals upon such matters allowed to come before the House."

[117] "Appeal Panel" is the term used in PD 3 and PD 13, although not in Pt 2 of the Rules.

[118] r.16(1); PD 3 para.3.1.1.

[119] See para.18–004.

[120] r.11(2).

[121] r.10(1). PD 3 para.3.1.1 states that it is "essential" that the application is made in the correct form. The application should be on A4 paper, securely bound on the left, using both sides of the paper in accordance with PD 3 para.3.1.2.

[122] PD 3 para.3.1.4.

[123] PD 3 para.3.1.2.

courts below, and subject matter catchwords for indexing (whether or not the case has been reported).[124]

Applications which are not legible or which are not produced in the required form will not be accepted.[125] Parties may consult the Registry at any stage of preparation of the application, and may submit applications in draft for approval. Amendments to applications are allowed where the registrar is satisfied that this will assist the appeal panel and will not unfairly prejudice the respondents or cause undue delay. Any amendments must be made in accordance with r.30(5) and served on the respondent.[126]

If the application for permission to appeal asks the Supreme Court to depart from one of its own decisions (or from a decision of the House of Lords), or seeks a declaration of incompatibility under the Human Rights Act 1998,[127] or seeks a reference to the Court of Justice of the European Communities,[128] then this must be clearly stated in the application together with full details.[129] The Human Rights Act 1998 applies to the Supreme Court and issues under that statute will often arise on appeals to the Supreme Court.[130] The Crown has the right to intervene in any appeal where the Court is considering whether to declare that a provision of primary or subordinate legislation is incompatible with a Convention right under r.40.[131]

Case title

18–027   Applications for permission to appeal (and appeals) should carry the same title as in the court below, except that the parties are described as appellant(s) and respondent(s). For reference purposes, the names of parties to the original proceedings who are not parties to the appeal should nevertheless be included in the title: their names should be enclosed in square brackets. The names of all parties should be given in the same sequence as in the title used in the court below.[132] In any application or appeal concerning children, or where the title used in the court below has been such as to conceal the identity of one or more parties to the proceedings, this fact should be clearly drawn to the attention of the Registry at the time of filing the application for permission, so that the title adopted in the Supreme

---

[124] PD 3 para.3.1.5.
[125] PD 3 para.3.1.2.
[126] PD 3 para.3.1.6.
[127] The practice in r.42 and PD 4 para.4.2.12 applies to cases where an appellant or respondent seeks a declaration of incompatibility or seeks to challenge an act of a public authority under the Human Rights Act 1998. See PD 9.
[128] The practice in r.42 and PD 4 para.4.2.13 applies to cases where an appellant seeks a reference to the Court of Justice of the European Court of Justice. See para.18–071.
[129] PD 3 para.3.1.3.
[130] PD 1 para.1.2.23. See also PD 9.
[131] The relevant procedure is set out in PD 9.
[132] PD 2 para.2.1.18. Further direction relating to case titles is given in PD 2 paras 2.1.19–2.1.22.

Court can take account of the need for anonymity.[133] The Supreme Court has power to make an anonymity order restraining publication of the identity of an individual named in the proceedings or judgments,[134] but in most cases as a general rule the parties will be named in judgments and in newspaper or law reports.

Service of application for permission to appeal

A copy of the application for permission to appeal must be served on every respondent (and on any person who was an intervener in the court below) before the application is filed.[135] **18–028**

Filing the application for permission to appeal

Four copies of the application must be filed with the Registry together with the certificate of service. Further, within seven days of filing the application,[136] the applicant should file four copies of[137]: **18–029**

(1) the order appealed against and (if separate) the order of the court below refusing permission to appeal to the Supreme Court (although if the order appealed from is not immediately available, the application should be filed without delay—and within the prescribed time limit—and the order filed as soon as it is available);

(2) the official transcript of the judgment of the court below;

(3) the final order(s) of all other courts below;

(4) any unreported judgment(s) cited in the application or judgment of a court below; and

(5) a document setting out the history of the proceedings.

These documents must comply with the requirements for documents set out at Practice Direction 5 para.5.1.2 (see para.18–017). Other than the documents prescribed by r.14(1) and Practice Direction 3 para.3.2.1, the Registry will not accept any other documents unless requested by the appeal panel. An applicant who wishes to provide documents other than those listed above must give a detailed explanation as to why they are needed. **18–030**

The Registry will not issue an application for permission to appeal (or other document) unless it has been properly served on the respondent(s), all

---

[133] PD 2 para.2.1.20; PD 3 para.3.1.11.
[134] The source of this power is s.6 of the Human Rights Act and s.37 of the Senior Court Act. This power fulfils the United Kingdom's positive obligation under art.8 of the European Convention: *Re Guardian News and Media Ltd* [2010] UKSC 1; [2010] 2 W.L.R. 325 SC.
[135] r.12; PD 2 para.2.1.23; PD 3 para.3.1.6.
[136] r.14(2).
[137] r.14(1); PD 3 para.3.2.1.

of the required documents have been supplied, and the prescribed fee has been paid (or a request for fee remission made).[138]

If the required documents are not filed within eight weeks after the filing of the application and no good reason is given for the delay, the registrar may refer the application to an appeal panel without the required accompanying papers; dismiss the application, or give such other directions as appear appropriate under r.8,[139] including summary dismissal of the appeal.[140]

Time limit

18–031 An application for permission to appeal must be filed within 28 days of the order or decision of the court below[141] (subject to any enactment which makes special provision with regard to any particular category of appeal[142]). The Supreme Court may extend this time limit on application by the applicant.[143]

Interventions

18–032 Rule 15(1) provides that any person, and in particular any official body or non-governmental organisation seeking to make submissions in the public interest, or any person with an interest in proceedings by way of judicial review, may make written submissions[144] to the Supreme Court in support of an application for permission to appeal and request that the Supreme Court take them into account. Any submissions made by an intervener will be referred to the panel of Justices which considers the application for permission to appeal.[145] If permission is granted, the intervener will be

---

[138] PD 2 para.2.1.11.

[139] PD 3 para.3.2.3.

[140] r.8(4).

[141] r.11(1); PD 1 para.1.2.9; PD 2 para.2.1.12. As set out at para.18–018, if an applicant has applied for public funding, the registrar must be informed in writing within the 28 day time limit that public funding has been applied for. The time limit for the application for permission will then be extended to 28 days after the final determination of the application for funding, including any appeals: r.5(5).

[142] For example, s.2 of the Administration of Justice Act 1960 provides that an application for permission to appeal to the Supreme Court in a case involving civil contempt of court must be filed within 14 days, beginning with the date on which the application for permission is refused by the court below. S.13 of the Administration of Justice Act 1969 provides that an application for permission to appeal to the Supreme Court in a "leapfrog appeal" from the High Court must be filed within one month from the date on which the High Court judge grants a certificate under s.12. Different time limits also apply in respect of habeas corpus (PD 1 para.1.2.9, PD 12 and PD 3 paras 3.6.17–3.6.18) and publicly funded matters (r.5(5) and PD 2 para.2.1.12(c)).

[143] PD 1 para.1.2.9.

[144] The submissions must be served in the appellant, every respondent, and any intervener in the court below before four copies of the submissions are filed in the Registry together with a certificate of service: r.15(2); PD 3 para.3.3.17.

[145] r.15(3); PD 3 para.3.3.18.

notified; however, if the intervener wishes to intervene in the appeal itself, they must apply to the Supreme Court for permission to intervene in the appeal under r.26 (see para.18–054).[146] Further, if the intervener's submissions were taken into account by the Supreme Court and permission is granted, the applicant should serve the re-sealed application for permission standing as the notice of appeal on the intervener.[147]

Notice of objection

If the respondent wishes to object to the application for permission to appeal, they must serve and file a notice of objection in Form 3,[148] and may (at the same time) submit written objections giving their reasons why permission to appeal should be refused.[149] A respondent who fails to file a notice of objection will not be permitted to participate in the application and will not be given notice of its progress,[150] nor will they be able to obtain an order for costs.[151] The notice of objection should be served on the applicant, any other respondent, and any person who was an intervener in the court below[152] before filing it in the Registry together with a certificate of service.[153]

18–033

Exceptionally, the appeal panel may ask the respondent to file more fully reasoned objections. The further objections should be filed within 14 days of the appeal panel's request. Further, the respondent may seek to file more fully reasoned objections if, for example, an oral hearing of the application for permission to appeal is ordered. In that case, the further objections should be filed within 14 days of the referral of the application for an oral hearing.[154] The respondent's further objections should set out briefly the reasons why the application should be refused, or make submissions as to the terms upon which permission should be granted (for example, on costs).[155] A copy of the respondents' objections should be sent to the solicitors for the other parties. In certain circumstances, the appeal panel may invite further submissions from the applicant in the light of the respondents' objections, but applicants are not encouraged to comment on respondents' objections. Where the appeal panel does not require further submissions to

---

[146] r.15(4)(a).
[147] r.18(2).
[148] r.13.
[149] PD 3 para.3.3.6.
[150] r.13(3).
[151] PD 3 para.3.1.10.
[152] r.13(2); PD 3 para.3.1.9.
[153] r.13(1); PD 3 para.3.1.8. The original notice together with three copies must be filed at the Registry together with the prescribed fee (set out in Annex 2 to PD 7). When a notice of objection is filed, it will be sealed by a member of staff in the Registry: r.7(4).
[154] PD 3 para.3.3.6. In either case, the Respondent may apply (in writing) to the registrar requesting an extension of time for filing written objections: PD 3 para.3.3.10.
[155] PD 3 para.3.3.7. One original and four copies of the respondents' written objections must be filed in the Registry. The objections must be produced on A4 paper, securely fastened, using both sides of the paper.

make its decision, the parties are sent a copy of the order sealed by the registrar which records the panel's decision.[156]

Consideration of the application

18–034   Every admissible[157] application for permission to appeal shall be considered, together with any intervener's submissions and any notice of objection from a respondent, on paper without a hearing by a panel of Justices—usually three.[158] If the appeal panel decides that the application is admissible, the appeal panel has a range of powers. It may[159]:

(1) refuse permission to advance all or any of the grounds of appeal[160];

(2) grant permission to advance all or any of the grounds of appeal[161];

(3) invite the parties to file written submissions within 14 days as to the grant of permission on terms (whether as to costs or otherwise)[162]; or

(4) direct an oral hearing of the application for permission to appeal.[163]

The permission process, from filing the application for permission to appeal at the Registry to consideration of the application under r.16, is normally completed within eight sitting weeks (excluding any oral hearing). The applicant or respondent may apply for an expedited disposal of the application for permission to appeal (in writing to the registrar under r.31) if the proceedings involve liberty of the subject, urgent medical intervention or the well-being of children, or if the proceedings are under the Hague Convention.[164]

---

[156] PD 3 para.3.3.8.

[157] An application will be admissible if the Supreme Court has jurisdiction to entertain an appeal (see paras 18–004 and 18–005). If the appeal panel determines that an application is inadmissible, it will refuse permission on that ground alone and not consider the content of the application. The appeal panel will give a reason for deciding that the application is inadmissible: PD 3 para.3.3.1.

[158] r.16(1).

[159] r.16(1). An order of the Supreme Court shall be prepared and sealed by the registrar to record any decision made under r.16(1): per r.16(5). The order will be sent to the appellant, any recognised intervener, and all respondents who have filed notice of objection under r.13: PD 3 para.3.3.19.

[160] r.16(2)(a); PD 3 paras 3.3.2(a) and 3.3.4.

[161] r.16(2)(a); PD 3 paras 3.3.2(b) and 3.3.5.

[162] r.16(2)(b); PD 3 paras 3.3.2(c) and 3.3.6 to 3.3.11.

[163] r.16(2)(c); PD 3 paras 3.3.2(d) and 3.3.12 to 3.3.16.

[164] r.31; PD 3 paras 3.4.3–3.4.7; PD 4 para.4.8.1; PD 6 para.6.2.4. The Convention on the Civil Aspects of International Child Abduction ("the Hague Convention") deals with the wrongful removal and retention of children from their habitual country of residence. The Revised Brussels II Regulation ("the Regulation") also deals with these matters. In the Supreme Court an expedited timetable applies. The parties must therefore inform the registrar that the proceedings fall under the Convention or Regulation. The Supreme Court normally gives judgment within six weeks of the commencement of proceedings but this can only be achieved with the fullest cooperation of the parties: PD 3 para.3.4.4.

Refusal of permission

If the appeal panel decides that permission should be refused, the parties are notified that the application is refused and they are sent a copy of the order sealed by the registrar which records the appeal panel's decision.[165] That is the end of the attempted appeal. **18–035**

Granting of permission

If the appeal panel decides that an appeal should be entertained, it grants permission outright and the parties are sent a copy of the order sealed by the registrar which records the panel's decision.[166] Where the appeal panel grants permission to advance limited grounds of appeal, it shall (unless it directs otherwise) be taken to have refused permission to advance the other grounds.[167] If permission to appeal is granted, the applicant must notify any person who was an intervener in the court below, regardless of whether or not that person made submissions on the application for permission to appeal under r.15(1).[168] **18–036**

Permission to appeal on terms

If the appeal panel is considering granting permission to appeal on terms, the appeal panel will propose terms and the parties have the right to make submissions on the proposed terms within 14 days of the date of the appeal panel's proposal.[169] The panel will then decide whether to grant permission (unconditionally or on terms). Prospective applicants who are granted permission to appeal subject to terms that they are unwilling to accept may decline to pursue the appeal. In an application for permission to appeal under the "leapfrog" procedure prospective appellants who decline to proceed on the basis of the terms proposed by the appeal panel may instead pursue an appeal to the Court of Appeal in the usual way.[170] Where the appeal panel has invited the parties' submissions as to terms, it shall reconsider the application on paper without a hearing, and may refuse permission or grant permission (either conditionally or on terms) to advance all or any of the grounds of appeal.[171] **18–037**

---

[165] PD 3 para.3.3.4.
[166] PD 3 para.3.3.5.
[167] r.16(4).
[168] r.15(4)(b).
[169] PD 3 para.3.3.11.
[170] *R. (Jones) v Ceredigion CC v Jones (No.2)* [2007] UKHL 24; [2009] 1 W.L.R. 1400 HL; see para.18–010.
[171] r.16(3).

Oral hearing

18–038   In all cases where further argument is required, the application for permission to appeal will be referred for an oral hearing. Respondents may seek to file more fully reasoned objections within 14 days of being informed that the application has been referred for a hearing.[172] When an application is referred for an oral hearing, the applicant and all respondents who have filed notice of objection under r.13 are notified of the date of the hearing before the appeal panel.[173] Parties may be heard before the appeal panel by counsel, by solicitor, or in person.[174] If counsel are briefed, solicitors should ensure that the Registry is notified of their names (in Form 4). Only a junior counsel's fee is allowed on assessment.[175] Oral permission hearings usually last for 30 minutes. The appeal panel will normally give its decision orally at the end of the hearing.[176] The appeal panel may refuse permission or grant permission (either conditionally or on terms) to advance all or any of the grounds of appeal.

Costs of application for permission to appeal

18–039   If permission is refused, any respondent seeking an order for costs must make an application for costs at the end of the hearing.[177] The reasonable costs of objecting to an unsuccessful application for permission to appeal will normally be awarded to the respondent, subject to any order for costs made by the appeal panel. Where permission to appeal is granted (either on paper or at an oral hearing), costs of the application for permission (including the costs of the respondent's objections) become costs in the appeal.[178]

---

[172] PD 3 paras 3.3.6(b) and 3.3.13.
[173] r.17(1); PD 3, paras 3.3.14 and 3.4.8.
[174] PD 3 paras 3.3.14 and 3.4.8.
[175] This is so even if a public funding or legal aid certificate provides for leading counsel. The only exception to this practice is where leading counsel who conducted the case in the court below are instructed by the Legal Services Commission or legal aid authorities to advise on the merits of an appeal: PD 3 para.3.4.8.
[176] PD 3 para.3.3.15.
[177] PD 3 para.3.5.3. No order for costs will be made unless a request is made at that time. The potential costs orders are set out at PD 3 para.3.5.1.
[178] PD 3 para.3.5.4.

COMMENCEMENT OF THE APPEAL

Notice to proceed

Where permission to appeal was required (as usually is the case for appeals   **18–040**
from England and Wales) and has been granted by the Supreme Court,[179]
the application for permission to appeal will stand as the notice of appeal
under r.18, and the grounds of appeal are limited to those on which permission has been granted.[180] The appellant must, within 14 days of the
grant by the Supreme Court of permission to appeal, file notice under
r.18(1)(c) that they wish to proceed with the appeal.[181] When the notice is
filed, the application for permission to appeal will be re-sealed and under
r.18(2) the appellant must then serve a copy on each respondent, on any
recognised intervener (that is, an intervener whose submissions have been
taken into account under r.15) and on any person who was an intervener in
the court below. The appellant must then file the original and three copies
together with a certificate of service.[182]

Where an appellant is unable to file notice under r.18 within the time
limit of 14 days, a formal application for an extension of time must be
made in Form 2.[183] The respondent's views on the extension of time should
be sought and, if possible, those views should be communicated to the
Registry. The application will be referred to the registrar and, if it is
granted, the appellant must then comply with r.18(2).

Notice of appeal

In all other cases where permission to appeal is not required, rr.19 and 20   **18–041**
apply. A notice of appeal must be filed in Form 1 within 42 days of the date
of the order or decision of the court below,[184] and a copy must be served on
each respondent and any intervener in the court below.[185] Further
requirements in cases where permission to appeal was not required are set
out in Practice Direction 4 paras 4.2.1 to 4.5.1.

---

[179] Where permission to appeal is not required, for example in most Scottish appeals, rr.19
and 20 apply. Appeals from courts in Scotland are outside the scope of this book. Rr.19
and 20 do not apply where permission to appeal is required (i.e. in appeals from courts in
England and Wales).

[180] r.18(1) and (2).

[181] See also PD 4 para.4.1.1.

[182] r.6(4); PD 2 para.2.1.24; PD 3 para.3.4.1; PD 4 para.4.1.1.

[183] PD 3 para.3.4.2; PD 7 para.7.1.

[184] r.19(2). Amendments to notices are allowed where the registrar is satisfied that this will
assist the court and will not unfairly prejudice the respondents or cause undue delay. Any
amendments must be served on the respondents (PD 4 para.4.2.15).

[185] r.20.

Acknowledgement by the respondent

18–042   Each respondent who intends to participate in the appeal must, within 14 days after service of the notice to proceed or the notice of appeal, file a notice under Form 3 together with a certificate of service in accordance with r.21(1).[186] The time limit for a respondent to give notice under r.21 runs from the date on which they are served with a resealed copy of the application.[187] Before filing the notice, the respondent's notice must be served on the appellant, any other respondent, and any intervener in the court below or whose submissions were taken into account when the application for permission was considered, under r.15.[188] A respondent who does not give notice under r.21(1) will not be permitted to participate in the appeal and will not be given notice of its progress.[189] An order for costs will not be made in favour of a respondent who has not given notice.[190]

Procedural applications

18–043   Procedural applications are governed by r.30, and the formal requirements and procedure are outlined in Practice Direction 7. They must be made in Form 2, as soon as it becomes apparent that an application is necessary or expedient.[191] They should set out the reasons for the application and, where necessary, should be supported by written evidence.[192] If a party wishes to oppose an application they must serve a notice of objection within seven days of service of the notice of application.[193] Applications will be dealt with without a hearing wherever possible.[194]

---

[186] The original notice together with three copies must be filed at the Registry (PD 4 para.4.6.3) with the prescribed fee set out in Annex 2 to PD 7. When Form 3 is filed, it will be sealed by a member of staff in the Registry under r.7(4). A certificate of service (giving the full name and address of the persons served) must be included in Form 3 and signed or a separate certificate of service must be provided: see r.6(4); PD 2 para.2.1.24 and PD 4 para.4.6.2.

[187] The time limit for the respondent's notice may be extended on application under r.5.

[188] r.21(2); PD 4 para.4.6.2.

[189] r.21(3); PD 4 para.4.6.4.

[190] PD 4 para .4.6.4.

[191] PD 7 para.7.1.1. The original and three copies of the application must be filed, with the prescribed fee. The original application must bear a certificate of service on the other parties and must clearly indicate whether the other parties consent or refuse to consent to the application. The original and three copies of the notice of objection must be filed, with the prescribed fee. The original notice must bear a certificate of service on the other parties: PD 7 para.7.1.7.

[192] PD 7 para.7.1.3. An application must state what order the applicant is seeking and, briefly, why the applicant is seeking the order: see r.30(2). Certain applications (e.g. for security) should be supported by written evidence. Although there may be no requirement to provide evidence in support, it should be borne in mind that, as a practical matter, the court will often need to be satisfied by evidence of the facts that are relied on in support of or for opposing the application. Evidence must be filed as well as served on the respondents.

[193] r.30(4); PD 7 para.7.1.4.

[194] PD 7 para.7.1.6.

PREPARATION OF THE APPEAL: DOCUMENTS

Rules 22 to 24 outline the documents which the parties must serve and file   **18–044**
prior to the appeal hearing.[195] Those documents are as follows.

A statement of relevant facts and issues

The appellant must submit this statement to every respondent, and agree it   **18–045**
with every respondent, before filing it within 112 days of the filing of the
notice to proceed (r.18(1)) or the notice of appeal (r.19).[196] The statement
must set out the relevant facts and, if the parties cannot agree as to any
matter, the statement should make clear what items are disputed. The
statement should contain references to every law report of the proceedings
below, and should state the duration of the proceedings below. It should be
signed by counsel for all parties.[197]

Because the statement must be agreed between the parties, the time
required to finalise it should not be underestimated. It is likely to be sensible
for the parties to agree between themselves a timetable for it to be agreed:
i.e. dates by which the first draft is to be produced, suggested amendments
made by other parties, and a final version produced. Further, it must be
finalised in advance of the deadline so that it can be signed by counsel, and
then reproduced.

An appendix of the essential documents which were in evidence before the court below, or which record the proceedings in the court below

The appellant must submit this appendix to every respondent, and agree it   **18–046**
with every respondent, before filing it within 112 days of the filing of the
notice to proceed (r.18(1)) or the notice of appeal (r.19).[198] The appendix

---

[195] These rules are supplemented by PD 5 and PD 6.

[196] r.22(1)(a); PD 5 para.5.1.3. The appellant may make an application for an extension of
this time limit in accordance with r.5. However, the time limit is considered by the
Supreme Court to be generous and so the application for an extension should set out in
detail why the appellant is unable to comply with the time limit (PD 5 para.5.2.4).
Respondents should not unreasonably withhold consent to any application for extension of
time, and appellants should indicate to the Registry on the application whether the
respondent(s) consents or objects to the application (PD 5 para.5.2.5).

[197] PD 5 para.5.1.3.

[198] r.22(1)(b); PD 5 para.5.1.4. The appellant may make an application for an extension of
this time limit in accordance with r.5. However, the time limit is considered by the
Supreme Court to be generous and so the application for an extension should set out in
detail why the appellant is unable to comply with the time limit (PD 5 para.5.2.4).
Respondents should not unreasonably withhold consent to any application for extension of
time, and appellants should indicate to the Registry on the application whether the
respondent(s) consents or objects to the application (PD 5 para.5.2.5).

should only contain such material as is necessary for understanding the legal issues and the argument to be presented to the Supreme Court.[199] It should not contain documents that were not in evidence in the court below, nor should it contain transcripts of the proceedings or evidence below unless they are essential to the legal argument. If necessary (i.e. in cases where there is a lot of documentation), the appendix should be in two or more parts, with the most essential documents in Pt 1, and only Pt 1 will be included in the core volumes (see para.18–050). All documents in the appendix must be numbered, and each part of the appendix must include a list of its contents. Again, since the appendix must be agreed, it may be worth agreeing a timetable between the parties for its production.

Documents should be included in the appendix in the following order[200]:

(1) the order appealed against;
(2) the order refusing permission to appeal to the Supreme Court (if separate);
(3) the official transcript of the judgment of the court below;
(4) the final order(s) of all other courts below;
(5) the official transcript of the final judgment(s) of all other courts below;
(6) the relevant documents filed in the courts below that are necessary for understanding the legal issues and the argument; and
(7) the relevant documents and correspondence relating to the appeal that are necessary for understanding the legal issues and the argument.

The appellant must file the original and seven additional copies of the statement, and eight copies of the appendix (or Pt 1 of the appendix if it is in two parts) and 10 copies of Pt 2 of the appendix (if any) at the Registry with the fee prescribed in Annex 2 to Practice Direction 7.[201]

Notice to the registrar that the appeal is ready for listing[202]

18–047 This notice must be given by every party within seven days of the filing of the statement and the appendix. The notice should specify the number of hours that the parties' respective counsel estimate to be necessary for oral submissions.[203] Any request for an expedited hearing should be made to the registrar at the same time (and where possible all parties' views should be

---

[199] PD 5 para.5.1.4.
[200] PD 5 para.5.1.5.
[201] PD 5 para.5.2.6.
[202] r.22(3); PD 5 para.5.2.7; PD 6 para.6.2.1.
[203] Parties are encouraged to offer agreed dates which are convenient to all counsel at an early stage, but there is no need to wait until after the filing of the statement of facts and issues to fix the hearing date. Time estimates must be as accurate as possible since, subject to the court's discretion, they are used as the basis for arranging the court's list (PD 6 para.6.2.1).

obtained before the request is made and communicated to the registrar).[204] On receipt of the notices, the registrar will inform the parties of the date fixed for the hearing,[205] and, on request, will inform the parties of the constitution of the Supreme Court for the appeal hearing.[206]

Written cases

The appellant, every respondent, and any intervener or advocate to the Supreme Court[207] must sequentially exchange their respective written cases.[208] The appellant must file at the Registry the original and seven additional copies of their written case, and serve it on the respondent(s), no later than five weeks before the proposed hearing date.[209] The respondent(s) and any intervener(s) or advocate to the Supreme Court must serve a copy of their written case in response on the appellant no later than three weeks before the hearing date, and file the original and seven additional copies at the Registry.[210]

    18–048

    The written case is the statement of the party's argument in the appeal. Following exchange of written cases, further arguments by either side may not be submitted in advance of the hearing without permission.[211] The Supreme Court does not prescribe any maximum length, but Practice Direction 6 para.6.3.1 provides that "the Court favours brevity and a case should be a concise summary of the submissions to be developed". The written case should be confined to the heads of argument that counsel proposes to submit at the hearing, and it should omit material already contained in the statement of facts and issues.[212]

    The guidance in Practice Direction 6 is consistent with (and, in places, expressly restates) Lord Diplock's detailed statement of the proper practice with regard to parties' written cases in *MV Yorke Motors v Edwards*.[213]

---

[204] r.31; PD 6 para.6.2.4. In fact, it is more usual to apply for an expedited appeal at the stage of applying for permission.

[205] PD 6 para.6.2.3. The registrar lists appeals taking into account the convenience of all the parties. Provisional dates are agreed with the parties well in advance of the hearing and every effort is made to keep to these dates. Counsel, solicitors and parties are, however, advised to hold themselves in readiness during the week before and the week following the provisional date given. Solicitors receive formal notification shortly before the hearing (PD 6 para.6.6.1).

[206] PD 6 para.6.6.7.

[207] The Supreme Court may request the appointment of an advocate to the Supreme Court to assist the court with legal submissions under r.35(1) (see also PD 8 paras 8.13.1–8.13.2). It may also appoint an independent specially qualified adviser to assist the court as assessor on a technical matter under r.35(2). The fees of the advocate or adviser will be costs in the appeal (r.35(3)).

[208] r.22(4).

[209] PD 6 para.6.3.9.

[210] PD 6 para.6.3.10.

[211] PD 6 para.6.3.12.

[212] PD 6 para.6.3.1.

[213] [1982] 1 W.L.R. 444 at 446–447. This passage was cited with approval by Lord Fraser in *G v G (Minors: Custody Appeal)* [1985] 1 W.L.R. 647 at 655.

That was a decision of the House of Lords pre-dating the new procedural code in the Supreme Court, but Lord Diplock's advice holds good:

> "It should be borne in mind that the members of the Appellate Committee will have also read the judgments in the courts below. The case should, accordingly, start with a statement of what the party conceives to be the issues that arise on the appeal. In an appeal to this House, these are generally questions of law or (as in the instant case) of the exercise of a judicial discretion, although occasionally a party may want to challenge a finding of fact. It should generally be possible to describe each issue (if there be more than one) in not more than a sentence or two...
>
> The case should set out the heads, but no more than the heads, of the argument upon each of the issues which it is intended should be advanced by counsel for the party at the oral hearing to challenge or support, as the case may be, the decision on that issue of the court from which the appeal is brought. Detailed or elaborate argument adds unnecessarily to the costs of preparing the case and is seldom helpful or time-saving at the oral hearing."

18–049   If either party is abandoning a point made in the court below, this should be made plain in the written case.[214] Similarly, if a party intends to take a new point not taken in the court below, this also should be indicated in the written case, and the registrar should be informed. If the new point involves the introduction of fresh evidence, an application for permission to adduce fresh evidence must be made either in the case or by filing an application notice in accordance with Practice Direction 7. If a party intends to invite the Supreme Court to depart from one of its own decisions or from a decision of the House of Lords, this intention must be clearly stated in a separate paragraph of their case, to which special attention must be drawn.[215] A respondent who wishes to contend that a decision of the court below should be affirmed on grounds other than those relied on by that court must set out the grounds for that contention in their case.

When citing authorities in the written case, the parties should have regard to the guidance from Lord Diplock in *MV Yorke Motors v Edwards*.[216]

> "Reference to authorities relied upon in support of the argument on any issue should be limited to key authorities (seldom numbering more than one or two on any one issue) which lay down the principle which it is contended is applicable, and the particular passage or passages in the judgments in which the principle is stated should be identified and,

---

[214] PD 6 para.6.3.3. This expressly restates the guidance given by Lord Diplock in *MV Yorke Motors v Edwards* [1982] 1 W.L.R. 444 at 446.

[215] PD 6 para.6.3.4.

[216] [1982] 1 W.L.R. 444 at 447. This passage was cited with approval by Lord Fraser in *G v G (Minors: Custody Appeal)* [1985] 1 W.L.R. 647 at 655.

unless unduly lengthy, may helpfully be quoted verbatim. But references to numerous other cases in which that principle has been previously applied by courts to particular facts which it is claimed may be regarded as presenting some analogies to the facts of the case under appeal are usually out of place in the written case and, I may add, more often than not turn out to be time-wasting in oral argument also. Where, however, it is intended to rely, as persuasive authority, on cases decided by courts in other countries or legal writings such as the American *Restatement*, it is of assistance to their Lordships if specific reference is made to these in the written case."

The written case must conclude with a numbered summary of the reasons upon which the argument is founded, and must bear the signature of at least one counsel for each party to the appeal who has appeared in the court below or who will be briefed for the hearing before the court.[217]

Parties who have only a passive interest in the appeal (for example, stakeholders, trustees, executors etc) are not required to file a separate written case, but they should ensure that their position is explained in one of the written cases filed.[218]

The core volumes

The core volumes are the equivalent of trial bundles. As soon as the parties   **18–050** have exchanged their written cases, and in any event not later than 14 days before the date is fixed for the hearing, the appellant[219] must file 10 bound copies of the core volumes, including the appendix (or Pt 1 of the appendix if it is in two or more parts); and (if necessary) additional volumes containing Pt 2 or further parts of the appendix.[220] In addition to the documents already filed, the core volumes must include the following documents in the following order[221]:

(1) Form 1—a copy of the notice of appeal or the re-sealed application for permission to appeal;
(2) notice of cross-appeal (if any);
(3) the statement of facts and issues;

---

[217] PD 6 para.6.3.6.
[218] PD 6 para.6.3.8.
[219] Respondents are not encouraged to provide additional documents of their own but, where it is necessary for a respondent to place documents before the Court, they should be provided to the Registry in advance of the hearing with an explanatory letter: PD 6 para.6.5.9.
[220] r.23; PD 6 para.6.4.1.
[221] PD 6 para.6.4.3.

(4) the appellants' and respondents' written cases,[222] with cross-references to the appendix and authorities volume(s);

(5) the written case of the advocate to the court or intervener, if any;

(6) Pt 1 of the appendix; and

(7) the index to the authorities volume(s) (see para.18–051).

The core volumes should be bound, preferably with plastic comb binding and with blue card covers[223]; they should include tabs for each of the documents set out in Practice Direction 6 para.6.4.3, preferably with the name of the document on the tab; they should show on the front cover a list of the contents and the names and addresses of the solicitors for all parties; and they must indicate (by, for example, a label attached to the plastic spine) the volume number (in arabic numerals) and the short title of the appeal.[224]

The authorities volumes

18–051   A joint set of the authorities that may be referred to during the hearing must be jointly produced and compiled for the appeal hearing, and 10 copies of the joint authorities volumes must be filed by the appellant at the same time as the core volumes,[225] although they should be filed in separate containers from the core volumes.[226] Supplemental or additional volumes of authorities should be avoided. The cost of preparing the volumes of authorities falls to the appellants, but is ultimately subject to the decision of the Supreme Court as to the costs of the appeal.

The authorities should be collected together into one or more volumes or folders. It should be noted, however, that folders should only be used with caution: a lever arch file in particular is likely to be unacceptable, as when documents are printed on both sides, the left hand page cannot be annotated or marked up by anyone right handed. The volumes of authorities should have a separate index and authorities should appear in alphabetical order. Authorities should (where appropriate) be further divided into the categories: domestic, Strasbourg, foreign and academic material. The volumes of authorities should[227]:

---

[222] To enable the appellants to produce the core volumes, the respondents must provide the appellants' solicitors with a further 10 copies of the respondents' case in addition to the cases already exchanged: PD 6 para.6.4.5.

[223] Criminal core volumes are in red card covers: PD 6 para.6.4.4(a).

[224] PD 6 para.6.4.4.

[225] r.24; PD 6 para.6.5.1. The appellants have the initial responsibility for producing the authorities volumes and for filing them at the Registry but, to enable the appellants to file the volumes, the respondents must provide the appellants with 10 copies of any authorities which the respondents require but which the appellants do not, or arrange with the appellants for their photocopying. Respondents should arrange with the appellants for the delivery to them of such authorities volumes as the respondents' counsel and agents require.

[226] PD 6 para.6.5.4.

[227] PD 6 para.6.5.2.

(1) Be A4 size reproduced as one page per view (with any authorities smaller than A4 being enlarged).
(2) Separate each authority by numbered dividers.
(3) Contain an index to that volume; the first volume must also contain an index to all the volumes.[228]
(4) Be numbered consecutively on the cover and spine with numerals at least point 72 in size for swift identification of different volumes during the hearing.
(5) Have printed clearly on the front cover the title of the appeal and the names of the solicitors for all parties.
(6) Have affixed to the spine a sticker indicating clearly the volume number and short title of the appeal.

The Law Reports should be cited if possible in preference to any other law report. Transcripts of unreported judgments should only be cited when they contain an authoritative statement of a relevant principle of law not to be found in a reported case or when they are necessary for the understanding of some other authority.[229] Where a case is not reported in the Law Reports or Session Cases, references to other recognised reports may be given. In Revenue appeals, Tax Cases or Simon's Tax Cases may be cited but, wherever possible, references to the case in the Law Reports or Session Cases should also be given.[230] In order to produce the volumes of authorities, parties may download text from electronic sources; but the volumes of authorities must be filed in paper form. It is suggested, however, that parties should not file authorities printed out from online resources unless the relevant database contains reproductions (in pdf form) of the printed page of the published reports. There should only be one page per view.   **18–052**

Cross-appeals

Permission is required for a cross-appeal. A respondent who wishes to argue that the order appealed from should be varied,[231] must apply for and obtain permission from the Supreme Court to cross-appeal in accordance with Pt 2 of the Rules,[232] after the appellant has obtained permission to appeal.[233] The same panel of Justices who considered the application for permission to appeal shall consider the application for permission to cross-appeal.[234]   **18–053**

---

[228] In an appeal where there is a large number of volumes of authorities, it is helpful to produce an index of indexes, separate from the index contained in the first authorities volume: PD 6 para.6.5.3.
[229] PD 6 para.6.3.5. This reflects the direction of Lord Diplock in *Roberts v Petroleum v Bernard Kenny Ltd* [1983] 2 A.C. 192 at 202.
[230] PD 6 para.6.5.5.
[231] r.25(2); PD 8 para.8.3.1.
[232] Unless an appeal lies to the Supreme Court as of right, which would be the case in many Scottish appeals.
[233] PD 8 para.8.3.2.
[234] r.25(3).

Where there is a cross-appeal, Pt 3 of the Rules also applies with appropriate modifications.[235] There shall be a single statement of facts and issues, a single appendix, and a single written case for each party dealing with both the appeal and the cross-appeal (and each written case should make it clear that both the appeal and cross-appeal are dealt with).[236] The appellant shall remain primarily responsible for the preparation of all papers for the appeal, and notifying the registrar under r.22(3), notwithstanding the cross-appeal.[237]

A respondent who wishes merely to argue that the order appealed from should be upheld on grounds different from those relied on by the court below need not bring a cross-appeal, although they must state clearly in their written case the grounds on which the order should be upheld.[238]

Intervention

18–054   A person who is not a party to an appeal may apply in accordance with r.26 for permission to intervene in the appeal, after permission to appeal has been granted. Rule 26(1) provides that "any person" may apply for permission to intervene, "in particular" any official body or non-governmental organization seeking to make submissions in the public interest, any person with an interest in proceedings by way of judicial review, and any person who was an intervener in the court below or whose submissions were taken into account under r.15. An intervener in the application for permission under r.15 who wishes to intervene in the appeal itself must still make a formal application under r.26 in Form 2.[239] The application should state whether permission is sought for both oral and written interventions or for written intervention only. The application should be filed with the prescribed fee and confirmation of the consent of the appellants and respondent(s) in the appeal. If their consent is refused, the application must be endorsed with a certificate of service, with a brief explanation of the reasons for the refusal.

Applications for permission to intervene should be filed at least six weeks before the date of hearing of the appeal. The application shall be considered on paper by a panel of Justices. The panel may refuse permission to intervene, or may permit intervention by written submission only, or by both written and oral submissions.[240] Any permission to make oral submissions may be limited to a specified duration. The guidelines by which the

---

[235] Where permission to cross-appeal is granted by the Supreme Court, the application for permission to cross-appeal will stand as the notice of appeal and the appellant must then comply with r.18 and para.3.4.1 of PD 3 (PD 8 para.8.3.2).

[236] r.25(4)(b); PD 8 paras 8.3.5–8.3.7.

[237] r.25(4)(c).

[238] r.25(1); PD 8 para.8.3.1.

[239] PD 6 paras 6.9.1 to 6.9.2. No permission will be required for an intervention by the Crown under s.5 of the Human Rights Act 1998 (r.26(3)(a)), or for an intervention by the relevant officer in a case where the Court is exercising its devolution jurisdiction (r.26(3)(b)).

[240] r.26(2).

Supreme court will be guided when considering applications for permission to intervene were set out by Lord Hoffman in *E v Chief Constable of the Royal Ulster Constabulary*.[241] He held that it is not the role of an intervener to be an additional counsel for one of the parties; an intervention will be of no assistance if it merely repeats points already made by the appellant or respondent. Interventions must be restricted to avoid unnecessarily taking up time on appeals.

All counsel instructed on behalf of an intervener with permission to address the court should attend the hearing unless specifically excused.[242] Orders for costs will not normally be made either in favour of or against interveners, but such orders may be made if the Supreme Court in the exercise of its discretion considers it just to do so (in particular, if an intervener has in substance acted as the sole or principal appellant or respondent).[243]

Applications

Except in cases involving alleged contempt of court,[244] the Supreme Court has discretion whether or not to hold an oral hearing of any application or procedural matter. Oral hearings on procedural matters are normally heard in open court or in a place to which the public are admitted.[245]   **18–055**

Security for costs

The Supreme Court has the power, on the application of a respondent, to order the appellant to give security for the costs of the appeal pursuant to r.36(1). This rule is supplemented by Practice Direction 4 paras 4.7.1–4.7.5. Orders for security for costs will be made sparingly, and will not be made in relation to cross-appeals. It will often be appropriate for a party seeking security to make that clear at the stage permission is sought, so that the Justices can consider making the provision of security a condition of permission being granted: see para.18–037.   **18–056**

Settlement

If the matter settles, or if an event occurs that arguably disposes of the dispute, it is the duty of counsel and solicitors in any pending appeal either   **18–057**

---

[241] [2008] 3 W.L.R. 1208 HL; see also PD 8 para.8.8.2 which draws attention to this judgment.
[242] PD 6 para.6.9.4.
[243] r.46(3); PD 6 para.6.9.5.
[244] In a case of an alleged contempt, an oral hearing must be held: PD 1 para.1.3.4.
[245] PD 1 para.1.3.7.

to ensure that the appeal is withdrawn by consent under r.34,[246] or, if there is no agreement on that course, to bring the facts promptly to the attention of the registrar and to seek directions.[247]

HEARING OF THE APPEAL

18–058　The presumption is that contested appeals will be heard in open court except, exceptionally, when it is necessary to sit in private for part of an appeal hearing in the interests of justice or in the public interest.[248] Only in wholly exceptional circumstances will the court consider sitting in private.[249]

Directions

18–059　Where it considers it to be appropriate, the court may decide that a directions hearing should be held prior to the hearing of the appeal.[250] A directions hearing will normally be held before three Justices. Any request for a directions hearing should be made to the registrar. Wherever possible the views of all parties should be obtained before a request is made.

Counsel

18–060　Each party who files a written case under r.22(4) has the right to be heard by two counsel.[251] The fees of only two counsel will be allowed for any party on assessment unless the Supreme Court orders otherwise on application at the hearing under Practice Direction 13 para.16.5. The costs officers have no discretion to allow fees for more than two counsel unless the Supreme Court has made such an order.

Time estimates

18–061　Subject to any directions by the court before or at the hearing, counsel are expected to confine their submissions to the time indicated in their estimates submitted in the notice issued under r.22(2). The registrar must be informed

---

[246] See also PD 8 paras 8.16.1–8.16.4.
[247] r.33(c); PD 8 para.8.5.1.
[248] r.27(1).
[249] PD 6 para.6.6.4. Any request for the court to sit in private should be addressed to the registrar and should be copied to the other parties. The request should set out fully the reasons why it is made and the request together with any objections filed by the other parties will normally be referred to the presiding Justice.
[250] PD 6 para.6.2.5.
[251] PD 6 para.6.3.7.

at once of any alteration to the original estimate. Not more than two days are normally allowed for the hearing of an appeal and appeals are listed for hearing on this basis. Estimates of more than two days must be fully explained in writing to the registrar and may be referred to the presiding Justice. Counsel should agree an order of speeches and timetable for the hearing and submit it to the Registry on the working day before the hearing.[252]

Transcripts

If a party wishes to have a stenographer present at the hearing, or wishes to   18–062
obtain a full transcript of the hearing, they must inform the registrar not less than seven days before the hearing.[253] The costs will be borne by the party or parties making the request.

Filming

Some of the proceedings of the Supreme Court will be filmed, and some-   18–063
times broadcast.[254] The Supreme Court is the only court in the United Kingdom to allow this.

JUDGMENT IN THE APPEAL

Powers of the Supreme Court

The Supreme Court has all the powers of the court below[255] and, under   18–064
r.29(1), may:

(1) affirm, set aside, or vary any order or judgment made or given by the court below;
(2) remit any issue for determination by the court below;
(3) order a new trial or hearing;
(4) make orders for the payment of interest; and
(5) make a costs order.

---

[252] PD 6 para.6.2.2.
[253] PD 6 para.6.6.6.
[254] PD 6 para.6.6.9; PD 8 para.8.17.1.
[255] This rule reflects the decision in *Grobbelaar v News Group Newspapers Ltd* [2002] 1 W.L.R. 3024 at 3037 and 3049 that the House of Lords has inherent jurisdiction to exercise any power that was exerciseable by the Court of Appeal.

The House of Lords 1966 Practice Statement

18–065 The House of Lords issued a Practice Statement on July 26, 1966 ("the Practice Statement") which stated that it would treat former decisions of the House as normally binding, but that it would depart from a previous decision when it appeared right to do so.[256] Lord Hope explained in *Austin v Mayor and Burgesses of the London Borough of Southwark* that the Supreme Court has not thought it necessary to re-issue the Practice Statement as a fresh statement of practice in the court's own name because "it has as much effect in this Court as it did before the Appellate Committee in the House of Lords".[257]

The Practice Statement is in the following terms[258]:

> "Their Lordships regard the use of precedent as an indispensable foundation upon which to decide what is the law and its application to individual cases. It provides at least some degree of certainty upon which individuals can rely in the conduct of their affairs, as well as a basis for orderly development of legal rules.
>
> Their Lordships nevertheless recognise that too rigid adherence to precedent may lead to injustice in a particular case and also unduly restrict the proper development of the law. They propose, therefore, to modify their present practice and, while treating former decisions of this House as normally binding, to depart from a previous decision when it appears right to do so.
>
> In this connection they will bear in mind the danger of disturbing retrospectively the basis on which contracts, settlements of property and fiscal arrangements have been entered into and also the especial need for certainty as to the criminal law."

18–066 The Supreme Court's power to depart from a previous decision of the Supreme Court or the House of Lords will be exercised sparingly,[259] in order to strike the appropriate balance between the interests of certainty on the one hand, and the interests of justice on the other hand. The Supreme Court will generally refuse to depart from earlier decisions that concern questions of construction of statute or other documents.[260] The Supreme Court will be astute to avoid departing from an earlier decision where to do

---

[256] *Practice Statement (Judicial Precedent)* [1966] 1 W.L.R. 1234. See also paras 3–017 to 3–020.

[257] [2010] UKSC 28 at [24]–[25].

[258] *Practice Statement (Judicial Precedent)* [1966] 1 W.L.R. 1234.

[259] *R. v National Insurance Commissioner Ex p. Hudson* [1972] A.C. 944 at 966.

[260] *R. v National Insurance Commissioner Ex p. Hudson* [1972] A.C. 944 at 966; *R. v Kansal (No.2)* [2001] 3 W.L.R. 1562; *Jindal Iron and Steel Co Ltd v Islamic Solidarity Shipping Co Jordan Inc* [2005] 1 W.L.R. 1363. However, one exception was *R. v Home Secretary Ex p. Khawaja* [1984] A.C. 74 which related to the construction of the Immigration Act 1971.

so would to usurp the role of Parliament.[261] The fact that a different con-stituted panel of Justices may consider that the earlier decision was wrong will not in itself amount to sufficient grounds to depart from it[262]: there must be special or unusual circumstances to justify departure from the earlier decision.[263] Special or unusual circumstances may exist where an old-established precedent has caused injustice and it cannot be said that persons may have acted in reliance on that old-established law.[264] Further, the Supreme Court may be prepared to exercise this exceptional power where the earlier decision does not reflect modern public policy or there has been a change of circumstances since that decision.[265]

The principal rationale for refusing to interfere with earlier decisions is that the law should be certain and consistent; if the Supreme Court were to change its mind this would undermine the interests of justice. However, where the earlier decision itself has created uncertainty and confusion, the Supreme Court will be more minded to depart from that decision. In *Murphy v Brentwood*[266] the House of Lords departed from the decision in *Anns v Merton LBC*[267] because it considered that earlier decision was wrong and (more importantly) had led to uncertainty about the application of the law. Lord Keith noted that *Anns* was inconsistent with long-estab-lished principles[268] regarding liability in the tort of negligence for economic loss; the decision had led to a vast spate of litigation in which the courts had been forced to distinguish Anns on creative and artificial grounds. He commented that: "There can be no doubt that to depart from the decision would re-establish a degree of certainty in this field of law which it has done a remarkable amount to upset."[269]

---

[261] *Miliangos v George Frank (Textiles) Ltd* [1976] A.C. 443 at 467.

[262] *Fitzleet Estates v Cherry*, 51 T.C. 708 at 717; *Paal Wilson & Co v Partenreederei (the Hannah Blumenthal)* [1983] 1 A.C. 854 at 917; *Vestey v Inland Revenue Commissioners* [1980] A.C. 1148 at 1176; *R. v Kansal (No.2)* [2001] 3 W.L.R. 1562; *Rees v Darlington Memorial Hospital NHS Trust* [2003] 3 W.L.R. 1091.

[263] *Paal Wilson & Co v Partenreederei (the Hannah Blumenthal)* [1983] 1 A.C. 854 at 917.

[264] *Dick v Burgh of Falkirk* [1976] S.C. (HL) 1 at 28.

[265] See in particular *Arthur JS Hall & Co v Simons* [2000] 3 W.L.R. 543 where the House of Lords reversed the decision in *Rondel v Worsley* [1969] 1 A.C. 191 on advocates' immunity from suit on the basis that "The world was different then ... public policy is not immutable and your Lordships must consider the arguments afresh" (at 575). See also *Miliangos v George Frank (Textiles) Ltd* [1976] A.C. 443 at 460; *Kuddus v Chief Con-stable of Leicestershire* [2001] 2 W.L.R. 1789. In such cases, it is not necessary for the earlier decisions to be doubted; on the contrary, they are generally considered to have been correctly decided at the time.

[266] [1991] 1 A.C. 398.

[267] [1978] A.C. 728.

[268] See also *Westdeutsche Landesbank v Islington BC* [1996] A.C. 669 where an earlier decision was over-ruled on the basis that it was contrary to accepted modern principles.

[269] [1991] 1 A.C. 398 at 471 to 472.

Reopening appeals

18–067   In addition, the Supreme Court has jurisdiction, in exceptional cases, to reopen an appeal to that Court which had been concluded.[270] The Supreme Court will not reopen any appeal save in circumstances where a party, through no fault of its own, has been subjected to an unfair procedure. It is not enough to demonstrate that the order made by the Supreme Court is wrong or may be wrong: unfairness in procedure must be established. The Supreme Court may rescind or vary its earlier order in order to correct any injustice caused. There is no relevant statutory limitation on the jurisdiction of the Supreme Court to reopen appeals, and therefore its jurisdiction remains unfettered.

In *Broome v Cassell & Co Ltd (No.2)* the House of Lords varied an order for costs made by the House in circumstances where the parties had not had a fair opportunity to address argument on the point.[271] In *R. v Bow Street Metropolitan Stipendiary Magistrate Ex p. Pinochet Ugarte* the House of Lords set aside an earlier order where an appearance of bias on the part of one of the members of the Committee that had determined the appeal could be demonstrated.[272] The House of Lords directed that the appeal be reheard by a differently constituted Committee.

Delivery of judgment

18–068   Judgment may be delivered in open court or, if the Supreme Court so directs, promulgated by the registrar.[273] Judgments are given on a day notified in advance. One week's notice is normally given.[274] One junior counsel for each party or group of parties who have filed a case may attend when judgment is delivered in open court, but the attendance of counsel is not required. If counsel do attend, they should be familiar with the subject matter of the appeal and with the options for its disposal. Where judgment is to be promulgated by the registrar, copies will be made available for collection by counsel or a solicitor at the Registry on a day notified in advance.[275]

---

[270] The House of Lords confirmed in *R. v Bow Street Metropolitan Stipendiary Magistrate Ex p. Pinochet Ugarte* [2000] 1 A.C. 119 at 132 that they have a long-standing inherent jurisdiction to reopen concluded appeals to the House of Lords in exceptional circumstances. It was observed that this inherent jurisdiction stems from the House of Lords' long-established inherent status as a final appellate court. Although the Supreme Court is a creature of statute, under s.40 of the Constitutional Reform Act 2005 it has taken over the powers of the former House of Lords and so has the same jurisdiction to reopen appeals to the House of Lords or the Supreme Court.

[271] [1972] A.C. 1136.

[272] *R. v Bow Street Metropolitan Stipendiary Magistrate Ex p. Pinochet Ugarte* [2000] 1 A.C. 119.

[273] r.28.

[274] PD 6 para.6.8.1.

[275] PD 6 para.6.8.2. Further directions are given in PD 6 at paras 6.8.3–6.8.5.

FEES AND COSTS

Fees

The fees payable in the Supreme Court are set out in Annex 2 to Practice Direction 7. The current fees order, the Supreme Court Fees Order 2009 came into force on October 1, 2009.[276] Under r.45, the registrar may refuse to accept a document, or refuse to allow a party to take a particular step in the appeal proceedings, if the appropriate fee is not paid.

18–069

Costs

Costs are in the discretion of the Supreme Court, who may make such orders as it considers just in respect of the costs of any appeal, application for permission to appeal, or any other application before the Supreme Court, in accordance with r.46. Costs orders can be made either at the final determination of the appeal or application, or during the course of the proceedings.[277] Detailed directions relating to costs are set out in Practice Direction 13. Detailed assessments of costs in the Supreme Court are conducted by Costs Officers appointed by the President of the Supreme Court under r.49.

18–070

The usual rule is that costs will follow the event. If a party seeks a different order, they may make written submissions or oral submissions at the conclusion of the relevant hearing. If a party wishes to defer making submissions as to costs until after judgment, the Supreme Court must be informed of this not later than at the close of the oral argument.[278] If the Committee accedes to the request it will give directions for submissions.[279]

The Supreme Court may assess costs on the standard basis or on the indemnity basis in accordance with r.50. The presumption is that costs will be assessed on the standard basis. Costs assessed on the standard basis will only be allowed if they are proportionate to the matters in issue, reasonably incurred, and in a reasonable amount.[280] Costs assessed on the indemnity basis need not satisfy the test of proportionality.[281] A party who is dissatisfied with the assessment of costs made at an oral hearing may apply for that decision to be reviewed by a single Justice within 14 days of the decision.[282]

---

[276] SI 2009/2131.
[277] r.46(2).
[278] r.47(1).
[279] r.47(2).
[280] r.51(1).
[281] r.51(3).
[282] r.53(1).

THE SUPREME COURT AND EUROPE

18-071   The Supreme Court must give effect to directly applicable European Union law, and interpret domestic law so far as possible consistently with European Union law. It must also give effect to the rights contained in the European Convention on Human Rights. Under the Treaty on the Functioning of the European Union (art.267), the Supreme Court must refer to the European Court of Justice ("ECJ") in Luxembourg any question of European Union law, where the answer is not clear and it is necessary for the ECJ to give judgment. When the Supreme Court refuses permission to appeal where the application includes a contention that a question of Community law is involved, the Court gives additional reasons for its decision not to grant permission to appeal pursuant to r.42(1) and in accordance with the decision of the European Court of Justice in *CILFIT v Ministry of Health*.[283]

In giving effect to rights contained in the European Convention on Human Rights ("ECHR"), the Supreme Court must take account of any decision of the ECHR in Strasbourg. No national court should "without strong reason dilute or weaken the effect of the Strasbourg case law" (Lord Bingham of Cornhill in *R. (Ullah) v Special Adjudicator*).[284]

An individual contending that their Convention rights have not been respected by a decision of a United Kingdom court (including the Supreme Court) against which they have no domestic recourse may bring a claim against the United Kingdom before the ECHR.[285]

---

[283] Case C-283/81.
[284] [2004] UKHL 26. See, however, Lord Hoffmann's Judicial Studies Board Annual Lecture 2009 "The Universality of Human Rights": "The Strasbourg court ... has no mandate to unify the laws of Europe on the many subjects which may arguably touch upon human rights."
[285] Such claims are outside the scope of this book. See further PD 11.

CHAPTER 19

Privy Council

INTRODUCTION

As Britain acquired colonies and dominions, the practice grew up that   **19–001**
Orders in Council or Acts of Parliament should provide for appeals as of
right from colonial courts to the King or Queen in Council; and there
should be conditions on which such appeals should be permitted.[1] But
outside these provisions, there had always been reserved a discretion to the
monarch in Council to grant special leave to appeal from a colonial court
irrespective of the limitations fixed by the colonial law. This discretion to
grant special leave to appeal was in practice described as the prerogative
right: it was a residuum of the Royal prerogative of the sovereign as the
fountain of justice. In England, the right for a subject to bring a petition to
the monarch for redress came to be brought instead to the King in Parliament, the origin of the modern judicial functions of the House of Lords, or
to the King in his Chancery, from which flowed the jurisdiction of the Court
of Chancery. But from the Courts of the Channel Islands and later from the
Courts of the Plantations or Colonies the petition went to the monarch in
Council, and this continued to be the practice after the jurisdiction of the
Privy Council in English common law cases had been abolished.

This appellate jurisdiction, along with other jurisdictions such as in
Admiralty or Ecclesiastical Causes, was affirmed and regulated by Parliament in the Privy Council Acts of 1833 and 1844. The present day Judicial
Committee of the Privy Council, also referred to as the Board, is a statutory
body established in 1833[2] to hear appeals to the King or Queen in Council
"... from the decisions of various courts of judicature in the East Indies,
and in the plantations, and colonies and other dominions of His Majesty
abroad ...".

Pursuant to the 1833 Act, a Committee of Her Majesty's Privy Council is
styled the Judicial Committee of the Privy Council; and all appeals, which

---

[1] This introduction closely follows the judgment of Viscount Sankey L.C. in *British Coal
Corp v The King* [1935] A.C. 500 at 510–511.
[2] The Judicial Committee Act 1833: "An Act for the better Administration of Justice in His
Majesty's Privy Council."

either by law, statute or custom may be brought before Her Majesty in Council from the order of any Court or judge are referred by Her Majesty to, and heard by, the Judicial Committee. The Committee must then make a report or recommendation, stated in open court, to Her Majesty in Council for her decision thereon. The Judicial Committee Act 1844[3] empowered Her Majesty in Council to override a colonial law limiting or excluding appeals to Her Majesty in Council from any colonial court. However, on a state's attainment of independence or fully responsible status within the Commonwealth, a relevant constitution or legislative instrument may prevail so as to negate the Judicial Committee's jurisdiction to hear an appeal under the 1844 Act.[4] The Committee is a judicial body or court, though all it can do is to report or recommend to Her Majesty in Council, since according to constitutional convention Her Majesty in Council will always give effect to the report of the Judicial Committee. The Committee is thus in truth an appellate court of law.[5]

19–002   With the demise of the British Empire, the Privy Council has lost much of its jurisdiction. In 1935 the Judicial Committee referred with approval to the Report of the Imperial Conference, 1926 which stated that:

> "it was no part of the policy of His Majesty's Government in Great Britain that questions affecting judicial appeals (i.e. to the Judicial Committee of the Privy Council) should be determined otherwise than in accordance with the wishes of the part of the Empire primarily affected."[6]

Even though the Empire no longer exists, that overall policy remains effective.[7] When it heard appeals from India, Australia, Canada and New Zealand it developed many and detailed rules of practice and procedure relating to appeals from foreign jurisdictions, and the latitude to be allowed to local courts in matters of local law and custom, which is now of only historical interest. Those countries have now all developed their own independent appellate systems, and the Privy Council is much quieter.

The Judicial Committee is authorised to hear appeals from some independent countries of the Commonwealth who no longer recognise the Queen as head of state and retains a jurisdiction to hear final appeals from countries which recognise the Queen as head of state, British Overseas Territories, Crown Dependencies, and civil cases from Brunei, heard by

---

[3] The Judicial Committee Act 1844.
[4] *Att Gen for St Christopher & Nevis v Rodionov* [2004] UKPC 38; [2004] 1 W.L.R. 2796. Cf. *Maharaj v Att Gen for Trinidad and Tobago* [1977] 1 All E.R. 411.
[5] *British Coal Corp v The King* [1935] 1 A.C. 500 at 510–511
[6] *British Coal Corp v The King* [1935] 1 A.C. 500 at 523. Report of the Imperial Conference (1926) at p.19.
[7] *Seaga v Harper (Jamaica)* [2009] UKPC 26 at [9].

agreement with the Sultan.[8] The Judicial Committee also hears occasional appeals from a number of ancient and ecclesiastical courts including the Church Commissioners, the Arches Court of Canterbury, the Chancery Court of York, prize courts and the Court of Admiralty of the Cinque Ports. The Judicial Committee deals with about 55–65 Commonwealth appeals a year.[9]

Five judges normally sit to hear Commonwealth appeals, and three for other matters.[10] Generally the judges are Justices of the Supreme Court, but they may be supplemented by any person who is a member of the Privy Council and who holds or who has held high judicial office: a judge of the Supreme Court, the Court of Appeal in England and Wales, the High Court in England and Wales, the Court of Session, the Court of Appeal in Northern Ireland, the High Court in Northern Ireland, or who has been appointed a Lord of Appeal in Ordinary.[11] A majority of the Judicial Committee must concur in the report or recommendation to Her Majesty.[12]

The Judicial Committee generally sat in the Council Chamber in Downing Street, London. Since 2009, it sits in the same building as The Supreme Court, in Parliament Square. Occasionally the Judicial Committee sits in the jurisdiction where the appeal originated; recent hearings have taken place in the Caribbean and Mauritius.

POWERS OF THE JUDICIAL COMMITTEE

The Privy Council has the power to admit new evidence, take oral evidence from witnesses on oath; and it may remit cases for rehearing.[13] It may require the attendance of any witnesses, and the production of any deeds, evidences or writings by writ to be issued by the President of the Privy Council in as near a form as may be to the writ of subpoena ad

19–003

---

[8] The following countries, overseas territories and crown dependencies send appeals to Her Majesty in Council: Antigua and Barbuda, Grenada, Bahamas, Jamaica, St Christopher and Nevis, Belize, Saint Lucia, the Cook Islands and Niue (Associated States of New Zealand), Saint Vincent and the Grenadines, Tuvalu (countries of which Her Majesty is head of State); Anguilla Gibraltar Bermuda, Montserrat, British Virgin Islands, Pitcairn Islands, Cayman Islands, St Helena and dependencies, Falkland Islands and the Turks and Caicos Islands (British Oversea Territories); the Sovereign Base Areas of Akrotiri and Dhekelia (in Cyprus); and the Crown Dependencies of Jersey, Guernsey and the Isle of Man. From the following independent republics within the Commonwealth an appeal lies to the Judicial Committee itself: the Republic of Trinidad and Tobago; the Commonwealth of Dominica; Mauritius; and Kiribati (only where it is alleged that certain constitutional rights of any Banaban or of the Rabi Council have been or are likely to be infringed).

[9] Judicial Committee PD 1 s.1.1.

[10] Judicial Committee PD 1 s.1.3. There must be a minimum of three members of the Committee: see Court of Chancery Act 1851 s.16.

[11] Judicial Committee Act 1833 s.1 as amended by Sch.16 to Constitutional Reform Act 2005. The judges who hold or have held "high judicial office" are defined in s.60(2)(a) of the Constitutional Reform Act. The upper age limit is 75: see s.1 of the Judicial Committee Act 1881 and s.3 of the Appellate Jurisdiction Act 1887. The monarch in Council may authorise judges from the court from which the appeal is brought to attend as an assessor: see s.1 of the Appellate Jurisdiction Act 1908.

[12] Judicial Committee Act 1833 s.5.

[13] Judicial Committee Act 1833 s.7–9.

testificandum or of subpoena duces tecum.[14] It may require notes of evidence taken in the courts of any colony or foreign settlement or foreign dominion of the crown, requiring the judge or judges of such court to transmit a note of evidence, and of the reasons given by the judge.[15]

The monarch in Council has the same powers of enforcing judgments, decrees and orders, both in personam and in rem, as are available to the High Court, Queen's Bench and Chancery Divisions.[16] Contempt of the Judicial Committee is subject to the same penalties and consequences as contempt of Court in the Queen's Bench Division of the High Court.[17] Any allegation of contempt of court will be considered and determined at an oral hearing before the Judicial Committee.[18] The Privy Council may direct new trials, either generally or on particular issues.[19] It may refer matters to the registrar in the same manner as matters may be referred to a master in Chancery.[20] Costs are in the discretion of the Committee.[21]

PROCEDURE OF THE PRIVY COUNCIL

19–004 The rules of the Privy Council have recently been amended, and may now be found in the Judicial Committee (Appellate Jurisdiction) Rules Order 2009.[22] Whereas the rules previously could differ by reference to the jurisdiction whence the appeal came, now the rules are intended to apply generally to all appeals. Thus, the new Rules repeal various instruments relating to appeals from different countries and territories "only and in so far as they relate to the powers of the Judicial Committee of the Privy Council and the procedure to be adopted by it with respect to proceedings before it."[23] The new Rules came into force on April 21, 2009; transitional provisions are set out in the Schedule to the Rules. The Rules govern both civil and criminal appeals to the Judicial Committee under its general appellate jurisdiction. Appeals under s.18 of the Vetinary Surgeons Act 1966 and s.1 of the Brunei (Appeals) Act 1989 have some slight different provisions, which are outside the scope of this book.

The Judicial Committee Rules are supplemented by various Practice Directions, made under Judicial Committee Rule r.1(1). Cases in the Privy Council must be Privy Council Agents.[24] Counsel who may appear include

---

[14] Judicial Committee Act 1833 s.19.
[15] Judicial Committee Act 1844 s.10.
[16] Judicial Committee Act 1833 s.28.
[17] Judicial Committee Act 1833 s.19. See also Judicial Committee Act 1844 s.12.
[18] Judicial Committee Rules r.9(6). See fn.22.
[19] Judicial Committee Act 1833 s.13.
[20] Judicial Committee Act 1833 s.17.
[21] Judicial Committee Act 1833 s.15.
[22] The Rules appear in the Schedule to the Judicial Committee (Appellate Jurisdiction) Rules Order 2009 and are referred to herein as the Judicial Committee Rules.
[23] Judicial Committee (Appellate Jurisdiction) Rules Order 2009 art.5.
[24] Judicial Committee Rules r.2(1), definition of "agent". The relevant Order in Council was made on March 6, 1896.

advocates having the right of audience in the court from which the appeal came or in an equivalent appeal to the Supreme Court.[25]

Many appellants to the Privy Council do not need to seek permission, because they have obtained permission, sometimes as of right, from the local court of appeal. Those who do need permission obtain it much more frequently than those who seek it from the Supreme Court: the statistics indicate that just under half of the applications made for permission to appeal from the Privy Council are successful. The grounds of appeal should be set out either in the successful application for permission to appeal, or in a notice. Respondents must file a notice if they are to take any part in the appeal. It should be noted that applications for permission to appeal, notices of appeal and respondents' notices must be served on the other parties before they are filed. Since generally the rules indicate the dates by which documents are to be filed, parties must take care to prepare the documents in sufficient time to serve them on other parties before they need to be filed.

Documents relevant to the appeal are filed in the Record. The parties file and exchange written cases, equivalent to skeleton arguments, well in advance of the hearing. The appellant's solicitors must then ensure that all documents, including authorities, are filed in preparation for the hearing. As in the Supreme Court, the general practice is for all documents and authorities to be filed in A4 sized comb bound volumes, printed on both sides and no more than approximately one inch thick; lever arch files are not, generally, acceptable.[26] The time taken to prepare and reproduce the bundles for an appeal to the Privy Council should not be underestimated. Generally, documents must be signed (in hand) by counsel, rather than, as has become the practice in the lower courts of England and Wales, simply bearing counsel's printed name.

19–005

As with appeals to the Supreme Court, the staff in the Registry are accustomed to the fact that lawyers representing the parties may not have much or indeed any experience of preparing cases for the Privy Council, and are happy to answer questions: if in doubt, ring them up. The Judicial Committee has a useful website, at *www.jcpc.gov.uk*, from which rules, practice directions and forms may be downloaded.

REGISTRAR OF THE PRIVY COUNCIL

The Privy Council Registrar was established in 1833 by statute.[27] Parties may consult the Registry at any stage of preparation of the application for permission to appeal, and may submit applications in draft for approval.[28]

19–006

---

[25] *Atkin's Court Forms* 2nd edn, 5(1), (2004 edn), para.9.
[26] Judicial Committee PD 5 s.5.1.2.
[27] Judicial Committee Act 1833 s.18.
[28] Judicial Committee PD 3 s.3.1.2

Any procedural question arising at any time other than in the course of a hearing will be considered by the registrar who may either determine the question or refer it to the Judicial Committee for determination.[29] The registrar will normally consider the question on paper but may direct an oral hearing.[30] A party may apply for a decision of the registrar to be reviewed by the Judicial Committee. Any application must be made in Form 2 in accordance with general rules for applications to the Privy Council, considered in para.19–011. It must be filed within 14 days of the registrar's decision.[31] Any question referred to the Judicial Committee will normally be considered on paper but the Judicial Committee may direct an oral hearing.[32]

SERVICE OF DOCUMENTS

19–007   A document may be served by personal service; first class post, or an alternative service which provides for delivery on the next working day; with the consent of the party to be served through a document exchange; with the consent of the party to be served or at the direction of the registrar by electronic means in accordance with the relevant practice direction.[33] Where the address of the person on whom a document is to be served is unknown, the registrar may direct that service is effected by an alternative method of service. A document served by first-class post or through a document exchange will be taken to have been served on the second day after it was posted or left at the document exchange, as the case may be (not including days which are not business days). A certificate of service must give details of the persons served, the method of service used and must state the date on which the document was served.[34]

FILING OF DOCUMENTS

19–008   A document may be filed by personal delivery; first class post (or an alternative service which provides for delivery on the next working day); through a document exchange; (with the consent of the registrar) by electronic means in accordance with the relevant practice direction. A document filed by first-class post or through a document exchange will be taken to have been filed on the second day after it was posted or left at the

---

[29] Judicial Committee Rules r.9(2).
[30] Judicial Committee Rules r.9(3).
[31] Judicial Committee PD 1 s.3.3.
[32] Judicial Committee Rules r.9(4)–(5).
[33] A party or agent will be taken to have consented to a particular method of service if, for example, their writing paper includes a fax number or a numbered box at a document exchange unless they have indicated in writing that they are not willing to accept service by that particular method: Judicial Committee PD 2 s.2.1.20.
[34] Judicial Committee Rules r.6.

document exchange, as the case may be (not including days which are not business days[35]). Except with the consent of the registrar, the contents of documents filed in hard copy must also be provided to the Registry by electronic means, and documents filed by electronic means must also be provided to the Registry in hard copy in accordance with the relevant practice direction.[36]

TIME LIMITS

The registrar may extend or shorten any time limit set by these Rules or any relevant practice direction (unless to do so would be contrary to any statutory provision). The registrar may exercise these powers either on an application by one or more parties or without an application being made. The registrar will notify the parties when a time limit is varied under this rule. An application for an extension may be granted after the time limit has expired. When the period specified by the Rules or a practice direction, or by any judgment or order for doing any act at the Registry ends on a day on which the Registry is closed, that act shall be in time if done on the next day on which the Registry is open.[37]   **19–009**

FAILURE TO COMPLY WITH THE RULES

Any failure by a party to comply with the Rules or any relevant practice direction shall not have the effect of making the proceedings invalid. Where any provision in these Rules or any relevant practice direction is not complied with, the registrar may give whatever directions appear appropriate having regard to the seriousness of the non-compliance and generally to the circumstances of the case including the summary dismissal of an appeal or debarring a respondent from resisting an appeal. The registrar may refuse to accept any document which does not comply with any provision in these Rules or any relevant practice direction and may give whatever directions appear appropriate.[38]   **19–010**

---

[35] Business days are days other than Saturdays, Sundays, Christmas Day, Good Friday, or a bank holiday under the Banking and Financial Dealings Act 1971 in England and Wales: see Judicial Committee PD 2 s.2.1.8.

[36] Judicial Committee Rules r.7

[37] Judicial Committee Rules r.5.

[38] Judicial Committee Rules r.8.

APPLICATIONS

19–011   Applications must be made as soon as it becomes apparent that an application is necessary or expedient. It must be made in Form 2 and served on all other parties before it is filed. The original and three copies of the application must be filed with the prescribed fee. The original application must bear a certificate of service on the other parties and must clearly indicate whether the other parties consent or refuse to consent to the application.[39]

The application must state what order the applicant is seeking and, briefly, why the applicant is seeking the order. Certain applications (e.g. for security) should be supported by written evidence. Although there may be no requirement to provide evidence in support, it should be borne in mind that, as a practical matter, the Judicial Committee will often need to be satisfied by evidence of the facts that are relied on in support of or for opposing the application. Evidence must be filed as well as served on the respondents.[40]

A party who wishes to oppose an application must, within 14 days after service, file notice of objection in Form 3 and must (before filing) serve a copy on the applicant and any other parties.[41] The original and three copies of the notice of objection must be filed, with the prescribed fee. The original notice must bear a certificate of service on the other parties.[42] A party who does not file notice of objection will not be permitted to participate in the application and will not be given notice of its progress.[43]

Applications will be dealt with without a hearing wherever possible. Unless the registrar directs otherwise, opposed incidental applications are referred to a panel and may be decided with or without an oral hearing. If the panel orders an oral hearing, the parties may seek permission to adduce affidavits, witness statements and such other documents as they may wish. Eight copies are required. Copies of such documents must be served on the other parties before the oral hearing. Authorities are not normally cited before the panel.[44]

The parties to an application for a consent order must ensure that they provide any material needed to satisfy the Judicial Committee that it is appropriate to make the order.[45]

---

[39] Judicial Committee PD 7 s.7.1.2 and 7.1.7.
[40] See Judicial Committee Rules r.31 and Judicial Committee PD 7 s.7.1.1–7.1.3.
[41] Judicial Committee Rules r.30(3) and Judicial Committee PD 7 s.7.1.4.
[42] Judicial Committee PD 7 s.7.1.7.
[43] Judicial Committee Rules r.30(4).
[44] Judicial Committee PD 7 s.7.1.6 and 7.1.8.
[45] Judicial Committee PD 7 s.7.1.5.

PERMISSION TO APPEAL

Generally an appellant will seek leave to appeal from the local Court of **19–012** Appeal, and in relation to that will have to comply with locally applicable rules. Leave can usually be obtained as of right from final judgments in civil disputes where the value of the dispute is greater than a stated amount, and in cases involving issues constitutional interpretation.[46] Further, most Courts of Appeal also have discretion to grant leave.

If he fails to do so, or fails to obtain leave, he will need to apply for special permission from the Privy Council. The Privy Council enjoys "complete discretion" whether to grant leave, though no doubt that discretion must be exercised judicially. Leave is sometimes granted in civil cases where the local Court of Appeal has refused,[47] though if there was good reason to refuse, that is of course less likely. If the lower court should have granted leave as of right, the Judicial Committee will grant permission save in exceptional circumstances, such as where the proposed appeal is wholly devoid of merit and bound to fail.[48] Under the former practice, leave to appeal was generally considered at an oral hearing. The new rules indicate that the general practice will now follow that of the Supreme Court, when permission is usually considered without an oral hearing. It should be noted that where permission is refused without a hearing, there is no right to an oral hearing to renew the application.

Applications to the Judicial Committee for permission to appeal should be produced in Form 1 on A4 paper, securely bound on the left, using both sides of the paper.[49] The application should set out briefly the facts and points of law; and include a summary of the reasons why permission should be granted. If an application for permission to appeal invites the Judicial Committee to depart from one of its own decisions or from one made by the House of Lords or the UK Supreme Court, this should be stated clearly in the application.[50] An application for permission to appeal must be signed by the appellant or his agent.[51]

Amendments to applications are allowed where the registrar is satisfied that this will assist the appeal panel and will not unfairly prejudice the respondents or cause undue delay. Any amendments must be served on the respondents.[52]

---

[46] Judicial Committee PD 1 s.2.1(1). Art.3(1) of The Cayman Islands (Appeals to Privy Council) Order 1984 (SI 1984/126), for example, provides that an appeal lies of right in civil disputes worth more than £300.

[47] Judicial Committee PD 2 s.2.1(2).

[48] *Crawford v Financial Institutions Services Ltd* [2003] UKPC 49; [2003] 1 W.L.R. 2147.

[49] Judicial Committee PD 3 s.3.1.2. See Annex 1 to PD 7 for Form 1.

[50] Judicial Committee PD 3 s.3.1.3.

[51] Judicial Committee PD 3 s.3.1.4

[52] Judicial Committee PD 3 s.3.1.2.

A copy of the application must be served on the respondents before it is filed. A signed certificate of service must be included in the original application or a separate certificate of service must be provided.[53]

19–013 In a major change from the old rules, which contained no express deadline, applications for permission to appeal must now be filed within 56 days from the date of the order or decision of the court below or the date of the court below refusing permission to appeal (if later).[54] The registrar may refuse to accept an application that contains no reasonable ground of appeal or is an abuse of process,[55] or where the application has not been properly served on the respondents.

The Registry may accept applications for permission to appeal which are out of time if the application or notice sets out the reasons why it was not filed within the time limit and it is in order in all other respects.[56] An application for an extension of time must be made in s.7 of Form 1. The respondent's views on the extension of time should be sought and, if possible, those views should be communicated to the Registry. The application for an extension of time will be referred to the registrar.[57]

In cases involving the liberty or life of the subject, urgent medical intervention or the well-being of children, a request for expedition may be made in writing to the registrar.[58] It may be that the registrar will consider other well founded reasons for expedition.

19–014 The following additional papers must be filed by the appellant for use by the appeal panel within 21 days after the filing of the application: (a) four copies of the application; (b) four copies of the order appealed against; (c) if separate from the order at (b) above, four copies of the order of the court below refusing permission to appeal to the Judicial Committee; (d) four copies of the official or approved transcript of the judgment of the court below; (e) four copies of the final order(s) of all other courts below; (f) four copies of the official or approved transcript of the final judgment(s) of all other courts below; (g) four copies of any unreported judgment(s) cited in the application or judgment of a court below; (h) four copies of a document which sets out the history of the proceedings.[59] No other papers are required and documents other than those listed above will not be accepted unless requested by the appeal panel. An appellant who wishes to provide documents other than those listed above must give a detailed explanation.[60] The additional documents must be (a) reproduced or printed (both as to font size and otherwise) so as to be easily legible; (b) reproduced on paper

---

[53] Judicial Committee PD 3 s.3.1.5.

[54] Judicial Committee Rules r.11(2); PD 2 s.2.1.12(a). If an appellant has applied to be treated as a financially assisted person (under r.38) the period for filing an application for permission to appeal is extended to 28 days after the final determination of the application for funding, including any appeals.

[55] Judicial Committee Rules r.11. See para.15 for appeals from decisions of the registrar.

[56] Judicial Committee PD 3 s.3.1.6 and PD 4 s.4.4.

[57] Judicial Committee PD 3 s.3.1.6

[58] Judicial Committee PD 3 s.3.1.19.

[59] Judicial Committee Rules r.14; PD 3 s.3.2.1.

[60] Judicial Committee PD 3 s.3.2.1.

of A4 size, printed on both sides; but they need not be bound. They must be properly labelled and indexed. Documents must be presented in a form which is robust, manageable and not excessively heavy. Duplication of material must be avoided particularly where two or more appeals are heard together.[61]

Each respondent who wishes to object to the application must, within 14 days after service, file notice of objection in Form 3 together with three certificates of service.[62] The original notice together with three copies must be filed at the Registry together with the prescribed fee. Before filing, a respondent must serve a copy of the notice on the appellant and any other respondent.[63] A signed certificate of service must be included in Form 3 or a separate certificate of service must be provided.[64] A respondent who files notice will be permitted to participate in the application and will be given notice of its progress. An order for costs will not be made in favour of a respondent who has not given notice.[65]

Practice Direction 3 provides that exceptionally a respondent could seek to file more fully reasoned objections or might be asked to do so by the appeal panel. In such circumstances further objections should be filed within 14 days of any invitation by the appeal panel to do so; or within 14 days of an application for permission to appeal being referred for an oral hearing. According to this provision, it appears that more fully reasoned objections should only be filed at the request of the appeal panel, or if there is to be an oral hearing. Respondents' objections should set out briefly the reasons why the application should be refused or make submissions as to the terms upon which permission should be granted (for example, on costs). The original and four copies of the respondents' written objections must be filed in the Registry. The objections must be produced on A4 paper, securely fastened, using both sides of the paper.[66]   **19–015**

A copy of the respondents' objections should be sent to the agents for the other parties. In certain circumstances the appeal panel may invite further submissions from the appellant in the light of the respondents' objections, but appellants do not have a right to comment on respondents' objections.[67]

Applications for permission to appeal are considered by an appeal panel of the Judicial Committee. Applications are generally decided on paper, without a hearing so it is essential that the application is in the correct form and that the basis on which and the relevant provisions under which the Judicial Committee is said to have jurisdiction are set out.[68] The appeal panel decides first whether an application for permission to appeal is admissible (that is, whether the Judicial Committee has jurisdiction to   **19–016**

---

[61] Judicial Committee PD 3 s.3.2.2 and PD 5 s.5.1.1.
[62] Judicial Committee r.13(1); PD 3.1.7. See Annex 1 to PD 7 for Form 3.
[63] Judicial Committee r.13(2); PD 3.1.8.
[64] Judicial Committee r. 6(4) and PD 2 s.2.1.21.
[65] Judicial Committee PD 3 s.3.1.9.
[66] Judicial Committee PD 3 s.3.3.6–3.3.7.
[67] Judicial Committee PD 3 s.3.3.8.
[68] Judicial Committee PD 3 para.3.1.1.

entertain an appeal). If the appeal panel determines that an application is inadmissible, it will refuse permission on that ground alone and not consider the content of the application. The appeal panel must give its reason(s) for deciding that the application is inadmissible.[69]

When considering an application for permission to appeal, the appeal panel may decide that permission should be granted or refused without further proceedings, in which case the parties are notified of the outcome and they are sent a copy of the order sealed by the registrar which records the panel's decision. The appeal panel may consider granting permission to appeal on terms, in which case the panel proposes the terms and the parties have the right to make submissions on the proposed terms within 14 days of the date of the panel's proposal. The panel will then decide whether to grant permission unconditionally or on terms; prospective appellants who are granted permission to appeal subject to terms that they are unwilling to accept may decline to pursue the appeal.

In all cases where further argument is required, an application for permission to appeal is referred for an oral hearing. As set out in para.19–015, respondents may seek to file more fully reasoned objections within 14 days of being informed that the application has been referred for a hearing. When an application is referred for an oral hearing, the appellant and all respondents who have filed notice of objection under r.13 are notified of the date of the hearing before the appeal panel. Parties may be heard before the appeal panel by counsel, by agent, or in person. If counsel are briefed, agents should ensure that the Registry is notified of their names. Appellants and respondents to an application for permission to appeal may instruct leading or junior counsel, according to the rules; whether they may instruct both is not clear. Oral permission hearings usually last for 30 minutes. The panel will normally give its decision orally at the end of the hearing. All the parties are sent a copy of the order sealed by the registrar which records the panel's decision. [70]

Where an application for permission to appeal is referred for an oral hearing and is dismissed, any application for costs must be made by the respondent at the end of the hearing. Where permission to appeal is granted, costs of the application for permission become costs in the appeal. The reasonable costs of objecting to an unsuccessful application for permission to appeal will normally be awarded to the respondent, subject to any order for costs made by the appeal panel.[71]

NOTICE OF APPEAL

19–017　The notice of appeal must set out the basis on which and the relevant provisions under which the Judicial Committee is said to have jurisdiction.

---

[69] Judicial Committee PD 3 s.3.3.1.
[70] Judicial Committee PD 3 ss.3.3.12–3.3.16.
[71] Judicial Committee PD 3 ss.3.5.1–3.5.3.

A notice of appeal should be produced in Form 1 on A4 paper, securely bound on the left, using both sides of the paper. Notices which are not legible or which are not produced in the required form will not be accepted. Parties may consult the Registry at any stage of preparation of the notice, and may submit notices in draft for approval. Amendments to notices are allowed where the registrar is satisfied that this will assist the Judicial Committee and will not unfairly prejudice the respondents or cause undue delay. Any amendments must be served on the respondents.[72]

If an appellant asks the Judicial Committee to depart from one of its own decisions or from one made by the House of Lords or the UK Supreme Court, this should be stated clearly in the notice of appeal and full details of the relevant decision must be given.

A copy of the notice of appeal must be served on the respondents before it is filed. A signed certificate of service must be included in Form 1 or a separate certificate of service must be provided.[73]

A notice of appeal must be filed within 56 days of the date of the order or decision of the court below or (if later) from the date of the order or decision of that court granting permission or leave.[74] If the order appealed from is not immediately available, the notice of appeal should be filed without delay and the order filed as soon as it is available.[75] Where an appellant is unable to file a notice of appeal within the relevant time limit, an application for an extension of time must be made in s.7 of Form 1. The respondent's views on the extension of time should be sought and, if possible, those views should be communicated to the Registry. The application for an extension of time will be referred to the registrar.[76]

Where permission to appeal has been granted by the Judicial Committee, the application for permission to appeal will stand as the notice of appeal and the grounds of appeal are limited to those on which permission has been granted.[77] The appellant must, within 14 days of the grant by the Judicial Committee of permission to appeal, file notice that he wishes to proceed with his appeal. When the notice is filed, the application for permission to appeal will resealed and the appellant must then serve a copy on each respondent and file the original and three copies.[78]

---

[72] Judicial Committee PD 4 s.4.2.1. See Annex 1 to PD 7 for Form 1.

[73] Judicial Committee Rules r.6(4); PD 2 s.2.1.21 and PD 4 s.4.2.6.

[74] Judicial Committee Rules r.18(2); PD 2 s.2.1.12(b). If an appellant has applied to be treated as a financially assisted person (under r.38) the period for filing an application for the appeal notice is extended to 28 days after the final determination of the application for funding, including any appeals.

[75] Judicial Committee Rules r.18(5) and PD 4 s.4.3.2

[76] Judicial Committee PD 4 s.4.4; see also s.4.3.1.

[77] Judicial Committee Rules r.17(1); PD 4 s.4.1.1

[78] Judicial Committee Rules r.17(2)–(3). See Annex 1 to PD 7 for Form 1.

RESPONDENT'S NOTICE

19–018 Each respondent who intends to participate in the appeal must give notice within 21 days after service of the resealed application for permission to appeal (if permission to appeal has been granted by the Judicial Committee) or the notice of appeal (if permission was not required, or granted by the lower court of appeal). The notice should be given using Form 3, produced on A4 paper, securely fastened, using both sides of the paper.[79] The notice must be served on the appellant and any other respondent before it is filed. A signed certificate of service should be included in Form 3 or a separate certificate of service must be provided.[80]

Note that Form 3 requires respondents to set out the respondent's grounds of appeal (if any), including reasons why the appeal should be allowed (or, presumably, dismissed). Respondents are to include information to explain what the respondent intends to ask the Judicial Committee to do.

The original notice together with three copies of Form 3 must be filed at the Registry together with the prescribed fee. A respondent who does not give notice under r.19 will not be permitted to participate in the appeal and will not be given notice of its progress. An order for costs will not be made in favour of a respondent who has not given notice.[81]

SECURITY FOR COSTS

19–019 In *Electrotec Services v Issa Nicholas Ltd* [81a] the defendant sought security for costs under s.548 of the Companies Act of Grenada. The Privy Council declined, holding that the particular statutory provision related only to proceedings at first instance. As for appeals, the West Indies Associated States (Appeals to Privy Council) (Grenada) Order 1967 and the Judicial Committee (General Appellate Jurisdiction) Rules Order 1982 were to be construed as a coherent code concerning a single system of appeals to the Judicial Committee from the Grenadian judicial system. The qualification in art.5 of the Order of 1967, whereby the Court of Appeal of Grenada was required to obtain security for costs in a sum not exceeding £500 "in the first instance" did not assume an inherent power in the Judicial Committee to require security in a greater amount on further application. Any inherent jurisdiction of the Board to require security should be exercised only in exceptional cases.

---

[79] Judicial Committee Rules r.19(1); PD 4 s.4.6.1. See Annex 1 to PD 7 for Form 3.
[80] Judicial Committee Rules r.19(2); PD 4 s.4.6.2
[81] Judicial Committee Rules r.19(3); PD 4 ss.4.6.3–4.6.4
[81a] [1998] 1 W.L.R. 202.

The new rules provide that where the court below grants permission to appeal, security for costs is a matter for the court below.[82] This provision is consistent with the decision in *Electrotec Services v Issa Nicholas Ltd*[82a] that no security for costs will generally be awarded in an appeal brought as of right, in particular where rules relating to permission also govern the issue of security for costs. No security for costs is required in cross-appeals, or where the appellant is a financially assisted person.[83]

Otherwise, where the Judicial Committee grants permission to appeal, the Judicial Committee has a discretion to grant security for costs.[84] An application for security must be made as soon as it becomes apparent that the application is necessary or expedient[85] in the general form of application, Form 2; and should be supported by evidence.[86] Both the application and the evidence in support should be served on all other parties before filing. The evidence should be filed as well as the application.[87] The original and three copies of the application must be filed, with the prescribed fee. The original application must bear a certificate of service on the other parties and must clearly indicate whether the other parties consent or refuse to consent to the application.[88]

If the appellant opposes the application for security for costs, it should serve and file a notice of objection and any evidence in accordance with Practice Direction 7, and as described in para.19–011.

In *Electrotec Services v Issa Nicholas Ltd*[88a] Lord Hoffmann held that the inherent jurisdiction to award security for costs would only be exercised in exceptional cases; for example, when it appears likely that the bringing of the appeal is an abuse of process. It may be that that dictum is limited to applications for security for costs in relation to appeals brought as of right. Nevertheless, the Practice Direction makes it clear that orders for security for costs will be made sparingly.[89] **19–020**

Where the Judicial Committee or the registrar orders an appellant to give security for the costs of the appeal and any order for security will determine (a) the amount of that security, and (b) the manner in which, and the time within which, security must be given.[90]

Deposits of security money may be made by banker's draft or cheque. Drafts and cheques for security money must be made payable to "Judicial Committee Security Fund Account".[91] Failure to provide security as required will result in the appeal being struck out by the registrar although

---

[82] Judicial Committee PD 4 s.4.7.4.
[82a] [1998] 1 W.L.R. 202.
[83] Judicial Committee PD 4 s.4.7.3
[84] See *Electrotec Services v Issa Nicholas Ltd* [1998] 1 W.L.R. 202 and *GFN SA v Bancredit Cayman Ltd* [2009] UKPC 39; [2010] Bus. L.R. 587.
[85] Judicial Committee PD 7 s.7.1.1
[86] Judicial Committee PD 4 s.4.7.1 and PD 7 s.7.1.3.
[87] Judicial Committee PD 7 s.7.1.3
[88] Judicial Committee PD 7 s.7.1.7
[88a] [1998] 1 W.L.R. 202.
[89] Judicial Committee PD 4 s.4.7.1.
[90] Judicial Committee Rules r.37; PD 4 s.4.7.1.
[91] Judicial Committee PD 7 s.7.9.1.

the appellant may apply to reinstate the appeal.[92] No doubt good reason would have to be shown why security had not been provided.

APPLICATIONS TO AMEND

19–021   An application for permission to appeal, a notice of appeal or any other document may be amended with the permission of the registrar on such terms as appear appropriate and the registrar may invite the parties' written submissions on any application to amend.[93]

THE RECORD

19–022   "The record" means all such documents (including originating process, pleadings, witness statement and affidavits,[94] transcripts of evidence, exhibits, judgments and orders) relating to the proceedings in the court below as are necessary for the hearing of the appeal by the Judicial Committee. As soon as permission to appeal has been granted or a notice of appeal has been filed, the appellant must without delay arrange for the record to be certified by the proper officer of the court below; transmitted to the registrar; and reproduced.[95]

If a transcript is not available, because the proceedings were not recorded, then the parties will have to try to obtain the judge's notes.

The record must be reproduced 12 times, on double sided A4 paper and comb bound.[96] It may well be cheaper to have the record reproduced in London to avoid excessive postage costs. The parties must endeavour to agree the contents of the reproduced record and in the event of a disagreement the registrar may give whatever directions appear appropriate.

In circumstances where the Record is or may be voluminous, it is in the parties' interests to seek to restrict it to documents which are relevant and necessary for the appeal. Accordingly, the practice direction provides that directions should be sought from the registrar in those cases in which the parties consider that the Judicial Committee will not be assisted by the record and that they are able to provide an agreed bundle of the documents which will be necessary for the determination of the appeal. Any request for directions should provide a detailed explanation of the reasons for the request and be signed by counsel for the parties. Similarly where the record is extensive and the provision of 12 copies will entail considerable expense, a request for directions should be made to the registrar.[97]

---

[92] Judicial Committee PD 4 s.4.7.5
[93] Judicial Committee Rules r.32.
[94] For witness statements and affidavits see Judicial Committee PD 5 s.5.1.3.
[95] Judicial Committee Rules r.20.
[96] Judicial Committee PD 5 ss.5.1.2–5.1.3.
[97] Judicial Committee PD 5 s.5.1.5.

The record may take some time to obtain from the court below, and therefore it is important that the appellant's advisers comply with the obligation to seek it without delay.

Any documents which are not in English must be accompanied by a translation into English. Every translation must be accompanied by a statement by the person making it that it is a correct translation, and that statement must include (a) the name of the person making the translation, (b) his address, and (c) his qualifications for making a translation.[98]

STATEMENT OF FACTS AND ISSUES

The appellant must draw up and agree a statement of facts and issues so that it is ready to be filed within 42 days after the filing of the re-sealed application for permission to appeal or of the filing of the notice of appeal.[99] **19–023**

The parties must seek to agree the statement of facts and issues. In the event that the parties disagree, the registrar may give such directions as appear appropriate.[100] Disagreements should be rare if the parties bear in mind that the statement of facts and issues is intended to be a neutral document to assist the Judicial Committee; no party should draft the statement in terms which advance one party's case over that of another. The statement should contain references to every law report of the proceedings below, and should state the duration of the proceedings below. It should be signed by counsel for both parties.[101]

Appellants who are unable to complete preparation of the statement within the time limit may apply to the registrar for an extension of that time under r.5. Any application must be made in the general form of application, Form 2 and should explain the reasons why an extension is needed. Since the time limits provided by the Rules are generous, applicants for an extension of time must set out in some detail why they are unable to comply with it. The registrar may grant an application for an extension of time, provided that it does not prejudice the preparation for the hearing or its proposed date.[102] When the statement is ready, the original and 12 copies of the statement, must be filed at the Registry.[103]

---

[98] Judicial Committee PD 5 s.5.1.9.
[99] Judicial Committee Rules r.21.
[100] Judicial Committee Rules r.21(3).
[101] Judicial Committee PD 5 s.5.1.7. The reference to duration of the proceedings probably relates primarily to the duration of the hearings from which the appeal is brought.
[102] Judicial Committee PD 5 s.5.2.2–5.2.3. For Form 2 see Annex 1 to PD 7.
[103] Judicial Committee PD 5 s.5.2.5

PRECIS

19-024 The statement of facts and issues must be accompanied by a précis of the case. This must be on no more than one side of A4 paper (in Arial point 12), and should be drafted initially by the appellant but submitted to, and agreed by, every respondent before filing. The précis should be filed with the statement of facts and issues and an electronic copy of the précis should be emailed to the Registry.[104] Like the statement of facts and issues, it should be uncontroversial.

DIRECTIONS

19-025 Where it considers it to be appropriate, the Judicial Committee may decide that a directions hearing should be held. A directions hearing will normally be held before three members of the Board. Any request for a directions hearing should be made to the registrar. Wherever possible the views of all parties should be obtained before a request is made.[105] The registrar may in any event ask the parties to agree directions, in accordance with the rules and the practice directions, so that the parties know exactly when each step needs to be taken.

EXPEDITION OF APPEALS

19-026 In relation to expediting applications for permission to appeal, see para.19-011. In relation to the appeal itself, the relevant practice direction says simply that any request for an expedited hearing should be made to the registrar; wherever possible the views of all parties should be obtained before a request is made.[106]

LISTING THE APPEAL

19-027 Within 14 days after the filing of the statement of facts and issues, and in order to enable the registrar to fix the date for the hearing of the appeal, the parties must notify the registrar that the appeal is ready to list, specify the number of hours that their respective counsel estimate to be necessary for their oral submissions and file the other required listing particulars. Notwithstanding the indication in r.22(1), the practice direction states that parties are encouraged to offer agreed dates which are convenient to all

---

[104] Judicial Committee PD 5 s.5.1.8
[105] Judicial Committee PD 6 s.6.2.5.
[106] Judicial Committee PD 6 s.6.2.4.

counsel at an early stage and there is no need to wait until after the filing of the statement of facts and issues to fix the hearing date. Time estimates must be as accurate as possible since, subject to the Judicial Committee's discretion, they are used as the basis for arranging the Judicial Committee's list.[107]

In relation to time estimates, not more than one day is normally allowed for the hearing of an appeal and appeals are listed for hearing on this basis. Estimates of more than one day must be fully explained in writing to the registrar.[108]

The registrar will inform the parties of the date fixed for the hearing.

CASES

The case is the statement of a party's argument in the appeal. The Judicial Committee does not prescribe any maximum length but the Committee favour brevity and a case should be a concise summary of the submissions to be developed.[109] The case should be confined to the heads of argument that counsel propose to submit at the hearing and omit material contained in the statement of facts and issues.[110]   **19–028**

Under the old practice parties exchanged cases, which meant that the respondent might have little idea what points were going to be argued. Under the new rules, cases are served and filed sequentially: the appellant must file and serve the case at least five weeks before the hearing date; and the respondent must file and serve the case at least three weeks before the hearing date.

If either party is abandoning any point taken in the courts below, this should be made plain in their case. If they intend to apply in the course of the hearing for permission to introduce a new point not taken below, this should also be indicated in their case and the registrar informed. If such a point involves the introduction of fresh evidence, application for permission must be made either in the case or by filing an application for permission to adduce the fresh evidence.[111]

If a party intends to invite the Judicial Committee to depart from one of its own decisions or from a decision of the House of Lords or the UK Supreme Court, this intention must be clearly stated in a separate paragraph of their case, to which special attention must be drawn.[112]

A respondent who wishes to contend that a decision of the court below should be affirmed on grounds other than those relied on by that court must set out the grounds for that contention in their case. In relation to citation

---

[107] Judicial Committee PD 6 s.6.2.1.
[108] Judicial Committee PD 6 s.6.2.2.
[109] Judicial Committee PD 6 s.6.3.1.
[110] Judicial Committee PD 6 s.6.3.2.
[111] Judicial Committee PD 6 s.6.3.3.
[112] Judicial Committee PD 6 s.6.3.4. This point should also have been made clear in either the application for permission to appeal or the notice of appeal: see paras 19–012 and 19–017.

of authority, transcripts of unreported judgments should only be cited when they contain an authoritative statement of a relevant principle of law not to be found in a reported case or when they are necessary for the understanding of some other authority.[113]

All cases must conclude with a numbered summary of the reasons upon which the argument is founded, and must bear the signature of at least one counsel for each party to the appeal who has appeared in the court below or who will be briefed for the hearing before the Judicial Committee.[114]

APPEALS FROM DECISIONS OF FACT

19–029 Whilst the Judicial Committee has jurisdiction to hear appeals on points of fact, by long established rule of conduct, the Privy Council will not interfere with concurrent findings of judgments of two courts on a pure question of fact: that is to say, where an appellate court has reviewed decisions on factual matters of a trial judge, it will decline to review the evidence for a third time.[115] The only exceptions to this rule of practice are if there are circumstances amounting to (a) some miscarriage of justice such as to make that which happened not in the proper sense of the word judicial procedure at all; or (b) violation of some principle of law which, if corrected, means that the finding cannot stand; or (c) violation of some principle of procedure which, likewise, if corrected, means that the finding cannot stand.

The Privy Council is also sensitive to the fact that local courts may be better placed to decide certain issues. Whether a state of local affairs is of sufficient notoriety to be a matter of judicial notice is something which is best decided by a local court.[116] The quantum of damages for personal injury cases may also best be decided by a court with knowledge of local social and economic conditions.[117]

APPEALS ON QUESTIONS OF LAW

19–030 The Privy Council applies the relevant local law, and parties need not adduce evidence of it.

---

[113] Judicial Committee PD 6 s.6.3.4.

[114] Judicial Committee PD 6 s.6.3.6. The filing of a case carries the right to be represented by two counsel. The fees of two counsel only for any party are allowed on assessment unless Judicial Committee orders otherwise on application at the hearing: PD 6 s.6.3.7.

[115] *Robins v National Trust Co Ltd* [1927] A.C. 515 at 517–518, *Devi v Roy* [1946] A.C. 508 at 521; *Bekoe v Broomes* [2005] UKPC 39 at [11]–[12].

[116] *Saunders v Adderley* [1999] 1 W.L.R. 884.

[117] *Selvanayagam v University of W Indies* [1983] 1 W.L.R. 585 (disapproved on another point in *Geest Plc v Lansiquot* [2002] 1 W.L.R. 3111).

AUTHORITIES

As noted above, the time required to put together and copy authorities   **19–031**
bundles should not be underestimated. The appellant is obliged to liaise
with the respondent to draw up an index of authorities referred to in the
cases and such other authorities to which the parties wish to refer. In an
appeal where there is a large number of volumes of authorities, it is helpful
to produce an index of indexes, separate from the index contained in the
first authorities volume.[118]

The Law Reports should be cited if possible in preference to any other
law report. Transcripts of unreported judgments should only be cited when
they contain an authoritative statement of a relevant principle of law not to
be found in a reported case or when they are necessary for the understanding of some other authority.[119] It is suggested that unreported first
instance decisions should be cited only for very good reasons. Parties should
not file authorities printed out from online resources unless the relevant
database contains reproductions (in pdf form) of the printed page of the
published reports. There should only be one page per view.

The authorities should be collected together into one or more volumes or
folders. It should be noted, however, that folders should only be used with
caution: a lever arch file in particular is likely to be unacceptable, as when
documents are printed on both sides, the left hand page cannot be annotated or marked up by anyone right handed. The volumes of authorities
should have a separate index and authorities should appear in alphabetical
order. The volumes of authorities should (a) be A4 size reproduced as one
page per view (with any authorities smaller than A4 being enlarged); (b)
separate each authority by numbered dividers; (c) contain an index to that
volume; the first volume must also contain an index to all the volumes; (d)
be numbered consecutively on the cover and spine with numerals at least
point 72 in size for swift identification of different volumes during the
hearing; (e) have printed clearly on the front cover the title of the appeal
and the names of the agents for all parties; (f) have affixed to the spine a
sticker indicating clearly the volume number and short title of the appeal.[120]

10 copies of the joint set of authorities must be filed at least 14 days
before the hearing. Respondents should arrange with the appellants for the
delivery to them of such authorities volumes as the respondents' counsel
and agents require.[121]

---

[118] Judicial Committee PD 6 s.6.4.3.
[119] Judicial Committee PD 6 s.6.3.5.
[120] Judicial Committee PD 6 s.6.4.2.
[121] Judicial Committee PD 6 s.6.4.1.

THE DAY BEFORE THE HEARING

19–032   Counsel should agree an order of speeches and timetable for the hearing and submit it to the Registry on the working day before the hearing.[122]

THE HEARING

19–033   The Judicial Committee usually hears appeals on Mondays from 11am–1pm and from 2–4pm, and on Tuesdays to Thursdays from 10.30am–1pm and 2–4pm.[123] The registrar will on request inform the parties of the intended constitution of the Judicial Committee for the hearing of a forthcoming appeal; this will be subject to possible alteration. Counsel should assume that the Judicial Committee will have read the printed cases and the judgment under appeal but not all the papers which have been filed.[124]

    Only in wholly exceptional circumstances will the Judicial Committee consider sitting in private. Any request for the Judicial Committee to sit in private should be addressed to the registrar and should be copied to the other parties. The request should set out fully the reasons why it is made and the request together with any objections filed by the respondents will normally be referred to the Judicial Committee.[125]

    If a party wishes to have a stenographer present at the hearing or to obtain a full transcript of the hearing, he must notify the registrar not less than seven days before the hearing. Any costs of the stenographer or of transcription must be borne by the party making such a request.[126]

    No more than two counsel will be heard on behalf of a party (or a single counsel on behalf of an intervener permitted to make oral submissions).[127]

HANDING DOWN JUDGMENT

19–034   Judgments are given on a day notified in advance. One week's notice is normally given.[128] It is usual for junior counsel to attend; leading counsel is not required and his or her costs will not be recoverable. The written judgment is usually available about half an hour before judgment is handed down.

---

[122] Judicial Committee PD 6 s.6.2.2.
[123] Judicial Committee PD 6 s.6.5.3.
[124] Judicial Committee PD 6 s.6.5.7.
[125] Judicial Committee PD 6 s.6.5.4.
[126] Judicial Committee PD 6 s.6.5.6.
[127] Judicial Committee PD 6 s.6.5.5. See Ch.9 on when parties may intervene in English appeals; it is thought that similar principles will apply to the Privy Council.
[128] Judicial Committee PD 6 s.6.7.1.

COSTS

Costs are in the discretion of the Committee.[129] The usual rule will be that costs follow the event. If a party seeks a different order, they may make written submissions in accordance with r.44 if the Judicial Committee so directs.[130] If a party wishes to defer making submissions as to costs until after judgment, the Committee must be informed of this not later than at the close of the oral argument. If the Committee accedes to the request it will give directions for submissions.

The Privy Council has a discretion to order costs against a non-party. Generally speaking, where a non-party promotes and funds proceedings by an insolvent company solely or substantially for his own financial benefit, he should be liable for the costs if his claim or defence or appeal fails. That is not to say, however, that orders will invariably be made in such cases, particularly, say, where the non-party is himself a director or liquidator who can realistically be regarded as acting rather in the interests of the company (and more especially its shareholders and creditors) than in his own interests.[131]

The registrar will normally direct an oral hearing for the purposes of assessing costs.[132] It is unlikely that, absent relevant local rules, a party will be entitled to recover an uplift pursuant to a conditional fee agreement, or an after-the-event insurance premium.[133]

There are detailed rules for the assessment of costs set out in Practice Direction 8. The assessment of costs may be conducted by the senior costs judge or any costs judge nominated by him.

---

[129] Judicial Committee Act 1833 s.15; Judicial Committee Act 1843 s.12.
[130] Judicial Committee PD 6 s.6.6.1.
[131] *Dymocks Franchise Systems (NSW) Pty Ltd v Todd* [2004] UKPC 39; [2004] 1 W.L.R. 2807 at [29].
[132] Judicial Committee Rules r.9(3).
[133] *Seaga v Harper (No.2)* [2010] 1 W.L.R. 312.

PART 5

Arbitration Appeals

CHAPTER 20

Background to Arbitration Appeals

INTRODUCTION

Although there is some overlap between arbitration appeals and other types **20–001**
of civil appeal, it is probably right to treat them as a separate topic. They
are subject to their own procedural code and their own (in some ways much
more codified) substantive rules and requirements.

The primary reason for this is obvious. Arbitration is a private form of
dispute resolution. Different considerations apply to the bringing of appeals
against the decisions reached by the tribunals appointed (in effect) by the
parties than apply to decisions reached by judges. The fact remains that,
while the *extent* to which it is open to the courts to entertain appeals
against the decisions of arbitrators varies, it is not possible (at least in
arbitrations with their seat in England and Wales and hence subject to the
supervision of the courts of England and Wales) for the right of appeal to be
excluded entirely. This chapter considers the statutory scheme for appealing
against arbitration awards and the procedural steps required in order to
exercise such a right of appeal.

The aim, however, is to restrict that consideration to appeals from
arbitration awards to the courts of England and Wales. Specifically, this
section will consider:

(1) the three possible grounds of appeal of an arbitrator's award,
namely:

    (a) error of law;
    (b) procedural unfairness; and
    (c) want of jurisdiction;

(2) together with the procedural requirements in relation to such
appeals.

This section will also consider the possibility of appealing from the High
Court to the Court of Appeal. Such appeals are not common under the new
regime:

"In reality the High Court is the court of last resort in arbitral proceedings. Whilst there is a theoretical right of appeal, it is only to be exercised by the High Court itself in quite exceptional circumstances."[1]

There will be no discussion of what might be described as "internal" appeals, as provided for by many established arbitration institutions,[2] whereby a further tribunal reviews or reconsiders the original award. Nor will this chapter address the other situations (some of which share features with appeals) in which the courts might become involved in an arbitration (e.g. protective measures, early references on questions of law and enforcement of awards). For these topics, readers should turn to a specialised work on arbitrations.[3]

THE ARBITRATION ACT 1996

20–002 The Arbitration Act 1996 (AA 1996) swept away the many and various means by which parties could challenge an arbitral award under the previous Arbitration Acts of 1950, 1975 and 1979. It was not intended to be a consolidation or a codification of the existing rules so much as a wholesale reconsideration of the manner in which arbitrations governed by English curial law (i.e. having their seat in England and Wales) are conducted and supervised, with the stated[4] intent of improving the law and making England a preferred jurisdiction in which international parties might choose to arbitrate their disputes. A very important aspect of that process was limiting the scope for "interference" by the courts, not least in terms of the scope and procedure for appeals. This is discussed in more detail below.

While it would be wrong to say that all of the pre-1996 jurisprudence was rendered irrelevant by the AA 1996, a number of authorities have emphasised that the AA 1996 represented a deliberate break with at least some of what had gone before. Certainly in the context of appeals, there has been a reluctance to assume that the pre-1996 approach forms any more than the background to the AA 1996.

In the years immediately following the coming into force of the AA 1996, there continued to be a number of arbitrations brought under the "old law",[5] with appeals therefrom dealt with by reference to the old procedural regime.[6] Inevitably, the number of these has dwindled over time and it has

---

[1] *Mousaka v Golden Seagull* [2001] Lloyd's Rep. 657 at [33], per David Steel J.

[2] Especially in commodities arbitrations and salvage arbitrations.

[3] Such as Professor Merkin's excellent looseleaf *Arbitration Law* published by Informa.

[4] Its preamble states that it is "an Act to restate and improve the law relating to arbitration pursuant to an arbitration agreement; to make other provision relating to arbitration and arbitration awards; and for connected purposes".

[5] Under the Arbitration Act 1996 (Commencement No.1) Order 1996, the "old law" still applies to arbitral proceedings commenced before the Arbitration Act 1996 was appointed, i.e. January 31, 1997, and to arbitration applications relating to arbitral proceedings commenced before the appointed day.

[6] See CPR rr.62.11–62.16.

now reached the stage where any detailed discussion of that regime is likely to be of historical interest only.[7] Accordingly, what follows assumes that the arbitration in question is governed by the AA 1996.[8]

THE NATURE OF ARBITRATION AND THE COURT'S APPROACH TO ARBITRATION APPEALS

Arbitration is a process of resolving disputes which operates separately from, and largely outside, the court system. It is, at least in one sense, a consensual process, with the arbitrators' jurisdiction and powers flowing from the parties' agreement.
    20–003

As such, the parameters of the arbitration process will be set out in the arbitration agreement between the parties. Parties may choose to give their arbitrator(s) exclusive power to determine all aspects of their dispute. The arbitration agreement can stipulate for (among other things) the applicable substantive and/or curial law, the seat, the procedure to be followed, and the extent of the parties' rights of appeal.

The courts of England and Wales have recognised that, where parties[9] choose to arbitrate their disputes, rather than submit them to the courts, that choice should be respected. That choice carries with it a decision to forego the mechanisms/rights/rules of the court system and, indeed, to take the risk that an arbitration tribunal doing its best might still get the answer wrong.

The importance of respecting that choice was a particular theme of the AA 1996 and forms the background to any consideration of arbitration appeals as can be seen from s.1 of the AA 1996.

In simple terms, the scope for appealing the decision of an arbitrator is very much more limited than the scope for appealing the decision of a judge. It is limited strictly to and by the words of the AA 1996, with the courts repeatedly declining to entertain any challenge which falls outside those words:

> (1) In *Surefire Systems Ltd v Guardian ECL Ltd*,[10] Jackson J. emphasised[11] that where the parties enter into an arbitration agreement, their rights thereafter to challenge the arbitrator's award are strictly limited by the AA 1996. With a particular eye to

---

[7] For a very comprehensive discussion of this topic, see Mustill and Boyd, *Commercial Arbitration*.

[8] It is observed that the AA 1996 applies to all arbitrations whose seat is in England or Wales or Northern Ireland. See s.2(1) of AA 1996.

[9] Especially international parties, whose only link with England might be its selection as a neutral forum for dispute resolution.

[10] [2005] EWHC 1860 (TCC); [2005] B.L.R. 534.

[11] At [42].

construction arbitrations,[12] he commented[13] that "[t]here are good commercial reasons for parties in the construction industry to choose arbitration. The parties obtain a resolution (almost always a final resolution) of their disputes by a suitably qualified individual of their own choosing. There is, however, a price to be paid. The parties cannot have their cake and eat it. The parties cannot refer their factual or technical disputes first to an arbitrator and then to a judge of the Technology and Construction Court".

(2) In *North Range Shipping v Seatrans Shipping*[14-15] in which the Court of Appeal decided that it did have a residual (i.e. outwith the AA 1996) jurisdiction to set aside a judge's decision for misconduct or unfairness, the Court emphasised that it was very conscious of the need for finality in arbitrations and to avoid a return to the "bad old days".

HUMAN RIGHTS AND ARBITRATION APPEALS

20–004   With the incorporation of the Convention for the Protection of Human Rights and Fundamental Freedoms (ECHR) into domestic law by the Human Rights Act 1998 (HRA), the protection of human rights has pervaded almost all aspects of English law. Arbitration appeals have not escaped. In this context particularly relevant is art.6(1) of the ECHR, which provides that:

> "In the determination of his civil rights and obligations or of any criminal charge against him, everyone is entitled to a fair and public hearing within a reasonable time by an independent and impartial tribunal established by law."

However, the impact of art.6(1) on arbitrations has been less dramatic than might have been anticipated. In particular, the European Court of Human Rights has held[16] that an arbitration agreement will have the effect of waiving the right of access to a court. This approach has been followed by the English Court:

(1) In *BLCT (13096) v J Sainsbury Plc*,[17] a challenge to s.69(5)[18] founded on art.6(1) was rejected by the Court of Appeal. They

---

[12] But no doubt only because that would be the type of arbitration appeal which would most frequently be before a judge of the TCC.

[13] At [43].

[14-15] [2002] EWCA Civ 405; [2002] 1 W.L.R. 2397.

[16] *De La Pradelle v France* [1992] E.C.H.R. 76.

[17] [2003] EWCA Civ 884.

[18] Which provides that the application for permission to appeal under s.69 is to be determined without a hearing unless it appears to the court that a hearing is required. See para.21–051.

confirmed that statutory provisions limiting the right of appeal from an arbitral award do not offend art.6 and that it is open to parties to agree to waive the protection of a public hearing.[19] Arden L.J. summarised the position thus[20]:

> "I do not accept the submission that it is a requirement of Article 6 that there should be an oral hearing unless there are exceptional circumstances in the case. The fact is that the parties have already had a full hearing before the arbitrator and Mr Barnes does not suggest that that process did not comply with Article 6. The hearing was before an independent tribunal. Each side had the opportunity to put its case and knew the evidence of the other party. The arbitrator gave reasons for his decision. The proceedings were in private. This is apparently contrary to Article 6, but the parties waived their right to assert that this was a violation by virtue of their agreement to arbitration."

(2) In *Sukuman v Commonwealth Secretariat*,[21] Colman J. did not accept that there was any inconsistency between an agreement ousting any right of appeal on questions of law and art.6(1). On the contrary, the parties were acting entirely consistently with art.6(1) in the sense that they were preferring the facility offered by s.69(1) of AA 1996 of finality and privacy to the prospect of subsequent supervisory court proceedings.[22]

This is not to say that art.6(1) is completely irrelevant to arbitration appeals. On the contrary, it has often been invoked and can be seen playing its part in the court's approach to procedural questions.[23] The important point is that art.6 has not been permitted to expand the limited scope for appealing arbitration awards set out in the AA 1996.

---

[19] See [33].
[20] At [36].
[21] [2006] EWHC 304 (Comm); [2006] 2 Lloyd's Rep. 53.
[22] See [26].
[23] Perhaps the best example being *North Range Shipping* [2002] EWCA Civ 405; [2002] 1 W.L.R. 2397.

CHAPTER 21

Appeal on Points of Law: Section 69

INTRODUCTION

21–001 The most familiar of the grounds for appealing an arbitration award is found in s.69 of the Arbitration Act 1996 (AA 1996):

"69 Appeal on point of law

(1) Unless otherwise agreed by the parties, a party to arbitral proceedings may (upon notice to the other parties and to the tribunal) appeal to the court on a question of law arising out of an award made in the proceedings. An agreement to dispense with reasons for the tribunal's award shall be considered an agreement to exclude the court's jurisdiction under this section.

(2) An appeal shall not be brought under this section except—

(a) with the agreement of all the other parties to the proceedings, or
(b) with the leave of the court.

The right to appeal is also subject to the restrictions in section 70(2) and (3).

(3) Leave to appeal shall be given only if the court is satisfied—

(a) that the determination of the question will substantially affect the rights of one or more of the parties,
(b) that the question is one which the tribunal was asked to determine,
(c) that, on the basis of the findings of fact in the award—

   (i) the decision of the tribunal on the question is obviously wrong, or
   (ii) the question is one of general public importance and the decision of the tribunal is at least open to serious doubt, and

(d) that, despite the agreement of the parties to resolve the matter by arbitration, it is just and proper in all the circumstances for the court to determine the question.

(4) An application for leave to appeal under this section shall identify the question of law to be determined and state the grounds on which it is alleged that leave to appeal should be granted.

(5) The court shall determine an application for leave to appeal under this section without a hearing unless it appears to the court that a hearing is required.

(6) The leave of the court is required for any appeal from a decision of the court under this section to grant or refuse leave to appeal.

(7) On an appeal under this section the court may by order—

(a) confirm the award,
(b) vary the award,
(c) remit the award to the tribunal, in whole or in part, for reconsideration in the light of the court's determination, or
(d) set aside the award in whole or in part.

The court shall not exercise its power to set aside an award, in whole or in part, unless it is satisfied that it would be inappropriate to remit the matters in question to the tribunal for reconsideration.

(8) The decision of the court on an appeal under this section shall be treated as a judgment of the court for the purposes of a further appeal. But no such appeal lies without the leave of the court which shall not be given unless the court considers that the question is one of general importance or is one which for some other special reason should be considered by the Court of Appeal."

The historical perspective

For the majority of the 20th century, recourse to the courts was readily available to a party to an arbitration seeking to appeal on a point of law. 21–002

The primary method of doing so was by requiring the arbitral tribunal to state a "special case", by reference to which the courts could then decide the point of law. There were virtually no restrictions on a party's right to seek a "special case", and the courts had no qualms about ordering a reluctant tribunal to put this procedure in motion. In *The Lysland*,[1] the Court of Appeal held that so long as the putative special case was "real and substantial ... such as to be open to serious argument", "clear cut", and "necessary for the proper determination of the case", it had to be stated.[2] In practice this was tantamount to there being a right of appeal on all points of law except the irrelevant or the unarguable.

---

[1] *Halfdan Grieg & Co A/S v Sterling Coal & Navigation Corp, The Lysland* [1973] Q.B. 843.
[2] [1973] Q.B. 843 at 862.

Nor could the parties agree in advance that their appointed tribunal's decision to be final and not subject to appeal to the courts on a point of law. In *Czarnikow Ltd v Roth, Schmidt and Co*,[3] it was held that an agreement between the parties not to apply for a special case to be stated was void as contrary to public policy.[4] Scrutton L.J. colourfully pronounced that there "must be no Alsatia in England where the King's writ does not run".[5]

By the 1970s, those involved in commercial arbitration increasingly favoured a more self-restrained approach. There was a serious concern that commercial parties would stop naming London in arbitration clauses in order to avoid judicial meddling in private arbitrations.[6] Many of the old justifications for requiring strict judicial oversight, such as a lack of legal expertise on the part of lay arbitrators, were no longer applicable, given the growing professionalism of experienced commercial and legal arbitrators, highly familiar with the latest legal developments relevant to their industry.

The product of this thinking was the Arbitration Act 1979 (the 1979 Act). The philosophy underlying it was that the supervision of commercial arbitration should give effect to the parties' decision to arbitrate, rather than litigate. Section 1 of the 1979 Act therefore did away with both the "special case" procedure and also the parallel procedure involving setting aside an award for an error on its face. These were replaced with a straightforward system of appeal on a point of law, with much stricter controls governing whether an appeal should be entertained at all.

Czarnikow v Roth was reversed by statute in s.3, which expressly recognised the validity of "exclusion agreements". Such agreements could oust the jurisdiction of the courts to hear appeals on a point of law altogether.

21–003   There was some initial uncertainty over the new requirements for leave to appeal. Some judges continued to approach applications on the basis that access to the appellate jurisdiction of the courts should be granted on a liberal basis.[7] But the intention behind the new regime was powerfully spelt out by the House of Lords in *The Nema*.[8] In the leading judgment, Lord Diplock emphasised the need to provide finality for the parties, and

---

[3] [1922] 2 K.B. 478 CA.

[4] The clause struck down in *Czarnikow v Roth* did not even go so far as to exclude the court's jurisdiction altogether, since the tribunal was still empowered to state a case of its own motion, and the award could still be set aside for errors on its face. It merely sought to restrain the parties from requiring the arbitrators to do so or applying to the court for an order to the same effect.

[5] ibid. at 488. "Alsatia" was the name given to an area of London lying north of the River Thames covered by the Whitefriars monastery, to the south of the west end of Fleet Street and adjacent to the Temple. Between the 15th and 17th centuries it had the privilege of a sanctuary and as a result it was famous for being the refuge of criminals.

[6] Mustill and Boyd describe the 1979 Act as "the first legal procedural reform ever introduced with the explicit aim of attracting business". See *Commercial Arbitration* at p.455.

[7] See, for example, *International Sea Tankers Inc v Hemisphere Shipping Co Ltd, The Wenjiang* [1981] 2 Lloyd's Rep. 308 (reversed in part on appeal: [1982] 1 Lloyd's Rep. 128 CA, after the House of Lords' decision in *The Nema*); *Schiffahrtsagentur Hamburg Middle East Line GmbH v Virtue Shipping Corp, The Oinoussian Virtue* [1981] 1 Lloyd's Rep. 533.

[8] *Pioneer Shipping Ltd v BTP Dioxide Ltd, The Nema (No.2)* [1982] A.C. 724.

accordingly set out a series of restrictive criteria which needed to be met before leave to appeal should be granted. These "*Nema* guidelines" were forcefully restated in *The Antaios*[9] and are largely (although not precisely) reproduced in the provisions in relation to permission to appeal in the AA 1996.[10]

Indeed, by the late 80s and early 90's, the debate had moved on to whether a qualified right of appeal on a point of law should exist at all. The first UNCITRAL Model Law on International Commercial Arbitration, published in 1985, allowed an arbitral award to be challenged for want of jurisdiction or procedural irregularity[11] but not for an error of law. This approach was, however, rejected by the Departmental Advisory Committee (the DAC): both in 1989 under the chairmanship of Sir Michael J. Mustill and in the later 1996 Report which formed the foundation stone of the AA 1996. In the later report, the DAC stated that "we are not persuaded that the right of appeal should be abolished ... a limited right of appeal is consistent with the fact that the parties have chosen to arbitrate rather than litigate".[12]

It is probably fair to say that this question remains contentious, arising for discussion in one form or another in most arbitration symposia. Detractors of the current position stress the importance of finality, cost, speed, and privacy, noting that the very existence of s.69 of the AA 1996 can end up depriving the parties of many of the greatest benefits of private arbitration.[13] The supporters of the current position reply with two arguments: that parties ought (at least unless they agree otherwise) to have some protection against errors of law on the part of their arbitration tribunal and that English commercial law needs to evolve by a process of new judicial precedents.[14]

In a finely-balanced debate, it is tentatively submitted that the current form of s.69 strikes a sensible balance between these competing considerations. It is always open to the parties to exclude the jurisdiction of the courts in relation to errors of law (see further below), and indeed the widespread usage of standard rules such as those issued by the ICC or LCIA has made it increasingly common for them to do so.[15]

---

[9] *Antaios Compania Naviera SA v Salen Rederierna AB, The Antaios* [1985] A.C. 191.
[10] Discussed in paras 21–033 to 21–040.
[11] i.e. loosely corresponding to ss.67 and 68 of the 1996 Act.
[12] See para.285 of the DAC Report.
[13] e.g. R. Holmes and M. O'Reilly, "Appeals from Arbitral Awards: Should Section 69 be Repealed?" (2003) 69 *Arbitration* 1, 1–9.
[14] e.g. H.R. Dundas, "Appeals on Questions of Law: Section 69 Revitalised" (2003) 69 *Arbitration* 3, 172–183; Mustill and Boyd at p.244.
[15] Both of these sets of rules exclude the right of appeal to the courts on a point of law.

EXCLUDING THE RIGHT TO APPEAL ON ISSUES OF LAW

21–004   As noted above, before the passage of the 1979 Act, there had been a protracted debate concerning whether parties to an arbitration agreement should be entitled to "contract out" of the right of appeal to the courts on a point of law.

The AA 1996 broadly reproduces the position under the 1979 Act by identifying "mandatory" sections and "non-mandatory" sections, the latter of which may be excluded if the parties so agree.[16]

Section 69 is "non-mandatory" and can therefore be excluded. This is also made clear by the pre-amble to s.69(1), which states that the right of appeal under this section is available "unless otherwise agreed by the parties".

The old regime

21–005   One of the unsatisfactory features of the regime governing exclusion agreements under the 1979 Act was the existence of parallel procedures for domestic and international arbitration agreements.[17]

An arbitration agreement was "domestic" if none of the parties involved was based outside the United Kingdom and the seat of the arbitration was the United Kingdom. Under the "domestic" regime, an exclusion agreement could only be valid if it was made *after* the commencement of the arbitral proceedings. By contrast, in "international" arbitrations (i.e. arbitrations which did not fall under the "domestic" heading), an exclusion agreement could be concluded before the dispute arose (and hence included in the arbitration agreement itself).

The position was further confused by the existence of three "special categories".[18] If the subject matter of an arbitration fell into one of these "special categories", the "domestic" regime would apply (and the right to appeal could not be excluded) even if the arbitration would ordinarily be termed an "international" one.

---

[16] s.4 of the 1996 Act. The full list of "mandatory" sections can be found in Sch.1 to that Act.

[17] ss.3(6)–3(7) of the 1979 Act.

[18] By s.4 of the 1979 Act, the three "special categories" were those arbitrations arising from: (a) questions or claims falling within the jurisdiction of the Admiralty Court, (b) disputes arising from contracts of insurance, and (c) disputes arising from commodity contracts.

The Arbitration Act 1996

Although the rationale behind it was undoubtedly laudable,[19] this confused **21–006** regime was not popular with practitioners and was dispensed with when the AA 1996 came into force. While this distinction between "domestic" and "international" arbitration can still be found in the text of the AA 1996 in ss.85–87, these sections were never brought into force.[20] It now seems unlikely that they ever will be.

Excluding the right to appeal

An agreement to exclude any right of appeal pursuant to s.69 must be made **21–007** in writing.[21] Aside from that, no particular form is required.

There are usually said to be four methods of agreeing to exclude the right of appeal:

(1) by express agreement;
(2) by dispensing with the tribunal's duty to give a reasoned award[22];
(3) by providing that the arbitration should be governed by foreign law[23]; and
(4) by incorporating an "equity clause" such that the tribunal is not to, or does not have to, conduct the arbitration using strict legal principles.[24]

Express provision

In determining whether any provision in a contract is indeed an exclusion **21–008** agreement, the court will apply the usual principles of construction.[25] Any clause stating on its face that it excludes the court's jurisdiction will have the effect of doing so.

---

[19] The rules governing "domestic" arbitrations were designed to tackle potential imbalances in bargaining power that was felt not to arise to the same extent in international arbitrations. The "special categories" were considered those areas most likely to be conducive to further the development of English commercial law, and similarly were most at risk of creating their own parallel set of laws.

[20] See art.3 of the Arbitration Act (Commencement No.1) Order 1996 (SI 1996/3146).

[21] s.5(1) of the 1996 Act. Note, however, that under s.5(3) of the 1996 Act: "Where parties agree otherwise than in writing by reference to terms which are in writing, they make an agreement in writing."

[22] s.69(1) of the 1996 Act.

[23] Since the court's jurisdiction only extends to hearing appeals on domestic law.

[24] The validity of such clauses is expressly acknowledged by s.46(1)(b) of the 1996 Act.

[25] *Essex CC v Premier Recycling Ltd* [2006] EWHC 3594 (TCC); [2007] B.L.R. 233; *Sumukan Ltd v Commonwealth Secretariat (No.1)* [2007] EWCA Civ 243; [2007] 2 Lloyd's Rep. 87 in which it was argued that the exclusion agreement was not incorporated as it was an onerous term to which the appellant's attention had not been drawn and which therefore did not form part of the agreement. Though ultimately unsuccessful, the argument illustrates the applicability of familiar contractual principles in determining whether or not an exclusion agreement is operative.

This is the case even when the clause is incorporated by reference to an established set of trade rules[26] or a separate document.[27]

There are conflicting authorities as to whether the use of the words "final and binding" or equivalent is sufficient to constitute an express exclusion agreement.

- In *The Rio Sun*,[28] Lord Denning M.R. stated that if both the owners and the charterers had been prepared to accept the tribunal's decision as final, there would be no prospects of an appeal. The court in that case was not, however, required to consider the effect of any particular wording.[29]
- H.H.J. Havelock-Allen QC considered this question in *Al Hadha Trading Co v Tradigrain SA*[30] and noted that the inclusion of the word "conclusive" in a clause might weigh more strongly in favour of an exclusion agreement. However, he did not need to decide the issue and declined to do so.
- In *Essex CC v Premier Recycling*,[31] Ramsey J. considered these authorities and concluded that the words "final and binding" did not exclude the right of appeal. His decision was based partly on the fact that, under s.58 of the Act, an award made by an arbitral tribunal "is final and binding", but that did not affect the right of any party to challenge it in accordance with s.69. Any exclusion of the right of appeal has to contain "sufficiently clear wording".[32]
- In *Shell Eygpt v Dana Gas*[33] Gloster J. decided that there was no agreement to exclude any appeal, despite the use of the phrase "final, conclusive and binding". She held that:

> "a phrase such as 'final, conclusive and binding' in the context of an arbitration agreement ... does no more than restate what has long been the rule in relation to arbitrations, namely that an award is final, conclusive and binding in the traditional sense, in that it creates a res judicata and issue estoppel. Such words, by

---

[26] Exclusion clauses appear in both the ICC rules (art.24.2) and the LCIA rules (art.26.9). The UNCITRAL Model Law also precludes any appeal on a point of law (see arts 5 and 34). The incorporation of these rules will accordingly oust the court's s.69 jurisdiction: *Arab African Energy Corp Ltd v Olieprodukten Nederland BV* [1983] 2 Lloyd's Rep. 419; *Marine Contractors Inc v Shell Petroleum Development Co of Nigeria* [1984] 2 Lloyd's Rep. 77 CA; *Sanghi Polyesters (India) Ltd v International Investor (KCFC) (Kuwait)* [2000] 1 Lloyd's Rep. 480. S.4(3) of the AA 1996 allows the parties to make arrangements to exclude non-mandatory provisions by agreeing to the application of institutional rules.

[27] *Sumukan Ltd v Commonwealth Secretariat (No.1)* [2007] EWCA Civ 243; [2007] 2 Lloyd's Rep. 87.

[28] [1982] 1 W.L.R. 158 CA.

[29] *The Rio Sun* was one of the earliest cases decided by the Court of Appeal under the regime introduced by the 1979 Act and it is possible to read Lord Denning's words as simply recognising the shift in the legal position under the Act.

[30] [2002] 2 Lloyd's Rep. 512.

[31] [2006] EWHC 3594 (TCC).

[32] At [25].

[33] [2009] EWHC 2097 (Comm).

themselves and absent any other contextual indicators, are not sufficient, in my judgment, to amount to an agreement to exclude rights of appeal under section 69 of the AA 1996."[34]

It seems therefore that parties wishing to exclude s.69 should ensure that their agreement makes this clear, rather than simply referring in some more general way to the finality of the arbitration award.

Excluding the duty to give reasons

A change under the AA 1996 was the creation of a free-standing duty on any arbitral tribunal to give a reasoned award, unless the parties agree otherwise.[35]   **21–009**

Prior to the passage of the AA 1996, reasons only had to be given if they were material to a possible appeal on a point of law: there was no jurisdiction to compel the giving of reasons generally.[36] If the parties excluded an appeal on a point of law, there were no restrictions on the tribunal giving an unreasoned award. This meant that the parties who wished to insulate any award against interference by the court had to run the (at least theoretical) risk of receiving an entirely unreasoned award. The existence of a "stand-alone" duty to give reasons ensures that the parties can have a reasoned, but still unappealable, award.[37]

The parties may nevertheless elect to exclude the duty to give reasons.[38] Such an election will preclude any right of appeal on a point of law under s.69.[39]

It should be noted that it is the agreement, rather than the absence of reasons, which has this effect. In the event that a reasoned award is given despite the parties having agreed to dispense with any requirement for reasons, the exclusion agreement will nevertheless remain effective.[40] The fact that the parties did not want a reasoned award is determinative; whether or not they actually get reasons is immaterial.

Foreign law

It has been a long-standing principle of arbitration law that the parties may choose the governing law. This entitlement is now found in s.46(1)(a) of the AA 1996. The court's jurisdiction to hear appeals on a point of law is   **21–010**

---

[34] See [47].

[35] See s.52(4) of the 1996 Act. If the tribunal fails to do so, the court can order that it provide reasons under s.70(4).

[36] *Universal Petroleum Co Ltd (In Liquidation) v Handels-Und Transport* [1987] 1 Lloyd's Rep. 517.

[37] Indeed, a failure to give reasons can now lead to award being set aside for failure to comply with s.68(2)(h) (serious procedural irregularity): *Benaim v Davies Middleton & Davies* [2005] EWHC 1370.

[38] s.52(4) of, and Sch.1 to, the 1996 Act.

[39] s.69(1) of the 1996 Act.

[40] This is clear from the wording of s.69(1), which focuses on the agreement to dispense with reasons rather than the giving of reasons themselves.

confined to questions of domestic law.[41] Thus, the parties' election of any law other than that of England and Wales, or Northern Ireland[42] will have the effect of excluding appeals under s.69. This is probably true even if the tribunal has assumed (in the absence of evidence) that there is no relevant difference between the relevant foreign law and English law; it would still be determining an issue of foreign law.[43]

Equity clauses

21–011   Under s.46(1)(b) of the AA 1996, it is possible for the parties not have the dispute settled according to fixed legal principles but instead to have it decided based on "other considerations". There does not appear to be any fixed list of considerations, and although s.46(1)(b) undoubtedly encompasses arbitrations to be decided on an *ex aequo et bono*[44–45] basis, the scope is potentially much broader. The only apparent limits are those imposed by the parties themselves. Any clause stipulating that the arbitration will be governed by "other considerations" seems likely to have the effect of excluding any appeal on legal grounds.

Appeals concerning exclusion agreements

21–012   As will be discussed in more detail below, the scope for appealing (e.g. to the Court of Appeal) from a decision at first instance as to whether or not to grant permission to appeal is very limited. There was some uncertainty as to whether the scope for appeal from a decision at first instance that the first instance court had *no jurisdiction* to grant permission to appeal (because of an exclusion agreement) was similarly limited.

In *Sumukan Ltd v The Commonwealth Secretariat (No.1)*,[46] the appellant sought to appeal against a ruling made by Colman J. that it had entered into an exclusion agreement. The Court of Appeal heard the appeal on the basis that there was a "distinction between a decision as to whether the parties have agreed to exclude the court and ... the decision as to whether to grant or refuse permission to appeal".[47]

---

[41] s.82(1) of the 1996 Act. See further para.21–022.

[42] For English or Welsh courts, and Northern Irish courts respectively. This has existed as a rule for many years and gave rise to an historic practice of specifying Scottish law which was technically "foreign" to the English courts.

[43] See *Reliance v Enron Oil & Gas* [2002] B.L.R. 36 at [27]–[33]. Nor is it possible to dress up an attempt to appeal against an award applying foreign law as a challenge under s.67 or 68 of AA 1996 for lack of jurisdiction or serious irregularity: see *B v A* [2010] EWHC (Comm) 1626.

[44–45] Literally "according to the right and good"—essentially a reference to broad equitable principles.

[46] [2007] EWCA Civ 243; [2007] 2 Lloyd's Rep. 87.

[47] [2007] EWCA Civ 243; [2007] 2 Lloyd's Rep. 87 at [30].

A QUESTION OF LAW?

Section 69(1) of the AA 1996 makes clear that the court may only consider   **21–013**
an appeal on a "question of law". As noted above,[48] the question of law
must concern the substantive law of England and Wales.

This restriction is easy to state, but the precise definition of a "question of
law" has always proven elusive. It may be easiest to identify by reference to
what it is not: it is not a procedural matter or a finding of fact. A more
comprehensive discussion of this topic, which is not specific to arbitration
appeals (even if the distinction is sometimes more rigorously applied in that
context) is found in Chapter 3.

Generally

The issue of whether a particular question could be considered one of law   **21–014**
for the purposes of an arbitral appeal was helpfully considered by Mustill J.
(as he then was) in *The Chrysalis*.[49] He answered this problem by reference
to the decision-making process undertaken by an arbitral tribunal when
making its award:

> "In a case such as the present, the answer is to be found by dividing the
> arbitrator's process of reasoning into three stages: (1) The arbitrator
> ascertains the facts. This process includes the making of findings on
> any facts which are in dispute. (2) The arbitrator ascertains the law.
> This process comprises not only the identification of all material rules
> of statute and common law, but also the identification and inter-
> pretation of the relevant parts of the contract, and the identification of
> those facts which must be taken into account when the decision is
> reached. (3) In the light of the facts and the law so ascertained, the
> arbitrator reaches his decision.
>
> In some cases, stage (3) will be purely mechanical. Once the law is
> correctly ascertained, the decision follows inevitably from the appli-
> cation of it to the facts found. In other instances, however, stage (3)
> involves an element of judgment on the part of the arbitrator. There is
> no uniquely "right" answer to be derived from marrying the facts and
> the law, merely a choice of answers, none of which can be described as
> wrong.
>
> Stage (2) of the process is the proper subject matter of an appeal under
> the Act of 1979. In some cases an error of law can be demonstrated by

---

[48] See para.21–010.
[49] [1983] 1 W.L.R. 1469. This formulation was cited with approval in *Covington Marine
Corp v Xiamen Shipbuilding Industry Co Ltd* [2005] EWHC 2912 (Comm); [2006] 1
Lloyd's Rep. 745; *Kershaw Mechanical Services Ltd v Kendrick Construction Ltd* [2006]
EWHC 727 (TCC) and *Penwith DC v VP Developments* [2007] EWHC 2544 (TCC).

studying the way in which the arbitrator has stated the law in his reasons. It is, however, also possible to infer an error of law in those cases where a correct application of the law to the facts found would lead inevitably to one answer, whereas the arbitrator has arrived at another; and this can be so even if the arbitrator has stated the law in his reasons in a manner which appears to be correct, for the court is then driven to assume that he did not properly understand the principles which he had stated."

Some examples

21-015 While the formulation in *The Chrysalis* provides a helpful starting point, it could hardly be said to enable practitioners to see at a glance whether the particular issue which they want to appeal can be categorised as a question of law.

It is more common to look for authorities dealing with analogous types of issue. The following are questions of law for the purpose of an arbitration appeal:

(1) the proper construction of a document,[50] statute,[51] or earlier judgment or award[52];

(2) whether or not certain documents had contractual force on their proper construction[53];

(3) the basis on which damages should be assessed,[54] including whether a head of loss is too remote[55];

---

[50] *Woodhouse AC Israel Cocoa Ltd SA v Nigerian Produce Marketing Co Ltd* [1972] A.C. 741; *The Lysland* [1973] Q.B. 843; *Pilgrim Shipping Co Ltd v The State Trading Corp of India, The Hadjitsakos* [1975] 1 Lloyd's Rep. 356; *The Oinoussian Virtue* [1981] 1 Lloyd's Rep. 533; *The Nema* [1982] A.C. 724, *Glafki Shipping Co SA v Pinios Shipping Co No.1, The Maira (No.2)* [1985] 1 Lloyd's Rep. 300; *André et Cie v Cook Industries Inc* [1986] 2 Lloyd's Rep. 200; *Cero Navigation Corp v Jean Lion & Cie, The Solon* [2000] 1 Lloyd's Rep. 292 (effect of an exclusion clause); *Covington Marine Corp v Xiamen Shipbuilding Industry Co Ltd* [2005] EWHC 2912 (Comm); [2006] 1 Lloyd's Rep. 745; *Stern Settlement v Levy* [2007] EWHC 1187 (TCC).

[51] *Cozens v Brutus* [1973] A.C. 854 (a defamation case), cited with approval in the context of an arbitration appeal in *Belgravia Navigation Co SA v Cantor Shipping, The Troll Park* [1988] 2 Lloyd's Rep. 423.

[52] *Lincoln National Life Insurance Co v Sun Life Assurance Co of Canada* [2004] EWCA Civ 1660; [2005] 1 Lloyd's Rep. 606.

[53] *Covington Marine Corp v Xiamen Shipbuilding Industry Co Ltd* [2005] EWHC 2912 (Comm); [2006] 1 Lloyd's Rep. 745.

[54] *Sealace Shipping Co Ltd v Oceanvoice Ltd, The Alecos M* [1990] 1 Lloyd's Rep. 82 (the actual decision of Steyn J. was reversed by the Court of Appeal, but the proposition that the correct measure of damages is a question of law stands); *Islamic Republic of Iran Shipping Lines v Ierax Shipping Co of Panama, The Forum Craftsman* [1991] 1 Lloyd's Rep. 81 (demurrage); *Stolt Tankers Inc v Landmark Chemicals SA* (running of laytime/demurrage); *Medora Shipping Inc v Navix Line Ltd and Navios Corp, The Timawra* [1996] 2 Lloyd's Rep. 166.

[55] *Islamic Republic of Iran Shipping Lines v Ierax Shipping Co of Panama, The Forum Craftsman* [1991] 1 Lloyd's Rep. 81.

(4) the circumstances under which an innocent party may decline to accept a repudiation[56];

(5) the sums properly due under a contract[57];

(6) whether a term should be implied into a contract[58];

(7) the test for frustration.[59]

By contrast, the following have been held to be findings of fact:

(1) the existence or otherwise of certain terms in a contract[60];

(2) whether or not a party is in breach of its obligations[61];

(3) whether VAT is recoverable[62];

(4) the date on which a contract was concluded[63];

(5) the quantum of damages, including questions of mitigation[64];

(6) the valuation of certain assets, including the appropriate method of valuation used[65];

(7) the proper value to be attributed to land or other assets[66];

(8) whether there has been adherence to the rules of an association.[67]

Questions of causation will usually be a mixture of fact and law.[68]

---

[56] *Clea Shipping Corp v Bulk Oil International Ltd, The Alaskan Trader (No.2)* [1984] 1 All E.R. 129; *Ocean Marine Navigation Ltd v Koch Carbon Inc, The Dynamic* [2003] EWHC 1936 (Comm); [2003] 2 Lloyd's Rep. 693.

[57] *Mooney v Henry Boot Construction Ltd, Balfour Beatty Construction v Kelston Sparkes Contractors Ltd* (1997) 80 B.L.R. 66.

[58] *Islamic Republic of Iran Shipping Lines v The Royal Bank of Scotland Plc, The Anna Ch* [1987] 1 Lloyd's Rep. 266; *The Zenovia* [2009] EWHC 739 (Comm) at [22].

[59] *Tsakiroglou & Co Ltd v Noblee Thorl GmbH* [1962] A.C. 93; *Kodros Shipping Corp v Empresa Cubana de Fletes, The Evia* [1981] 2 Lloyd's Rep. 613; *The Nema* [1982] A.C. 724.

[60] *Surefire Systems Ltd v Guardian ECL Ltd* [2005] EWHC 1860 (TCC); [2005] B.L.R. 534 (whether a contract was varied or not); *Plymouth City Council v DR Jones (Yeovil) Ltd* [2005] EWHC 2356 (TCC); *Chattan Developments Ltd v Reigill Civil Engineering Contractors Ltd* [2007] EWHC 305 (TCC).

[61] *Portunus Navigation Co Inc v Avin Chartering SA* [1982] 1 Lloyd's Rep. 60 (short delivery); *Athenian Tankers Management SA v Pyrena Shipping Inc, The Arianna* [1987] 2 Lloyd's Rep. 376 (seaworthiness/suitability of a vessel); *Demco Investments & Commercial SA v SE Banken Forsakring Holding Aktiebolag* [2005] EWHC 1398 (Comm); [2005] 2 Lloyd's Rep. 650 (gross negligence).

[62] *Mirpuri v Jass* (1997) 56 Con. L.R. 31.

[63] *Plymouth City Council v DR Jones (Yeovil) Ltd* [2005] EWHC 2356 (TCC).

[64] *Famosa Shipping Co Ltd v Armada Bulk Carriers Ltd, The Fanis* [1994] 1 Lloyd's Rep. 633; *Glencore International AG v Beogradska Plovidba, The Avala (No.2)* [1996] 2 Lloyd's Rep. 311.

[65] *Marklands Ltd v Virgin Retail Ltd* [2003] EWHC 3428 (Ch).

[66] *Beaconscross Ltd v Norris* [1992] A.D.R.L.J. 161; *Amego Litho Ltd v Scanway Ltd* [1994] 2 E.G. 110; *Surefire Systems Ltd v Guardian ECL Ltd* [2005] B.L.R. 534.

[67] *Moran v Lloyd's* [1983] 1 Lloyd's Rep. 51.

[68] *Sinclair v Woods of Winchester (No.2)* [2006] EWHC 3003 (TCC).

Findings of fact

21–016   Outside the field of arbitration law, where a tribunal makes a finding of primary fact that is subsequently held could not properly have been made on the evidence, that will constitute an error of law.[69] This is not the case in the field of arbitration, at least for those arbitrations conducted under the auspices of the AA 1996. An arbitral tribunal's findings of fact cannot be impeached by the courts.[70]

In particular, the court will not entertain any appeal (at least under s.69 of the AA 1996) based on the argument that an arbitral tribunal weighed the evidence in an inappropriate manner, since the parties are taken to have agreed to the tribunal being the sole finder of fact. The provisions of s.34(2)(f)[71] when read with para.170 of the DAC Report[72] prevent the parties from seeking to reopen the evidence before the tribunal at the appellate stage. This prohibition is underscored by the introductory words to s.69(3)(c),[73] para.286(iii) of the DAC Report,[74] and a number of post-1996 authorities.[75]

The courts have also disapproved of litigants seeking to challenge findings of fact under the guise of pursuing other avenues of appeal, such as under ss.67 and 68.[76]

21–017   Having said that, there remains some uncertainty as to whether it could be an error of law for an arbitral tribunal to make a finding of fact based upon no evidence whatsoever:

---

[69] *Edwards (Inspector of Taxes) v Bairstow* [1956] A.C. 14.

[70] *The Baleares (No.2)* [1993] 1 Lloyd's Rep .215 at 227 :"it is inconsistent with the thrust and purpose of the 1979 Act to allow findings of fact to be reviewed by means of any examination which involves reference being made to the evidence which was before the arbitrators", per Neill L.J. See also *Blexen v G Percy Trentham* (1990) 21 Con. L.R. 61 CA; *How Engineering Services Ltd v Lindner Ceilings Floors Partitions Plc* (1999) 64 Con. L.R. 67; *Fence Gate Ltd v NEL Construction Ltd* (2001) 82 Con. L.R. 41; *Hallamshire Construction v South Holland DC* [2003] EWHC 8 (TCC); *Demco Investments & Commercial SA v SE Banken Forsakring Holding Aktiebolag* [2005] EWHC 1398 (Comm); [2005] 2 Lloyd's Rep. 650.

[71] "It shall be for the tribunal to decide ... whether to apply strict rules of evidence (or any other rules) as to the admissibility, relevance or weight of any material (oral, written or other) sought to be tendered on any matters of fact or opinion, and the time, manner and form in which such material should be exchanged and presented."

[72] In the guidance to cl.34(2)(f), the DAC explains that "clause 34(2)(f) helps to put an end to any arguments that it is a question of law whether there is material to support a fact".

[73] In which an appeal on the law is stated to be "on the basis of the findings of fact in the award".

[74] Explaining that s.69(3)(c) is designed to tackle the potential abuse of litigants "dress[ing] up questions of fact as questions of law".

[75] *Hallamshire Construction v South Holland DC* [2003] EWHC 8 (TCC); *Demco Investments & Commercial SA v SE Banken Forsakring Holding Aktiebolag* [2005] EWHC 1398 (Comm); [2005] 2 Lloyd's Rep. 650; *London Underground v Citylink Telecommunications* [2007] EWHC 1749 (TCC); [2007] B.L.R. 931; *Penwith DC v VP Developments Ltd (In Company Voluntary Arrangement)* [2007] EWHC 2544 (TCC).

[76] e.g. *The Baleares (No.2)* [1993] 1 Lloyd's Rep. 215, especially Steyn L.J. at 228.

(1) In *The Baleares (No.2)*,[77] Steyn L.J. implied that the arbitrator's findings of fact had to stand even if they were completely unsupported by evidence.[78] However, Neill L.J., whilst opining that it would be inconsistent with the object and purposes of the 1979 Act to permit an appeal based on a review of the evidence before the arbitrators, refused to make a positive ruling on this question. Ralph Gibson L.J. simply agreed with the judgment of Neill L.J. Although Steyn L.J.'s comment has been subsequently applied,[79] its status remains unclear.

(2) In the post-1996 case of *Fence Gate Ltd v NEL Construction Ltd*,[80] H.H.J. Thornton QC held that as a matter of English law no decision could be reached if there was no evidence to support it.[81] Thus, where the arbitrator has made a purported finding of fact in the absence of any evidence (as opposed to merely misjudging what weight to put on the evidence before him) this would be susceptible to appeal. *Fence Gate* was followed in *Newfield Construction Ltd v Tomlinson*[82] and this distinction was also accepted to be correct in *Benaim (UK) Ltd v Davies Middleton & Davies Ltd*.[83]

(3) By contrast, *Fence Gate* was rejected by Cooke J. in *Demco Investments v SE Banken*,[84] relying upon a careful consideration of the AA 1996 and the DAC Report. *Demco Investments* was subsequently followed in *London Underground v Citylink Telecommunications*,[85] which in turn was applied in *Penwith DC v VP Developments Ltd*.[86] It was also applied in *Sinclair v Woods of Winchester Ltd (No.2)*[87], in which H.H.J. Coulson QC (as he was) stated the principle simply thus: "it is simply not possible for a party to seek permission to appeal on Arbitrator's findings of fact no matter how wrong they might seem to be".[88]

(4) Since the decision in *Demco Investments*, no reported case has applied the reasoning in *Fence Gate*. It is submitted that a court

---

[77] [1993] 1 Lloyd's Rep. 215. This case was under the 1979 Act regime.
[78] See 228.
[79] *Demco Investments & Commercial SA v SE Banken Forsakring Holding Aktiebolag* [2005] EWHC 1398 (Comm); [2005] 2 Lloyd's Rep. 650, *London Underground v Citylink Telecommunications* [2007] EWHC 1749 (TCC); [2007] B.L.R. 931.
[80] (2001) 82 Con. L.R. 41.
[81] (2001) 82 Con. L.R. 4 at [38]–[44].
[82] [2004] EWHC 3051; 97 Con. L.R. 148.
[83] [2005] EWHC 1370 (TCC); 102 Con. L.R. 1. The court noted the difference between the arbitrators placing an inappropriate amount of weight on particular evidence (which could not be the subject of an appeal) and where a finding of fact was made on the basis of no evidence whatsoever. It emphasised that such a jurisdiction would be exceptional.
[84] [2005] EWHC 1542 (Comm); [2005] 2 Lloyd's Rep. 650.
[85] [2007] EWHC 1749 (TCC); [2007] B.L.R. 931, per Ramsey J.
[86] [2007] EWHC 2544 (TCC).
[87] [2006] EWHC 3003 (TCC).
[88] [2006] EWHC 3003 (TCC) at [9]. H.H.J. Coulson QC's statement is a little surprising given that he had given the judgments in both *Newfield v Tomlinson* and *Benaim v Davies Middleton & Davies* which supported *Fence Gate*.

faced with a similar situation would prefer the approach in *Demco Investments* over that in *Fence Gate*, although the position will obviously remain uncertain until clarified by the decision of a higher court.

(5) Of course, it may be that deciding a case on the basis of a point which was not raised as an issue or argued, without giving the parties the opportunity to deal with it, will be a procedural irregularity.[89] See para.22–010.

Findings of combined fact and law

21–018 If a finding is a combined one of fact and law, the court will only interfere if the conclusion reached by the tribunal is one that was outside the permissible range, assuming the correct approach as a matter of law.[90] The appellant will have to show that there must have been a failure by the arbitrators to apply the correct legal test by demonstrating that their conclusion was necessarily inconsistent with the proper application of that test.[91]

Application of the law

21–019 Finally, it appears that a failure to apply the law correctly to the given facts is not an "error of law". Hence, in *Benaim v Davies Middleton & Davies*, H.H.J. Coulson QC (as he was) decided that "an error of law arises where the arbitrator errs in ascertaining the legal principle which is to be applied to the factual issues in the dispute, and does not arise if the arbitrator, having identified the correct legal principle, goes on to apply it incorrectly".[92–93]

Errors in procedure

21–020 Procedural defects, as distinct from true questions of law, cannot be appealed under s.69. If they are open to appeal at all, they fall within ss.67 and 68, which deal with the substantive jurisdiction of the tribunal and serious misconduct, respectively.

---

[89] e.g. *London Underground v Citylink* (supra) at [37].

[90] *Cosemar SA v Marimarna Shipping Co Ltd ("The Mathew")* [1990] 2 Lloyd's Rep. 323; *Benaim (UK) v Davies Middleton Davies* [2005] EWHC 1370 (TCC); *Plymouth City Council v DR Jones (Yeovil) Ltd* [2005] EWHC 2356 (TCC); *Sinclair v Woods of Winchester Ltd (No.2)* [2006] EWHC 3003 (TCC).

[91] See *The Nema* [1982] A.C. 724; *The Aegean Dolphin* [1992] 2 Lloyd's Rep. 178, especially at 184; *Sylvia Shipping v Progress Bulk Carriers* [2010] EWHC 542 (Comm) at [52]–[55].

[92–93] [2005] EWHC 1370 (TCC) at [107]. See also *Northern Elevator Manufacturing Sdn Bhd v United Engineers (Singapore) Pte Ltd (No.2)* [2004] 2 S.L.R. 494 (Singapore Court of Appeal); [2004] 1 All E.R. (Comm) 59.

This reflects the position prior to 1996: "Section 1 and the 1979 Act are not concerned with procedural matters nor with misconduct".[94] That this remains the position under s.69 of the AA 1996 was confirmed in *Icon Navigation Corp v Sinochem*.[95]

Exercise of discretion

However, the exercise of a discretion (such as a discretion on the part of the tribunal to extend time for the commencement of proceedings) can involve an error of law, at least where it can be shown that extraneous matters were taken into account, or that the tribunal has failed to exercise its discretion on any identifiable grounds at all.[96] **21–021**

Foreign law

Section 82(1) of the AA 1996 defines a "question of law" as: **21–022**

"(a) for a court in England and Wales, a question of the law of England and Wales, and

(b) for a court in Northern Ireland, a question of the law of Northern Ireland."

Issues of foreign law are therefore not subject to appeal under s.69 and the provision that an arbitration is to be conducted by foreign law will exclude this section.[97]

One rationale for this might be that under English law, the existence and terms on foreign law are findings of fact. However, the rule appears to go wider than that. In *Egmatra AG v Marco Trading Corp*,[98] the appellant submitted that the construction of a document in accordance with Swiss law was a finding of law even if the actual terms of Swiss law were questions of fact. This was rejected by Tuckey J.: "But that is not the point here. The Judge may be deciding questions of law but he would obviously not be deciding questions of the law of England and Wales."[99]

---

[94] *President of India v Jadranska Slobodna Plovidna* [1992] 2 Lloyd's Rep. 274 at 278, per Hobhouse J. Before the 1996 Act came into force, procedural irregularities and misconduct were addressed by ss.22 and 23 of the Arbitration Act 1950.
[95] [2002] EWHC 2812 (Comm); [2003] 1 All E.R. (Comm) 405.
[96] See *SOS Corp Alimentaria v Inerco Trade* [2010] EWHC 162 (Comm) at [30]–[33]. It is clear from this decision that only very extreme facts would give rise to a successful appeal against the exercise of a discretion.
[97] *Egmatra AG v Marco Trading Corp* [1999] 1 Lloyd's Rep. 862; *Sanghi Polyesters Ltd (India) v The International Investor (KCFC) Kuwait* [2000] 1 Lloyd's Rep. 480; *Reliance Industries Ltd v Enron Oil and Gas India Ltd* [2002] 1 Lloyd's Rep. 645; *Athletic Union of Constantinople v National Basketball Association* [2002] 1 Lloyd's Rep. 305.
[98] [1999] 1 Lloyd's Rep. 862.
[99] [1999] 1 Lloyd's Rep. 862 at 865.

The rule that there is no jurisdiction to hear appeals from arbitrations governed by foreign law is simple and absolute. Indeed, it even applies if the foreign law in question is identical to English law on the particular issue in dispute.[100] The arbitrators would still be applying foreign law, but simply a foreign law "which happened to be the same as English law on this topic".[101]

"ARISING OUT OF AN AWARD"

21–023   The question of law to be appealed must be one arising out of an award. The award in question may be either an interim or final award, but it appears that purely procedural matters, such as orders for disclosure, will not be susceptible of appeal pursuant to s.69 of the Act.[102]

Where a tribunal has only made a provisional award and has (for the purposes of doing so) declined to take into account a particular issue, that issue cannot be said to arise out of that provisional award. It therefore cannot be considered by the courts on appeal.[103] In *Universal Petroleum Co Ltd v Handels und Transport GmbH*,[104] Kerr L.J. stressed that the question of law must arise out of the award and not simply out of the arbitration.

It seems unlikely, however, that the effect of this limitation is to prevent legal arguments being pursued which are advanced before the arbitration tribunal but then not do not feature in the award.[105]

However, in *Checkpoint Ltd v Strathclyde Pension Fund*,[106] the arbitrator engaged in post-award correspondence in which he answered questions put to him concerning the reasons for his award. The appellant sought

---

[100] *Reliance Industries Ltd v Enron Oil and Gas India Ltd* [2002] 1 Lloyd's Rep. 645.

[101] [2002] 1 Lloyd's Rep. 645 at [30], per Aikens J.

[102] *Urban Small Space Ltd v Burford Investment* [1990] 28 E.G. 116, a case decided under the 1979 Act. On a narrow reading of *Urban Small Space*, it is more obviously an authority for the proposition that no appeal will be entertained unless it substantially affects the rights of the parties, consistent with *The Nema* guidelines and (now) s.69(3)(a) of the 1996 Act. However, the judgment implies that a question of law is only susceptible to appeal if it would necessarily arise at the substantive hearing, and it is thus generally accepted that this would support the contention that only questions arising out of the award may be appealed: e.g. Merkin, *Arbitration Law*. One potential importance of such a distinction is that consensual appeals need not clear the hurdles erected under s.69(3).

[103] *BMBF (No.12) Ltd v Harland and Wolff Shipbuilding and Heavy Industries Ltd* [2001] EWCA Civ 862. The court will not grant permission to appeal on a question of law not raised before the tribunal: s.69(3)(b), addressed at para.21–035, but that might be said to be a slightly different point.

[104] [1987] 1 W.L.R. 1178.

[105] In *Marklands v Virgin Retail* [2003] EWHC 3428 (Ch); [2004] 2 E.G.L.R. 43 at [22], Lewison J. said that if the alleged point of law is not dealt with in the award, he did not see how it could be said that the question of law arises out of the award; further, it was impossible in those circumstances to say that that the determination of the question "will" substantially affect the rights of the parties, as required by s.69(3)(a). However, the judge acknowleged that his approach might be thought "over-technical" and went on to consider the challenge on its merits.

[106] [2002] EWHC 439 (Ch). The point did not arise on appeal ([2003] EWCA Civ 84; [2003] 1 E.G.L.R. 1).

to appeal the award on the basis of this correspondence, alleging that the answers it contained disclosed a misunderstanding of the law on the arbitrator's part. Park J. refused to grant leave to appeal, but in doing so he considered (a little reluctantly) some parts of this post-award correspondence and appeared to accept that it was theoretically possible for an error of law in the reasoning underlying the award to be "revealed" by explanations provided by the tribunal after the award and the accompanying reasons were published. If that is right, it would follow that "arising out of an award" does not necessarily mean "apparent on the face of the award".

ONLY PARTIES TO THE ARBITRATION MAY BRING AN APPEAL

Any appeal to be brought under the AA 1996 must be brought by a party to the arbitration.   21–024

The arbitration tribunal itself is not to be considered to be a party for the purposes of bringing an appeal.[107]

PRE-CONDITIONS

Section 69(2)

Once the court's jurisdiction has been established under s.69(1) of the AA 1996, it must then consider whether an appeal may actually be brought. Section 69(2) identifies certain pre-conditions: 21–025

> "(2) An appeal shall not be brought under this section except—
>
> (a) with the agreement of all the other parties to the proceedings, or
> (b) with the leave of the court.
>
> The right to appeal is also subject to the restrictions in section 70(2) and (3)."

The requirement that either the parties agree (i.e. consensual appeals), or the court gives leave (appeals with permission of court), is addressed immediately below.

---

[107] *Vascroft (Contractors) Ltd v Seeboard Plc* (1996) 78 B.L.R. 132, a case decided under the 1979 Act. The proposition that a tribunal should be considered a "party" was described as "fanciful" by H.H.J. Lloyd QC, since—carried to its logical but extreme conclusion—it would mean that an arbitrator could send his own award to be appealed in the face of the opposition of those parties actually affected by the award.

Section 70(2): exhausting options

21–026 Some further preconditions to the making of an appeal are imposed by s.70(2). This provides that:

> "(2) An application or appeal may not be brought if the applicant or appellant has not first exhausted—
>
> (a) any available arbitral process of appeal or review, and
> (b) any available recourse under section 57 (correction of award or additional award)."

Appellate body

21–027 The parties are required by s.70(2)(a) to exhaust any arbitral process of appeal or review. If the arbitration is being conducted pursuant to fixed set of institutional rules, and that institution has an appellate body (such as the GAFTA Board of Appeal), any scope to appeal to that body must first be exhausted.

It is only when these "internal" appeals have run their course that the parties can seek recourse to the courts.

Correcting awards

21–028 Section 70(2)(b) requires the parties to first seek any available recourse under s.57 before lodging an appeal.[108] Section 57 re-enacts the power to correct slips which had previously existed in s.17 of the Arbitration Act 1950. It allows the arbitrators to rectify clerical mistakes or errors in an award, and has been held to encompass errors in mathematical calculations.[109] It may also be that, where the problem is that the reasons given by the tribunal are inadequate, the solution is for an application to be made under s.57 for further and better reasons—and possibly even that, if this is not done, a challenge or appeal premised on the inadequacy of the reasons will not be available.

This "slip rule" power under s.57 is, however, a non-mandatory provision within the meaning of the Act. It is open to the parties to exclude it. This is further made clear by the wording of s.57(1).[110] Should the parties decide to do so, it must follow that there is no available recourse under s.57 and this aspect of s.70(2) ceases to be relevant.

---

[108] This section was applied to bar appeals in *Groundshire v VHE Construction* [2001] EWHC 8 (TCC). See also *Torch Offshore LLC v Cable Shipping Inc* [2004] EWHC 787 (Comm); [2004] 2 Lloyd's Rep. 446.

[109] *Danae Air Transport SA v Air Canada* [2000] 1 W.L.R. 395.

[110] "The parties are free to agree on the powers of the tribunal to correct an award or make an additional award."

CONSENSUAL APPEALS: NO NEED FOR PERMISSION

Should the parties wish, s.69(2)(a) of the AA 1996 allows them to dispense **21–029** with the need to obtain permission to appeal. This can be agreed before the award is given; indeed, for obvious reasons, it is unusual for the successful party to consent to his opponent having permission to appeal *after* the award has been published.

Where parties have agreed to allow appeal of the award, then provided there is a point of English law involved, the court has no discretion to refuse to hear the appeal (e.g. because it takes the view that the decision was probably correct). However, it is submitted that all of the other pre-conditions to an appeal (e.g. ss.69(1), 70(2) and 70(3)) will still need to be met including that the appeal concern a question of English law.[110a]

In the arbitration clause

Mutual agreement to the bringing of an appeal is usually arrived at by the **21–030** inclusion of express words evincing this intention, and this practice is common in certain standard form contracts, particularly in the construction industry.[111] In *Vascroft (Contractors) Ltd v Seeboard Plc*,[112] the parties used a DOM/2 standard form contract which contained, at cl.38.7, the following words:

> "The parties hereby agree and consent pursuant to sections 1(3)(a) and 2(1)(b) of the Arbitration Act 1979 that either party ... may appeal to the High Court on a point of law arising out of an award."

H.H.J. Lloyd QC held that these words were sufficient to dispense with the need for leave.[113] The effect of such wording will be to allow the appeal to be heard without the need to meet the tests imposed by s.69(3) and (4).[114]

[110a] See *Guangzhou Dockyards v ENE Aegiali* [2010] EWHC 2826 (Comm).

[111] The JCT standard forms of contract have long specified that, where the parties agree to arbitration of disputes, they also agree that they should be entitled to appeal points of law: see cl.41.6.1 of the JCT Standard Form Contract, 1980 edn, cl.41B.4 of the 1998 edn and cl.9.7 of the 2005 edn.

[112] (1996) 78 B.L.R. 132, a case decided under s.1(3)(a) of the 1979 Act, the predecessor to s.69(2)(a) of the 1996 Act.

[113] It is interesting to note that H.H.J. Lloyd QC indicated that he would not have granted leave to appeal if it had been required—notwithstanding the fact that the appeal was actually successful.

[114] *The Trade Nomad* [1998] 1 Lloyd's Rep. 57 (a rare example of such a clause outside the construction industry); *Taylor Woodrow Civil Engineering Ltd v Hutchison IDH Development Ltd* (1998) 75 Con. L.R. 1 (in which it was held that the agreement that the parties should have leave to appeal in a JCT standard form should have effect under the 1996 Act although it referred to the 1979 Act); *Robin Ellis Ltd v Vinexsa International* [2003] EWHC 1352 (TCC); [2003] B.L.R. 373 (following *Taylor Woodrow v Hutchison); BR Cantrell v Wright & Fuller Ltd* [2003] EWHC 1545 (TCC); [2003] B.L.R. 412, *Kershaw Mechanical Services Ltd v Kendrick Construction Ltd* [2006] EWHC 727 (TCC).

No particular form of words is required. The suggestion that (given the wider policy of the AA 1996) an agreement pursuant to s.69(2) must be "expressed in the clearest terms" has been rejected; rather the court should apply ordinary principles of construction to determine what has been agreed.[115]

Once the arbitration is underway

21–031   Agreement to an appeal being made can also be reached at a later stage,[116] although it is fair to say that this is much less common.

Effect of agreement

21–032   It seems that the approach taken by a court to an appeal from an award brought pursuant to an agreement of this type is not fundamentally different from its approach to any other arbitration appeal.[117]

PERMISSION TO APPEAL

Introduction

21–033   In the absence of agreement, permission to appeal is required.

In order for permission to appeal to be granted, the court must be satisfied[118]:

(1) that the determination of the question will substantially affect the rights of one or more of the parties,
(2) that the question is one which the tribunal was asked to determine,
(3) that, on the basis of the findings of fact in the award—

---

[115] See *RSA v BAE Systems* [2008] 1 Lloyd's Rep. 712 at [30].

[116] In *The Chrysalis* [1983] 1 Lloyd's Rep. 503, it appears that the parties reached an agreement before the award was published that each should have the right to appeal to the High Court on any question of law arising out of any award made by the arbitrator.

[117] In *The Chysalis* [1983] 1 Lloyd's Rep. 503, Mustill J. rejected the submission that a different approach should be taken because the parties had agreed in advance that there should be an appeal. See also *Kershaw Mechanical Services Ltd v Kendrick Construction Ltd* [2006] EWHC 727 (TCC), in which Jackson J. held (again in the context of a consensual appeal) that where the arbitrator's experience assists him in determining a question of law, such as the interpretation of contractual documents or correspondence passing between members of his own trade or industry, the court will accord some deference to the arbitrator's decision on that question. The court will only reverse that decision if it is satisfied that the arbitrator, despite the benefit of his relevant experience, has come to the wrong answer. See especially [57].

[118] AA 1996 s.69(3).

(a) the decision of the tribunal on the question is obviously wrong, or

(b) the question is one of general public importance and the decision of the tribunal is at least open to serious doubt, and

(4) that, despite the agreement of the parties to resolve the matter by arbitration, it is just and proper in all the circumstances for the court to determine the question.

These criteria represent a codification (albeit with some new features[119]) of the House of Lords' guidelines in *The Nema*,[120] which were restated in *The Antaios*.[121]

Substantial effect on the rights of the parties

The first requirement is that "the determination of the question will sub- **21–034** stantially affect the rights of one or more of the parties". The "rights" in question must be those at issue in the arbitration.[122]

This means that the appeal must have the potential[123] to affect the substantive outcome of the arbitration.[124] Permission will not be given if the award will stand on other grounds, such that the question of law becomes hypothetical.[125] Nor are procedural orders ever likely to be able to pass this test.[126]

The size of the overall sum at stake is often invoked by one side or another in this context, although it seems unlikely that the precise figure will ever be the deciding factor.[127]

Question which the tribunal was asked to determine

The next requirement is that: "the question is one which the tribunal was **21–035** asked to determine."[128]

---

[119] *The Northern Pioneer* [2002] EWCA Civ 1878. See also the discussion in *The Agios Dimitrios* [2005] 1 Lloyds Rep. 23.
[120] [1982] 1 A.C. 724.
[121] [1985] A.C. 191.
[122] *The Northern Pioneer* [2002] EWCA Civ 1878 at [17].
[123] But (it is submitted) not that they inevitably would, whatever might be implied by Lewison J. in *Marklands v Virgin Retail* [2003] EWHC 3428 (Ch) at [22]. If the tribunal has made an error in relation to the legal test to be applied, that would appear sufficient, even if it is impossible to predict whether, if and when the correct test is applied, a different result would be obtained.
[124] *DDT Trucks v DDT Holdings* [2007] 2 Lloyd's Rep. 213 at [33]–[34].
[125] *Torch Offshore LLC v Cable Shipping Inc* [2004] 2 All E.R. (Comm) 365.
[126] *Urban Small Spaces Ltd v Burford Investment Co* [1990] 28 E.G. 116.
[127] In *Miranos International Trading v VOC Steel Services* [2005] EWHC 1812 (Comm), Cooke J. was satisfied that the appeal would substantially affect the rights of the parties despite acknowledging that the sums involved were not large (US$38,322.90).
[128] AA 1996 s.69(3)(b).

This means that the would-be appellant cannot raise by way of appeal a point which was not canvassed at all before the tribunal.[129] Of course, that should not prevent a party appealing on an issue of law which was raised, but not properly dealt with in the award.

It also appears that, if the tribunal does in fact decide a point which was not put to it, that will qualify for this purpose as a question the arbitration tribunal was asked to determine.[130]

This restriction does not apply to the respondent to an arbitration appeal. A party which is responding to an application for permission to appeal may rely on reasons which were not expressed (or not fully expressed) in the award.[131] However, it is necessary to be careful where a party has lost on one issue, but won on another, so as to make the outcome of the other issue irrelevant to the final result. If the court overturns the decision of the tribunal on the second issue, it is not clear whether the respondent can successfully contend by way of response that the result on the first issue was wrong without making an application of his own.[132]

Question of general public importance and the decision is "at least open to serious doubt"

21–036 Next, the court must be satisfied either that:

(1) the question is one of general public importance and the decision of the tribunal is at least open to serious doubt; or
(2) the decision of the tribunal on the question is obviously wrong.

General public importance

21–037 The threshold is lower in relation to cases of "general public importance" (as it was in *The Nema*) because these will be cases in which the guidance of the court is likely to be more valuable. In *The Nema* the distinction was justified on the basis that it was required "to add to the certainty and clarity of the common law".[133]

---

[129] *The Northern Pioneer*, in which (at [34]) it was held that, although leading counsel had virtually conceded the point, he did enough to prevent being shut out under s.69(3)(b) from seeking to appeal against the arbitrators' finding. Contrast this with *Surefire Systems v Guardian ECL* [2005] B.L.R. 534 in which there was no mention in the arbitration of the clause on which reliance was subsequently placed (see [37]–[38]).

[130] See *Omnibridge Consulting Ltd v Clearsprings (Management) Ltd* [2004] EWHC 2276 (Comm). This might also found a challenge pursuant to s.68. See para.22–010.

[131] See, by way of illustration, CPR PD 62 para.12.3.

[132] The respondent to the appeal in *The Mary Nour* [2008] 1 Lloyd's Rep. 250 was unable to do so, but was advancing the (rather unlikely) proposition that, in this context, even findings of fact could be challenged. Field J. made clear (at [13]) that a respondent must show that the tribunal erred in law so that, if any of the relevant findings are mixed findings of fact and law, there will only be an error of law if the tribunal misdirected itself or no tribunal properly instructed as to the relevant law could have come to the determination reached.

[133] [1982] A.C. 724 at 743, per Lord Diplock.

This suggests that the purpose behind a finding of "general public importance" must be to add to the jurisprudence on a question, rather than merely providing another factual illustration of an established principle. It has also been observed that the "public" in this context may not be the man on the Clapham omnibus, so much as the man in the Baltic Exchange.[134]

The construction of standard form contracts will generally be of general public importance,[135] as will broader points of law relating to, e.g. frustration, or the way in which a particular (and recurrent) type of notice is to be given.[136] By contrast, where the case concerns events unlikely to recur or a "one-off" case,[137] or the meaning of individually negotiated clauses,[138] the test of general public importance will not be met.

An issue of general public importance may arise where there can be seen to be a divergence of opinion on the legal question by experienced commercial arbitrators.[139] But it cannot be enough in itself that the judge disagrees with the particular tribunal (else the test might become rather circular).

Value is not necessarily a guide to "public importance". A relatively low value claim can still be of public importance.[140]

Open to serious doubt

This threshold is generally considered to be fairly low, although it still requires the judge to feel some uncertainty about the correctness of the decision arrived at.

21–038

In *The Northern Pioneer*[141] it was held that this new test was less restrictive than Lord Diplock's "strong prima facie case". Indeed, it was suggested that the fact that there was a difference of view between experienced arbitrators provided in itself grounds for contending the majority decision was at least open to serious doubt.[142] Certainly where an issue has been the subject of differing views in different arbitrations and has become a "hot topic" for articles in the trade press for the particular market sector, it is common for permission to be given even where one suspects that the judge considering the application agrees with the decision reached by the arbitration tribunal in the award under appeal.

---

134 *The Antaios* [1985] A.C. 191.
135 *The Lipa* [2001] 2 Lloyd's Rep. 17.
136 *The Rio Sun* [1981] 2 Lloyd's Rep. 489 at 495 and 497.
137 *The Kelaniya* [1988] 1 Lloyd's Rep. 30 at 32, per Lord Donaldson.
138 *The Nema* [1982] A.C. 724 at 736–738.
139 *Aden Refinery v Ugland* [1986] 2 Lloyd's Rep. 336 at 341, per Lord Donaldson M.R.— albeit just expressing a view.
140 *The Livanita* [2008] 1 Lloyd's Rep. 86 at [11]—Langley J. citing Tomlinson J.'s reasons for granting permission.
141 [2002] EWCA Civ 1878.
142 See [64].

Obviously wrong

21–039 More often, however, the potential appeal concerns an issue of no general public importance (albeit perhaps of considerable importance to the party who believes it to have been wrongly decided). In such a case, the court will only give permission for an appeal if the decision can be said to be "obviously wrong". This is a very much higher hurdle for the party seeking to appeal to clear.

The essence of the test seems to be that it should not require any careful consideration for the error of law to be apparent to the judge considering the application.

The error must normally be apparent on the face of the award itself, albeit that the court may also look at documents expressly referred to in the award which the court needs to read in order to determine a question of law arising out of the award.[143] The court is looking for a clear and obvious error on the face of the award. This should not require minute textual analysis of the award to emerge.[144]

It should be noted that the courts will usually be very deferential to an experienced arbitral panel, especially when industry experience can be said to have a bearing on the issue.[145]

Just and proper in all the circumstances

21–040 The court retains a residual discretion to refuse to grant permission to appeal.[146] This discretion was established in authorities decided under the 1979 Act, but which are generally understood to remain good law. It appears to remain possible for permission to be refused despite the judge considering the application reaching the view that, for example, the arbitrators were obviously wrong.[147]

In practice, it is rare to see permission refused when the test for obtaining permission is otherwise met. However, the courts have shown reluctance in the past to grant permission to appeal:

(1) where the parties have agreed to hold a quick arbitration to ascertain their rights for the purposes of future performance of the relevant contract[148];

---

[143] *Kershaw v Kendrick* [2006] EWHC 727 (TCC); [2006] 4 All E.R. 79; *The VOC Gallant* [2009] 1 Lloyd's Rep. 418.

[144] *Kershaw v Kendrick* [2006] EWHC 727 (TCC); [2006] 4 All E.R. 79 at [57], per Jackson J.

[145] *Kershaw v Kendrick* at [57]) and *Braes of Doune Wind Farm v Alfred McAlpine* [2008] 1 B.L.R. 321 at [31] (where it appears to have been linked to the question of whether it is just and proper for there to be an appeal—see the next section). See also *Novologistics v Five Ocean* [2009] EWHC 3046 (Comm) at [13]–[15].

[146] For a discussion of the reasons for this, see the DAC Report, paras 289–290.

[147] See *Braes of Doune Wind Farm v Alfred McAlpine* [2008] 1 B.L.R. 321 at [31].

[148] *The Nema* [1982] A.C. 724, followed in *National Rumour Co SA v Lloyd-Libra Navegacao SA* [1982] 1 Lloyd's Rep. 472, in which it was decided that both sides were seeking a quick arbitration in order that they might know what their rights were so as to regulate their future conduct.

(2) where it appears that the intention of the parties was that the award would be final, even in the absence of a clear exclusion agreement. Thus, where there was a stipulation that the tribunal's award was to be "final and binding", this was taken into account by the court when determining whether it would be "just and proper" to grant leave to appeal[149];

(3) where it appears to the court that the party seeking permission is "hell bent on taking almost every point and to avail themselves of every procedure" to challenge the decisions of the arbitrator, irrespective of cost and resources.[150] There may also be cases in which the real aim appears to be delay by the party ordered to pay money, although it is difficult to identify any reported case in which permission has been refused on this basis. It is also true to say that there are other ways of addressing this last problem, at least in the extreme case in which there is clear evidence of an intention to use delay caused by the appeal to dissipate assets.[151]

In one very unusual case, it was suggested that permission might be refused where the result of reaching a different decision on an issue of law from that reached by the arbitration tribunal would be to create a serious injustice (e.g. because the arbitration tribunal had allowed a new point to be taken at the very last minute and then decided that point, wrongly, against the party raising it).[152]

Conditional leave/security

The court can impose conditions upon the grant of permission to appeal.[153] **21–041**
These include providing security for costs on the usual grounds,[154] or even requiring that any money payable under the award be brought into court. It has been pointed out, however, that "the Court is in most cases rather unlikely to find it appropriate to impose such a condition under s.69,

---

[149] *Essex CC v Premier Recycling* [2006] EWHC 3594 (TCC); [2007] B.L.R. 233. This obviously assumes that those words are insufficiently clear to oust the court's jurisdiction altogether pursuant to s.69(1), since if they could do so the question would never arise. See generally paras 21–007 and 21–008.

[150] *Trustees of Edward Stern Settlement v Levy (No.2)* [2009] 1 Lloyd's Rep. 345 at [29], per Akenhead J.

[151] e.g. giving conditional leave, or even awarding a freezing injunction.

[152] See *Icon Navigation v Sinochem* [2004] 1 All E.R. (Comm) 405. If a respondent wished to take a point like this, it might be appropriate for there to be an oral hearing of the permission application. See especially at [27].

[153] ss.70(6)–(8) of AA 1996.

[154] e.g. CPR r.25.13 (but not on the ground that applicant is based outside the UK). See *Azov Shipping v Baltic Shipping (No.2)* [1999] 2 Lloyd's Rep. 39 (where an order was made in a s.67 case on the basis that there was considerable doubt as to the existence of any arrangements in the Ukraine for the enforcement of foreign costs orders including costs orders of this court; and the involvement of a foreign creditor would make an enforcement a more difficult and time consuming exercise; see at 44).

bearing in mind the stringency of the criteria which must be satisfied by an applicant for leave to appeal under that section".[155]

Footnote: lower threshold for appeals on points of EU law

21–042   The test for granting permission to appeal may however be slightly different if it concerns a point of EU law. In *Nordsee*[156] the European Court of Justice held that domestic courts have a duty, when considering appeals against arbitration awards, to ensure the uniform application of EU law.

This was applied in *Bulk Oil (Zug) AG v Sun International (No.1)*,[157] in which the Court of Appeal found that it would not be appropriate to apply the *Nema* guidelines where a case raised a difficult point of EU law, of importance to a range of countries. In such a case, it was sufficient for permission to be given if it could be shown that the disputed point of EU law was "capable of serious argument".

It is suggested that this position has not been affected by the Arbitration Act 1996.

THE APPLICATION FOR LEAVE TO APPEAL

21–043   The application for leave to appeal must be made in accordance with CPR Pt 49.

Timing

21–044   The application must be made within 28 days of the making of the award, or (where there is scope for an appeal within the arbitration procedure itself) notification to the applicant of the result of the appeal.[158]

It seems likely that, if an application for clarification is made under the slip rule (s.57 of AA 1996), time does not run for the purpose of an appeal until the arbitration tribunal has responded to that application in one way or another.[159]

An application may be made to the court for an extension of time under s.80(5) of AA 1996, although it appears to be necessary to show that the

---

[155] See *Peterson Farms v C&M Farming* [2003] EWHC 2298 (QB) at [18].

[156] Case 102/81 [1982] ECR 1095

[157] [1983] 1 Lloyd's Rep. 587.

[158] AA 1996 s.70(3): "Any application or appeal must be brought within 28 days of the date of the award or, if there has been any arbitral process of appeal or review, of the date when the applicant or appellant was notified of the result of that process."

[159] See *Al Hadha Trading Co v Tradigrain SA* [2002] 2 Lloyd's Rep. 512 and *Surefire v Guardian* [2005] EWHC 1860 (TCC); [2005] 1 B.L.R. 534 at [27], although this is not as clear as might be expected because s.70(3) of AA 1996 mentions appeals and arbitral process of review, but not the s.57 procedure. See, for a different perspective, *RC Pillar v Edwards*, January 11, 2001, an unreported decision of H.H.J. Thornton QC.

appeal is a strong one and that there was a good reason for the delay.[160] The application for an extension can be made without notice if the 28 day period has not yet expired.[161] Once the 28 day period has expired, the application for an extension must be made in the arbitration claim form.[162]

Procedural requirements

An arbitration claim must include a concise statement of the remedy claimed and the question on which the decision of the court is sought, making clear under which section of AA 1996 it is brought.[163]

21–045

In an application pursuant to s.69, the claim form must identify the question of law to be determined and the grounds on which it is alleged permission to appeal should be granted.[164] It is necessary to identify precisely the arbitration award challenged and, if appropriate, the parts or points of the award which are challenged and the grounds for that challenge.

It does seem that the court can reformulate the question identified, if it appears necessary, and is not compelled to dismiss the application just because the question identified is not properly a question of law.[165] But it is probably also true to say that the court is not obliged to do so and could simply refuse the application on the basis that the question of law has not been sufficiently clearly identified.

If any other order is sought (e.g. an order requiring the arbitration tribunal to provide reasons for its award), this would usually be sought together with the application for permission to appeal. The claim form should also identify against which (if any) defendant a costs order is sought.[166] In the usual way, a Statement of Truth will need to be signed by the applicant or his solicitor.

An Arbitration Claim Form may be issued at any of the following courts:

(1) the Admiralty and Commercial Registry at the RCJ in London, in which case it will be entered into the Commercial list;
(2) the TCC Registry at St Dunstan's House, London, where it will be entered into the TCC list;

---

[160] The requirements in this regard seem very similar to those for extensions of time in relation to other types of arbitration applications. See *Surefire v Guardian* [2005] EWHC 1860 (TCC); [2005] 1 B.L.R. 534 at [28] which refers to *AOOT Kalmmneft v Glencore* [2002] 1 Lloyd's Rep. 128 (a s.68 case).

[161] See CPR r.62.9(2). It should be made by way of CPR Pt 23 application—see CPR 62 PD para.11.1(1).

[162] CPR r.62.9(3).

[163] See generally CPR r.62.4(1).

[164] AA 1996 s.69(4) and CPR r.62.4(1).

[165] See, for example, *HOK Sport v Aintree Racecourse* [2003] B.L.R. 155.

[166] CPR r.62.4(1)(e).

(3) a District Registry of the High Court where there is a Mercantile Court, in which case the application will be entered into the Mercantile list;

(4) the District Registry of the High Court for a local TCC List.[167]

Appeals in arbitrations with an IT or construction element, and especially those in which the applicant is represented by counsel or solicitors who regularly practice in the TCC, are often issued in the main TCC list. Most other arbitration appeals will be listed in the Commercial Court.

Where an arbitration relates to a landlord and tenant or partnership dispute, however, the arbitration claim form must be issued in the Chancery Division.[168]

It should also be noted that the Commercial Court retains primary responsibility for the administration and monitoring of arbitrations.

An arbitration claim form can only be inspected with the permission of the court.[169-170]

The approach to settling the application for permission

21–046   Given that the decision as to whether or not to grant permission is made on paper and is final (see below), practitioners have to argue the case at some length in the application notice, rather than simply setting out the grounds in the manner which might once have been preferred (when the grounds were simply going to be the jumping-off point for an oral application). This tendency towards prolix applications has been addressed in the new Practice Direction at paras 12.1–12.3. It is provided that the claim form must be accompanied by a skeleton argument of no more than 15 pages in length.

It has been suggested by the Court of Appeal that the intention behind the statutory requirement that application for permission to appeal should be dealt with on paper unless the court otherwise directed was to simplify the procedure and save the court's time. It was said that, as a result, any written submission placed before the court in support of an application for permission to appeal from findings in an arbitral award should normally be capable of being read and digested by the judge within the half-hour that used to be allotted for such applications.[171]

On the other hand, it is certainly insufficient simply to assert that the arbitrator was wrong and it is probably fair to say that the vast majority of applications for permission are more fully argued than this reference to the material being read and digested by the judge within 30 minutes would suggest. However, the limit of 15 pages (and requirement that, if a longer

---

[167] CPR PD 62 para.2.3(1).
[168] CPR PD 62 para.2.3(2).
[169-170] See CPR PD 62 para.5.1.
[171] See *The Northern Pioneer* [2002] EWCA Civ 1878 at [23]. But this is obviously not to be understood as an absolute restriction. See *Braes of Doune Wind Farm v Alfred McAlpine* [2008] 1 B.L.R. 321 at [28].

document is prepared, the writer must explain in court why) may bring practice back into line with what the court obviously wants.

Evidence in support

Evidence which is admissible on an application for leave to appeal is strictly limited, and will generally comprise only: **21–047**

(1) the award itself;
(2) any evidence related to the issue of whether the question of law is of general public importance[172]; and
(3) evidence to show that the issue substantially affects the rights of the parties.[173]

Pleadings and evidence from the underlying arbitration should not usually be provided, but it may be appropriate to exhibit a complete copy of any contract which falls to be construed and any other document which the court would need to read in order properly to consider the question of law arising out of the award.[174]

It may be necessary to show (by reference to the "pleadings", or written submissions in the arbitration) that the question was one which the arbitrator was asked to determine,[175] although it is not usual to deal with this until the point is put in issue by the respondent.

It had become common for parties to file evidence in support of (or in opposition to) the appeal which is directed to the issue of whether the decision itself was wrong as a matter of law.[176]

Judges disapproved of this practice:

"... submissions need not be set out in a witness statement since that is a document that places admissible evidence and not legal argument before the court (see CPR 32.4(1)). All that the witness statement served by the parties should do is to identify the evidence relied on for the purpose of showing that the requirements of section 69(3) of the Arbitration Act 1996 are or are not met and that served by the defendant should additionally state the grounds of opposing the grant

---

[172] e.g. copies of standard form contracts with equivalent or analogous clauses.

[173] See CPR PD 62 para.12.4.

[174] See *Kershaw v Kendrick* [2006] EWHC 727 (TCC); [2006] 4 All E.R. 79 at [45], per Jackson J. See also *Sylvia Shipping v Progress Bulk Carriers* [2010] EWHC 542 (Comm) at [85]–[88]. See also CPR PD 62 para.12.5.

[175] *Surefire Systems Ltd v Guardian ECL Ltd* [2005] EWHC 1860 (TCC) at [22]. By contrast, it was emphasised in that case that the court should not be burdened with vast tracts of inadmissible evidence, nor should the court be burdened with many pages of intricate argument about the factual issues which the arbitrator has decided. It was said that the preparation of such material was a waste of time, effort and costs.

[176] This often takes the form of the statement maker expressing his or her amazement at the decision and predicting reverberations around the "industry" as a result.

of permission. Thus, the witness statements should be succinct and confined to evidence" (per H.H.J. Thornton in *HOK Sport v Aintree Racecourse* [2003] 1 B.L.R. 155 at [19]).

This has now been addressed in para.12.4 of the Practice Direction to Pt 62.[176a]

Service

21–048   The application must be served on the other party to the arbitration, who is made a respondent to the application.[177] Once issued, the arbitration claim form is valid for one month and must be served within that period.[178]

Service can be effected out of the jurisdiction if the seat of the arbitration was in England, Wales or Northern Ireland.[179]

Responding to an application

21–049   If the respondent to an appeal wishes to contend that the award should be upheld for reasons not expressed (or not fully expressed) in the award, he must make this clear.[180]

More generally, the respondent has 21 days[181] from the date of service of the arbitration claim form[182] or the date on which he was required to acknowledge service to file his notice and supporting evidence setting out any material which it is suggested the court should take into account for the purposes of deciding the application for permission. The only evidence which it is appropriate for a respondent to put forward at this stage would be any *factual* material directly relevant to whether the pre-conditions to the grant of permission to appeal are fulfilled, such as whether the legal questions identified arise out of the award, were live before the tribunal, will substantially affect the rights of the parties, are of general public importance, etc.

Of course, a respondent must have regard to the fact that, if permission is granted, the next document he puts before the court is likely to be a skeleton argument shortly before the appeal hearing. As such, if his arguments more generally are likely to require reference to documents which the

---

[176a] See also the provision covering cost penalties at CPR PD 62 para.12.11.

[177] See CPR r.62.6.

[178] CPR r.62.4(2).

[179] CPR r.62.5(1). The application must be supported by written evidence stating the grounds on which the application is made and showing in what place or country the respondent is or probably may be found. See CPR r.62.5(2).

[180] See CPR PD 62 para.12.6(2).

[181] It should be noted that there is a shorter seven day period for entering evidence opposing an application for an extension of time—see CPR r.62.9(3).

[182] Or from the date of service of any order granting a retrospective extension of time. See CPR r.62.9(3)(c).

applicant has not put in evidence, it may be appropriate to exhibit them now.[182a]

Replying

If evidence in response is served, the applicant has seven days to provide any   **21–050**
evidence in reply.[183] There is usually only real value in entering a reply if an
issue of substance is raised (e.g. that a point was not taken in the arbitration
and thus does not qualify as a question arising out of the award), in which
case it may be necessary to obtain a short extension to this time period.

In practice, however, applicants are often unable to resist the temptation
to respond to arguments raised in relation to the merits of the appeal in the
respondent's witness statement, even if it seems unlikely that the judge will
find this of any assistance.[183a]

Oral hearing

Under s.69(5), the court can determine an application for leave to appeal on   **21–051**
paper and without any oral hearing, unless it appears to the court that a
hearing is required.

This procedure was challenged in *BLCT (13096) v J Sainsbury Plc.*[184] It
was said that it was contrary to art.6(1) of the ECHR. But this argument
was rejected by the Court of Appeal. It was held that the parties, in opting
for arbitration, had waived the protection of a public hearing, and that as
long as the original arbitration provided a fair hearing there was no obligation under art.6 for an appeal to be provided under the general law.

In practice, applications for permission are now almost invariably dealt
with on paper. In exceptional cases, some oral argument might be
allowed,[185] most commonly if the application for permission pursuant to
s.69 has been combined with an appeal on other grounds (e.g. ss.67 and 68
of the AA 1996).[186] But if a party seeks to use a s.68 application as "cover"
in order to have the opportunity to argue the detail of its s.69 application,
that will not be permitted.[187]

[182a] But note CPR PD 62 para.12.10.

[183] CPR PD 62 para.6.3.

[183a] It remains to be seen whether CPR PD 62 para.12.9 will curb this practice.

[184] [2003] EWCA Civ 884.

[185] As the Court of Appeal acknowledged in *BLCT (13096) v J Sainsbury* [2003] EWCA Civ
884.

[186] *The Pamphilos* [2002] EWHC 2292 (Comm). But one also very occasionally sees the
application for leave combined with the substantive appeal—e.g. *HOK Sport v Aintree
Racecourse* [2003] 1 B.L.R. 155 (described by H.H.J. Thornton on that case as a "practice
is one which, in an appropriate case, is desirable since it saves costs, time and resources"—
see [3]).

[187] *Newfield v Tomlinson* [2004] EWHC 3051 (TCC)

The giving of reasons

21–052   It has now been established that the court must give short reasons when refusing permission to appeal[188]:

> (1) In *Mousaka Inc v Golden Seagull*,[189] it was suggested that the provision of reasons might satisfy curiosity but would be completely worthless.
>
> (2) However, the Court of Appeal in *North Range Shipping*[190] disagreed and decided that art.6(1) of the ECHR required that reasons be given when refusing permission to appeal under s.69. These reasons must be sufficient for a party to understand the decision, but could be very short. Indeed, it may be enough simply to identify which of the statutory tests the applicant has failed to meet.[191]

THE HEARING OF THE SUBSTANTIVE APPEAL

Material

21–053   It has often been said that, since the appeal cannot go behind the tribunal's findings of fact, there is no good reason for putting before them bundles containing material such as the submissions and evidence that were before the tribunal, or transcripts of the live evidence at the arbitration hearing. Rather, the focus ought to be on the award itself.[192]

While the principal and, often, sole document which should be considered in any appeal under s.69 of the AA 1996 is the award itself, the court should also be provided with any document (most obviously a contract or the equivalent) referred to in the award which the court needs to read in order to determine a question of law arising out of the award.[193]

An agreed indexed and paginated bundle should be prepared by the claimant.[194] The standard directions provide for the claimant to provide a chronology and skeleton argument two clear days before the hearing, with the respondent's skeleton due one clear day before the hearing (e.g. by 4pm on Wednesday for a hearing on the Friday).[195]

---

[188] PD 62 para.12.5.

[189] [2002] 2 Lloyd's Rep. 657 at [35].

[190] [2002] EWCA Civ 405.

[191] [2002] EWCA Civ 405 at [27].

[192] See *Sylvia Shipping v Progress Bulk Carriers* [2010] EWHC 542 (Comm) at [85]–[88].

[193] See *Kershaw Mechanical Services Ltd v Kendrick Construction Ltd* [2006] EWHC 727 (TCC) at [45]; *The VOC Gallant* [2009] 1 Lloyd's Rep. 418 at [6]. See CPR PD 62 para.12.15.

[194] CPR PD 62 para.6.4.

[195] See CPR PD 62 paras 6.6–6.7.

Listing

It is understood that the court will usually[196] seek to ensure that a different   **21–054**
judge will hear the substantive appeal than granted permission. This is due
to a concern that the judge granting permission would be likely to have
formed at least preliminary views as to the merits. It is probably particularly
important in cases found to have met the "obviously wrong" test
(s.69(3)(c)(i) of the AA 1996).

In public

Under CPR r.62.10, the court may order that an arbitration appeal be heard   **21–055**
either in public or in private. Subject to a contrary order by the court, an
appeal under s.69 will be heard in public.[197]

The Court of Appeal set out the considerations which are material to
deciding whether an appeal should be heard in public or in private in
Moscow City Council v Bankers Trust Co.[198]

Approach

It is probably fair to say that, once permission has been granted, an arbi-   **21–056**
tration appeal hearing does not have a great deal to distinguish it from any
other appeal hearing:

(1) the issue is whether the decision of the tribunal was wrong in
law—it is a review, not a re-hearing. But it is not necessary to show
that, for example, the decision was "obviously wrong". Once that
hurdle has been cleared for the purposes of obtaining permission
to appeal, it ceases to be relevant[199];

(2) the appellant will usually go first, with the respondent (if called
upon) answering those submissions and the appellant traditionally
granted a right of reply. But it is not uncommon for judges to alter
this order; to ask to hear what one party or another has to say
about a particular point, or even inviting the respondent to go first
if the award seems difficult to defend at first sight.

---

[196] Unless, exceptionally, the application for permission is being heard together with the
substantive appeal—see *HOK Sport v Aintree Racecourse* [2003] 1 B.L.R. 155.

[197] But not any oral hearing of the application for permission. See CPR r.62.10(4)(b).

[198] [2004] EWCA Civ 314; [2004] 2 Lloyds Rep. 179.

[199] See *Finelvet AG v Vinava Shipping Co Ltd (The Chrysalis)* [1983] 1 Lloyd's Rep. 503 at
506–507.

It should be noted that the judge hearing the appeal is not bound by the decision on any aspect of the judge granting permission.[200]

However, in much the same way as with the application for permission, the court will endeavour to read the award as a whole in a fair and reasonable way, rather than looking to pick holes in the reasoning.[201]

On the hearing of an appeal from an arbitral award, the court:

(1) will show considerable deference for the views of those perceived to be arbitrators with experience in the particular industry. There is a sense, for example, that the arbitrators selected by the parties are better placed than the court to decide how a particular risk ought to be allocated in the industry in question[202]; and

(2) will be particularly conscious that they are not to be drawn into reconsideration of issues of fact, over which the tribunal has exclusive jurisdiction.

Powers of the court

Ordering the giving of reasons

21–057   If the award does not contain any/sufficient reasons, under s.70(4) the court can require the arbitrator to give reasons.[203]

Orders in relation to the award

21–058   Under s.69(7), on an appeal, the court may confirm the award, vary the award, remit the award to the tribunal, in whole or in part, for reconsideration in the light of the court's determination or set aside the award in whole or in part.

The section further provides that the court shall not exercise its power to set aside an award, in whole or in part, unless it is satisfied that it would be inappropriate to remit the matters in question to the tribunal for reconsideration.

It does not seem that the court has a discretion to ignore what it has found to be an error of law, for example on the basis that there had been an substantial irregularity in allowing the particular issue to be raised at all.[204]

---

[200] See *Owners of the Vessel Ocean Crown v Five Oceans Salvage* [2009] EWHC 3040 (Admlty) at [53], in which Gross J. rejected the submission that he was bound by the decision on the application for permission that a question of law had arisen.

[201] *Kershaw Mechanical Services Ltd v Kendrick Construction Ltd* [2006] EWHC 727 (TCC) at [57]; *Dalwood v Nordana* [2009] EWHC 3394 (Comm) at [37].

[202] On the other hand, this may not apply if the court forms the view that the arbitration tribunal was operating under a particular disadvantage: such as where the legal issue has been decided on paper and without the benefit of oral argument (see *The Florida* [2007] 1 Lloyd's Rep. 1 at [8]).

[203] *Petroships Pte Ltd v Petec Trading & Investment Corp* [2001] 2 Lloyd's Rep. 348. This applies to applications under ss.67 and 68 as well as s.69, although the need for reasons is more obvious when the focus of the appeal is an error of law.

[204] See *Icon Navigation v Sinochem* [2004] 1 All E.R. (Comm) 405 at [22].

The effect of those possible orders is further expanded upon at s.71 of AA 1996:

> "**Section 71 Challenge or appeal: effect of order of court**
>
> (1) The following provisions have effect where the court makes an order under section 67, 68 or 69 with respect to an award.
>
> (2) Where the award is varied, the variation has effect as part of the tribunal's award.
>
> (3) Where the award is remitted to the tribunal, in whole or in part, for reconsideration, the tribunal shall make a fresh award in respect of the matters remitted within three months of the date of the order for remission or such longer or shorter period as the court may direct.
>
> (4) Where the award is set aside or declared to be of no effect, in whole or in part, the court may also order that any provision that an award is a condition precedent to the bringing of legal proceedings in respect of a matter to which the arbitration agreement applies, is of no effect as regards the subject matter of the award or, as the case may be, the relevant part of the award."

Setting aside

The power to set aside an award is rarely exercised in the context of an appeal under s.69; awards are more commonly varied or remitted to the arbitration tribunal. It is not entirely clear what happens if an award is set aside as a result of an error of law. In particular, it is not clear whether new arbitrators need to be appointed to begin the process again, whether the jurisdiction of the panel whose award has been set aside is revived, or whether the whole arbitration clause ceases to bind.   **21–059**

FURTHER APPEALS

Appealing to the Court of Appeal

For most practical purposes, the first instance judge is the only forum for an appeal pursuant to s.69 of the AA 1996.[205]   **21–060**

There is jurisdiction to grant permission to appeal to the Court of Appeal, found in:

(1) s.69(6) against the court's grant or refusal of permission to appeal from tribunal[206];

---

[205] *Mousaka* [2002] 2 Lloyd's Rep. 657 at [33], per David Steel J.
[206] Although this would now require some extraordinary circumstances to be justified. See *North Range Shipping v Seatrans Shipping* [2002] EWCA Civ 405; [2002] 1 W.L.R. 2397.

(2) s.69(8) against the substantive appeal by the court:

> "The decision of the court on an appeal under this section shall be treated as a judgment of the court for the purposes of a further appeal. But no such appeal lies without the leave of the court which shall not be given unless the court considers that the question is one of general importance or is one which for some other special reason should be considered by the Court of Appeal".

However, in either case only "the court" can grant that permission and s.105(1) makes clear that this means the court of first instance. Accordingly, there is no scope for seeking permission from the Court of Appeal if the judge has refused it.[207]

The only exceptions to this scheme are that a failure to "act judicially" has been said to justify the Court of Appeal in reconsidering a decision to grant or refuse leave[208] and that a decision which the first instance judge had no jurisdiction to make could probably also be re-considered on appeal.[209] But it would take some rather remarkable facts to justify the exercise of that "residual jurisdiction" by the Court of Appeal.

The criteria to be applied by the judge

21–061 In terms of making the decision to permit or refuse leave to appeal to the Court of Appeal, s.69(8) of the AA 1996 makes clear that it: "shall not be given unless the court considers that the question is one of general importance or is one which for some other special reason should be considered by the Court of Appeal". The aim appears to be to limit very considerably the scope for further appeals; it does not make sense to argue that, because only the judge can give permission, he or she should be willing to do so more frequently than in cases in which permission could be sought from the Court of Appeal.

In general, it is points which can genuinely be said to require appellate authority in respect of which permission should be granted, such as recurring issues,[210] issues concerning arbitrations generally, the construction of a common term in standard contract, or a point of general law.[211]

---

[207] *Henry Boot v Malmaison Hotel* [2001] Q.B. 388; *CGU Insurance v AstraZeneca Insurance* [2007] 1 Lloyd's Rep. 142 and *Kazakhstan v Istil* [2007] EWCA Civ 471; [2007] 2 Lloyd's Rep. 548.

[208] *North Range Shipping v Seatrans Shipping* [2002] EWCA Civ 405; [2002] 1 W.L.R. 2397; *BLCT (13096) Ltd v J Sainsbury Plc* [2003] EWCA Civ 884; *CGU Insurance v Astra-Zeneca Insurance* [2007] 1 Lloyd's Rep. 142.

[209] See *Cetelem v Roust* [2005] 1 W.L.R. 3555.

[210] *Aden Refinery v Ugland* [1987] Q.B. 650 (divergence in judicial opinion giving rise to need for CA to intervene).

[211] e.g. *The Agathon (No.2)* [1984] 1 Lloyd's Rep. 183 at 193.

By contrast, neither the size of the sum at stake,[212] nor the fact that judge has overturned the decision of experienced arbitrators,[213] ought to be enough. In practice, however, these are undoubtedly factors which can influence the decision.[214]

In the Court of Appeal

It should be noted that the Court of Appeal may not allow the appeal on any point not raised before the judge (see s.69(8)), but can uphold the judge's decision for different reasons.[215]   **21–062**

The Supreme Court

There is some uncertainty as to whether a further appeal can be made from the Court of Appeal to the Supreme Court (previously the House of Lords) in respect of an arbitration award. In *The Baleares*[216] it was decided (under the 1979 Act) that there was no appeal to the House of Lords against a decision of the Court of Appeal to grant or refuse permission to appeal.   **21–063**

But where there has been a substantive decision of the Court of Appeal, the issue would appear to be governed by the usual rules in respect of such an appeal. In particular, it seems that, if permission is refused by the Court of Appeal, the Supreme Court can be petitioned in the usual way. However, it seems likely that permission would only be given (whether by the Court of Appeal or the Supreme Court) in the most extreme of cases.

---

[212] *Prudential Assurance v 99 Bishopsgate* [1992] 1 E.G.L.R. 119 (concerned with s.2(3) of the 1979 Act).

[213] *The Pera* [1985] 2 Lloyd's Rep. 103 at 105.

[214] e.g. in *BMBF (No.12) v Harland & Wolff* Unreported November 17, 2000, Tomlinson J. noted that the issue he had decided was a short point of construction worth US$40m on which he had differed from an experienced panel including an ex-member of the Court of Appeal, and on this basis gave leave despite the fact that the clauses in question were "one-offs".

[215] *Vitol v Norelf* [1996] 3 All E.R. 193.

[216] [1991] 1 Lloyd's Rep. 318 HL.

CHAPTER 22

Challenging Serious Irregularity: Section 68

INTRODUCTION

22–001 A further ground for challenging an arbitration award is found in s.68 of the AA 1996 and is directed to the manner in which the tribunal has conducted itself, rather than the content of its decision:

> **"68 Challenging the award: serious irregularity**
>
> (1) A party to arbitral proceedings may (upon notice to the other parties and to the tribunal) apply to the court challenging an award in the proceedings on the ground of serious irregularity affecting the tribunal, the proceedings or the award. A party may lose the right to object (see section 73) and the right to apply is subject to the restrictions in section 70(2) and (3).
>
> (2) Serious irregularity means an irregularity of one or more of the following kinds which the court considers has caused or will cause substantial injustice to the applicant—
>
> (a) failure by the tribunal to comply with section 33 (general duty of tribunal);
> (b) the tribunal exceeding its powers (otherwise than by exceeding its substantive jurisdiction: see section 67);
> (c) failure by the tribunal to conduct the proceedings in accordance with the procedure agreed by the parties;
> (d) failure by the tribunal to deal with all the issues that were put to it;
> (e) any arbitral or other institution or person vested by the parties with powers in relation to the proceedings or the award exceeding its powers;
> (f) uncertainty or ambiguity as to the effect of the award;
> (g) the award being obtained by fraud or the award or the way in which it was procured being contrary to public policy;

(h) failure to comply with the requirements as to the form of the award; or

(i) any irregularity in the conduct of the proceedings or in the award which is admitted by the tribunal or by any arbitral or other institution or person vested by the parties with powers in relation to the proceedings or the award.

(3) If there is shown to be serious irregularity affecting the tribunal, the proceedings or the award, the court may—

(a) remit the award to the tribunal, in whole or in part, for reconsideration,

(b) set the award aside in whole or in part, or

(c) declare the award to be of no effect, in whole or in part.

The court shall not exercise its power to set aside or to declare an award to be of no effect, in whole or in part, unless it is satisfied that it would be inappropriate to remit the matters in question to the tribunal for reconsideration.

(4) The leave of the court is required for any appeal from a decision of the court under this section."

The concept of "serious irregularity" is not to be understood as containing any moral censure. The arbitration proceedings can be affected by a "serious irregularity" without there being any bias or deliberate misconduct on the part of the tribunal—although s.68 embraces that type of situation as well. **22–002**

Section 68 is mandatory,[1] so the parties cannot "contract out" of the right to challenge an award for serious irregularity.

However, a party can lose the right to object under s.68 if the objection is not made promptly.[2]

On the other hand, the parties can only invoke s.68 after an award has been rendered. There is no scope for the court to intervene during the course of an arbitration.

LIMITING SCOPE FOR OBJECTION

Listing the grounds

Section 68(2) sets out a number of grounds of "appeal" (or perhaps more accurately "objections"), under the description "serious irregularity". **22–003**

---

[1] See s.4 of AA 1996 and Sch.1.
[2] See AA 1996 s.73.

By setting out such an exhaustive list, the AA 1996 for the first time expressly limits the scope for judicial intervention. The English court has no freestanding jurisdiction to overturn procedural decisions.[3]

This list encompasses matters which would previously have been referred to as "misconduct" by the tribunal, and also grounds which might previously have justified remission (such as patently defective awards and admitted mistakes). But some grounds which were previously available appear now to have been deleted. Most obviously, none of the grounds permit an award to be challenged on the basis that evidence has come to light after it was made which is inconsistent with the award.[4] The only exception would appear to be where the evidence had in effect been suppressed by the other party (see discussion of s.68(2)(g) below). Of course, if the evidence came to light before the award was made (but, say, after the hearing), a refusal by a tribunal to admit that evidence might (depending on the circumstances) permit a challenge under s.68(2)(a) of AA 1996.[5]

It is also difficult see how the older cases in which a procedural mishap had been the result of an error by the party affected[6] fit into the new scheme. Indeed, there have been strong indications that errors by the parties or their representatives will not now permit any relief. In *The Magdalena Oldendorff*,[7] the Court of Appeal was not impressed by the suggestion that the tribunal ought to have alerted leading counsel to the fact that they considered a particular point to be important.

It has been repeatedly emphasised that s.68 is only for extreme cases,[8] and certainly not for challenging the substantive conclusions of the arbitration tribunal.[9]

22–004   In *Sinclair v Woods of Winchester*,[10] H.H.J. Peter Coulson QC (as he was) set out a useful procedural checklist for applications under s.68 (entertainingly, the particular application with which he was concerned fell at every hurdle):

   (1) an aggrieved party in an arbitration must raise its objections to the arbitration or the award forthwith or lose its right to object[11];

---

[3] See *Fletamentos Maritimos SA v Effjohn International BV (No.2)* [1997] 2 Lloyd's Rep. 302.

[4] In other words, the equivalent of *Ladd v Marshall* situation in the context of litigation.

[5] See the discussion in paras 22–010 and 22–011.

[6] Such as *The Aristides Xilas (No.2)* [1975] 2 Lloyd's Rep. 402 or *Krohn & Co v PT Tulung Agung Indah* [1992] 1 Lloyd's Rep. 377.

[7] [2007] EWCA Civ 998.

[8] See *Petroships Pte Ltd v Petec Trading and Investment Corp ("The Petro Ranger")* [2001] 2 Lloyd's Rep. 348 at 351, col.1; *ABB AG v Hochtief* [2006] EWHC 388 (Comm) (not a ground for intervention that the court considered that it might have done things differently or expressed its conclusions on the essential issues at greater length—see [67]).

[9] *Lesotho Highlands v Impregilo* [2005] UKHL 43.

[10] [2005] EWHC 1631 (QB), relying on his own unreported decision of *Benaim v Davies Middleton Davies*, June 15, 2005; [2005] EWHC 1370 (TCC).

[11] *Margulead Ltd v Exide Technologies* [2004] EWHC 1019 (Comm); *Thyssen Canada Ltd v Mariana Maritime SA* [2005] EWHC 219 (Comm).

(2) the aggrieved party cannot make an application under s.68 unless he has exhausted any available arbitral process of appeal or review or any available recourse under s.57 as to the correction of ambiguities and so on[12];

(3) the removal of an arbitrator is a "most serious step" which will only be ordered if the arbitrator's misconduct was so serious that he could not be trusted "to complete the arbitration fairly and properly even with the benefit of an examination of his conduct by the parties and their representatives and guidance from the court ..."[13]; the mere fact that one party has lost confidence in an arbitrator will not without evidence of real and substantial injustice lead to an order removing the arbitrator under s.24[14];

(4) intervention under s.68 is only permissible after an award has been made where there has been a serious irregularity which has caused or will cause substantial injustice to the applicant and falls within the closed list of categories set out in paras (a) to (i)[15];

(5) the arbitrator needs to ensure that the issues are reasonably defined by the parties or himself before he produces an award on those issues, and a failure so to do may in an extreme case be a breach of s.33[16];

(6) an arbitrator is obliged to decide only those matters which are relevant to his ultimate decision. He does not have to decide every issue put to him[17]; and

(7) it is always necessary for an applicant in the position of the Claimants to show substantial injustice as a result of the alleged serious irregularity. Substantial injustice can only be demonstrated where what has happened simply cannot on any view be defended

---

[12] *Torch Offshore LLC v Cable Shipping Inc* [2004] 2 All E.R. (Comm) 365 at [28].

[13] *Groundshire v VHE Construction* [2001] B.L.R. 395.

[14] *Conder Structures v Kavaerner Construction Ltd* [1999] A.D.R.L.J. 305. H.H.J. Coulson QC referred by way of example to *Damond Lock Grabowski v Laing Investments (Bracknell) Ltd*, 60 Build. L.R. 112 in which the judge reviewed the conduct of an arbitrator who even the party resisting the application to remove him described as "eccentric, autocratic and obsessive" and concluded: "Looking at the whole sorry history of the matter, it seems to me clear that the arbitrator has unquestionably pointed the finger at the Applicants and repeatedly accused them, in my judgment unfairly, of deliberate delay. Above all, he has not paid proper heed to their objections and has insisted that the hearing must start on the day he ordered, when they cannot be in a position to conduct their case properly. In my judgment he must be removed. I therefore grant the order asked in paragraph 1 of the notice of motion."

[15] *Lesotho Highlands Development Authority v Impregilo SPA* [2006] 1 A.C. 221 at [28] per Lord Steyn. H.H.J. Coulson QC also referred to the judgment of H.H.J. Humphrey Lloyd QC in *Weldon Plant Ltd v The Commission for the New Towns* [2000] B.L.R. 496 at [28]–[29], approved by Colman J. in *World Trade Corp v Czarnikow Sugar Ltd* [2005] 1 Lloyd's Rep. 422.

[16] *RC Pillar v Edwards*, January 11, 2001, unreported decision of H.H.J. Thornton QC.

[17] *Checkpoint Ltd v Strathclyde Pension Fund* [2003] EWCA Civ 84; *World Trade Corp v Czarnikow Sugar Ltd* [2005] 1 Lloyd's Rep. 422.

as an acceptable consequence of the choice that the parties made to arbitrate.[18]

"Substantial injustice"

22–005   In addition to listing (and thereby limiting) the grounds upon which a challenge can be based, s.68(2) also requires that the applicant has or will suffer "substantial injustice" as a result of the procedural irregularity.

This was an innovation in the AA 1996, introduced to emphasise the fact that the courts should intervene as little as possible and only where substantial injustice has/will occur. As the DAC explained in their report of February 1996, at para.280:

> "The test of [substantial injustice] is not what would have happened had the matter been litigated. To apply such a test would be to ignore the fact that the parties have agreed to arbitrate, not litigate. Having chosen arbitration, the parties cannot validly complain of substantial injustice unless what has happened simply cannot on any view be defended as an acceptable consequence of that choice. In short [section 68 of the Arbitration Act 1996] is really designed as a long stop, available only in extreme cases where the tribunal has gone wrong in its conduct that justice calls out for it to be corrected."

Burden of proof

22–006   The burden is on the applicant to show that the outcome could have been different had the irregularity not occurred.[19]

Financial loss is often used as a guide to injustice and it appears to be appropriate to test the financial impact of the irregularity against the cost of remitting the award, etc.[20]

It seems a number of minor matters cannot be joined together; if they would not meet the test individually, they will not do so collectively.[21]

However, there is no need to determine precisely what the outcome would actually have been, so long as the irregularity is shown to have "real effect".[22] Indeed, it appears that in determining whether there had been substantial injustice the court is not required to decide for itself what would have happened in the arbitration had there been no irregularity. Provided

---

[18]   para.280 of the DAC Report of February 1996; *Egmatra AG v Marco Trading Corp* [1999] 1 Lloyd's Rep. 862; *Petroships Pte Ltd of Singapore v Petec Trading and Investment Corp* [2001] 2 Lloyd's Rep. 348.

[19]   *Lesotho Highlands Authority v Impregilo SpA* [2006] 1 A.C. 221; [2005] 2 Lloyd's Rep. 310.

[20]   *Groundshire Ltd v VHE Construction* and *Mohsin v Commonwealth Secretariat* [2002] EWHC 377 (Comm), per David Steel J.

[21]   *London Underground v Citilink* [2007] EWHC 1749 (TCC). But see also *Hussman v Al Ameen Development* [2000] 2 Lloyd's Rep. 83.

[22]   *Groundshire Ltd v VHE Construction Plc* [2001] B.L.R. 395.

that the point was one on which the arbitration tribunal might well have reached a different view had it not been for the irregularity, the court should enquire no further.[23-24]

Certainly once there are held to be justifiable doubts about the impartiality of an arbitrator, it does not appear that the court will need to be persuaded that this will cause substantial injustice. In *ASM Shipping v TTMI*,[25] Morison J. expressed the view that,

> "if the properly informed independent observer concluded that there was a real possibility of bias, then I would regard that as a species of 'serious irregularity' which has caused substantial injustice to the applicant ... It is contrary to fundamental principles to hold that an arbitral award made by a tribunal which was not impartial is to be enforced unless it can be shown that the bias has caused prejudice. The problem with unconscious bias is that it is inherently difficult to prove and the statements made about it by the judges themselves cannot be tested. Nor can the court know whether the bias actually made any difference or not."

That said, where the judge is able to reach the conclusion the tribunal actually reached on the basis of evidence which is undisputed, an irregularity affecting the evidence more generally would not give rise to substantial injustice.[26] Similarly, where the complaint is that the tribunal failed to address an issue on which the party making the complaint was bound to fail, that would not give rise to substantial injustice.[27]

THE SPECIFIC GROUNDS

What follows is not intended to be a detailed discussion of the specific grounds on which an arbitration award can be challenged on the basis of a serious irregularity. Whether or not such a challenge will be successful will depend upon the particular facts of the case and detailed consideration of the standards against which those facts will be tested is better suited to an arbitration textbook than a discussion of arbitration appeals. 22–007

However, it is useful to look briefly at each of the specific grounds, if only to illustrate further the general propositions that the court will be very slow to uphold a s.68 challenge and that anything other that the most extreme

---

[23-24] See *Vee Networks Ltd v Econet Wireless International Ltd* [2004] EWHC 2909 (Comm) at [90]; *ABB AG v Hochtief Airport GmbH* [2006] 2 Lloyd's Rep. 1 at 17; *Van der Giessen-de-Noord v Imtech* [2008] EWHC 2904 (Comm); [2009] 1 Lloyd's Rep. 273 at [13].

[25] [2006] 1 Lloyd's Rep. 375 at [39(3)]. See also *Norbrook Laboratories Ltd v Tank* [2006] 1 Lloyd's Rep. 375; *ASM Shipping v Harris* [2008] 1 Lloyd's Rep. 61.

[26] *Compania Sud-Americana v Nippon Yusen Kaisha* [2009] EWHC 1606 (Comm) at [70] (where the irregularity was a failure to allow cross-examination on a particular issue).

[27] See *Buyuk Camlica Shipping v Progress Bulk Carriers* [2010] EWHC 442 (Comm) at [47].

facts is unlikely to be considered sufficient to justify interference with the agreed dispute resolution process.

Section 68(2)(a): duty to act fairly

22–008   This ground is often invoked but rarely successful. What might seem to the losing party (and even his or her representatives) the most egregiously one-sided behaviour by the tribunal may not have quite the same appearance to the court, which will be giving the tribunal the benefit of every doubt.

The starting point for consideration of the duty to act fairly is s.33(1) of the AA 1996, which imposes two general duties upon the arbitrator, namely to:

(1)   act fairly and impartially between the parties; and
(2)   adopt suitable procedures, avoiding unnecessary delay or expense.

Challenges under this ground usually take one of two forms:

(1)   "bias" cases; and
(2)   cases focussed on procedural failures.

Bias

22–009   Challenges on grounds of bias are usually likened to challenges under s.24(1) of the Act, which provides:

"A party to arbitral proceedings may ... apply to the court to remove an arbitrator on any of the following grounds—(a) that circumstances exist that give rise to justifiable doubts as to his impartiality."

The test has been stated to be as follows: "whether the fair-minded and informed observer, having considered the facts, would conclude that there was a real possibility that the tribunal was biased. The test was 'real possibility' and not 'real danger'."[28]

In *ASM Shipping v TTMI*,[29] Morison J. arrived at the (to some, surprising) conclusion that the fact that the arbitrator (a QC) had had some limited involvement as advocate in a previous case involving one of the witnesses to be called in this arbitration meant that the independent observer would experience a "feeling of discomfort" and concluded that there was a real possibility that the arbitrator was biased. This was despite the fact that Morison J. rejected out of hand the complaints made about particular procedural decisions made by the tribunal in that case (e.g. refusing a last minute adjournment sought as a result of a bereavement).

---

[28] *ASM Shipping v TTMI* [2006] 2 Lloyd's Rep. 485 at [39], based on *Porter v Magill* [2002] A.C. 357.
[29] [2006] 1 Lloyd's Rep. 375.

By contrast, in the subsequent case of *ASM Shipping v Harris*,[30] Andrew Smith J. did not accept that the other members of the panel had been "tainted" by the QC's apparent bias.

Mere loss of confidence in the arbitrator is not sufficient; indeed, it has been described as "irrelevant".[31]

Procedural failures

If the complaint concerns the procedure adopted by the tribunal, only something obviously unfair or inappropriate will usually suffice. The complaint needs to involve more than a "procedural mishap".[32]   **22–010**

The examples usually involve a genuine denial of the right of the party making a complaint properly to present his or her case, or deciding against a party on grounds not raised by the other party, without giving that party any reasonable opportunity to put forward arguments in answer to those grounds.[33] For example:

(1) failing to give a party a proper opportunity to deal with the evidential foundations of a case[34] or a proper chance to make representations[35];

(2) deciding the amount of a bonus using a mechanism for which neither party contended and on which they had not made any submissions[36];

(3) contacting parties independently without notice to the other party, or contacting potential witnesses without involving the parties[37];

(4) deciding the case on grounds of its own devising, without giving the parties an opportunity to make any submissions on these matters[38];

would all appear to qualify.

However, it is well established that arbitrators are not obliged to hear evidence which they decide is not material just because one of the parties thinks otherwise.[39] Absent agreement to the contrary, the tribunal has the right to determine its procedure, and decisions about this are not lightly to

---

[30] [2008] 1 Lloyd's Rep. 61.
[31] *Conder Structures v Kvaerner Construction Ltd* [1999] A.D.R.L.J. 305.
[32] *Weldon Plant Ltd v Commission for the New Towns* [2000] B.L.R. 496.
[33] *The Bunga Saga Lima* [2005] 2 Lloyd's Rep. 1 at [19].
[34] *Compania Sud-Americana v Nippon Yusen Kaisha* [2009] EWHC 1606 (Comm), where the tribunal had allowed a party to run a case which had been implicitly abandoned after that party's witnesses had been cross-examined.
[35] *Gbangbola v Smith & Sheriff Ltd* [1998] 3 All E.R. 730 (which concerned representations in relation to costs).
[36] *Omnibridge Consulting v Clearsprings (Management) Ltd* [2004] EWHC 2276 (Comm).
[37] *Norbrook Laboratories Ltd v Tank* [2006] EWHC 1055 (Comm).
[38] See *F Ltd v M Ltd* at [9]–[11], citing *Zermalt Holdings SA v Nu-Life Upholstery Repairs Ltd* [1985] 2 E.G.L.R. 14 and *London Underground Ltd v Citylink Telecommunications* [2007] EWHC 1749 (TCC); [2007] B.L.R. 931.
[39] *Egmatra AG v Marco Trading Corp* [1999] 1 Lloyd's Rep. 826; *ABB AG v Hochtief* [2006] EWCH 388 (Comm).

be declared to have involved a party having been deprived of a fair hearing.[40] For example, a refusal to hold an oral hearing is not a serious irregularity.[41]

22–011 More generally, it needs to be remembered that only extreme cases qualify as serious irregularities. For example, in *Petroships v Petec Trading*, Cresswell J. referred to something "so far removed from what can reasonably be expected of the arbitral process" as representing the trigger for intervention by the court. That the arbitration tribunal has not behaved precisely in the way which the court might have done, or has chosen to express itself in a different, or more succinct, way is not going to suffice. For example, unless it were apparent to the tribunal that counsel for one of the parties had missed an important point, there was no need for the panel to check that counsel had understood what was being said by the other side.[42]

It is also regularly pointed out that s.68 in general and this section in particular, is concerned with the procedure by which the decision was reached, and not the substantive decision itself. Errors of law can only be dealt with under s.69 of the AA 1996 and, while a case might in principle fall within both ss.68 and 69, it was not appropriate to use s.68 to challenge substantive rulings.[43] The temptation to repackage a complaint about the outcome as a complaint about the fairness of the procedure[44] in order to get around a term excluding any right of appeal, or to avoid the need to obtain permission to appeal, is powerful, but should be resisted.

Section 68(2)(b): excess of powers

22–012 This ground is concerned with the tribunal exceeding its powers. It should be noted that issues about the substantive jurisdiction of the arbitrators fall under s.67 of the AA 1996.[45] But an error in the application of the chosen law would fall under s.68(2)(b), not s.67.[46]

The leading authority on the role of s.68(2)(b) is *Lesotho Highlands Authority v Impregilo SpA* [2005] 2 Lloyd's Rep. 310.[47] The majority of the House of Lords identified a difference between the misapplication or erroneous use of powers which the tribunal does have (which is a substantive error of law) and the purported exercise of a power which the tribunal does not in fact have (which would fall within s.68(2)(b)). This is

---

[40] See, e.g. *AOOT Kalmneft v Glencore International AG* [2002] 2 All E.R. (Comm) 577 and *Brandeis (Brokers) v Black* [2001] 2 Lloyd's Rep. 359.
[41] See *O'Donoghue v Enterprise Inns Plc* [2008] EWHC B15 (Ch).
[42] See *The Magdalena Oldendorff* [2007] EWCA Civ 998.
[43] *Weldon Plant Ltd v Commission for the New Towns* [2000] B.L.R. 496.
[44] e.g. on the basis that a decision so perverse can only have been the product of some failure to follow a fair procedure!
[45] As the bracket in s.68(2)(b) makes clear.
[46] See *B v A* [2010] EWHC 1626 (Comm) at [28]. It seems, however, that only a conscious disregard of the provisions of the chosen law would suffice; a mistaken application would not. See [25]–[27].
[47] Also [2006] 1 A.C. 221.

not an easy distinction to draw in practice, especially having regard to the fact that jurisdictional issues fall within s.67. In *Lesotho*, the examples given by their Lordships of decisions which might fall foul of s.68(2)(b) included appointing an expert where the parties had agreed that the tribunal should not do so and awarding compound interest where the arbitration agreement permitted only the award of simple interest.[48]

Certainly in the majority of cases, the complaint is about the decision to exercise a particular procedural power, rather than that the tribunal did not have such a power at all.

Section 68(2)(c): conduct of proceedings in accordance with parties' agreement

This ground is concerned with express agreements about the manner in which the arbitration is to be conducted. It is rarely invoked, since it is relatively rare for there to be such an agreement and, where there is, tribunals are usually scrupulous about complying with it.
    22–013

However, the ground has been said to extend to a failure by the tribunal to make its decision by reference to the shape of the cases presented by the parties.[49] Specifically, it was suggested that a mischaracterisation by the tribunal (in the context of making an award of costs) of the shape of a dispute as identified in the parties' pleadings would trigger s.68(2)(c). It might be thought slightly artificial to describe the parties' pleadings as representing an agreement as to the conduct of proceedings and this decision seems slightly out of line with the more general policy of limiting the scope for challenges pursuant to s.68.

Section 68(2)(d): failure to deal with all issues before it

This ground is concerned with a failure by the tribunal to deal with the issues presented to it.
    22–014

Fidelity Management SA v Myriad International Holdings BV[50] offers a useful summary of the three most important points:

    (1) s.68(2)(d) is concerned with issues the determination of which were essential to a decision on the claims or specific defences raised in the course of the reference. The court will intervene only to remedy a situation in which a claim has been overlooked or a key

---

[48] See Lord Steyn at 319, col.2. Of course, if there was (for example) a dispute as to whether or not, properly construed, the arbitration agreement permitted the award of compound interest, the lines between substantive error and procedural failing might again begin to blur.

[49] *Newfield v Tomlinson* [2004] EWHC 3051 (TCC).

[50] [2005] 2 Lloyd's Rep. 508, per Morison J., especially at [9].

issue not been addressed, because only in these circumstances will the failure be capable of causing substantial injustice[51];

(2) it is not to be used as a means of launching a detailed enquiry into the manner in which the tribunal considered the various issues. It is concerned with a failure, that is to say where the arbitral tribunal has not dealt at all with the case of a party so that substantial injustice has resulted, e.g. where a claim has been overlooked or where the decision cannot be justified as a particular key issue has not been decided that is crucial to the result. It is not concerned with a failure to arrive at the right answer to an issue[52];

(3) arbitrators do not have to deal with every argument on every point raised; they should deal with essential issues.

The Court of Appeal has emphasised that "issues" mean the very disputes which the arbitration has to resolve. In order fairly to resolve those disputes, a tribunal may have subsidiary questions to decide. Some will be critical to the decision. Once some are decided one way or the other, others may fade away (in the sense of being matters which, while being points of dispute, do not require resolution).[53] A tribunal does not have to deal explicitly with every argument raised by counsel in support of his case. Provided that the tribunal decides all those issues put to it that were essential to be dealt with for the tribunal to come fairly to its decision on the dispute or disputes between the parties, it will probably have complied with the requirements of s.68(2)(d).[54]

For the avoidance of doubt, a failure by the tribunal to give reasons should be dealt with under s.70(4) of the AA 1996, not by way of a challenge under s.68(2)(d).[55] Similarly, where it is genuinely unclear as to whether or not an issue had been considered, the applicant should first seek that clarification from the tribunal.[56] But there would be serious irregularity if the arbitrators failed to address all of the substantive issues put to them under s68(2)(d), overlooking the argument rather than just failing to explain their reasons adequately.[57] Nor, it seems, can the court assume that an issue has been addressed, and the argument rejected, just because the answer appears obvious to the judge hearing the application.[58]

It has been held to satisfy s.68(2)(d) where an arbitrator has failed to recognise that an element of profit needed to be included in a calculation,

---

[51] See *World Trade Corp v Czarnikow Sugar* [2005] 1 Lloyd's Rep 422, per Colman J.
[52] See also *Weldon Plant Ltd v The Commission for New Towns* [2001] 1 All E.R. (Comm) 264.
[53] *Checkpoint Ltd v Strathclyde Pension Fund* [2003] EWCA Civ 84 at [49] and [51].
[54] See *Buyuk Camlica Shipping v Progress Bulk Carriers* [2010] EWHC 442 (Comm) at [28]–[30].
[55] *Fidelity Management* (supra) at [9]; *Margulead Ltd v Exide Technologies* [2005] 1 Lloyd's Rep. 324; *World Trade Corp Ltd v C Czarnikow Sugar Ltd* [2005] 1 Lloyd's Rep. 422.
[56] See *Torch Offshore v Cable Shipping* [2004] EWHC 787 (Comm). But note also *Buyuk Camlica Shipping v Progress Bulk Carriers* [2010] EWHC 442 (Comm) at [42]–[46].
[57] See *Van Der Giessen-De-Noord Shipbuilding v Imtech Marine* [2008] EWHC 2904 (Comm).
[58] See *Buyuk Camlica Shipping v Progress Bulk Carriers* [2010] EWHC 442 (Comm) at [38].

even though this was not a submission which the appellant had actually made to the arbitrator.[59] However, this is probably a decision which turns on its particular facts rather than being authority for a broader proposition that arbitrators must deal with every possible contention, whether or not advanced before them.

Section 68(2)(e): excess of powers

This provision extends the effect of s.68(2)(b) and (c) to other bodies exercising equivalent powers to arbitrator, such as arbitral institutions with powers to hear appeals from arbitration awards.   22–015

See paras 22–012 and 22–013 for a discussion of the effect of s.68(2)(b) and (c).

Section 68(2)(f): uncertainty or ambiguity as to the effect of the award

An award can be challenged if there is some genuine (and important) uncertainty or ambiguity in relation to its meaning.   22–016

However, such uncertainties/ambiguities can (and should) usually be dealt with under the slip rule at s.57 of the AA 1996.[60]

Section 68(2)(g): fraud or public policy

An award which has been procured by fraud, or is otherwise void as a matter of public policy, can be challenged under this ground.   22–017

Obviously, this is directed to the extreme rather than the ordinary case. It has been said that "it will normally be necessary to satisfy the court that some form of reprehensible or unconscionable conduct ... has contributed in a substantial way to obtaining an award". By way of example, if the complaint is about a non-disclosure of relevant documents, it would have to be shown to be fraudulent (i.e. deliberately withholding documents which were known to be relevant and disclosable), otherwise every inadvertent or negligent non-disclosure could lead to the award being challenged, despite the fact that the successful party has acted innocently.[61] Inadvertent conduct, however careless, would not suffice.[62]

It has been emphasised that the conduct under scrutiny must be that of a party to the arbitration, on the basis that it is a party to an arbitration that

---

[59] See *Metropolitan Property Realizations Ltd v Atmore Investments Ltd* [2008] EWHC 2925 (Ch).

[60] See para.22–023.

[61] *Profilati Italia Srl v Paine Webber Inc* [2001] 1 All E.R. (Comm) 1065.

[62] *Cuflet Chartering v Carousel Shipping Co Ltd ("The Marie H")* [2001] 1 Lloyd's Rep. 707; *Protech Projects v Al-Kharafi* [2005] 2 Lloyd's Rep. 779.

obtains an award in its favour or has one made against it: "The words 'obtained by fraud' must refer to an award being obtained by the fraud of a party to the arbitration or by the fraud of another to which a party to the arbitration was privy."[63] Where such fraud is alleged, the onus is on the applicant to make good the application by cogent evidence.[64]

Further, there is some doubt as to the extent to which "mere" lying by witnesses would qualify as a serious irregularity. It was described as "not uncommon in arbitration or in civil proceedings in general" by Akenhead J. in *Brown v Crosby*.[65] This is especially true if the credibility of the witness had been a feature of the arbitration (because in those circumstances one would be challenging the factual finding of the arbitrator—namely that the witness in question was credible).

It may be necessary, in cases in which the fraud in question is said to be perjury by a witness, to show that the evidence which demonstrates that lies have been told could not have been produced at the arbitration with reasonable diligence.[66]

Section 68(2)(h): form of the award

22–018　This ground concerns the form taken by the award. The form of the award can be agreed by the parties. Failing agreement, the default situation is provided for at s.52 of the AA 1996 (namely, signed, dated, with a statement identifying the seat, and reasons).

Again, it is unusual for tribunals to make any substantial error in this regard, especially bearing in mind that the slip rule (s.57 of the AA 1996) should be used first to permit minor matters to be corrected.[67]

In practice, applications pursuant to s.68(2)(h) are usually directed to a failure to give reasons (or complaints about the sufficiency of those reasons).

Section 68(2)(i): admitted irregularity

22–019　As with some of the other heads of s.68, it is difficult even to imagine circumstances which might result in an arbitration tribunal admitting an

---

[63] See *Elektrim SA v Vivendi Universal* [2007] 1 Lloyd's Rep. 693 at [80], per Aikens J. and *Double K v Neste Oil* [2009] EWHC 3380 (Comm) at [36].

[64] *Cuflet Chartering v Carousel Shipping Co Ltd* [2001] 1 Lloyd's Rep. 707 at [12]; *Elektrim* [2007] 1 Lloyd's Rep. 693 at [81]; *Double K v Neste Oil* at [33].

[65] [2008] EWHC 817 (TCC); [2008] 1 B.L.R. 366.

[66] See *DDT Trucks v DDT Holdings* [2007] 2 Lloyd's Rep. 213 at [22]–[23], in which Cooke J. makes reference to and relies upon the judgment of Waller L.J. in *Westacre v Jugoimport* [2000] Q.B. 288 (at 306 to 309) in relation to setting aside a court judgment. This was followed in *Double K v Neste Oil* [2009] EWHC 3380 (Comm).

[67] *Groundshire v VHE Construction* [2001] B.L.R. 395; *Al Hadha Trading Co v Tradigrain SA* [2002] 2 Lloyd's Rep. 512; *Torch Offshore LLC v Cable Shipping Inc* [2004] 2 All E.R. (Comm) 365.

irregularity, but being unable or unwilling to put it right themselves. Mere errors in the award can be put right with the slip rule and time can be extended for this purpose if necessary.[68]

It is perhaps no surprise, therefore, that the authorities which touch on the application of s.68(2)(i) have often been decided on other grounds. For example, in *Gannet v Eastrade*,[69] Langley J. expressed the view that, if for some reason the arbitrator had been prevented from correcting his award in relation to costs in the light of the correction he had made to the award on the substance of the claim, the gap could have been filled by the Court making an order pursuant to s.68(2)(i) and remitting the award to the Tribunal. But, in the event, there was no need to do so, because the arbitrator was entitled to make the correction pursuant to s.57.

As a result of the dearth of authority, it remains unclear what is to be considered as an "irregularity" in this context. In particular, it is unclear whether that irregularity has to be one which arguably falls within s.68(2)(a)–(h) (i.e. a "serious irregularity"), or whether it can be some lesser procedural failure, so long as it is admitted by the arbitration tribunal and has or is likely to cause substantial injustice. In *CNH Global v PGN Logistics*,[70] Burton J. identified the competing arguments and expressed the view that "[i]t must by definition be an irregularity other than those defined in (a) to (h), which falls within s.68(2) because of the admission by the Tribunal". However, he acknowledged the point to be "entirely free of authority"[71] and declined to decide whether an error of fact or law which was not otherwise susceptible of appeal might be challenged using s.68(2)(i), since the point did not ultimately arise for decision.

There is a further uncertainty as to whether, if the irregularity could be linked to an error by the party affected in the presentation of their case, this would prevent a challenge being made. This appears to have been the intention of the Departmental Advisory Committee.[72] However, in *Gannet v Eastrade* Langley J. indicated that he could not "see why that failure, if it is correct to describe it as such, should preclude the charterers from asserting a substantial injustice has resulted as a consequence of a wholly and understandably unforeseen mistake in the amount of the award". That said, the judgment does not suggest that Langley J. had been referred to para.281 of the DAC report.

---

[68] See *Gold Coast v Naval Gijon* [2006] EWHC 1044 (Comm); [2006] 2 Lloyd's Rep. 400, in which the Tribunal had held that he had made a mistake of calculation which he would have wanted to put right, but that time had expired for the correction of that error using s.57 of the Act. The Court exercised its discretion to extend time (pursuant to s.79 of the Act).

[69] [2002] 1 Lloyd's Rep. 713.

[70] [2009] EWHC 977 (Comm).

[71] At [50].

[72] See para.281 of the DAC report.

LOSING THE RIGHT TO CHALLENGE

22–020 Section 73(1) of the Act provides that, if a party continues to take part in proceedings without making any objection forthwith (or within any relevant time limit) that the proceedings have been improperly conducted; that there has been a failure to comply with the arbitration agreement or any other section of the Act; or that there has been any other irregularity affecting the tribunal or the proceedings, he may not raise that objection later, unless he did not know and could not have discovered the grounds for the objection.

Objection

22–021 At least in the context of an irregularity coming to light before the award, an objection does not necessarily mean commencing court proceedings.[73] It does not appear that any particular form is required,[74] but the objection needs to embrace the particular irregularity about which complaint is subsequently made, because s.73(1) says "he may not raise *that* objection later" (emphasis added).[75]

Usually, the party wishing to make the objection will send a letter to the tribunal and the other parties to the reference identifying the alleged irregularity and expressly reserving the right to challenge the award.[76] It should not be assumed that raising the issue in some more general way, or with the arbitral institution, will suffice.[77] Nor is it enough for the purpose of s.73 that a party indicates that an objection might be made, or "puts down a marker" to that effect. He must either make his objection or risk losing any right subsequently to challenge the award.[78]

Timing

22–022 Section 73(1) provides that the objection must be made forthwith or "within such time as is allowed by the arbitration agreement or the tribunal

---

[73] See *Wicketts v Brine Builders* (Unreported, 2001) at p.11.

[74] There is no express provision in the Act that the objection be in writing, although there is obviously much greater scope for dispute about what was said if the objection is not put in writing.

[75] This appears to have been common ground in *AEK v NBA* [2002] 1 Lloyd's Rep. 305 (see [20]–[21]).

[76] Of course, a party taking this step will be alive to the offence it may cause to the arbitration tribunal and will not take it lightly. But it has no real alternative if it wishes to preserve the right to make a challenge.

[77] In *Rustal Trading v Gill & Duffus* [2000] 1 Lloyd's Rep. 14, it was common ground that a letter to the Refined Sugar Association raising a concern about the suitability of one of the arbitrators it had appointed did not involve raising that objection in a manner that would satisfy the requirements of s.73.

[78] See *ASM Shipping v Harris* [2008] 1 Lloyd's Rep. 61 at [53].

or by any provision of this Part". A number of the rules of arbitration institutions provide for waiver in the event that objection is not made "promptly" (or the equivalent) but it is unusual for an express timetable (i.e. a particular period of hours, days or weeks) within which to register the objection to be fixed.

Assuming there is no specific timetable fixed by the arbitration agreement, applicable arbitral rules or the tribunal, the objection must be made "forthwith". This probably means "promptly", "without unnecessary delay" or "as soon as reasonably possible", rather than "within a matter of seconds".[79]

Certainly, however, an objection must be raised when the issue comes to light, rather than only once the award is received. Continuing to take part in the arbitration may not require any positive step to be taken by the party intending to raise the objection, so he must either object in clear terms or state that he is withdrawing from proceedings.[80] In a case where there is knowledge or reasonable means of knowledge of the grounds for objection at the hearing the point must be raised then.[81] If the matter comes to light after the hearing, but before the award, the objection may still have to be made before the award is published.[82]

It should also be noted that it is possible for any right to challenge to be waived following an award, if a party with knowledge of the irregularity conducts himself in such a way as to indicate that he will not make a challenge.[83] In general, however, the time limits applicable to a challenge under s.68[84] are the most immediate potential barrier to a challenge in respect of an irregularity which comes to light upon receipt of the award.

PROCEDURE

Preliminaries

A challenge to an award pursuant to s.68 of the Act is made by way of an arbitration claim (Pt 8 procedure) following CPR Pt 62 and the Practice Direction to CPR Pt 62.   **22–023**

The courts in which such a claim can be commenced are the same as for the other types of arbitration appeals.[85]

---

[79] See *Wicketts v Brine Builders* (Unreported, 2001) at p.11; *Margulead v Exide* [2005] 1 Lloyd's Rep. 324 at [35].

[80] See *Rustal Trading* [2000] 1 Lloyd's Rep. 14 at p.20; *ASM Shipping v Harris* [2008] 1 Lloyd's Rep. 61 at [54].

[81] See *Margulead v Exide* [2005] 1 Lloyd's Rep. 324 at [35].

[82] See *Thyssen Canada v Mariana Maritime* [2005] 1 Lloyd's Rep. 640 at [20]–[21].

[83] For example, in *The Vimeira* [1985] 2 Lloyd's Rep. 377, the owners had sought and obtained an order under s.26 of the Arbitration Act 1950 enforcing the award. Hirst J. held (at 405) that such action was an unequivocal act of approbation and they could not subsequently seek to challenge the award.

[84] See paras 22–024 and 22–025.

[85] See para.21–045.

As with s.69, no application can be made unless all available arbitral procedures (including any possible application under s.57 of the Act or any other slip rule) have been exhausted.[86]

Time limit

22–024   The application must be made within 28 days of the date of the award.[87]

This time limit can be extended. See s.80(5) of the Act.[88] In the context of a s.68 application, an applicant seeking an extension of time will probably need to show a good reason for the delay (addressing the extent to which he or his legal advisors were responsible for it), a good arguable case on the challenge itself, and that the balance of prejudice favours granting the extension.

In *AOOT Kalmneft v Glencore*,[89] Colman J. attempted to summarise the considerations which a judge would take into account on such an application (see [59]–[60]):

"Accordingly, although each case turns on its own facts, the following considerations are, in my judgment, likely to be material:

(i) the length of the delay;

(ii) whether, in permitting the time limit to expire and the subsequent delay to occur, the party was acting reasonably in all the circumstances;

(iii) whether the respondent to the application or the arbitrator caused or contributed to the delay;

(iv) whether the respondent to the application would by reason of the delay suffer irremediable prejudice in addition to the mere loss of time if the application were permitted to proceed;

(v) whether the arbitration has continued during the period of delay and, if so, what impact on the progress of the arbitration or the costs incurred in respect of the determination of the application by the Court might now have;

(vi) the strength of the application;

(vii) whether in the broadest sense it would be unfair to the applicant for him to be denied the opportunity of having the application determined."

22–025

---

[86] See paras 21–026 to 21–028.
[87] See s.70(3) of the Act and *UR Power v Kuok Oils* [2009] EWHC 1940 (Comm).
[88] See also CPR r.62.9 and CPR PD 62 para.11.1.
[89] [2002] 1 Lloyd's Rep.128.

This summary has since been approved by the Court of Appeal, with some   22–025
comments made about the relative importance of the different considerations.[90] In particular, the strength of the underlying challenge will not
usually be investigated in detail,[91] but it has been suggested that an
intrinsically weak case will count against the application for extension
whilst a strong case would positively assist the application.[92]

Of course, if the facts on which the challenge is based only come to light
after the time period for making the challenge has expired, that is likely to
be a powerful justification for extending time.[93]

A common reason for delay in practice is that the parties have not collected the award promptly, often because of difficulties finding the money
to pay the tribunal's fees. In *The Amer Energy*[94] the principal reason given
for the delay was that the applicants were unable to provide funds to their
solicitors to collect the award. Flaux J. commented that he would not
usually regard impecuniosity as a sufficient reason to extend time for
making an application under s.68 or 69 of the Act, but accepted that, on the
particular facts of that case, the applicants had acted reasonably.[95]

Where it appears to the court that a party has deliberately chosen not to
take up the award until after the expiry of the time limit for challenge, he
will find it difficult to show that he was acting reasonably in all the circumstances. Such parties will be "the conscious authors of their own
predicament".[96]

Documents

Claim form

The application is made on a Pt 8 Claim Form (although there is now a   22–026
special form—N8—for arbitration claims). It is usually drafted so that the
claim form itself is limited to a short summary of the grounds of challenge
and the relief claimed, with the more detailed explanation of the grounds
set out in an accompanying witness statement.

In practice, this means alleging that there has been a serious irregularity
which has caused or will cause substantial injustice, identifying the subsection or subsections of s.68(2) on which reliance is placed and listing out

---

[90] See *Nagusina Naviera v Allied Maritime* [2002] EWCA Civ 1147; [2003] 2 C.L.C. 1 at [38]–[42].
[91] See *Thyssen Canada Ltd v Mariana Maritime SA* [2005] EWHC 219 (Comm) at [56].
[92] See *Brown v Crosby* [2008] EWHC 817 (TCC); [2008] 1 B.L.R. 366 at [32]; *Squirrel Films v SPP Opportunities* Unreported March 5, 2010.
[93] See *Elektrim AS v Vivendi Universal* [2007] EWHC 11 (Comm); [2007] 1 Lloyd's Rep. 693. Aikens J. also observed that, in a case in which perjury was alleged, it was reasonable for newly instructed solicitors to investigate the matter before making the application for an extension of time, since they would need to set out the grounds of the application.
[94] [2009] 1 Lloyd's Rep. 293.
[95] See [14]–[15].
[96] See *Buyuk Camlica Shipping v Progress Bulk Carriers* [2010] EWHC 442 (Comm) at [62]–[64].

the remedy or remedies sought.[97] If the circumstances permit, it is good practice to summarise in a few short sentences the facts which are said to give rise to the irregularity, but often reference will simply be made to the accompanying witness statement.

Witness statement

22–027   The accompanying witness statement must in any event contain (or exhibit) all of the evidence required for the applicant to make good his challenge. It must prove the facts necessary to show that there was an irregularity falling within one of the subsections of s.68(2), that the irregularity caused or will cause substantial injustice, etc. Many would take the view that it is best to deal upfront with all potential barriers to a challenge; showing that an objection was made at the earliest possible juncture, that all alternative avenues of appeal have been exhausted, etc.

In practice, it is relatively rare for the underlying facts of a challenge to be controversial. In the more usual case, there will be agreement about what the tribunal did or did not do, and the dispute will centre on whether or not this amounted to an irregularity, whether it caused substantial injustice, and the suchlike. Perhaps as a reflection of the likely shape of the dispute, it is common for the accompanying witness statement to be made by the solicitor having conduct of the application, whether or not he or she had first hand evidence to give about the events in question. If, however, there are likely to be facts in dispute, there does not seem to be any obvious reason why more than one witness statement in support could not be filed.

Reasons

22–028   In some situations, the parties agree (as part of the arbitration procedure) not to make use of the reasons provided by the arbitration tribunal. This will not prevent the court looking at the reasons in the context of a s.68 application and the reasons can be put in evidence for this purpose.[98]

Parties

22–029   The other parties to the arbitration must be made respondents to the application. They have to be served with the arbitration claim form and supporting evidence.[99]

Notice must also be given to the arbitrators, but they are not usually made parties to the application. See s.68(1) of the Act. They can enter evidence of their own[100] to assist the court and will often do so if the

---

[97] Usually, this simply means listing all of the alternatives, so as to offer maximum flexibility in the event the challenge succeeds.
[98] See *The Easy Rider* [2004] 2 Lloyd's Rep. 626, especially at [28].
[99] See s.68(1) of the Act and CPR r.62.6(2)–(3).
[100] See CPR PD 62 paras 4.1–4.3.

challenge concerns procedural decisions they have made. But they are not under any obligation to take part.[101]

Security

For the award

Under s.70(7) of the Act, the court can order the applicant to provide security for the sum awarded in the challenged award as a condition of hearing the application. It seems that the purpose for such an order is to prevent the time obtained by making the application diminishing (by design or otherwise) the ability of the applicant to meet the challenged award and it might thus not be appropriate to make such an order where the practical effect would be to require a third party to put up security.[102]

22–030

For costs

The court may order the applicant to put up security for the respondent's costs of the challenge.[103] However, such an order cannot be made solely on the basis that the applicant is a foreign company.[104]

22–031

Form of hearing

An application brought pursuant to s.68 will be heard at an oral hearing, usually in private.[105]

22–032

It should be noted that, where an application pursuant to s.68 is combined with an application under s.69, the usual (but not invariable) practice is to have short oral submissions on the issue of permission to appeal (pursuant to s.69) at the substantive hearing of the s.68 application, rather

---

[101] See *Port Sudan v Chettiar* [1977] 1 Lloyd's Rep. 166, in which Donaldson J. explained (at 178) that the practice of notifying arbitrators when a challenge of this kind was made was based upon the consideration of natural justice that no one should have his conduct criticised without being given an opportunity for replying or explaining. He also made clear that it was not the practice to make an order for costs against an umpire or arbitrator unless the facts are wholly exceptional, e.g. fraud by the arbitrator, or where the arbitrator takes an active part in the court proceedings. By contrast, merely attending by counsel or giving the court information (in a witness statement or affidavit) which is thought to be helpful would not usually involve the arbitrator in any risk of liability for the costs of the court proceedings.

[102] See *Peterson Farms v C&M Farming* [2003] EWHC 2298 (QB); [2004] 1 Lloyd's Rep. 614 at [19], in which Tomlinson J. declined to order the provision of security in relation to a jurisdictional challenge under s.67 of the Act which he did not think was "flimsy". He also appears to have been influenced by the fact that enforcement proceedings were already underway in Arkansas and would offer a measure of protection against the dissipation of assets.

[103] See s.70(6) of the Act.

[104] See s.70(6) of the Act.

[105] Although it has been said judgment should usually be given in public in s.68 cases. See *Department of Economic Policy v Bankers Trust* [2005] Q.B. 207. This guidance appears to have been followed in *Double K v Neste Oil* [2009] EWHC 3380 (Comm) (see [14]).

than dealing with permission to appeal on paper.[106] Judges have warned, however, that this should not encourage putative appellants to include applications pursuant to s.68 in the hope of being able to argue the detail of the s.69 application for permission to appeal application orally.[107]

Remedies

22–033   If a challenge pursuant to s.68 is upheld, the court can remit the award to the tribunal for further consideration, set it aside or declare it to be of no effect.

Section 68(3) expressly provides that remission is to be preferred to setting aside the award, unless the court is satisfied that it would be inappropriate to remit the matters in question to the tribunal for reconsideration. In those circumstances (e.g. where the irregularity concerns the manner in which the tribunal has conducted itself and especially cases about bias), the problem is often dealt with by removing one or more members of the panel before remitting the award for further consideration.[108] Setting aside the whole of an award is rarely appropriate because this may simply mean the parties having to start the arbitration again from scratch, which would only make sense in the most extreme cases.

The award can be remitted in whole or in part (see s.68(3)(a)), so where the challenge concerns only one aspect of the dispute, the court can remit only the affected part of the award. In those circumstances, the tribunal would only have power to revisit the part of the award which has been remitted; they cannot take into account other new arguments affecting other issues.[109] Meanwhile, the rest of the award remains valid and binding,[110] although there is some doubt as to whether it is enforceable, at least where the remission affects the substance of the award.[111]

---

[106] *Bulfracht (Cyprus) Ltd v Boneset Shipping Co Ltd* [2002] EWHC 2292 (Comm); *Newfield v Tomlinson* [2004] EWHC 3051 (TCC). But see also *The Amer Energy* [2009] 1 Lloyd's Rep. 293 in which a different route was taken, with Flaux J. determining the s.69 application on paper and then making some robust comments about the apparent merits of the s.68 application, which he reserved to himself, if the applicants should (despite these comments) be minded to pursue it.

[107] See *Newfield v Tomlinson* [2004] EWHC 3051 (TCC) at [6].

[108] Although this probably requires a parallel application to remove the arbitrators pursuant to s.24 of the Act, and is a topic which falls outside the scope of this work.

[109] See *The Avala (No.2)* [1996] 2 Lloyd's Rep. 311 in which Rix J. made clear that once an arbitrator had made his award he was functus officio and his jurisdiction was revived only to the extent of the court's remission. When a court remitted an award to an arbitrator it was not remitting a whole dispute unless on the terms of the order it expressly did so; it generally remitted something narrower, and where it did so against the background of an arbitration which had already been defined by pleadings and argument before an arbitrator, it was one or more of the issues as so defined within the scope of the reference that must be considered to be the subject matter of the remission.

[110] See *Carter v Simpson Associates* [2004] UKPC 29; [2004] 2 Lloyd's Rep. 512.

[111] See Mustill & Boyd, *Commercial Arbitration*, p. 567.

Section 71(3) of the Act provides that the tribunal shall make a fresh award within three months of the date of the order providing for remission, or such longer or shorter period as the court may direct.

Costs

In general, the costs of the application challenging the award will follow the event. If it succeeds, the applicant might expect to obtain an order for costs; if it fails, the respondent ought to obtain an order.

22–034

The court will not make an order for costs against an umpire or arbitrator unless the facts are wholly exceptional, e.g. fraud by the arbitrator, or where the arbitrator has taken an active part in the court proceedings.[112] By contrast, merely attending by counsel or giving the court information (in a witness statement or affidavit) which is intended to be helpful would probably not involve the arbitrator in any risk of liability for the costs of the court proceedings.[113]

It is less clear whether the arbitrators can recover the costs of such limited "participation" in the event that the challenge is rejected. The answer must be that it depends on the circumstances.

It is also unclear whether the court can make an order for costs against an arbitrator on the basis that his conduct has resulted in the particular application. This might arise, for example, in the context of (successful) applications for remission for the production of further reasons pursuant to s.68(2)(h), especially where the other party to the arbitration does not contest the application, or even consents to it. The general consensus appears to be that the immunity conferred on arbitrators by s.29 of the Act[114] extends to immunity against orders for the payment of costs.[115]

---

[112] As in *Wicketts v Brine Builders* Unreported 2001, an application for the removal of an arbitrator.

[113] See *Port Sudan v Chettiar* [1977] 1 Lloyd's Rep. 166, 178.

[114] Immunity for act or omissions in the discharge or purported discharge of their duties, unless bad faith is demonstrated.

[115] See Merkin, *Arbitration Law*, para.21.26.

CHAPTER 23

Challenging the Substantive Jurisdiction: Section 67

INTRODUCTION

23–001   A challenge to the substantive jurisdiction of the arbitration tribunal to make an award is brought under s.67 of the AA 1996:

> **"67 Challenging the award: substantive jurisdiction**
>
> (1) A party to arbitral proceedings may (upon notice to the other parties and to the tribunal) apply to the court—
>
> (a)   challenging any award of the arbitral tribunal as to its substantive jurisdiction; or
>
> (b)   for an order declaring an award made by the tribunal on the merits to be of no effect, in whole or in part, because the tribunal did not have substantive jurisdiction.
>
> A party may lose the right to object (see section 73) and the right to apply is subject to the restrictions in section 70(2) and (3).
>
> (2) The arbitral tribunal may continue the arbitral proceedings and make a further award while an application to the court under this section is pending in relation to an award as to jurisdiction.
>
> (3) On an application under this section challenging an award of the arbitral tribunal as to its substantive jurisdiction, the court may by order—
>
> (a)   confirm the award,
>
> (b)   vary the award, or
>
> (c)   set aside the award in whole or in part.
>
> (4) The leave of the court is required for any appeal from a decision of the court under this section."

23–002   It might be said that such a challenge is not properly to be described as an "appeal" at all. The objection is not to the decision itself, but rather to the entitlement of the arbitrator to make the decision. Indeed, there is an important conceptual (and practical) uncertainty as to the status of the tribunal's decision when a challenge is made to its substantive jurisdiction to make that decision. This affects both the way in which any challenge is categorised and the manner in which challenges to jurisdiction fall to be resolved. It means that this type of challenge has very little in common with civil appeals more generally and has some important procedural differences by comparison with appeals under s.69 or s.68.

It is for this reason that this type of "appeal" is addressed last,[1] even though its place in the AA 1996,[2] and in most practitioners' consideration of their options when challenging an award,[3] might suggest that it should come first.

"Kompetenz-Kompetenz"

The conceptual uncertainty flows from the fact that, in arbitration, the tribunal's power is premised upon the existence of an agreement by the parties to abide by the decision of that tribunal. Whether or not the arbitrators have power to determine a particular dispute depends upon the proper construction of the arbitration agreement. If there is in fact no such agreement, it might appear to follow that the tribunal has no more power to bind the parties than any passer-by in the street and that, as a result, to have a tribunal deciding its own jurisdiction is akin to lifting oneself up using one's own bootstraps.

23–003

The paradigm case for a challenge under s.67 of the Act would be one in which A alleges that an agreement was reached with B for the purchase of a quantity of a product and that the agreement contains an arbitration clause. B disputes the existence of the agreement. A appoints (or purports to appoint) an arbitrator, C, who in due course decides that there was an agreement. Logically, if the true position is that there was no agreement, then there is no arbitration clause and B has no more agreed to abide by the decisions of C than he has agreed to sell A the product in question. It might seem to follow that, where there is a challenge to the substantive jurisdiction of the arbitration tribunal to make the decision in question, as opposed to a challenge to the way in which the decision is made by a tribunal with jurisdiction, or to the content of that decision, it must fall to someone other than C to resolve that challenge.

In fact, under the internationally recognised doctrine of "kompetenz-kompetenz", an arbitration tribunal has the power to rule on its own

---

[1] It should also be noted that what follows is concerned with the procedure and practice associated with a challenge pursuant to s.67 of AA 1996, not the substantive question of the jurisdiction of arbitration tribunals.

[2] At s.67, and hence before s.68 and s.69.

[3] Logically, the first question in relation to any award must be "did the tribunal have jurisdiction to decide this?", even if in practice issues about jurisdiction will usually have crystallised (or been waived) at an earlier stage.

jurisdiction, unless the parties agree otherwise. This means that the question of jurisdiction can, in the first instance, be resolved by the tribunal itself and an allegation that the tribunal lacks jurisdiction does not of itself require a stay of the arbitration for the matter to be resolved by the court. In accordance with this doctrine, s.30 of the AA 1996 provides that a tribunal is entitled to determine its own substantive jurisdiction "unless otherwise agreed by the parties".

However, there are differences between the status of a tribunal's decision as to its own jurisdiction and the status of its decisions (in the absence of a challenge to its jurisdiction) on other issues. These differences have informed the drafting of s.67 of the AA 1996 and also impact upon the procedure followed when an application pursuant to s.67 is made. By way of summary:

(1) there is no need for the court's permission to make an application pursuant to s.67[4]; and

(2) the court is not limited to a review of the tribunal's decision, but can take whatever course (including the hearing or re-hearing of live evidence) is considered appropriate for the purpose of resolving for itself the issue as to the tribunal's jurisdiction.[5]

CHALLENGING SUBSTANTIVE JURISDICTION

23–004 A challenge to the tribunal's jurisdiction is a challenge to its entitlement to make the decision which it has made. Section 67 of the AA 1996 is not concerned with the content of the decision or the manner in which it has been arrived at, unless either of those matters affects the tribunal's entitlement to make the decision. A decision which is obviously correct and has been reached with scrupulous fairness will nevertheless be set aside if the tribunal did not have jurisdiction to make it.

As such, an application pursuant to s.67 is always concerned (and concerned only) with questions of jurisdiction. As illustrated by s.30 of the AA 1996, this means issues as to:

"(a) whether there is a valid arbitration agreement,

(b) whether the tribunal is properly constituted, and

(c) what matters have been submitted to arbitration in accordance with the arbitration agreement."

It should be noted that an error in the application of the chosen law does not involve a lack of substantive jurisdiction. It has been held[6] that a breach

---

[4] Compare s.67 of the AA 1996 with s.69(2) of the AA 1996.
[5] See paras 23–020 and 23–021.
[6] In *B v A* [2010] EWHC 1626 (Comm) at [28].

of s.46 of the AA 1996 (concerned with the substantive law applied to the dispute) can only be addressed by an application under s.68(2)(b).[7]

It should be remembered that it does not follow that the award which is the subject matter of the "appeal" will inevitably have been directed exclusively (or, for that matter, have touched upon) such jurisdictional issues. Subject to the rules about losing the right to object,[8] it is entirely possible to have an "appeal" pursuant to s.67 in relation to an award which does not deal at all with the jurisdictional issues which are to be canvassed before the court.

In practice, "appeals" on jurisdictional grounds can arise in at least three different ways: 23–005

(1) Where a party has objected to the jurisdiction of the tribunal at the outset and the tribunal has ruled on that issue as a preliminary issue. In these circumstances, it would be open to the party challenging jurisdiction to appeal against this award on jurisdiction under s.67 of the Act.

(2) A party objects to the tribunal's jurisdiction and the tribunal decides to deal with that issue along with the other substantive issues, such that a single award is produced at the end of proceedings. In such circumstances, the party disputing jurisdiction could appeal against the whole award (based on jurisdictional grounds) under s.67 of the Act.

(3) A party objects to jurisdiction and declines to take any part in the arbitration proceedings. The tribunal either produces an award on jurisdiction, or a substantive award. In either event, the party which has not taken part in proceedings could challenge the award relying on s.67 of AA 1996.

As is immediately apparent, there is scope for complexity here. Where an   23–006 award embraces jurisdictional and other issues, the court (under s.67 of AA 1996) can only concern itself with the jurisdictional aspect. This can be more difficult than it appears at first sight, because often the jurisdictional aspects overlap to a considerable degree with substantive questions.[9] This might suggest that the tidier course would be for the tribunal to always deal with issues of jurisdiction at the outset. However, in practice the tribunal has a complete discretion as to what course to take and often it will be more convenient in terms of conduct of the arbitration reference to defer a decision on jurisdiction. A party cannot rely upon s.67 of the Act to challenge a tribunal's ruling as to what course to take.[10]

---

[7] See para.22–012.
[8] See paras 23–009 to 23–011.
[9] This arises most obviously when the jurisdictional objection is that the contract containing the arbitration clause relied upon was not in fact agreed.
[10] See *Kalmneft v Glencore* [2001] 2 All E.R. (Comm) 577 at [70]–[71].

APPLICABILITY

23–007 Section 67 of the AA 1996 applies to all arbitrations where the seat of the arbitration is in England, no matter what the applicable law is or indeed whether the arbitration is governed by public international law.[11] It applies whether the party wishes to challenge a ruling by the tribunal that it has substantive jurisdiction, a ruling that it does not, or a ruling on the merits on the basis that the tribunal lacked jurisdiction to determine the merits.[12]

However, where the parties have concluded an ad hoc agreement to confer jurisdiction on the tribunal to determine the issue of jurisdiction, s.67 does not apply.[13] Such an agreement exists independently of the underlying contract or arbitration agreement[14] and any challenge has to be made under s.68 or s.69 of the AA 1996 instead.

CONTRACTING OUT

23–008 Section 67 is a mandatory provision. The parties cannot contract out of the right to challenge the tribunal's decision on jurisdiction.[15]

LOSING THE RIGHT TO OBJECT

23–009 A concern which looms large where there is an issue (or potential issue) about jurisdiction is the danger of losing the right to object by virtue of the regime contained in ss.67(1) and 73 of the AA 1996. The statutory effect of a loss of the right to object is no different from a finding that the tribunal does have substantive jurisdiction.[16] It follows that it is of significant importance.

"73 Loss of right to object

(1) If a party to arbitral proceedings takes part, or continues to take part, in the proceedings without making, either forthwith or within

---

[11] See *Republic of Ecuador v Occidental Exploration and Production Co* [2005] EWCA Civ 1116; [2006] Q.B. 432, where the Court of Appeal held that the court had jurisdiction to entertain an application under s.67 where the arbitration in question had been provided for in a bilateral investment treaty. See also *Czech Republic v European Media Ventures* [2007] All E.R. (D) 75.

[12] AA 1996 s.67(1)(a)–(b); *Caltex Gas Co Ltd v China National Petroleum Corp* [2001] EWCA Civ 788; [2001] 1 W.L.R. 1892.

[13] Subject, of course, to challenging the tribunal's finding that there was such an ad hoc agreement.

[14] *Caltex Gas Co Ltd v China National Petroleum Corp* [2001] EWCA Civ 788; [2001] 1 W.L.R. 1892 at [13] and [50].

[15] See s.4 of, and Sch.1 to, the Act.

[16] At least for the purposes of any further issue in this regard before the English court. It may not have the same effect for the purposes of enforcement in other jurisdictions, but that is a topic falling outside the scope of this work.

such time as is allowed by the arbitration agreement or the tribunal or by any provision of this Part, any objection—

   (a) that the tribunal lacks substantive jurisdiction,
   (b) that the proceedings have been improperly conducted,
   (c) that there has been a failure to comply with the arbitration agreement or with any provision of this Part, or
   (d) that there has been any other irregularity affecting the tribunal or the proceedings,

he may not raise that objection later, before the tribunal or the court, unless he shows that, at the time he took part or continued to take part in the proceedings, he did not know and could not with reasonable diligence have discovered the grounds for the objection.

(2) Where the arbitral tribunal rules that it has substantive jurisdiction and a party to arbitral proceedings who could have questioned that ruling—

   (a) by any available arbitral process of appeal or review, or
   (b) by challenging the award,

does not do so, or does not do so within the time allowed by the arbitration agreement or any provision of this Part, he may not object later to the tribunal's substantive jurisdiction on any ground which was the subject of that ruling."

A party taking part or continuing to take part in the arbitration proceedings[17] must state his objection to the tribunal's jurisdiction "forthwith or within such time as is allowed by the arbitration agreement or the tribunal or by any provision of this Part".[18] A party is not precluded from raising an objection by the mere fact that he has appointed or participated in the appointment of an arbitrator.[19]   **23–010**

Section 31 of the AA 1996 requires an objection on jurisdictional grounds at the outset of the proceedings to be raised by a party no later than the time it takes the first step in the proceedings to contest the merits of any matter in relation to which it challenges the tribunal's jurisdiction[20] and any such objection during the course of the arbitral proceedings to be made as soon as possible after the matter alleged to be beyond its jurisdiction is raised.[21] The tribunal may admit an objection later than the time specified if

---

[17] See *Rustal Trading Ltd v Gill & Duffuss* [2000] 1 Lloyd's Rep. 14 at 20 as to what may constitute taking part in the proceedings.

[18] AA 1996 s.73(1).

[19] AA 1996 s.31(1).

[20] AA 1996 s.31(1). Where it is an arbitration procedure which has more than one "tier" (e.g. there is a built in appeal process), this probably means the objection must be raised before the "first-tier" arbitrators. See *UR Power v Kuok Oils and Grains* [2009] EWHC 1940 (Comm) at [30].

[21] AA 1996 s.31(2).

it considers the delay to have been justified.[22] If a party discovers grounds of objection after the conclusion of the hearing but before publication of the award, it is still expected to raise that objection promptly.[23]

The objection should be recorded in writing and sent to the tribunal and the other parties. It should make clear the nature of the jurisdictional objection and also state plainly that any further participation in the arbitration will be without prejudice to the objection.

The rule is that *each* ground of objection raised before the court must have been raised before the arbitral tribunal. Section 73 of AA 1996 provides that a party to arbitral proceedings who does not raise an objection to the tribunal's jurisdiction at the appropriate time may not normally raise "that objection" later (either before the tribunal or the court). It has been held that this is to be read as "that *ground* of objection", meaning that any objection raised before the court must fall within the scope of an original ground of objection raised before the tribunal.[24] The purpose of this provision is to ensure that a party does not keep a point "up his sleeve" and wait to see what happens while considerable expense is incurred.[25]

23–011   However, it seems that the court will take a broad approach to what constitutes an objection, allowing different aspects of an objection to be raised on "appeal" even though those aspects of the objection were not specifically raised before the tribunal.[26]

If a party wishes to raise a wholly new point before the court, it will need to bring itself with the exception to the general rule in s.73(1) of the AA 1996, namely that, at the time the party took part or continued to take part in the proceedings it "did not know and could not with reasonable diligence have discovered the grounds for the objection".[27]

In *Vee Networks Ltd v Econet Wireless International Ltd*[28] the court held that the jurisdictional objection had to be an express challenge to the validity of the arbitration agreement. It was not enough that the main agreement had been challenged without reference to the arbitration agreement itself. This conclusion is based on the principle of separability found in s.7 of AA 1996.

The principle of separability means that the invalidity or rescission of the main contract does not necessarily entail the invalidity or rescission of the arbitration agreement. The arbitration agreement must be treated as a distinct agreement and can be void or voidable only on grounds which relate directly to the arbitration agreement.[29] For example, if the main

---

[22] AA 1996 s.31(3).

[23] *Rustal Trading Ltd v Gill & Duffuss* [2000] 1 Lloyd's Rep. 14.

[24] *Primetrade Ag v Ythan Ltd* [2006] 1 Lloyd's Rep. 457 at [59]; *JSC Zestafoni G Nikoladze Ferroalloy Plant v Ronly Holdings* [2004] 2 Lloyd's Rep. 335 at [64]; *Athletic Union of Constantinople v National Basketball Association* [2002] 1 All E.R. 70

[25] *Rustal Trading Ltd v Gill & Duffuss* [2000] 1 Lloyd's Rep. 14 at 20; *Hussmann Europe v Al Ameen* [2000] 2 Lloyd's Rep. 83 at 91

[26] *Primetrade Ag v Ythan Ltd* [2006] 1 Lloyd's Rep. 457 at 474.

[27] AA 1996 s.73(1).

[28] [2005] 1 Lloyd's Rep. 192.

[29] *Premium Nafta Products v Fili Shipping Co Ltd* [2007] Bus. L.R. 1725 at [17].

agreement is challenged as being voidable on ground of duress,[30] or is impeached by bribery,[31] the principle of separability means that the arbitration agreement will still be binding unless it is alleged that the arbitration agreement itself was induced by duress or should itself be impeached for bribery.

There will of course be some cases in which the ground upon which the main agreement is challenged is identical to the ground on which the arbitration agreement is challenged,[32] but parties need to be alive to the possibility that the right to "appeal" to the court may be lost if the objection raised before the tribunal did not necessarily amount to an objection that the *arbitration agreement* itself was not binding.

It is worth noting that s.73 of AA 1996 refers to an objection "that the tribunal lacks substantive jurisdiction". It does not apply to an application challenging a finding by the tribunal that it *does not* have substantive jurisdiction.[33]

PARTIES CHOOSING NOT TO PARTICIPATE IN THE ARBITRAL PROCEEDINGS

A person alleged to be a party to arbitral proceedings, but choosing *not* to participate, will not lose the right to object as long as it acts within the time limits[34] for bringing the application to challenge the award once it is published.   **23–012**

"72 Saving for rights of person who takes no part in proceedings

(1) A person alleged to be a party to arbitral proceedings but who takes no part in the proceedings may question—

(a)   whether there is a valid arbitration agreement,
(b)   whether the tribunal is properly constituted, or
(c)   what matters have been submitted to arbitration in accordance with the arbitration agreement,

by proceedings in the court for a declaration or injunction or other appropriate relief.

(2) He also has the same right as a party to the arbitral proceedings to challenge an award—

---

[30] See for example *El Nasharty v J Sainsbury Plc* [2008] 1 Lloyd's Rep. 360.
[31] See for example *Premium Nafta Products Ltd v Fili Shipping Co Ltd* [2007] Bus. L.R. 1725.
[32] For example where it is alleged that the entire document containing the alleged agreements has been forged: *Premium Nafta Products v Fili Shipping Co Ltd* [2007] Bus. L.R. 1725 at [17].
[33] See *Caltex Gas Co Ltd v China National Petroleum Corp* [2001] EWCA Civ 788; [2001] 1 W.L.R 1892 at [79].
[34] See para.23–016.

(a) by an application under section 67 on the ground of lack of substantive jurisdiction in relation to him, or

(b) by an application under section 68 on the ground of serious irregularity (within the meaning of that section) affecting him;

and section 70(2) (duty to exhaust arbitral procedures) does not apply in his case."

Participating means participating either by way of challenge to the jurisdiction, or in relation to the merits of the underlying claim.[35]

PREVIOUS PROCEEDINGS BEFORE A FOREIGN COURT

23–013   The right to object can also be lost where the matter has been resolved in proceedings in a foreign court. If a jurisdictional challenge has already been raised in and determined by a foreign court of competent jurisdiction, that decision may raise an issue estoppel in relation to that particular challenge.[36] However, it should still be open to a party to raise other jurisdictional points not already dealt with by that foreign court.

THE TIMING OF THE APPLICATION TO THE COURT

Requirement for there to have been an award

23–014   An application to the court under s.67 of the AA 1996 can only be made *after* an award has been made by the arbitral tribunal which determines whether the tribunal has jurisdiction over the dispute.

In this sense, a challenge under s.67 of the AA 1996 should be distinguished from an objection during the arbitration proceedings that the Tribunal lacks substantive jurisdiction and the procedure for the determination by the court of jurisdictional issues during the arbitration under s.32 or s.72(1) of the AA 1996 (all of which falls outside the scope of this work).[37]

---

[35] See *Broda Agro Trade v Alfred C Toepfer* [2010] EWCA Civ 1100.

[36] *Leibinger v Stryker Trauma GmbH* [2006] EWHC 690 (Comm); *Kazakhstan v Istil Group Inc* [2006] EWHC 448 (Comm); [2006] 2 Lloyd's Rep. 370.

[37] s.32 gives jurisdiction to the court to determine preliminary points of jurisdiction only where all the parties have agreed in writing, or it is made with the permission of the tribunal and the court is satisfied that the determination of the question is likely to produce substantial savings in costs, the application was made without delay and that there is good reason why the matter should be decided by the court. S.72(1) is addressed in para.23–012: it provides that a party who takes no part in proceedings shall not lose the right to challenge an award under ss.67 or 68 by reason of having failed to exhaust arbitral proceedings.

In most cases it will be appropriate to allow the tribunal to determine its own jurisdiction first and then bring an "appeal" by way of s.67. The DAC Report provides that s.32 was only intended to be used in "exceptional" cases[38] (possibly where the jurisdictional challenge will involve lengthy examination of witnesses of fact and/or expert witnesses[39]) and was not intended to detract from the basic rule in s.30 that the arbitral tribunal may in the first instance rule on its own substantive jurisdiction. Hence, in *Fiona Trust v Privalov*[40] the Court of Appeal emphasised that "it will in general be right for the arbitrators to be the first tribunal to consider whether they have jurisdiction to determine the dispute".

The question whether an award determining jurisdiction has been made raises two sub-questions:

(1) Has there been an "award"?
(2) If so, did the award "determine jurisdiction"?

In *Michael Wilson v Emmott*,[41] Teare J. considered whether an order of the   23–015
tribunal entitled "Sixth Procedural Order" was an "award" for the purposes of s.67. He held that whether or not a decision was an award was a question of substance and not of form, and the test to be applied was whether the reasonable recipient of the decision would have viewed it as an award. On the facts of the case he concluded that the decision was not an award: neither party had requested the tribunal to issue an award as to jurisdiction, the language used was not the formal language usually found in an award finally determining a dispute as to jurisdiction and the content mainly concerned two procedural questions.

If the decision can properly be regarded as an "award", it does not have to determine jurisdiction *expressly* in order to fall within the scope of s.67. It is sufficient if the award implicitly determines jurisdiction.[42]

Time limit for making the application

Section 70(3) of the AA 1996 requires that the application to the court be   23–016
brought within 28 days of the date of the relevant award, unless there is an arbitral process of appeal or review, in which case the 28 day period will begin to run from the date on which the applicant was notified of the result of the appeal or review on the question of the tribunal's jurisdiction. The application must include all of the grounds of objection on which the

---

[38] See also *Azov Shipping Co v Baltic Shipping Co* [1999] 1 Lloyd's Rep. 68 at 69.
[39] *Azov Shipping Co v Baltic Shipping Co (No.3)* [1999] 2 Lloyd's Rep. 159 at 161.
[40] [2007] 2 Lloyd's Rep. 267 at [34].
[41] [2008] EWHC 2684 (Comm); [2009] 1 Lloyd's Rep. 162 at [17]–[20].
[42] *Vee Networks Ltd v Econet Wireless* [2005] 1 Lloyd's Rep. 192, in which Colman J. held that the implication of a determination by the arbitrator of his substantive jurisdiction depends crucially on whether the issue of substantive jurisdiction has been specifically raised by either of the parties—see [31].

applicant proposes to rely and which are known to it at the time. A party will not be allowed to introduce new grounds of challenge following the expiry of the 28 day time limit if it was aware of the grounds within that period.[43]

Where the arbitral tribunal deals with a jurisdictional issue as a preliminary matter, it may be that the preliminary ruling on that issue takes effect as an award. In such a case the parties need to be alive to the possibility that the time limit may start to run from the date of that ruling as opposed to the date of any final award dealing with the substantive merits.

Further, where a tribunal withholds an award under s.56 of the AA 1996 as security for payment of fees and expenses, the time limit for making the application may expire before the award is even released. In those circumstances, the court might be more likely to exercise its powers to grant an extension of time,[44] unless the non-payment appears to have been a tactical decision by the party wishing to make a challenge.[45]

It will be noted that the 28 day time period is for the making of the application. Notice of the application to the other party is required to be given "promptly", but not necessarily within the 28 day period.[46]

Court's power to extend time

23–017　The court has the power to extend the period of 28 days fixed by the Act.[47] The considerations[48] relevant to an application to extend time in relation to an appeal under s.68 of the AA 1996 are similarly applicable here.[49]

PROCEDURE FOR THE APPLICATION

Notice

23–018　Unlike an appeal under s.69 of the AA 1996, an application under s.67 does not require the permission of the court. It simply requires notice to be given

---

[43] *Westland Helicopters Ltd v Sheikh Salah Al-Hejailan* [2004] 2 Lloyd's Rep. 523; *Tradigrain v State Trading Corp of India* [2006] 1 Lloyd's Rep. 216; *Leibinger v Styker Trauma GmbH* [2005] EWHC 690 (Comm).

[44] *Dulwich Estates v Baptiste* [2007] EWHC 410 (Ch).

[45] As in *Buyuk Camlica Shipping v Progress Bulk Carriers* [2010] EWHC 442 (Comm) at [62]–[64].

[46] AA 1996 s.67(1).

[47] AA 1996 s.80(5), CPR r.62.9 and CPR PD 62 para.11.1.

[48] See *AOOT Kalmneft v Glencore International AG* [2002] 1 Lloyd's Rep. 128 at [53]–[60]; *Nagusina Naveira v Allied Maritime Inc* [2002] EWCA Civ 1147; [2003] 2 C.L.C. 1 and also paras 22–024 and 22–025.

[49] See *Peoples Insurance Co of China v Vysanthi Shipping Co Ltd (The Joanna V)* [2003] 2 Lloyd's Rep. 617 at [27]. Thomas J. expressed the view that the criteria should perhaps be applied more strictly in s.67 cases because AA 1996 itself gives notice that in s.67 cases the right might be lost if not exercised in time. See also *Broda Agro Trade v Alfred C Toepfer* [2009] EWHC 3318 (Comm) in which a delay of 14 months was held to be too long.

to the other parties to the proceedings, including the tribunal. Whilst the application must be made within the 28 day time period[50-51] it is sufficient if notice of the application is given to the other parties "promptly".

Stay of the arbitration proceedings

Whilst the arbitral tribunal may continue the arbitral proceedings and make a further award while the s.67 application is pending,[52] it will often be in the interests of the parties to stay the arbitral proceedings until the jurisdictional issue is resolved. However, everything depends on the circumstances and there may be a good reason to proceed with the arbitration notwithstanding the risk of wasted costs and the difficult decision of the party challenging as to whether to participate in the arbitration.

23–019

The hearing

A challenge under s.67 involves a re-hearing rather than a review.[53] Whereas decisions of an arbitral tribunal that might be challenged under ss.68 and 69 of the AA 1996 have presumptive validity, decisions challenged under s.67 do not.[54] They are either made by a tribunal which has jurisdiction or they are not. It follows that the task of the court is to determine whether the tribunal reached the right answer on the jurisdictional issue and not simply to decide whether the tribunal was entitled to reach the decision it did, as would be the case with a challenge under s.68 and s.69 or in other civil appeals.

23–020

Because the hearing is a full re-hearing, the court will hear oral evidence if there are substantial issues of fact to be determined, including issues of foreign law.[55] The evidence is not restricted to the evidence that was before the arbitral tribunal. The parties are entitled to adduce additional evidence.[56] The reasoning behind this principle is that the s.67 procedure is available to a party that took no part in the arbitral proceedings but wishes to object to the tribunal's jurisdiction. If such a party were not able to adduce fresh evidence, it would significantly undermine the ability of such a party to challenge the award.

[50-51] See para.23–011.

[52] AA 1996 s.67(2).

[53] *Azov Shipping Co v Baltic Shipping Co (No.1)* [1999] 1 Lloyd's Rep. 68 at 70; *Astra SA Insurance and Reinsurance Co v Sphere Drake Insurance Ltd* [2000] 2 Lloyd's Rep. 550 at 551; *AOOT Kalmneft v Glencore* [2002] 1 Lloyd's Rep. 128 at 141; *Electrosteel Castings Ltd v Scan-Trans Shipping & Chartering SDN BHD* [2003] 1 Lloyd's Rep. 190 at [22]; *Peterson Farms v C&M Farming*, ibid. at [18]; *Primetrade AG v Ythan Ltd, The Ythan* [2006] 1 Lloyd's Rep. 457; *The Botnica* [2006] EWHC 1360 (Comm) at [4].

[54] See *Peterson Farms v C&M Farming Ltd* [2003] EWHC 2298 (QB); [2004] 1 Lloyd's Rep. 614 at [26].

[55] *Astra SA Insurance and Reinsurance Co v Sphere Drake Insurance Ltd* [2000] 2 Lloyd's Rep. 550.

[56] e.g. *AOOT Kalmneft v Glencore* [2002] 1 Lloyd's Rep. 128 at [91].

This does not mean that a party who did take part in the arbitral proceedings is completely free to adduce whatever new evidence it likes at the re-hearing. On the contrary, it has been emphasised that, so far as possible, a party must bring forward all its evidence at the hearing before the arbitrators and that if a party wishes to adduce new evidence before the court it must give notice to the other side. If the other side does not agree, the party wishing to adduce the new evidence must seek permission from the court, and the court may decide not to permit the new evidence where to do so would result in substantial prejudice to the other side which cannot fairly be dealt with either by appropriate orders for costs or by an adjournment.[57] The introduction of new evidence is closely linked to the restriction that a party cannot raise grounds of objection that have not previously been raised before the arbitral tribunal.[58]

23–021 The principle that the hearing needs to be a full re-hearing is still controversial among arbitration practitioners. The effect can be to require the parties to go through two identical (and often very expensive) hearings on jurisdiction.

There are two possible solutions to this but neither is very satisfactory. The first would be to remove the tribunal's power to resolve issues as to its own jurisdiction. In practice, this would mean more arbitrations being derailed by jurisdiction objections. The second would be to limit the court's power to a review (rather than re-hearing) of a tribunal's ruling on its substantive jurisdiction. This runs into the juridical objection addressed at the outset of this chapter that it is permitting a tribunal to pull itself up by its own boot straps.

Instead, it is submitted that, where it is anticipated that the jurisdictional challenge will involve lengthy examination of evidence, the parties should be alive to the possibility of asking the tribunal for permission to make an application under s.32 of AA 1996. Section 32 allows a party to make an application to the court to determine any question as to the substantive jurisdiction of the tribunal[59] and, unlike s.67, the application can be made before any award is handed down.

POWERS OF THE COURT

Decision on jurisdiction

23–022 On an application under s.67 of the AA 1996, the court is to determine whether the award as to jurisdiction should be confirmed, varied or set aside in whole or in part.[60]

---

[57] *Primetrade AG v Ythan Ltd, The Ythan* [2006] 1 Lloyd's Rep. 457 at [62]–[63].
[58] See paras 23–009 to 23–011.
[59] AA 1996 s.32(1). S.32 is not an appeal; rather it is a preliminary ruling on jurisdiction made by the court. For this reason it falls outside the scope of this work.
[60] AA 1996 s.67(3).

The general principle is that if the court considers that the award was made entirely without jurisdiction, or if a substantial, non-severable part of the award was made without jurisdiction, the whole of the award should be set aside. However, the court will, wherever possible, just sever the offending part of the award.[61]

Where only part of the award is set aside, the arbitral proceedings may be able to continue and the tribunal may be entitled to make further awards within its jurisdiction.[62] Whilst an order to set aside an award or part or of an award deprives that award or part of any legal effect, the arbitration can still continue unless the jurisdictional objection which has been upheld by the court relates to the appointment of the arbitration tribunal or the validity of the agreement to arbitrate, so as to deprive the appointed arbitration tribunal of any further role.[63]

Ordering the provision of security

Where an application is made under s.67 (as with applications under ss. 68 and 69), the court may make an order requiring: 23–023

(1) the applicant to provide security for costs[64]; and/or
(2) any money payable under the award to be paid into court or otherwise secured.[65]

The court may direct that the application be dismissed if the order is not complied with.

In relation to an order that the applicant provide security for costs, it would appear that the usual criteria for securing costs will apply.[66]

In relation to securing the money payable under the award, the court has indicated that such an order should only be made in exceptional circumstances (given that an application can be made pursuant to s.67 as of right) and that the purpose of the order is purely to prevent the applicant from putting his assets beyond the reach of the respondent and is not intended to be used a method for enforcing an award (e.g. by compelling a third party to make a payment as a condition of allowing a challenge to the jurisdiction).[67]

---

[61] See for example *Peterson Farms v C&M Farming Ltd* [2004] 1 Lloyd's Rep. 603.
[62] *Hussmann (Europe) Ltd v Pharaon* [2003] 1 All E.R. (Comm) 879 at [83].
[63] *Hussmann (Europer) Ltd v Pharaon* [2003] 1 All E.R. (Comm) 879. See also *Vee Networks Ltd v Econet Wireless International Ltd* [2004] EWHC 2909 (Comm) at [21].
[64] AA 1996 s.70(6).
[65] AA 1996 s.70(7).
[66] Although it should be noted that AA 1996 s.70(6) excludes the application of CPR r.25.13.
[67] *Peterson Farms v C&M Farming Ltd* [2003] EWHC 2298 (QB); [2004] Lloyd's Rep. 614.

Having said that, it seems that the court can make a preliminary assessment of the strength of the challenge and that such orders can and will be made when a feeble jurisdictional challenge is made in an effort to defer payment.[68]

Power to order tribunal to give reasons

23–024   As with appeals under s.68 and s.69 of the AA 1996, a court considering an application under s.67 has the power to order the arbitral tribunal to state the reasons for its decision in sufficient detail to enable the court to properly consider the application, where either[69]:

(1) The award does not contain the tribunal's reasons; or
(2) The award does not set out the tribunal's reasons in sufficient detail to enable the court properly to consider the application.

However, given that the "appeal" under s.67 is a re-hearing rather than a review of the arbitral tribunal's decision and that the award being challenged may not have even touched upon the jurisdictional issues, it is doubted whether there will be many cases where the court will need to exercise this power in relation to an application under s.67.

FURTHER APPEALS

23–025   The leave of the court is required for any appeal from the decision of the court under s.67.[70] The procedure is the same as for an appeal from the decision of the court under s.68 of the AA 1996. It is settled that the court whose leave is required is the trial judge. If the judge refuses permission, the Court of Appeal has no jurisdiction to grant it.[71]

In *Republic of Kazakhstan v Istil Group Ltd*[72] the Court of Appeal rejected the argument that s.67(4) should be read as implying a right to appeal to the Court of Appeal in order to be compatible with art.6 of the European Convention on Human Rights. The Court held that art.6 was satisfied because the rule supported the objective that only second appeals which had a reasonable prospect of success should be allowed.

---

[68] See *Tajik Aluminium Plant v Hydro Aluminium* [2006] EWHC 11 35 (Comm), in which Morison J. clearly had considerable doubts about Tajik's jurisdictional challenge and misgivings about allowing it to have another bite of the cherry in the form of a second full trial on its arguments about the validity of the agreement. He assuaged these doubts by ordering Tajik to provide security for the US$150m award.

[69] AA 1996 s.70(4).

[70] AA 1996 s.67(4).

[71] See *Henry Boot Construction (UK) Ltd v Malmaison Hotel (Manchester) Ltd* [2001] 1 Q.B. 388 and *Athletic Union of Constantinople v National Basketball Association* [2002] 1 W.L.R. 2863.

[72] [2007] EWCA Civ 471; [2007] 2 Lloyd's Rep. 548 at [26].

There is an exception to the general rule that the permission of the trial judge must be obtained, whereby the Court of Appeal may give permission where there has been a failure by the judge to act judicially in reaching the decision on permission to appeal.[73] However, the Court of Appeal has noted that:

> "It is all too easy to dress up an argument on paper seeking to persuade this court that the process of the hearing in respect of the permission to appeal has been unfair or that the judge has not engaged properly with the submission made but it is an application that is only very rarely going to succeed."[74]

More generally, first instance judges have been discouraged by the Court of Appeal from granting permission for an expensive second appeal in relation to jurisdiction. In *Amec Civil Engineering Ltd v Secretary of State for Transport*[75] it was observed that:

> "The policy of the 1996 Act does not encourage such further appeals which in general delay the resolution of disputes by the contractual machinery of arbitration. The judge and Mr Akenhead had reached the same conclusion for substantially the same reasons. Their combined experience and authority was, I think, sufficient to conclude the matter without an expensive second appeal."

23–026

---

[73] *CGU v AstraZeneca* [2007] 1 Lloyd's Rep. 142.
[74] *Republic of Kazakhstan v Istil Group Ltd (No.3)* [2007] EWCA Civ 471 at [33], per Longmore L.J.
[75] [2005] 1 W.L.R. 2339 at [9].

APPENDIX ONE

Part 52 Appeals

Contents of this Part

I GENERAL RULES ABOUT APPEALS

52.1 Scope and interpretation

App 1–001   (1) The rules in this Part apply to appeals to—
(a) the civil division of the Court of Appeal;

(b) the High Court; and

(c) a county court.

(2) This Part does not apply to an appeal in detailed assessment proceedings against a decision of an authorised court officer.

(Rules 47.20 to 47.23 deal with appeals against a decision of an authorised court officer in detailed assessment proceedings)

(3) In this Part—

(a) 'appeal' includes an appeal by way of case stated;

(b) 'appeal court' means the court to which an appeal is made;

(c) 'lower court' means the court, tribunal or other person or body from whose decision an appeal is brought;

(d) 'appellant' means a person who brings or seeks to bring an appeal;

(e) 'respondent' means—

    (i) a person other than the appellant who was a party to the proceedings in the lower court and who is affected by the appeal; and

    (ii) a person who is permitted by the appeal court to be a party to the appeal; and

(f) 'appeal notice' means an appellant's or respondent's notice.

(4) This Part is subject to any rule, enactment or practice direction which sets out special provisions with regard to any particular category of appeal.

52.2 Parties to comply with Practice Directions 52

All parties to an appeal must comply with Practice Direction 52.   App 1–002

52.3 Permission

(1) An appellant or respondent requires permission to appeal—   App 1–003

(a) where the appeal is from a decision of a judge in a county court or the High Court, except where the appeal is against—

    (i) a committal order;

    (ii) a refusal to grant habeas corpus; or

    (iii) a secure accommodation order made under section 25 of the Children Act 1989[1]; or

(b) as provided by Practice Direction 52.

(Other enactments may provide that permission is required for particular appeals)

(2) An application for permission to appeal may be made—

(a) to the lower court at the hearing at which the decision to be appealed was made; or

(b) to the appeal court in an appeal notice.

(Rule 52.4 sets out the time limits for filing an appellant's notice at the appeal court. Rule 52.5 sets out the time limits for filing a respondent's notice at the appeal court. Any application for permission to appeal to the appeal court must be made in the appeal notice (see rules 52.4(1) and 52.5(3))

---

[1] 1989 c.41.

(Rule 52.13(1) provides that permission is required from the Court of Appeal for all appeals to that court from a decision of a county court or the High Court which was itself made on appeal)

(3) Where the lower court refuses an application for permission to appeal, a further application for permission to appeal may be made to the appeal court.

(4) Subject to paragraph (4A), where the appeal court, without a hearing, refuses permission to appeal, the person seeking permission may request the decision to be reconsidered at a hearing.

(4A) Where the Court of Appeal refuses permission to appeal without a hearing, it may, if it considers that the application is totally without merit, make an order that the person seeking permission may not request the decision to be reconsidered at a hearing.

(4B) Rule 3.3(5) will not apply to an order that the person seeking permission may not request the decision to be reconsidered at a hearing made under paragraph (4A).

(5) A request under paragraph (4) must be filed within 7 days after service of the notice that permission has been refused.

(6) Permission to appeal may be given only where—
(a) the court considers that the appeal would have a real prospect of success; or
(b) there is some other compelling reason why the appeal should be heard.

(7) An order giving permission may—
(a) limit the issues to be heard; and
(b) be made subject to conditions.

(Rule 3.1(3) also provides that the court may make an order subject to conditions)

(Rule 25.15 provides for the court to order security for costs of an appeal)

52.4 Appellant's notice

App 1–004 (1) Where the appellant seeks permission from the appeal court it must be requested in the appellant's notice.

(2) The appellant must file the appellant's notice at the appeal court within—
(a) such period as may be directed by the lower court (which may be longer or shorter than the period referred to in sub-paragraph (b)); or
(b) where the court makes no such direction, 21 days after the date of the decision of the lower court that the appellant wishes to appeal.

(3) Unless the appeal court orders otherwise, an appellant's notice must be served on each respondent—
(a) as soon as practicable; and
(b) in any event not later than 7 days,
after it is filed.

52.5 Respondent's notice

(1) A respondent may file and serve a respondent's notice.

App 1–005

(2) A respondent who—
(a) is seeking permission to appeal from the appeal court; or
(b) wishes to ask the appeal court to uphold the order of the lower court for reasons different from or additional to those given by the lower court, must file a respondent's notice.

(3) Where the respondent seeks permission from the appeal court it must be requested in the respondent's notice.

(4) A respondent's notice must be filed within—
(a) such period as may be directed by the lower court; or
(b) where the court makes no such direction, 14 days after the date in paragraph (5).

(5) The date referred to in paragraph (4) is—
(a) the date the respondent is served with the appellant's notice where—
 (i) permission to appeal was given by the lower court; or
 (ii) permission to appeal is not required;
(b) the date the respondent is served with notification that the appeal court has given the appellant permission to appeal; or
(c) the date the respondent is served with notification that the application for permission to appeal and the appeal itself are to be heard together.

(6) Unless the appeal court orders otherwise a respondent's notice must be served on the appellant and any other respondent—
(a) as soon as practicable; and
(b) in any event not later than 7 days, after it is filed.

52.6 Variation of time

(1) An application to vary the time limit for filing an appeal notice must be made to the appeal court.

App 1–006

(2) The parties may not agree to extend any date or time limit set by—
(a) these Rules;
(b) Practice Direction 52; or
(c) an order of the appeal court or the lower court.

(Rule 3.1(2)(a) provides that the court may extend or shorten the time for compliance with any rule, practice direction or court order (even if an application for extension is made after the time for compliance has expired))

(Rule 3.1(2)(b) provides that the court may adjourn or bring forward a hearing)

52.7 Stay

Unless—
(a) the appeal court or the lower court orders otherwise; or

App 1–007

(b) the appeal is from the Immigration and Asylum Chamber of the Upper Tribunal, an appeal shall not operate as a stay of any order or decision of the lower court.

52.8 Amendment of appeal notice

App 1–008

An appeal notice may not be amended without the permission of the appeal court.

52.9 Striking out appeal notices and setting aside or imposing conditions on permission to appeal

App 1–009

(1) The appeal court may—
(a) strike out the whole or part of an appeal notice;
(b) set aside permission to appeal in whole or in part;
(c) impose or vary conditions upon which an appeal may be brought.

(2) The court will only exercise its powers under paragraph (1) where there is a compelling reason for doing so.

(3) Where a party was present at the hearing at which permission was given he may not subsequently apply for an order that the court exercise its powers under sub-paragraphs (1)(b) or (1)(c).

52.10 Appeal court's powers

App 1–010

(1) In relation to an appeal the appeal court has all the powers of the lower court.

(Rule 52.1(4) provides that this Part is subject to any enactment that sets out special provisions with regard to any particular category of appeal—where such an enactment gives a statutory power to a tribunal, person or other body it may be the case that the appeal court may not exercise that power on an appeal)

(2) The appeal court has power to—
(a) affirm, set aside or vary any order or judgment made or given by the lower court;
(b) refer any claim or issue for determination by the lower court;
(c) order a new trial or hearing;
(d) make orders for the payment of interest;
(e) make a costs order.

(3) In an appeal from a claim tried with a jury the Court of Appeal may, instead of ordering a new trial—
(a) make an order for damages; or
(b) vary an award of damages made by the jury.

(4) The appeal court may exercise its powers in relation to the whole or part of an order of the lower court.

(Part 3 contains general rules about the court's case management powers)

(5) If the appeal court—
(a) refuses an application for permission to appeal;
(b) strikes out an appellant's notice; or
(c) dismisses an appeal,
and it considers that the application, the appellant's notice or the appeal is totally without merit, the provisions of paragraph (6) must be complied with.

(6) Where paragraph (5) applies—
(a) the court's order must record the fact that it considers the application, the appellant's notice or the appeal to be totally without merit; and
(b) the court must at the same time consider whether it is appropriate to make a civil restraint order.

52.11 Hearing of appeals

(1) Every appeal will be limited to a review of the decision of the lower court unless— **App 1–011**
(a) a practice direction makes different provision for a particular category of appeal; or
(b) the court considers that in the circumstances of an individual appeal it would be in the interests of justice to hold a re-hearing.

(2) Unless it orders otherwise, the appeal court will not receive—
(a) oral evidence; or
(b) evidence which was not before the lower court.

(3) The appeal court will allow an appeal where the decision of the lower court was—
(a) wrong; or
(b) unjust because of a serious procedural or other irregularity in the proceedings in the lower court.

(4) The appeal court may draw any inference of fact which it considers justified on the evidence.

(5) At the hearing of the appeal a party may not rely on a matter not contained in his appeal notice unless the appeal court gives permission.

52.12 Non-disclosure of Part 36 offers and payments

(1) The fact that a Part 36 offer or payment into court has been made must not be disclosed to any judge of the appeal court who is to hear or determine— **App 1–012**
(a) an application for permission to appeal; or
(b) an appeal,
until all questions (other than costs) have been determined.

(2) Paragraph (1) does not apply if the Part 36 offer or payment into court is relevant to the substance of the appeal.

(3) Paragraph (1) does not prevent disclosure in any application in the appeal proceedings if disclosure of the fact that a Part 36 offer or payment into court has been made is properly relevant to the matter to be decided.

(Rule 36.3 has the effect that a Part 36 offer made in proceedings at first instance will not have consequences in any appeal proceedings. Therefore, a fresh Part 36 offer needs to be made in appeal proceedings. However, rule 52.12 applies to a Part 36 offer whether made in the original proceedings or in the appeal.)

52.12A Statutory appeals—court's power to hear any person

App 1–013

(1) In a statutory appeal, any person may apply for permission—
(a) to file evidence; or
(b) to make representations at the appeal hearing.

(2) An application under paragraph (1) must be made promptly.

II SPECIAL PROVISIONS APPLYING TO THE COURT OF APPEAL

52.13 Second appeals to the court

App 1–014

(1) Permission is required from the Court of Appeal for any appeal to that court from a decision of a county court or the High Court which was itself made on appeal.

(2) The Court of Appeal will not give permission unless it considers that—
(a) the appeal would raise an important point of principle or practice; or
(b) there is some other compelling reason for the Court of Appeal to hear it.

52.14 Assignment of appeals to the Court of Appeal

App 1–015

(1) Where the court from or to which an appeal is made or from which permission to appeal is sought ('the relevant court') considers that—
(a) an appeal which is to be heard by a county court or the High Court would raise an important point of principle or practice; or
(b) there is some other compelling reason for the Court of Appeal to hear it, the relevant court may order the appeal to be transferred to the Court of Appeal.

(The Master of the Rolls has the power to direct that an appeal which would be heard by a county court or the High Court should be heard instead by the Court of Appeal—see section 57 of the Access to Justice Act 1999)[1]

(2) The Master of the Rolls or the Court of Appeal may remit an appeal to the court in which the original appeal was or would have been brought.

52.15 Judicial review appeals

App 1–016

(1) Where permission to apply for judicial review has been refused at a hearing in the High Court, the person seeking that permission may apply to the Court of Appeal for permission to appeal.

---

[1] 1999 c.22.

(2) An application in accordance with paragraph (1) must be made within 7 days of the decision of the High Court to refuse to give permission to apply for judicial review.

(3) On an application under paragraph (1), the Court of Appeal may, instead of giving permission to appeal, give permission to apply for judicial review.

(4) Where the Court of Appeal gives permission to apply for judicial review in accordance with paragraph (3), the case will proceed in the High Court unless the Court of Appeal orders otherwise.

52.16 Who may exercise the powers of the Court of Appeal

(1) A court officer assigned to the Civil Appeals Office who is—   **App 1–017**
(a) a barrister; or
(b) a solicitor
   may exercise the jurisdiction of the Court of Appeal with regard to the matters set out in paragraph (2) with the consent of the Master of the Rolls.

(2) The matters referred to in paragraph (1) are—
(a) any matter incidental to any proceedings in the Court of Appeal;
(b) any other matter where there is no substantial dispute between the parties; and
(c) the dismissal of an appeal or application where a party has failed to comply with any order, rule or practice direction.

(3) A court officer may not decide an application for—
(a) permission to appeal;
(b) bail pending an appeal;
(c) an injunction;
(d) a stay of any proceedings, other than a temporary stay of any order or decision of the lower court over a period when the Court of Appeal is not sitting or cannot conveniently be convened.

(4) Decisions of a court officer may be made without a hearing.

(5) A party may request any decision of a court officer to be reviewed by the Court of Appeal.

(6) At the request of a party, a hearing will be held to reconsider a decision of—
(a) a single judge; or
(b) a court officer,
   made without a hearing.

(6A) A request under paragraph (5) or (6) must be filed within 7 days after the party is served with notice of the decision.

(7) A single judge may refer any matter for a decision by a court consisting of two or more judges.

(Section 54(6) of the Supreme Court Act 1981[1] provides that there is no appeal from the decision of a single judge on an application for permission to appeal)

---

[1] 1981 c.54; section 54 was amended by section 59 of the Access to Justice Act 1999 (c.22).

(Section 58(2) of the Supreme Court Act 1981[1] provides that there is no appeal to the Supreme Court from decisions of the Court of Appeal that—

(a) are taken by a single judge or any officer or member of staff of that court in proceedings incidental to any cause or matter pending before the civil division of that court; and

(b) do not involve the determination of an appeal or of an application for permission to appeal, and which may be called into question by rules of court. Rules 52.16(5) and (6) provide the procedure for the calling into question of such decisions)

III PROVISIONS ABOUT REOPENING APPEALS

52.17 Reopening of final appeals

App 1–018

(1) The Court of Appeal or the High Court will not reopen a final determination of any appeal unless—

(a) it is necessary to do so in order to avoid real injustice;

(b) the circumstances are exceptional and make it appropriate to reopen the appeal; and

(c) there is no alternative effective remedy.

(2) In paragraphs (1), (3), (4) and (6), "appeal" includes an application for permission to appeal.

(3) This rule does not apply to appeals to a county court.

(4) Permission is needed to make an application under this rule to reopen a final determination of an appeal even in cases where under rule 52.3(1) permission was not needed for the original appeal.

(5) There is no right to an oral hearing of an application for permission unless, exceptionally, the judge so directs.

(6) The judge will not grant permission without directing the application to be served on the other party to the original appeal and giving him an opportunity to make representations.

(7) There is no right of appeal or review from the decision of the judge on the application for permission, which is final.

(8) The procedure for making an application for permission is set out in Practice Direction 52.

---

[1] 1981 c.54; section 58 was amended by section 60 of the Access to Justice Act 1999 (c.22).

IV STATUTORY RIGHTS OF APPEAL

52.18 Appeals under the Law of Property Act 1922[1]

An appeal lies to the High Court against a decision of the Secretary of State under paragraph 16 of Schedule 15 to the Law of Property Act 1922[2].

App 1–019

52.19 Appeals from certain tribunals

(1) A person who was a party to proceedings before a tribunal referred to in section 11(1) of the Tribunals and Inquiries Act 1992[3] and is dissatisfied in point of law with the decision of the tribunal may appeal to the High Court.

App 1–020

(2) The tribunal may, of its own initiative or at the request of a party to the proceedings before it, state, in the form of a special case for the decision of the High Court, a question of law arising in the course of the proceedings.

52.20 Appeals under certain planning legislation

(1) Where the Secretary of State has given a decision in proceedings on an appeal under Part VII of the Town and Country Planning Act 1990[4] against an enforcement notice—
(a) the appellant;
(b) the local planning authority; or
(c) another person having an interest in the land to which the notice relates, may appeal to the High Court against the decision on a point of law.

App 1–021

(2) Where the Secretary of State has given a decision in proceedings on an appeal under Part VIII of that Act against a notice under section 207 of that Act—
(a) the appellant;
(b) the local planning authority; or
(c) any person (other than the appellant) on whom the notice was served, may appeal to the High Court against the decision on a point of law.

(3) Where the Secretary of State has given a decision in proceedings on an appeal under section 39 of the Planning (Listed Buildings and Conservation Areas) Act 1990() against a listed building enforcement notice—
(a) the appellant;
(b) the local planning authority; or
(c) any other person having an interest in the land to which the notice relates, may appeal to the High Court against the decision on a point of law.

---

[1] 1922 c. 16.
[2] 1922 c. 16. Schedule 15, paragraph 16 was amended by the Law of Property (Amendment) Act 1924 (c. 5), section 2 and Schedule 2, paragraph 5(8) and S.I. 2002/794, article 5(1) and Schedule 1, paragraph 1(d).
[3] 1992 c. 53.
[4] 1990 c. 8.

APPENDIX 2

Practice Direction
Appeals

This Practice Direction supplements Part 52

Contents of this Practice Direction

App 2–001   **1.1**   This Practice Direction is divided into five sections:

- Section I—General provisions about appeals
- Section II—General provisions about statutory appeals and appeals by way of case stated
- Section III—Provisions about specific appeals
- Section IV—Provisions about reopening appeals
- Section V—Transitional provisions relating to the abolition of the Asylum and Immigration Tribunal.

SECTION I—GENERAL PROVISIONS ABOUT APPEALS

App 2–002   **2.1**   This practice direction applies to all appeals to which Part 52 applies except where specific provision is made for appeals to the Court of Appeal.

2.2   For the purpose only of appeals to the Court of Appeal from cases in family proceedings this Practice Direction will apply with such modifications as may be required.

ROUTES OF APPEAL

App 2–003   **2A.1**   The court or judge to which an appeal is to be made (subject to obtaining any necessary permission) is set out in the tables below:

Table 1[1] addresses appeals in cases other than insolvency proceedings and those cases to which Table 3 applies;

Table 2 addresses insolvency proceedings; and

Table 3 addresses certain family cases to which CPR Part 52 may apply.

The tables do not include so-called 'leap frog' appeals either to the Court of Appeal pursuant to s. 57 of the Access to Justice Act 1999 or to the House of Lords pursuant to s 13 of the Administration of Justice Act 1969.

(An interactive routes of appeal guide can be found on the Court of Appeal's website at http://www.hmcourts-service.gov.uk/infoabout/coa_civil/routes_app/index.htm)

TABLE 1

In this Table, reference to—

App 2–004

(a) a 'Circuit judge' includes a recorder or a district judge who is exercising the jurisdiction of a circuit judge with the permission of the designated civil judge in respect of that case (see Practice Direction 2B (Allocation of cases to levels of judiciary), paragraph 11.1(d));

(b) 'the Destinations of Appeal Order' means the Access to Justice Act 1999 (Destination of Appeals) Order 2000; and

(c) 'final decision' has the meaning for the purposes of this table as set out in paragraphs 2A.2 and 2A.3.

Court	Track/nature of claim	Judge who made the decision	Nature of the decision under appeal	Apeal Court
County	Part 7 claim	District judge	Interim decision	Circuit judge in the county court
County	Part 7 claim, other than a claim allocated to the multi-track	District judge	Final decision	Circuit judge in the county
County	Part 7 claim, allocated to the multi-track	District judge	Final decision	Court of Appeal
County	Part 8 claim	District judge	Any decision	Circuit judge in the county court
County	Claims or originating or pre-action applications started otherwise than by a Part 7 or Part 8 claim (for example an application under Part 23)	District judge	Any decision	Circuit judge in the county court

---

[1] Reproduced with the kind permission of Tottel Publishing, publisher of *Manual of Civil Appeals*.

Court	Track/nature of claim	Judge who made the decision	Nature of the decision under appeal	Apeal Court
County	Specialist proceedings (under the Companies Act 1985 or the Companies Act 1989 or to which Sections I or II of Part 57 or any of Parts 60, 62 or 63 apply)	District judge	Interim decision	Circuit judge in the county court
County	Specialist proceedings (under the Companies Act 1985 or the Companies Act 1989 or to which Sections I or II, of Part 57 or any of Parts 60, 62 or 63 apply)	District judge	Final decision	Court of Appeal
County	Part 7 claim	Circuit judge	Interim decision	Single judge of the High Court
County	Part 7 claim, other than a claim allocated to the multi-track	Circuit judge	Final decision	Single judge of the High Court
County	Part 7 claim, allocated to the multi-track	Circuit judge	Final decision	Court of Appeal
County	Part 8 claim	Circuit judge	Any decision	Single judge of the High Court
County	Claims or originating or pre-action applications started otherwise than by a Part 7 or Part 8 claim (for example an application under Part 23)	Circuit judge	Any decision	Single judge of the High Court
County	Specialist proceedings (under the Companies Act 1985 or the Companies Act 1989 or to which Sections I or II of Part 57 or any of Parts 60, 62 or 63 apply)	Circuit judge	Interim decision	Single judge of the High Court

Court	Track/nature of claim	Judge who made the decision	Nature of the decision under appeal	Apeal Court
County	Specialist proceedings (under the Companies Act 1985 or the Companies Act 1989 or to which Sections I or II of Part 57 or any of Parts 60, 62 or 63 apply)	Circuit judge	Final decision	Court of Appeal
High	Part 7 claim	Master, district judge sitting in a district registry or any other judge referred to in article 2 of the Destination of Appeals Order (where appropriate)	Interim decision	Single judge of the High Court
High	Part 7 claim, other than a claim allocated to the multi-track	Master, district judge sitting in a district registry or any other judge referred to in article 2 of the Destination of Appeals Order (where appropriate)	Final decision	Single judge of the High Court
High	Part 7 claim, allocated to the multi-track	Master, district judge sitting in a district registry or any other judge referred to in article 2 of the Destination of Appeals Order (where appropriate)	Final decision	Court of Appeal

Court	Track/nature of claim	Judge who made the decision	Nature of the decision under appeal	Apeal Court
High	Part 8 claim	Master, district judge sitting in a district registry or any other judge referred to in article 2 of the Destination of Appeals Order (where appropriate)	Any decision	Single judge of the High Court
High	Claims or originating or pre-action applications started otherwise than by a Part 7 or Part 8 claim (for example an application under Part 23)	Master, district judge sitting in a district registry or any other judge referred to in article 2 of the Destination of Appeals Order (where appropriate)	Any decision	Single judge of the High Court
High	Specialist proceedings (under the Companies Act 1985 or the Companies Act 1989 or to which Sections I, II, or III of Part 57 or any of Parts 58 to 63 apply)	Master, district judge sitting in a district registry or any other judge referred to in article 2 of the Destination of Appeals Order (where appropriate)	Interim decision	Single judge of the High Court
High	Specialist proceedings (under the Companies Act 1985 or the Companies Act 1989 or to which Sections I, II or III of Part 57 or any of Parts 58 to 63 apply)	Master, district judge sitting in a district registry or any other judge referred to in article 2 of the Destination of Appeals Order (where appropriate)	Final decision	Court of Appeal
High	Any	High Court judge	Any decision	Court of Appeal

TABLE 2

Insolvency proceedings Circuit In this Table references to a 'Circuit judge' include a recorder or a district judge who is exercising the jurisdiction of a circuit judge with the permission of the designated civil judge in respect of that case (see: Practice Direction 2B, paragraph 11.1(d)).

App 2–005

Court	Track/nature of claim	Judge who made the decision	Nature of the decision under appeal	Apeal Court
County	*Insolvency*	*District judge or circuit judge*	Any	*Single judge of the High Court*
High Court	Insolvency	Registrar	Any	Single judge of the High Court
High Court	Insolvency	High Court judge	Any	Court of Appeal

TABLE 3

Proceedings which may be heard in the Family Division of the High Court and to which the CPR may apply. Appeal Centres The proceedings to which this table will apply include proceedings under the Inheritance (Provision for Family and Dependants) Act 1975 and proceedings under the Trusts of Land and Appointment of Trustees Act 1996.

App 2–006

For the meaning of 'final decision' for the purposes of this table see paragraphs 2A.2 and 2A.3 below.

Court	Track/nature of claim	Judge who made the decision	Nature of the decision under appeal	Apeal Court
High Court Principal Registry of the Family Division	*District judge*	*Proceedings under CPR Pt 8 (if not allocated to any track or if simply treated as allocated to the multi-track under CPR 8.9(c))*	*Any decision*	*High Court judge of the Family Division*
High Court Principal Registry of the Family Division	District judge	Proceedings under CPR Pt 8 specifically allocated to the multi-track by an order of the court.	Any decision	High Court judge of the Family Division
High Court Principal Registry of the Family Division	District judge	Proceedings under CPR Part 7	Any decision other than a final decision	High Court judge of the Family Division

Court	Track/nature of claim	Judge who made the decision	Nature of the decision under appeal	Apeal Court
High Court Principal Registry of the Family Division	District judge	Proceedings under CPR Part 7 and allocated to the multi-track	Final decision	Court of Appeal
High Court Family Division	High Court Judge	Proceedings under CPR Part 7 or 8	Any	Court of Appeal

2A.2 A 'final decision' is a decision of a court that would finally determine (subject to any possible appeal or detailed assessment of costs) the entire proceedings whichever way the court decided the issues before it. Decisions made on an application to strike-out or for summary judgment are not final decisions for the purpose of determining the appropriate route of appeal (Art. 1 Access to Justice Act 1999 (Destination of Appeals) Order 2000). Accordingly:
  (1) a case management decision;
  (2) the grant or refusal of interim relief;
  (3) a summary judgment;
  (4) a striking out,
  are not final decisions for this purpose.

2A.3 A decision of a court is to be treated as a final decision for routes of appeal purposes where it:
  (1) is made at the conclusion of part of a hearing or trial which has been split into parts; and
  (2) would, if it had been made at the conclusion of that hearing or trial, have been a final decision.
  Accordingly, a judgment on liability at the end of a split trial is a 'final decision' for this purpose and the judgment at the conclusion of the assessment of damages following a judgment on liability is also a 'final decision' for this purpose.

2A.4 An order made:
  (1) on a summary or detailed assessment of costs; or
  (2) on an application to enforce a final decision,
  is not a 'final decision' and any appeal from such an order will follow the routes of appeal set out in the tables above.

  (Section 16(1) of the Supreme Court Act 1981 (as amended); section 77(1) of the County Courts Act 1984 (as amended); and the Access to Justice Act 1999 (Destination of Appeals) Order 2000 set out the provisions governing routes of appeal).

2A.5
  (1) Where an applicant attempts to file an appellant's notice and the appeal court does not have jurisdiction to issue the notice, a court officer may notify the applicant in writing that the appeal court does not have jurisdiction in respect of the notice.
  (2) Before notifying a person under paragraph (1) the court officer must confer—
  (a) with a judge of the appeal court; or,

(b) where the Court of Appeal, Civil Division is the appeal court, with a court officer who exercises the jurisdiction of that Court under rule 52.16.

(3) Where a court officer in the Court of Appeal, Civil Division notifies a person under paragraph (1), rule 52.16(5) shall not apply.

GROUNDS FOR APPEAL

3.1 Rule 52.11(3) (a) and (b) sets out the circumstances in which the appeal court will allow an appeal.   **App 2–007**

3.2 The grounds of appeal should—
(1) set out clearly the reasons why rule 52.11(3)(a) or (b) is said to apply; and
(2) specify, in respect of each ground, whether the ground raises an appeal on a point of law or is an appeal against a finding of fact.

PERMISSION TO APPEAL

4.1 Rule 52.3 sets out the circumstances when permission to appeal is required.   **App 2–008**

4.2 The permission of—
(1) the Court of Appeal; or
(2) where the lower court's rules allow, the lower court,
is required for all appeals to the Court of Appeal except as provided for by statute or rule 52.3.

(The requirement of permission to appeal may be imposed by a practice direction—see rule 52.3(b))

4.3 Where the lower court is not required to give permission to appeal, it may give an indication of its opinion as to whether permission should be given.

(Rule 52.1(3)(c) defines 'lower court')

4.3A
(1) This paragraph applies where a party applies for permission to appeal against a decision at the hearing at which the decision was made.
(2) Where this paragraph applies, the judge making the decision shall state—
(a) whether or not the judgment or order is final;
(b) whether an appeal lies from the judgment or order and, if so, to which appeal court;
(c) whether the court gives permission to appeal; and
(d) if not, the appropriate appeal court to which any further application for permission may be made.

(Rule 40.2(4) contains requirements as to the contents of the judgment or order in these circumstances.)

4.3B Where no application for permission to appeal has been made in accordance with rule 52.3(2)(a) but a party requests further time to make such an application, the court may adjourn the hearing to give that party the opportunity to do so.

Appeals from case management decisions

App 2–009   4.4   Case management decisions include decisions made under rule 3.1(2) and decisions about:
(1) disclosure
(2) filing of witness statements or experts reports
(3) directions about the timetable of the claim
(4) adding a party to a claim
(5) security for costs.

4.5   Where the application is for permission to appeal from a case management decision, the court dealing with the application may take into account whether:
(1) the issue is of sufficient significance to justify the costs of an appeal;
(2) the procedural consequences of an appeal (e.g. loss of trial date) outweigh the significance of the case management decision;
(3) it would be more convenient to determine the issue at or after trial.

Court to which permission to appeal application should be made

App 2–010   4.6   An application for permission should be made orally at the hearing at which the decision to be appealed against is made.

4.7   Where:
(a) no application for permission to appeal is made at the hearing; or
(b) the lower court refuses permission to appeal,
an application for permission to appeal may be made to the appeal court in accordance with rules 52.3(2) and (3).

4.8   There is no appeal from a decision of the appeal court to allow or refuse permission to appeal to that court (although where the appeal court, without a hearing, refuses permission to appeal, the person seeking permission may request that decision to be reconsidered at a hearing). See section 54(4) of the Access to Justice Act and rule 52.3(2), (3), (4) and (5).

Second appeals

App 2–011   4.9   An application for permission to appeal from a decision of the High Court or a county court which was itself made on appeal must be made to the Court of Appeal.

4.10   If permission to appeal is granted the appeal will be heard by the Court of Appeal.

Consideration of Permission without a hearing

App 2–012   4.11   Applications for permission to appeal may be considered by the appeal court without a hearing.

4.12   If permission is granted without a hearing the parties will be notified of that decision and the procedure in paragraphs 6.1 to 6.6 will then apply.

4.13 If permission is refused without a hearing the parties will be notified of that decision with the reasons for it. The decision is subject to the appellant's right to have it reconsidered at an oral hearing. This may be before the same judge.

4.14 A request for the decision to be reconsidered at an oral hearing must be filed at the appeal court within 7 days after service of the notice that permission has been refused. A copy of the request must be served by the appellant on the respondent at the same time.

Permission hearing

4.14A App 2–013
- (1) This paragraph applies where an appellant, who is represented, makes a request for a decision to be reconsidered at an oral hearing.
- (2) The appellant's advocate must, at least 4 days before the hearing, in a brief written statement—
- (a) inform the court and the respondent of the points which he proposes to raise at the hearing;
- (b) set out his reasons why permission should be granted notwithstanding the reasons given for the refusal of permission; and
- (c) confirm, where applicable, that the requirements of paragraph 4.17 have been complied with (appellant in receipt of services funded by the Legal Services Commission).

4.15 Notice of a permission hearing will be given to the respondent but he is not required to attend unless the court requests him to do so.

4.16 If the court requests the respondent's attendance at the permission hearing, the appellant must supply the respondent with a copy of the appeal bundle (see paragraph 5.6A) within 7 days of being notified of the request, or such other period as the court may direct. The costs of providing that bundle shall be borne by the appellant initially, but will form part of the costs of the permission application.

Appellants in receipt of services funded by the Legal Services Commission applying for permission to appeal

4.17 Where the appellant is in receipt of services funded by the Legal Services App 2–014
Commission (or legally aided) and permission to appeal has been refused by the appeal court without a hearing, the appellant must send a copy of the reasons the appeal court gave for refusing permission to the relevant office of the Legal Services Commission as soon as it has been received from the court. The court will require confirmation that this has been done if a hearing is requested to re-consider the question of permission.

Limited permission

4.18 Where a court under rule 52.3(7) gives permission to appeal on some issues App 2–015
only, it will—
- (1) refuse permission on any remaining issues; or
- (2) reserve the question of permission to appeal on any remaining issues to the court hearing the appeal.

4.19 If the court reserves the question of permission under paragraph 4.18(2), the appellant must, within 14 days after service of the court's order, inform the appeal court and the respondent in writing whether he intends to pursue the reserved issues. If the appellant does intend to pursue the reserved issues, the parties must include in any time estimate for the appeal hearing, their time estimate for the reserved issues.

4.20 If the appeal court refuses permission to appeal on the remaining issues without a hearing and the applicant wishes to have that decision reconsidered at an oral hearing, the time limit in rule 52.3(5) shall apply. Any application for an extension of this time limit should be made promptly. The court hearing the appeal on the issues for which permission has been granted will not normally grant, at the appeal hearing, an application to extend the time limit in rule 52.3(5) for the remaining issues.

4.21 If the appeal court refuses permission to appeal on remaining issues at or after an oral hearing, the application for permission to appeal on those issues cannot be renewed at the appeal hearing. See section 54(4) of the Access to Justice Act 1999.

Respondents' costs of permission applications

App 2–016   **4.22** In most cases, applications for permission to appeal will be determined without the court requesting—
   (1) submissions from, or
   (2) if there is an oral hearing, attendance by
 the respondent.

4.23 Where the court does not request submissions from or attendance by the respondent, costs will not normally be allowed to a respondent who volunteers submissions or attendance.

4.24 Where the court does request—
   (1) submissions from; or
   (2) attendance by the respondent,
 the court will normally allow the respondent his costs if permission is refused.

APPELLANT'S NOTICE

App 2–017   **5.1** An appellant's notice must be filed and served in all cases. Where an application for permission to appeal is made to the appeal court it must be applied for in the appellant's notice.

Human Rights

App 2–018   **5.1A**
   (1) This paragraph applies where the appellant seeks—
   (a) to rely on any issue under the Human Rights Act 1998; or
   (b) a remedy available under that Act,
 for the first time in an appeal.

(2) The appellant must include in his appeal notice the information required by paragraph 15.1 of Practice Direction 16.

(3) Paragraph 15.2 of Practice Direction 16 applies as if references to a statement of case were to the appeal notice.

5.1B CPR rule 19.4A and Practice Direction 19A shall apply as if references to the case management conference were to the application for permission to appeal.

(Practice Direction 19A provides for notice to be given and parties joined in certain circumstances to which this paragraph applies)

Extension of time for filing appellant's notice

5.2 Where the time for filing an appellant's notice has expired, the appellant must—

App 2–019

(a) file the appellant's notice; and

(b) include in that appellant's notice an application for an extension of time.
The appellant's notice should state the reason for the delay and the steps taken prior to the application being made.

5.3 Where the appellant's notice includes an application for an extension of time and permission to appeal has been given or is not required the respondent has the right to be heard on that application. He must be served with a copy of the appeal bundle (see paragraph 5.6A). However, a respondent who unreasonably opposes an extension of time runs the risk of being ordered to pay the appellant's costs of that application.

5.4 If an extension of time is given following such an application the procedure at paragraphs 6.1 to 6.6 applies.

Applications

5.5 Notice of an application to be made to the appeal court for a remedy incidental to the appeal (e.g. an interim remedy under rule 25.1 or an order for security for costs) may be included in the appeal notice or in a Part 23 application notice.

App 2–020

(Rule 25.15 deals with security for costs of an appeal)
(Paragraph 11 of this practice direction contains other provisions relating to applications)

Documents

5.6

App 2–021

(1) This paragraph applies to every case except where the appeal—

(a) relates to a claim allocated to the small claims track; and

(b) is being heard in a county court or the High Court.

(Paragraph 5.8 applies where this paragraph does not apply)

(2) The appellant must file the following documents together with an appeal bundle (see paragraph 5.6A) with his appellant's notice—

(a) two additional copies of the appellant's notice for the appeal court; and

(b) one copy of the appellant's notice for each of the respondents;

   (c)   one copy of his skeleton argument for each copy of the appellant's notice that is filed (see paragraph 5.9);

   (d)   a sealed copy of the order being appealed;

   (e)   a copy of any order giving or refusing permission to appeal, together with a copy of the judge's reasons for allowing or refusing permission to appeal;

   (f)   any witness statements or affidavits in support of any application included in the appellant's notice.

   (g)   a copy of the order allocating a case to a track (if any).

5.6A

   (1)   An appellant must include in his appeal bundle the following documents:

   (a)   a sealed copy of the appellant's notice;

   (b)   a sealed copy of the order being appealed;

   (c)   a copy of any order giving or refusing permission to appeal, together with a copy of the judge's reasons for allowing or refusing permission to appeal;

   (d)   any affidavit or witness statement filed in support of any application included in the appellant's notice;

   (e)   a copy of his skeleton argument;

   (f)   except where sub-paragraph (1A) applies a transcript or note of judgment (see paragraph 5.12), and in cases where permission to appeal was given by the lower court or is not required those parts of any transcript of evidence which are directly relevant to any question at issue on the appeal;

   (g)   the claim form and statements of case (where relevant to the subject of the appeal);

   (h)   any application notice (or case management documentation) relevant to the subject of the appeal;

   (i)   in cases where the decision appealed was itself made on appeal (eg from district judge to circuit judge), the first order, the reasons given and the appellant's notice used to appeal from that order;

   (j)   in the case of judicial review or a statutory appeal, the original decision which was the subject of the application to the lower court;

   (k)   in cases where the appeal is from a Tribunal, a copy of the Tribunal's reasons for the decision, a copy of the decision reviewed by the Tribunal and the reasons for the original decision and any document filed with the Tribunal setting out the grounds of appeal from that decision;

   (l)   any other documents which the appellant reasonably considers necessary to enable the appeal court to reach its decision on the hearing of the application or appeal; and

   (m)   such other documents as the court may direct.

   (1A)   Where the appeal relates to a judgment following a determination on the papers under Part 8 in accordance with Practice Direction 8B, the appellant must include in the appeal bundle the order made by the court containing the reasons for the award of damages. A transcript of the judgment is not required.

   (2)   All documents that are extraneous to the issues to be considered on the application or the appeal must be excluded. The appeal bundle may include affidavits, witness statements, summaries, experts' reports and exhibits but only where these are directly relevant to the subject matter of the appeal.

   (3)   Where the appellant is represented, the appeal bundle must contain a certificate signed by his solicitor, counsel or other representative to the effect that he has read and understood paragraph (2) above and that the composition of the appeal bundle complies with it.

   5.7   Where it is not possible to file all the above documents, the appellant must indicate which documents have not yet been filed and the reasons why they are not currently available. The appellant must then provide a reasonable estimate of when the missing document or documents can be filed and file them as soon as reasonably practicable.

Small claims

5.8

App 2–022

(1) This paragraph applies where—

(a) the appeal relates to a claim allocated to the small claims track; and

(b) the appeal is being heard in a county court or the High Court.

(1A) An appellant's notice must be filed and served in Form N164.

(2) The appellant must file the following documents with his appellant's notice—

(a) a sealed copy of the order being appealed; and

(b) any order giving or refusing permission to appeal, together with a copy of the reasons for that decision.

(3) The appellant may, if relevant to the issues to be determined on the appeal, file any other document listed in paragraph 5.6 or 5.6A in addition to the documents referred to in sub-paragraph (2).

(4) The appellant need not file a record of the reasons for judgment of the lower court with his appellant's notice unless sub-paragraph (5) applies.

(5) The court may order a suitable record of the reasons for judgment of the lower court (see paragraph 5.12) to be filed—

(a) to enable it to decide if permission should be granted; or

(b) if permission is granted to enable it to decide the appeal.

Skeleton arguments

5.9

App 2–023

(1) The appellant's notice must, subject to (2) and (3) below, be accompanied by a skeleton argument. Alternatively the skeleton argument may be included in the appellant's notice. Where the skeleton argument is so included it will not form part of the notice for the purposes of rule 52.8.

(2) Where it is impracticable for the appellant's skeleton argument to accompany the appellant's notice it must be filed and served on all respondents within 14 days of filing the notice.

(3) An appellant who is not represented need not file a skeleton argument but is encouraged to do so since this will be helpful to the court.

Content of skeleton arguments

5.10

App 2–024

(1) A skeleton argument must contain a numbered list of the points which the party wishes to make. These should both define and confine the areas of controversy. Each point should be stated as concisely as the nature of the case allows.

(2) A numbered point must be followed by a reference to any document on which the party wishes to rely.

(3) A skeleton argument must state, in respect of each authority cited—

(a) the proposition of law that the authority demonstrates; and

(b) the parts of the authority (identified by page or paragraph references) that support the proposition.

(4) If more than one authority is cited in support of a given proposition, the skeleton argument must briefly state the reason for taking that course.

(5) The statement referred to in sub-paragraph (4) should not materially add to the length of the skeleton argument but should be sufficient to demonstrate, in the context of the argument—

(a) the relevance of the authority or authorities to that argument; and

(b) that the citation is necessary for a proper presentation of that argument.

(6) The cost of preparing a skeleton argument which—

(a) does not comply with the requirements set out in this paragraph; or

(b) was not filed within the time limits provided by this Practice Direction (or any further time granted by the court),

will not be allowed on assessment except to the extent that the court otherwise directs.

(7) A skeleton argument filed in the Court of Appeal, Civil Division on behalf of the appellant should contain in paragraph 1 the advocate's time estimate for the hearing of the appeal.

5.11 The appellant should consider what other information the appeal court will need. This may include a list of persons who feature in the case or glossaries of technical terms. A chronology of relevant events will be necessary in most appeals.

Suitable record of the judgment

App 2–025 5.12 Where the judgment to be appealed has been officially recorded by the court, an approved transcript of that record should accompany the appellant's notice. Photocopies will not be accepted for this purpose. However, where there is no officially recorded judgment, the following documents will be acceptable:

Written judgments

(1) Where the judgment was made in writing a copy of that judgment endorsed with the judge's signature.

Note of judgment

(2) When judgment was not officially recorded or made in writing a note of the judgment (agreed between the appellant's and respondent's advocates) should be submitted for approval to the judge whose decision is being appealed. If the parties cannot agree on a single note of the judgment, both versions should be provided to that judge with an explanatory letter. For the purpose of an application for permission to appeal the note need not be approved by the respondent or the lower court judge.

Advocates' notes of judgments where the appellant is unrepresented

(3) When the appellant was unrepresented in the lower court it is the duty of any advocate for the respondent to make his/her note of judgment promptly available, free of charge to the appellant where there is no officially recorded judgment or if the court so directs. Where the appellant was represented in the lower court it is the duty of his/her own former advocate to make his/her note available in these circumstances. The appellant should submit the note of judgment to the appeal court.

Reasons for Judgment in Tribunal cases

(4) A sealed copy of the Tribunal's reasons for the decision.

5.13 An appellant may not be able to obtain an official transcript or other suitable record of the lower court's decision within the time within which the appellant's notice must be filed. In such cases the appellant's notice must still be completed to the best of the appellant's ability on the basis of the documentation available. However it may be amended subsequently with the permission of the appeal court.

Advocates' notes of judgments

5.14   Advocates' brief (or, where appropriate, refresher) fee includes:

   (1)   remuneration for taking a note of the judgment of the court;

   (2)   having the note transcribed accurately;

   (3)   attempting to agree the note with the other side if represented;

   (4)   submitting the note to the judge for approval where appropriate;

   (5)   revising it if so requested by the judge,

   (6)   providing any copies required for the appeal court, instructing solicitors and lay client; and

   (7)   providing a copy of his note to an unrepresented appellant.

App 2–026

Transcripts or Notes of Evidence

5.15   When the evidence is relevant to the appeal an official transcript of the relevant evidence must be obtained. Transcripts or notes of evidence are generally not needed for the purpose of determining an application for permission to appeal.

App 2–027

Notes of evidence

5.16   If evidence relevant to the appeal was not officially recorded, a typed version of the judge's notes of evidence must be obtained.

App 2–028

Transcripts at public expense

5.17   Where the lower court or the appeal court is satisfied that—

   (1)   an unrepresented appellant; or

   (2)   an appellant whose legal representation is provided free of charge to the appellant and not funded by the Community Legal Service;
is in such poor financial circumstances that the cost of a transcript would be an excessive burden the court may certify that the cost of obtaining one official transcript should be borne at public expense.

App 2–029

5.18   In the case of a request for an official transcript of evidence or proceedings to be paid for at public expense, the court must also be satisfied that there are reasonable grounds for appeal. Whenever possible a request for a transcript at public expense should be made to the lower court when asking for permission to appeal.

Filing and service of appellant's notice

5.19   Rule 52.4 sets out the procedure and time limits for filing and serving an appellant's notice. The appellant must file the appellant's notice at the appeal court within such period as may be directed by the lower court which should not normally exceed 35 days or, where the lower court directs no such period, within 21 days of the date of the decision that the appellant wishes to appeal.

App 2–030

(Rule 52.15 sets out the time limit for filing an application for permission to appeal against the refusal of the High Court to grant permission to apply for judicial review)

5.20 Where the lower court judge announces his decision and reserves the reasons for his judgment or order until a later date, he should, in the exercise of powers under rule 52.4(2)(a), fix a period for filing the appellant's notice at the appeal court that takes this into account.

5.21
(1) Except where the appeal court orders otherwise a sealed copy of the appellant's notice, including any skeleton arguments must be served on all respondents in accordance with the timetable prescribed by rule 52.4(3) except where this requirement is modified by paragraph 5.9(2) in which case the skeleton argument should be served as soon as it is filed.
(2) The appellant must, as soon as practicable, file a certificate of service of the documents referred to in paragraph (1).

5.22 Unless the court otherwise directs a respondent need not take any action when served with an appellant's notice until such time as notification is given to him that permission to appeal has been given.

5.23 The court may dispense with the requirement for service of the notice on a respondent. Any application notice seeking an order under rule 6.28 to dispense with service should set out the reasons relied on and be verified by a statement of truth.

5.24
(1) Where the appellant is applying for permission to appeal in his appellant's notice, he must serve on the respondents his appellant's notice and skeleton argument (but not the appeal bundle), unless the appeal court directs otherwise.
(2) Where permission to appeal—
(a) has been given by the lower court; or
(b) is not required,
the appellant must serve the appeal bundle on the respondents with the appellant's notice.

Amendment of Appeal Notice

App 2–031 5.25 An appeal notice may be amended with permission. Such an application to amend and any application in opposition will normally be dealt with at the hearing unless that course would cause unnecessary expense or delay in which case a request should be made for the application to amend to be heard in advance.

PROCEDURE AFTER PERMISSION IS OBTAINED

pp 2–032 6.1 This paragraph sets out the procedure where:
(1) permission to appeal is given by the appeal court; or
(2) the appellant's notice is filed in the appeal court and—
(a) permission was given by the lower court; or
(b) permission is not required.

6.2 If the appeal court gives permission to appeal, the appeal bundle must be served on each of the respondents within 7 days of receiving the order giving permission to appeal.

(Part 6 (service of documents) provides rules on service)

6.3 The appeal court will send the parties—
(1) notification of—
(a) the date of the hearing or the period of time (the 'listing window') during which the appeal is likely to be heard; and
(b) in the Court of Appeal, the date by which the appeal will be heard (the 'hear by date');
(2) where permission is granted by the appeal court a copy of the order giving permission to appeal; and
(3) any other directions given by the court.

6.3A
(1) Where the appeal court grants permission to appeal, the appellant must add the following documents to the appeal bundle—
(a) the respondent's notice and skeleton argument (if any);
(b) those parts of the transcripts of evidence which are directly relevant to any question at issue on the appeal;
(c) the order granting permission to appeal and, where permission to appeal was granted at an oral hearing, the transcript (or note) of any judgment which was given; and
(d) any document which the appellant and respondent have agreed to add to the appeal bundle in accordance with paragraph 7.11.
(2) Where permission to appeal has been refused on a particular issue, the appellant must remove from the appeal bundle all documents that are relevant only to that issue.

Appeal Questionnaire in the Court of Appeal

6.4 The Court of Appeal will send an Appeal Questionnaire to the appellant when it notifies him of the matters referred to in paragraph 6.3.   **App 2–033**

6.5 The appellant must complete and file the Appeal Questionnaire within 14 days of the date of the letter of notification of the matters in paragraph 6.3. The Appeal Questionnaire must contain:
(1) if the appellant is legally represented, the advocate's time estimate for the hearing of the appeal;
(2) where a transcript of evidence is relevant to the appeal, confirmation as to what parts of a transcript of evidence have been ordered where this is not already in the bundle of documents;
(3) confirmation that copies of the appeal bundle are being prepared and will be held ready for the use of the Court of Appeal and an undertaking that they will be supplied to the court on request. For the purpose of these bundles photocopies of the transcripts will be accepted;
(4) confirmation that copies of the Appeal Questionnaire and the appeal bundle have been served on the respondents and the date of that service.

Time estimates

6.6 The time estimate included in an Appeal Questionnaire must be that of the   **App 2–034**
advocate who will argue the appeal. It should exclude the time required by the court to give judgment. If the respondent disagrees with the time estimate, the respondent must inform the court within 7 days of receipt of the Appeal Questionnaire. In the absence of such notification the respondent will be deemed to have accepted the estimate proposed on behalf of the appellant.

RESPONDENT

App 2–035   **7.1**   A respondent who wishes to ask the appeal court to vary the order of the lower court in any way must appeal and permission will be required on the same basis as for an appellant.

(Paragraph 3.2 applies to grounds of appeal by a respondent.)

7.2   A respondent who wishes only to request that the appeal court upholds the judgment or order of the lower court whether for the reasons given in the lower court or otherwise does not make an appeal and does not therefore require permission to appeal in accordance with rule 52.3(1).

(Paragraph 7.6 requires a respondent to file a skeleton argument where he wishes to address the appeal court)

7.3
(1)   A respondent who wishes to appeal or who wishes to ask the appeal court to uphold the order of the lower court for reasons different from or additional to those given by the lower court must file a respondent's notice.
(2)   If the respondent does not file a respondent's notice, he will not be entitled, except with the permission of the court, to rely on any reason not relied on in the lower court.

7.3A   Paragraphs 5.1A, 5.1B and 5.2 of this practice direction (Human Rights and extension for time for filing appellant's notice) also apply to a respondent and a respondent's notice.

Time limits

App 2–036   **7.4**   The time limits for filing a respondent's notice are set out in rule 52.5 (4) and (5).

7.5   Where an extension of time is required the extension must be requested in the respondent's notice and the reasons why the respondent failed to act within the specified time must be included.

7.6   Except where paragraph 7.7A applies, the respondent must file a skeleton argument for the court in all cases where he proposes to address arguments to the court. The respondent's skeleton argument may be included within a respondent's notice. Where a skeleton argument is included within a respondent's notice it will not form part of the notice for the purposes of rule 52.8.

7.7
(1)   A respondent who—
(a)   files a respondent's notice; but
(b)   does not include his skeleton argument within that notice,
  must file and serve his skeleton argument within 14 days of filing the notice.
(2)   A respondent who does not file a respondent's notice but who files a skeleton argument must file and serve that skeleton argument at least 7 days before the appeal hearing.

(Rule 52.5(4) sets out the period for filing and serving a respondent's notice)

7.7A
(1) Where the appeal relates to a claim allocated to the small claims track and is being heard in a county court or the High Court, the respondent may file a skeleton argument but is not required to do so.
(2) A respondent who is not represented need not file a skeleton argument but is encouraged to do so in order to assist the court.

7.7B The respondent must—
(1) serve his skeleton argument on—
(a) the appellant; and
(b) any other respondent,
at the same time as he files it at the court; and
(2) file a certificate of service.

Content of skeleton arguments

7.8 A respondent's skeleton argument must conform to the directions at paragraphs 5.10 and 5.11 with any necessary modifications. It should, where appropriate, answer the arguments set out in the appellant's skeleton argument. **App 2–037**

Applications within respondent's notices

7.9 A respondent may include an application within a respondent's notice in accordance with paragraph 5.5 above. **App 2–038**

Filing respondent's notices and skeleton arguments

7.10 **App 2–039**
(1) The respondent must file the following documents with his respondent's notice in every case:
(a) two additional copies of the respondent's notice for the appeal court; and
(b) one copy each for the appellant and any other respondents.
(2) The respondent may file a skeleton argument with his respondent's notice and—
(a) where he does so he must file two copies; and
(b) where he does not do so he must comply with paragraph 7.7.

7.11 If the respondent wishes to rely on any documents which he reasonably considers necessary to enable the appeal court to reach its decision on the appeal in addition to those filed by the appellant, he must make every effort to agree amendments to the appeal bundle with the appellant.

7.12
(1) If the representatives for the parties are unable to reach agreement, the respondent may prepare a supplemental bundle.
(2) If the respondent prepares a supplemental bundle he must file it, together with the requisite number of copies for the appeal court, at the appeal court—
(a) with the respondent's notice; or
(b) if a respondent's notice is not filed, within 21 days after he is served with the appeal bundle.

7.13 The respondent must serve—
(1) the respondent's notice;
(2) his skeleton argument (if any); and
(3) the supplemental bundle (if any),
on—
(a) the appellant; and
(b) any other respondent,
at the same time as he files them at the court.

APPEALS TO THE HIGH COURT

Application

App 2–040 **8.1** This paragraph applies where an appeal lies to a High Court judge from the decision of a county court or a district judge of the High Court.

8.2 The following table sets out the following venues for each circuit—
(a) Appeal centres—court centres where appeals to which this paragraph applies may be filed, managed and heard. Paragraphs 8.6 to 8.8 provide for special arrangements in relation to the South Eastern Circuit.
(b) Hearing only centres—court centres where appeals to which this paragraph applies may be heard by order made at an appeal centre (see paragraph 8.10).

		Hearing Only Centres
Midland Circuit	Birmingham	Lincoln
	Nottingham	Leicester
		Northampton
		Stafford
North Eastern Circuit	Leeds	Teesside
	Newcastle	
	Sheffield	
Northern Circuit	Manchester	Carlisle
	Liverpool	
	Preston	
	Chester	
Wales Circuit	Cardiff	
	Swansea	
	Mold	Caernarfon
Western Circuit	Bristol	Truro
	Exeter	Plymouth
	Winchester	
South Eastern Circuit	Royal Courts of Justice	
	Lewes	

Hearing Only Centres

Luton

Norwich

Reading

Chelmsford

St Albans

Maidstone

Oxford

Venue for appeals and filing of notices on circuits other than the South Eastern Circuit

8.3 Paragraphs 8.4 and 8.5 apply where the lower court is situated on a circuit other than the South Eastern Circuit. **App 2–041**

8.4 The appellant's notice must be filed at an appeal centre on the circuit in which the lower court is situated. The appeal will be managed and heard at that appeal centre unless the appeal court orders otherwise.

8.5 A respondent's notice must be filed at the appeal centre where the appellant's notice was filed unless the appeal has been transferred to another appeal centre, in which case it must be filed at that appeal centre.

Venue for appeals and filing of notices on the South Eastern Circuit

8.6 Paragraphs 8.7 and 8.8 apply where the lower court is situated on the South Eastern Circuit. **App 2–042**

8.7 The appellant's notice must be filed at an appeal centre on the South Eastern Circuit. The appeal will be managed and heard at the Royal Courts of Justice unless the appeal court orders otherwise. An order that an appeal is to be managed or heard at another appeal centre may not be made unless the consent of the Presiding Judge of the circuit in charge of civil matters has been obtained.

8.8 A respondent's notice must be filed at the Royal Courts of Justice unless the appeal has been transferred to another appeal centre, in which case it must be filed at that appeal centre.

General provisions

8.9 The appeal court may transfer an appeal to another appeal centre (whether or not on the same circuit). In deciding whether to do so the court will have regard to the criteria in rule 30.3 (criteria for a transfer order). The appeal court may do so either on application by a party or of its own initiative. Where an appeal is transferred under this paragraph, notice of transfer must be served on every person on whom the appellant's notice has been served. An appeal may not be transferred to an appeal centre on another circuit, **App 2–043**

589

either for management or hearing, unless the consent of the Presiding Judge of that circuit in charge of civil matters has been obtained.

8.10 Directions may be given for—
(a) an appeal to be heard at a hearing only centre; or
(b) an application in an appeal to be heard at any other venue,
instead of at the appeal centre managing the appeal.

8.11 Unless a direction has been made under 8.10, any application in the appeal must be made at the appeal centre where the appeal is being managed.

8.12 The appeal court may adopt all or any part of the procedure set out in paragraphs 6.4 to 6.6.

8.13 Where the lower court is a county court:
(1) subject to paragraph (1A), appeals and applications for permission to appeal will be heard by a High Court Judge or by a person authorised under paragraphs (1), (2) or (4) of the Table in section 9(1) of the Supreme Court Act 1981 to act as a judge of the High Court;
(1A) an appeal or application for permission to appeal from the decision of a Recorder in the county court may be heard by a Designated Civil Judge who is authorised under paragraph (5) of the Table in section 9(1) of the Supreme Court Act 1981 to act as a judge of the High Court; and
(2) other applications in the appeal may be heard and directions in the appeal may be given either by a High Court Judge or by any person authorised under section 9 of the Supreme Court Act 1981 to act as a judge of the High Court.

8.14 In the case of appeals from Masters or district judges of the High Court, appeals, applications for permission and any other applications in the appeal may be heard and directions in the appeal may be given by a High Court Judge or by any person authorised under section 9 of the Supreme Court Act 1981 to act as a judge of the High Court.

APPEALS TO A JUDGE OF A COUNTY COURT FROM A DISTRICT JUDGE

App 2–044   **8A.1** The Designated Civil Judge in consultation with his Presiding Judges has responsibility for allocating appeals from decisions of district judges to circuit judges.

RE-HEARINGS

pp 2–045   **9.1** The hearing of an appeal will be a re-hearing (as opposed to a review of the decision of the lower court) if the appeal is from the decision of a minister, person or other body and the minister, person or other body—
(1) did not hold a hearing to come to that decision; or
(2) held a hearing to come to that decision, but the procedure adopted did not provide for the consideration of evidence.

APPEALS TRANSFERRED TO THE COURT OF APPEAL

10.1   Where an appeal is transferred to the Court of Appeal under rule 52.14 the Court of Appeal may give such additional directions as are considered appropriate.

App 2–046

APPLICATIONS

11.1   Where a party to an appeal makes an application whether in an appeal notice or by Part 23 application notice, the provisions of Part 23 will apply.

App 2–047

11.2   The applicant must file the following documents with the notice
(1)   one additional copy of the application notice for the appeal court and one copy for each of the respondents;
(2)   where applicable a sealed copy of the order which is the subject of the main appeal;
(3)   a bundle of documents in support which should include:
(a)   the Part 23 application notice; and
(b)   any witness statements and affidavits filed in support of the application notice.

DISPOSING OF APPLICATIONS OR APPEALS BY CONSENT

Dismissal of applications or appeals by consent

12.1   These paragraphs do not apply where—
(1)   any party to the proceedings is a child or protected party; or
(2)   the appeal or application is to the Court of Appeal from a decision of the Court of Protection.

App 2–048

12.2   Where an appellant does not wish to pursue an application or an appeal, he may request the appeal court for an order that his application or appeal be dismissed. Such a request must contain a statement that the appellant is not a child or protected party and that the appeal or application is not from a decision of the Court of Protection. If such a request is granted it will usually be on the basis that the appellant pays the costs of the application or appeal.

12.3   If the appellant wishes to have the application or appeal dismissed without costs, his request must be accompanied by a consent signed by the respondent or his legal representative stating—
(1)   that the respondent is not a child or protected party and that the appeal or application is not from a decision of the Court of Protection; and
(2)   that he consents to the dismissal of the application or appeal without costs.

12.4   Where a settlement has been reached disposing of the application or appeal, the parties may make a joint request to the court stating that—
(1)   none of them is a child or protected party; and
(2)   the appeal or application is not from a decision of the Court of Protection, and asking that the application or appeal be dismissed by consent. If the request is granted the application or appeal will be dismissed.
('Child' and 'protected party' have the same meaning as in rule 21.1(2).)

Allowing unopposed appeals or applications on paper

App 2–049 **13.1** The appeal court will not normally make an order allowing an appeal unless satisfied that the decision of the lower court was wrong, but the appeal court may set aside or vary the order of the lower court with consent and without determining the merits of the appeal, if it is satisfied that there are good and sufficient reasons for doing so. Where the appeal court is requested by all parties to allow an application or an appeal the court may consider the request on the papers. The request should state that none of the parties is a child or protected party and that the application or appeal is not from a decision of the Court of Protection and set out the relevant history of the proceedings and the matters relied on as justifying the proposed order and be accompanied by a copy of the proposed order.

Procedure for consent orders and agreements to pay periodical payments involving a child or protected party or in applications or appeals to the Court of Appeal from a decision of the Court of Protection

App 2–050 **13.2** Where one of the parties is a child or protected party or the application or appeal is to the Court of Appeal from a decision of the Court of Protection—
- (1) a settlement relating to an appeal or application;
- (2) in a personal injury claim for damages for future pecuniary loss, an agreement reached at the appeal stage to pay periodical payments; or
- (3) a request by an appellant for an order that his application or appeal be dismissed with or without the consent of the respondent,
  requires the court's approval.

Child

App 2–051 **13.3** In cases involving a child a copy of the proposed order signed by the parties' solicitors should be sent to the appeal court, together with an opinion from the advocate acting on behalf of the child.

Protected party

App 2–052 **13.4** Where a party is a protected party the same procedure will be adopted, but the documents filed should also include any relevant reports prepared for the Court of Protection.

('Child' and 'protected party' have the same meaning as in rule 21.1(2).)

Periodical payments

App 2–053 **13.5** Where periodical payments for future pecuniary loss have been negotiated in a personal injury case which is under appeal, the documents filed should include those which would be required in the case of a personal injury claim for damages for future pecuniary loss dealt with at first instance. Details can be found in Practice Direction 21.

Summary assessment of costs

14.1 Costs are likely to be assessed by way of summary assessment at the fol- **App 2–054**
lowing hearings:
(1) contested directions hearings;
(2) applications for permission to appeal at which the respondent is present;
(3) dismissal list hearings in the Court of Appeal at which the respondent is
present;
(4) appeals from case management decisions; and
(5) appeals listed for one day or less.

14.2 Parties attending any of the hearings referred to in paragraph 14.1 should be
prepared to deal with the summary assessment.

OTHER SPECIAL PROVISIONS REGARDING THE COURT OF APPEAL

Filing of documents

15.1 **App 2–055**
(1) The documents relevant to proceedings in the Court of Appeal, Civil Division
must be filed in the Civil Appeals Office Registry, Room E307, Royal Courts
of Justice, Strand, London, WC2A 2LL.
(2) The Civil Appeals Office will not serve documents and where service is
required by the CPR or this practice direction it must be effected by the
parties.

15.1A
(1) A party may file by email—
(a) an appellant's notice;
(b) a respondent's notice;
(c) an application notice, in the Court of Appeal, Civil Division, using the email
account specified in the 'Guidelines for filing by Email' which appear on the
Court of Appeal, Civil Division website at www.civilappeals.gov.uk.
(2) A party may only file a notice in accordance with paragraph (1) where he is
permitted to do so by the 'Guidelines for filing by Email'.

15.1B
(1) A party to an appeal in the Court of Appeal, Civil Division may file—
(a) an appellant's notice;
(b) a respondent's notice; or
(c) an application notice, electronically using the online forms service on the
Court of Appeal, Civil Division website at www.civilappeals.gov.uk.
(2) A party may only file a notice in accordance with paragraph (1) where he is
permitted to so do by the 'Guidelines for filing electronically'. The Guidelines
for filing electronically may be found on the Court of Appeal, Civil Division
website.
(3) The online forms service will assist the user in completing a document
accurately but the user is responsible for ensuring that the rules and practice
directions relating to the document have been complied with. Transmission
by the service does not guarantee that the document will be accepted by the
Court of Appeal, Civil Division.
(4) A party using the online forms service in accordance with this paragraph is
responsible for ensuring that the transmission or any document attached to it
is filed within any relevant time limits.

(5) Parties are advised not to transmit electronically any correspondence or documents of a confidential or sensitive nature, as security cannot be guaranteed.

(6) Where a party wishes to file a document containing a statement of truth electronically, that party should retain the document containing the original signature and file with the court a version of the document on which the name of the person who has signed the statement of truth is typed underneath the statement.

Core bundles

App 2–056 15.2 In cases where the appeal bundle comprises more than 500 pages, exclusive of transcripts, the appellant's solicitors must, after consultation with the respondent's solicitors, also prepare and file with the court, in addition to copies of the appeal bundle (as amended in accordance with paragraph 7.11) the requisite number of copies of a core bundle.

15.3
(1) The core bundle must be filed within 28 days of receipt of the order giving permission to appeal or, where permission to appeal was granted by the lower court or is not required, within 28 days of the date of service of the appellant's notice on the respondent.
(2) The core bundle—
(a) must contain the documents which are central to the appeal; and
(b) must not exceed 150 pages.

Preparation of bundles

App 2–057 15.4 The provisions of this paragraph apply to the preparation of appeal bundles, supplemental respondents' bundles where the parties are unable to agree amendments to the appeal bundle, and core bundles.

(1) **Rejection of bundles.** Where documents are copied unnecessarily or bundled incompletely, costs may be disallowed. Where the provisions of this Practice Direction as to the preparation or delivery of bundles are not followed the bundle may be rejected by the court or be made the subject of a special costs order.

(2) **Avoidance of duplication.** No more than one copy of any document should be included unless there is a good reason for doing otherwise (such as the use of a separate core bundle—see paragraph 15.2).

(3) **Pagination**
(a) Bundles must be paginated, each page being numbered individually and consecutively. The pagination used at trial must also be indicated. Letters and other documents should normally be included in chronological order. (An exception to consecutive page numbering arises in the case of core bundles where it may be preferable to retain the original numbering).
(b) Page numbers should be inserted in bold figures at the bottom of the page and in a form that can be clearly distinguished from any other pagination on the document.

(4) **Format and presentation**
(a) Where possible the documents should be in A4 format. Where a document has to be read across rather than down the page, it should be so placed in the bundle as to ensure that the text starts nearest the spine.
(b) Where any marking or writing in colour on a document is important, the document must be copied in colour or marked up correctly in colour.

(c) Documents which are not easily legible should be transcribed and the transcription marked and placed adjacent to the document transcribed.

(d) Documents in a foreign language should be translated and the translation marked and placed adjacent to the document translated. The translation should be agreed or, if it cannot be agreed, each party's proposed translation should be included.

(e) The size of any bundle should be tailored to its contents. A large lever arch file should not be used for just a few pages nor should files of whatever size be overloaded.

(f) Where it will assist the Court of Appeal, different sections of the file may be separated by cardboard or other tabbed dividers so long as these are clearly indexed. Where, for example, a document is awaited when the appeal bundle is filed, a single sheet of paper can be inserted after a divider, indicating the nature of the document awaited. For example, 'Transcript of evidence of Mr J Smith (to follow)'.

(5) Binding

(a) All documents, with the exception of transcripts, must be bound together. This may be in a lever arch file, ring binder or plastic folder. Plastic sleeves containing loose documents must not be used. Binders and files must be strong enough to withstand heavy use.

(b) Large documents such as plans should be placed in an easily accessible file. Large documents which will need to be opened up frequently should be inserted in a file larger than A4 size.

(6) Indices and labels

(a) An index must be included at the front of the bundle listing all the documents and providing the page references for each. In the case of documents such as letters, invoices or bank statements, they may be given a general description.

(b) Where the bundles consist of more than one file, an index to all the files should be included in the first file and an index included for each file. Indices should, if possible, be on a single sheet. The full name of the case should not be inserted on the index if this would waste space. Documents should be identified briefly but properly.

(7) Identification

(a) Every bundle must be clearly identified, on the spine and on the front cover, with the name of the case and the Court of Appeal's reference. Where the bundle consists of more than one file, each file must be numbered on the spine, the front cover and the inside of the front cover.

(b) Outer labels should use large lettering eg 'Appeal Bundle A' or 'Core Bundle'. The full title of the appeal and solicitors' names and addresses should be omitted. A label should be used on the front as well as on the spine.

(8) Staples etc. All staples, heavy metal clips etc, must be removed.

(9) Statements of case

(a) Statements of case should be assembled in 'chapter' form—i.e claim followed by particulars of claim, followed by further information, irrespective of date.

(b) Redundant documents, eg particulars of claim overtaken by amendments, requests for further information recited in the answers given, should generally be excluded.

(10) New Documents

(a) Before a new document is introduced into bundles which have already been delivered to the court, steps should be taken to ensure that it carries an appropriate bundle/page number so that it can be added to the court documents. It should not be stapled and it should be prepared with punch holes for immediate inclusion in the binders in use.

(b) If it is expected that a large number of miscellaneous new documents will from time to time be introduced, there should be a special tabbed empty loose-leaf file for that purpose. An index should be produced for this file, updated as necessary.

(11) **Inter-solicitor correspondence.** Since inter-solicitor correspondence is unlikely to be required for the purposes of an appeal, only those letters which will need to be referred to should be copied.

(12) **Sanctions for non-compliance.** If the appellant fails to comply with the requirements as to the provision of bundles of documents, the application or appeal will be referred for consideration to be given as to why it should not be dismissed for failure to so comply.

Master in the Court of Appeal, Civil Division

App 2–058 **15.5** The Master of the Rolls may designate an eligible officer to exercise judicial authority under rule 52.16 as Master. Other eligible officers may also be designated by the Master of the Rolls to exercise judicial authority under rule 52.16 and shall then be known as Deputy Masters.

Respondent to notify Civil Appeals Office whether he intends to file respondent's notice

App 2–059 **15.6** A respondent must, no later than 21 days after the date he is served with notification that—

(1) permission to appeal has been granted; or

(2) the application for permission to appeal and the appeal are to be heard together, inform the Civil Appeals Office and the appellant in writing whether—

(a) he proposes to file a respondent's notice appealing the order or seeking to uphold the order for reasons different from, or additional to, those given by the lower court; or

(b) he proposes to rely on the reasons given by the lower court for its decision.

(Paragraph 15.11B requires all documents needed for an appeal hearing, including a respondent's skeleton argument, to be filed at least 7 days before the hearing)

Listing and hear-by dates

App 2–060 **15.7** The management of the list will be dealt with by the listing officer under the direction of the Master.

15.8 The Civil Appeals List of the Court of Appeal is divided as follows:

• *The applications list*—applications for permission to appeal and other applications.

• *The appeals list*—appeals where permission to appeal has been given or where an appeal lies without permission being required where a hearing date is fixed in advance. (Appeals in this list which require special listing arrangements will be assigned to the special fixtures list)

• *The expedited list*—appeals or applications where the Court of Appeal has directed an expedited hearing. The current practice of the Court of Appeal is summarised in *Unilever plc. v. Chefaro Proprietaries Ltd. (Practice Note)* [1995]1 W.L.R. 243.

- *The stand-out list*—Appeals or applications which, for good reason, are not at present ready to proceed and have been stood out by judicial direction.

- *The second fixtures list*—[see paragraph 15.9A(1) below].

- *The second fixtures list*—if an appeal is designated as a 'second fixture' it means that a hearing date is arranged in advance on the express basis that the list is fully booked for the period in question and therefore the case will be heard only if a suitable gap occurs in the list.

- *The short-warned list*—appeals which the court considers may be prepared for the hearing by an advocate other than the one originally instructed with a half day's notice, or such other period as the court may direct.

Special provisions relating to the short-warned list

15.9 App 2–061
(1) Where an appeal is assigned to the short-warned list, the Civil Appeals Office will notify the parties' solicitors in writing. The court may abridge the time for filing any outstanding bundles in an appeal assigned to this list.
(2) The solicitors for the parties must notify their advocate and their client as soon as the Civil Appeals Office notifies them that the appeal has been assigned to the short-warned list.
(3) The appellant may apply in writing for the appeal to be removed from the short-warned list within 14 days of notification of its assignment. The application will be decided by a Lord Justice, or the Master, and will only be granted for the most compelling reasons.
(4) The Civil Appeals Listing Officer may place an appeal from the short-warned list 'on call' from a given date and will inform the parties' advocates accordingly.
(5) An appeal which is 'on call' may be listed for hearing on half a day's notice or such longer period as the court may direct.
(6) Once an appeal is listed for hearing from the short warned list it becomes the immediate professional duty of the advocate instructed in the appeal, if he is unable to appear at the hearing, to take all practicable measures to ensure that his lay client is represented at the hearing by an advocate who is fully instructed and able to argue the appeal.

Special provisions relating to the special fixtures list

15.9A App 2–062
(1) The special fixtures list is a sub-division of the appeals list and is used to deal with appeals that may require special listing arrangements, such as the need to list a number of cases before the same constitution, in a particular order, during a particular period or at a given location.
(2) The Civil Appeals Office will notify the parties' representatives, or the parties if acting in person, of the particular arrangements that will apply. The notice—
(a) will give details of the specific period during which a case is scheduled to be heard; and
(b) may give directions in relation to the filing of any outstanding documents.

(3) The listing officer will notify the parties' representatives of the precise hearing date as soon as practicable. While every effort will be made to accommodate the availability of counsel, the requirements of the court will prevail.

Requests for directions

App 2–063 15.10 To ensure that all requests for directions are centrally monitored and correctly allocated, all requests for directions or rulings (whether relating to listing or any other matters) should be made to the Civil Appeals Office. Those seeking directions or rulings must not approach the supervising Lord Justice either directly, or via his or her clerk.

Bundles of authorities

App 2–064 15.11

(1) Once the parties have been notified of the date fixed for the hearing, the appellant's advocate must, after consultation with his opponent, file a bundle containing photocopies of the authorities upon which each side will rely at the hearing.

(2) The bundle of authorities should, in general—

(a) have the relevant passages of the authorities marked;

(b) not include authorities for propositions not in dispute; and

(c) not contain more than 10 authorities unless the scale of the appeal warrants more extensive citation.

(3) The bundle of authorities must be filed—

(a) at least 7 days before the hearing; or

(b) where the period of notice of the hearing is less than 7 days, immediately.

(4) If, through some oversight, a party intends, during the hearing, to refer to other authorities the parties may agree a second agreed bundle. The appellant's advocate must file this bundle at least 48 hours before the hearing commences.

(5) A bundle of authorities must bear a certification by the advocates responsible for arguing the case that the requirements of sub-paragraphs (3) to (5) of paragraph 5.10 have been complied with in respect of each authority included.

Supplementary skeleton arguments

App 2–065 15.11A

(1) A supplementary skeleton argument on which the appellant wishes to rely must be filed at least 14 days before the hearing.

(2) A supplementary skeleton argument on which the respondent wishes to rely must be filed at least 7 days before the hearing.

(3) All supplementary skeleton arguments must comply with the requirements set out in paragraph 5.10.

(4) At the hearing the court may refuse to hear argument from a party not contained in a skeleton argument filed within the relevant time limit set out in this paragraph.

Papers for the appeal hearing

15.11B　　　　　　　　　　　　　　　　　　　　　　　　　　　**App 2–066**

(1) All the documents which are needed for the appeal hearing must be filed at least 7 days before the hearing. Where a document has not been filed 10 days before the hearing a reminder will be sent by the Civil Appeals Office.

(2) Any party who fails to comply with the provisions of paragraph (1) may be required to attend before the Presiding Lord Justice to seek permission to proceed with, or to oppose, the appeal.

Disposal of bundles of documents

15.11C　　　　　　　　　　　　　　　　　　　　　　　　　　　**App 2–067**

(1) Where the court has determined a case, the official transcriber will retain one set of papers. The Civil Appeals Office will destroy any remaining sets of papers not collected within 21 days of—

(a) where one or more parties attend the hearing, the date of the court's decision;

(b) where there is no attendance, the date of the notification of court's decision.

(2) The parties should ensure that bundles of papers supplied to the court do not contain original documents (other than transcripts). The parties must ensure that they—

(a) bring any necessary original documents to the hearing; and

(b) retrieve any original documents handed up to the court before leaving the court.

(3) The court will retain application bundles where permission to appeal has been granted. Where permission is refused the arrangements in sub-paragraph (1) will apply.

(4) Where a single Lord Justice has refused permission to appeal on paper, application bundles will not be destroyed until after the time limit for seeking a hearing has expired.

Reserved Judgments

15.12 Practice Direction 40E contains provisions relating to reserved judgments.　　**App 2–068**

SECTION II—GENERAL PROVISIONS ABOUT STATUTORY APPEALS AND APPEALS BY WAY OF CASE STATED

16.1 This Section contains general provisions about statutory appeals (paragraphs 17.1–17.11) and appeals by way of case stated (paragraphs 18.1–18.20).　　**App 2–069**

16.2 Where any of the provisions in this Section provide for documents to be filed at the appeal court, these documents are in addition to any documents required under Part 52 or section 1 of this Practice Direction.

STATUTORY APPEALS

17.1 This part of this section—　　　　　　　　　　　　　　　　**App 2–070**

(1) applies where under any enactment an appeal (other than by way of case stated) lies to the court from a Minister of State, government department, tribunal or other person ('statutory appeals'); and

(2) is subject to any provision about a specific category of appeal in any enactment or Section III of this practice direction.

Part 52

App 2–071 17.2 Part 52 applies to statutory appeals with the following amendments:

Filing of appellant's notice

App 2–072 17.3 Subject to paragraph 17.4A, the appellant must file the appellant's notice at the appeal court within 28 days after the date of the decision of the lower court being appealed.

17.4 Where a statement of the reasons for a decision is given later than the notice of that decision, the period for filing the appellant's notice is calculated from the date on which the statement is received by the appellant.

17.4A
(1) Where the appellant wishes to appeal against a decision of the Administrative Appeals Chamber of the Upper Tribunal, the appellant's notice must be filed within 42 days of the date on which the Upper Tribunal's decision on permission to appeal to the Court of Appeal is given.
(2) Where the appellant wishes to appeal against a decision of any other Chamber of the Upper Tribunal, the appellant's notice must be filed within 28 days of the date on which the Upper Tribunal's decision on permission to appeal to the Court of Appeal is given.

Service of appellant's notice

App 2–073 17.5
(1) Subject to sub-paragraph (1A), in addition to the respondents to the appeal, the appellant must serve the appellant's notice in accordance with rule 52.4(3) on the chairman of the tribunal, Minister of State, government department or other person from whose decision the appeal is brought.
(1A) Sub-paragraph (1) does not apply to an appeal against a decision of the Upper Tribunal.
(2) In the case of an appeal from the decision of a tribunal that has no chairman or member who acts as a chairman, the appellant's notice must be served on the member or members of the tribunal.

Right of Minister etc. to be heard on the appeal

App 2–074 17.6 Where the appeal is from an order or decision of a Minister of State or government department, the Minister or department, as the case may be, is entitled to attend the hearing and to make representations to the court.

Rule 52.12A Statutory appeals—court's power to hear any person

App 2–075 17.7 Where all the parties consent, the court may deal with an application under rule 52.12A without a hearing.

17.8 Where the court gives permission for a person to file evidence or to make representations at the appeal hearing, it may do so on conditions and may give case management directions.

17.9 An application for permission must be made by letter to the relevant court office, identifying the appeal, explaining who the applicant is and indicating why and in what form the applicant wants to participate in the hearing.

17.10 If the applicant is seeking a prospective order as to costs, the letter must say what kind of order and on what grounds.

17.11 Applications to intervene must be made at the earliest reasonable opportunity, since it will usually be essential not to delay the hearing.

APPEALS BY WAY OF CASE STATED

18.1 This part of this section—   App 2–076
  (1) applies where under any enactment—
  (a) an appeal lies to the court by way of case stated; or
  (b) a question of law may be referred to the court by way of case stated; and
  (2) is subject to any provision about to a specific category of appeal in any enactment or Section III of this practice direction.

Part 52

18.2 Part 52 applies to appeals by way of case stated subject to the following   App 2–077
amendments.

Case stated by Crown Court or Magistrates' Court

Application to state a case

18.3 The procedure for applying to the Crown Court or a Magistrates' Court to   App 2–078
have a case stated for the opinion of the High Court is set out in the Crown Court Rules 1982 and the Magistrates' Courts Rules 1981 respectively.

Filing of appellant's notice

18.4 The appellant must file the appellant's notice at the appeal court within 10   App 2–079
days after he receives the stated case.

Documents to be lodged

18.5 The appellant must lodge the following documents with his appellant's   App 2–080
notice:
  (1) the stated case;
  (2) a copy of the judgment, order or decision in respect of which the case has been stated; and
  (3) where the judgment, order or decision in respect of which the case has been stated was itself given or made on appeal, a copy of the judgment, order or decision appealed from.

Service of appellant's notice

App 2–081   **18.6**   The appellant must serve the appellant's notice and accompanying documents on all respondents within 4 days after they are filed or lodged at the appeal court.

Case stated by Minister, government department, tribunal or other person

Application to state a case

App 2–082   **18.7**   The procedure for applying to a Minister, government department, tribunal or other person ('Minister or tribunal etc.') to have a case stated for the opinion of the court may be set out in—

(1) the enactment which provides for the right of appeal; or

(2) any rules of procedure relating to the Minister or tribunal etc.

Signing of stated case by Minister or tribunal etc.

App 2–083   **18.8**

(1) A case stated by a tribunal must be signed by—

(a) the chairman;

(b) the president; or

(c) in the case where the tribunal has neither person in sub-paragraph (a) or (b) nor any member who acts as its chairman or president, by the member or members of the tribunal.

(2) A case stated by any other person must be signed by that person or by a person authorised to do so.

Service of stated case by Minister or tribunal etc.

App 2–084   **18.9**   The Minister or tribunal etc. must serve the stated case on—

(1) the party who requests the case to be stated; or

(2) the party as a result of whose application to the court, the case was stated.

18.10   Where an enactment provides that a Minister or tribunal etc. may state a case or refer a question of law to the court by way of case stated without a request being made, the Minister or tribunal etc. must—

(1) serve the stated case on those parties that the Minister or tribunal etc. considers appropriate; and

(2) give notice to every other party to the proceedings that the stated case has been served on the party named and on the date specified in the notice.

Filing and service of appellant's notice

App 2–085   **18.11**   The party on whom the stated case was served must file the appellant's notice and the stated case at the appeal court and serve copies of the notice and stated case on—

(1) the Minister or tribunal etc. who stated the case; and

(2) every party to the proceedings to which the stated case relates, within 14 days after the stated case was served on him.

18.12   Where paragraph 18.10 applies the Minister or tribunal etc. must—

(1) file an appellant's notice and the stated case at the appeal court; and

(2) serve copies of those documents on the persons served under paragraph 18.10 within 14 days after stating the case.

18.13   Where—

(1) a stated case has been served by the Minister or tribunal etc. in accordance with paragraph 18.9; and

(2) the party on whom the stated case was served does not file an appellant's notice in accordance with paragraph 18.11,
any other party may file an appellant's notice with the stated case at the appeal court and serve a copy of the notice and the case on the persons listed in paragraph 18.11 within the period of time set out in paragraph 18.14.

18.14 The period of time referred to in paragraph 18.13 is 14 days from the last day on which the party on whom the stated case was served may file an appellant's notice in accordance with paragraph 18.11.

Amendment of stated case

18.15 The court may amend the stated case or order it to be returned to the Minister or tribunal etc. for amendment and may draw inferences of fact from the facts stated in the case.   **App 2–086**

Right of Minister etc. to be heard on the appeal

18.16 Where the case is stated by a Minister or government department, that Minister or department, as the case may be, is entitled to appear on the appeal and to make representations to the court.   **App 2–087**

Application for order to state a case

18.17 An application to the court for an order requiring a minister or tribunal etc. to state a case for the decision of the court, or to refer a question of law to the court by way of case stated must be made to the court which would be the appeal court if the case were stated.   **App 2–088**

18.18 An application to the court for an order directing a Minister or tribunal etc. to—

(1) state a case for determination by the court; or

(2) refer a question of law to the court by way of case stated, must be made in accordance with Part 23.

18.19 The application notice must contain—

(1) the grounds of the application;

(2) the question of law on which it is sought to have the case stated; and

(3) any reasons given by the minister or tribunal etc. for his or its refusal to state a case.

18.20 The application notice must be filed at the appeal court and served on—

(1) the Minister, department, secretary of the tribunal or other person as the case may be; and

(2) every party to the proceedings to which the application relates, within 14 days after the appellant receives notice of the refusal of his request to state a case.

SECTION III—PROVISIONS ABOUT SPECIFIC APPEALS

20.1 This Section of this Practice Direction provides special provisions about the appeals to which the following table refers. This section is not exhaustive and does not create, amend or remove any right of appeal.   **App 2–089**

20.2 Part 52 applies to all appeals to which this section applies subject to any special provisions set out in this section.

20.3 Where any of the provisions in this section provide for documents to be filed at the appeal court, these documents are in addition to any documents required under Part 52 or sections I or II of this practice direction.

APPEALS TO THE COURT OF APPEAL	*Paragraph*
Articles 81 and 82 of the EC Treaty and Chapters I and II of Part I of the Competition Act 1998	21.10A
Asylum and Immigration Appeals	21.7
Civil Partnership—conditional order for dissolution or nullity	21.1
Competition Appeal Tribunal	21.10
Contempt of Court	21.4
Court of Protection	21.12
Decree nisi of divorce	21.1
Lands Tribunal	21.9
Nullity of marriage	21.1
Patents Court on appeal from Comptroller	21.3
Proscribed Organisations Appeal Commission	21.11
Revocation of patent	21.2
Special Commissioner (where the appeal is direct to the Court of Appeal)	21.8
Value Added Tax and Duties Tribunals (where the appeal is direct to the Court of Appeal)	21.6

APPEALS TO THE HIGH COURT	*Paragraph*
Agricultural Land Tribunal	22.7
Architects Act 1997, s. 22	22.3
Charities Act 1993	23.8A
Chiropractors Act 1994, s. 31	22.3
Clergy Pensions Measure 1961, s. 38(3)	23.2
Commons Registration Act 1965	23.9
Consumer Credit Act 1974	22.4
Dentists Act 1984, s. 20 or s. 44	22.3
Employment Tribunals Act 1996	22.6E
Extradition Act 2003	22.6A
Friendly Societies Act 1974	23.7
Friendly Societies Act 1992	23.7
Industrial and Provident Societies Act 1965	23.2, 23.7
Industrial Assurance Act 1923	23.2, 23.7

APPEALS TO THE HIGH COURT	*Paragraph*
Industrial Assurance Act 1923, s. 17	23.6
Inheritance Tax Act 1984, s. 222	23.3
Inheritance Tax Act 1984, s. 225	23.5
Inheritance Tax Act 1984, ss. 249(3) and 251	23.4
Land Registration Act 1925	23.2
Land Registration Act 2002	23.2, 23.8B
Law of Property Act 1922, para. 16 of Sched. 15	23.2
Medical Act 1983, s. 40	22.3
Medicines Act 1968, ss. 82(3) and 83	(2)22.3
Mental Health Review Tribunal	22.8
Merchant Shipping Act 1995	22.2
National Health Service Act 1977	22.6D
Nurses, Midwives and Health Visitors Act 1997, s. 12	22.3
Opticians Act 1989, s. 23	22.3
Osteopaths Act 1993, s. 31	22.3
Pensions Act 1995, s. 97	23.2
Pension Schemes Act 1993, ss. 151 and 173	23.2
Pharmacy Act 1954	22.3
Planning (Listed Buildings and Conservation Areas) Act 1990, s. 65 (appeal)	22.6C
Planning (Listed Buildings and Conservation Areas) Act 1990, s. 65 (case stated)	22.8A
Social Security Administration Act 1992	22.6
Stamp Duty Reserve Tax Regulations 1986, reg. 10	23.5
Taxes Management Act 1970, ss. 53 and 100C	(4)23.4
Taxes Management Act 1970, s. 56A	23.5
Town and Country Planning Act 1990, s. 289 (appeal)	22.6C
Town and Country Planning Act 1990, s. 289 (case stated)	22.8A
Value Added Tax and Duties Tribunal	23.8
Water Resources Act 1991, s. 205	(4)23.2

APPEALS TO THE COUNTY COURT	*Paragraph*
Local Government (Miscellaneous Provisions) Act 1976	24.1
Housing Act 1996, ss. 204 and 204A	24.2

Immigration and Asylum Act 1999, Part II	24.3
Representation of the People Act 1983, s. 56	24.4 to 24.6
UK Borders Act 2007, s.11	24.7

APPEALS TO THE COURT OF APPEAL

Appeal against decree nisi of divorce or nullity of marriage or conditional dissolution or nullity order in relation to civil partnership

App 2–090 **21.1**

    (1) The appellant must file the appellant's notice at the Court of Appeal within 28 days after the date on which the decree was pronounced or conditional order made.

    (2) The appellant must file the following documents with the appellant's notice—

    (a) the decree or conditional order; and

    (b) a certificate of service of the appellant's notice.

    (3) The appellant's notice must be served on the appropriate district judge (see sub-paragraph (6)) in addition to the persons to be served under rule 52.4(3) and in accordance with that rule.

    (4) The lower court may not alter the time limits for filing of the appeal notices.

    (5) Where an appellant intends to apply to the Court of Appeal for an extension of time for serving or filing the appellant's notice he must give notice of that intention to the appropriate district judge (see sub-paragraph 6) before the application is made.

    (6) In this paragraph 'the appropriate district judge' means, where the lower court is—

    (a) a county court, the district judge of that court;

    (b) a district registry, the district judge of that registry;

    (c) the Principal Registry of the Family Division, the senior district judge of that division.

Appeal against order for revocation of patent

App 2–091 **21.2**

    (1) This paragraph applies where an appeal lies to the Court of Appeal from an order for the revocation of a patent.

    (2) The appellant must serve the appellant's notice on the Comptroller-General of Patents, Designs and Trade Marks (the 'Comptroller') in addition to the persons to be served under rule 52.4(3) and in accordance with that rule.

    (3) Where, before the appeal hearing, the respondent decides not to oppose the appeal or not to attend the appeal hearing, he must immediately serve notice of that decision on—

    (a) the Comptroller; and

    (b) the appellant

    (4) Where the respondent serves a notice in accordance with paragraph (3), he must also serve copies of the following documents on the Comptroller with that notice—

    (a) the petition;

    (b) any statements of claim;

    (c) any written evidence filed in the claim.

(5) Within 14 days after receiving the notice in accordance with paragraph (3), the Comptroller must serve on the appellant a notice stating whether or not he intends to attend the appeal hearing.

(6) The Comptroller may attend the appeal hearing and oppose the appeal—

(a) in any case where he has given notice under paragraph (5) of his intention to attend; and

(b) in any other case (including, in particular, a case where the respondent withdraws his opposition to the appeal during the hearing) if the Court of Appeal so directs or permits.

Appeal from Patents Court on appeal from Comptroller

21.3 Where the appeal is from a decision of the Patents Court which was itself made on an appeal from a decision of the Comptroller-General of Patents, Designs and Trade Marks, the appellant must serve the appellant's notice on the Comptroller in addition to the persons to be served under rule 52.4(3) and in accordance with that rule. **App 2–092**

Appeals in cases of contempt of court

21.4 In an appeal under section 13 of the Administration of Justice Act 1960 (appeals in cases of contempt of court), the appellant must serve the appellant's notice on the court or the Upper Tribunal from whose order or decision the appeal is brought in addition to the persons to be served under rule 52.4(3) and in accordance with that rule. **App 2–093**

Omitted

21.5 **App 2–094**

Appeals from Value Added Tax and Duties Tribunals

21.6 **App 2–095**

(1) An application to the Court of Appeal for permission to appeal from a value added tax and duties tribunal direct to that court must be made within 28 days after the date on which the tribunal certifies that its decision involves a point of law relating wholly or mainly to the construction of—

(a) an enactment or of a statutory instrument; or

(b) any of the Community Treaties or any Community Instrument, which has been fully argued before and fully considered by it.

(2) The application must be made by the parties jointly filing at the Court of Appeal an appellant's notice that—

(a) contains a statement of the grounds for the application; and

(b) is accompanied by a copy of the decision to be appealed, endorsed with the certificate of the tribunal.

(3) The court will notify the appellant of its decision and—

(a) where permission to appeal to the Court of Appeal is given, the appellant must serve the appellant's notice on the chairman of the tribunal in addition to the persons to be served under rule 52.4(3) within 14 days after that notification.

(b) where permission to appeal to the Court of Appeal is refused, the period for appealing to the High Court is to be calculated from the date of the notification of that refusal.

Asylum and Immigration Appeals

21.7

(1) This paragraph applies to appeals from the Immigration and Asylum Chamber of the Upper Tribunal under section 13 of the Tribunals, Courts and Enforcement Act 2007.

(2) The appellant is not required to file an appeal bundle in accordance with paragraph 5.6A of this practice direction, but must file the documents specified in paragraphs 5.6(2)(a) to (f) together with a copy of the Tribunal's determination.

(3) The appellant's notice must be filed at the Court of Appeal within 14 days after the appellant is served with written notice of the decision of the Tribunal to grant or refuse permission to appeal.

(4) The appellant must serve the appellant's notice in accordance with rule 52.4(3) on—

(a) the persons to be served under that rule; and

(b) the Immigration and Asylum Chamber of the Upper Tribunal.

(5) On being served with the appellant's notice, the Immigration and Asylum Chamber of the Upper Tribunal must send to the Court of Appeal copies of the documents which were before the relevant Tribunal when it considered the appeal.

21.7A Omitted

21.7B

(1) This paragraph applies to appeals from the Immigration and Asylum Chamber of the Upper Tribunal which—

(a) would otherwise be treated as abandoned under section 104(4A) of the Nationality, Immigration and Asylum Act 2002 (the '2002 Act'); but

(b) meet the conditions set out in section 104(4B) or section 104(4C) of the 2002 Act.

(2) Where section 104(4A) of the 2002 Act applies and the appellant wishes to pursue his appeal, the appellant must file a notice at the Court of Appeal—

(a) where section 104(4B) of the 2002 Act applies, within 28 days of the date on which the appellant received notice of the grant of leave to enter or remain in the United Kingdom for a period exceeding 12 months; or

(b) where section 104(4C) of the 2002 Act applies, within 28 days of the date on which the appellant received notice of the grant of leave to enter or remain in the United Kingdom.

(3) Where the appellant does not comply with the time limits specified in paragraph (2) the appeal will be treated as abandoned in accordance with section 104(4) of the 2002 Act.

(4) The appellant must serve the notice filed under paragraph (2) on the respondent.

(5) Where section 104(4B) of the 2002 Act applies, the notice filed under paragraph (2) must state—

(a) the appellant's full name and date of birth;

(b) the Court of Appeal reference number;

(c) the Home Office reference number, if applicable;

(d) the date on which the appellant was granted leave to enter or remain in the United Kingdom for a period exceeding 12 months; and

  (e) that the appellant wishes to pursue the appeal in so far as it is brought on the ground relating to the Refugee Convention specified in section 84(1)(g) of the 2002 Act.

(6) Where section 104(4C) of the 2002 Act applies, the notice filed under paragraph (2) must state—

  (a) the appellant's full name and date of birth;

  (b) the Court of Appeal reference number;

  (c) the Home Office reference number, if applicable;

  (d) the date on which the appellant was granted leave to enter or remain in the United Kingdom; and

  (e) that the appellant wishes to pursue the appeal in so far as it is brought on the ground relating to section 19B of the Race Relations Act 1976 specified in section 84(1)(b) of the 2002 Act.

(7) Where an appellant has filed a notice under paragraph (2) the Court of Appeal will notify the appellant of the date on which it received the notice.

(8) The Court of Appeal will send a copy of the notice issued under paragraph (7) to the respondent.

Appeal from Special Commissioners

21.8   **App 2–097**

(1) An application to the Court of Appeal for permission to appeal from the Special Commissioners direct to that court under section 56A of the Taxes Management Act 1970 must be made within 28 days after the date on which the Special Commissioners certify that their decision involves a point of law relating wholly or mainly to the construction of an enactment which has been fully argued before and fully considered before them.

(2) The application must be made by the parties jointly filing at the Court of Appeal an appellant's notice that—

  (a) contains a statement of the grounds for the application; and

  (b) is accompanied by a copy of the decision to be appealed, endorsed with the certificate of the tribunal.

(3) The court will notify the parties of its decision and—

  (a) where permission to appeal to the Court of Appeal is given, the appellant must serve the appellant's notice on the Clerk to the Special Commissioners in addition to the persons to be served under rule 52.4(3) within 14 days after that notification.

  (b) where permission to appeal to the Court of Appeal is refused, the period for appealing to the High Court is to be calculated from the date of the notification of that refusal.

Appeal from Lands Tribunal

21.9 The appellant must file the appellant's notice at the Court of Appeal within 28 days after the date of the decision of the tribunal.   **App 2–098**

Appeal from Competition Appeal Tribunal

21.10   **App 2–099**

(1) Where the appellant applies for permission to appeal at the hearing at which the decision is delivered by the tribunal and—

  (a) permission is given; or

(b) permission is refused and the appellant wishes to make an application to the Court of Appeal for permission to appeal,

the appellant's notice must be filed at the Court of Appeal within 14 days after the date of that hearing.

(2) Where the appellant applies in writing to the Registrar of the tribunal for permission to appeal and—

(a) permission is given; or

(b) permission is refused and the appellant wishes to make an application to the Court of Appeal for permission to appeal,

the appellant's notice must be filed at the Court of Appeal within 14 days after the date of receipt of the tribunal's decision on permission.

(3) Where the appellant does not make an application to the tribunal for permission to appeal, but wishes to make an application to the Court of Appeal for permission, the appellant's notice must be filed at the Court of Appeal within 14 days after the end of the period within which he may make a written application to the Registrar of the tribunal.

Appeals relating to the application of Articles 81 and 82 of the EC Treaty and Chapters I and II of Part I of the Competition Act 1998

App 2–100   21.10A

(1) This paragraph applies to any appeal to the Court of Appeal relating to the application of—

(a) Article 81 or Article 82 of the Treaty establishing the European Community; or

(b) Chapter I or Chapter II of Part I of the Competition Act 1998.

(2) In this paragraph—

(a) 'the Act' means the Competition Act 1998;

(b) 'the Commission' means the European Commission;

(c) 'the Competition Regulation' means Council Regulation (EC) No. 1/2003 of 16 December 2002 on the implementation of the rules on competition laid down in Articles 81 and 82 of the Treaty;

(d) 'national competition authority' means—

(i) the Office of Fair Trading; and

(ii) any other person or body designated pursuant to Article 35 of the Competition Regulation as a national competition authority of the United Kingdom;

(e) 'the Treaty' means the Treaty establishing the European Community.

(3) Any party whose appeal notice raises an issue relating to the application of Article 81 or 82 of the Treaty, or Chapter I or II of Part I of the Act, must—

(a) state that fact in his appeal notice; and

(b) serve a copy of the appeal notice on the Office of Fair Trading at the same time as it is served on the other party to the appeal (addressed to the Director of Competition Policy Co-ordination, Office of Fair Trading, Fleetbank House, 2-6 Salisbury Square, London EC4Y 8JX).

(4) Attention is drawn to the provisions of article 15.3 of the Competition Regulation, which entitles competition authorities and the Commission to submit written observations to national courts on issues relating to the application of Article 81 or 82 and, with the permission of the court in question, to submit oral observations to the court.

(5) A national competition authority may also make written observations to the Court of Appeal, or apply for permission to make oral observations, on issues relating to the application of Chapter I or II.

(6) If a national competition authority or the Commission intends to make written observations to the Court of Appeal, it must give notice of its

intention to do so by letter to the Civil Appeals Office at the earliest opportunity.

(7) An application by a national competition authority or the Commission for permission to make oral representations at the hearing of an appeal must be made by letter to the Civil Appeals Office at the earliest opportunity, identifying the appeal and indicating why the applicant wishes to make oral representations.

(8) If a national competition authority or the Commission files a notice under sub-paragraph (6) or an application under sub-paragraph (7), it must at the same time serve a copy of the notice or application on every party to the appeal.

(9) Any request by a national competition authority or the Commission for the court to send it any documents relating to an appeal should be made at the same time as filing a notice under sub-paragraph (6) or an application under sub-paragraph (7).

(10) When the Court of Appeal receives a notice under sub-paragraph (6) it may give case management directions to the national competition authority or the Commission, including directions about the date by which any written observations are to be filed.

(11) The Court of Appeal will serve on every party to the appeal a copy of any directions given or order made—

(a) on an application under sub-paragraph (7); or

(b) under sub-paragraph (10).

(12) Every party to an appeal which raises an issue relating to the application of Article 81 or 82, and any national competition authority which has been served with a copy of a party's appeal notice, is under a duty to notify the Court of Appeal at any stage of the appeal if they are aware that—

(a) the Commission has adopted, or is contemplating adopting, a decision in relation to proceedings which it has initiated; and

(b) the decision referred to in (a) above has or would have legal effects in relation to the particular agreement, decision or practice in issue before the court.

(13) Where the Court of Appeal is aware that the Commission is contemplating adopting a decision as mentioned in sub-paragraph (12)(a), it shall consider whether to stay the appeal pending the Commission's decision.

(14) Where any judgment is given which decides on the application of Article 81 or 82, the court shall direct that a copy of the transcript of the judgment shall be sent to the Commission.

Judgments may be sent to the Commission electronically to comp-amicus@cec.eu.int or by post to the European Commission—DG Competition, B–1049, Brussels.

Appeal from Proscribed Organisations Appeal Commission

21.11　　　　　　　　　　　　　　　　　　　　　　　　　　　　　　　App 2–101

(1) The appellant's notice must be filed at the Court of Appeal within 14 days after the date when the Proscribed Organisations Appeal Commission—

(a) granted; or

(b) where section 6(2)(b) of the Terrorism Act 2000 applies, refused permission to appeal.

Appeal from the Court of Protection

21.12　　　　　　　　　　　　　　　　　　　　　　　　　　　　　　　App 2–102

(1) In this paragraph—

   (a) 'P' means a person who lacks, or who is alleged to lack, capacity within the meaning of the Mental Capacity Act 2005 to make a decision or decisions in relation to any matter that is subject to an order of the Court of Protection;

   (b) 'the person effecting notification' means—
     (i)   the appellant;
     (ii) an agent duly appointed by the appellant; or
     (iii) such other person as the Court of Protection may direct,

   (c) 'final order' means a decision of the Court of Appeal that finally determines the appeal proceedings before it.

   (2) Where P is not a party to the proceedings, unless the Court of Appeal directs otherwise, the person effecting notification must notify P—

   (a) that an appellant's notice has been filed with the Court of Appeal and—
     (i)   who the appellant is;
     (ii) what final order the appellant is seeking;
     (iii) what will happen if the Court of Appeal makes the final order sought by the appellant; and
     (iv) that P may apply under rule 52.12A by letter for permission to file evidence or make representations at the appeal hearing;

   (b) of the final order, the effect of the final order and what steps P can take in relation to it; and

   (c) of such other events and documents as the Court of Appeal may direct.
     (Paragraphs 17.7 to 17.11 of this practice direction contain provisions on how a third party can apply for permission to file evidence or make representations at an appeal hearing.)

   (3) The person effecting notification must provide P with the information specified in sub-paragraph (2)—

   (a) within 14 days of the date on which the appellant's notice was filed with the Court of Appeal;

   (b) within 14 days of the date on which the final order was made; or

   (c) within such time as the Court of Appeal may direct,
     as the case may be.

   (4) The person effecting notification must provide P in person with the information specified in sub-paragraph (2) in a way that is appropriate to P's circumstances (for example, using simple language, visual aids or any other appropriate means).

   (5) Where P is to be notified as to—

   (a) the existence or effect of a document other than the appellant's notice or final order; or

   (b) the taking place of an event, the person effecting notification must explain to P—
     (i)   in the case of a document, what the document is and what effect, if any, it has; or
     (ii) in the case of an event, what the event is and its relevance to P.

   (6) The person effecting notification must, within 7 days of notifying P, file a certificate of notification (form N165) which certifies—

   (a) the date on which P was notified; and

   (b) that P was notified in accordance with this paragraph.

   (7) Where the person effecting notification has not notified P in accordance with this paragraph, he must file with the Court of Appeal a certificate of non-notification (form N165) stating the reason why notification has not been effected.

   (8) Where the person effecting notification must file a certificate of non-notification with the Court of Appeal, he must file the certificate within the following time limits—

(a) where P is to be notified in accordance with sub-paragraph (2)(a) (appellant's notice), within 21 days of the appellant's notice being filed with the Court of Appeal;

(b) where P is to be notified in accordance with sub-paragraph (2)(b) (final order), within 21 days of the final order being made by the Court of Appeal; or

(c) where P is to be notified of such other events and documents as may be directed by the Court of Appeal, within such time as the Court of Appeal directs.

(9) The appellant or such other person as the Court of Appeal may direct may apply to the Court of Appeal seeking an order—

(a) dispensing with the requirement to comply with the provisions of this paragraph; or

(b) requiring some other person to comply with the provisions of this paragraph.

(10) An application made under sub-paragraph (9) may be made in the appellant's notice or by Part 23 application notice.

(Paragraph 12 contains provisions about the dismissal of applications or appeals by consent. Paragraph 13 contains provisions about allowing unopposed appeals or applications on paper and procedures for consent orders and agreements to pay periodical payments involving a child or protected party or in appeals to the Court of Appeal from a decision of the Court of Protection.)

Appeals in relation to serious crime prevention orders

21.13   App 2–103

(1) This paragraph applies where the appeal is in relation to a serious crime prevention order and is made under section 23(1) of the Serious Crime Act 2007 or section 16 of the Supreme Court Act 1981.

(2) The appellant must serve the appellant's notice on any person who made representations in the proceedings by virtue of section 9(1), (2) or (3) of the Serious Crime Act 2007 in addition to the persons to be served under rule 52.4(3) and in accordance with that rule.

APPEALS TO THE HIGH COURT—QUEEN'S BENCH DIVISION

22.1 The following appeals are to be heard in the Queen's Bench Division.   App 2–104

Statutory Appeals

Appeals under the Merchant Shipping Act 1995

22.2   App 2–105

(1) This paragraph applies to appeals under the Merchant Shipping Act 1995 and for this purpose a re-hearing and an application under section 61 of the Merchant Shipping Act 1995 are treated as appeals.

(2) The appellant must file any report to the Secretary of State containing the decision from which the appeal is brought with the appellant's notice.

(3) Where a re-hearing by the High Court is ordered under sections 64 or 269 of the Merchant Shipping Act 1995, the Secretary of State must give reasonable notice to the parties whom he considers to be affected by the re-hearing.

Appeals against decisions affecting the registration of architects and health care professionals

App 2–106 **22.3**

  (1) This paragraph applies to an appeal to the High Court under—

  (a) section 22 of the Architects Act 1997;
  (b) section 82(3) and 83(2) of the Medicines Act 1968;
  (c) section 12 of the Nurses, Midwives and Health Visitors Act 1997;
  (cc) article 38 of the Nursing and Midwifery Order 2001;
  (d) section 10 of the Pharmacy Act 1954;
  (e) section 40 of the Medical Act 1983;
  (f) section 29 or section 44 of the Dentists Act 1984;
  (g) sections 23 of the Opticians Act 1989;
  (h) section 31 of the Osteopaths Act 1993; and
  (i) section 31 of the Chiropractors Act 1994.

  (2) Every appeal to which this paragraph applies must be supported by written evidence and, if the court so orders, oral evidence and will be by way of re-hearing.

  (3) The appellant must file the appellant's notice within 28 days after the decision that the appellant wishes to appeal.

  (4) In the case of an appeal under an enactment specified in column 1 of the following table, the persons to be made respondents are the persons specified in relation to that enactment in column 2 of the table and the person to be served with the appellant's notice is the person so specified in column 3.

1 *Enactment*	2 *Respondents*	3 *Person to be served*
Architects Act 1997, s. 22	The Architects' Registration Council of the United Kingdom	The registrar of the Council
Medicines Act 1968, s. 82(3) and s. 83(2)	The Pharmaceutical Society of Great Britain	The registrar of the Society
Nurses, Midwives and Health Visitors Act 1997, s. 12; Nursing and Midwifery Order 2001, art. 38	The Nursing and Midwifery Council	The Registrar of the Council
Pharmacy Act 1954, s. 10	The Royal Pharmaceutical Society of Great Britain	The registrar of the Society
Medical Act 1983, s. 40	The General Medical Council	The Registrar of the Council
Dentists Act 1984, s. 29 or s. 44	The General Dental Council	The Registrar of the Council
Opticians Act 1989, s. 23	The General Optical Council	The Registrar of the Council
Osteopaths Act 1993, s. 31	The General Osteopathic Council	The Registrar of the Council
Chiropractors Act 1994, s. 31	The General Chiropractic Council	The Registrar of the Council

Consumer Credit Act 1974: appeal from Secretary of State

22.4

App 2–107

(1) A person dissatisfied in point of law with a decision of the Secretary of State on an appeal under section 41 of the Consumer Credit Act 1974 from a determination of the Office of Fair Trading who had a right to appeal to the Secretary of State, whether or not he exercised that right, may appeal to the High Court.

(2) The appellant must serve the appellant's notice on—

(a) the Secretary of State;

(b) the original applicant, if any, where the appeal is by a licensee under a group licence against compulsory variation, suspension or revocation of that licence; and

(c) any other person as directed by the court.

(3) The appeal court may remit the matter to the Secretary of State to the extent necessary to enable him to provide the court with such further information as the court may direct.

(4) If the appeal court allows the appeal, it shall not set aside or vary the decision but shall remit the matter to the Secretary of State with the opinion of the court for hearing and determination by him.

Omitted

22.5

App 2–108

The Social Security Administration Act 1992

22.6

App 2–109

(1) Any person who by virtue of section 18 or 58(8) of the Social Security Administration Act 1992 ('the Act') is entitled and wishes to appeal against a decision of the Secretary of State on a question of law must, within the prescribed period, or within such further time as the Secretary of State may allow, serve on the Secretary of State a notice requiring him to state a case setting out—

(a) his decision; and

(b) the facts on which his decision was based.

(2) Unless paragraph (3) applies the prescribed period is 28 days after receipt of the notice of the decision.

(3) Where, within 28 days after receipt of notice of the decision, a request is made to the Secretary of State in accordance with regulations made under the Act to furnish a statement of the grounds of the decision, the prescribed period is 28 days after receipt of that statement.

(4) Where under section 18 or section 58(8) of the Act, the Secretary of State refers a question of law to the court, he must state that question together with the relevant facts in a case.

(5) The appellant's notice and the case stated must be filed at the appeal court and a copy of the notice and the case stated served on—

(a) the Secretary of State; and

(b) every person as between whom and the Secretary of State the question has arisen, within 28 days after the case stated was served on the party at whose request, or as a result of whose application to the court, the case was stated.

(6) Unless the appeal court otherwise orders, the appeal or reference shall not be heard sooner than 28 days after service of the appellant's notice.

(7) The appeal court may order the case stated by the Secretary of State to be returned to the Secretary of State for him to hear further evidence.

Appeals under the Extradition Act 2003

App 2–110 **22.6A**

(1) In this paragraph, 'the Act' means the Extradition Act 2003.

(2) Appeals to the High Court under the Act must be brought in the Administrative Court of the Queen's Bench Division.

(3) Where an appeal is brought under section 26 or 28 of the Act—

(a) the appellant's notice must be filed and served before the expiry of 7 days, starting with the day on which the order is made;

(b) the appellant must endorse the appellant's notice with the date of the person's arrest;

(c) the High Court must begin to hear the substantive appeal within 40 days of the person's arrest; and

(d) the appellant must serve a copy of the appellant's notice on the Crown Prosecution Service, if they are not a party to the appeal, in addition to the persons to be served under rule 52.4(3) and in accordance with that rule.

(4) The High Court may extend the period of 40 days under paragraph (3)(c) if it believes it to be in the interests of justice to do so.

(5) Where an appeal is brought under section 103 of the Act, the appellant's notice must be filed and served before the expiry of 14 days, starting with the day on which the Secretary of State informs the person under section 100(1) or (4) of the Act of the order he has made in respect of the person.

(6) Where an appeal is brought under section 105 of the Act, the appellant's notice must be filed and served before the expiry of 14 days, starting with the day on which the order for discharge is made.

(7) Where an appeal is brought under section 108 of the Act the appellant's notice must be filed and served before the expiry of 14 days, starting with the day on which the Secretary of State informs the person that he has ordered his extradition.

(8) Where an appeal is brought under section 110 of the Act the appellant's notice must be filed and served before the expiry of 14 days, starting with the day on which the Secretary of State informs the person acting on behalf of a category 2 territory, as defined in section 69 of the Act, of the order for discharge.

(Section 69 of the Act provides that a category 2 territory is that designated for the purposes of Part 2 of the Act).

(9) Subject to paragraph (10), where an appeal is brought under section 103, 105, 108 or 110 of the Act, the High Court must begin to hear the substantive appeal within 76 days of the appellant's notice being filed.

(10) Where an appeal is brought under section 103 of the Act before the Secretary of State has decided whether the person is to be extradited—

(a) the period of 76 days does not start until the day on which the Secretary of State informs the person of his decision; and

(b) the Secretary of State must, as soon as practicable after he informs the person of his decision, inform the High Court—

(i) of his decision; and

(ii) of the date on which he informs the person of his decision.

(11) The High Court may extend the period of 76 days if it believes it to be in the interests of justice to do so.

(12) Where an appeal is brought under section 103, 105, 108 or 110 of the Act, the appellant must serve a copy of the appellant's notice on—

(a) the Crown Prosecution Service; and

(b) the Home Office,

if they are not a party to the appeal, in addition to the persons to be served under rule 52.4(3) and in accordance with that rule.

Appeals from decisions of the Law Society or the Solicitors Disciplinary Tribunal to the High Court

22.6B

(1) This paragraph applies to appeals from the Law Society or the Solicitors Disciplinary Tribunal ('the Tribunal') to the High Court under the Solicitors Act 1974, the Administration of Justice Act 1985, the Courts and Legal Services Act 1990, the European Communities (Lawyer's Practice) Regulations 2000 or the European Communities (Recognition of Professional Qualifications) Regulations 2007.

(2) The appellant must file the appellant's notice in the Administrative Court.

(3) The appellant must, unless the court orders otherwise, serve the appellant's notice on—

(a) every party to the proceedings before the Tribunal; and

(b) the Law Society.

Appeals under s 289(6) of the Town and Country Planning Act 1990 and s 65(5) of the Planning (Listed Buildings and Conservation Areas) Act 1990

22.6C

(1) An application for permission to appeal to the High Court under section 289 of the Town and Country Planning Act 1990 ('the TCP Act') or section 65 of the Planning (Listed Buildings and Conservation Areas) Act 1990 ('the PLBCA Act') must be made within 28 days after notice of the decision is given to the applicant.

(2) The application—

(a) must be in writing and must set out the reasons why permission should be granted; and

(b) if the time for applying has expired, must include an application to extend the time for applying, and must set out the reasons why the application was not made within that time.

(3) The applicant must, before filing the application, serve a copy of it on the persons referred to in sub-paragraph (11) with the draft appellant's notice and a copy of the witness statement or affidavit to be filed with the application.

(4) The applicant must file the application in the Administrative Court Office with—

(i) a copy of the decision being appealed;

(ii) a draft appellant's notice;

(iii) a witness statement or affidavit verifying any facts relied on; and

(iv) a witness statement or affidavit giving the name and address of, and the place and date of service on, each person who has been served with the application. If any person who ought to be served has not been served, the witness statement or affidavit must state that fact and the reason why the person was not served.

(5) An application will be heard—

(a) by a single judge; and

(b) unless the court otherwise orders, not less than 21 days after it was filed at the Administrative Court Office.

(6) Any person served with the application is entitled to appear and be heard.

(7) Any respondent who intends to use a witness statement or affidavit at the hearing—

(a) must file it in the Administrative Court Office; and

(b) must serve a copy on the applicant as soon as is practicable and in any event, unless the court otherwise allows, at least 2 days before the hearing.

(8) The court may allow the applicant to use a further witness statement or affidavit.

(9) Where on the hearing of an application the court is of the opinion that a person who ought to have been served has not been served, the court may adjourn the hearing, on such terms as it directs, in order that the application may be served on that person.

(10) Where the court grants permission—

(a) it may impose terms as to costs and as to giving security;

(b) it may give directions; and

(c) the relevant appellant's notice must be served and filed within 7 days of the grant.

(11) The persons to be served with the appellant's notice are—

(a) the Secretary of State;

(b) the local planning authority who served the notice or gave the decision, as the case may be, or, where the appeal is brought by that authority, the appellant or applicant in the proceedings in which the decision appealed against was given;

(c) in the case of an appeal brought by virtue of section 289(1) of the TCP Act or section 65(1) of the PLBCA Act, any other person having an interest in the land to which the notice relates; and

(d) in the case of an appeal brought by virtue of section 289(2) of the TCP Act, any other person on whom the notice to which those proceedings related was served.

(12) The appeal will be heard and determined by a single judge unless the court directs that the matter be heard and determined by a Divisional Court.

(13) The court may remit the matter to the Secretary of State to the extent necessary to enable him to provide the court with such further information in connection with the matter as the court may direct.

(14) Where the court is of the opinion that the decision appealed against was erroneous in point of law, it will not set aside or vary that decision but will remit the matter to the Secretary of State for re-hearing and determination in accordance with the opinion of the court.

(15) The court may give directions as to the exercise, until an appeal brought by virtue of section 289(1) of the TCP Act is finally concluded and any re-hearing and determination by the Secretary of State has taken place, of the power to serve, and institute proceedings (including criminal proceedings) concerning—

(a) a stop notice under section 183 of that Act; and

(b) a breach of condition notice under section 187A of that Act.

National Health Service Act 1977: appeal from tribunal

App 2–113   **22.6D**

(1) This paragraph applies to an appeal from a tribunal constituted under section 46 of the National Health Service Act 1977.

(2) The appellant must file the appellant's notice at the High Court within 14 days after the date of the decision of the tribunal.

Employment Tribunals Act 1996: appeal from tribunal

App 2–114   **22.6E**

(1) This paragraph applies to an appeal from a tribunal constituted under section 1 of the Employment Tribunals Act 1996.

(2) The appellant must file the appellant's notice at the High Court within 42 days after the date of the decision of the tribunal.

(3) The appellant must serve the appellant's notice on the secretary of the tribunal.

Appeals by way of case stated

Reference of question of law by Agriculture Land Tribunal

22.7 App 2–115

(1) A question of law referred to the High Court by an Agricultural Land Tribunal under section 6 of the Agriculture (Miscellaneous Provisions) Act 1954 shall be referred by way of case stated by the Tribunal.

(2) Where the proceedings before the tribunal arose on an application under section 11 of the Agricultural Holdings Act 1986, an—

(a) application notice for an order under section 6 that the tribunal refers a question of law to the court; and

(b) appellant's notice by which an appellant seeks the court's determination on a question of law, must be served on the authority having power to enforce the statutory requirement specified in the notice in addition to every other party to those proceedings and on the secretary of the tribunal.

(3) Where, in accordance with paragraph (2), a notice is served on the authority mentioned in that paragraph, that authority may attend the appeal hearing and make representations to the court.

Case stated by Mental Health Review Tribunal

22.8 App 2–116

(1) In this paragraph 'the Act' means the Mental Health Act 1983 and 'party to proceedings' means—

(a) the person who initiated the proceedings; and

(b) any person to whom, in accordance with rules made under section 78 of the Act, the tribunal sent notice of the application or reference or a request instead notice of reference.

(2) A party to proceedings shall not be entitled to apply to the High Court for an order under section 78(8) of the Act directing the tribunal to state a case for determination by court unless—

(a) within 21 days after the decision of the tribunal was communicated to him in accordance with rules made under section 78 of the Act he made a written request to the tribunal to state a case; and

(b) either the tribunal
    (i) failed to comply with that request within 21 days after it was made; or
    (ii) refused to comply with it.

(3) The period for filing the application notice for an order under section 78(8) of the Act is—

(a) where the tribunal failed to comply with the applicant's request to state a case within the period mentioned in paragraph 2(b)(i), 14 days after the expiration of that period;

(b) where the tribunal refused that request, 14 days after receipt by the applicant of notice of the refusal of his request.

(4) A Mental Health Review Tribunal by whom a case is stated shall be entitled to attend the proceedings for the determination of the case and make representations to the court.

(5) If the court allows the appeal, it may give any direction which the tribunal ought to have given under Part V of the Act.

Case stated under section 289 of the Town and Country Planning Act 1990 or section 65 of the Planning (Listed Buildings and Conservation Areas) Act 1990

22.8A A case stated under section 289(3) of the Town and Country Planning Act App 2–117
1990 or section 65(2) of the Planning (Listed Buildings and Conservation

Areas) Act 1990 will be heard and determined by a single judge unless the court directs that the matter be heard and determined by a Divisional Court.

APPEALS TO THE HIGH COURT—CHANCERY DIVISION

App 2–118   23.1   The following appeals are to be heard in the Chancery Division.

Determination of appeal or case stated under various Acts

App 2–119   23.2   Any appeal to the High Court, and any case stated or question referred for the opinion of that court under any of the following enactments shall be heard in the Chancery Division—

(1) paragraph 16 of Schedule 15 to the Law of Property Act 1922;
(2) the Industrial Assurance Act 1923;
(3) the Land Registration Act 1925;
(4) section 205(4) of the Water Resources Act 1991;
(5) section 38(3) of the Clergy Pensions Measure 1961;
(6) the Industrial and Provident Societies Act 1965;
(7) section 151 of the Pension Schemes Act 1993;
(8) section 173 of the Pension Schemes Act 1993;
(9) section 97 of the Pensions Act 1995;
(10) The Charities Act 1993.
(11) section 13 and 13B of the Stamp Act 1891;
(12) section 705A of the Income and Corporation Taxes Act 1988;
(13) regulation 22 of the General Commissioners (Jurisdiction and Procedure) Regulations 1994;
(14) section 53, 56A or 100C(4) of the Taxes Management Act 1970;
(15) section 222(3), 225, 249(3) or 251 of the Inheritance Tax Act 1984;
(16) regulation 8(3) or 10 of the Stamp Duty Reserve Tax Regulations 1986;
(17) the Land Registration Act 2002;
(18) regulation 74 of the European Public Limited-Liability Company Regulations 2004.
(This list is not exhaustive)

Statutory Appeals

Appeal under section 222 of the Inheritance Tax Act 1984

App 2–120   23.3
(1) This paragraph applies to appeals to the High Court under section 222(3) of the Inheritance Tax Act 1984 (the '1984 Act') and regulation 8(3) of the Stamp Duty Reserve Tax Regulations 1986 (the '1986 Regulations').
(2) The appellant's notice must—
(a) state the date on which the Commissioners for HM Revenue and Customs (the 'Board') gave notice to the appellant under section 221 of the 1984 Act or regulation 6 of the 1986 Regulations of the determination that is the subject of the appeal;
(b) state the date on which the appellant gave to the Board notice of appeal under section 222(1) of the 1984 Act or regulation 8(1) of the 1986 Regulations and, if notice was not given within the time permitted, whether the Board or the Special Commissioners have given their consent to the appeal being brought out of time, and, if they have, the date they gave their consent; and

(c) either state that the appellant and the Board have agreed that the appeal may be to the High Court or contain an application for permission to appeal to the High Court.

(3) The appellant must file the following documents with the appellant's notice—

(a) 2 copies of the notice referred to in paragraph 2(a);

(b) 2 copies of the notice of appeal (under section 222(1) of the 1984 Act or regulation 8(1) of the 1986 Regulations) referred to in paragraph 2(b); and

(c) where the appellant's notice contains an application for permission to appeal, written evidence setting out the grounds on which it is alleged that the matters to be decided on the appeal are likely to be substantially confined to questions of law.

(4) The appellant must—

(a) file the appellant's notice at the court; and

(b) serve the appellant's notice on the Board, within 30 days of the date on which the appellant gave to the Board notice of appeal under section 222(1) of the 1984 Act or regulation 8(1) of the 1986 Regulations or, if the Board or the Special Commissioners have given consent to the appeal being brought out of time, within 30 days of the date on which such consent was given.

(5) The court will set a date for the hearing of not less than 40 days from the date that the appellant's notice was filed.

(6) Where the appellant's notice contains an application for permission to appeal—

(a) a copy of the written evidence filed in accordance with paragraph (3)(c) must be served on the Board with the appellant's notice; and

(b) the Board—

  (i) may file written evidence; and

  (ii) if it does so, must serve a copy of that evidence on the appellant, within 30 days after service of the written evidence under paragraph (6)(a).

(7) The appellant may not rely on any grounds of appeal not specified in the notice referred to in paragraph (2)(b) on the hearing of the appeal without the permission of the court.

Appeals under section 53 and 100C(4) of the Taxes Management Act 1970 and section 249(3) or 251 of the Inheritance Tax Act 1984

23.4

App 2–121

(1) The appellant must serve the appellant's notice on—

(a) the General or Special Commissioners against whose decision, award or determination the appeal is brought; and

(b) (i) in the case of an appeal brought under section 100C(4) of the Taxes Management Act 1970 or section 249(3) of the Inheritance Tax Act 1984 by any party other than the defendant in the proceedings before the Commissioners, that defendant; or

  (ii) in any other case, the Commissioners for HM Revenue and Customs.

(2) The appellant must file the appellant's notice at the court within 30 days after the date of the decision, award or determination against which the appeal is brought.

(3) Within 30 days of the service on them of the appellant's notice, the General or Special Commissioners, as the case may be, must—

(a) file 2 copies of a note of their findings and of the reasons for their decision, award or determination at the court; and

(b) serve a copy of the note on every other party to the appeal.

(4) Any document to be served on the General or Special Commissioners may be served by delivering or sending it to their clerk.

Appeals under section 56A of the Taxes Management Act 1970, section 225 of the Inheritance Tax Act 1984 and regulation 10 of the Stamp Duty Reserve Tax Regulations 1986

App 2–122 **23.5**
  (1) The appellant must file the appellant's notice—
  (a) where the appeal is made following the refusal of the Special Commissioners to issue a certificate under section 56A(2)(b) of the Taxes Management Act 1970, within 28 days from the date of the release of the decision of the Special Commissioners containing the refusal;
  (b) where the appeal is made following the refusal of permission to appeal to the Court of Appeal under section 56A(2)(c) of that Act, within 28 days from the date when permission is refused; or
  (c) in all other cases within 56 days after the date of the decision or determination that the appellant wishes to appeal.

Appeal under section 17 of the Industrial Assurance Act 1923

App 2–123 **23.6** The appellant must file the appellant's notice within 21 days after the date of the Commissioner's refusal or direction under section 17(3) of the Industrial Assurance Act 1923.

Appeals affecting industrial and provident societies etc.

App 2–124 **23.7**
  (1) This paragraph applies to all appeals under—
  (a) the Friendly Societies Act 1974;
  (b) the Friendly Societies Act 1992;
  (c) the Industrial Assurance Act 1923; and
  (d) the Industrial and Provident Societies Act 1965
  (2) At any stage on an appeal, the court may—
  (a) direct that the appellant's notice be served on any person;
  (b) direct that notice be given by advertisement or otherwise of—
    (i) the bringing of the appeal;
    (ii) the nature of the appeal; and
    (iii) the time when the appeal will or is likely to be heard; or
  (c) give such other directions as it thinks proper to enable any person interested in—
    (i) the society, trade union, alleged trade union or industrial assurance company; or
    (ii) the subject matter of the appeal,
    to appear and be heard at the appeal hearing.

Appeal from Value Added Tax and Duties Tribunal

App 2–125 **23.8**
  (1) A party to proceedings before a Value Added Tax and Duties Tribunal who is dissatisfied in point of law with a decision of the tribunal may appeal under section 11(1) of the Tribunals and Inquiries Act 1992 to the High Court.
  (2) The appellant must file the appellant's notice—
  (a) where the appeal is made following the refusal of the Value Added Tax and Duties Tribunal to grant a certificate under article 2(b) of the Value Added Tax and Duties Tribunal Appeals Order 1986, within 28 days from the date of the release of the decision containing the refusal;
  (b) in all other cases within 56 days after the date of the decision or determination that the appellant wishes to appeal.

Appeal against an order or decision of the Charity Commissioners

23.8A App 2–126

(1) In this paragraph—
'the Act' means the Charities Act 1993; and
'the Commissioners' means the Charity Commissioners for England and Wales.

(2) The Attorney-General, unless he is the appellant, must be made a respondent to the appeal.

(3) The appellant's notice must state the grounds of the appeal, and the appellant may not rely on any other grounds without the permission of the court.

(4) Sub-paragraphs (5) and (6) apply, in addition to the above provisions, where the appeal is made under section 16(12) of the Act.

(5) If the Commissioners have granted a certificate that it is a proper case for an appeal, a copy of the certificate must be filed with the appellant's notice.

(6) If the appellant applies in the appellant's notice for permission to appeal under section 16(13) of the Act—

(a) the appellant's notice must state—
  (i) that the appellant has requested the Commissioners to grant a certificate that it is a proper case for an appeal, and they have refused to do so;
  (ii) the date of such refusal;
  (iii) the grounds on which the appellant alleges that it is a proper case for an appeal; and
  (iv) if the application for permission to appeal is made with the consent of any other party to the proposed appeal, that fact;

(b) if the Commissioners have given reasons for refusing a certificate, a copy of the reasons must be attached to the appellant's notice;

(c) the court may, before determining the application, direct the Commissioners to file a written statement of their reasons for refusing a certificate;

(d) the court will serve on the appellant a copy of any statement filed under sub-paragraph (c).

Appeal against a decision of the adjudicator under section 111 of the Land Registration Act 2002

23.8B App 2–127

(1) A person who is aggrieved by a decision of the adjudicator and who wishes to appeal that decision must obtain permission to appeal.

(2) The appellant must serve on the adjudicator a copy of the appeal court's decision on a request for permission to appeal as soon as reasonably practicable and in any event within 14 days of receipt by the appellant of the decision on permission.

(3) The appellant must serve on the adjudicator and the Chief Land Registrar a copy of any order by the appeal court to stay a decision of the adjudicator pending the outcome of the appeal as soon as reasonably practicable and in any event within 14 days of receipt by the appellant of the appeal court's order to stay.

(4) The appellant must serve on the adjudicator and the Chief Land Registrar a copy of the appeal court's decision on the appeal as soon as reasonably practicable and in any event within 14 days of receipt by the appellant of the appeal court's decision.

Appeals under regulation 74 of the European Public Limited-Liability Company Regulations 2004

23.8C App 2–128

(1) In this paragraph—

(a) 'the 2004 Regulations' means the European Public Limited-Liability Company Regulations 2004;

(b) 'the EC Regulation' means Council Regulation (EC) No 2157/2001 of 8 October 2001 on the Statute for a European company (SE);

(c) 'SE' means a European public limited-liability company (Societas Europaea) within the meaning of Article 1 of the EC Regulation.

(2) This paragraph applies to appeals under regulation 74 of the 2004 Regulations against the opposition—

(a) of the Secretary of State or national financial supervisory authority to the transfer of the registered office of an SE under Article 8(14) of the EC Regulation; and

(b) of the Secretary of State to the participation by a company in the formation of an SE by merger under Article 19 of the EC Regulation.

(3) Where an SE seeks to appeal against the opposition of the national financial supervisory authority to the transfer of its registered office under Article 8(14) of the EC Regulation, it must serve the appellant's notice on both the national financial supervisory authority and the Secretary of State.

(4) The appellant's notice must contain an application for permission to appeal.

(5) The appeal will be a review of the decision of the Secretary of State and not a re-hearing. The grounds of review are set out in regulation 74(2) of the 2004 Regulations.

(6) The appeal will be heard by a High Court judge.

Appeals by way of case stated

Proceedings under the Commons Registration Act 1965

App 2–129 23.9

(1) A person aggrieved by the decision of a Commons Commissioner who requires the Commissioner to state a case for the opinion of the High Court under section 18 of the Commons Registration Act 1965 must file the appellant's notice within 42 days from the date on which notice of the decision was sent to the aggrieved person.

(2) Proceedings under that section are assigned to the Chancery Division.

APPEALS TO A COUNTY COURT

Local Government (Miscellaneous Provisions) Act 1976

App 2–130 24.1 Where one of the grounds upon which an appeal against a notice under sections 21, 23 or 35 of the Local Government (Miscellaneous Provisions) Act 1976 is brought is that—

(a) it would have been fairer to serve the notice on another person; or

(b) that it would be reasonable for the whole or part of the expenses to which the appeal relates to be paid by some other person,

that person must be made a respondent to the appeal, unless the court, on application of the appellant made without notice, otherwise directs.

Appeals under sections 204 and 204A of the Housing Act 1996

App 2–131 24.2

(1) An appellant should include appeals under section 204 and section 204A of the Housing Act 1996 in one appellant's notice.

(2) If it is not possible to do so (for example because an urgent application under section 204A is required) the appeals may be included in separate appellant's notices.

(3) An appeal under section 204A may include an application for an order under section 204A(4)(a) requiring the authority to secure that accommodation is available for the applicant's occupation.

(4) If, exceptionally, the court makes an order under section 204A(4)(a) without notice, the appellant's notice must be served on the authority together with the order. Such an order will normally require the authority to secure that accommodation is available until a hearing date when the authority can make representations as to whether the order under section 204A(4)(a) should be continued.

Appeal under Part II of the Immigration and Asylum Act 1999 (carriers' liability)

24.3   App 2–132

(1) A person appealing to a county court under section 35A or section 40B of the Immigration and Asylum Act 1999 ("the Act") against a decision by the Secretary of State to impose a penalty under section 32 or a charge under section 40 of the Act must, subject to paragraph (2), file the appellant's notice within 28 days after receiving the penalty notice or charge notice.

(2) Where the appellant has given notice of objection to the Secretary of State under section 35(4) or section 40A(3) of the Act within the time prescribed for doing so, he must file the appellant's notice within 28 days after receiving notice of the Secretary of State's decision in response to the notice of objection.

(3) Sections 35A and 40B of the Act provide that any appeal under those sections shall be a re-hearing of the Secretary of State's decision to impose a penalty or charge, and therefore rule 52.11(1) does not apply.

Representation of the People Act 1983—appeals against decisions of registration officers

24.4   App 2–133

(1) This paragraph applies in relation to an appeal against a decision of a registration officer, being a decision referred to in section 56(1) of the Representation of the People Act 1983 ('the Act').

(2) Where a person ('the appellant') has given notice of such an appeal in accordance with the relevant requirements of section 56, and of the regulations made under section 53 ('the Regulations'), of the Act, the registration officer must, within 7 days after he receives the notice, forward—

(a) the notice; and

(b) the statement required by the Regulations,
    by post to the county court.

(3) The respondents to the appeal will be—

(a) the registration officer; and

(b) if the decision of the registration officer was given in favour of any other person than the appellant, that other person.

(4) On the hearing of the appeal—

(a) the statement forwarded to the court by the registration officer, and any document containing information submitted to the court by the registration officer pursuant to the Regulations, are admissible as evidence of the facts stated in them; and

(b) the court—
   (i) may draw any inference of fact that the registration officer might have drawn; and
   (ii) may give any decision and make any order that the registration officer ought to have given or made.

(5) A respondent to an appeal (other than the registration officer) is not liable for nor entitled to costs, unless he appears before the court in support of the registration officer's decision.

(6) Rule 52.4, and paragraphs 5, 6 and 7 of this practice direction, do not apply to an appeal to which this paragraph applies.

Representation of the People Act 1983—special provision in relation to anonymous entries in the register

App 2–134 **24.5**

(1) In this paragraph—
'anonymous entry' has the meaning given by section 9B(4) of the Representation of the People Act 1983;
'appeal notice' means the notice required by regulation 32 of the Representation of the People (England and Wales) Regulations 2001.

(2) This paragraph applies to an appeal to a county court to which paragraph 24.4 applies if a party to the appeal is a person—

(a) whose entry in the register is an anonymous entry; or

(b) who has applied for such an entry.

(3) This paragraph also applies to an appeal to the Court of Appeal from a decision of a county court in an appeal to which paragraph 24.4 applies.

(4) The appellant may indicate in his appeal notice that he has applied for an anonymous entry, or that his entry in the register is an anonymous entry.

(5) The respondent or any other person who applies to become a party to the proceedings may indicate in a respondent's notice or an application to join the proceedings that his entry in the register is an anonymous entry, or that he has applied for an anonymous entry.

(6) Where the appellant gives such an indication in his appeal notice, the court will refer the matter to a district judge for directions about the further conduct of the proceedings, and, in particular, directions about how the matter should be listed in the court list.

(7) Where the court otherwise becomes aware that a party to the appeal is a person referred to in sub-paragraph (2), the court will give notice to the parties that no further step is to be taken until the court has given any necessary directions for the further conduct of the matter.

(8) In the case of proceedings in a county court, the hearing will be in private unless the court orders otherwise.

(9) In the case of proceedings in the Court of Appeal, the hearing may be in private if the court so orders.

Representation of the People Act 1983—appeals selected as test cases

App 2–135 **24.6**

(1) Where two or more appeals to which paragraph 24.4 applies involve the same point of law, the court may direct that one appeal ('the test-case appeal') is to be heard first as a test case.

(2) The court will send a notice of the direction to each party to all of those appeals.

(3) Where any party to an appeal other than the test-case appeal gives notice to the court, within 7 days after the notice is served on him, that he desires the appeal to which he is a party to be heard—

(a) the court will hear that appeal after the test-case appeal is disposed of;

(b) the court will give the parties to that appeal notice of the day on which it will be heard; and

(c) the party who gave the notice is not entitled to receive any costs of the separate hearing of that appeal unless the judge otherwise orders.

(4) Where no notice is given under sub-paragraph (3) within the period limited by that paragraph—

(a) the decision on the test-case appeal binds the parties to each of the other appeals;

(b) without further hearing, the court will make, in each other appeal, an order similar to the order in the test-case appeal; and

(c) the party to each other appeal who is in the same interest as the unsuccessful party to the selected appeal is liable for the costs of the test-case appeal in the same manner and to the same extent as the unsuccessful party to that appeal and an order directing him to pay such costs may be made and enforced accordingly.

(5) Sub-paragraph (4)(a) does not affect the right to appeal to the Court of Appeal of any party to an appeal other than the test-case appeal.

Appeals under section 11 of the UK Borders Act 2007

24.7 App 2–136

(1) A person appealing to a county court under section 11 of the UK Borders Act 2007 ('the Act') against a decision by the Secretary of State to impose a penalty under section 9(1) of the Act, must, subject to paragraph (2), file the appellant's notice within 28 days after receiving the penalty notice.

(2) Where the appellant has given notice of objection to the Secretary of State under section 10 of the Act within the time prescribed for doing so, the appellant's notice must be filed within 28 days after receiving notice of the Secretary of State's decision in response to the notice of objection.

SECTION IV—PROVISIONS ABOUT REOPENING APPEALS

REOPENING OF FINAL APPEALS

25.1 This paragraph applies to applications under rule 52.17 for permission to reopen a final determination of an appeal. App 2–137

25.2 In this paragraph, "appeal" includes an application for permission to appeal.

25.3 Permission must be sought from the court whose decision the applicant wishes to reopen.

25.4 The application for permission must be made by application notice and supported by written evidence, verified by a statement of truth.

25.5 A copy of the application for permission must not be served on any other party to the original appeal unless the court so directs.

25.6 Where the court directs that the application for permission is to be served on another party, that party may within 14 days of the service on him of the copy of the application file and serve a written statement either supporting or opposing the application.

25.7 The application for permission, and any written statements supporting or opposing it, will be considered on paper by a single judge, and will be allowed to proceed only if the judge so directs.

App 2–138   **SECTION V—TRANSITIONAL PROVISIONS RELATING TO THE ABOLITION OF THE ASYLUM AND IMMIGRATION TRIBUNAL**

(1) Rules 52.7 and 54.28 to 54.36, paragraphs 21.7, 21.7A and 21.7B of Practice Direction 52 and the whole of Practice Direction 54B in force immediately before the 15 February 2010 will continue to apply to the applications, references, orders and cases, as appropriate, set out in paragraphs 5, 7, 9,10, 11 and 13(1) (c) of Schedule 4 to the Transfer of Functions of the Asylum and Immigration Tribunal Order 2009 as if—
  (i) rule 52.7 and paragraphs 21.7 and 21.7B of Practice Direction 52 had not been amended; and
  (ii) paragraph 21.7A of Practice Direction 52, rules 54.28 to 54.36 and Practice Direction 54B had not been revoked.

(2) For the purpose of service of any claim form issued before 15 February 2010 paragraph 6.2 of Practice Direction 54A shall apply with modification so that the reference in that paragraph to the Immigration and Asylum Chamber of the First-tier Tribunal shall be treated as a reference to the Asylum and Immigration Tribunal.

(3) For ease of reference, the amended and revoked provisions are reproduced below in italics:

Stay

52.7

Unless—
(a) the appeal court or the lower court orders otherwise; or
(b) the appeal is from the Asylum and Immigration Tribunal,
an appeal shall not operate as a stay of any order or decision of the lower court.

Applications for Statutory Review under Section 103A of the Nationality, Immigration and Asylum Act 2002

Scope and Interpretation

54.28
(1) This Section of this Part contains rules about applications to the High Court under section 103A of the Nationality, Immigration and Asylum Act 2002 for an order requiring the Asylum and Immigration Tribunal to reconsider its decision on an appeal.
(2) In this Section—
(a) 'the 2002 Act' means the Nationality, Immigration and Asylum Act 2002;
(b) 'the 2004 Act' means the Asylum and Immigration (Treatment of Claimants, etc.) Act 2004;

(c) 'appellant' means the appellant in the proceedings before the Tribunal;

(d) 'applicant' means a person applying to the High Court under section 103A;

(e) 'asylum claim' has the meaning given in section 113(1) of the 2002 Act;

(ea) 'fast track case' means any case in relation to which an order made under section 26(8) of the 2004 Act provides that the time period for making an application under section 103A(1) of the 2002 Act or giving notification under paragraph 30(5) of Schedule 2 to the 2004 Act is less than 5 days;

(f) 'filter provision' means paragraph 30 of Schedule 2 to the 2004 Act;

(g) 'order for reconsideration' means an order under section 103A(1) requiring the Tribunal to reconsider its decision on an appeal;

(h) 'section 103A' means section 103A of the 2002 Act;

(i) 'Tribunal' means the Asylum and Immigration Tribunal.

(3) Any reference in this Section to a period of time specified in—

(a) section 103A(3) for making an application for an order under section 103A(1); or

(b) paragraph 30(5)(b) of Schedule 2 to the 2004 Act for giving notice under that paragraph, includes a reference to that period as varied by any order under section 26(8) of the 2004 Act.

(4) Rule 2.8 applies to the calculation of the periods of time specified in—

(a) section 103A(3); and

(b) paragraph 30(5)(b) of Schedule 2 to the 2004 Act.

(5) Save as provided otherwise, the provisions of this Section apply to an application under section 103A regardless of whether the filter provision has effect in relation to that application.

Representation of applicants while filter provision has effect

54.28A

(1) This rule applies during any period in which the filter provision has effect.

(2) An applicant may, for the purpose of taking any step under rule 54.29 or 54.30, be represented by any person permitted to provide him with immigration advice or immigration services under section 84 of the Immigration and Asylum Act 1999.

(3) A representative acting for an applicant under paragraph (2) shall be regarded as the applicant's legal representative for the purpose of rule 22.1 (Documents to be verified by a statement of truth) regardless of whether he would otherwise be so regarded.

Service of documents on appellants within the jurisdiction

54.28B

(1) In proceedings under this Section, rules 6.7 and 6.23(2)(a) do not apply to the service of documents on an appellant who is within the jurisdiction.

(2) Where a representative is acting for an appellant who is within the jurisdiction, a document must be served on the appellant by—

(a) serving it on the appellant's representative; or serving it on the appellant personally or sending it to the appellant's address by first class post (or an alternative service which provides for delivery on the next business day),

but if the document is served on the appellant under sub-paragraph (b), a copy must also at the same time be sent to the appellant's representative.

Application for review

52.29

(1) Subject to paragraph (5), an application for an order for reconsideration must be made by filing an application notice—
(a) during a period in which the filter provision has effect, with the Tribunal at the address specified in the relevant practice direction; and
(b) at any other time, at the Administrative Court Office.
(2) During any period in which the filter provision does not have effect, the applicant must file with the application notice—
(a) the notice of the immigration, asylum or nationality decision to which the appeal related;
(b) any other document which was served on the appellant giving reasons for that decision;
(c) the grounds of appeal to the Tribunal;
(d) the Tribunal's determination on the appeal; and
(e) any other documents material to the application which were before the Tribunal.
(2A) During any period in which the filter provision has effect, the applicant must file with the application notice a list of the documents referred to in paragraph (2)(a) to (e).
(3) The applicant must also file with the application notice written submissions setting out—
(a) the grounds upon which it is contended that the Tribunal made an error of law which may have affected its decision; and
(b) reasons in support of those grounds.
(4) Where the applicant—
(a) was the respondent to the appeal; and
(b) was required to serve the Tribunal's determination on the appellant,
the application notice must contain a statement of the date on which, and the means by which, the determination was served.
(5) Where the applicant is in detention under the Immigration Acts, the application may be made either—
(a) in accordance with paragraphs (1) to (3); or
(b) by serving the documents specified in paragraphs (1) to (3) on the person having custody of him.
(6) Where an application is made in accordance with paragraph (5)(b), the person on whom the application notice is served must—
(a) endorse on the notice the date that it is served on him;
(b) give the applicant an acknowledgment in writing of receipt of the notice; and
(c) forward the notice and documents within 2 days
    (i) during a period in which the filter provision has effect, to the Tribunal; and
    (ii) at any other time, to the Administrative Court Office.

Application to extend time limit

54.30

An application to extend the time limit for making an application under section 103A(1) must—
(a) be made in the application notice;
(b) set out the grounds on which it is contended that the application notice could not reasonably practicably have been filed within the time limit; and
(c) be supported by written evidence verified by a statement of truth.

Procedure while filter provision has effect

54.31

(1) This rule applies during any period in which the filter provision has effect.
(2) Where the applicant receives notice from the Tribunal that it—
(a) does not propose to make an order for reconsideration; or
(b) does not propose to grant permission for the application to be made outside the relevant time limit,
and the applicant wishes the court to consider the application, the applicant must file a notice in writing at the Administrative Court Office in accordance with paragraph 30(5)(b) of Schedule 2 to the 2004 Act.
(2A) The applicant must file with the notice—
(a) a copy of the Tribunal's notification that it does not propose to make an order for reconsideration or does not propose to grant permission for the application to be made outside the relevant time limit (referred to in CPR rule 54.31(2));
(b) any other document which was served on the applicant by the Tribunal giving reasons for its decision in paragraph (a);
(c) written evidence in support of any application by the applicant seeking permission to make the application outside the relevant time limit, if applicable;
(d) a copy of the application for reconsideration under section 103A of the 2002 Act (Form AIT/103A), as submitted to the Tribunal (referred to in Rule 54.29(1)(a).
(3) Where the applicant—
(a) was the respondent to the appeal; and
(b) was required to serve the notice from the Tribunal mentioned in paragraph (2) on the appellant,
the notice filed in accordance with paragraph 30(5)(b) of Schedule 2 to the 2004 Act must contain a statement of the date on which, and the means by which, the notice from the Tribunal was served.
(4) A notice which is filed outside the period specified in paragraph 30(5)(b) must—
(a) set out the grounds on which it is contended that the notice could not reasonably practicably have been filed within that period; and
(b) be supported by written evidence verified by a statement of truth.
(5) If the applicant wishes to respond to the reasons given by the Tribunal for its decision that it—
(a) does not propose to make an order for reconsideration; or
(b) does not propose to grant permission for the application to be made outside the relevant time limit,
the notice filed in accordance with paragraph 30(5)(b) of Schedule 2 to the 2004 Act must be accompanied by written submissions setting out the grounds upon which the applicant disputes any of the reasons given by the Tribunal and giving reasons in support of those grounds.

Procedure in fast track cases while filter provision does not have effect

54.32

(1) This rule applies only during a period in which the filter provision does not have effect.
(2) Where a party applies for an order for reconsideration in a fast track case—

(a) the court will serve copies of the application notice and written submissions on the other party to the appeal; and
(b) the other party to the appeal may file submissions in response to the application not later than 2 days after being served with the application.

Determination of the application by the Administrative Court

54.33

(1) This rule, and rules 54.34 and 54.35, apply to applications under section 103A which are determined by the Administrative Court.
(2) The application will be considered by a single judge without a hearing.
(3) Unless it orders otherwise, the court will not receive evidence which was not submitted to the Tribunal.
(4) Subject to paragraph (5), where the court determines an application for an order for reconsideration, it may—
(a) dismiss the application;
(b) make an order requiring the Tribunal to reconsider its decision on the appeal under section 103A(1) of the 2002 Act; or
(c) refer the appeal to the Court of Appeal under section 103C of the 2002 Act.
(5) The court will only make an order requiring the Tribunal to reconsider its decision on an appeal if it thinks that—
(a) the Tribunal may have made an error of law; and
(b) there is a real possibility that the Tribunal would make a different decision on reconsidering the appeal (which may include making a different direction under section 87 of the 2002 Act).
(6) Where the Court of Appeal has restored the application to the court under section 103C(2)(g) of the 2002 Act, the court may not refer the appeal to the Court of Appeal.
(7) The court's decision shall be final and there shall be no appeal from that decision or renewal of the application.

Service of order

54.34

(1) The court will send copies of its order to—
(a) the applicant and the other party to the appeal, except where paragraph (2) applies; and
(b) the Tribunal.
(2) Where the appellant is within the jurisdiction and the application relates, in whole or in part, to an asylum claim, the court will send a copy of its order to the Secretary of State.
(2A) Paragraph (2) does not apply in a fast track case.
(3) Where the court sends an order to the Secretary of State under paragraph (2), the Secretary of State must—
(a) serve the order on the appellant; and
(b) immediately after serving the order, notify—
    (i)   the court; and
    (ii) where the order requires the Tribunal to reconsider its decision on the appeal, the Tribunal,
on what date and by what method the order was served.
(4) The Secretary of State must provide the notification required by paragraph (3)(b) no later than 28 days after the date on which the court sends him a copy of its order.

(5) If, 28 days after the date on which the court sends a copy of its order to the Secretary of State in accordance with paragraph (2), the Secretary of State has not provided the notification required by paragraph (3)(b)(i), the court may serve the order on the appellant.

(5A) Where the court serves an order for reconsideration under paragraph (5), it will notify the Tribunal of the date on which the order was served.

(6) If the court makes an order under section 103D(1) of the 2002 Act, it will send copies of that order to—

(a) the appellant's legal representative; and

(b) the Legal Services Commission.

(7) Where paragraph (2) applies, the court will not serve copies of an order under section 103D(1) of the 2002 Act until either—

(a) the Secretary of State has provided the notification required by paragraph (3)(b); or

(b) 28 days after the date on which the court sent a copy of its order to the Secretary of State, whichever is the earlier.

Costs

54.35

The court shall make no order as to the costs of an application under this Section except, where appropriate, an order under section 103D(1) of the 2002 Act.

Continuing an application in circumstances in which it would otherwise be treated as abandoned

54.36

(1) This rule applies to an application under section 103A of the 2002 Act which—

(a) would otherwise be treated as abandoned under section 104(4A) of the 2002 Act; but

(b) meets the conditions set out in section 104(4B) or section 104(4C) of the 2002 Act.

(2) Where section 104(4A) of the 2002 Act applies and the applicant wishes to pursue the application, the applicant must file a notice at the Administrative Court Office—

(a) where section 104(4B) of the 2002 Act applies, within 28 days of the date on which the applicant received notice of the grant of leave to enter or remain in the United Kingdom for a period exceeding 12 months; or

(b) where section 104(4C) of the 2002 Act applies, within 28 days of the date on which the applicant received notice of the grant of leave to enter or remain in the United Kingdom.

(3) Where the applicant does not comply with the time limits specified in paragraph (2), the application will be treated as abandoned in accordance with section 104(4) of the 2002 Act.

(4) The applicant must serve the notice filed under paragraph (2) on the other party to the appeal.

(5) Where section 104(4B) of the 2002 Act applies, the notice filed under paragraph (2) must state—

(a) the applicant's full name and date of birth;

(b) the Administrative Court reference number;

(c) the Home Office reference number, if applicable;

(d) the date on which the applicant was granted leave to enter or remain in the United Kingdom for a period exceeding 12 months; and

(e) that the applicant wishes to pursue the application insofar as it is brought on grounds relating to the Refugee Convention specified in section 84(1)(g) of the 2002 Act.

(6) Where section 104(4C) of the 2002 Act applies, the notice filed under paragraph (2) must state—

(a) the applicant's full name and date of birth;

(b) the Administrative Court reference number;

(c) the Home Office reference number, if applicable;

(d) the date on which the applicant was granted leave to enter or remain in the United Kingdom; and

(e) that the applicant wishes to pursue the application insofar as it is brought on grounds relating to section 19B of the Race Relations Act 1976 specified in section 84(1)(b) of the 2002 Act.

(7) Where an applicant has filed a notice under paragraph (2) the court will notify the applicant of the date on which it received the notice.

(8) The court will send a copy of the notice issued under paragraph (7) to the other party to the appeal.

PRACTICE DIRECTION 52—APPEALS

Asylum and Immigration Appeals

21.7

(1) This paragraph applies to appeals—

(a) from the Immigration Appeal Tribunal under section 103 of the Nationality, Immigration and Asylum Act 2002 ('the 2002 Act'); and

(b) from the Asylum and Immigration Tribunal under the following provisions of the 2002 Act—

　　(i)　section 103B (appeal from the Tribunal following reconsideration); and

　　(ii)　section 103E (appeal from the Tribunal sitting as a panel).

(2) The appellant is not required to file an appeal bundle in accordance with paragraph 5.6A of this practice direction, but must file the documents specified in paragraphs 5.6(2)(a) to (f) together with a copy of the Tribunal's determination.

(3) The appellant's notice must be filed at the Court of Appeal within 14 days after the appellant is served with written notice of the decision of the Tribunal to grant or refuse permission to appeal.

(4) The appellant must serve the appellant's notice in accordance with rule 52.4(3) on—

(a) the persons to be served under that rule; and

(b) the Asylum and Immigration Tribunal.

(5) On being served with the appellant's notice, the Asylum and Immigration Tribunal must send to the Court of Appeal copies of the documents which were before the relevant Tribunal when it considered the appeal.

21.7A

(1) This paragraph applies to appeals from the Asylum and Immigration Tribunal referred to the Court of Appeal under section 103C of the Nationality, Immigration and Asylum Act 2002.

(2) On making an order referring an appeal to the Court of Appeal, the High Court shall send to the Court of Appeal copies of—

(a) that order and any other order made in relation to the application for reconsideration; and

(b) the application notice, written submissions and other documents filed under rule 54.29

(3) Unless the court directs otherwise, the application notice filed under rule 54.29 shall be treated as the appellant's notice.

(4) The respondent may file a respondent's notice within 14 days after the date on which the respondent is served with the order of the High Court referring the appeal to the Court of Appeal.

(5) The Court of Appeal may give such additional directions as are appropriate.

21.7B

(1) This paragraph applies to appeals from the Asylum and Immigration Tribunal which—

(a) would otherwise be treated as abandoned under section 104(4A) of the Nationality, Immigration and Asylum Act 2002 (the '2002 Act'); but

(b) meet the conditions set out in section 104(4B) or section 104(4C) of the 2002 Act.

(2) Where section 104(4A) of the 2002 Act applies and the appellant wishes to pursue his appeal, the appellant must file a notice at the Court of Appeal—

(a) where section 104(4B) of the 2002 Act applies, within 28 days of the date on which the appellant received notice of the grant of leave to enter or remain in the United Kingdom for a period exceeding 12 months; or

(b) where section 104(4C) of the 2002 Act applies, within 28 days of the date on which the appellant received notice of the grant of leave to enter or remain in the United Kingdom.

(3) Where the appellant does not comply with the time limits specified in paragraph (2) the appeal will be treated as abandoned in accordance with section 104(4) of the 2002 Act.

(4) The appellant must serve the notice filed under paragraph (2) on the respondent.

(5) Where section 104(4B) of the 2002 Act applies, the notice filed under paragraph (2) must state—

(a) the appellant's full name and date of birth;

(b) the Court of Appeal reference number;

(c) the Home Office reference number, if applicable;

(d) the date on which the appellant was granted leave to enter or remain in the United Kingdom for a period exceeding 12 months; and

(e) that the appellant wishes to pursue the appeal in so far as it is brought on the ground relating to the Refugee Convention specified in section 84(1)(g) of the 2002 Act.

(6) Where section 104(4C) of the 2002 Act applies, the notice filed under paragraph (2) must state—

(a) the appellant's full name and date of birth;

(b) the Court of Appeal reference number;

(c) the Home Office reference number, if applicable;

(d) the date on which the appellant was granted leave to enter or remain in the United Kingdom; and

(e) that the appellant wishes to pursue the appeal in so far as it is brought on the ground relating to section 19B of the Race Relations Act 1976 specified in section 84(1)(b) of the 2002 Act.

(7) Where an appellant has filed a notice under paragraph (2) the Court of Appeal will notify the appellant of the date on which it received the notice.

(8) The Court of Appeal will send a copy of the notice issued under paragraph (7) to the respondent.

Practice direction 54A—Rule 54.7—Service of claim form

6.2

Where the defendant or interested party to the claim for judicial review is—
(a) the Asylum and Immigration Tribunal, the address for service of the claim form is the Asylum and Immigration Tribunal, Official Correspondence Unit, PO Box 6987, Leicester, LE1 6ZX or fax number 0116 249 4131;
(b) the Crown, service of the claim form must be effected on the solicitor acting for the relevant government department as if the proceedings were civil proceedings as defined in the Crown Proceedings Act 1947.

(The practice direction supplementing Part 66 gives the list published under section 17 of the Crown Proceedings Act 1947 of the solicitors acting in civil proceedings (as defined in that Act) for the different government departments on whom service is to be effected, and of their addresses.)

(Part 6 contains provisions about the service of claim forms.)

PRACTICE DIRECTION 54B—APPLICATIONS FOR STAUTUTORY REVIEW UNDER SECTION 103A OF THE NATIONALITY, IMMIGRATION AND ASYLUM ACT 2002

This Practice Direction supplements Section III of CPR Part 54

Contents of this Practice Direction
The Court

Access to court orders served on the appellant by the Secretary of State
Referral to Court of Appeal

1

Attention is drawn to:
(1) Sections 103A, 103C and 103D of the Nationality, Immigration and Asylum Act 2002 (inserted by section 26(6) of the Asylum and Immigration (Treatment of Claimants, etc.) Act 2004); and
(2) Paragraph 30 of Schedule 2 to the 2004 Act.

The Court

2.1

Applications for review under section 103A(1) of the 2002 Act are dealt with in the Administrative Court, subject to the transitional filter provision in paragraph 30 of Schedule 2 of the 2004 Act which provides that they shall initially be considered by a member of the Tribunal.

2.2

During any period in which the filter provision has effect, the address for filing section 103A applications shall be the Asylum and Immigration Tribunal, P.O. Box 6987, Leicester LE1 6ZX.

2.3   *Where a fast track order within the meaning of Rule 54.32(3) applies to a section 103A application, paragraph 2.2 shall not apply and the address for filing the application shall be the address specified in the Tribunal's determination of the appeal.*

Access to court orders served on the appellant by the Secretary of State

3.1   *Where the court sends a copy of its order on a section 103A application to the Secretary of State but not the appellant in accordance with Rule 54.34(2), then Rules 5.4(3)(b) and 5.4(5)(a)(ii) are modified as follows.*

3.2

Neither the appellant nor any other person may obtain from the records of the court a copy of the court's order on the section 103A application, or of any order made under section 103D(1) of the 2002 Act in relation to that application, until either the Secretary of State has given the court the notification required by Rule 54.34(3)(b) or 28 days after the date on which the court sent a copy of the order to the Secretary of State, whichever is the earlier.

Referral to Court of Appeal

4.1

Where the court refers an appeal to the Court of Appeal, its order will set out the question of law raised by the appeal which is of such importance that it should be decided by the Court of Appeal.

4.2

Paragraph 21.7A of the practice direction supplementing Part 52 makes provision about appeals which are referred to the Court of Appeal.

INDEX

LEGAL TAXONOMY
FROM SWEET & MAXWELL

This index has been prepared using Sweet and Maxwell's Legal Taxonomy. Main index entries conform to keywords provided by the Legal Taxonomy except where references to specific documents or non-standard terms (denoted by quotation marks) have been included. These keywords provide a means of identifying similar concepts in other Sweet & Maxwell publications and online services to which keywords from the Legal Taxonomy have been applied. Readers may find some minor differences between terms used in the text and those which appear in the index. Suggestions to *sweet&maxwell.taxonomy@thomson.com*.